CHORL
GILES' SHIPPING LAW

EIGHTH EDITION

N J J GASKELL · C DEBATTISTA
AND R J SWATTON

Institute of Maritime Law
University of Southampton

PITMAN
150
YEARS

PITMAN PUBLISHING
128 Long Acre London WC2E 9AN

© O C Giles, N J J Gaskell, C Debattista and R J Swatton 1987

First published in Great Britain 1987

British Library Cataloguing in Publication Data

Chorley, Robert Samuel Theodore Chorley, *Baron*
Chorley and Giles' Shipping Law – 8th ed.
1. Maritime Law – England
I. Title   II. Giles, Otto Charles
III. Gaskell, N.J.J.   IV. Debattista, C
V. Swatton, Richard J.
344.203'96   KD1819

ISBN 0-273-02194-X

Typeset by Belmont Press, Northampton.
Printed and bound in Great Britain

CONTENTS

iii

PART TWO: THE CARRIAGE OF GOODS BY SEA

PREFACE TO THE EIGHTH EDITION

O.C. Giles the surviving co-author of *Chorley and Giles* died in 1980 shortly after the publication of the seventh edition. Together with Lord Chorley, he established the book as a leading text on the basic principles of shipping law. Consequently, we are extremely pleased to have been asked to produce the eighth edition of this much loved work, and have striven to maintain its established tradition of clarity and readability, while at the same time providing a thorough and accurate updating of the work.

In the last six years there have been many changes and developments in shipping law. Apart from the many new cases, Statutes and a host of Statutory Instruments, we have also referred to significant developments in the international scene which reflect the universal nature of shipping law. Further, to enhance the practical nature of the work, we have referred wherever possible to standard contracts which commonly form the basis of unofficial legal codes created and understood by those in the trade.

Particular reference has been made to new Statutes such as the Merchant Shipping Acts 1981, 1983, 1984, the Pilotage Act 1983, the Dangerous Vessels Act 1985, and the Merchant Shipping (Liner Conferences) Act 1982, as well as to the amendments to the jurisdiction of the courts brought about by the Supreme Court Act 1981 and the Civil Jurisdiction and Judgments Act 1982. Developments with international conventions such as SOLAS and MARPOL have required the virtual rewriting of the chapter on construction, maintenance and equipment to take account of resulting Statutory Instruments. The chapter on limitation of liability now emphasizes the enactment in the UK of the 1976 Limitation Convention, on 1 December 1986, and the bringing into force of the relevant provisions of the Merchant Shipping Act 1979. The field of carriage of goods by sea has been marked by a prolific amount of case law, and detailed treatment of developments here has had to be selective lest the generalist nature of the book be seriously impaired. Within this constraint, we have attempted to make due mention of *The Evia*, *The Scaptrade*, and *The Chicuma* in charterparty law; *The New York Star*, *The Elli 2*, *Mayhew Foods* v. *OCL* and *The Morviken* in the law relating to bills of lading; *The Varenna* and *The*

Miramar in the area of bills of lading under charterparties; *The Aliakmon* on the right of receivers of goods to sue carriers; and finally the possible impact of *Photo Production* v. *Securicor* on the law of carriage of goods generally. In our coverage of marine insurance, we have included for the first time a discussion of the new MAR policy form and its various associated Institute clauses, including the Institute Cargo Clauses 1982 and the Institute Time Clauses (Hulls) 1983. Reference has also been made to the Lloyds Act 1982 and recent cases such as *The Salem, The Popi M, The Bamburi* and *General Reinsurance* v. *Forsäkringsaktiebolaget Fennia Patria.*

It was not our original intention to make radical changes to such an established and well respected work, particularly in view of the time available for the revision. However, in view of the many developments in the law referred to above, it has been found necessary to rewrite a larger portion of the text than was at first intended. In this context, the opportunity has also been taken to divide the existing work into smaller, more manageable chapters with a uniform system of subheadings which we hope will clarify the overall structure. There is a new introductory chapter on legal disputes concerning ships which draws together material from a variety of locations in the previous edition, as does the new chapter on time bars. The treatment of limitation of liability has been moved from the beginning of the book so that it can be considered after the main liability issues. Despite such changes, we hope that the book retains the imprint of the original co-authors.

Although we accept joint responsibility for the whole, the revision of Parts 1 and 3 were undertaken by Nick Gaskell, Part 2 by Charles Debattista and Part 4 by Richard Swatton.

We would like to thank our long suffering families and friends, especially Louise and Maryann. We should also like to make special mention of our colleagues in the Institute of Maritime Law, particularly David Jackson, Alison Clarke and Richard Holt for their advice and assistance. We are also grateful to Pitmans for their patience and understanding throughout the production of this edition.

Although we aimed to state the law as at 1 January 1986, we have endeavoured to take into account developments up to 1 January 1987.

NJJG
Southampton   CD
February 1986   RJS

PREFACE TO THE FIRST EDITION

The need of a general elementary textbook on the law relating to shipping has long been felt by students of the subject and, particularly, by those embarking upon a commercial rather than a legal career; to these the technicalities in the numerous excellent practitioners' works on various aspects of the subject present a formidable obstacle. We have endeavoured in this volume to fill the gap, and we have had in mind the commerce rather than the professional legal student.

This book deals in an elementary way with all the aspects of the law with which those engaged in the business of owning and managing ships are likely to meet. The text was completed early in the war, when printing difficulties prevented publication. Wartime decisions and legislation affecting points of general importance have been noticed, and we are particularly grateful to Sir William McNair, K.C., of the commercial bar, for giving us his valuable advice in regard to these developments.

We have made no attempt to deal with the special wartime controls and regulations. It is not improbable that some of these have come to stay, but we have considered it too early to deal with such developments which, in any event, are not likely to change the permanent framework of the law as described in these pages.

CHORLEY
O.C. GILES
*London School of Economics
and Political Science*

ACKNOWLEDGEMENTS

We should like to thank the following for permitting us to reproduce materials in this work and for assisting in various other ways.

Part 1
The Controller of Her Majesty's Stationery Office (Bill of Sale; Mortgage to Secure Account Current). Both forms are Crown copyright.
The Norwegian Shipbrokers Association (SALEFORM 1983)

Part 2
Atlantic Container Line Services Ltd (ACL Bill of Lading)
The Baltic and International Maritime Council (Gencon Charterparty)
The General Council of British Shipping (GCBS Waybill)

Part 3
The British Tugowners Association (UKSTC 1983)
The Committee of Lloyd's (LOF 1980)

Part 4
CBC London (printers of the Lloyd's S.G. and MAR Forms)
The Institute of London Underwriters (Institute Insurance Clauses)
Lloyd's Underwriters Association, in particular Mr R. H. Jones (Lloyd's S.G. and MAR Policies)
Willis, Faber and Dumas Ltd, in particular Mr Colin Dennis
Witherby and Co. Ltd (publishers of the Institute Insurance Clauses)

We also owe a special debt of gratitude to our colleagues on the secretarial staff of the Institute of Maritime Law and of the Faculty of Law at Southampton, particularly Marion Dalton, Alison Lampard and Margaret Newton.

TABLE OF CASES

[Numbers in bold type indicate cases illustrated in the text]

TABLE OF
STATUTES

TABLE OF STATUTORY INSTRUMENTS

ABBREVIATED BOOK TITLES

The following books are referred to elsewhere in the text by means of the abbreviated forms indicated in bold type below.

Arnould (1981): M. Mustill and J. Gilman, *Arnould's Law of Marine Insurance and Average,* 16th edn, Sweet & Maxwell (1981), with 1986 Supplement.

Atiyah (1985): P.S. Atiyah, *The Sale of Goods,* 7th edn, Pitman (1985).

Benjamin (1981): *Benjamin's Sale of Goods* (ed. A.G. Guest), 2nd edn, Sweet & Maxwell (1981).

Brice (1983): G. Brice, *Maritime Law of Salvage,* Stevens (1983).

Carver (1982): R.P. Colinvaux, *Carver's Carriage by Sea,* 13th edn, Stevens (1982)

Chitty (1983): *Chitty on Contracts* (ed. A.G. Guest), 25th edn, 2 vols, Sweet & Maxwell (1983), with 1986 Supplement.

Clerk and Lindsell (1982): *Clerk and Lindsell's Law of Torts* (ed. R.W. M. Dias), 15th edn, Sweet & Maxwell (1982), with 1985 Supplement.

Dicey and Morris (1980): J.H.C. Morris, *Dicey and Morris on the Conflict of Laws,* 10th edn, Stevens (1980), with 1985 Cumulative Supplement.

Douglas (1983): R.P.A. Douglas, *Harbour Law,* 2nd edn, Lloyd's of London Press (1983).

Geen and Douglas (1983): G.K. Geen and R.P.A. Douglas, *The Law of Pilotage,* 2nd edn, Lloyd's of London Press (1983).

Goode (1982): R. Goode, *Commercial Law,* Penguin (1982) (Reprinted 1985 with minor additions).

Herman (1983): A. Herman, *Shipping Conferences,* Lloyd's of London Press (1983).

Ivamy (1985): E.R.H. Ivamy, *Marine Insurance*, 4th edn, Butterworths (1985).

Jackson (1985): D.C. Jackson, *Enforcement of Maritime Claims,* Lloyd's of London Press (1985).

Kennedy (1985): D. Steel, F. Rose and R. Shaw, *Kennedy's Law of Salvage,* 5th edn, Stevens (1985).

Kitchen (1980): J.S. Kitchen, *The Employment of Merchant Seamen*, Croom Helm (1980).

Lowndes and Rudolf (1975): J.Donaldson, C.S. Staughton and D.J. Wilson, *The Law of General Average and the York-Antwerp Rules* 10th edn, Stevens (1975).

Marsden (1961): *Marsden's Law of Collisions at Sea*, 11th edn, Sweet & Maxwell (1961), with Supplement 1973. [12th edition in preparation]

Northrup and Rowan (1983): H. Northrup and R. Rowan, *The International Transport Workers Federation and Flag of Convenience Shipping*, University of Pennsylvania Industrial Research Unit (1983).

Packard (1981): W.V. Packard, *Sale and Purchase*, Fairplay Publications (1981).

Pollard (1977): D.W. Pollard, *Social Welfare Law*, Oyez (1977), with Supplements.

Rose (1984): F.Rose, *The Modern Law of Pilotage*, Sweet & Maxwell (1984).

Sassoon (1984): D. Sassoon and H.O Merren, *CIF and FOB Contracts*, 3rd edn, Stevens (1984).

Scrutton (1984): A.A. Mocatta, M.J. Mustill and S.C. Boyd, *Scrutton on Charterparties*, 19th edn, Sweet & Maxwell (1984).

Singh (1983): N. Singh, *International Maritime Conventions*, 4 vols, Stevens (1983).

Singh and Colinvaux (1967): N. Singh and R.P. Colinvaux, *Shipowners*, Stevens (1967).

Sturt (1984): R.H.B. Sturt, *The Collision Regulations*, 2nd edn, Lloyd's of London Press (1984).

Temperley (1976): M. Thomas and D. Steel, *Temperley's Merchant Shipping Acts*, 7th edn, Sweet & Maxwell (1976).

Templeman (1986): R.J. Lambeth, *Templeman on Marine Insurance*, Pitman (1986).

Thomas (1980): D. R. Thomas, *Maritime Liens*, Sweet & Maxwell (1980).

Wood (1980): P. Wood, *Law and Practice of International Finance*, Sweet & Maxwell (1980).

PART ONE
THE SHIP

1
LEGAL DISPUTES
INVOLVING SHIPS

1.1 INTRODUCTION

DURING the course of commercial activities involving ships many legal questions will arise. They will be handled by the parties and their advisers as part of their day to day business, without any wish to get involved in litigation. Inevitably, disputes will occur. Most will be settled more or less amicably, taking into account commercial considerations such as the need to continue existing trading arrangements and the desire to avoid the expense and delay involved in going to court.

The role of the law in this context is to define the basic obligations of the parties – to provide a basis for negotiation. Sometimes the parties cannot, or will not, agree but submit themselves to the legal process and allow somebody else to resolve the dispute. The law is then a tool in that person's hands.

It is convenient at this stage to examine, in outline only, the structure of the legal decision-making process which will apply in shipping cases.

1.2 ARBITRATION

Many shipping disputes are referred for arbitration before arbitrators who will have particular experience (commercial or legal) in the area in question.[1] Arbitration clauses will be found in many shipping contracts, such as charterparties and bills of lading, as well as in ship sale, ship-building and salvage contracts. Where there is such a clause the judges will not usually permit a party to go to court until the arbitrator has heard the disputes and may order a 'stay' (i.e. suspension) of the court proceedings.[2] For certain non-domestic arbitrations the court must

---

1 See generally M. Mustill, S. Boyd, *Commercial Arbitration* (1982).
2 Arbitration Act 1950, s. 4.

order a stay.[3] Except in those cases where it was mandatory the court was able to order a stay on conditions, e.g. that the security provided by arrest of the ship be allowed to stand.[4] The Civil Jurisdiction and Judgments Act 1982, s. 26 now makes it clear that, whenever Admiralty proceedings are dismissed or stayed for the purposes of arbitration, the court has power to order that any ship arrested (or alternative security) be retained. It may attach conditions to the stay, e.g. to make the claimant commence the arbitration as soon as possible.

In many countries the arbitrator's decision is final. In England the courts always exercised a power of review and defendants sometimes used this facility as a means of delaying the payment of money owed. The Arbitration Act 1979 has greatly restricted this abuse and appeals on points of law will only be allowed where the arbitrator is clearly wrong or some point of general importance is at stake.[5]

1.3 JURISDICTION OF THE COURTS

In England and Wales most shipping cases will be heard in the High Court of Justice, usually in the Queens Bench Division.[6] The latter contains a specialist Commercial Court and an Admiralty Court.[7] The Admiralty Court exercises a wide jurisdiction over admiralty matters and can hear cases on claims relating to matters as diverse as ownership; mortgages; damage done by, or to, a ship; cargo damage; personal injury and death involving ships; salvage; towage; pilotage; general average; wages; marine pollution damage.[8]

---

3 Arbitration Act 1975, s. 1; e.g., where there is a written agreement between two foreign nationals to arbitrate abroad.
4 *The Rena K* [1979] Q.B. 377. *Cf. The Vasso* [1984] 1 Lloyd's Rep. 235, *The Tuyuti* [1984] 2 Lloyd's Rep. 51; for arrest, see Section 1.4, *infra*.
5 *The Nema* [1981] 2 All E.R. 1030. The Arbitration Act 1979, s. 2 allows a preliminary point of law to be referred to the court with the consent of all the parties (or of the arbitrator).
6 Some smaller claims may be heard in the County Court, County Courts Act 1984, ss. 26–31. The value of property salved cannot exceed £15 000 in salvage claims and claims in other cases cannot exceed £5000, s. 27(2). For Scotland, see the Administration of Justice Act 1956, Part V; for Northern Ireland, s. 55 and the Judicature (Northern Ireland) Act 1978.
7 Supreme Court Act 1981, s. 6.
8 See s. 20 (Appendix 1) for the full list.

1.3.1 ACTIONS *IN PERSONAM*

Where the plaintiff has been the victim of some legal wrong committed by a natural, or a legal,[9] person he is entitled to sue that other person *in personam*. In the shipping world the practical problem is that this individual defendant may be outside the plaintiff's country. Collisions, for instance, could occur anywhere in the world between ships of various nationalities. The International Convention on Certain Rules Concerning Civil Jurisdiction in Matters of Collision 1952[10] laid down restrictions on the exercise of jurisdiction over collision cases and is reflected in s.22 of the Supreme Court Act 1981. Thus the Admiralty Court can only hear collision actions brought *in personam* (i.e. against an individual or a legal person such as a company) if the defendant has his habitual residence or place of business in England and Wales; or if the facts giving rise to the claim[11] occurred in English or Welsh waters; or if an action arising from the same incident is already before the Court.

The Civil Jurisdiction and Judgments Act 1982[12] imposes restrictions on actions *in personam* by making jurisdiction depend, in respect of defendants domiciled in an EEC state, primarily on the domicile[13] of the defendant. For instance, in most commercial matters, a Frenchman must be sued in a French court. However, this is only the basic rule and there are many alternatives. Under Art. 5 contract disputes can be heard where the contract should have been performed; tort disputes (e.g., where collision damage is caused negligently) can be heard in the place where the harmful event occurred; and salvage disputes concerning cargo can be heard where the cargo was arrested. Limitation of shipowners' liability[14] may also be dealt with by the court trying the issue of liability (e.g., for a collision). There is a section devoted entirely to insurance. Policy holders are allowed to sue in their place of domicile.[15] Special provisions are made for marine insurance to allow

9 Such as a company.
10 Cmnd 8954, Singh (1983) Vol. 4, p.3107; enacted first in English law in the Administration of Justice Act 1956; see now the Supreme Court Act 1981, ss. 21, 22.
11 The 'cause of action', in legal terminology.
12 Enacting the EEC Convention on Jurisdiction and the Enforcement of Judgments on Civil and Commercial Matters 1968, and Protocol 1971, which are found in the Schedules to the Act. The Act enters into force on 1 January 1987.
13 Ss. 41–46 define domicile. For an individual it means residence in a country with which he has a substantial connection: for companies it is where the company has the 'seat', e.g. the place where it has its registered office or from which it is controlled.
14 See Chapter 22, *infra*.
15 Art. 8.

insurers, such as Lloyd's, to insert terms in their policies choosing the jurisdiction of a particular country.[16]

1.3.2 ACTIONS *IN REM*

Maritime law has long allowed a plaintiff to proceed not only *in personam* (e.g., against a shipowner) but also *in rem* (against the thing itself, e.g., the ship). The jurisdiction of the Admiralty Court *in rem* is very wide. For instance, in collision cases it can be exercised against the defendant ship wherever the collision occurred and whatever the nationality of its owner.[17]

The *in rem* jurisdiction is theoretically affected by the restrictions in the Civil Jurisdiction and Judgments Act 1982, already mentioned. Fortunately for those maritime lawyers who do not like change, the provisions of that Act are subject to existing Conventions dealing with jurisdiction, of which the Arrest Convention 1952 is one.[18] That Convention gives jurisdiction over the merits of a claim if the domestic law of the country of arrest gives jurisdiction.[19] This brings us back full circle to English domestic law which, it seems, would do so for most maritime claims *in rem*.

In English law the jurisdiction issue is hopelessly intertwined with the questions of when a ship can be arrested and how claimants can exercise rights of lien in order to obtain security for their claims.[20]

The Supreme Court Act 1981 allows actions *in rem* to be brought for ownership and ship mortgage claims and where there is a maritime lien (e.g., for collision or salvage).[21] An action *in rem* can also be brought for many other maritime claims (e.g., for towage, pilotage, shiprepair or personal injury) specified in the Statute – so called 'statutory rights *in rem*'.[22]

The English theory is that the action *in rem* is a mere device to get the real defendant (e.g., the owner) into court. Once he has acknowledged the service of the writ he submits himself personally to the jurisdiction

16 Arts 7–12A. For the circumstances in which a court can grant leave for a writ to be served outside the jurisdiction, see Rules of the Supreme Court (R.S.C.) Order 11, *Amin Rasheed Shipping Corporation* v. *Kuwait Insurance Co.* [1984] A.C. 50, *The Spiliada* [1986] 3 W.L.R. 972.

17 S. 20(7), Supreme Court Act 1981.

18 Art. 57 and see Section 1.4, *infra*.

19 Art. 7.

20 Readers are advised to refer to a specialist book, e.g. Jackson (1985).

21 Ss. 21(2), 21(3). For maritime liens see Section 7.1, *infra*.

22 S. 21(4). See further Section 7.2, *infra*.

of the Admiralty Court and from then on the action continues against him not only as an action *in rem*, but also as an action *in personam*.[23]

1.4 ARREST

Once a plaintiff has obtained a writ in an action *in rem* he can apply for a warrant to arrest the ship.[24] This is a very special feature of English shipping law. After a car crash on land the plaintiff is not allowed to 'arrest' the defendant's car! Nor in such an ordinary *in personam* action against a defendant could the latter be arrested to force him to pay the claim. It is only *after* judgment on the merits of the claim that the defendant's property may be seized to satisfy that claim.

The main purpose of arresting a vessel is to obtain security before judgment for the claim.[25] While the ship is under arrest it cannot be moved.[26] This means that the owner will not be able to fulfil the contracts which enable him to earn profits, but at the same time he will continue to incur expenses. To break out of this vicious circle the owner can put up bail for the ship. In practice, however, it is more usual for shipowners to arrange that security, in the form of a guarantee or undertaking, be provided by their banks or Protection and Indemnity (P & I) Clubs.

The court has the power to order the arrest of a ship even though the real purpose of the arrest is to obtain security for arbitration proceedings taking place elsewhere and not for the action in the Admiralty Court.[27] However, the court has a discretion to order the release of the

---

23 *The August 8th* [1983] 1 Lloyd's Rep. 351, 355; also *The Rena K* [1979] Q.B. 377.
24 See R.S.C. Order 75, in *The Supreme Court Practice* (1985) – the 'White Book'. On average about 175 ships are arrested each year, of which 25 are appraised and sold by court order and 150 are released after security is provided, *The Myrto (No.2)* [1984] 2 Lloyd's Rep. 341, 347. The 'ship' includes all property on board, apart from that owned by persons other than the shipowner, *The Silia* [1981] 2 Lloyd's Rep. 534.
25 Although in England it is also a way of obtaining jurisdiction. Arrest may also be used to enforce the judgments of foreign courts, *The Despina G.K.* [1982] 2 Lloyd's Rep. 555; *cf. The Alletta* [1974] 1 Lloyd's Rep. 40, *The Daien Maru No. 2* [1986] 1 Lloyd's Rep. 387.
26 A master who takes an arrested ship out of the jurisdiction is guilty of contempt of court and can be imprisoned, *The Jarlinn* [1965] 3 All E.R. 36; *The Merdeka* [1982] 1 Lloyd's Rep. 401.
27 *The Vasso* [1984] 1 Lloyd's Rep. 235 and *The Tuyuti* [1984] 2 Lloyd's Rep. 51.

vessel[28] and, as has already been noted, it may impose conditions for doing so which include the provision of security.[29]

If there is more than one claimant there is no need for each to take the arrest procedure. Once the vessel has been arrested claimants can protect their interests by entering a 'caveat' in the Admiralty Registrar's Caveat book.[30]

Under the International Convention for the Unification of Certain Rules Relating to the Arrest of Seagoing Ships 1952[31] ships can be arrested in any Contracting State for any of the maritime claims listed in Art. 1 – essentially those enacted in the Supreme Court Act 1981, s. 20.[32] Any security given can be used to meet a judgment given in another country if, e.g., the country where the ship was arrested did not have jurisdiction to decide the merits of the underlying dispute.[33] Under Art. 3 of the Convention a claimant may be able to arrest not only the ship which gave rise to the claim, but also a sister ship.[34]

1.5 MAREVA INJUNCTIONS

Mention should be made briefly of a remedy, fashioned by the courts in recent years, which looks similar to arrest but is very different.[35] The

---

28 *The Vanessa Ann* [1985] 1 Lloyd's Rep. 5. Where a limitation fund has been established in another country the court will usually allow the vessel to be released, provided that the shipowner had shown that he was prima facie entitled to limit; *The Wladyslaw Lokietek* [1978] 2 Lloyd's Rep. 520, and see Sections 22.2.4 and 22.3.4, *infra*.

29 *The Vasso, supra* and the Civil Jurisdiction and Judgments Act 1982, s. 26. The security should be for an amount that represents the plaintiff's reasonably arguable best case, *The Gulf Venture* [1984] 2 Lloyd's Rep. 445. Where no security is provided the court could order that the vessel be sold *pendente lite* (during the litigation), *The Gulf Venture* [1985] 1 Lloyd's Rep. 131.

30 The vessel cannot then be released without the consent of the claimant or court, R.S.C. Order 75, Rules 13, 14.

31 Cmnd 8952, Singh (1983) Vol. 4, p. 3101. The Supreme Court Act 1981 has given effect to most of the provisions of this Convention.

32 Under the Nuclear Installations Act 1965, s. 14 no ship carrying irradiated nuclear fuel on behalf of a 'licensee' of a nuclear site may be arrested. This is because, under the Act, the licensee alone is responsible for nuclear damage.

33 Art. 7.

34 See the Supreme Court Act 1981, s. 21(4), Appendix 1. Reference should be made to Section 7.2, *infra*, for the ability to arrest a sister ship in English law.

35 For a detailed analysis of the Mareva injunction, see Jackson (1985), Chapter 10, especially p. 198; A. Colman, *The Practice and Procedure of the Commercial Court* 2nd edn, (1986), Chapter 6.

idea is to stop defendants removing assets from (or dissipating them within) England before the plaintiff has managed to get judgment on his claim. The courts have long had the power to grant pre-trial injunctions to preserve the status quo. The Mareva injunction derives its name from a 1975 case[36] in which shipowners who were owed hire were able to get an injunction to prevent the time charterers from removing assets from the country. Those assets consisted of freight paid by sub-charterers into a London bank account. Without the order the foreign defendant would probably have removed the money and ceased trading.

However, the injunction is not restricted in any way to maritime claims. Under s. 37(3), Supreme Court Act 1981 the injunction may be issued whether or not the defendant is resident in the jurisdiction. The English courts must have jurisdiction over the underlying dispute.[37] It is, at present, not generally possible to obtain a Mareva injunction to support foreign proceedings.[38] The precise extent of the Mareva injunction is still under development by the courts, but it operates *in personam*, as an order to a named person not to permit specified assets to be removed. Failure to obey is a contempt of court which could result in imprisonment. It is not available as of right and the plaintiff must convince the court that there is a danger of dissipation of assets[39] and that he, himself, has made a full and frank disclosure.[40] This is because the application is usually made *ex parte* (by one party alone), in the first instance.

The plaintiff usually has to give an undertaking to pay damages for any expense caused, particularly to third parties such as banks who may have great difficulty in tracing accounts.[41] It is sometimes very difficult for plaintiffs to get accurate information about the exact whereabouts and extent of the assets of evasive defendants. Accordingly, the courts do have power to order defendants and others to disclose documents and provide information so that assets may be traced.[42]

Sometimes the effects of an injunction on a third party will be so drastic that the court will refuse the injunction altogether. In one case a Mareva injunction was issued against a cargo-owner who was also the voyage charterer. The effect of the injunction would have been to

36 *Mareva Compañia Naviera S.A.* v. *International Bulkcarriers S.A.* [1975] 2 Lloyd's Rep. 509.
37 *The Siskina* [1979] A.C. 210.
38 But note the Civil Jurisdiction and Judgments Act 1982, ss. 24, 25.
39 *Z Ltd* v. *A.* [1982] Q.B. 558.
40 *Third Chandris Shipping Corporation* v. *Unimarine S.A.* [1979] Q.B. 645.
41 *Z Ltd* v. *A., supra.*
42 *A. Bekhor & Co. Ltd* v. *Bilton* [1981] 1 Q.B. 923.

prevent the innocent owner, on whose ship the cargo was loaded, removing his ship from the jurisdiction. The plaintiff had no claim against the shipowner, but wanted to retain the cargo as security for an earlier claim against its owner. The injunction would have interfered seriously in the shipowner's commercial arrangements and inconvenienced the crew. The Court of Appeal lifted the injunction.[43]

The final point to note is that the injunction does not attach assets: it is directed at individuals. It does not create any form of preferred claim or priority.[44]

1.6 SOVEREIGN IMMUNITY

Opinion on whether ships run by foreign governments for ordinary commercial purposes could be arrested in proceedings *in rem* varied according to the dominant philosophy during the era in question.[45] The issue of 'sovereign immunity' became one of real importance in the present century when many states with centrally planned economies made laws reserving foreign trade to the state.

Actually, the first English case arose earlier. A state-owned Belgian ship used for the public purpose of carrying mail, but also carrying passengers as a business, collided in Dover harbour with another vessel, and the latter brought proceedings *in rem* and arrested her. The action failed.[46] Forty years later, a Portuguese state-owned ship engaged solely in ordinary trade also escaped arrest.[47] In both cases the 'absolute theory' of state immunity prevailed. Later, the House of Lords, without having to decide the precise point, cast doubt on the 'absolute theory'.[48]

This was natural for, with government-owned merchant ships having greatly multiplied since the matter was first judicially considered, it seemed inequitable that they should enjoy immunity in respect of arrest when they had caused loss or damage to privately owned ship- and cargo-owners. After all, state immunity is a concept reflecting the view of the majesty of the state, but a state engaging in the mundane business of trading must in fairness submit to the general rules applicable to traders; majesty cannot be asserted in the market

43 *The Eletherios* [1982] 1 Lloyd's Rep. 351.
44 *The Cretan Harmony* [1978] 1 Lloyd's Rep. 425, Jackson (1985), p. 187. See also Section 7.3, *infra*.
45 Jackson (1985), pp. 117–122.
46 *The Parlement Belge* (1880) 5 P.D. 197.
47 *The Porto Alexandre* [1920] P. 30.
48 *Compañia Naviera Vascongada* v. *SS Cristina* [1938] A.C. 485.

place. At last, some forty years later, the Judicial Committee of the Privy Council decisively rejected the absolute theory.[49] The time had come, the Board held, for the 'restrictive theory', restricting state immunity to ships engaged on public missions, to prevail. It granted actions *in rem* to charterers for breach of the charterparty and to ship's agents for goods supplied and disbursements, although the ship was owned by a company which in reality was an agent of the Philippine Government. In 1981, the House of Lords extended the restrictive theory to actions *in personam* as well.[50]

This state of affairs has been put on a statutory footing by the State Immunity Act 1978, by which the Government has at last been able to ratify the International Convention for the Unification of Certain Rules Concerning the Immunity of State-owned Ships, 1926 and a Protocol of 1934.[51] The Statute assumes the general principle of state immunity and then sets out a number of exceptions.[52] It provides that no state is immune as respects Admiralty proceedings, both actions *in rem* and *in personam*, against one of its ships, and also hovercraft if, when the cause of action arose, it was in use or intended for use, for commercial purposes.[53] The same applies to proceedings in respect of commercial cargoes carried in ships used for commercial purposes. The privileges and immunities may be extended or restricted by Order.[54]

1.7 FORUM SHOPPING

As already noted, the English Admiralty Court has long exercised a wide jurisdiction in maritime cases, e.g. involving collisions. Foreign plaintiffs often sue in that Court for collisions (or other shipping disputes) occurring abroad. This is no doubt convenient if the suit is, in

---

49 *The Philippine Admiral* [1977] A.C. 373.

50 *The I Congreso del Partido* [1981] 2 Lloyd's Rep. 367.

51 Cmnd 5672 and 5673, Singh (1983) Vol. 4, p. 3096. C. Lewis, *State and Diplomatic Immunity* (2nd edn 1985).

52 Jackson (1985), p. 119.

53 S. 10.

54 S. 15. In relation to the ships and cargoes of the USSR a warrant of arrest must be preceded by a notice to a Soviet consul. However, judgments cannot be enforced against such ships and cargoes: State Immunity (Merchant Shipping) (USSR) Order 1978 (S.I. No. 1524), in accordance with the Protocol to the Treaty on Merchant Navigation, London 3 August 1968.

reality, between insurers based in London. However, defendants sometimes object and apply for the English proceedings to be stayed so that
the action can proceed in the foreign court.[55]

At one time the English courts took the rather chauvinistic view that
the plaintiff could choose English justice – no matter how inconvenient
this was for the defendant. In 1972 Lord Denning went so far as to say,
'You may call this "forum-shopping" if you please, but if the forum is
England, it is a good place to shop in, both for the quality of the goods
and the speed of service'.[56] The House of Lords disagreed with Lord
Denning's approach in that case[57] and has now adopted the doctrine of
forum non conveniens from Scottish law.[58] Essentially this means that the
applicant for a stay of the English proceedings must satisfy the court
that there is another forum (i.e. court) to whose jurisdiction he is
amenable in which justice can be done between the parties at substantially less inconvenience or expense. The stay must not deprive the
plaintiff of a legitimate personal or legal advantage which would be
available to him if he invoked the jurisdiction of the English courts.

Illustration: *The Abidin Daver*[59]

A collision occurred between Turkish and Cuban vessels in the Bosporus. The
Turkish shipowners arrested the Cuban vessel and started a collision action
in a Turkish court. Three months later the Cuban shipowners arrested, in
England, a sister ship of the Turkish vessel and started an action *in rem* in the
Admiralty Court. The Turkish shipowners applied to stay the English action.

Neither party had any connection with England. The collision took place in
Turkish territorial waters. The respective crews were Cuban and Turkish, but
the latter lived in the Bosporus region and the pilot on the Cuban vessel was
Turkish. Court-appointed surveyors reported on the collision within a few
days of its occurrence and the Turkish ship was surveyed in a local Turkish
port. It was more convenient for the Turkish witnesses to give other evidence
in Turkey while, for the Cubans, there was little to choose between England
and Turkey. The Turkish proceedings were no more expensive than the
English. There was no cogent evidence of any possible injustice because of

55 Under the Civil Jurisdiction and Judgments Act 1982, s. 26 a court which does
    submit the dispute to another country can order that property arrested be retained
    as security, or that some equivalent security (e.g., a bank guarantee) be provided.
56 *The Atlantic Star* [1973] 1 Q.B. 364, 382.
57 [1974] A.C. 436, especially per Lord Reid at p. 453: 'that seems to me to recall the
    good old days, the passing of which many may regret, when inhabitants of this
    island felt an innate superiority over those unfortunate enough to belong to other
    races'.
58 *The Abidin Daver* [1984] A.C. 398, *The Spiliada* [1986] 3 W.L.R. 972.
59 *Ibid.*

ideological or political reasons, or the inexperience or inefficiency of the judiciary, or excessive delay, or the unavailability of remedies. The Turks offered to supply security for any Cuban cross-claim.

Held: The court would exercise its discretion to grant a stay as, on balance, Turkey was the most natural and convenient forum.

The jurisdiction in which a tort is committed is, prima facie, the natural forum for the determination of the dispute.[60]

1.8 JURISDICTION CLAUSES

In order to avoid quarrels as to where legal disputes should be heard parties to contracts sometimes agree in advance that the courts of a particular country should have jurisdiction. For obvious reasons such clauses are not really relevant to collision cases where the parties have no existing relationship, but they are common in bills of lading, charterparties, and agreements for ship sale, repair, towage and salvage.

The principles to be applied by the court have been summarized as follows.[61]

(1) Where plaintiffs sue in England in breach of an agreement to refer disputes to a foreign court, and the defendants apply for a stay, the English court, assuming the claim to be otherwise in its jurisdiction, is not bound to grant a stay, but has a discretion whether to do so or not. (2) The discretion would be exercised by granting a stay unless strong cause for not doing so is shown. (3) The burden of proving such strong cause is on the plaintiffs. (4) In exercising its discretion the court should take into account all the circumstances of the particular case. (5) In particular, but without prejudice to (4), the following matters, where they arise, may properly be regarded: (a) In what country the evidence on the issues of fact is situated, or more readily available, and the effect of that on the relative convenience and expense of trial as between the English and foreign courts. (b) Whether the law of the foreign court applies and, if so, whether it differs from English law in any material respects. (c) With what country either party is connected and how closely. (d) whether the defendants generally desire trial in the foreign country, or are only seeking procedural advantages. (e) Whether the

---

60 *The Albaforth* [1984] 2 Lloyd's Rep. 91. That assumption may be easily displaced in a case where the tort is committed by a member of the crew on board a ship as it passed through territorial waters when neither crew nor ship have any connection with the country in whose waters the ship was then being navigated; see *The Forum Craftsman* [1985] 1 Lloyd's Rep. 291.

61 *The El Amria* [1981] 2 Lloyd's Rep. 119, *per* Brandon LJ at pp. 123–4, approving his earlier statement in *The Eleftheria* [1969] 1 Lloyd's Rep. 237.

plaintiffs would be prejudiced by having to sue in the foreign court because they would: (i) be deprived of security for their claim; (ii) be unable to enforce any judgment obtained; (iii) be faced with a time bar not applicable in England; or (iv) for political, social, religious or other reasons be unlikely to get a fair trial.'

It will be noted that many of the factors are similar to those discussed in relation to *forum non conveniens*. The essential point is that the court will normally uphold the choice of the parties,[62] unless there is some good practical reason, or it is prevented from so doing by law.[63]

1.9   CHOICE OF LAW CLAUSES

Similarly, contracting parties from different states may wish to avoid disputes about the 'conflict of laws', i.e. as to whose law is to apply.[64] They may specify which is to be the 'proper law' of the contract, i.e. the law that governs the interpretation, validity and mode of performance of the contract and the consequences of breaching it.[65] English law gives the parties to a contract a wide liberty to choose the law by which the contract is to be governed.[66] Assuming that the choice is bona fide, legal and not contrary to public policy it will generally be upheld.[67]

Where the parties have not made an express choice of law the court will try to ascertain their intentions from the contract and will apply the system of law with which the transaction has its closest and most real connection.[68]

62 See, e.g. *The Forum Craftsman* [1985] 1 Lloyd's Rep. 291.
63 E.g., *The Morviken* [1983] 1 Lloyd's Rep. 1: cf. *The Benarty* [1984] 2 Lloyd's Rep. 244. See generally Section 10.2.1, *infra*. For the effect of a jurisdiction clause in a bill of lading and the EEC Jurisdiction Convention (fn. 12, *supra*.), see *Partenreederei Ms. Tilly Russ* v. *Haven Vervoerbedrijf Nova N.V.* [1985] 3 W.L.R 179.
64 For this complex subject see Jackson (1985) Chapter 19 and J.H.C. Morris (ed.), *Dicey and Morris on the Conflict of Laws*, 10th edn, (1980).
65 *Amin Rasheed Shipping Corporation* v. *Kuwait Insurance Co.* [1984] A.C. 50, 60.
66 *Ibid.*, at p. 61.
67 *Vita Food Products Inc.* v. *Unus Shipping Co. Ltd* [1939] A.C. 277; cf. *The El Amria* [1981] 2 Lloyd's Rep. 119 (fn. 61, *supra*). But note the effect of the Carriage of Goods by Sea Act 1971 (Section 10.2, *infra* and the cases cited in fn. 63, *supra*) and the Unfair Contract Terms Act 1977, s. 27.
68 *Compagnie d'Armement Maritime S.A.* v. *Compagnie Tunisienne de Navigation S.A.* [1971] A.C. 572, *Amin Rasheed Shipping Corporation* v. *Kuwait Insurance Co.* [1984] A.C. 50, *Coast Lines* v. *Hudig and Veder Chartering N.V.* [1972] 2 Q.B. 34. For the proper law of torts, see Jackson (1985) pp. 334–339.

2

INTERNATIONAL LAW
AND SHIPS

SHIPS operating on international voyages will pass by and visit many different states. States exercise sovereign rights in what they claim as territorial waters and ships must obey the laws of those states while in such areas. This takes us into the realm of international law, that body of law which regulates the relations between states. When a Convention is agreed, states assume rights and obligations between themselves. However, a convention signed by the UK Government generally has no direct effect in UK national law until there has been an act of ratification, or accession, *and* the Convention has been incorporated by statute.

2.1 THE LAW OF THE SEA

Four Conventions on the International Law of the Sea were agreed at Geneva in 1958. The UK is a party to these but in 1982 a UN Conference on the Law of the Sea (UNCLOS III) produced a new Convention after many years work and much dispute. This Convention (which to confuse matters is also referred to as UNCLOS) was an attempt to codify the international law of the sea. It contains some 320 articles plus annexes and is too long and complex to discuss here.[1] However, many of its non-controversial provisions may already be regarded as customary international law. International law recognizes that the high seas are no one's domain, that no state exercises sovereign rights there. For instance, Art. 87 of UNCLOS preserves the freedom of the high seas.

---

1 See Singh (1983) Vol. 4, p.2671. For further reading see D. O'Connell, *The International Law of the Sea*, Vol. II (1984) and R.R. Churchill and A.V. Lowe, *The Law of the Sea*, (1982). The existing 1958 Geneva Conventions are on the Continental Shelf, the High Seas, Fishing and Conservation of the Living Resources of the High Seas, Territorial Sea and Contiguous Zone: see Singh (1983) Vol. 4, p. 2626.

On the other hand, in the sea close to the shore, the littoral (i.e. coastal) state has sovereign rights; these waters are known as territorial waters.

In the years following the 1939 – 45 war the area of the high seas has shrunk, not from natural causes, but through the political acts of man. The extent of territorial waters was never defined by international treaty, but most states used to claim a three-mile limit, thought to have been determined by the range of early shore-based guns. In more modern times, wider limits have been claimed, most states settling for twelve miles, some for less and a few for considerably more. Article 3 of UNCLOS, for instance, allows states to establish the breadth of the territorial sea up to a limit not exceeding 12 nautical miles. So far, the UK has maintained the three-mile limit, although in 1987 a Territorial Sea Bill is expected to extend it to twelve miles.[2]

But that is not the only modern encroachment on the high seas, for countries depending on fishing are anxious to reserve a wider exclusive area to their fishing fleets, so as to conserve stocks and protect the livelihood of their fishermen. Of even greater importance has been the discovery of mineral resources on and below the sea bed, which littoral states are anxious to exploit. Most states agreed that there was a need to recognize an exclusive economic zone, extending beyond the territorial sea, in whose waters a coastal state has rights and duties in relation to natural resources. Article 57 of UNCLOS fixed the zone at up to 200 nautical miles.

In the exclusive economic zone there is the same freedom of navigation as on the high seas.[3] However, the Convention recognized that the increasing use of offshore installations, such as oil platforms, meant that coastal states may need to restrict navigation in the interests of safety. Article 60 allows coastal states to establish reasonable safety zones (not

---

2 Territorial Waters Jurisdiction Act 1878; Territorial Waters Order in Council (15 September 1964), Territorial Waters (Amendment) Order in Council (23 May 1979). Second Report from the Expenditure Committee 1978-9 H.C. 105-I, and the Government's non-committal response, Cmnd 7525 (April 1979): G. Marston, *The Marginal Seabed: United Kingdom Legal Practice* (1981). Pirate radio stations broadcasting within UK territorial waters may commit an offence against the Wireless Telegraphy Act 1949, s. 1; see *Post Office* v. *Estuary Radio Ltd* [1967] 3 All E.R. 663. However, the Marine &c., Broadcasting Act 1967, s. 4 makes it an offence to facilitate illegal broadcasting by ships on the high seas, e.g. by supplying goods or equipment to them.

3 Art. 58.

exceeding 500 metres) around them. The UK makes extensive use of such zones in North Sea oil and gas exploration.[4]

Even more ambitious claims are being advanced, as technological development makes their realization more and more possible, namely, the exploitation of the mineral resources in an even wider area, the continental margin. This is the comparatively steep slope leading down from the continental shelf, until it meets the more gentle rise from the deep ocean, the abyssal floor, which some geologists actually include in the continental margin. These claims are resisted, in particular, by land-locked and continental shelf-locked states. They argue that resources in those areas, and those beyond, are the common heritage of mankind and should be adminstered for the common good by an international sea-bed authority.

It was over this exploitation issue that the greatest disputes occurred at UNCLOS because some Western countries, and the USA in particular, were anxious to preserve their existing investments in ocean-floor prospecting. Land-locked and continental shelf states, on the other hand, argued that the sea-bed and its subsoil should be available to all.[5] Article 136 of UNCLOS did declare these areas to be the common heritage of mankind and, in Art. 156, authorized the establishment of an International Sea-bed Authority to administer their resources.[6] But the precise future of the Convention must be in some doubt because of the objections of certain industrialized countries such as the USA and the UK. However, the Deep Sea Mining (Temporary Provisions) Act 1981[7] prohibits the unlicensed deep sea exploration or mining of hard

---

4 Originally under the Continental Shelf Act 1964 and now under the Oil and Gas (Enterprise) Act 1982, ss. 21-23, 37. The Offshore Installations (Safety Zones) Order 1982 (S.I. No. 1606) designates the particular installations. Further orders have added or removed zones according to the movements of the installations concerned, e.g. 1985 (S.I. Nos 690, 765). See also the Continental Shelf (Designation of Additional Areas) Orders, e.g. 1982 (S.I. No 1072), designating areas of the UK continental shelf in which UK rights with respect to the sea-bed and their natural resources are exercisable and the Continental Shelf (Jurisdiction) Order 1980 (S.I. No. 184), amended 1982 (S.I. No. 1523), assigning to those areas the appropriate jurisdiction and civil law of England and Wales, Scotland or Northern Ireland.

5 For further reading in this huge and complex area, T.G. Kronmiller, *The Lawfulness of Deep Seabed Mining*, 3 Vols 1980; R. Platzoder, *Third United Nations Conference on the Law of the Sea: Documents*, VII Vols, 1982-4.

6 Art. 186 also provided for disputes to be settled by an international tribunal on the law of the sea.

7 In force 25 January 1982. Deep Sea Mining (Temporary Provisions) Act 1981 (Appointed Day) Order 1982 (S.I. No. 52).

mineral resources[8] by UK nationals who are resident in the UK. The Secretary of State can issue exploration or exploitation licences, although the latter can only be granted for periods after 1 January 1988.[9] The licences can contain a wide variety of terms and conditions relating to, e.g., health and safety, processing of minerals, waste material, samples, speed of operations and protection of the environment.[10] Not surprisingly the Government wants to increase its revenue! The licences may require payments to be made to the Treasury[11] and the holder of an exploitation licence must pay a Deep Sea Mining Levy on minerals he has recovered.[12] The sums are paid into a Deep Sea Mining Fund. This will be held open until 1992 in case a Deep Sea Bed Organization is established under UNCLOS and accepted by the UK. If it is, the money in the Fund may be paid over to that Organization: if no such organization is designated by the Secretary of State then the Fund will be wound up and the money paid into central funds.[13]

It is possible to recognize licences granted by designated reciprocating countries.[14] For countries which adopt discriminatary practices against UK ships the Secretary of State may impose restrictions in the term of licences granted to ships registered in those countries.[15] There are powers to appoint inspectors to oversee licensees' operations.[16] It is

8 That is, deposits of modules containing elements of manganese, nickel, cobalt, copper, phosphorus and molybdenum; see s. 1(6)

9 S. 2

10 Ss. 2, 5. The Deep Sea Mining (Exploration Licences) Regulations 1984 (S.I. No. 1230) which came into operation on 3 September 1984 provide for the form and content of the exploration licences. They are to last for an initial period of 10 years, with the possibility of 5-year extensions. There are a set of model clauses which shall be included in the licence, unless the Secretary of State has some reason to alter them. The clauses set out in more detail the obligations of the licensee and include an indemnity to protect the Secretary of State from third party claims and an arbitration clause. There is a continuous obligation to monitor and record environmental conditions.

11 S. 2(3)(g), Deep Sea Mining (Exploration Licences) (Applications) Regulations 1982 (S.I. No. 58). Regulation 5 of the 1984 Regulations (S.I. No. 1230) requires £15 000 and £25 000 to be paid one and six years respectively after its grant. A 5-year extension will cost another £25 000.

12 Equal to 3.75% of the value of minerals recovered or, if that is impossible to calculate, 0.75% of the value of the specific elements recovered (such as manganese, etc.), s. 9.

13 S. 10. The Act may also be repealed by order, s. 18.

14 S. 3. The Deep Sea Mining (Reciprocating Countries) Order 1985 (S.I. No. 2000), when in force, designates France, the Federal Republic of Germany, Italy, Japan and the USA.

15 S. 8.

16 For which, of course, a fee must be paid, see 1984 (S.I. No. 1230).

an offence to conduct unlicensed operations,[17] interfere with licensed operations,[18] or to disclose information received under the Act.[19]

It is interesting to observe that, long before the resources of the sea-bed were thought of, the distinguished American naval historian, Alfred Thayer Mahan, described the sea 'from the political and social point of view [as] a great highway; or better, perhaps, [as] a wide common, over which men may pass in all directions, but on which some well-worn paths [exist] … called trade routes'.[20]

Even within the territorial waters where innocent passage of ships is allowed, states can, and do, impose restrictions to ensure safety. For instance, the United States Ports and Waterways Safety Act 1972 imposed on all tankers entering United States waters the duty to equip themselves with Loran C navigational gear; without it the coastguard would turn them away. Canada established the Eastern Canada Traffic System (ECAREF), under which ships arriving at the twelve-mile limit had to report to the coastguard such matters as the nature of cargo they were carrying, particulars relating to the master of the vessel and defects in hull and navigational equipment, so that serious matters could be put right before the ship entered territorial waters.[21]

Students of the law of merchant shipping require no detailed knowledge of the international law of the sea, although they must know that such rules exist. But that is not the end of the matter. Without special rules a ship, while at sea, would find itself in a legal vacuum. To fill that vacuum, states give their ships a nationality, the outward sign of which is a ship's right to sail under the national flag, so as to be recognized as belonging to a particular state and entitled, for instance, in an emergency to appeal for help to naval vessels of its state.

2.2 NATIONALITY

Since the ship is accorded a nationality it follows that, even in another state's territorial waters, those on board live under the law of the state whose flag the ship flies. Births, deaths and marriages on board rank as events happening in the country whose nationality the ship is accorded. Again, offences committed on board a ship are triable by the courts of

17 S. 1.
18 S. 4.
19 S. 13.
20 *The Influence of Sea Power upon History,* 1965 edition, p. 25; first published in 1890.
21 [1977] 3 L.M.C.L.Q. 463.

the country of the ship's nationality and according to the criminal law of that country.

British ships are in a peculiar position. Strictly, there is no British criminal law – England, Scotland and, to a certain extent, Northern Ireland living under different systems, which the Act of Union has not merged. But before the Union, the English Admiralty exercised a wide jurisdiction over crimes committed on board ships at sea, not only on what is now called the high seas, but also in 'all waters below low-water mark where great ships can go',[22] in other words, also in the territorial waters of another state. The criminal law applied was the English law and this continues to this day in respect of all British ships. Thus a theft committed on board a British ship, wherever its home port, is judged under the Theft Act 1968 which, according to s. 36, does not apply to Scotland or Northern Ireland.

Of course, littoral states can claim concurrent jurisdiction in respect of offences committed on ships while sailing in territorial waters, but unless interests of the state are affected no jurisdiction is claimed in respect of offences which affect only life on board. Littoral states also assume jurisdiction in the exclusive economic zone when ships disregard its exclusiveness, e.g. by fishing there.

Seeing that important events of legal significance occurring on board a British ship are dealt with according to British law it is not surprising that s. 1 of the Merchant Shipping Act 1894 provides that a British ship or a share therein can be owned only by British subjects by birth or by naturalization. Likewise, such persons alone are entitled to have a beneficial interest in the ship, e.g. as beneficiaries under a trust. Defining a British subject can be very difficult as the British Nationality Act 1981 mainly uses the term citizenship.[23]

Corporations such as companies, incorporated under the Companies Act 1985, present some difficulties, and these have gained in importance as the ownership of ships has passed from individuals to shipping companies. The nationality of such companies is determined by their

---

22　The above quotation is taken from *Oteri* v. *The Queen* [1977] 1 Lloyd's Rep. 105, at p. 108, a Privy Council case which anyone requiring more detailed knowledge of this subject should consult, together with the other cases cited there.

23　And see s. 37(4). Under s. 51(1) it seems that the definitions of a British subject (for the 1894 Act) will differ in relation to any time before or after the commencement of the 1981 Act. For the former period, reference must be made to a person's status under the old legislation (British Nationality Act 1948, s. 1, Commonwealth Immigrants Act 1962, s. 21(2)): for the latter period the British subject is a person who has the status of 'Commonwealth Citizen' under the 1981 Act. See I. MacDonald, N. Blake, *The New Nationality Law,* (1982).

registered offices – by the law under which they are incorporated. Section 1(d) of the Merchant Shipping Act 1894 prescribes that companies, in order to qualify for the ownership of British ships, must not only be incorporated, but must also have their principal place of business within Her Majesty's Dominions. It was held during the Great War, 1914-18, that, where a shipping company was registered in England under the Companies Act, but its affairs were directed from Hamburg by the chairman of the Board of Directors who owned the majority of the shares, the principal place of business was in Hamburg, and the ship was forfeited as enemy property.[24] But the mere holding of shares in a British shipping company by a foreigner does not disqualify the company, for the company is a legal entity independent of its shareholders.[25] Were it otherwise, shipping shares would be impossible investments for foreigners, and the legal situation would become uncertain. Still, in time of war British courts have endeavoured to look behind the screen, and have condemned as prizes ships owned by non-enemy companies, but controlled by enemy shareholders.[26] If any foreigner acquires voluntarily as legal or beneficial owner a British ship or a share therein,[27] he forfeits his interest.

A British ship alone is entitled to fly the national flag, and where this flag is used otherwise, the ship is forfeited.[28] Only where a foreign ship hoists the British flag for the purpose of avoiding capture by the enemy or by some foreign ship of war exercising belligerent rights does the law allow a temporary exception. Moreover, British ships are bound to show the British flag when requested by one of Her Majesty's ships, when entering or leaving a foreign port, and if of 50 tons gross tonnage or over also when entering or leaving a British port.[29] The necessary complement of this provision is the prohibition of concealment of British, or the assumption of a foreign, character.[30] Contravention is punished by forfeiture of the ship, and fine or imprisonment of the master if he commits, or is privy to, the offence.

24 *The Polzeath* [1916] P. 117, 241.
25 *Salomon* v. *Salomon* [1897] A.C. 22. Note that the British Fishing Boats Act 1983 restricts the operations of certain British fishing boats if less than 75% of the crew are British citizens. This was partly to deal with attempts by foreign nationals to evade fishing restrictions: also the British Fishing Boats Order 1983 (S.I. No 482)
26 *The St Tudno* [1916] P. 291; *The Hamborn* [1919] A.C. 993; *Kuenigl* v. *Donnersmarck* [1955] 1 All E.R. 46, deals with an English company acquiring enemy character.
27 As distinct from a share in a shipping company.
28 Merchant Shipping Act 1894, s. 69; on precedure, see s. 76.
29 Merchant Shipping Act 1894, ss. 73, 74.
30 Merchant Shipping Act 1894, s. 70

2.3 FLAG DISCRIMINATION

Every country wants its shipping industry to thrive, a goal often
attainable to the desired extent only by hurting the shipping industries
of other countries. They may, for instance, charge higher harbour dues
to foreign vessels than they do to their own, or they may fix quotas for
imports and exports to be carried exclusively by their own ships.[31] In
this way shipowners can become involved in trade warfare which they
cannot survive without the help of their own governments. England
and the Netherlands engaged in such undesirable practices in the seventeenth century, and Spain earlier. Nowadays we find countries doing so
among those wishing to build up a merchant fleet of their own. In the
United Kingdom the Government has power to counter such flag
discrimination, if it threatens to damage or in fact damages British
shipping.[32] Traders may be required to give information on the basis of
which appropriate action to protect British sea carriers can be decided
upon.

On a more general level, the UK has acted to counter legislation in
other countries which try to control international trade outside their
territories to the detriment of UK trading interests. The legislation is
largely aimed at the USA and the extra territorial effects of its anti-trust
(anti-competitive) laws.[33] Under the Protection of Trading Interests
Act 1980 the Government has power to prohibit compliance with
foreign requirements, prohibitions[34] or orders for the discovery of
documents.[35] Failure to comply with the Secretary of State's requirements or directions is an offence.[36] Certain foreign judgments for
punitive multiple damages are unenforceable in the UK.[37] Moreover, if,
e.g., a UK company has to pay multiple damages in a foreign court
then it can recover in the UK any excess over the real compensation it
should have paid.[38]

These are rather extreme measures for a state to adopt, and may have
more of a diplomatic rather than a legal significance as the UK is trying

31 Singh and Colinvaux (1967), Chapter 11.
32 Merchant Shipping Act 1974, ss. 14, 15, Sched. 4, Merchant Shipping Act, 1979,
    s. 40. See the Merchant Shipping (Protection of Shipping and Trading Interests)
    (USSR) Order 1986 (S.I. No. 310).
33 The Act replaces the Shipping Contracts and Commercial Documents Act 1964.
34 S. 1.
35 S. 2.
36 S. 3. The powers were used recently in *British Airways Board* v *Laker Airways Ltd*
    [1984] 3 All E.R. 39.
37 S. 5. Multiple damages are where the real compensation is increased by, e.g., two
    or three times as a kind of deterrent, see s. 5(3).
38 S. 6.

to encourage the USA to change the law. The matter is not unimportant to the shipping industry, as major UK container operators were fined nearly US$2 million for anti-trust offences in 1979.[39]

2.4 CODE OF CONDUCT FOR LINER CONFERENCES

The 1970s saw a growth in the movement for many less developed countries to participate in world shipping. The United Nations Conference on Trade and Development (UNCTAD) produced, in 1974, the Convention on a Code of Conduct for Liner Conferences. 'Conferences' are groups of shipowners who come together to provide a regular cargo service in which there are uniform freight rates and shared sailings. Outsiders are often excluded from a particular trade by means of loyalty agreements given to regular customers of the conference.[40]

The UNCTAD Liner Code sought to share the right to carry cargo between two countries by giving their shipping fleets an equal share of the freight and traffic generated by that trade: 20 per cent of the trade could be left for third country shipping lines, the so-called 'cross-traders' (the 40:40:20 formula). The Code caused some consternation to British shipping companies, as so much of their earnings was from cross-trading. In 1979 the EEC produced a compromise[41] to ensure that there was no discrimination between the shipping lines of EEC member states and certain other OECD countries while at the same time granting developing countries the full benefit of the Code.[42] The UK passed the Merchant Shipping (Liner Conferences) Act 1982 in order to implement the Code's provisions, subject to the EEC reservations. The Code entered into force on 6 October 1983: the Act was brought into force on 14 March 1985,[43] but the implementation of the Code has been

39 *US* v. *Atlantic Container Line Ltd* 1979 Trade Reg. Rep. (Trans Binder) 45 079 (Cases 2705-6).
40 See Herman (1983).
41 Council Regulation (EEC) No. 954/79, of 15 May 1979 (O.J. 1979 L121/1). The Regulation is directly applicable in the UK by virtue of the European Communities Act 1972, s. 2. The Regulation encouraged EEC member states to ratify the Code, but subject to a number of reservations made in the Regulation; e.g. it rejects the 40:40:20 formula as between member states.
42 Herman (1983), pp. 188-192.
43 Merchant Shipping (Liner Conferences) Act 1982 (Commencement) Order 1985 (S.I. No. 182). See Singh (1983) Vol. 4, p 3229.

achieved by the Merchant Shipping (Liner Conferences) (Mandatory Provisions) Regulations 1985.[44]

The 1982 Act applies to conferences based in the UK which serve the trade between contracting parties to the Code. It also applies to conferences not based in the UK which serve the trade between the UK and another contracting party.[45] The Secretary of State is given wide powers to make regulations to clarify or supplement the Code[46] and indeed, the 1985 Regulations do so.

The 1985 Regulations take account of the EEC compromise and list provisions contained in the Code which are to be treated as mandatory. The provisions are enforceable either as statutory duties or as implied terms in contracts. The Regulations specify the persons to whom and by whom the various statutory duties are owed. The Code itself regulates many conference practices such as loyalty arrangements, freight rates and surcharges.[47] But, for instance the Regulations make Art. 16.1 of the Code a mandatory provision; there is a statutory duty, enforceable by shippers against conferences, to impose surcharges for sudden increases in costs only as a temporary measure. Likewise, the rights given to a shipper, under Art. 8 of the Code, to use non-conference shipping (if a conference line fails to provide a ship on time) are made implied terms of any contract containing a loyalty arrangement between the conference and the shipper.

The Code provides for mandatory 'conciliation' in the event of disputes between conferences, shipping lines or shippers: but the 'recommendations' of the conciliators are only binding if they have been accepted by the parties involved.[48] A binding recommendation is enforceable in the UK unless, e.g., it was obtained by fraud.[49] Where proceedings arise out of the Code, in respect of damage or loss suffered by any person, the liability of the conference member must be in proportion to his responsibility.[50] No legal proceedings can be brought

---

44 (S.I. No. 406); also the Merchant Shipping (Liner Conferences) (Conditions for Recognition) Regulations 1985 (S.I. No. 405), which lay down the conditions for recognition of shipping lines and shippers organizations. These Regulations came into force in December 1985.

45 S. 2.

46 Ss. 2,3; and also to restrict the application of Code for lack of reciprocity by other states, s. 4.

47 Arts 7-17.

48 Art. 37.

49 Merchant Shipping (Liner Conferences) Act 1982, s. 9.

50 Ss. 5-9. Thus one member cannot be sued for the losses caused by the conference as a whole. Under s. 7(3) a court must stay English proceedings if the conciliation procedure has not been followed.

in the UK after two years from the date when the claim arose or, if later, six months from the end of conciliation proceedings.[51] As long ago as 1891 an excluded shipowner failed in an attempt to have a conference's activities declared in restraint of trade.[52] Section 11 of the 1982 Act excludes the application of restrictive trade practices law to most conference agreements.

51 S. 8.
52 *Mogul Steamship Company* v. *McGregor, Gow & Co.* [1892] A.C. 25.

3

REGISTRATION OF SHIPS

3.1 INTRODUCTION

3.1.1 THE REGISTER

THE same reason for which ownership of Britain ships is limited to British subjects or corporations makes it imperative that a record of British ships be kept. To achieve this purpose the Register of British Ships has been created. This is used as evidence of the right to fly the flag of the State as well as of the right of ownership and of mortgages,[1] in much the same way as is the case with the registration of title to land.[2]

Ship registers are kept by the Registrar of British Ships. For any port in the UK the Registrars are any officers (whether at that port or elsewhere) appointed for that purpose by the Commissioner of Customs and Excise (CCE), elsewhere in the British Isles corresponding officers; in overseas possessions it is usually the Governor.[3] Registrars are protected against actions for damages on account of their acts or omissions in their capacity of Registrar, unless they are guilty of negligence or a wilful act,[4] a somewhat cryptic provision, for it is

---

1 *Liverpool Borough Bank* v. *Turner* (1860) 29 L.J. Ch., at p. 830. Registration is not conclusive as to ownership, e.g., *The Vanessa Ann* [1985] 1 Lloyd's Rep. 549.

2 Compulsory registration of ships dates back to Oliver Cromwell's Navigation Acts. Their purpose was restricting commerce by sea to English ships, a policy in line with the seventeenth century economic doctrine of mercantilism, also practised in the Netherlands and in France. When this policy was abandoned the register of ships was retained for the purposes set out in the text. For an international survey, see L. Hagberg (ed.), *Handbook on Marine Law: Registration of Vessels, Mortgages on Vessels*, Vols III-A, III-B (1983).

3 Merchant Shipping Act 1894, s. 4(1) and (2). Merchant Shipping Act 1983, s. 6. In the Isle of Man it is an officer of the Isle of Man Harbour Board, as appointed by the Governor in Council, Isle of Man Act 1979, the Isle of Man (Transfer of Functions) Order 1980 (S.I. No. 399). See M.S. Notice No. M. 1162, H.M. Customs & Excise Notice No. 382.

4 Merchant Shipping Act 1894, s. 4(3).

difficult to imagine liability in the absence of negligence or intention. There is no relevant case law.

Register books are open for inspection against payment of a fee fixed by the CCE.[5] Thus anybody who desires to deal with the owner of the ship, for instance, as a prospective buyer or mortgagee, can satisfy himself about the property or encumbrances. If this facility is to be of any use all relevant matters must be contained in the register, and the Act provides that the owner or owners and the ship itself be most carefully described.

The registration of hovercraft, or air-cushion vehicles, which can operate on the water or be airborne over water or land is effected, like that of aircraft, with the Secretary of State.[6] Application for registration is made to the Civil Aviation Authority.[7] In the field of private law, the Carriage of Goods by Sea Act 1971 applies to the carriage of goods by hovercraft, and the Carriage by Air Act 1961 to the carriage of passengers and their luggage. These craft are also subject to Admiralty jurisdiction as provided for in the Supreme Court Act 1981.[8] All British fishing boats must be entered in a separate fishing boat register, unless exempted.[9]

3.1.2   FLAGS OF CONVENIENCE

Several states allow, indeed encourage, registration of foreign-owned ships, this being a source of revenue. Notably some Central American and African states attract foreign shipowners; taxes there are lower than in their own countries, and labour laws and safety requirements less strict, allowing ships to be run at substantially lower costs, which makes them more competitive in the international freight market. Accordingly many foreign shipowners choose a *marriage de convenance*, as it were, and flags of those states are indeed called flags of convenience. Because of lower safety standards those ships, which often

5 Merchant Shipping Act 1894, s. 64(1).
6 Hovercraft Act 1968, s. 1; Hovercraft (General) Order 1972 (S.I. No. 674), Art. 5; Civil Aviation Act 1982, s. 100; and see Section 18.4, *infra*.
7 Air Navigation Order 1980 (S.I. No. 1965); amended 1982 (S.I. No. 161), 1983 (S.I. No. 1905), 1984 (S.I. No. 1988), 1985 (S.I. No. 458).
8 Ss. 20, 24, Hovercraft (Application of Enactments) Order 1972 (S.I. No. 971); amended 1978 (S.I. No. 1913), 1979 (S.I. No. 1309), 1982 (S.I. No. 715), 1983 (S.I. No. 769).
9 Merchant Shipping Act 1894, Part IV, Merchant Shipping (Fishing Boats Registry) Order 1981 (S.I. No. 740), M.S. Notice No. M. 1100; British Fishing Boats Act 1983, British Fishing Boats Order 1983 (S.I. No. 482).

never touch their home ports, have tended to have an unsatisfactory casualty record, but some flag of convenience states have taken action to correct this shortcoming, which has caused anxiety.

Both Art. 5 of the 1958 Geneva High Seas Convention and Art. 91 of UNCLOS 1982 recognize that there should exist a 'genuine link' between the ship and the state. A UN body, UNCTAD (United Nations Conference on Trade and Development) has been considering the meaning of 'genuine link' for many years. The aim was to come up with some sort of international agreement which would regulate the activities of some of the countries with 'open' registries. These countries, along with many Western countries, were concerned that any mandatory convention might interfere with their sovereign rights.[10] In February 1986 final agreement was reached on the UN Convention on Conditions of Registration of Ships.[11] This lays down basic principles on matters such as: the functions of national administrations; the identification and accountability of shipowners; manning; the control of shipowning companies and ships; the details to be recorded on the Register; the position of bareboat charters and joint ventures. One of the most important themes of the Convention is the need for flag states to exercise effective jurisdiction and control over their ships. This could help to reduce fraud and increase safety. Article 10 tries to introduce a 'genuine link' by requiring owners to be incorporated, or to have a principal place of business in the territory of the flag state. It also requires local representatives who are able to meet the owners' legal responsibilities. Flag states should ensure that the owners can meet their financial obligations, e.g. by checking that insurance has been arranged.

3.1.3 SMALL SHIPS REGISTER

Because of the complication and expense of the registry system, s. 5 of the Merchant Shipping Act 1983 set up a separate register for small ships, i.e. (non-fishing) vessels which are under 24 metres in length. Such small ships are usually exempt from registry under the 1894 Act, but they must be owned wholly by persons qualified to be owners of British ships. Regulations establishing the Register have been made[12]

10 PC/3, pp. 13-17, 18 May 1983.
11 TD/RS/CONF/L.19, 7 February 1986. This Convention is not yet in force. And see Section 9.4.6(b), *infra*.
12 Merchant Shipping (Small Ships Register) Regulations 1983 (S.I. No. 1470); M.S. Notice No. M. 1162.

and it is run by the Royal Yachting Association on behalf of the DoT. Applicants must supply details of the ship (including a description along with the overall length and name) and the name and address of the owner.[13] The Register will record these details as well as the registration number of the ship, the date of registration and date of expiry of registration.[14] The Certificate of Registration is valid for five years.[15] Any existing registration under Part I of the 1894 Act can be closed, provided that there is no registered mortgage or certificate of mortgage or sale affecting the ship, or a share in it.[16] Within one month of registration the registered owner must mark the registration number after the letters 'SSR'.[17] Failure to make or maintain the mark is an offence.[18] There are also offences for making false statements to gain registration or for using the certificate with intent to deceive.[19]

3.2   CO-OWNERSHIP

As with all objects of property commanding a certain value and involving a certain risk, co-ownership in ships is a familiar phenomenon. This may arise either by a number of persons acquiring a ship by purchase, or by inheriting it together, in which case we speak of acquisition by operation of law.

In the case of ships, moreover, ownership in common takes a somewhat unusual form, since each ship is notionally divided into sixty-four parts.[20] This is an arbitrary figure, but it was found practically convenient; possibly the reason for this limitation was to prevent the Register of Ships from becoming too unwieldy and to simplify dealings with the ship. There is, of course, nothing to prevent a person from owning several, or even all, parts of a ship. A corporation may be registered as owner by its corporate name[21] and, apart from small vessels, it is now customary for shipowners to form a limited company,

13 Reg. 3(2).
14 Reg. 3(5).
15 Reg. 5, although it may be renewed.
16 Reg. 3(6).
17 Reg. 4.
18 Reg. 9.
19 Ibid.
20 Merchant Shipping Act 1894, s. 5(i).
21 Merchant Shipping Act 1894, s. 5(v). The Companies Act 1985, Part VII, Chapter II, ss. 257–266 and Schedule 9 make particular provisions for the accounts of certain special categories of companies, such as shipping companies.

so as to restrict their risk still further than is already provided for by the
Merchant Shipping Act 1894.[22] For this reason it will suffice to give
quite a brief description of the position of individuals as shipowners.

It is provided that not more than sixty-four persons, individuals or
corporations, shall be registered as owners, or one person for each part
or share. Though the name may lead to an opposite conclusion the
several owners do not necessarily constitute a partnership. They need
not, in the words of s. 1(1) of the Partnership Act 1890, 'carry on a
business in common with a view to profit'. If no partnership exists the
position of part-owners of a ship is much the same, apart from the
question of liability, as that of shareholders in a limited company. Just as
normally only one person is registered as holder of any one share in a
company, only one person shall be registered as holder of a ship's part.
This restriction is a matter of convenience in order to simplify transfers
of ships. A ship is not a corporation like a company and, when it is
transferred to another owner, all part-owners must join in the conveyance, each part-owner conveying his part; clearly, the Act, by
setting up the limitations just stated, simplifies this procedure.

If two or more persons do own one part they are regarded not as
several owners of a portion, but as joint owners of the undivided part,
and for purposes of transfer are regarded as one person.[23] It is possible to
be joint owners of the whole of, or a single share in, a ship. But the
register will not take notice of more than five joint owners[24] and in no
case will equities, such as rights arising from trusts, find a place on it.[25]

At this stage it is convenient to notice the position *inter se* of the part-
owners. Though they are not necessarily partners with regard to the
ship permanently, they may, and generally will be, partners in any
individual adventure;[26] this entails their sharing in any profit or loss,
and their obligation to honour liabilities incurred by the managing
owner or ship's husband within the scope of his authority. The managing owner, who need not himself own a part but may be a servant, must
be registered, but such registration serves only for the convenience of
public authorities, who naturally cannot make sixty-four part-owners
responsible for the manifold obligations of a public character which a
ship must comply with in the course of its career. In the absence of
additional evidence, registration does not amount to a holding-out of

22 It is customary for the company to own all 64 shares. If part interests are required
    this is usually achieved by the allocation of shares in the company.
23 S. 5(iii) and (iv).
24 This may arise, e.g., on transmission: see Merchant Shipping Act 1894, s. 27.
25 Merchant Shipping Act 1894, ss. 5(ii) and 56.
26 Partnership Act 1890, s. 2(1).

the managing owner as the part-owner's agent generally.[27] The questions to be asked in each case are: did the owners hold out the person as their agent or was there in fact authority?[28] The managing owner may pledge the credit of those co-owners who have appointed him, or have assented to his appointment, or held him out. But this authority is limited. The managing owner may only pledge the credit of the co-owners for necessary repairs where communication is impossible. He may also procure charters and make contracts to carry them out, but he has no power to alter or cancel charters. In principle, all part-owners must consent to a voyage but, as this may unduly hamper the profitable employment of the ship, the law allows the majority to employ the ship 'upon any probable design',[29] but excludes in such a case the minority from any share in the profit and loss of the voyage, and the Admiralty Court will secure the dissentients' rights by a bond to be given by the majority part-owners either to restore the ship in safety or to pay them the value of their shares.[30] Besides there is nothing to prohibit a dissentient part-owner from selling his part, if he can.

3.3 NAME

In addition to the names of the owners, the name of the ship must be registered, so that it can be identified, and the Department of Transport (DoT)[31] can refuse to register a name that is identical with, or similar to, that of another British ship, and so cause confusion.[32] At the same time, once the name of a ship is registered, the owner has no property right in it, and when the register is closed because the ship is lost or broken up the name becomes free for anybody's use. Thus an owner anxious to retain the name for future use must resort to a subterfuge. The Cunard-White Star Company did that in 1936. In those great days of transatlantic passenger traffic many ships were household words and enjoyed the special affection of passengers. The liner *Mauretania* was one of those great ships, and when her age made breaking up advisable, Cunard, to

---

27 *Frazer* v. *Cuthbertson* (1880) 6 Q.B.D. 93, 97 *et seq.*
28 *Ibid.*; *Barker* v. *Highley* (1863) 15 C.B. N.S. 27; *Thomas* v. *Lewis* (1878) 4 Ex. D. 18; *Guion* v. *Trask* (1860) 1 De G.F. & J. 373.
29 Molloy, *De Jure Maritimo*, 9th edn (1769), Book 2, Chapters 1 and 2.
30 Supreme Court Act 1981, s. 20(2)(b), s. 20(4).
31 All shipping functions were transferred to the Secretary of State for Transport by the Transfer of Functions (Trade and Industry) Order 1983 (S.I. No. 1127).
32 Merchant Shipping Act 1894, s. 47; Merchant Shipping Act 1906, s. 50; The Merchant Shipping (Ships' Names) Regulations 1979 (S.I. No. 341).

retain the famous name for future use, arranged with the company that ran a service round the Isle of Wight that one of their little steamers should be named *Mauretania* and give back the name when Cunard had built a worthy successor to the old ship. Alas, that day never dawned; the Second World War intervened and then transatlantic liners had to yield their passengers to aircraft.

The name has to be painted on both bows and stern, together with the port of registry, and any interference with this marking is an offence.[33] Where a foreign ship on transfer to British ownership is first registered in the UK the last name previous to such transfer shall be entered on the register.[34]

3.4   TONNAGE

Tonnage, measurements, and all other particulars necessary for identification, as certified by a DoT or Lloyd's Register of Shipping surveyor, must be registered, and any substantial[35] alterations must likewise be recorded.[36]

On 18 July 1982 the IMO International Convention on Tonnage Measurement of Ships 1969 entered into force. This has produced a more balanced and uniform system of tonnage measurement. The tonnage measurement is important for a number of purposes. Harbour and lighthouse dues are calculated on it, as well as a host of contractual payments, such as towage.[37] Tonnage is also used in many legal instruments.[38]

In general terms, gross tonnage is meant to represent the size of the vessel, as it is based on the total of enclosed space. The net tonnage essentially represents the earning capacity of the vessel, as it is based on the amount of space available for cargo or passengers, e.g., it does not include space occupied by engines. Under the 1969 Convention certain

33 Merchant Shipping Act 1894, s. 7. Fishing boats on the Fishing Boat Register are exempted from this provision.

34 *Ibid.*, s. 47(7), but a mere English adaptation will probably not do any harm. *Bell* v. *Bank of London* (1858) 28 L.J. (Ex.) 116 (*City of Bruxelles* registered as *City of Brussels*).

35 Merchant Shipping Act 1894, s. 6; Merchant Shipping Act 1965, s. 1; Merchant Shipping (Tonnage) Regulations 1982 (S.I. No. 841).

36 Merchant Shipping Act 1894, ss. 48–53; Merchant Shipping Act 1965, s. 1.

37 See generally, M. Corkhill, *The Tonnage Measurement of Ships*, 2nd edn, (1980).

38 See especially Chapter 8, *infra.*

ships, such as Roll on: Roll off (Ro-Ro) container ships, will cease to have artificially low tonnages.

The 1969 Convention applies to all new ships (or whose keels were laid) on or after 18 July 1982.[39] It also applies to existing ships which undergo substantial alterations, or whose owners want them to be remeasured. There is a transitional 12-year period for other ships.[40]

3.5 BEGINNING AND END OF REGISTRATION

The Act does not expressly provide when a ship must be registered. Section 2 of the Merchant Shipping Act 1894 only says that every British ship requires registration, and according to s. 742 of the Act, a ship 'includes every description of vessel used in navigation not propelled by oars'. It seems to follow that the material time for registration of a new ship is neither the laying of the keel, nor the launching, but the moment when she is actually 'used', in other words when she is finished and commissioned. In the case of foreign-built ships, the material time is the transfer of property to the British owner.

Likewise the register is closed when the ship is transferred to a foreign owner,[41] and when it is wrecked or otherwise lost, actually or constructively.[42] Though the House of Lords regarded a ship broken in two with the parts remaining severed for months as a ship,[43] it is certainly no longer 'used in navigation' and the register relating to it would have to be closed by the Registrar at the instance of the owner.

3.6 BRITISH SHIPS REQUIRING REGISTRATION

The purpose of the shipping register is to provide a record of ships enjoying the privileges of British ships, to enable administrative regulations to be enforced and to evidence the title of owners where the ship is of some value. Accordingly, compulsion to register only exists where

---

39 Art. 3, Merchant Shipping (Tonnage) Regulations 1982 (S.I. No. 841), reg. 3.
40 *Ibid.*
41 Merchant Shipping Act 1894, ss. 21, 44(10).
42 Merchant Shipping Act 1894, s. 21. The meaning of 'constructively lost' is the same as in marine insurance; see *Manchester Ship Canal Co.* v. *Horlock* [1914] 2 Ch. 199, see Section 31.2, *infra.*
43 *British S.S. Owners' Association* v. *Chapman & Son* (1935) 52 Ll. L. Rep. 169, 171.

at least one of those considerations prevails. The general principle was
that all sea-going vessels were bound to register. But, because the
registration system was rather burdensome in relation to certain vessels, the 1894 Act provided various exemptions from registry. Thus,
vessels propelled by oars were exempt, on the basis that such craft were
no longer used for sea-going traffic.[44] There was also an exemption for
ships not exceeding 15 tons burden and employed solely on rivers and
coasts of the United Kingdom or of some British possessions within
which the managing owners reside. To simplify matters the Merchant
Shipping Act 1983, s.4, substituted for this measurement by tonnage
one based on *length*, namely 13.7 metres.[45]

Further exemptions from registry relate to lighters, barges and other
like vessels used exclusively in non-tidal waters, except harbours[46] and
to ships registered under the small ships register set up under s.5 of the
Merchant Shipping Act 1983.

It is worth mentioning here the new modes of water transport
introduced in the 1970s, the lighter carried aboard ship (LASH) and the
barge aboard a catamaran (BACAT). In either case, the cargo-carrying
craft comes down to the sea on inland waters, is then carried across the
sea much like a container, and then set down to complete its mission on
inland waterways. Although such lighters and barges cross the sea they
are not sea-going vessels, since they do not navigate but are carried on a
sea-going ship. This was decided in a case concerned, not with registration, though it is relevant in that context, but with harbour dues.
Where such dues are levied on sea-going ships, barges carried by the
latter are exempt.[47]

Ships belonging to Her Majesty's Navy do not come within the
purview of the Act, and other ships belonging to the Government are
dealt with by Order in Council.[48]

44 Merchant Shipping Act 1894, ss. 3, 742.
45 The 1983 Act left untouched another exemption relating to certain fishing and
   coasting ships not exceeding 30 tons burden and trading solely in various Canadian
   waters around Newfoundland and the Gulf of St. Lawrence. Presumably few, if
   any, of these vessels now operate. And see M.S. Notice No. M. 1162.
46 Merchant Shipping Act 1921, s. 1(1) proviso.
47 *British Transport Docks Board* v. *Barge aboard Catamaran (UK) Ltd* [1976] 2 Lloyd's
   Rep. 410.
48 Merchant Shipping Act 1894, s. 741; Merchant Shipping Act 1906, s. 80: Order in
   Council 22nd March 1911 (S.I. No. 338), amended 1964 (S.I. No. 489), 1978 (S.I.
   No. 1533).

3.7 EFFECT OF REGISTRATION

According to its purpose the registration of a ship has a dual effect. It gives an entitlement to all the privileges of a British ship,[49] but an owner cannot, by failing to register, evade duties cast on such vessels. Indeed, an essential object of registration is the enforcement of such duties. As regards fines and forfeitures, the payment of dues and the punishment of offences committed on board, or by persons belonging to her, non-registered ships are nevertheless regarded as British.[50] Thus owners are prevented from creating a private no-man's-land where they might be exempt from any national jurisdiction.[51]

Apart from these public matters, registration is also important as proof of title. It is not conclusive but furnishes at least prima facie evidence of the registered owner being the true owner, thus resulting in a shifting of the burden of proof. Whoever, without being registered, claims ownership must displace that prima facie evidence.

Illustration: *The Bineta*[52]
S sold the motor yacht *Bineta*, of which he was the registered owner, to G. G was registered as owner, but S retained possession pending payment of the purchase price; that is, he exercised the unpaid seller's lien under s.48, Sale of Goods Act 1893 [now 1979]. Eventually, since G failed to pay, S, as he was entitled to do under that section, sold the yacht to the plaintiff; but G, relying on the fact that he was the registered owner, objected to the plaintiff's registration.

Held: Although S was no longer the registered owner he had conferred a good title on the plaintiff, who was entitled to registration as owner in place of G.

3.8 MEANS OF REGISTRATION

Application must be made to the Registrar of the port desired to be the home port by one or more of the owners. In the case of the application being made by an agent the authority must be in writing and signed,

49 Merchant Shipping Act 1894, ss. 2(2), 72.
50 Merchant Shipping Act 1894, s. 72. *Oteri* v. *The Queen* [1977] 1 Lloyd's Rep. 105.
51 *Baumwoll Manufactur von Carl Scheibler* v. *Furness* [1893] A.C. 8, 20; Merchant Shipping Act 1894, s. 2(3): power to detain a ship that ought to be registered.
52 [1966] 2 Lloyd's Rep. 419.

and in the case of a corporation sealed with the common seal.[53] The
surveyor's certificate must be produced,[54] together with a declaration of
ownership, which must set out the qualification to own a British ship, a
statement of time and place of building or, where the ship is foreign-
built and these particulars are not known, a statement to this effect. The
declaration must also make known the name of ship and master, and the
number of shares in the ship held by the applicant; finally a declaration
is necessary that to the best of the applicant's knowledge and belief, no
unqualified person or body of persons is entitled as owner to any legal
or beneficial interest in the ship or any share therein.[55] On a first
registration a builder's certificate has to be lodged together with the
application. The purchaser of a foreign-built ship who is unable to
produce the builder's certificate must produce to the Registrar the bill
of sale, and he must state at the same time that he is unable to produce
the certificate.[56]

When the registration is effected the Registrar retains the surveyor's
and builder's certificates, any previous bill of sale, the copy of the
condemnation as a prize, if any, and all declarations of ownership.[57] He
thereupon issues a certificate of registration,[58] which fulfils to a certain
extent the function of a title deed. But more than that, the certificate is a
public document, which shows that the ship is entitled to the privileges
and is subject to the duties of a British ship, and that the master is the
lawfully appointed master. For this reason the registration certificate
must not be removed from the ship or be used as a means of private
security by the owner, mortgagee, or any person entitled to a lien on the
ship;[59] it may only be used in connection with its lawful use, i.e.
navigation. Any change of the master or owner shall be endorsed on the
certificate by the Registrar, or other competent officer, as soon as
possible.[60] In the event of the ship becoming lost or ceasing to be
British-owned, the certificate shall be delivered up to the Registrar,
who thereupon closes the Register.[61]

53 Merchant Shipping Act 1894, s. 8.
54 *Ibid.*, ss. 6, 9.
55 *Ibid.*, s. 9.
56 *Ibid.*, s. 10.
57 *Ibid.*, s. 12.
58 *Ibid.*, s. 14.
59 *Ibid.*, s. 15.
60 *Ibid.*, s. 19, (as amended by s. 100(3) of the Merchant Shipping Act 1970), and
   s. 20.
61 *Ibid.*, s. 21.

4

ACQUIRING OWNERSHIP

4.1   MISCELLANEOUS METHODS

BEFORE considering the ordinary commercial purchase of a ship, mention must be made of three other ways of obtaining ownership.

4.1.1   TRANSMISSION

It may happen that a person has property in a ship transmitted to him involuntarily, e.g., by inheritance or bankruptcy. A British subject must regularize his position by proving his title to the Registrar and, furnishing him with a declaration of transmission containing the necessary particulars of the ship.[1]

Where a foreigner becomes the owner the ship does not cease to be British. But as he cannot own a British ship he must apply to the court quickly for an order that the ship be sold and the proceeds paid to him (less the expenses of sale). If he does not apply within four weeks of the transmission the ship is forfeited to the Crown. The court examines the case and may grant the application, appointing nominees[2] to transfer the ship to a purchaser and to pay over the proceeds of sale to the foreign seller.[3] Fortunately, such anachronistic provisions are unlikely to be relevant today to trading ships, for such ships are now usually owned by limited companies who are unaffected by death and whose liquidator, in the event of a winding-up, will normally be a British subject.

4.1.2   CAPTURE

For the sake of completeness it may be mentioned that property in a ship may also be acquired by capture of an enemy ship in times of war. A Prize Court can then transfer property in the ship to the captor by

---

1 Merchant Shipping Act 1894, s. 27.
2 For a foreigner cannot execute a bill of sale in respect of a British ship.
3 Ss. 28, 29.

'condemning' it.[4] A subsequent purchaser of the ship will obtain a good title.[5] However, the right of capture is vested solely in the Crown. Letters of marque, entitling private shipowners to capture enemy ships, are no longer granted. The subject of the Law of Prize is a specialist branch of international law and cannot be dealt with here.[6]

4.1.3   JUDICIAL SALE

Where a court orders the sale of a ship any purchaser will get a good title to the ship and can transfer her as if he were the registered owner.[7] The ship will be free of all claims, encumbrances or liens, these being transferred to the proceeds of sale.[8] The court has the power to order that the ship may be sold in a foreign currency, e.g. US dollars, particularly if the principal debts are in that currency.[9]

4.2   SALE AND PURCHASE

4.2.1   INTRODUCTION

The next question requiring discussion is how you acquire a ship.[10] This is done, in the first place, by purchase either of an existing ship or of a new one built to order. With two exceptions the law relating to the sale and purchase of ships tallies with that of all other moveable property, for all vessels afloat, from the giants measuring several hundred thousand tons down to the cockleshell or coracle, are 'goods' within the meaning of the Sale of Goods Act 1979.

The law relating to the sale of goods is a subject of some complexity and this is not the place to go into every detail; that is best studied in a book devoted to the subject.[11] We must be content with devoting a few /

4 *The Purissima Conception* 6 C. Rob. 45, 165 E.R. 844
5 The High Court exercises the prize jurisdiction, Supreme Contract 1981, s. 27.
6 See, *Halsbury's Laws of England* (4th edn, 1982), Volume 37 pp. 819-864. C. Colombos, *Law of Prize*, (3rd edn, 1949). Note that the Armed Forces Act 1981, s. 25 has abolished the 5% deduction formerly made from all prizes, grants and bounty money distributed to officers and crew of HM ships.
7 Merchant Shipping Act 1894, s. 29.
8 *The Acrux* [1962] 1 Lloyd's Rep. 405. For the sale of a mortgaged ship, see Section 6.3. See also the Insolvency Act 1986, ss. 15, 43, 283.
9 *The Halcyon the Great* [1975] 1 All E.R. 882.
10 See, I. Goldrein, *Ship Sale and Purchase* (1985), Packard, *Sale and Purchase* (1981).
11 For instance, Atiyah, (1985).

pages to those provisions which are likely to affect a seller and buyer of a ship or boat. Even this limited task presents difficulties for, in the course of legislating to protect the 'consumer', much of the law relating to the sale of goods has been divided into compartments, that which comprises buyers in the course of business and that where buyers act in their private capacity as consumers.

Our first task, though, is to explain two provisions which relate to all registered ships. We have already noticed that only British-owned ships can be entered in the Register of British Ships, Now, s. 1, Sale of Goods Act, distinguishes between a sale and an agreement to sell. Under the former, the property in goods passes at the time when the contract is made. Under the latter, property passes at some future time which buyer and seller have in mind; for instance, when certain agreed alterations have been made to the goods.

This has its bearing on the sale to a foreigner, or a foreign corporation, of a ship on the British Register. To make sure that this contains no foreign-owned ships s. 71, the Merchant Shipping Act 1894 provides that where property in a British-registered ship purports to be passed to a foreign buyer the latter forfeits his interest. On the other hand, if the contract with a foreign buyer is an agreement to sell, the British seller can get the ship struck off the British Register and, that being done, safely pass the property in the ship into foreign hands. Where the contract makes it at all possible, courts will construe it as an agreement to sell so as to make the sale a valid one.[12] The seller of a British ship to foreign owners requires a certificate of sale granted by the Registrar.[13]

British buyers of foreign ships do not normally run into this difficulty. Most foreign laws do not distinguish between a sale and an agreement to sell, nor are sales of ships to aliens impeded, the only

---

12 *N.V. Stoomvaart Maatschappij Vredobert* v. *European Shipping Co. Ltd*, (1926) 25 Ll. L. Rep. 210. The Uniform Laws on International Sales Act 1967 (based on a Convention of 1964) does not govern sales of registered ships, Sch. 1, Art. 5(1) (b): nor does the U.N. Convention on Contracts for the International Sale of Goods, Art. 2(e). The SALEFORM 1983, Section 4.2.2, *infra*, is clearly an agreement to sell: see also *The Blankenstein* [1985] 1 Lloyd's Rep. 93.

13 Merchant Shipping Act 1894, s. 39.

consequence of such a transaction being the loss of the ship's right to fly the flag of the seller's state.[14]

The other provision peculiar to registered ships is s. 3, Merchant Shipping Act 1894. Clearly, to effect registration the applicant must furnish evidence of his ownership, evidence moreover that specifically refers to the transfer of property. The contract of sale, which can be oral, provides no such suitable evidence. A document is needed, the bill of sale, by which the seller declares that he transfers the property of the ship to the buyer.[15] This document has nothing whatever to do with that identically named and regulated in the Bills of Sale Acts 1878 – 91. The seller need not prepare a bill of sale where the ship was registered though there was no obligation to do so because it was too small; where a shipbuilder transfers a new ship, which was never registered, to an alien; or where a ship 'constructively lost' within the meaning of s. 21, Merchant Shipping Act 1894, is sold, since this is no longer a ship used in navigation.[16]

4.2.2   SALE OF GOODS ACT 1979

We must now turn to those provisions of the general law of sale of goods which are of special interest to the buyers and sellers of ships and boats.

In the contract of sale, buyers and sellers will make each other a number of promises. For instance, the buyer will give various undertakings as to payment and the seller will promise that the article sold has certain features. In case the parties omit basic matters from their express agreement the law provides that certain terms shall be *implied* into

14 For a survey see G. Schaps and H. Abraham, *Das Deutsche Seerecht,* 3rd edn, Vol. 1, p. 242. It is an intriguing possibility that such restrictions are contrary to the Treaty of Rome, Art. 7 (prohibiting discrimination on grounds of nationality), or Art. 34 (prohibiting quantitative restrictions on exports and measures of equivalent effect, subject to Art. 36): cf. Regulation 141/62/EEC and note the European Communities Act 1972. The EEC Commission is already examining problems of transfer between member states which result in wasteful re-examining of ships. Sometimes owners are forced to replace equipment certified by the original flag state. It seems likely that there is to be a Community list of approved equipment: see 'Progress Towards a Common Transport Policy, Maritime Transport', Com. (85) Final, 14 March 1985, 48.
15 S. 24.
16 *Benyon* v. *Cresswell* (1848) 12 Q.B.D. 899, *Union Bank of London* v. *Lenanton* (1878) 3 C.P.D. 243; *Manchester Ship Canal Co.* v. *Horlock* [1914] 2 Ch. 199. Singh and Colinvaux (1967), paras 125 *et seq.*

contracts.[17] That is, that certain obligations be fulfilled although the contract includes no *express* terms to that effect. Thus under the Sale of Goods Act 1979 the seller impliedly promises that he has the right to sell the goods and confer a good title on the buyer;[18] that if the sale is by description the goods shall correspond with the description;[19] and – most important, but applying only to sellers in the course of a business – that the goods are of merchantable quality, except for defects specifically indicated to the buyer or defects which a buyer who actually examines the goods ought to discover.[20] Merchantable quality has not been authoritatively defined; broadly, it means the quality which the buyer has the right to expect. Where the buyer makes known to the seller a particular purpose for which the goods are required, the seller also impliedly undertakes that the goods are fit for that purpose.[21]

There is no need to illustrate the working of these sections, as their application is often a matter of common sense. However, the parties will want to know what their rights are if the other is in breach of an express or implied term. The innocent party will usually be entitled to damages. But a buyer may want to reject the goods if they are defective and a seller may prefer not to deliver if payment is not made on time. In other words, they may want to put an end to the bargain (or, more precisely, to any unperformed obligations). The Sale of Goods Act 1979 categorizes certain terms as either 'conditions' or 'warranties'. Thus, breach of a condition entitles the buyer to reject the goods, while breach of a warranty entitles the buyer to claim damages only, normally in the form of paying a reduced price. Whether a promise is a condition or warranty usually depends on the intention of the parties. However, the implied terms as to title, description and merchantability, above, are stated by the Act to be conditions. Normally, unless the contract is clearly expressed otherwise, stipulations as to time of payment are not conditions.[22]

17 Terms may be implied by statute or by the courts. A recent statute implying terms into hire or service contracts is the Supply of Goods and Services Act 1982. But the courts will not rewrite the contract for the parties and will only imply a term where it is *necessary* to give business sense to the contract, see *Liverpool City Council* v. *Irwin* [1977] A.C. 239 and *Chitty* (1983) Vol. 1.

18 S. 12.

19 S. 13.

20 S. 14(2).

21 S. 14(3).

22 See ss. 10, 11. However, the courts have held other stipulations as to time in commercial contracts to be of 'the essence', i.e., conditions, see *Bunge Corp.* v. *Tradax S.A.* [1981] 1 W.L.R. 711.

Even where a stipulation is in the nature of a condition the buyer, on discovering its breach, is not compelled to terminate the contract; he can change his mind, waive the breach altogether or treat the breach of condition as a breach of warranty.[23] Thus where it is a condition that the ship has a specified shallow draft, but it turns out that the draft exceeds the one specified, the buyer may, on consideration, keep it and claim compensation.

At one time it was thought that *all* the terms of a sale of goods contract could be classified as either conditions or warranties. But it is now clear that this is no longer so.[24] There is an intermediate category of terms[25] whose breach will only entitle the innocent party to 'terminate' the contract where the effect of that breach is to deprive him of substantially the whole benefit of the contract.[26] This is now a rather unsettled area of law.[27] But the idea is that the courts will not be anxious to allow an innocent party to 'terminate' performance under the contract on the grounds of a trivial breach,[28] unless they are compelled to do so by statute,[29] previous case law,[30] or the specific choice of the parties.[31]

There is one further general matter on which we must concentrate.

4.2.3 EXEMPTION CLAUSES

In principle, seller and buyer can agree that stipulations implied by the Sale of Goods Act shall be excluded.[32] This is where the modern

23 S. 11(2) as regards England and Northern Ireland; s. 11(5) as regards Scotland.
24 *The Hansa Nord: Cehave* v. *Bremer Handelsgesellschaft m.b.H.* [1975] 3 All E.R. 739
25 Described in *The Hong Kong Fir; Hongkong Fir Shipping Co. Ltd* v. *Kawasaki Kisen Kaisha Ltd* [1962] 2 Q.B. 26: see further, 'seaworthiness' in Section 11.3, *infra.*
26 This is properly called a 'fundamental breach', *Photo Production Ltd* v. *Securicor Transport Ltd* [1980] A.C. 827. Where the innocent party chooses to terminate for breach the entire contract is not ended, only the future performance of both parties. Thus, exemption and arbitration clauses may continue to apply, *Photo Production Ltd* v. *Securicor Transport Ltd, supra, Heyman* v. *Darwins Ltd* [1942] A.C. 356.
27 A student should consult a contract textbook, e.g. *Chitty* (1983), Vol. 1, Chapter 24.
28 *The Diana Prosperity: Reardon-Smith Line* v. *Hansen-Tangen* [1976] 1 W.L.R. 989, 998.
29 E.g., Sale of Goods Act 1979, s. 14.
30 *The Mihalis Angelos: Maredelanto Compania Naviera S.A.* v. *Bergbau-Handel G.m.b.H.* [1971] 1 Q.B. 164. It is doubtful whether a buyer could reject a ship described in the contract as lying in Berth No. 1 if, in fact, she was in Berth No. 2, alongside. The buyer would always have the right to damages, e.g. shifting expenses.
31 See Section 4.2.4, *infra*, and SALEFORM 1983 clauses 13 and 14, Appendix 3.
32 S. 55.

legislative protection of the buyer, mainly the private buyer, the 'consumer', bites as a result of the Unfair Contract Terms Act 1977.

No seller can any longer contract out of his duty to confer a good title on the buyer.[33] Where the seller runs a business and sells in the course of that business, and the buyer contracts for his private use for the purchase of goods ordinarily supplied for private use or consumption, i.e., where the buyer is a 'consumer',[34] the seller cannot reduce or exclude his implied liability in respect of description, merchantable quality and fitness set out above.[35] This benefits the buyer of yachts of a size requiring registration and, in particular, of boats.

Illustration: *Rasbora Ltd* v. *J.C.L. Mason Ltd*[36]

A contract for the building of a powerboat contained a clause limiting the seller's liability to the terms of a warranty certificate, under which the builder undertook to replace defective items, but which excluded all implied conditions. Within 27 hours of delivery, while off Dungeness, the boat caught fire and became a total loss.

Held: The evidence showed that the boat was not of merchantable quality, that this was a consumer sale, that the clause excluding the implied condition to deliver a boat of merchantable quality was invalid, and that the sellers were liable.

Of course, the private seller is free to contract out of the implied conditions of description, merchantable quality or fitness, though not of conferring a good title. If the private owner of a sailing yacht sells his boat 'as she lies' or 'with all faults', the buyer has no redress when he finds even a serious fault.[37]. The business seller can only rely on such a clause to the extent that any faults fall short of making the boat unmerchantable.

Where the business seller sells to a business buyer, the implied conditions can be cut down or excluded by a term in the contract, but only as far as the extent of contracting out is reasonable in the circumstances.[38] Such exemption clauses to be upheld by the court must pass a stiff test. The term must be fair and reasonable to be included in the contract, taking into account what the parties contemplated at the time

33 S. 6(1).
34 S. 12(1).
35 S. 6(2).
36 [1972] 1 Lloyd's Rep. 645; this case was decided under the Sale of Goods Act 1893, s. 55(4), (5), (7) and (8), since replaced by the almost identical Unfair Contract Terms Act 1977, s.6.
37 To this extent *Sullivan* v. *Constable* (1932) 48 T.L.R. 369 is still law.
38 S. Unfair Contract Terms Act 1977, s. 6(3).

of the contract. Even if the exemption clause was commonly used in the trade it would be relevant to ask if it had been freely negotiated between representatives of buyers and sellers or whether one party could more easily cover the loss by insurance.[39]

In the above case of *Rasbora* v. *Mason*, Lawson J said *obiter* that the would have struck down the particular exemption clause for un-reasonableness even if that had not been a sale to a consumer. But a clause in a business sale excluding economic losses, such as lost time if the vessel broke down, might not be unreasonable.[40]

Particular note should be taken that where there is an international supply contract[41] the parties are freed from the restrictions of the Unfair Contract Terms Act. The idea, presumably, is that international business transactions do not need regulating. The paradox is that a British owner needs to make his ship sale contract fair and reasonable if he sells to another British owner, but not if he sells to a foreign buyer!

Certain exemption clauses in all contracts, including sales, are also void, unless reasonable in the circumstances, by virtue of s. 3, Unfair Contract Terms Act; namely, when the sale is to a consumer or, even when the sale is to a business, if the parties contract on the basis of the seller's written or printed standard terms. This includes a term by which the seller limits or excludes his liability in the event of his own breach of contract.

Students of this subject should also bear in mind the far-reaching provisions governing credit and hire-purchase agreements, which may affect, in particular, the purchase of pleasure craft. The Consumer Credit Act 1974 governs such agreements made by consumers and it came fully into force in May 1985. A consumer credit agreement under the Act is a personal credit agreement by which the creditor provides the debtor with credit not exceeding £15 000.[42] The Act provides a detailed framework of protection for consumers,[43] with provisions as

---

39 *George Mitchell (Chesterhall) Ltd* v. *Finney Lock Seeds Ltd* [1983] A.C. 803.
40 *The Zinnia: Stag Line Ltd* v. *Tyne Shiprepair Group* [1984] 2 Lloyd's Rep. 211. This was a shiprepair case, but the judge would have found unreasonable a clause depriving an owner of all remedy if he did not return the vessel to a particular yard (wherever the ship might be).
41 I.e., where the parties selling the ship have places of business in different states and e.g., (i), the acts of offer and acceptance were done in different states (e.g. by telex) or (ii), the contract provides for the goods to be delivered to a state other than that where those acts were done; Unfair Contract Terms Act 1977, s. 26.
42 Consumer Credit Act 1974 s. 8(2); Consumer Credit (Increase of Monetary Limits) Order 1983 (No. 1878).
43 It is fleshed out by a mass of regulations. Students should consult, R. Goode, *Consumer Credit Legislation* (1984, with supplements).

to, e.g., the form and content of agreements,[44] the information to be given to the consumer,[45] the right to cancel the agreement if not signed at business premises[46] and a cooling off period.[47]

Sellers sometimes fail to deliver the promised goods. The remedy of the disappointed buyer is an action for damages for non-delivery.[48] On rare occasions this fails to satisfy the buyer, as the article he bought is unique and damages will not compensate him. In that event the court has power to make a decree of specific performance.[49]

4.2.4 THE SALEFORM AGREEMENT

In practice, most sales of commercial ships are agreed on the basis of standard forms such as SALEFORM 1966 or 1983, or NIPPONSALE 1974, although market conditions may enable buyers, or sellers, to insist on terms more favourable to them. The agreements are, of course, subject to the general law.

(A) TIME WHEN AGREEMENT IS BINDING

This distinction between an agreement to sell and a sale has already been noted.[50] The SALEFORM is headed 'Memorandum of Agreement'. This emphasizes the fact that it usually *records* an agreement that has already been made, often by an exchange of telexes. These will fix all the basic terms, such as price and date of delivery, and will often incorporate the SALEFORM agreement. The actual signing of such a memorandum is not normally considered in the market as a prerequisite to the conclusion of a binding contract:[51] nor is the payment of

---

44 S. 60.
45 Ss. 55, 62–64, 69.
46 S. 67.
47 S. 68.
48 Sale of Goods Act 1979, s. 31.
49 S. 52. See also Section 4.2.4(c), *infra*, for specific examples.
50 Section 4.2.1 *supra*.
51 *The Blankenstein: Damon Compania Naviera S.A.* v. *Hapag-Lloyd International S.A.* [1985] 1 Lloyd's Rep. 93, 97–98. Where the parties contract 'subject details' this shows that they are not normally bound until all the details of the sale have been agreed, see, e.g. *The Nissos Samos* [1985] 1 Lloyd's Rep. 378. If the agreement is expressed to be 'subject to satisfactory survey' it seems there is no binding contract: but even if there is, the buyer can reject the survey if his dissatisfaction is reasonable, or at least bona fide, *Astra Trust, Ltd* v. *Adams and Williams* (1969) 1 Lloyd's Rep. 80. *Cf The Merak: Varverakis* v. *Compagnia de Navegacion Artico S.A.* [1976] 2 Lloyd's Rep. 250.

the deposit.[52] A binding agreement may also be reached even though the persons conducting the negotiations do not intend to buy the vessels personally, but expect to nominate a company in their control as the real purchasers. When the company's name is inserted in the Memorandum a new contract comes into existence between the sellers and the company.[53]

(B) SELLERS' RIGHTS

The SALEFORM 1983[54] requires a 10 per cent deposit of the purchase price to be paid within an agreed time of signing the form.[55] Payment of the purchase money has to be made within three days of the date on which the vessel is ready for delivery.[56] What happens if the buyer pays a day late? Under the 1966 and 1983 versions of SALEFORM the seller has the express right to 'cancel' the contract, retain the deposit and, if this does not cover his losses, claim further compensation.[57] However, under the 1966 SALEFORM there was no express provision dealing with what happened when the *deposit* was paid late. It is obviously vital for the seller to get his deposit early, as that is his security against nonperformance. In *The Selene G*[58] it was held that the time of payment of the deposit was 'of the essence', i.e., a 'condition' and not an 'intermediate term'.[59] The seller was allowed to terminate the contract. Clause 13 of SALEFORM 1983 now makes it clear that non-payment of deposit is treated like non-payment of purchase price.

Where the seller does exercise this right to cancel, his damages will normally be the loss he suffered by selling the vessel in the market. In *The Blankenstein*[60] the contract price was $2 365 000 and the sellers lost $60 000 on the resale after cancelling. The sellers, however, claimed instead the $236 500 representing the 10 per cent deposit which had not

52 *The Blankenstein, supra.*
53 *Ibid.*
54 See Appendix 3. See Goldrein, fn. 10 *supra* for the London Ship Sale Contract 1985.
55 Clause 2. this is returnable if the buyer is not satisfied with the survey afloat (Clause 4) or if the ship is lost before delivery (Clause 5). A deposit would be returnable if the sellers wrongfully repudiate the contract, see *The Hazelmoor: Anchor Line Ltd* v. *Keith Howell Ltd* [1980] 2 Lloyd's Rep. 351.
56 Clause 3.
57 Clause 13 of both.
58 [1981] 2 Lloyd's Rep. 180.
59 See Section 4.2.2, *supra.*
60 *Damon Compania Naviera S.A.* v. *Hapag-Lloyd International S.A.* [1985] 1 Lloyd's Rep. 93.

been paid. The Court of Appeal held that they were entitled to this sum as it had become due before the cancellation. Although Clause 2 of SALEFORM 1966 required the deposit to be paid 'on signing this contract' (which the buyers never did) the Court held that the buyers were in breach for failing to sign it in a reasonable time. Clause 2 of SALEFORM 1983 now requires the deposit to be paid within an agreed number of days 'from the date of this agreement'. This should remove the difficulty in *The Blankenstein* if the number of days have been agreed.

(c) BUYERS' RIGHTS

SALEFORM 1983 also has specific provisions on when the buyer may cancel, e.g., where the seller fails to deliver the vessel with everything belonging to her in the manner and time agreed.[61]

But the form cannot specify the consequences of every breach. Is the buyer entitled to terminate if the seller fails to deliver immediately one plan which is on board the ship,[62] or if he does not forward promptly a single technical document?[63] Perhaps a court would treat these obligations as intermediate terms. Failure to deliver a detailed engine plan could be very serious, but a failure to deliver the instructions for the crew's refrigerator might not. If those breaches caused losses, e.g. by delay, the buyer would have a right to damages. But the right to terminate would depend on how serious were the consequences of the breach.

Although the SALEFORM allows the buyer to claim compensation[64] as well as to cancel, it leaves the assessment of that compensation to the general law of damages. It is a general principle that a plaintiff must do what is reasonable to mitigate (i.e., reduce) the loss resulting from the breach – at least if he wants to claim damages. In one case, the seller arranged to deliver the ship on 31 August, but was two days late because he had squeezed in a final cargo carrying voyage. The buyer cancelled and, as the market price of the vessel was £500 000 more than the contract price, he claimed the difference in damages.[65] The court held that the buyer did not act reasonably and was not entitled to

---

61 Clause 14. See *The Al Tawfiq* [1984] 2 Lloyd's Rep. 598.
62 Clause 8, line 95.
63 Clause 8, line 94.
64 Where the seller is proved to be negligent, Clause 14, see *The Al Tawfiq* (1984) 2 Lloyd's Rep. 598.
65 A buyer would not normally cancel on such a rising market.

damages. He should have made the sellers an offer for the vessel, as they would probably have agreed to sell it at the contract price.[66]

The buyer may not want to cancel if he needs that particular ship. It had been thought that, if a seller failed to deliver, the buyer of a ship could normally obtain an order of specific performance (i.e. an order that the seller must hand over the ship in exchange for the price).[67] But the remedy is discretionary. In *The Stena Nautica*[68] Canadian charterers exercised an option to buy a ferry which was a sister to two other ferries operated by them. The owner had meanwhile chartered the ship to a Belgian company. The court refused specific performance, largely because the owners were 'good' for any damages, but also because alternative tonnage was probably available and the Belgians had spent £150 000 on conversions. It would be different if no other vessels of the same type were available for sale.[69]

The SALEFORM 1983 obliges the seller to drydock the vessel at the port of delivery where it can be properly inspected by the buyer, or a Classification Society such as Lloyds Register of Shipping.[70] Basically, the seller pays if there are any defects discovered then, but if the vessel is sound the expenses of the dry-docking will be for the buyer's account. However, market conditions may enable the seller to insist that the sale takes place 'as is', without a prior dry-docking inspection.[71] It is apparently common to have a clause added to the SALEFORM to the effect that the vessel is to be delivered 'free of average damage affecting class'. This means damage caused by a peril normally covered by insurance[72] which prevents the vessel being in class, or which results in the surveyor imposing some qualification on class.[73]

---

66 *The Solholt* [1983] 1 Lloyd's Rep. 605.
67 Sale of Goods Act 1979, s. 52. See Atiyah (1985) p. 438. This remedy is not
   normally available if damages would be adequate compensation, see, e.g. *Behnke* v.
   Bede Shipping Co. Ltd [1927] 1 K.B. 649, where the ship 'was of peculiar and
   practically unique value' to the German plaintiff buyer: cheap, with practically new
   engines and boilers, so as to satisfy German regulations and thus qualify for
   immediate placing on the German Register.
68 *C.N. Marine Inc.* v. *Stena Line A/B* [1982] 2 Lloyd's Rep. 336.
69 *The Oro Chief* [1983] 2 Lloyd's Rep. 509.
70 Clause 6. A seller will be in breach if he fails to provide proper facilities for
   inspection, see *The Merak: Varverakis* v. *Compagnia de Navegacion Artico S.A.* (1976)
   2 Lloyd's Rep. 250.
71 See Packard (1981), p. 58 *et seq.*
72 E.g., peril of the sea, and not defects arising from old age, see generally Section
   30.3 *infra*.
73 *The Alfred Trigon: Piccinini* v. *Partrederiet Trigon II* [1981] 2 Lloyd's Rep. 333. *cf. The
   Star of Kuwait* [1986] 2 Lloyd's Rep. 641.

(D) ENCUMBRANCES

The buyer is not concerned only with the physical condition of the vessel: he will want to be sure that she is free from encumbrances such as liens and debts.[74] Clause 9 of SALEFORM 1983 contains two obligations.[75] First, the seller undertakes that the vessel is free on delivery from all encumbrances, maritime liens or any other debts. Secondly, he undertakes that he will indemnify the buyer against claims made against the vessel in respect of liability incurred prior to delivery.

Illustration: *The Barenbels*[76]
The vessel was delivered in December 1980. In February 1982 it called at Qatar and was arrested by local agents for debts incurred by *other* vessels belonging to the sellers. The buyers were obliged to put up a P&I Club guarantee which was valid until 1988. They claimed under Clause 9 for damages, or an indemnity.

Held: That the two obligations in Clause 9 were separate.
'Encumbrances' could refer to ships' mortgages and possessory liens. 'Other debts' only refers to debts giving rise to actual existing rights affecting property in, or the use of, the ship at the time of delivery. It did not refer to *any* debts which could make the vessel liable to arrest. However, there was a claim 'against the vessel' within the second sentence, as there was a threat that the vessel would be sold by court order unless security was put up. the buyers were entitled to the indemnity.

The result is that an operator of a large fleet of ships who sells one of them may find himself facing indemnity claims for a number of years.

---

74 See Chapter 7, *infra.*
75 See Appendix 3, *infra:* note also the documentary obligations in Clause 8.
76 *Athens Cape Naviera S.A.* v. *Deutsche Dampfschiffartsgesellschaft* [1985] 1 Lloyd's Rep. 528.

5

SHIPBUILDING
CONTRACTS

WE now turn to the legal aspects of the shipbuilding contract.[1] This case differs from the purchase of an existing ship, since work and labour are involved, and new legal questions might arise, as e.g. the shipbuilder's copyright in the plans. In essence, however, this contract too is a sale of goods, and in this chapter it is proposed to discuss but a few points of interest, with regard to which the purchase of an existing ship and the order for the construction of a new one are at variance.[2]

5.1   PROPERTY IN THE SHIP

To begin with, when a person gives such an order he makes an agreement for the purchase of a ship not yet in existence, he buys what are called future goods.[3] It needs little imagination to realize that as no property exists when the contract is concluded, none can pass at that time. Legally speaking, where future goods are bought or, more specifically, where an order is given for the construction of a vessel, no sale is possible, but the contract will always constitute an agreement to sell.[4] This being so, the passing of the property will normally not occur until the completion of the vessel, but the parties may provide for its

---

1 For a detailed international analysis see, M. Clarke, *Shipbuilding Contracts,* (1982): also, Packard (1981). The contract may be concluded by telex, but of course the parties can agree not to be bound unless a formal agreement is signed, see *Okura & Co. Ltd* v. *Navara Shipping Corporation S.A.* [1982] 2 Lloyd's Rep. 537.

2 The person ordering a ship to be built is not free to have it designed as he pleases. As explained in Chapter 8, ships must comply with high standards of safety, hygiene and comfort to protect passengers and crews. For the use of exemption clauses see Section 4.2.3, *supra.* Note that s. 26, Unfair Contract Terms Act is unlikely to apply to an international shipbuilding agreement as the contract, and delivery, will usually be made in one state; see Chapter 4, fn 41, *supra.*

3 See Sale of Goods Act 1979, s. 61.

4 *Ibid.,* ss. 2(5), 5(3); see Section 4.2.1, *supra.*

transfer by stages as building proceeds. Indeed a great number of shipbuilding disputes have turned on such provisions.

The problems underlying those cases must be sought for in the province of business. The larger the vessel, the greater are the costs involved, and the longer is the time the builder has to wait for the payment of the purchase price. As often as not he will not be able to finance the whole construction himself and he will be obliged to apply to other quarters for help. These other quarters will be either the purchaser or third parties. The latter will usually be banks and they will require a security for their advance. Unless they are content with debentures charging the whole undertaking of the builder, a specific equitable mortgage of the existing ship must be arranged; for we shall see in Chapter 6 that registered mortgages can only be effected when the ship is completed and registered. The builder may also require the buyer to arrange for third parties to guarantee payment of the purchase price.[5] Our present problem is concerned with advances on the price by the purchaser. He, too, must safeguard himself against the builder's possible supervening insolvency. This is usually done by a term in the building agreement, providing for the passing of the property to the purchaser of portions of the ship as construction goes on, in accordance with the instalments he pays on the price. Compared with the sale of an existing thing by instalments, the position is just the reverse. In instalment sales the vendor retains the property until the last instalment is paid, in our present case the purchaser with each instalment acquires portions of property.

That this effect is possible was laid down by the House of Lords a long time ago,[6] and it was expressly recognized in the original 1893 Sale of Goods Act, now s.18, Rule 5(1), of the Sale of Goods Act 1979. According to this Rule the property in future goods, in the absence of evidence to the contrary, will pass to the purchaser under two conditions,

(i) goods complying with the contractual description must exist in such a state that the buyer is bound under the contract to take delivery of them,[7]

(ii) such goods must be unconditionally appropriated to the contract by the consent of the parties

5 See e.g., *Hyundai Shipbuilding & Heavy Industries Co. Ltd* v. *Pournaras* (1978) 2 Lloyd's Rep. 502.

6 *Seath* v. *Moore* (1886) 11 App. Cas. 350, 370, 380.

7 Sale of Goods Act 1979, s. 18, Rule 5(1) and s. 61(5).

Moreover the buyer will not only desire that as building proceeds the vessel shall become his, but that if the builder becomes insolvent the completion shall take place in due course. He will usually attempt to secure this by a term in the contract that the materials brought into the shipyard for the purpose of constructing the ship shall become his property.[8]

The desired effect is not always wholly achieved. One has to bear in mind that whatever is thus transferred to the buyer ceases to be available to the builder's general creditors. Justice and common sense require that there should be strong evidence that materials or portions of a ship in construction in the builder's yard, and ostensibly his property, have been excluded from his assets. Therefore the parties are not deemed to have intended the passing of the property in stages by merely agreeing that instalments of the purchase price be paid in advance.[9] Likewise, in one case a contract for the building of two ships on the Clyde provided, in addition to the payment of the price by instalments, that the materials be passed by the purchasers' superintendent, but delivery to the Italian principals should take place after trials off the Italian coast. It was held that the contract was for the sale of two complete ships, and the property until completion remained in the builders.[10]

On the other hand, a contract providing for the payment of instalments at particular stages of construction, for inspection by the purchasers or their agents,[11] and for the passing of the property in the completed sections of the ship is effective.[12] In a case like that, the contract is construed not as an agreement to sell a completed ship, but as 'a contract for the sale from time to time of a ship in its various stages of construction, or of materials to be used in the construction of a ship, the

8 For a good example of such a clause see *Reid* v. *Macbeth & Gray* [1904] A.C. 223. *Cf. Romalpa* Clauses, p.53 *infra*.

9 *Seath* v. *Moore* (1886) 11 App. Cas. 350.

10 *Sir James Laing & Sons, Ltd* v. *Barclay, Curle & Co., Ltd* [1908] A.C. 35.

11 Lloyd's surveyors' approval, which is desirable, as it will enable or facilitate a Lloyd's survey prior to registration, is not inspection by the purchaser, as Lloyd's surveyors do not act as the purchaser's agent. See *Reid* v. *Macbeth & Gray* [1904] A.C. 223.

12 *In re Blyth Shipbuilding & Dry Docks Co. Ltd* [1926] Ch. 494; *Howden Bros* v. *Ulster Bank* [1924] 1 I.R. 117; 19 Ll. L.R. 199. Where, before delivery, a shipbuilder accepts a repudiation of the contract by the buyer or (apparently) where the shipbuilder 'cancels' on the basis of an express cancellation clause in the contract he is entitled to claim any instalments already due, *Hyundai Heavy Industries Co. Ltd* v. *Papadopoulos* [1980] 1 W.L.R. 1129. As the instalments will often be guaranteed by a third party, such as a bank, this remedy may be better than a claim for damages against a (possibly insolvent) buyer.

seller, however, being under an obligation of working up the things sold into a complete ship for the purpose of putting them into a deliverable state.[13]

This does not mean that property in materials intended to be built into the vessel and approved by the purchaser passes to the latter whenever it is mentioned in the contract. To produce this effect the material has to be 'appropriated' within the meaning of s.18, Rule 5(1), of the Sale of Goods Act. If the court comes to the conclusion that the whole contract is not for materials to be worked up into a ship, a case which will rarely arise, but a contract for the sale 'from time to time of a ship in its various forms of construction', or for a complete ship, something more than intention, however definite, is necessary for the appropriation of material not yet worked into the vessel. In addition, 'there must be some definite act, such as the affixing of the property to the vessel itself, or some definite agreement between the parties which amounts to an assent to the property in the materials passing from the builders to the purchasers'.[14]

Those who supply materials to shipbuilders may try to protect themselves against defaults in payment by using retention of title, or *Romalpa*,[15] clauses. A seller is generally entitled to do this under the Sale of Goods Act 1979, s.19(1) and the theory is that the seller retains ownership in the goods until paid. Thus he does not need to register the clause as a charge under the Companies Act 1985 as the goods are still his.[16] However, where the shipbuilder incorporates those materials into the ship the purchaser gets a perfectly good title to those goods, provided that he has acted in good faith and without any knowledge of the rights of the original supplier.[17]

When the ship is finally completed, and not delivered to foreign buyers,[18] the builder has to give a certificate in accordance with s.10 of

---

13 *Per* Romer J, *in re Blyth, supra,* p. 500. Wherever such arrangements are made it is usual to preserve the builder's lien for unpaid purchase money under the Sale of Goods Act 1979, s. 41, which enables him to retain possession of the ship in case the price is not paid or the purchaser becomes insolvent. Such possessory lien also attaches in favour of the builder who has effected repairs, and he is in possession of the ship though it be in a public dry dock, and the presence on board of ship's officers during repairs is by itself no reason why the repairer should not have possession; see *The Rellim* (1922) 39 T.L.R. 41, and Chapter 7, *infra.*

14 *Per* Sargant LJ, *in re Blyth, supra,* p. 518; cf. Lord Watson in *Seath* v. *Moore, supra,* 381.

15 After *Aluminium Industrie* v. *Romalpa Aluminium Ltd* [1976] 1 W.L.R. 676; see Atiyah (1985) pp. 358-364.

16 *Clough Mill Ltd* v. *Martin* [1985] 1 W.L.R. 111.

17 Sale of Goods Act 1979, s. 25.

18 *Union Bank of London* v. *Lenanton* (1878) 3 C.P.D. 243.

the Merchant Shipping Act 1894. And, where the property has not already vested in the purchaser (in stages, or under any other special contract as first described) the builder must apply for registration and transfer property to the purchaser by bill of sale.

5.2   PRICE INCREASES

In recent years inflation has been a particular problem for shipbuilders as their costs can rise dramatically after a fixed-price contract has been agreed. The best way to protect themselves is by means of some form of price escalation clause. If they do not do so they may have to bear the extra costs themselves. The same sort of problems are caused by currency instability.

Illustration: *The Atlantic Baron* [19]
In 1972 Company A agreed to build a large tanker for Company B for US$31 million payable in 5 instalments. A agreed to open a letter of credit, in B's favour, as a form of guarantee of repayment if the contract was terminated. After the first instalment was paid the US dollar was devalued by 10 per cent in February 1973. A claimed that all subsequent instalments should be increased by 10 per cent, although there was no legal basis in the contract for this, and threatened to terminate the contract. B was placed in great difficulty because it had already agreed a 3 year time charter for the vessel with important clients and no other vessels were available. Under pressure B agreed in June 1973 to the extra payment provided that A correspondingly increased by 10 per cent the letter of credit in B's favour. B eventually claimed repayment of the $3 million extra payments.

Held: That the June 1973 agreement was prima facie binding as each party had provided consideration (i.e. some new obligation in return for that of the other). However, A was guilty of 'economic duress' by insisting on the increased price without legal justification. This entitled B to avoid the June agreement. But, as the vessel had been delivered in November 1974 and A had continued to make payments, without protest, until June 1975 A had affirmed the June agreement and was bound by it. [20]

5.3   SELLERS' OBLIGATIONS

It remains to be mentioned that, of course, the shipbuilder is a person on whose skill or judgment the purchaser relies so that the builder gives

19 *North Ocean Shipping Co. Ltd* v. *Hyundai Construction Co. Ltd,* [1979] 1 Lloyd's Rep. 89.
20 See further *Chitty* (1983), Vol. 1, Chapter 3 (on consideration) and Chapter 7 (on duress).

an implied undertaking as to fitness for a particular purpose within the meaning of s.14(1) of the Sale of Goods Act 1979. In the same way, where a builder orders ship's parts from a subcontractor the latter will usually give an implied undertaking as to the fitness of the part for the particular ship.[21]

Mention should be made of an EEC Council Directive of 25 July 1985 on Products Liability.[22] This is designed to make producers of defective products strictly liable for damage which causes personal injury or death, or damage to property intended or used for private use or consumption.[23] The Directive has to be enacted by member states by 30 July 1988.[24] They are allowed to have provisions limiting the producer's liability to 70 million European Currency Units (ECU).[25]

The Directive will be of particular relevance to shipbuilders and the suppliers of components, as any defects in their products could easily cause a casualty giving rise to death or personal injury. However, their liability for property damage would still be based on fault, except, for example, where the product was used in pleasure craft.

If the producer cannot be identified the supplier will be liable,[26] so it will be no use for a shipbuilder to claim that the defective part came from a supplier whose identity he had forgotten. However, there are a number of defences allowed, e.g. that the defect was due to compliance with mandatory regulations, or that the scientific and technical 'state of the art' would not have allowed the defect to be discovered;[27] or that a component was made according to the design of the main producer.[28]

---

21 *Cammell Laird & Co. Ltd* v. *Manganese Bronze & Brass Co. Ltd* [1934] A.C. 402.
22 85/374/EEC (O.J. No. L 210, 7/8/85, p. 29).
23 Arts 1, 9. A manufacturer of defective goods is not liable at common law for pure economic loss suffered by the ultimate purchaser unless there was a very close proximity or relationship and real reliance by the purchaser on the manufacturer rather than the vendor, *Muirhead* v. *Industrial Tank Specialities Ltd* [1985] 3 All E.R. 705. *Cf. M/S Aswan Engineering Establishment Co.* v. *Lupdine* Ltd [1986] 2 Lloyd's Rep. 347.
24 Art. 19.
25 Equivalent to £39 893 280 on the date of the adoption of the Directive, Art. 16. The limit would be for a producer's total liability arising from identical items with the same defect. The UK government has announced that the enacting legislation will not contain a financial limit. See the Consumer Protection Bill.
26 Art. 3.
27 Art. 7. This defence would not have been available to the shipbuilders in *The Amoco Cadiz*, Section 5.4, *infra*, as, even if the design of the steering represented the 'state of the art', certain parts were below specification.
28 Art. 7(g).

In certain circumstances shipbuilders may be entitled to limit their liabilities by statute, either because they are owners of a vessel launched but uncompleted, or because they operate a dock.[29]

Finally, it is worth noting, in passing, that shipbuilders owe a duty of safety to their workmen and employees and other users of the shipyard under the Health and Safety at Work Act 1974 and regulations made thereunder.[30]

6.4 RESPONSIBILITY OF PURCHASER FOR DEFECTS

Suppose that the purchaser of a new vessel engages in trade and persons or property suffer damage by reason of any defect in the design or construction of the ship. It might be thought that the purchaser could rely on the skill of the shipbuilder so far as third parties are concerned, but this may not be wholly true. If the cargo being carried is damaged the carrier may not be liable if he has employed builders of repute and if he himself has adopted all reasonable precautions in the nature of appropriate surveys.[31] The position might be different if the shipowner has some hand in the design process, e.g., where his own naval architect fails to detect a fault in the design. Likewise, the same might apply if his own inspectors negligently pass bad work.

Illustration: *The Amoco Cadiz*[32]

The VLCC *Amoco Cadiz* went aground as a result of steering failure and caused enormous pollution damage on the French coast. The French claimants sued the shipbuilders (A) and shipowners (B) for over US $2 billion. Five (7 cm long) studs had fractured under pressure. Their design called for a thickness of half an inch as opposed to the three-quarters of an inch necessary to withstand possible pressure. Some of the studs were also below specification. The detailed design specifications were made by A who were

29 See Sections 22.2.6 and 22.3.6.

30 See also *McPhail* v. *London Graving Dock Co., Ltd* (1936) 54 Ll. L.R. 152; *MacColl* v. *Vickers-Armstrongs, Ltd* (1936) 53 Ll. L.R. 299; *Day* v. *Harland & Wolff* [1953] 2 Lloyd's Rep. 58. *The H.M.S. Glasgow* [1981] 2 Lloyd's Rep. 605. See Section 8.7,*infra*.

31 *Angliss* v. *P. & O. Steam Navigation Co.* [1927] 2 K.B. 456, 461, as he would have exercised due diligence under the Hague Rules: but see *The Riverstone Meat Co. Pty Ltd* v. *Lancashire Shipping Co. Ltd* [1961] A.C. 807, Section 11.3.6, *infra*, for the situation where *ship repairers* are used.

32 [1984] 2 Lloyd's Rep. 304 (Northern District Illinois). See Chapter 25 for pollution aspects.

reputable shipbuilders. The design was checked for B by the American Bureau of Shipping. B also had a naval architect to check general compliance with specifications. The general design was common for such ships at that date. B later tried to cut costs by delaying essential maintenance work on the steering.

Held: (US District Court) A and B were respectively liable for failure to meet specification and to carry out proper maintenance. A *and* B were also liable for the faulty design and construction. B was also liable for operating the ship without a secondary steering system.

The *Amoco Cadiz* decision in the USA is a significant extension of liability so far as owners are concerned. For it suggests that an owner may still be liable for defects even if he employs one of the recognized classification societies and a reputable shipbuilder who uses 'state of the art' technology. It is unlikely that an English court would go so far but, even so, students should be aware that claimants may 'forum shop'. That is, they may try to sue in the country whose laws are most favourable to them. This often involves claimants suing in the USA because her courts often give very large awards of damages.[33] In *The Amoco Cadiz* the shipbuilders were Spanish and the claimants French, but the shipbuilders were forced to litigate in the USA essentially because they signed the contract there.[34]

Where a crew member is injured by a defect in the ship's equipment, the shipowner may be deemed negligent under the Employer's Liability (Defective Equipment) Act 1969.[35] The shipowner will retain a right of contribution from the builder, or other person, negligent.

33 *Cf. Castanho* v. *Brown & Root (UK)* [1981] 1 All E.R. 143, and see Section 1.7.
34 *In re Oil Spill by the Amoco Cadiz off the Coast of France* 699 F. 2d 909 (1983, 7 Cir) 915.
35 *The Derbyshire* [1986] 1 Lloyd's Rep. 418 (reversed 190 L.M.N.L., 12 February 1987).

6

SHIP MORTGAGES

6.1 FINANCING AND SECURITY

WE HAVE seen how an owner acquires his ship. Next we must consider encumbrances that may arise with his consent. In the international shipping market purchases are, in nearly every case, effected by means of large loans from bankers and others.[1] Further loans may be effected during the course of the ship's life. The bankers will want to make sure that their money is as secure as possible and they will achieve this in a number of ways, the most prominent of which is to take a mortgage. The best summary of methods of securing financial advances was given by Roskill LJ in 1977:

'The bank advances to one or more owning companies a large sum of money. It of course requires security. It will take a mortgage on the ship for that security. It may take other mortgages on other ships for the same security. If the ship, as often happens, is about to be time chartered, then the bank will take an assignment of the time charter in order that the bank as assignee can benefit from the time charter in order to reduce the mortgage debt. In addition it will almost invariably in my experience take an assignment of insurance policies and P and I Club cover in order that in the event of total or partial loss of the ship the bank as the lender may be suitably secured.'[2]

The result of all this has been that the bank is almost completely secured against the insolvency of the borrower and may well have achieved priority over other creditors. The total indebtedness could even exceed the value of the ship. This is because lenders to 'one-ship' companies will often require alternative security to a mortgage on that ship alone. This could include all sorts of cross guarantees from associated companies which may also own one ship.

1 See generally, Wood (1980), Chapter 16.
2 *The Panglobal Friendship* [1978] 1 Lloyd's Rep. 368, 371.

If the ship is lost, it follows that the mortgagee loses his primary protection secured by the mortgage. Indeed ships might be thought a rather risky security because of the possibility of sinking, damage or obsolescence. This is why insurance is so important. The mortgagee can take out insurance himself against loss of, or damage to, the ship.[3] This can be expensive, although the mortgagee may provide expressly that the premiums are to be chargeable to the mortgagor. Alternatively, he can arrange for the insurance to be effected jointly with the owner.

The usual practice is for the owner to arrange and maintain specified insurance cover at his own expense. In the event of the loss of the ship the insurer would then pay the owner directly. This sum would also be at the disposal of all the other unsecured creditors. For that reason it is important for the mortgagee to insist on an assignment of the insurance,[4] or a pledge of the policy. Then the insurers will pay the sum assured to the mortgagee directly,[5] and this withdraws it from the grasp of the general creditors.

6.2 NATURE OF THE MORTGAGE

A mortgage is a charge or encumbrance which the borrower of money, the mortgagor, creates in favour of the lender, the mortgagee.[6] The latter thereby obtains a hold on the property mortgaged, which prevents the general creditors of the owner from selling the ship in satisfaction of their claims. It also enables the mortgagee to recoup himself for the mortgagor's failure to repay the loan, or the interest on it, by selling the ship or taking possession of her. On the other hand the ship remains in the mortgagor's possession and use. Thus, the mortgage would seem to constitute an ideal security, since it allows the mortgagor to continue his business as a going concern, while protecting the mortgagee's security in the event of default by the owner-debtor.

3 Under the Marine Insurance Act 1906, s. 14(1), (2) he has an insurable interest; see Section 28.1 *infra*.
4 As permitted by the Marine Insurance Act 1906, s. 50.
5 Mortgagees usually require some form of undertaking from the broker who arranges the insurance to ensure that the underwriters will pay the mortgagee and not the owner. See Wood (1980) pp. 396-399. It is in respect of this sum in the hands of brokers and insurers that other claimants may try to issue Mareva injunctions, e.g. *The Angel Bell* [1979] 2 Lloyd's Rep. 491, see Section 1.5, *supra*.
6 For an excellent general analysis of commercial credit and security see Goode (1982), Part 5; also Crossley Vaines, *Personal Property*, (5th edn, 1973). For an international survey, see L. Hagberg (ed.), *Handbook on Marine Law: Registration of Vessels, Mortgages on Vessels*, Vols III-A, III-B (1983).

Under the system of mortgaging established by the Merchant Shipping Act 1894, which is eminently practical and sensible, the mortgagor remains the owner of the ship or shares therein, which he has mortgaged. Thus the mortgagee does not incur any liabilities as against third parties, and he need not be a British subject. This is in accordance with the general scheme of the Act, for the mortgagor who remains in possession is the person whom the authorities can control.[7]

6.3   CREATION AND REGISTRATION

The mortgage must be in one of the two forms prescribed by the Act.[8] The first form is for securing the 'Principal Sum and Interest' and the second is to secure 'Account Current'. In practice the latter is used more often because it is more flexible and can cover sums other than the original purchase price.[9] By the form the mortgagor acknowledges receipt of the loan, promises to make repayment with interest and creates a 'mortgage ... in the ship above particularly described, and in her boats, guns, ammunitions, small arms and appurtenances'.[10]

When the mortgage has been 'executed' the mortgagee has a valid mortgage as between himself and the mortgagor, but he is not yet protected against the possibility of the owner obtaining further advances on the security of the same vessel. The mortgagee should advertise his mortgage to anyone proposing to become interested in the vessel. He does this by registering the mortgage.

On production of the form the Registrar of the ship's port of registry will record it in the register book.[11] In fact, the form will not tell an enquirer a great deal. The real substance of the mortgage is usually contained in a collateral 'Deed of Covenant'. This will contain details of

---

7 Merchant Shipping Act 1894, s. 34.

8 S. 31(1), First Sch. Part 1, Forms B(i) and (ii). See Appendix 4 *infra*.

9 Wood (1980), p. 362.

10 See Appendix 4 issued by the CCE with the consent of the DoT: see s. 65. The expression 'appurtenances' usually refers to things belonging to a ship and necessary for her use, but this issue is a question of fact. Certain rules were laid down in *The Humorous, The Mabel Vera* [1933] P. 109. Supposing a fishing vessel is mortgaged and at the time of the execution of the mortgage deed nets are not only on board, but are 'appropriated' by the owner to that particular ship, then the nets are mortgaged together with the ship. In course of time the nets are replaced by new ones, the latter becoming subject to the mortgage. On the other hand, if no nets were appropriated to the ship at the time when the mortgage was made, nets brought on board later do not form part of the security.

11 S. 31(1). He also notes the date and hour of the record. Mortgages are recorded in the order in which they are produced to him, s. 31(2).

the owner's personal obligations under the mortgage, e.g. to keep the ship seaworthy and in classification and not to sell or charge the vessel, or allow her to become subject to other mortgages.[12]

This Deed of Covenant cannot be registered. However, if created by a company, the mortgagee must register the mortgage as a charge under the Companies Act 1985.[13] Failure to do so within 21 days makes the charge void against a liquidator or other creditors.[14] This requirement to notify the company registrar also applies to charges created by foreign companies which have an established place of business in England and Wales.[15]

The mortgagee can transfer the registered mortgage,[16] although this does not appear to happen much in practice. Failure to register the mortgage does not affect its validity as between mortgagor and mortgagee,[17] but it does affect its priority. The Registrar cannot enter on the register interests in the ship created by trusts.[18]

6.4 PRIORITY OF REGISTERED MORTGAGES

From the date of registration the mortgagee has priority over all other mortgages registered after his and all unregistered mortgages or charges even if created before his registration.[19] Moreover, the registered mortgagee is unaffected by any later act of bankruptcy of the shipowner and is protected against all later secured creditors.[20]

---

12 Wood (1980), pp. 371-2. The fact that this detail is not in the statutory form does not affect the validity of the mortgage, *The Benwell Tower* (1895) 8 Asp. 13.

13 Ss. 395, 396(1)(h). The Companies Registry is entirely separate from the other registers mentioned and is situated in Cardiff.

14 S. 395.

15 S. 409. It may extend to charges created while the property in question (e.g. the ship) is abroad, see *N.V. Slavenburg's Bank* v. *Intercontinental National Resources Ltd* [1980] 1 All E.R. 955, 966.

16 Merchant Shipping Act 1894, s. 37.

17 See s. 57.

18 S. 56.

19 Merchant Shipping Act 1894, s. 33, *Black* v. *Williams* [1895] 1 Ch. 408.

20 S. 36, excluding ships from the bankruptcy doctrine of reputed ownership, will be repealed by the Insolvency Act 1985, Sch. 10. As the 1985 Act abolishes this doctrine there would appear to be no substantive change as a result of the repeal. The general rules of the Insolvency Act 1985 (e.g., as to preferences under ss. 174, 101) would apply to ship mortgages and a trustee in bankruptcy would take a bankrupt's property subject to existing rights, secured or not (s. 130(6)). Note also ss. 34, 49, 154(4), 157(3). From 29 December 1986, see the equivalent provisions in the consolidating Insolvency Act 1986.

However, the mortgagee ranks after previously registered mortgages, possessory liens[21] and maritime liens whenever created.[22] Maritime liens, as will appear later, are by no means uncommon, so that the ship as security for a loan is not an altogether satisfactory object.

Most mortgages tend to prohibit the taking of second mortgages. In any event prospective second mortgagees would probably not lend any money unless some sort of separate deed of priority was agreed between them and the first mortgagees. On general principles further advances can be covered by the original mortgages. Where a second registered mortgage intervenes between the further advance and the first mortgage the position is unclear but it seems as though the second mortgage will rank before the further advance.[23]

6.5   CERTIFICATES OF MORTGAGE

Before lending money to a shipowner it is obviously important for the lender to check the register carefully. This is not always possible without great inconvenience if the loan is to be made, and the mortgage to be executed, at a place other than the port of registry of the ship.

When the parties negotiate beyond the frontiers, the law has devised a method of facilitating the inspection by making the register, as it were, mobile, thus enabling the lender to make his inspection in distant parts of the world. This is effected in this way. The owner applies to the Registrar at the port of registry for a certificate of mortgage.[24] This is nothing but a document describing the ship and stating existing encumbrances, if any.[25] The certificate is sent to the lender abroad and, after execution of the mortgage, particulars of it are endorsed on the certificate by any British registrar or consular officer.[26] Such endorsement functions as registration and ranks in priority to any mortgage registered in the register after the certificate was issued, though prior to the actual endorsement of the certificate.[27] Thus, notice in the register

---

21 Such as those of a shipbuilder, or repairer, *Williams* v. *Allsup* (1861) 10 C.B.N.S. 417, 142 E.R. 514; *The Sherbro* (1885) 5 Asp. M.C. 88. See Thomas, (1980), p. 257.
22 See Chapter 7, *infra.*
23 *The Benwell Tower* (1895) 8 Asp. M.C. 13; *Liverpool Marine Credit Co.* v. *Wilson* (1872) L.R. 7 Ch. App. 507.
24 S. 39.
25 S. 42.
26 S. 43.
27 *Ibid.*

that a certificate of mortgage has been issued operates as a warning to all later lenders, and such persons should await the ultimate registration of the mortgage endorsed on the certificate before risking any money on the ship in question.

If the place where the transaction occurs is within the country of the port of registry, the prospective mortgagee must nevertheless inspect the register itself.[28]

6.6 REMEDIES OF THE MORTGAGEE

6.6.1 GENERAL

The realization of a registered mortgagee presents no legal difficulties. If the owner defaults on the loan or does anything that tends to jeopardize the security, the mortgagee has two primary remedies. These are to take possession of the ship,[29] or to sell her.[30] It depends on the circumstances of the case whether the owner jeopardizes the security. The courts have come to this conclusion in a case where the mortgagor failed to repair the ship so as to make her capable of performing a chartered voyage;[31] likewise, where he allowed the ship to be burdened by maritime liens for an unreasonably long time.[32] This is because such conduct showed the reduced circumstances of the owner and such liens ranked in priority to the mortgage.[33]

The mortgagee retains, of course, his right to enforce the personal obligation of the mortgagor to repay the loan. But this will often be of little practical value and that is why it is buttressed by taking security on the ship itself.

The mortgage may also be enforced by an action *in rem*. As part of these proceedings the ship may be arrested and, if necessary, later sold by judicial sale.[34]

28 See s. 41.
29 *De Mattos v. Gibson* (1868) 4 De G. & J. 276, 45 E.R. 108.
30 S. 35.
31 *De Mattos v. Gibson, supra.*
32 *The Manor* [1907] P. 339, 361.
33 See Sections 6.4 *supra* and 6.6.4, *infra.*
34 See Sections 4.1, *supra*, and 6.3, *infra.*

6.6.2   USE OF THE SHIP BY THE MORTGAGEE

The mortgagee is not entitled to do with the ship whatever he likes. He must consider the interests of the mortgagor and any other mortgagees. The law requires him to take reasonable steps and precautions, having regard to all the circumstances.[35]

When a mortgagee does take possession he is entitled to any freight which the ship might earn, but not to freight which was already due before he took possession.[36] But he will be liable to the mortgagor for any loss sustained through the imprudent use he makes of her.[37] For instance, in one case a mortgagee took possession of the ship and ran her on an entirely speculative trade. This resulted in financial loss and deterioration of the ship and the mortgagee subsequently effected a disadvantageous sale. It was held that he had to bear the loss; he was charged with the value of the vessel at the time he took possession of her.[38]

6.6.3   SALE OF A MORTGAGED SHIP

If the mortgagee sells the vessel he must hold the proceeds of sale (in excess of principal, interest and costs) in trust for later mortgagees, if any, and the owner. A second or third mortgagee can only effect a sale with the consent of prior mortgagees or by authority of the court.[39]

The order of appraisement (valuation) and sale will normally be made after judgment on the mortgagee's case. Where the claims greatly exceed the value of the ship it would not make much sense to allow all the costs of maintaining it continue and reduce the security available. In such a case the court has power to order sale pending the trial of the action.[40]

One question which often arises where an owner defaults and the mortgagee wishes to use the power of sale is whether the costs of

35 *The Calm C* [1975] 1 Lloyd's Rep. 188.
36 See *Scrutton* (1984), pp. 355–6. The owner, of course, may have already assigned all freight to the mortgagee as part of the earlier security arrangements, see e.g., *The Myrto* [1977] 2 Lloyd's Rep. 243.
37 *Temperley* (1976), para. 75.
38 *Marriott* v. *The Anchor Reversionary Co.* (1861) 30 L.J. (Ch.) 571.
39 S. 35.
40 E.g., *The Myrto* [1977] 2 Lloyd's Rep. 243, [1978] 1 Lloyd's Rep. 11. For an unsuccessful attempt to argue that the mortgagee had breached his implied obligation to take reasonable care in exercising the power of sale by selling at an undervalue and inflating the cost of repairs, see *The Jocelyne* [1984] 2 Lloyd's Rep. 569.

discharging any cargo on board should be deducted from the proceeds of sale available to the mortgagee. Cargo-owners will argue that the ship could not be sold unless the cargo is discharged. But in one case the discharging costs were £150 000 while the ship was only expected to fetch £640 000 – well below the amount owing to the mortgagees. It seems as though the correct course is for cargo-owners to pay for the removal of their own cargo and then make a claim against the shipowners for breach of the contract of carriage.[41]

6.6.4 RIGHTS OF CHARTERERS

In the last decade the shipping market has seen many shipowners default on loans. One problem of continuing importance is the effect on existing charterparties of the exercise by the mortgagee of his rights to take possession of, and sell, the ship. The charterers may demand the release of the vessel from arrest, or an injunction stopping its sale, on the basis that the mortgagee is interfering with the contract between them and the shipowner. The legal position is unsettled, but it seems that where the mortgagee has knowledge of the charter at the time of the grant of the mortgage he can be restrained from exercising his rights under the mortgage.[42] He will not be allowed to interfere unless his security has been impaired, or the owner is unwilling (or unable) to perform the charter.[43] Wrongful interference may be a tort which the charterer can restrain by obtaining an injunction.[44] It seems that the mortgagee does not commit a tort unless he has *actual* knowledge of the existence of the charter when the mortgage is granted.[45]

41 *The Jogoo* [1981] 1 Lloyd's Rep. 513, 517. See also *The Myrto (No. 3)* [1985] 2 Lloyd's Rep. 567. for the attempts by a mortgagee to recover discharging expenses from cargo-owners. For the practical problems faced by the Admiralty Marshal when a ship is arrested, see *The Myrto (No. 2)* [1984] 2 Lloyd's Rep. 341. But the mortgagee's claim will be subject to any other claims having a higher priority, see Section 7.3, *infra*. Thus, the Admiralty Marshal's expenses (including fees paid to a classification society to maintain the ship in class) would be met before the mortgagee's claim, see *The Honshu Gloria* [1986] 2 Lloyd's Rep. 63.
42 *De Mattos* v. *Gibson, supra. Lord Strathcona S.S. Co. Ltd* v. *Dominion Coal Co. Ltd* [1926] A.C. 108.
43 *The Myrto* [1977] 2 Lloyd's Rep. 243, 253-254.
44 *Ibid.* Of course, he will not be entitled to the injunction if it is clear the owner would have been unable to complete the charter, *De Mattos* v. *Gibson, supra*. It seems unlikely that the *owner* would be entitled to an injunction particularly where the mortgage allows a sale free of charter; see *The Arietta and the Julia* [1985] 2 Lloyd's Rep. 50.
45 *Swiss Bank Corporation* v. *Lloyds Bank Ltd* [1979] 1 Ch. 548, 569-575: *cf. Port Line Ltd* v. *Ben Line Steamers Ltd* [1958] 2 Q.B. 146.

6.7 UNREGISTERED MORTGAGES

6.7.1 GENERAL

As already noted, registration of a mortgage is not necessary to make it valid in English law although it does affect its priority.[46] Unregistered mortgages – usually referred to as equitable mortgages – may exist by accident or design. A ship which is exempt from registration under the Merchant Shipping Acts[47] may be mortgaged, although it might, of course, be registered in order to enable the creation of a registered mortgage. Low values may make this impractical. Parties might create an equitable mortgage where money is needed urgently, or where a foreign ship is involved and the lender does not want to go through the cumbersome process of registering a mortgage abroad.[48] In one case the court ordered that an equitable mortgage be created by two co-owners as a security for the claim of a third co-owner who objected to a proposed voyage.[49] However, it is more likely in practice that different means of security will be used.[50] Equitable mortgages may need to be registered under the Companies Act 1985,[51] but they may be enforced by an action *in rem*.[52]

6.7.2 UNFINISHED SHIPS

The necessity to mortgage a ship under construction may arise in several different ways. We noticed earlier[53] that where the purchaser of a

---

46 Ss 57, 33. Registered mortgages are sometimes described, perhaps inaccurately, as 'legal' mortgages. For the practical difficulties caused by the need to rely on an equitable mortgage, see *The Angel Bell* [1979] 2 Lloyd's Rep. 491. The enforceability of unregistered mortgages may differ in other countries, see Wood (1980), p. 358. The International Convention for the Unification of Certain Rules Relating to Maritime Liens and Mortgages 1967, although not in force, applies only to registered mortgages.

47 See Chapter 3, *supra*.

48 The lender may be content to take an equitable mortgage until one can be registered. He could accept the deposit of a mortgage registered in favour of the borrower, *Lacon* v. *Liffen* [1862] 32 L.J. (Ch.) 25, or agree to the execution of a registered mortgage.

49 *The Vanessa Ann* [1985] 1 Lloyd's Rep. 549. A registered mortgage could not be created immediately as there were technical defects in a previous owner's registration.

50 See Section 6.6.1, *supra*.

51 See Section 6.3, *supra*.

52 Supreme Court Act 1981, ss. 30(2)(c), 20(7)(c), 21(2). See Section 1.3.2, *supra*.

53 See Section 5.1, *supra*.

ship pays the price by instalments he usually stipulates for the passing to him of the property in the ship as far as it is built from time to time. Now if such purchaser has to borrow the money for the instalments and has no other suitable property to offer but the unfinished ship, the lender may be inclinded to accept this torso as security.

Conversely the builder may be anxious to get the order although the purchaser refuses to pay instalments in advance of completion. The builder's economic position will usually prevent him from financing the building out of his own resources. In such a case it will be he who wishes to use the not yet completed structure as collateral for a loan until such time as a purchaser pays the price.

In both cases, alternative means of security may be available to the parties, such as guarantees from banks or governments. But in the UK no mortgage can be registered on the unfinished ship because ordinary ship registration, under Part I of the Merchant Shipping Act 1894, is only possible for completed ships.[54] Many maritime countries have introduced legal mortgages on ships under construction so as to facilitate the financing of new ships. If the mortgage is not paid when the completed ship is registered, the mortgage is transferred to the ordinary ship's register.[55]

As no similar machinery exists in the UK, the purchaser or builder must rely on an equitable mortgage, or some other security such as a floating charge.[56] The equitable mortgagee can obtain his preferential right over the ship by informal agreement or by transfer of a builder's certificate.[57]

If the borrower is a limited company, an equitable mortgage may be created by the issue of a debenture charging all the company's assets and thus also binding the ship in the builder's yard.[58]

---

54 In certain circumstances owners may limit their liabilities for uncompleted vessels, see Chapter 22, *infra*.

55 E.g. Germany, see, *Schaps-Abraham: Das Seerecht,* (ed. H.J. Abraham) 4th edn, (1978) Part I, pp. 81, 85; H. Prüssmann and D. Rabe, Seehandelsrecht, 2nd edn, (1983) also Wood (1980), p. 399. The Convention Relating to Registration of Rights in Respect of Vessels Under Construction, 1957, which is not yet in force, provided for a separate official public register for such ships; see Art. 1.

56 See Goode (1982), pp. 787-803.

57 *Ex parte Hodgkin* [1875] L.R. 20 Eq. 746. A bill of sale, under the Bills of Sale Act 1878, may also be necessary: see Goode (1982), p. 740.

58 See, on debentures, L.C.B. Gower, *Modern Company Law* (4th edn, 1980) pp. 401-402, 409-412, 468-492.

6.8 BOTTOMRY AND RESPONDENTIA

The mortgages so far described do not differ from mortgages on other kinds of property. Two special kinds of ship's mortgage, bottomry and respondentia, are now almost obsolete and only require a passing notice. Before submarine cables, radio and satellites established a close network of communications throughout the world, ships' masters in foreign ports had to be given authority to act on behalf of their owners and of cargo-owners when in an emergency they could not communicate with them. They might have had to order repairs quickly to bring a perishable cargo home and had no money or credit in those distant parts. In such circumstances, the master, as agent of necessity, could borrow money, to be repaid with interest if the ship arrived safely at her destination. The ship – the ship's bottom, hence the name 'bottomry' – and possibly also cargo and freight, were mortgaged by a bond given to the lender. Where cargo only was available as security the lender received a respondentia bond. Both bonds provided security only while the property mortgaged remined in existence. The bond itself, and also the borrower's personal obligation, were discharged if ship and cargo were afterwards lost, the lender's risk being the completion of the adventure.[59]

7
LIENS[1]

SO FAR we have dealt with the modes of voluntarily employing the ship as a security for long- and short-term advances made to the owner. But a ship may also serve as a security for a money loan by operation of law. The seller of a ship may have a possessory lien for unpaid purchase money[2] and the shipbuilder one for the execution of repairs.[3] In other words he is entitled to keep hold of the ship until paid. Liens may also be created by contract, e.g. in charterparties or bills of lading.[4] One should also note the existence of equitable liens, or charges such as a floating charge over company assets.[5]

But one should bear in mind the peculiar character of a ship both in her capacity as an asset to the owner and with regard to the events she may encounter in the course of her career. To begin with a ship, as a rule, represents an unusually large proportion of the owner's general property; it may frequently cause unforeseeable damage by collision or otherwise; conversely, nobody can forecast where the ship might need unexpected assistance from strangers when encountering perils of the sea. If we add to these considerations the fact that a ship is an elusive sort of property which may easily slip out of the hands of a person damaged, or of a person having incurred expenses on her behalf, and that a ship may well escape any particular jurisdiction, we cannot wonder that

1 See Jackson (1985) Chapters 11-17.
2 Sale of Goods Act 1979, s. 41.
3 See *Williams* v. *Allsup* (1861) 142 E.R. 514, cited in Section 6.4, *supra*. To exercise the possessory lien the repairer must *have* possession – a question of fact. He does not obtain possession by sending his employees to work on the vessel while she is berthed at another yard. If a repairer does have possession he must enforce his lien by obtaining a court injunction or arresting the vessel. He is not entitled to exercise self-help, e.g. by removing the vessel's cylinder heads, *The Gregos* (1985) 2 Lloyd's Rep. 347.
4 See Part 3, *infra,* and Jackson (1985), Chapter 16. In *The Ugland Trailor: Re Welsh Irish Ferries* [1985] 2 Lloyd's Rep. 372 it was held that an owner's lien on cargoes and sub-freights under the NYPE form of charterparty was registerable as a charge under the Companies Act 1985: and see Section 6.3, *supra*.
5 Goode (1982), Chapter 28, Jackson (1985), Chapter 15: and see Chapter 6.7, *infra*.

from early days special methods were devised of protecting persons and property coming into contact with the ship and suffering damage thereby. The owner is often far away, his financial standing unknown and the courts of the country of registry may be inefficient or expensive to approach. Thus personal actions for damages may not be a satisfactory remedy.

7.1   MARITIME LIENS[6]

7.1.1   GENERAL

A valuable and effective method of enabling the injured party to make the vessel herself available as security for his claim has been devised in the so-called 'maritime lien'. A maritime lien is a claim against a ship or other maritime property which can be made effective by the seizure of the property in question.[7] It exists independently of the possession of the object over which it is claimed, but is attached to it in the sense that it is unaffected by change of ownership. It is therefore called by lawyers a right *in rem*, i.e. a right enforceable against the world at large, in this case against the thing itself, as opposed to a right *in personam,* against a particular person, say, the owner.

Illustration: *The Bold Buccleugh: Harmer* v. *Bell*[8]
The *Bold Buccleugh* ran down the plaintiff's vessel. Before proceedings in the Admiralty Court were taken the ship was sold to a purchaser without notice of the incident.

Held: the lien operated against a *bona fide* purchaser for value; it related back to the time when it attached. The lien is lost only by negligence or delay, neither of which was proved in this case.

The privilege of maritime lien arises as soon as the particular injury is sustained or right of payment accrues, but it is 'inchoate' (i.e., incomplete) until the action *in rem* is commenced. As part of those proceedings the property may be arrested and, if necessary, sold.[9]

---

6 See Jackson (1985), Chapter 12; Thomas (1980).
7 Including a hovercraft operating on land; Hovercraft Act 1968, s. 2(2).
8 (1850), 7 Moo. P.C.C. 267, 13 E.R. 884.
9 Supreme Court Act 1981, s. 21(2), and see Section 1.3.2, *supra.* Liens, and the claims on which they are based, may be subject to time bars, see Chapter 26, *infra.*

A person who voluntarily pays off a debt (e.g., wages) secured by a maritime lien does not thereby acquire the right to enforce it: but if he applies to the court for leave to pay the debt, the maritime lien may be preserved by order of the court.[10]

There is no English statute whch lists the maritime liens. They are to be found in the decisions of the Admiralty Court. English law recognizes a very limited number of maritime liens, and these are: damage done by a ship; salvage; seamens' and masters' wages; masters' disbursements; bottomry and respondentia.

It is doubtful whether pilotage gives rise to a maritime lien. On principle, it would seem that no such maritime lien would be justified, as it is an ordinary commercial transaction. Of course, where a pilot performs salvage services he will have a maritime lien under that head.[11] The same considerations would seem to apply to towage.[12]

It should be noted that other states, particularly the USA, recognize many more.[13] The International Convention for the Unification of Certain Rules Relating to Maritime Liens and Mortgages 1967 would have added port, canal, waterway and pilotage dues, as well as personal injury claims, to the list of maritime liens.[14] The Convention has never achieved the support necessary to enter into force. This is due to fundamental disagreements between states in part as to which claims should give rise to maritime liens and also as to the priority to be accorded to each claim.[15] The same difficulties are being faced by the UN body UNCTAD which has been trying to produce a new Convention for a number of years.

7.1.2   CATEGORIES OF MARITIME LIEN

The maritime liens may be grouped under two broad headings: first, those for remuneration or money due under some contract or consensual arrangement; and secondly, those for damage suffered from some tortious act. The purpose of categorizing maritime liens is partly

10 *The Petone* [1917] P. 198; *The Vasilia* [1972] 1 Lloyd's Rep. 51.
11 See Chapter 26, *infra*.
12 *Westrup* v. *Great Yarmouth Steam Carrying Co.* (1889) 43 Ch. D. 241; *The Heinrich Bjorn* (1886) 11 App. Cas. 270; Thomas (1980), pp. 16-17.
13 See *The Halcyon Isle* [1981] A.C. 221, see Section 7.3.1, *infra*.
14 Art. 4. A similar Convention of 1926 is in force but many maritime nations are not party to it.
15 See Section 7.3, *infra*.

in order to identify them, but mainly to resolve issues of priority between them.[16]

Into the heading of contract maritime liens fall the liens created by:
(i) Bottomry and respondentia.[17]
(ii) Salvage.[18]
(iii) Seamens' and masters' wages.[19]

The courts have interpreted the expression very broadly so as not to draw artificial distinctions about wages earned on board ship or not.[20] Thus, wages include contributions to a pension fund, whether deductible from wages, or to be contributed by the employer:[21] likewise for national insurance contributions;[22] damages for wrongful dismissal.[23] A master is given the same protection as a seaman.[24]

(iv) Masters' disbursements.

These have been defined as expenses

'By the master, which he makes himself liable for in respect of necessary things for the ship, for the purposes of navigation, which he, as master of the ship, is there to carry out – necessary in that they must be had immediately – and when the owner is not there, able to give the order, and he is not so near to the master that the master can ask for his authority, and the master is therefore obliged, necessarily, to render himself liable in order to carry out his duty as master.'[25]

It is not very likely that such claims will arise today with modern methods of communication.[26] In any event the master must have authority to pledge his owners' credit.[27] This, rather harsh rule may apply because of the exceptional priority accorded to maritime liens which can operate to the detriment of other claimants on the same fund. Moreover, it is reasonable to limit the number of claims

---

16 See Section 7.3, *infra*.
17 See Section 6.8, *supra*.
18 Salvage is usually performed as a result of some agreement, contractual or otherwise, but not necessarily so: see Chapter 24, *infra*.
19 See Chapter 9, *infra*.
20 *The Halcyon Skies* [1976] 1 All E.R. 856.
21 *Ibid*.
22 *The Gee-Whiz* [1951] 1 Lloyd's Rep. 145.
23 *The British Trade* [1924] P. 104. as explained in *The Halcyon Skies, supra*.
24 Merchant Shipping Act 1970, s. 18.
25 *The Orienta* [1895] P. 49, *per* Lord Esher MR, at p. 55.
26 The conditions which must prevail are similar to those required for him to sign a bottomry bond, see Section 6.8, *supra*.
27 *The Castlegate: Morgan v. Castlegate Steamship Company Ltd* [1893] A.C. 38, where a master had no maritime lien when he paid for bunkers which were for the account of charterers.

to which the vessel may be made liable when in the hands of a later owner.

The other heading concerns liens created by:
(v) Damage done by a ship.

Collisions are the most important example here, but two points should be borne in mind. First, the damage must be done by the ship. When, therefore, the crew of the *Dunlossit* cut the cables of the *Easdale* in order to get to sea and the *Easdale* suffered damage, her owners had no maritime lien on the *Dunlossit*.[28] Direct physical contact is probably not necessary as a ship may cause 'wash' damage through excess speed.[29]

Secondly, although the damage must be caused by the ship, the lien does not arise except in support of a personal action. Thus, if a lien is claimed, a liability of the owners for their own, or their employees', wrongful acts or neglects must first be proved.[30] However, justice and common sense call for a wide view of the term 'owner'. This expression covers not merely the registered owner, but any other person in control of the ship with the former's concurrence. Thus, when the owners let out the ship on demise charter[31] it is the demise charterer who appoints the crew: they are his servants and not the owners'. If a collision occurs through their negligence the demise charterers are treated as 'disponent' owners: they will be liable and a maritime lien arises.[32]

---

28 *Currie* v. *M'Knight* [1897] A.C. 97.
29 See *The Escherscheim* [1976] 2 Lloyd's Rep. 1, where there was damage 'done by' a salvage tug when it cast off a ship in such a way as to beach her on an exposed shore.
30 'No doubt at the time of action brought, a ship may be made liable in an action *in rem*, though its then owners are not, because by reason of the negligence of the owners, or their servants, causing a collision, a maritime lien on their vessel may have been established, and that lien binds the vessel in the hands of subsequent owners. But the foundation of the lien is the negligence of the owners or their servants at the time of the collision, and if that be not proved no lien comes into existence, and the ship is no more liable than any other property of which the owners at the time of the collision may have possessed'. *The Utopia* [1893] A.C. 492, *per* Sir F. Jeune, at p. 499.
31 See Section 10.3, *infra*.
32 Maritime Conventions Act 1911, s. 9(4). *The Father Thames* [1979] 2 Lloyd's Rep. 364.

7.2   STATUTORY RIGHTS *IN REM*[33]

7.2.1   INTRODUCTION

The whole question of liens in shipping law is bound up with the ability of the claimant to arrest a ship to satisfy the claim which gives rise to the lien.[34] We have seen that the importance of the maritime lien was that it gave a right to arrest, proceed against and ultimately sell a ship, even if it had been sold after the claim arose.

The nineteenth century saw great advances in trade and technology and it became clear that there were many new maritime claims, based on ordinary commercial transactions such as 'towage' charged by steam tugs, which did not give rise to maritime liens. Nevertheless it was realized that some of those transactions, though not justifying a maritime lien, should enjoy some additional protection compared with ordinary claims. Accordingly the Admiralty Court Act 1840 s. 6 created statutory rights of action *in rem* for towage and necessaries supplied to foreign ships.[35] Further rights of the same kind have been added over the years.[36] The current list of claims giving rise to such rights is contained in the Supreme Court Act 1981.[37]

7.2.2   WHEN THE RIGHTS MAY BE EXERCISED

An action *in rem* may be brought against the ship for claims relating to ownership, co-ownership, mortgages or forfeiture.[38]

An action *in rem* may also be brought against the ship for many other specific claims listed in s. 21(4).[39] However, to be able to exercise that right the claimant must be able to show (1) that the person (D) who

---

33 Sometimes called 'statutory liens', or 'statutory liens in Admiralty' or 'statutory rights of action *in rem*': see Jackson (1985), p. 251; Thomas (1980), pp. 31-32.

34 Reference should be made to Chapter 1.

35 No new maritime liens were created, *The Two Ellens: Johnson v. Black* (1872) L.R. 4 P.C. 161.

36 See *The Monica S.* [1968] p. 741, 749-50.

37 Ss. 20(2), 21(2) and (4). For the text of ss. 20-2 see Appendix 1.

38 S. 21(2).

39 And s. 20(2), e.g., damage done by a ship; loss or personal injury; loss of, or damage to goods; agreements concerning the carriage of goods, or hire; salvage; towage; pilotage; materials supplied; construction or repair; dock charges or dues; wages; disbursements; general average; bottomry. A claim which attracts a maritime lien may be enforced either as a maritime or statutory lien.

would be liable in an action *in personam* was the owner or charterer[40] of the ship when the cause of action arose, and (2) that when the writ was issued D was the beneficial owner or demise charterer of the whole ship.[41] For these specific claims the claimant may, in the alternative, bring an action *in rem* against any other ship 'beneficially' owned by D: this is the called 'sister ship' provision.

7.2.3 EFFECT OF THE PROVISIONS

Understanding this part of the Act is rather like trying to work out a difficult riddle, although the underlying idea is clear enough. It is to allow actions *in rem* to be brought for a wide category of maritime claims, but to ensure that the person whose ship is to be arrested should be the real culprit. It will be remembered that on issue of a writ *in rem* an inchoate maritime lien will attach from the event creating it. A lien attached to a claim under s. 21(4) will attach only from the issue of a writ and a purchaser will be affected thereby only if a writ has been issued before he bought the ship.[42] To that extent one might say that the statutory lien only attaches when the writ is issued and not when the claim arises – as with a maritime lien.[43]

The ability to arrest a sister ship is an additional right which was not available historically to holders of maritime liens. However, all the claims giving right to maritime liens are listed in s. 21(4) and so sister ship arrest would be possible for these claims under that section.

7.2.4 CHARTERERS

Section 21(4) made one change in the law which had applied since 1957. It is now possible to have the action *in rem* where D is the demise

40 Or person in possession or control of the ship. A shipowner would normally be liable *in personam* to the ship's agents for expenses incurred by them, thus allowing arrest of the vessel, e.g. *The Gulf Venture* [1984] 2 Lloyd's Rep. 445.

41 And not a part of it, *The Aventicum* [1978] 1 Lloyd's Rep. 184. In *The Munster* [1983] 1 Lloyd's Rep. 370 a demise charterparty was repudiated nine days before the issue of the writ *in rem* in respect of oil fuel supplied to the demise charterer. As the latter had thus ceased to be demise charterers at the date of the writ, it was set aside.

42 *The Aneroid* (1877) 2 P.D. 189, where the purchaser even had notice of the claim of the 'necessaries' men. Although, of course, the purchaser may have no notice of this writ until it is served, *The Monica S., supra*.

43 See *Re Aro Co. Ltd* [1980] 1 All E.R. 1067: the matter is important because the claimant becomes a secured creditor from this time and not from the service of the writ or the actual arrest of the vessel.

charterer at the date of the writ, and not only where he is the owner. This makes sense because demise charterers operate ships, to all intents and purposes, as if they are owners. Where D incurs a liability as a time charterer he may face the arrest of ships actually owned by him.[44]

7.2.5   CLAIMS GIVING RISE TO THE RIGHTS

The Supreme Court Act 1981 does not give the statutory right *in rem* for *every* maritime claim: the list in the Act must be considered closely. The House of Lords has recently decided in a Scottish case that there is no statutory right *in rem* where a marine insurance premium is unpaid,[45] adopting a narrow meaning to the words 'relating to' in the equivalent of s. 20(2)(b). Unfortunately for legal certainty, four months later the House, in an English case, gave a wide meaning to the expression 'arising out of' in the same provision![46] It seems that the 'agreement' must have a reasonably *direct* connection with the activities (such as carriage of goods, or hire).[47] But, once that hurdle has been jumped then *any* claim having some connection with the agreement will give rise to a statutory right *in rem*.[48]

Similar arguments would apply to a damages claim resulting from the breach of a minor term of a salvage contract.[49] Of course, it would be different if there was a claim for salvage reward (as that gives rise to a maritime lien as well as a statutory right *in rem*); or if the shipowner claimed for loss to his ship by the negligence of the salvors (as, although this could be a breach of the salvage contract, it could also be damage 'done by' the salvage tug within the Act).[50]

44   *The Span Terza* [1982] 1 Lloyd's Rep. 225, where an owner arrested a time charterer's ship for unpaid hire.

45   *The Sandrina: Gatoil Intenational Inc.* v. *Arkwright-Boston, Mutual Insurance Co. & Others,* [1985] 1 Lloyd's Rep. 181. That case concerned unpaid war risk premiums on cargo, but the same principle would apply to, e.g., unpaid P & I Club calls, *The Aifanourios* [1980] 2 Lloyd's Rep. 403.

46   *The Antonis P. Lemos: Samick Lines Co. Ltd* v. *Owners of the Ship 'Antonis P. Lemos'* [1985] 1 Lloyd's Rep. 283.

47   *The Sandrina, supra,* this would exclude container hire agreements, per Lord Keith at p. 188.

48   *The Antonis P. Lemos, supra,* allowing a sub-charterer to sue an owner in tort for delay, even though the only 'agreement' was the charterparty between the owner and the 'head' charterer.

49   *The Tesaba* [1982] 1 Lloyd's Rep. 397 where a salvor claimed damages from a shipowner for allowing the cargo to be removed before security had been provided to the salvors under the LOF 1980 salvage agreement. See Chapter 24, *infra*.

50   *The Eschersheim* [1976] 2 Lloyd's Rep. 1. See also *The Conoco Britannia* [1972] 1 Lloyd's Rep. 342 (towage indemnity).

7.2.6 PROCEDURE

A claimant can keep watch on all the ships in a fleet by use of a commercial organization such as Lloyd's Intelligence Service which can report on all ship movements, or by consulting Lloyd's List daily. The 'sister ship' provision is very important because, although the offending ship may be kept well clear of British ports, the claimant can 'pounce' on any of the sisters. Of course, he can only arrest one ship per claim and not the whole fleet.[51] However, he is entitled to have a writ issued naming more than one ship and to keep this ready until one of the ships is available for arrest.[52] The writ is valid for 12 months, after which it may be renewed.[53] Renewal of a writ *in rem* will not be allowed unless there had been no reasonable opportunity of serving it, e.g. where the relevant ship had not called at a British port.[54] But a change of ownership *after* a writ has been issued will not stop its being renewed.[55]

7.2.7 'BENEFICIAL' OWNERSHIP

We have seen that one of the grounds on which the statutory right of action *in rem* may be invoked is that D was the 'beneficial owner' of all the shares in the ship when the writ was issued.[56] A court is entitled to look to the 'real' owner and not a nominee.[57] This may involve looking beyond the registered owner or the legal owner of the 64 shares in the ship and, in an appropriate case, 'lifting the corporate veil'.[58] It seems that a court might lift the 'veil' if it was being used as some deliberate attempt to obscure the true ownership, or if the company structure was a sham.[59]

---

51 *The Banco* [1971] 1 All E.R. 524. The Supreme Court Act 1981, s. 21(8) provides that once a ship has been arrested no other ship may be arrested to enforce the same claim. This would not apply if the first ship had been arrested by mistake, i.e. where its owners could not be liable *in personam*, see *The Stephen J.* [1985] 2 Lloyd's Rep. 344.

52 *Ibid.*, and Supreme Court Act 1981, s. 21(8).

53 R.S.C. Order 6, 1.8.

54 *The Berny* [1978] 1 All E.R. 1065. A fresh writ could, of course, be issued if the relevant time bar had not expired, *ibid.* and see Chapter 26, *infra*.

55 *The Helene Roth* [1980] 1 All E.R. 1078. This is because the statutory right *in rem* attaches on the issuing of the writ, as discussed earlier.

56 Supreme Court Act 1981, s. 21(4).

57 *The Saudi Prince* [1982] 2 Lloyd's Rep. 255.

58 *The Aventicum* [1978] 1 Lloyd's Rep. 184, 187; *The Saudi Prince, supra* at p. 260: *cf.* ss. 57, 58, Merchant Shipping Act 1894.

59 *The Maritime Trader* [1981] 2 Lloyd's Rep. 153, 157; *The Aventicum, supra*.

The technical legal difficulty is that a company is not normally the beneficial owner of the assets of its subsidiary. This is a particular problem with one-ship subsidiary companies. It is very difficult to arrest sister ships as, by definition, there are no 'sisters' owned by D: each ship is owned by a separate limited company.

7.3 PRIORITY[60]

One of the most difficult tasks, but very important in practice, is to explain the priority of the various claims which have been discussed. It is obvious that several different claims, each giving rise to a maritime, or other, lien, may exist at the same time against one ship, or other maritime property. For instance, a ship may collide with another vessel through negligent navigation and be salved by a third one; the owners of the salved vessel may become insolvent and fail to discharge their obligations to pay the wages and disbursements of master and crew; in addition, there may be mortgages on the ship and after all these happenings a possessory lien of a repairer may have attached. Such circumstances, taken together, may exceed the value of the ship. In what order should they be discharged?

7.3.1 PRIORITY BETWEEN DIFFERENT TYPES OF LIEN

The first point to note is that there is no *general* statutory provision setting out the priorities for maritime claims. Sometimes statutes give harbour authorities an express right to detain vessels for a variety of causes, e.g. damage to quays,[61] and these rights are usually treated as having priority over other claims, e.g. cargo claims.[62] Otherwise, general principles are to be found largely in the case law, but it should be remembered that deciding priority is very much a matter for the discretion of the court.[63] The expenses of the Admiralty Marshal are normally paid first, but in general, maritime liens will be accorded the

---

60 See Thomas (1980), Chapter 9; Jackson (1985), Chapter 17; K. McGuffie,
    P. Fugeman, V. Gray, *Admiralty Practice* (1964, with supplement), Chapter 29. For
    priority of registered mortgages, see Section 6.4, *supra*.
61 See, e.g. the Harbour, Docks, and Piers Clauses Act 1847, s. 74, and Section
    20.2.4, *infra*.
62 *The Charger* [1966] 1 Lloyd's Rep. 670.
63 See, e.g., *The Royal Wells* [1984] 2 Lloyd's Rep. 255.

highest priority, e.g. over mortgages and statutory rights *in rem*. Statutory rights *in rem* are subject to maritime liens whenever created and possessory liens and mortgages created prior to them, e.g. a salvage claim, would be paid before a towage claim. As between themselves statutory liens probably rank *pari passu* (i.e. they are treated as of equal rank).

The common law possessory lien of a shiprepairer must stand back in favour of maritime liens that had attached before the ship came into his yard, for he must be taken to have admitted the vessel with all encumbrances when he consented to repair her. However, the possessory lien will rank before any later claims, including maritime liens. It should be noted that the possessory lien does depend on possession and will be lost when the repairer allows the vessel to leave the repair yard.[64] Even though out of possession, the repairer will continue to have his statutory right *in rem*.

We have already noted that different states recognize different maritime liens. What should a British court do when faced with a claim subject to a maritime lien in, e.g., the USA but not in the UK?

Illustration: *The Halcyon Isle*[65]

A mortgage dated April 1973 but registered in May 1974 was arranged by an English bank on the British registered *Halcyon Isle*. In March 1974 an American shiprepairer carried out work and supplied materials to the ship. Under US law a shiprepairer has a maritime lien but not in English (or Singaporean) law. The mortgagees arrested the ship in Singapore in September 1974 and she was sold by the court in 1975 for a sum insufficient to satisfy all the creditors.

Held: (Privy Council) an English court would be bound to apply English law (the law of the forum) which did not recognize the repairer's maritime lien. Accordingly, the mortgage took priority over the shiprepairer's statutory right *in rem*. Any possessory lien had been lost when the ship left the USA.

The result of this decision is that 'a ship will attract and shed maritime liens as she journeys around the world'.[66]

---

64 *The Gustaf* (1862) Lush. 506, 167 E.R. 230; *The Russland* [1924] P. 55. The possessory lien only extends to the cost of repairs: if he claims damages for occupation of his dock after repairs are completed, no lien attaches, *The Katingaki: Bristol Channel Shiprepairers Co.* v. *The Katingaki* [1976] 2 Lloyd's Rep. 372.
65 *Bankers Trust International Ltd.* v. *Todd Shipyards Corporation* [1980] 2 Lloyd's Rep. 325.
66 Jackson (1985), at p. 345.

7.3.2   PRIORITY BETWEEN MARITIME LIENS

Next we must consider the priority among the maritime liens.

(A)   CONTRACT LIENS

In the group of maritime liens arising from a contract, salvage[67] comes first, since by the salvage service the ship has been preserved and thereby the fund out of which any other claimants are paid.[68]

Next come wages, followed by the master's disbursements and bottomry.[69] At one time the master was personally liable to pay seamen their wages, but this is no longer the case.[70] The old rule justified the crew's wages being paid before the master. In *The Royal Wells*[71] it was held that this special treatment was no longer justified and all claims for wages now rank *pari passu*.

The priority of the salvage lien has been confirmed in *The Lyrma (No. 2)*[72] where a salvage lien and crew's wages and master's disbursements liens competed for a fund only large enough to meet the salvage claim. When salvage was complete the salved vessel's value was enough to satisfy all three claims, but by the time the Marshal sold the vessel its value, for various reasons, had fallen appreciably. No distinction could be made between wages earned and disbursements made before and after the salvage services. It was true that, in the absence of a salvage agreement, the court would never make a salvage award swallowing the entire salved value. Where, however, as in this case, a valid agreement for fixed remuneration had been made, the salvors were entitled to the full amount, even if this meant leaving nothing for other claimants.

Finally, among several contractual liens, unless special exceptions apply, and especially among several liens for salvage services, the later lien ranks first. Again, this can be readily explained by considering that it was the later act that preserved the ship for earlier claimants.

---

67 As already noted, although not strictly contractual salvage is generally considered as quasi-contractual in this group.
68 *The Gustaf, supra.*
69 *The Union* (1860) Lush, 128, 167 E.R. 60: *cf. The Hope* (1873) 1 Asp. M.C. 563.
70 Except where the master is, e.g. a part-owner. See Chapter 9, *infra*.
71 [1984] 2 Lloyd's Rep. 255.
72 [1978] 2 Lloyd's Rep. 30.

(B)   DAMAGE LIENS

On the other hand, maritime liens for damage arising from tort (*ex delicto*), principally by collision, rank *pari passu* even if it can be proved that the various damage liens arose at different times.[73] This is fair since the court, in whose hands the ship is when the action is tried, will see that the proceeds be divided equally, unless very special reasons exist to the contrary.

(C)   CONFLICTING CONTRACT AND DAMAGE LIENS

In respect of conflicting claims arising between both groups, no hard and fast rule exists, and it is curious that until late in the day the case law did not even allow a reliable forecast of what would be done in an individual case.[74] Generally speaking, the matter is dealt with on an equitable basis, and it has now been laid down[75] that the court will be guided by the following type of consideration. Much though seamen, lenders on bottomry and salvors[76] have worked to preserve the fund, they have meddled with the ship of their own free will:[77] therefore the owners of a ship damaged in a subsequent collision have a better right to the fund.[78] Thus, maritime liens arising from tort have priority over those arising from contract which accrued before the tort. On the other hand, a salvage lien attaching to the ship after a collision will take precedence over the damage liens resulting from that collision.[79] Wages liens are postponed to subsequent damage liens and, probably, to earlier damage liens as well.[80]

---

73 See the very careful judgement of Bateson J in *The Stream Fisher*, [1927] P. 73, where there were four successive collisions.

74 Procedure is regulated by R.S.C. Order 75, r. 22.

75 *The Inna* [1938] P. 148.

76 And if it is ever held that pilots and tugs have a maritime lien the same will apply to them.

77 It has become doubtful whether this consideration is still valid in respect of salvage liens, as ships are bound to go to the assistance of vessels in distress: Maritime Conventions Act 1911, s. 6.; Merchant Shipping (Safety Convention) Act 1949, s. 22; see Chapter 21.3.

78 *The Stream Fisher, supra.*

79 *The Inna, supra.*

80 *The Elin* (1882) 8 P.D. 39, 129. An additional reason for postponing wages claims to subsequent damage liens might be that the crew could have caused the collision through negligence.

8

CONSTRUCTION, MAINTENANCE AND EQUIPMENT

8.1 BACKGROUND

THE problems discussed in this chapter were not recognized before the eighteenth century, when the design of ships was first scientifically studied. Until then shipwrights proceeded by rule of thumb, though most skilfully, for the ships they built performed marvellous feats, as demonstrated by the great sea voyages of past ages, in particular in the sixteenth and seventeenth centuries. Of course, disasters happened as, for instance, when in 1628 the Swedish flagship, the *Vasa*, went down in Stockholm harbour, the victim of a sudden squall, forcing her to heel over, so that water entered through the lower gun ports and prevented her from righting herself.

That something was amiss with ship construction was known to the shipbuilders in those days. In England, James I granted a charter to the Worshipful Company of Shipwrights in 1612, a body formed to raise the standard of knowledge and practice among shipbuilders, who included such eminent men as the members of the Pett family and Sir Anthony Deane, who designed ships used by Raleigh, but of course also many not so good practitioners of the craft.

Not until the nineteenth century was the knowledge gained in the eighteenth applied in practice. A few dates are useful in this context. In 1855, Lloyd's Register published rules for iron shipbuilding, and followed this up in 1877 with rules for steel shipbuilding. Meanwhile, in 1860, the Royal Institution of Naval Architects was formed.

That century, too, witnessed the effect of humanitarian considerations, when people began to realize the shocking conditions under which passengers and crews lived on board ships, as described, for instance, in Robert Louis Stevenson's *The Wrecker*, in Great Britain, and by Richard Henry Dana's *Two Years before the Mast*, in America. The

Merchant Shipping Act 1854 established state supervision by the Board of Trade, now provided by the Department of Trade (DoT).

The present law is contained in the Merchant Shipping Acts, 1894–1984, supplemented by a mass of Statutory Instruments issued under them.[1] Most of the safety provisions are the fruit of international Conventions, through which maritime nations have made this branch of the law more or less uniform, prompted by humanitarian motives and the realization that without international standards real safety could not be achieved.

The international movement gathered strength after the 1939–45 war. In 1948, the London Conference for Safety of Life at Sea agreed on a Convention, embodied in the Merchant Shipping (Safety Convention) Act 1949. The safety provisions were revised at conferences of 1960 and 1974 convened by the Inter-governmental Maritime Consultative Organization (IMCO), now known as the International Maritime Organization (IMO). IMO co-ordinates all the international maritime safety legislation. The current international rules are those under the International Convention for the Safety of Life at Sea (SOLAS) 1974, which led to the Merchant Shipping (Safety Convention) Act 1977 and the Merchant Shipping Act 1979. The conventions and statutes reflect the progress of marine engineering and inventions of importance to shipping – buoyant apparatus, radiotelegraphy, radar, and giant tankers, to mention only some.

State supervision extends to ships generally, and passenger ships and oil tankers in particular, to which, more recently, have been added submersible craft, known popularly as midget submarines; and to care for the crews. Unfortunately, history has shown that the international community tends to react on safety matters *after* disasters, such as those to the *Titanic* in 1912 and the *Amoco Cadiz* in 1978. After the former incident watertight compartments were made compulsory. After the latter went aground because of steering failure, an IMO International Conference on Tanker Safety and Pollution Prevention agreed, in 1978, on a Protocol to SOLAS 1974 requiring improved steering gear on tankers. SOLAS 1974 has a special 'tacit acceptance' procedure

---

1 See, e.g., Merchant Shipping Act 1979, ss. 21, 22 as amended by the Safety at Sea Act 1986, s. 11. Students are advised to consult *Halsbury's Statutory Instruments*, Vol. 20 and Cumulative Supplements for comprehensive information. For hovercraft, see Hovercraft (General) Order 1972 (S.I. No. 674), Arts 8-12, which also provide for annual safety certificates, Civil Aviation Act 1982, s. 85; Hovercraft (Application of Enactments) Order 1972 (S.I. No. 971): amendments 1978 (S.I. No. 1913), 1979 (S.I. No. 1309) 1982 (S.I. No. 715), 1983 (S.I. No. 769).

whereby amendments can be agreed comparatively quickly without the
bother of reconvening a diplomatic conference.[2]

8.2 UNSEAWORTHINESS

The general aim is expressed in s. 44, Merchant Shipping Act 1979,
enacting a clause in the SOLAS Protocol 1978. This section provides as
follows: Both owner and master of a ship in a port in the UK, or of a
British-registered ship in any port commit an offence if the ship 'is unfit
... to go to sea without serious danger to human life'. The unfitness
must be caused by the defective condition of hull, machinery or equipment or by overloading or improper loading. Master and owner have a
valid defence if they can prove that they had made arrangements to
restore the vessel's fitness before going to sea or that it was reasonable
not to have made such arrangements – possibly because no adequate
repair facilities were available. Prosecution in England and Wales or in
Northern Ireland requires the consent of the Secretary of State or the
Director of Public Prosecutions.

It may be noticed in passing that a particular danger to ships in the
North Atlantic, that of icebergs, is guarded against by the North
Atlantic ice patrol, of which the UK is a member. This gives warning of
icebergs near the shipping routes,[3] and masters of ships anywhere have
a duty to report to the nearest coast station: tropical storms; ice;
temperatures below freezing-point associated with gale-force winds
causing severe ice accretion on superstructures; Beaufort Scale 10 winds
when no storm warning has been received; or any other direct dangers
to navigation. Failure to report is an offence.[4]

---

2 This procedure has been used for further amendments to the steering gear
   provisions of SOLAS 1974, see Resolution MSC. I (XLV) adopted on 20
   November 1981; and the Merchant Shipping (Modification of Enactments)
   Regulations 1985 (S.I. No. 212). For SOLAS 1974/78 see Singh (1983) Vol. 2,
   p. 1052 *et seq.*
3 Merchant Shipping (Safety Convention) Act 1949, s. 25.
4 Merchant Shipping (Safety and Load Line Conventions) Act 1932, s. 24; Merchant
   Shipping Act 1964, s. 16; Merchant Shipping (Navigational Warnings) Regulations
   1980 (S.I. No. 534), amended 1981 (S.I. No. 406); Merchant Shipping Notice No.
   M.1108.

8.3   CONSTRUCTION AND EQUIPMENT

Returning to the safety of the ship itself, it must be understood that a far more effective way of ensuring seaworthiness is to provide in great detail what should be done and, after appropriate inspection and survey, to prove by internationally acceptable certificates that what is required has been done.

The process of supervision begins at the construction stage. Hull, machinery and equipment of UK registered sea-going ships measuring not less than 500 gross tons, or even smaller vessels where the DoT has made an appropriate order, must comply with stringent standards.[5] 3The detailed provisions are contained in Regulations made under the Merchant Shipping Acts. The Regulations run into hundreds of pages and are often amended to take into account international developments. The main Regulations in use now give effect to SOLAS 1974/78, as amended, and include the following: the Merchant Shipping (Cargo Ship Construction and Survey) Regulations 1984;[6] the Merchant Shipping (Passenger Ship Construction and Survey) Regulations 1984;[7] the Merchant Shipping (Navigational Equipment) Regulations 1984;[8] the

5 Merchant Shipping Act 1964, s. 2, as amended by the Merchant Shipping (Safety Convention) Act 1977, Merchant Shipping (Modification of Merchant Shipping (Safety Convention) Act 1949 and Merchant Shipping Act 1964) Regulations 1980 (S.I. No. 539); Merchant Shipping (Modification of Enactments) Regulations 1981 (S.I. No. 568) – dealing with the SOLAS Protocol 1978, and the Merchant Shipping (Modification of Enactments) Regulations 1985 (S.I. No. 2120) – dealing with the SOLAS amendments of 1981; Merchant Shipping Act 1979, s. 22(2).

6 S.I. No. 1217, M.S. Notices Nos M. 1133, 1134. Like the other recent regulations these apply to new ships (here ships whose keels were laid or were at a similar stage of construction on or after 1 September 1984). For existing ships, reference should be made to the previous regulations as amended, e.g., the Merchant Shipping (Cargo Ship Construction and Survey) Regulations 1981 (S.I. No. 572), amended 1984 (No. 1219), 1986 (No. 1067): M.S. Notices Nos M. 964, 965. For non-UK ships, see the Merchant Shipping (Application of Construction and Survey Regulations to other Ships) Regulations 1985 (S.I. No. 661), also the Merchant Shipping (Cargo Ship Construction and Survey) Regulations 1981 (Amendment) Regulations 1985 (S.I. No. 663).

7 S.I. No. 1216, amended 1985 (No. 1216), 1986 (No. 1074): M.S. Notice No. M. 1132. For ships built before 1 September 1984, see the Merchant Shipping (Passenger Ship Construction) Regulations 1980 (S.I. No. 535), amended 1985 (S.I. No. 660): M.S. Notices Nos M. 932, 945. For non-UK ships see 1985 (S.I. No. 660), the Merchant Shipping (Application of Construction and Survey Regulations to other Ships) Regulations 1985 (S.I. No. 661).

8 S.I. No. 1203, amended 1985 (S.I. No. 659); M.S. Notice No. M. 1138. The previous regulations will only apply to non-UK ships: Merchant Shipping (Navigational Equipment) Regulations 1980 (S.I. No. 530), amended 1981 (S.I. No. 579), 1984 (S.I. No. 1203), 1985 (S.I. No. 659).

Merchant Shipping (Radio Installations) Regulations 1980;[9] the Merchant Shipping (Radio Installations Survey) Regulations 1981;[10] the Merchant Shipping (Fire Protection) Regulations 1984;[11] the Merchant Shipping (Life Saving Appliances) Regulations 1980);[12] the Merchant Shipping (Cargo Ship Safety Equipment Survey) Regulations 1981.[13]

There are also special rules for fishing vessels.[14]

The Cargo Ship Construction and Survey Regulations provide for such matters as structural strength; watertight bulkheads and doors; boilers and steering gear; fuel specification and installations; control, monitoring and alarm systems; electrical installations for lighting systems and emergency power; means of escape; surveys. On completion there is a full survey, as a result of which the DoT issues a Cargo Ship Construction Certificate. Intermediate, periodic and annual surveys are also required.[15] This ensures that the ship is kept up to standard by regular checks.

The Passenger Ship Construction and Survey Regulations deal with similar issues, but pay particular attention to safety and damage control matters, such as watertight subdivisions, pumping arrangements, means of escape and guard rails. The Regulations create six main categories of passenger ships and the requirements differ according to the length of voyages, including excursions, on which they sail and the

9 S.I. No. 529, amended 1981 (S.I. No. 582), 1984 (S.I. Nos 346, 1223), 1985 (S.I. No. 1216), (No. 1075); M.S. Notices Nos M. 928, 948, 1119.

10 S.I. No. 583.

11 S.I. No. 1218, amended 1985 (S.I. No. 1193), 1986 (S.I. No. 1070). For non-UK ships built between 25 May 1980–31 August 1984, see the Merchant Shipping (Fire Appliances) Regulations 1980 (S.I. No. 544), amended 1981 (S.I. Nos 1472, 1747), 1984 (S.I. No. 97), 1985 (S.I. No. 1194). For ships built before 25 May 1980, see the consolidating Merchant Shipping (Fire Protection) (Ships Built Before 25 May 1980) Regulations 1985 (S.I. No. 1218). Also 1986 (S.I. No. 1248).

12 S.I. No. 538, amended 1981 (S.I. Nos, 577, 1472), 1984 (S.I. No. 97), 1986 (S.I. No. 1072): and see now the Merchant Shipping (Life Saving Appliances) Regulations 1986 (S.I. No. 1066). Note also the Merchant Shipping (Medical Stores) Regulations 1986 (S.I. No. 144).

13 S.I. No. 573, amended 1985 (S.I. No. 211).

14 Fishing Vessels (Safety Provisions) Act 1970, Safety at Sea Act 1986, Fishing Vessels (Safety Provisions) Rules 1975 (S.I. No. 330), amended 1974 (S.I. No 471), 1976 (S.I. No. 432), 1978 (S.I. Nos 1598, 1873), 1979 (S.I. Nos 252, 313, 498), 1981 (S.I. No. 567); The Ard Aidham and Nordland [1985] 2 Lloyd's Rep. 412. The UK has ratified the Torremolinos International Convention for the Safety of Fishing Vessels 1977, but it is not yet in force.

15 The extent and frequency of the surveys varies according to the type of ship and machinery involved. Intermediate and annual surveys are carried out according to procedures specified in M.S. Notice No. M. 1134.

number of passengers they are licensed to carry. All ships must be surveyed at least once a year.[16] Those engaged on international voyages (Classes I and II) must have a Passenger and Safety Certificate. The others (Classes III–VI) must have a Passenger Certificate. The Certificate states the number of passengers permitted.[17]

The Cargo Ship Safety Equipment Survey Regulations require that the ship's safety equipment complies with the requirements of the various safety regulations. After a satisfactory survey (which must be repeated annually) a Cargo Ship Safety Equipment Certificate is issued.

All ships must observe high standards regarding radio installations, life-saving appliances and equipment for detecting, controlling and extinguishing fire.[18] The Radio Installations Survey Regulations require the radiotelegraph and radiotelephone facilities of passenger and cargo ships to comply with the requirements of the Radio Installations Regulations. Again, after a satisfactory survey (repeated annually) the DoT will issue a Cargo Ship Radiotelegraphy Certificate or a Cargo Ship Radiotelephony Certificate, as appropriate.

Of particular interest, perhaps, are the Life Saving Appliance Regulations. These deal with the number of lifeboats, motor lifeboats, inflatable boats, life-rafts, buoyant apparatus, lifebuoys, lifejackets, smoke signals and line-throwing equipment, as well as detailed specifications for them. They also provide for the positioning and capacity of lifeboats, bearing in mind that ships with a heavy list cannot launch the boats positioned on one of their sides. The very great detail of these regulations is indicated, e.g., by the provision in Sch. 13 that thread for the sewing of kapok lifejackets must comply with British Standards Specification. The requirements vary, again, with the type of ship. The

---

16 Merchant Shipping Act 1894, s. 271, as amended by the Merchant Shipping Act 1964, s. 17, but steam ferry boats working on chains are exempted. Passenger ships are ships carrying more than 12 passengers: Merchant Shipping Act 1894, s. 267; Merchant Shipping (Safety Convention) Act 1949, s. 26; Merchant Shipping Act 1964, s. 17; Merchant Shipping (Passenger Ship Construction and Survey) Regulations 1984 (S.I. 1216) reg. 1. *Duncan* v. *Graham* [1951] 1 K.B. 68 held that a fishing vessel carrying more than 12 passengers on one occasion gratuitously to visit a warship lying offshore was not a passenger ship. But drivers of goods vehicles on a roll-on, roll-off ferry are passengers, even if carried free of charge: *Clayton* v. *Albertsen* [1972] 3 All E.R. 364 (a pilotage case). Nor do persons cease to be passengers by signing a statement describing their capacity as 'unpaid crewing participation': *The Biche, Secretary of State for Trade* v. *Booth* [1984] 1 Lloyd's Rep. 26.

17 Merchant Shipping Act 1894, s. 274; Merchant Shipping (Safety Convention) Act 1949, s. 17.

18 Merchant Shipping Act 1964, ss. 8, 10; Merchant Shipping Act 1894, s. 427.

Regulations create 12 main classes of ship, including the six classes of passenger ships already mentioned. These vary from liners like the *Queen Elizabeth 2* (Class I) engaged on long international voyages, down to pleasure craft of 13.7 metres length (Class XII). Following disasters at holiday resorts, passenger ships of Class VI which are under 21.3 metres long and plying not more than three miles from their starting points shall carry liferafts, buoyant apparatus and lifebuoys sufficient for the total number of persons the ship is certified to carry. At one time the requirement extended only to 70 per cent of the certified number.

Other relevant Regulations include the Merchant Shipping (Closing of Openings in Hulls and Watertight Bulkheads) Regulations 1980[19] and the Merchant Shipping (Dangerous Goods) Regulations 1981.[20] There are special rules dealing with the testing and marking of anchors and chain cables.[21] Regulations also exist to ensure the safety of means of access to vessels, such as gangways and ladders.[22] Freight containers should comply with the International Convention for Safe Containers 1972.[23]

Failure to observe the various Regulations is punishable. For instance, the owner or master of a cargo ship not carrying a Cargo Ship Safety Construction Certificate when going to sea, or in the case of ships not registered in the UK, an 'accepted Safety Convention Certificate' of another country, is liable to a fine.[24] Disregard of the construction and

19 S.I. No. 540.
20 S.I. No. 1747, amended 1986 (S.I. No. 1069). Note also the Merchant Shipping (Grain) Regulations requirements 1985 (S.I. No. 2017) which ensure compliance with the SOLAS 1974 (as amended in 1981) as to the carriage of grain in bulk. The shifting of grain in rough seas can be very dangerous, see M.S. Notice No. M.1044.
21 Anchors and Chain Cables Act 1967; Anchors and Chain Cables Rules 1970 (S.I. No. 1453); Merchant Shipping (Cargo Ship Construction and Survey) Regulations 1984 (S.I. No. 1217), reg. 51.
22 Merchant Shipping (Means of Access) Regulations 1981 (S.I. No. 1729).
23 Freight Containers (Safety Convention) Regulations 1984 (S.I. No. 1890).
24 Merchant Shipping Act 1964, ss. 3, 5 and 6, Merchant Shipping (Safety Convention) Act 1949, s. 14: as modified by the Merchant Shipping (Modification of Enactments) Regulations 1981 (S.I. No. 568), 1985 (S.I. No. 212). Many fines were increased by the Merchant Shipping Act 1979, s. 43. Note that the Criminal Justice Act 1982 created a standard scale for fines with a general power to increase the relevant sums: see ss. 37-40, 46-49.

safety rules themselves is also an offence that is punishable by fine.[25]

Failure to observe rules relating to passenger ships, e.g. carrying more passengers than permitted and going to sea without the appropriate certificates, is also an offence punishable by a fine which, on indictment, can be heavy.[26] In this context, a provision in the Firearms Act 1968, is worth mentioning. This Act provides that persons wishing to have a firearm and ammunition must hold a police certificate. But no such certificate is needed for persons on board a ship requiring the firearm as part of the ship's equipment.[27]

For historical reasons it is worth mentioning that at one time special rules were made to counter abuses prevailing in emigrant ships.[28] These floating slums, as they were called, carried poor European emigrants from ports in the UK, the Netherlands and Germany to America. During the voyage these steerage passengers had to put up with overcrowded accommodation and unsanitary conditions, though there were exceptions, as recorded by Charles Dickens in *The Uncommercial Traveller*. Subsequently, improved general rules for all passenger ships rendered the emigrant ship provisions obsolete, and they were finally repealed in 1972.

8.4   LOAD LINES

One of the factors recognized relatively early on as influencing safety is the degree of submersion of a ship in water. This recognition was due to

25 See e.g., 1984 (S.I. No. 1217) reg. 64; 1980 (S.I. No. 538) reg. 53. Interestingly, the criminal statistics for 1983 (the latest available) show that for all offences of endangering life at sea (including contravention of the construction and survey rules) there were only four persons proceeded against. All were convicted and fined, (three in the magistrates' court and one at the Crown Court): *Criminal Statistics England and Wales,* Supplementary Tables 1983 Vol. 4, pp. 10-11. In the previous year there were only nine convictions and all were fined, 1982 *Statistics* Vol. 1, p.8, Vol. 2, p.6.

26 Merchant Shipping Act 1894, ss. 281, 283; Merchant Shipping Act 1906, s. 21; Merchant Shipping (Safety Convention) Act 1949, s. 12; Merchant Shipping (Load Lines) Act 1967, s. 25; 1984 (S.I. No. 1216) reg. 86.

27 S. 13. Presumably this allows ships to carry weapons to repel the growing number of armed pirates operating in some parts of the world.

28 Merchant Shipping Act 1894, s. 268.

one of the social reformers in nineteenth century England, Samuel Plimsoll, of Bristol. He exposed the 'coffin ships', vessels putting to sea though unseaworthy and overloaded – and over-insured into the bargain, so that their owners, risking the lives of the men sailing these ships, were sure of exorbitant profits whether the ship arrived or foundered. Plimsoll campaigned in and out of Parliament for the fixing of load lines for each vessel, showing the permitted degree of submersion, and in 1876 he succeeded. These load lines are still colloquially known as Plimsoll lines.

The modern law is contained in the Merchant Shipping (Load Lines) Act 1967, which gives effect to the International Convention on Load Lines of 1966. Detailed provisions are contained in the Merchant Shipping (Load Line) Rules 1968,[29] made by the DoT. They apply to all ships, except ships of war, fishing boats and pleasure yachts, and to ships carrying an exemption certificate because they ply in sheltered waters.[30] Attached to the Rules is a map, showing areas and seasonal periods, for load lines must, of course, differ according to whether the ship sails in fresh water or saltwater, in the tropics or the North Atlantic, in summer or in winter. According to Sch. 1 of the Rules, ships have painted on their hulls load lines marked F for freshwater, T for tropical zone, S for summer, W for winter, and WNA for winter in the North Atlantic. Timber shipments call for special marking, indicated by an L, for instance, LW for timber shipments in winter. Owners must provide their masters with information relating to the loading and ballasting of their ships.[31]

The new provisions distinguish between old and new ships, the latter being those with keels laid since the country of their nationality acceded to the Convention,[32] the reason being that construction requirements for new ships are stricter, so that a greater degree of submersion can be permitted without endangering buoyancy.[33] These rules apply in particular to new, very long ships. Their great length, exceeding that of the longest waves, is a safeguard against the ship breaking its back, additional protection being the strengthening of the centre section of the keel.

Before commissioning a ship, the owner must apply for the assigning of its freeboard to the DoT, or to Lloyd's Register of Shipping, or the

---

29 S.I. No. 1053, amended 1970 (S.I. No. 1003), 1979 (S.I. 1267), 1980 (S.I. No. 641). For the 1966 Load Lines Convention, see Singh (1983) Vol. 2, p. 982.
30 Ss. 18, 19 of the 1967 Act, and Rule 11.
31 Rule 31.
32 S. 32.
33 Schs 4 and 5 of the Rules.

British Committee of Bureau Veritas, or the British Technical Committee of the American Bureau of Shipping, or the British Committee of Det Norske Veritas, or the British Committee of Germanischer Lloyd,[34] and after survey and tests the assigning authority issues a load-line certificate.[35]

On this basis, the DoT issues an 'International Load Line Certificate (1966)' for existing ships of not less than 150 gross tons and for new ships not less than 24 metres long. Other ships are issued with a 'United Kingdom Load Line Certificate'.[36] The DoT also has the power to issue certificates in respect of ships registered in, or flying the flag of, a Convention country, if requested to do so by the government of the parent country.[37]

If a ship sails or attempts to sail without load-line marks, it can be detained and the owner or master is liable to a fine.[38] The fine may be raised, having regard to the earning capacity of the ship as a result of overloading.[39]

8.5   SPECIAL SHIPS

Three other types of ship also require special rules, which must be discussed: tankers, nuclear-powered vessels and what are colloquially known as midget submarines.

8.5.1   TANKERS

The size of oil tankers, the frequency of disasters involving them,[40] and international public concern over oil pollution has led to much work at IMO in improving tanker design and construction.

In accordance with SOLAS 1974/78 (as amended) the Merchant Shipping (Cargo Ship Construction and Survey) Regulations 1984[41] provide general rules for ships' construction but there is a special part

34 Rule 2.
35 Rules 3, 5, 6.
36 S. 6.
37 S. 12.
38 S. 3.
39 S. 4.
40 E.g. the *Amoco Cadiz* in 1978, and Chapter 25, *infra*.
41 S.I. No. 1217.

for the construction of tankers, dealing, e.g., with cargo tank ventilation.[42] Similarly, the Merchant Shipping (Fire Protection) Regulations 1984,[43] Part IV, deals with fire prevention and fire appliances on board tankers. In particular it requires every tanker of 500 GRT and above to have a fixed deck foam system.[44] Tankers of 20 000 DWT or more must have an inert gas system in order to reduce the risk of explosions caused by flammable gases in empty cargo tanks.[45] These provisions do not apply to ships having Certificates of Fitness issued in compliance with the Codes of Construction and Equipment of Ships carrying Liquified Gases in Bulk or Dangerous Chemicals in Bulk.[46] Tankers over 500 GRT also have to be provided with cargo tank purging or gas freeing arrangements.[47]

After SOLAS 1974 the Secretary of State was given power by the Merchant Shipping Act 1974,[48] to make specific oil tanker construction rules providing for surveys and certification and placing restrictions on uncertificated tankers entering or leaving ports. These provisions have now been repealed[49] to enable the UK to give effect to the International Convention for the Prevention of Pollution from Ships (MARPOL) 1973 and its Protocol 1978.[50] MARPOL 1973/78 came into force on 2 October 1983 and is very wide ranging. Its treatment of matters such as operational pollution will be dealt with later,[51] but MARPOL 1973/78, with its Annex I (dealing with oil pollution), has been implemented in the UK by the Merchant Shipping (Prevention of Oil Pollution) Regulations 1983.[52] These are 164 pages long, but some of the provisions relating to construction and equipment may be noted here.

UK tankers of 150 GRT and above and other UK ships of 400 GRT and over must be surveyed by a surveyor appointed by the Secretary of State before the ship is put into service and then at intervals not exceeding five years. He must be satisfied that the ship's structure, equipment, systems, fittings, arrangements and material comply with

42 Part IIB, reg. 12.
43 S.I No. 1218.
44 Reg. 49(1), Sch. 13.
45 Reg. 49(2), Sch. 14. See *The Tojo Maru* [1972] A.C. 242, Sections 22.2.3, 24.7.2 *infra*.
46 Reg. 49.
47 Reg. 50.
48 Ss. 10-13, Schs 2 and 3.
49 Merchant Shipping (Prevention of Oil Pollution) Order 1983 (No. 1106), made under the Merchant Shipping Act 1979, s. 20. The Order was amended as from 7 January 1986 by 1985 (S.I. No. 2002).
50 Cmnd 5748, 7347: see Singh (1983) Vol. 3, pp. 2272, 2414.
51 Chapter 25, *infra*.
52 S.I. No. 1398.

the Regulations.[53] The Secretary of State then issues an International Oil Pollution Prevention (IOPP) Certificate if the ship is going to other countries which are party to MARPOL 1973/78. For other ships a UK Oil Pollution Prevention (UKOPP) Certificate is issued.[54] There must be annual surveys and an intermediate survey half-way through the life-span of the IOPP Certificate.[55] The IOPP Certificate ceases to be valid if there are significant alterations to the ship without the approval of the Secretary of State, or if the intermediate survey is not carried out.[56] It may also be suspended if corrective action is not carried out according to the specifications of the Certifying Authority (such as Lloyd's Register).[57]

Inspections to see if there is an IOPP or UKOPP Certificate on board may take place in UK ports or offshore terminals. If there is no such Certificate the inspector can take such steps as he thinks necessary to stop the ship sailing, until it can do so without presenting an unreasonable threat of harm to the marine environment.[58] Moreover, a harbour master may deny entry to ships which he has reason to believe do not comply with the Regulations.[59] A ship suspected of contravening the Regulations may also be detained.[60] But in the case of a non-UK vessel detained (or denied entry) the Secretary of State must inform the flag state immediately.[61]

The Regulations require ships to carry certain anti-pollution equipment. Thus ships of 400 GRT and above, but less than 10 000 GRT, must carry oily-water separating equipment.[62] Ships over 10 000 GRT (and any ship that carries ballast water in its fuel tanks) must also have an oil discharge monitoring and control system and oil filtering equipment.[63]

53 Reg. 4. The surveys must be in accordance with the procedures laid down in Merchant Shipping Notice No. M. 1076; reg. 4(4).
54 Reg. 7.
55 Regs 5, 6.
56 Regs 7(6), 8(2).
57 Reg. 9.
58 Reg. 32. See also Section 8.8.1, infra.
59 Reg. 33(1). See also Section 8.8.3, infra.
60 Reg. 33(2).
61 Reg. 33(3).
62 Reg. 14(1), Sch. 3.
63 Reg. 14(2), Sch. 3, Merchant Shipping Notice No. M. 1081. There are exceptions for ships which operate in special areas or are not required to hold an IOPP Certificate. But even ships under 400 GRT must be equipped as far as practicable and reasonable with installations for the satisfactory storage and discharge of oil; reg. 14(3). For oil tankers over 150 GRT see reg. 15. The requirements apply to existing ships from 2 October 1986; reg. 14(4).

A surprising amount of oil can cling to the ship's tanks or remain as an unpumpable mass at the bottom of a hold. So oil tankers of over 150 GRT must have facilities for dealing with this oil retained on board. There must be means to clear tanks and a slop tank must be provided for the oil residues.[64] The slop tank has to have the capacity of not less than 3 per cent of the cargo carrying capacity of the ship.[65] However, this figure is reduced to 2 per cent if the ship has segregated or dedicated clean ballast tanks or a crude oil washing system, and to 1 per cent in the case of combination carriers with smooth cargo walls.[66] Indeed, new crude oil tankers of 20 000 DWT and above must have segregated ballast tanks and crude oil washing system.[67] The idea is that ships can operate safely on ballast voyages without the need to put sea water into dirty cargo tanks.

Altering existing ships can be very expensive and so MARPOL 1973/78 and the Regulations[68] allowed some transitional provisions. Existing oil tankers of 40 000 DWT and above had to have segregated ballast tanks by 2 October 1983, or fit a crude oil washing system. A short-term alternative to these solutions was offered in the form of dedicated ballast tanks.[69] However, this option was only made available until 2 October 1985 (for oil tankers of 70 000 DWT and above), or until 2 October 1987 (for oil tankers between 40 000 and 70 000 DWT).[70] Moreover, no ballast water can be carried in the oil fuel tanks of new oil tankers of 150 GRT and above, or any other new ship of 4000 GRT and above.[71] Other ships must comply so far as it is reasonable and practicable to do so.[72] There are also requirements as to oil residue (sludge) tanks,[73] and pumping arrangements.[74]

64 Reg. 15. New oil tankers of 70 000 DWT and over must have two slop tanks, reg. 15(2).
65 Reg. 15(2). There must also be an oil discharge monitoring and control system, and effective oil/water interface detectors, reg. 3, Schs 4, 5.
66 Reg. 15(2).
67 Reg. 18, subject to regs 19, 20, Sch. 7.
68 Regs 18(7), 18(8), 22, 23.
69 Subject to reg. 20, Sch. 6.
70 Reg. 18(9). The definition of what is a new, as opposed to an existing, ship is rather complicated and depends on its size, when the building contract was made, or when the keel was laid, or when the ship was delivered, or when major conversion work took place. But a ship of 70 000 DWT and over could be 'new' if its shipbuilding contract was placed after 31 December 1975: a ship under 70 000 DWT could be new if the building contact was placed after 1 June 1979; regs 1(2), 17.
71 Reg. 24, although there are exceptions, e.g. where there are abnormal conditions.
72 Reg. 24(3).
73 Reg. 25.
74 Reg. 26.

Part 5 of the Regulations deals with special constructional require-ments for minimizing oil pollution from oil tankers due to side and bottom damage.[75] Part 6 requires offshore installations such as mobile or fixed drilling or production platforms to comply with the Regu-lations applicable to non-tankers over 400 GRT.[76]

Responsibilities are put on the owner and the master to ensure that the condition of the ship and its equipment is maintained so as to comply with the Regulations.[77] If any ship fails to comply with the Regulations the owner *and* the master can each be guilty of an offence,[78] which could lead to an unlimited fine if a prosecution is brought in the Crown Court.[79]

International concern has also been expressed about pollution from noxious liquid substances carried in bulk other than oil, e.g. bulk chemicals. Annex II of MARPOL 1973/78 regulates this but has not yet been implemented – partly due to the practical problems of making chemical tankers comply with its provisions. Implementation is expected in April 1987.[80]

The IMO International Codes for the Construction and Equipment of Ships Carrying Dangerous Chemicals or Liquefied Gases in Bulk – made under the 1983 Amendments to SOLAS 1974 – became manda-tory for new and converted chemical tankers and gas carriers as from 1 July 1986.[81]

8.5.2   NUCLEAR POWERED SHIPS

Following SOLAS 1974 the DoT was given power to make rules on such matters as annual surveys and safety certificates for ships having

75 Regs 27-29.
76 As well as having the equipment mentioned in regs 14, and 25(1) and (2): reg. 30.
77 Reg. 8(1).
78 This overcomes the problems of interpretation in the earlier legislation, see *The Huntingdon* [1974] 2 All E.R. 97 and Section 25.1.2, fn 24 *infra*
79 Reg. 34. In the magistrates' court the fine would be limited to £1000, or £50 000 in the case of a discharging offence: see Section 25.1.2, *infra*.
80 It will be brought into effect in the UK by an order under the Merchant Shipping Act 1979, ss. 20–22.
81 See the Merchant Shipping (Chemical Tankers) Regulations 1986 (S.I. No. 1068), the Merchant Shipping (Gas Carriers) Regulations 1986 (S.I. No. 1073): M.S. Notices Nos M. 1168-70. MARPOL 1973/78, reg. 13, puts an obligation on states to have requirements equivalent to the Bulk Chemical and Gas Carrier Codes. Ships which conform to these Codes are exempt from the special tanker construction rules in Part IIB of the Merchant Shipping (Cargo Ship Construction and Survey) Regulations 1984 (S.I. No. 1217), regs 1, 9.

nuclear power plants.[82] SOLAS 1974 came into force on 25 May 1980 but no rules have yet been made – probably because there are no British nuclear powered commercial ships.

8.5.3   SUBMERSIBLE CRAFT

Many of the tankers are giants, but the Merchant Shipping Act 1974 also deals with pygmies – submersible craft and apparatus.[83] The provisions are another example of new shipping law being created by a particular incident.

In August 1973, a Vickers Oceanic midget submarine, *Pisces III*, failed to surface, and its two-man crew was trapped 1600 feet down on the Atlantic sea-bed, one hundred miles off southern Ireland before being rescued after three days. Fortunately a disaster was averted. But very detailed regulations were made[84] and they apply to craft launched from a UK registered ship in, or adjacent to, UK waters. They provide for the safety of craft and supporting apparatus, and the safety, health and welfare of personnel. Certain operations are prohibited: for instance, no craft must be launched while the supporting vessel is under way. Special rules apply to work at varying depths; and no one must dive for more than three hours in any twenty-four. Diving craft must be registered, a diving manual must be provided to all engaged in operations, casualties must be reported, a diving log book kept, and emergency services have to be on call. Owners and master of the launching vessel commit offences by disregarding the Regulations.

We may also note, in passing, that a number of diving tragedies – particularly in the North Sea – have led to stricter control of diving operations generally. There must be a diving contractor for each operation and he has a number of duties imposed, such as providing specified plant and machinery.[85] Divers themselves must have certificates of training and medical fitness.[86] However, the Regulations do not apply

---

82 Merchant Shipping (Safety Convention) Act 1977, s. 2.
83 Ss. 16, 17, and Sch. 5.
84 Merchant Shipping (Diving Operations) Regulations 1975 (S.I. No. 116), amended 1975 (S.I. No. 2062), 1979 (S.I. 1519), 1981 (S.I. No. 399); Merchant Shipping (Registration of Submersible Craft) Regulations 1976 (S.I. No. 940), amended 1979 (S.I. 1519); J. Kitchen, (1975) 4 *Industrial Law Journal* 234.
85 Diving Operations at Work Regulations 1981 (S.I. No. 399), reg. 12.
86 *Ibid.*, regs 7, 10, 11.

to diving operations carried out by training schools, or persons involved in archaeological or other non-commercial research.[87]

8.6 CREW ACCOMMODATION

The days when crews had cramped quarters in the forecastle have passed for good. An International Labour Conference, held in Seattle in 1946, concluded Conventions on accommodation, food and catering for crews, and in the UK they were given effect by the Merchant Shipping Act 1948, since replaced by Merchant Shipping Act 1970, s. 20, and s. 96 in respect of non-sea-going ships. The Merchant Shipping (Crew Accommodation) Regulations 1978[88] provide in great detail the duties owed by shipowners to those manning their ships.

The process of procuring adequate accommodation begins at the construction stage. When a ship is being built to the order of a person qualified to own a British ship, a plan has to be submitted to the classification surveyor before the laying of the keel, showing the crew accommodation – its position, its height, and its proposed heating, lighting and furniture. The accommodation must in the ordinary way be above the summer load line, although on passenger and some other ships a different position may be agreed.

The Regulations also provide for high standards in older UK registered ships. All ships, in addition to the sleeping-rooms and mess rooms for members of the crew, must have adequate sanitary and hospital accommodation, and recreation facilities. The hospitals in ships regularly engaged in voyages to areas within the Persian Gulf must be air-conditioned. The sleeping-room for the first or only Radio Officer must be as near as practicable to the radio telegraph room, but in new ships it must not be in that room. Even the showers must operate within a given temperature range.

The DoT also has power to say what should be done in respect of provisions and water and also medical stores for the crew.[89]

---

87 Merchant Shipping (Diving Operations) Regulations 1975 (S.I. No. 116) amended 1981 (No. 399).
88 S.I. No. 795, amended 1979 (S.I. No. 491), 1984 (S.I. No. 41). Merchant Shipping (Crew Accommodation) (Fishing Vessels) Regulations 1975 (S.I. No. 2220). For the 1946 ILO Conventions, see Singh (1983) Vol. 2, p. 2143 *et seq.*
89 Merchant Shipping (Safety Convention) Act 1977, ss. 21 and 24; Merchant Shipping (Provisions and Water) Regulations 1972 (S.I. No. 1871), amended 1975 (S.I. No. 733), 1978 (S.I. No. 36), laying down special scales to take account of the different dietary needs of seamen ordinarily resident in countries such as India, Pakistan, Bangladesh, Singapore and Hong Kong.

Any three or more seamen may complain to the master that water or provisions are insufficient or unfit for consumption. Failure to take appropriate action gives a right to complain to the mercantile marine superintendent or consular officer, who may fine the master.[90] Any seaman has the right to complain to the master about his actions or about other seamen or conditions aboard the ship.[91] Masters have an obligation to make weekly inspections of accommodation and to record their findings in the log book.[92]

8.7 HEALTH AND SAFETY ON BOARD SHIP

Employers' duties to provide safe working conditions were placed on a new footing by the Health and Safety at Work Act 1974, a measure designed to prevent injuries in the first place. Premises, where health and safety must be provided for, include any vessel or hovercraft,[93] and so the Act concerns the shipowner. As far as is reasonably practicable he must maintain plant and systems of work in a condition that protects his employees, who must also be given information, instruction, training and competent supervision.[94]

The 1974 Act set up a special Health and Safety Commission and Executive. However, the DoT has much experience in the shipping field and the Merchant Shipping Act 1979, ss. 21 and 22, gave the Secretary of State wide powers to make regulations for securing the health and safety of persons on ships.[95] Some of the Regulations have been mentioned already in this chapter. But of particular note are the Merchant Shipping (Health and Safety: General Duties) Regulations 1984,[96] which give effect, in part, to the ILO Merchant Shipping

90 Merchant Shipping Act 1970, s. 22.
91 S. 23.
92 1978 (S.I. No. 795) reg. 38(2); 1975 (S.I. No. 2220), reg. 35(2); Merchant Shipping (Official Log Books) Regulations 1981 (S.I. No. 569), Schs 21, 22, Merchant Shipping (Official Log Books) (Fishing Vessels) Regulations 1981 (S.I. No. 570), Schs. 17, 18: see Section 9.3.2, *infra*.
93 S. 53.
94 S. 2. Corresponding duties are placed on employees; s. 7. Failure to discharge duties under the Act is an offence; s. 33.
95 For the protection of persons on land, see The Health and Safety at Work Act 1974. In 1984 there were over 1000 accidents to crew members, M.S. Notice No. M. 1174.
96 S.I. No. 408, in force 24 April 1984. See also the Merchant Shipping (Protective Clothing and Equipment) Regulations 1985 (S.I. No. 1664), dealing with clothing and equipment for hazardous work.

(Minimum Standards) Convention 1976.[97] The Regulations impose a general duty on an employer of persons on UK ships to ensure the health and safety of employees and other persons aboard who might be affected by his acts and omissions. Regulation 4(2) lists particular instances of this duty relating to, e.g.: the provision and maintenance of plant, machinery, and equipment; the use, handling, stowage and transport of articles and substances;[98] the provision of information, training and supervision to employees; the maintenance of work places in the ship; the collaboration with the employers of other persons who work on board ship (e.g. stevedores). The employer also has to prepare a written statement of his general health and safety policy on board and bring it to his employees' notice.[99] Safety is also something to which *employees* can contribute and reg. 5 puts a duty on them to take reasonable care for themselves and others on board and to co-operate with the employer in the fulfilment of his health and safety duties.

An employer can face a fine of up to £1000, and an employee of up to £50, for breach of duty, but it is a defence to show that all reasonable precautions and all due diligence were exercised to avoid the offence.[1] Anyone who intentionally or recklessly interferes with, or misuses, safety equipment faces a fine of up to £200 – which might deter vandals who discard lifebelts or let off fire hoses.

There are also powers of inspection and detention of ships not conforming to the Regulations. This power also applies to non-UK ships in a UK port on business, but the flag state must be notified.[2] In any event the ship should not be delayed unreasonably.[3]

The Merchant Shipping (Safety Officials and Reporting of Accidents and Dangerous Occurrences) Regulations 1982[4] require employers of persons on board most UK seagoing ships[5] to appoint a safety officer

97 Cmnd 7183. Singh (1983) Vol. 2, p. 2208.
98 Regulations may already deal with specific problems, such as the stowage of deck cargo, e.g. the Merchant Shipping (Load Lines) (Deck Cargo) Regulations 1968 (S.I. No. 1098); Merchant Shipping (Load Lines) Act 1967; M.S. Notice No. M. 1110.
99 Reg. 4(3). This does not apply to an employer with less than five employees in total on board UK ships.
1 Reg. 8. If a company director, or similar senior officer, is involved in the breach of duty by the company then he can be convicted as well, reg. 10. See also Section 9.6, *infra* for compensation for injuries at work.
2 Regs 12, 13. See Section 8.8.1, *infra*.
3 Merchant Shipping Act 1894, s. 460 allows for compensation to be given in this case: see also s. 692.
4 S.I. No. 876 amended 1984 (S.I. No. 93).
5 Fishing vessels, offshore installations at their working stations and pleasure craft are excluded, as are ships on which there are five crew or less, reg. 2(1).

and enable the crew to elect safety representatives.[6] The employer then has to appoint a safety committee.[7] The safety officer has the duty of using his best endeavours to ensure compliance with the employers' safety policies, and in particular with the DoT's 'Code of Safe Working Practices'.[8] He must also make reports to the DoT.[9] The employer and master must co-operate with the safety officer, representatives and committees, e.g. by providing information, or time off for training.[10]

The cynic might wonder if all these Regulations are simply pious hopes, but there is no doubt that at the very least they serve to enhance safety *consciousness* – among owners and crews.

8.8   POLICING THE REGULATIONS

8.8.1   INSPECTION AND DETENTION

The Merchant Shipping Act 1894, s. 728, gave the Secretary of State power to appoint inspectors to report on a number of matters, such as whether safety and other regulations under the Act had been complied with, or whether the hull and machinery of ships were in good condition. The power to appoint inspectors was extended by the Merchant Shipping Act 1979,[11] and the powers of the inspectors themselves were set out in great detail in s. 27. In order to perform their functions they may: board any UK ship, or any non-UK ship in UK waters; take equipment on board; make examinations and investigations; direct that the ship be left undisturbed during investigations; take measurements, photographs and samples; dismantle or test dangerous articles; remove such articles to test them or preserve them for inspection or as evidence; require persons to attend, answer questions and sign a declaration; require production of certain books and documents; inspect and take copies of such documents; require persons to provide them with facilities or assistance.

6 Reg. 3(1).
7 Reg. 3(5).
8 Reg. 5.
9 See Section 8.9 *infra*.
10 Reg. 8. Merchant Shipping (Code of Safe Working Practices) Regulations 1980 (S.I. No. 686). The Code is amended to take account of new information as to e.g. the hazards of asbestos on board ship: M.S. Notice No. M. 1155. Note also the Merchant Shipping (Musters and Training) Regulations 1986 (S.I. No. 1071).
11 S. 26.

Wilfully obstructing an inspector, or failing without reasonable excuse to comply with his requirements is an offence.[12]

There are some safeguards built into s. 27, e.g. to consult persons about the actions they propose to take with dangerous articles or substances.[13] In particular, the inspector is not authorized to detain a ship unnecessarily.[14] If he does so, the DoT may be liable to pay costs and compensation to the owner.[15]

There are many specific powers given to inspect and detain ships to see whether they comply with safety and other regulations. Some of them are mentioned elsewhere in the text, but the following list, by no means exhaustive, gives some idea of their range and number: Merchant Shipping (Cargo Ship Construction and Survey) Regulations 1984;[16] Merchant Shipping (Fire Protection) Regulations 1984;[17] Merchant Shipping (Passenger Ship Construction and Survey) Regulations 1984;[18] Merchant Shipping (Life-Saving Appliances) Regulations 1980;[19] Merchant Shipping (Medical Examination) Regulations 1983;[20] Merchant Shipping (Prevention of Oil Pollution) Regulations 1983;[21] Merchant Shipping (Means of Access) Regulations 1981;[22] Merchant Shipping (Certification and Watchkeeping) Regulations 1982;[23] the Dangerous Vessels Act 1985[24] and the Prevention of Oil Pollution Act 1971, ss. 12-16.[25]

The DoT may appoint surveyors[26] who are given powers of inspection and detention.[27] In particular they may require a ship to be taken to a dry dock for a survey of the hull or machinery.[28]

---

12 S. 28.
13 S. 27(5).
14 S. 27(2). *Cf. The Mihalis: Micosta S.A.* v. *Shetland Island Council* [1984] 2 Lloyd's Rep. 525.
15 Merchant Shipping Act 1894, s. 460.
16 S.I. No. 1217, reg. 65.
17 S.I. No. 1218, reg. 147.
18 S.I. No. 1216, reg. 87.
19 S.I. No. 538, reg. 54.
20 S.I. No. 808, regs 12–14.
21 S.I. No. 1398, reg. 33.
22 S.I. No. 1729, regs 15, 16.
23 S.I. No. 1699, reg. 12.
24 Section 8.8.3, *infra*.
25 Considered in Section 25.1.3, *infra*.
26 Merchant Shipping Act 1894, s. 724.
27 Merchant Shipping Act 1970, s. 76, as amended by the Merchant Shipping Act 1979, s. 37(5).
28 Merchant Shipping Act 1970, s. 76(2).

Wide powers are also given to sea fisheries officers to board fishing boats, to examine fish and to require the production of documents, in order to enforce EEC fishing restrictions.[29]

8.8.2   IMPROVEMENT AND PROHIBITION NOTICES

The Merchant Shipping Act 1984 allows DoT inspectors to issue improvement notices to persons in breach of their statutory duties under the Merchant Shipping Acts 1894–1984 requiring them to remedy matters.[30] If activities are taking place on board ship which might involve serious personal injury or serious pollution of any navigable waters then an inspector can issue a prohibition notice.[31] This may direct that the activities cease and/or that the ship shall not go to sea until matters are put right. The improvement and prohibition notice may go so far as to include directions as to the way in which it is to be complied with. Although, for instance, it cannot force an owner to take measures more expensive than the minimum necessary to fulfil his statutory duty.[32]

Contravention of a notice is a criminal offence[33] and recipt of one could involve an owner in much difficulty and expense. The Act allows[34] the recipient of the notice to dispute its basis before an arbitrator,[35] provided that a complaint is made to the inspector within 21 days of the service of the notice. The arbitrator can cancel or affirm the notice, but where matters of health and safety are concerned he must listen to trade union representatives. Obviously it could take time to arrange an arbitration so the effect of the notices is suspended until the publication of the arbitration decision.[36] If there was no valid basis

---

29 See Fisheries Act 1981; Sea Fisheries (Enforcement of Community Control Measures) Order 1985 (S.I. No. 487), enacted to make provision for EEC Council and Commission Regulations.

30 S. 1.

31 S. 2

32 S. 3.

33 S. 6, which can lead to a fine (up to an amount specified in the Criminal Justice Act 1982, s. 74, or £1000 in Northern Ireland), or to imprisonment for up to 2 years.

34 S. 4.

35 Who must be qualified as a master mariner, naval architect, lawyer or have other relevant experience, s. 4(5). The arbitrator has the same powers as an inspector under s. 27 of the Merchant Shipping Act 1979.

36 Although a specific application must be made to the arbitrator to suspend a prohibition notice.

on which the inspector's opinion was based and the inspector had no reasonable grounds for it the arbitrator may award compensation.[37]

8.8.3   DANGEROUS VESSELS

It is convenient to consider here the position of a harbour master who has to deal with a dangerous vessel. Previously his powers were somewhat uncertain. Now the Dangerous Vessels Act 1985 allows a harbour master[38] to give directions prohibiting the entry into, or requiring the removal from, the harbour of any vessel.[39] The powers can only be exercised if, in his opinion, the condition of the vessel, or its contents, is such that its presence might involve two types of risk: first, grave and imminent danger to the safety of any person or property; or, secondly, grave and imminent risk that the vessel may, by sinking or foundering in the harbour, prevent or seriously prejudice the use of the harbour by other vessels.

The directions may be given to the owner; any person in possession of the vessel (e.g. a ship-repairer); the master; a salvor in possession.[40] There is no particular form for the directions, so long as they are given in a reasonable manner along with the grounds on which they are based.[41] The harbour master must take into account the safety of all persons and vessels.[42] Contravening, or failing to comply with, directions is an offence.[43] It is a defence for a person to show that he took all reasonable precautions and exercised all due diligence to avoid commission of the offence.[44]

Other local powers, e.g. relating to wreck raising,[45] are unaffected by the Act, as are the powers of receivers of wreck.[46]

The Secretary of State has wide powers to intervene to prevent pollution damage under the Prevention of Oil Pollution Act 1971,

37 S. 8.
38 Including a dock or pier master and their deputies.
39 S. 1. The power does not extend to Crown vessels or pleasure boats of 24 metres or less, s. 6.
40 S. 1(2).
41 S. 1(4), s. 1(5).
42 S. 1(3).
43 S. 5(1) which could lead to a £25 000 fine in a magistrates' court or an unlimited fine in the Crown Court.
44 S. 5(2).
45 S. 1(1). See Section 20.2.3, *infra*, for details and note the power under s. 530, Merchant Shipping Act 1894 to destroy wrecks which are an obstruction or danger to navigation: see, *The Crystal* [1984] A.C. 508.
46 S. 4(2). See Section 24.12, *infra*.

s. 12.[47] The 1985 Act does not affect these powers,[48] but it does give him power to give directions to the harbour master countermanding or altering the latter's directions.[49] In particular, the Secretary of State can direct that the vessel enter, or remain in the harbour.

It follows that an aggrieved owner should 'appeal' to the Secretary of State although the Act makes no specific provision for this. If the harbour master exceeds his powers the harbour authority could be liable to pay damages, but it would be entitled to limit its liability.[50] Although no doubt welcomed by harbour masters, this Act will not please salvors who are trying to salve an 'international leper' that nobody wants. The leaking tanker *Christos Bitas* was refused entry to a number of UK ports and eventually had to be sunk. One port would only allow entry if the ship was fully repaired there. Such a refusal under the 1985 Act could only be made if there was 'grave and imminent' danger or risk.[51]

8.9   REPORTING

At one time there was a voluntary system for the reporting of accidents on ships. Now Regulations require the notification of accidents on board UK ships (other than fishing vessels and pleasure craft).[52] The requirement applies to: every accident on board or during access to any person employed or carried in the ship resulting in personal injury (involving more than three days incapacity) or death; every dangerous occurrence on board or during access.[53] The master, or the most senior officer available, is required to report these accidents involving death or personal injury to the DoT as quickly as possible and no later than 24

---

47 See Section 25.1.3, *infra*.

48 S. 4(1).

49 S. 3.

50 Deliberate misuse of statutory powers could result in liability; see *The Mihalis: Micosta S.A.* v. *Shetland Island Council* [1984] 2 Lloyd's Rep. 525 and Section 20.2.1, *infra*. For limitation, see Sections 22.2.6 and 22.3.6, *infra*.

51 See Chapter 24 and Section 25.1.3.

52 Merchant Shipping (Safety Officials and Reporting of Accidents and Dangerous Occurrences) Regulations 1982 (S.I. No. 876), amended 1984 (S.I. No. 93). For fishing vessels see the Fishing Vessels (Reporting of Accidents) Regulations 1985 (S.I. No. 855).

53 Reg. 10. The Schedule provides an extended definition of 'dangerous occurrences' which are notifiable. The definition includes matters varying from the parting of a tow rope to a boiler explosion.

hours after the arrival of the ship at its next port.[54] Every accident and
dangerous occurrence must also be reported in writing to the DoT
within seven days of the ship's arrival at the next port of call. Failure to
comply with the Regulations is an offence, but there is the usual defence
that the person may show he took all reasonable steps.[55]

There are a variety of other provisions requiring reporting, e.g. in
relation to offshore installations or divers.[56]

A master is under a duty to report to the DoT any shipping casualty
which will justify a shipping inquiry.[57] But it is often vital that such
casualties be notified to competent authorities as quickly and clearly as
possible. Much work has been going on recently at IMO to tighten up
ship reporting procedures with a view to improving safety and preventing pollution.

The *Amoco Cadiz* disaster in 1978 added impetus to the move for
changes in reporting procedures.[58] MARPOL 1973/78 puts an obligation on masters to report incidents involving actual or threatened loss
into the sea of harmful substances.[59] UK Regulations require notification of such incidents by all ships within 200 miles of the UK; all UK
ships within 200 miles of the nearest land; all UK oil tankers when fully
or partly laden; and all UK ships of 10 000 GRT and above.[60]

The Regulations go further. Whenever an accident occurs to a UK
ship or a defect is discovered, either of which could affect the safety of
the ship or her equipment, then the master or owner must notify the
Secretary of State who may decide that a survey is needed.[61] If the ship
is in the port of a country party to MARPOL then a report must also be
made to the appropriate authorities there.[62] Non-UK ships in UK ports

54 Reg. 11.
55 Reg. 12.
56 Offshore Installations (Inspectors and Casualties) Regulations 1973 (S.I. No. 1842);
    Merchant Shipping (Diving Operations) Regulations 1975 (S.I. No. 116) reg. 21,
    amended 1975 (No. 2062), 1981 (No. 399); Submarine Pipelines (Inspectors etc.)
    Regulations 1977 (S.I. No. 835), amended 1982 (No. 1513).
57 Merchant Shipping Act 1970, s. 73. Failure to report is an offence. See Section
    8.10, *infra*.
58 The French were anxious that changes should allow coastal states to be kept fully
    informed of the progress of salvage operations.
59 Art. 8, Protocol I.
60 Merchant Shipping (Prevention of Oil Pollution) Regulations 1983 (S.I. No. 1398),
    reg. 31, M.S. Notice No. M. 1141.
61 Reg. 8(3). Although the context of the Regulations shows that it is intended to
    prevent marine pollution, reg. 8(3) seems to go further than MARPOL as it
    requires notification of incidents threatening the integrity of the ship generally —
    whether or not marine pollution may result.
62 *Ibid.*

must also report such accidents to the Secretary of State and to the authority which issued the IOPP Certificate.[63] Until the owner or master has reported the results of that authority's investigation or survey the Secretary of State may detain the ship.[64] If he is not satisfied that a full and proper report has been made to that authority – or the action taken has been ineffective – he can take steps to ensure that the ship does not sail until it can do so without presenting an unreasonable threat of harm to the marine environment.

There has been much concern recently about drums of dangerous chemicals being washed off the decks of ships. As Annex III of MAR-POL 1973/78 (dealing with packaged goods) is not yet in force IMO has issued a circular, 'Guidelines for reporting incidents involving dangerous goods in packaged form'.[65] The DoT has therefore urged masters voluntarily to report incidents with packaged dangerous goods.[66]

Following an EEC directive in 1979, sea-going tankers of 1600 GRT or more entering or leaving Community ports must notify the harbour master in advance of particulars of the ship and cargo.[67] If the circumstances of the tanker change after initial notification, or if defects occur while in port, these facts must also be notified.[68] Masters have to give pilots a check list which details such matters as the safety installations on board and the certification applicable to the ship and crew.[69] If the pilot does not receive the check list he should inform the harbour master of this fact – if he is aware that the master himself has failed to do so.[70] The owner and master of the tanker, and the pilot, can all be guilty of offences.[71]

63 Reg. 8(4)(a).
64 Reg. 8(4)(b) giving partial effect to the ILO Merchant Shipping (Minimum Standards) Convention 1976, Cmnd 7163.
65 MSC/Circ. 360, 13 January 1984.
66 M.S. Notice No. M. 1152. For the reporting of inadequate oily waste reception facilities see MARPOL 1973/78, Annex I, reg. 12, M.S. Notice No. M. 1142.
67 Merchant Shipping (Tankers) (EEC Requirements) Regulations 1981 (S.I. No. 1077), reg. 4.
68 Ibid., regs 5,6.
69 Ibid., reg. 7.
70 Merchant Shipping (Tankers) (EEC Requirements) (Amendments) Regulations 1982 (S.I. No. 1637), reg. 2 (inserting new Regulations 6A and 7A into the principal Regulations).
71 Ibid., and 1981 (S.I. No. 1077) reg. 8.

8.10 INQUIRIES INTO CASUALTIES

Various international instruments deal with the holding of inquiries. SOLAS 1974[72] allows flag states to conduct investigations into casualties where these may help to discover gaps in the Convention. These reports are kept confidential.[73] MARPOL 1973/78 obliges states to conduct investigations into casualties causing major harm to the marine environment.[74] The ILO Convention Concerning Minimum Standards in Merchant Ships 1974, Art. 2(g), requires states to hold an official inquiry into any serious marine casualty, particularly those involving injury and/or loss of life, the final report of which should normally be made public.

Part VI of the Merchant Shipping Act 1894 set up a system of formal inquiries into shipping casualties, but this has now been replaced by ss. 55-58, Merchant Shipping Act 1970.[75]

The 1970 Act envisages that an inquiry may take place where there has been a casualty, including: loss or stranding of, or damage to, the ship; loss of life or serious personal injury caused by fire or accident; damage caused by a ship.[76] But there may also be an inquiry where there has been an incident which could have caused a casualty, e.g. a 'near miss',[77] as well[78] as where there has been a discharge from a ship which might have been in contravention of the Merchant Shipping (Prevention of Oil Pollution) Regulations 1983.[79]

The DoT may order a preliminary inquiry by one person, to be followed, where it appears desirable, by a formal investigation. The latter (which is also allowed without a preliminary inquiry) is held by a wreck commissioner (or in Scotland, by a sheriff).[80] He has wide powers[81] and can compel the attendance of witnesses in the same way as

---

72 Chapter I, reg. 21.
73 *Ibid.*
74 Art. 12.
75 As from 1 July 1983; see 1982 (S.I. No. 1617). For inquiries into fitness and conduct, see Section 9.2.8, *infra.*
76 S. 55, as amended by the Merchant Shipping Act 1979, s. 32. Note also the power given in s. 61 of the 1970 Act (as amended by ss. 28, 29 of the 1979 Act) to hold an inquiry into the death of any person on board.
77 *Ibid.*
78 Merchant Shipping (Prevention of Oil Pollution) Order 1983 (S.I. No. 1106) Art. 5.
79 S.I. No. 1398. See Chapter 25, *infra.*
80 S. 55(1).
81 S. 55(2), as amended by s. 28 of the 1979 Act.

magistrates.[82] As a result of the investigation he has power to cancel or suspend certificates or censure the officer concerned.[83] The wreck commissioner may award legal costs in favour of, or against, the officers.[84] But he must use this power judicially. In one case a master who was exonerated at an inquiry incurred £3600 legal costs, but for no apparent reason was awarded £1500 costs against the DoT. The High Court quashed this award and ordered the commissioner to reconsider and, if he awarded a lesser sum, to give reasons.[85]

82 S. 56(2); Magistrates' Courts Act 1980, s. 97. Shipping Casualties and Appeals and Re-hearing Rules 1923 (S.R. and O. No. 752). Merchant Shipping (Formal Investigations) Rules 1985 (S.I. No. 1001).
83 See further, on this and appeals, Section 9.2.8. Because the general functions of the formal investigation are disciplinary and investigatory, a shipowner found to blame is not stopped from disputing his fault in a later collision damages action, *The Speedline Vanguard and European Gateway*, [1986] 2 Lloyd's Rep. 265 and see Chapter 21, *infra*.
84 S. 56(5) and (6).
85 *R. v. A Wreck Commissioner, ex p. Knight* [1976] 3 All E.R. 8.

9
MASTER AND CREW

9.1   EMPLOYMENT AND WELFARE LAW

THIS CHAPTER deals with the law relating to the employment and welfare of seamen. It is an area in which public regulation is increasing every year. This results, unfortunately, in a mass of complex statutes and regulations which are very difficult to digest. The modern tendency in Merchant Shipping legislation is for the statute to lay down a general framework. Students must expect to find the details in statutory instruments often supplemented by Merchant Shipping Notices. This provides a welcome flexibility for government departments, although it is sometimes difficult to keep track of developments.

9.1.1   GENERAL EMPLOYMENT LAW

The law of employment is a very big subject, much of it beyond the scope of this volume.[1] Yet even the general law cannot be ignored. Many of its provisions apply to mariners; others have been adapted to suit their working environment; some apply only to them.

Several factors call for that special treatment. Mariners' engagements are often for voyages to distant parts, in the course of which they are exposed to special hazards. When sick they may have to be left behind at a foreign port but, of course, they must not be abandoned. Thus mariners' service agreements contain welfare terms, not required in purely domestic surroundings where the existing services provided for the community at large can be called upon in case of need. Many of these welfare provisions are the result of international conventions.

Another important factor shaping the mariner's employment is his confinement on board his ship also when off duty and the danger of the

---

1 For more detail see Kitchen (1980), or *Encyclopaedia of Labour Relations Law* (1972, with supplements).

elements to which ships are exposed, frequently at places far removed from outside help, such as the fire brigade readily available on land. This factor has led to provisions relating to discipline which would be intolerable, and are indeed unnecessary, on land.

Statutes on this subject provide for minimum safeguards for those employed on ships. More generous and more detailed provisions have been worked out by the National Maritime Board (NMB), a body representing both sides of industry, established in 1919,[2] The NMB publishes a Summary of Agreements which is regularly updated and provides information on standard rates of pay, conditions of employment and decisions on such varied matters as catering, electric light, death or injury during warlike operations, repatriation in the event of dangerous illness, absence without leave and training allowances, to mention only a few. Perhaps the Board's most useful achievement is the Established Service Scheme for registered seafarers, designed to create a stable and attractive career, regularity of employment and to provide efficient and reliable personnel to shipping companies.

Employment law was consolidated in the Employment Protection (Consolidation) Act 1978,[3] but reference must also be made to a number of Acts introduced since. These have been designed, in particular, to regulate trade union activities and amend the 1978 Act: see the Employment Act 1980, the Employment Act 1982, the Trade Union Act 1984. Students should note that the law relating to matters such as employment or social security varies greatly along with the existing political climate — much more so than most non-controversial shipping law issues.

Among other matters, the legislation regulates the rights of employees, including remedies for unfair dismissal, whether with or without notice, with the possibility of reinstatement, if desired and practicable, and the right to compensation.[4] The 1978 Act also lays down the procedure for handling redundancies, that is, cases where employees have to lose their jobs because of changes in, or the demise of, the business in which they are employed. The shock of dismissal is cushioned by a lump sum payment, calculated on the basis of the last wage or salary and length of service.[5] Special provisions, however, apply to personnel employed on ships required to observe NMB

2 Bonwick and Steer, *Ship's Business* (5th edn, 1963), p. 51.
3 Which embodied the greater part of the Employment Protection Act 1975 and also the whole of the Contracts of Employment Act 1972 and the Redundancy Payments Act 1965.
4 Employment Protection (Consolidation) Act 1978 ss. 54–63, 67–75A (as amended).
5 S. 81 (as amended), Schs 4, 13, 14.

terms.[6] These terms compare favourably with those obtaining in other employments.

General provisions regulating periods of notice and the duty of employers to furnish employees with written particulars of their terms of employment and conditions of service[7] do not apply to the masters and seamen in seagoing British ships of 80 tons or over, to apprentices or to the skipper and crew of fishing vessels;[8] later in this chapter we shall encounter the special rules governing these categories of employee.[9]

Two categories are excepted from a wide range of general employee rights, namely, skippers and crews of fishing vessels remunerated exclusively by a share in gross earnings or gross profits, essentially self-employed earners, and personnel serving in ships registered in Great Britain but wholly employed outside the country or not ordinarily resident there.[10] Rights not enjoyed by these men and women include that of guaranteed payment if no work is available on a work day;[11] certain remuneration when suspended on medical grounds;[12] certain payments when absent on the ground of pregnancy;[13] reasonable time off for trade union activities or for such public duties as service as magistrates or local government councillors,[14] or for ante-natal care;[15] and reasonable time off when under notice to look for other work or make arrangements for training.[16] Some of these rights are, however, conferred on those concerned by legislation applying to merchant seamen or by collective agreements.

Not excluded are the provisions relating to unfair dismissal,[17] a very involved subject. One writer has stated that while the basis of the relevant provisions is simple, their interpretation has led to hundreds of decisions 'which have laid down guidelines varying from legal ingenuity, through sound common sense, and ending up, on occasions, with

6 Redundancy (Merchant Seamen Exclusion) Order 1973 (S.I. No. 1281). See *NMB Summary of Agreements,* pp. 35–47.

7 Ss. 1, 2 and 4.

8 Ss. 144(1), 144(5).

9 See also Merchant Shipping Act 1894, ss. 108, 373.

10 Employment Protection (Consolidation) Act 1978, ss. 144(2), 141(2), (5).

11 S. 12.

12 S. 19.

13 S. 33, as amended.

14 Ss. 27-29, 32.

15 S. 31A, inserted by the Employment Act 1980, s. 13.

16 S. 31.

17 Part V, s. 54 *et seq.*

cabalistic mystery'.[18] In one case,[19] relevant in this context, a shipping
company rule, embodying company policy, provided that no one with
a cardiac disease was to be employed as a radio officer at sea. A radio
officer was dismissed following two heart attacks, and that dismissal
was held to be fair, although the man had made what the medical
evidence described as an excellent recovery.

Reverting for a few moments to redundancy, it is worth mentioning
one rule of general application which produced a case concerning the
master of a merchant ship.

Since, as we have just said, the size of the lump sum depends partly on
the length of the employee's service, it is important to determine the
continuity of that service. What counts is service in a business irrespective of who owns it. Thus where a business is sold as a going concern,
with employees taken over by the new owner, the length of service,
should the employees later become redundant, is that under the old and
new owners combined.[20]

A similar, but not identical situation may arise in the following way.
The business moves to another place, and certain assets at the old place,
for instance, a warehouse, are sold off. An employee reasonably refuses
to move with the business, but the new owner of the warehouse
employs him on comparable terms. Here continuity is broken. The
business that has moved must make a redundancy payment to the
employee and, in the event of the new owner of the warehouse later
making him redundant, the length of service counts from entering the
employment of the new employer. Now let us look at the case of the
ship's master.

Illustration: *Watts, Watts and Co. Ltd v. Steeley*[21]

The Queen's Navigation Company sold its ships to Watts, Watts in October
1965. Steeley, who had been with Queen's since 1941, accepted the post of
master of one of the ships bought by Watts, which was employed in coastal
trade. Steeley was on prolonged sick leave, and on return to work was

18 N. Selwyn, *Law of Employment* (5th edn, 1985), p. 210.
19 *W. G. Jeffries* v. *B.P. Tanker Co. Ltd* [1974] I.R.L.R. 260.
20 See s. 94, Schs 4 and 13, Note the effect of the Transfer of Undertakings
   (Protection of Employment) Regulations 1981 (S.I. No. 1794), implementing an
   EEC directive. They safeguard continuity of employment on the transfer of a
   business. They do not affect a seaman's rights under the Merchant Shipping Act
   1970, s. 5, when a ship ceases to be British registered. But fishermen on a series of
   individual contracts for individual voyages (as opposed to one global contract) may
   not have continuity of employment: see *Hellyer Bros Ltd* v. *McLeod* [1986] I.C.R.
   122, *cf. Boyd Lines* v. *Pitts* [1986] I.C.R. 244.
21 [1968] 2 Lloyd's Rep. 179.

dismissed on the ground that his ship was now employed on voyages to West Africa, for which Steeley was not qualified. He claimed redundancy payment, with a length of service since 1941. One of the grounds on which Watts resisted the claim was that they had not taken over the business of Queen's, but only some of Queen's assets, the ships.

Held: The claim succeeded. Watts had taken over not only some ships, but the entire business of Queen's. The claimant had proved continuity since 1941.

9.1.2   UNLAWFUL DISCRIMINATION

An employer is no longer able to engage or dismiss anyone he chooses or to agree terms of employment entirely of his own making. Quite apart from collective agreements with trade unions, which are outside the scope of this work, stringent legislation prevents discrimination on several grounds. At the same time, because shipping presents its own particular problems, the general law has in some respects been modified in respect of employment on ships.

First, we must notice the Race Relations Act 1976. This imposes on employers the duty not to discriminate on the grounds of colour, race, nationality or ethnic or national origin by restricting the field of applicants, engagements, opportunities for promotion or terms of employment, or by dismissals.[22]

This duty exists where the person concerned is employed 'at an establishment in Great Britain'.[23] These words require elucidation in respect of ships which, of course, are apt to move in and out of the UK. Accordingly, it is provided that the following means of transport are establishments in Great Britain: ships registered at a port in Great Britain; and hovercraft (and aircraft) operated by persons who have their principal place of business, or are ordinarily resident, in Great Britain. Ships registered at British ports do, however, at any rate for certain periods, ply exclusively between foreign ports, and a special regimen was considered fair for such vessels. They are exempt from the non-discrimination duty in respect of ship's personnel employed 'wholly' outside the country. Other employers are not bound where the employment is 'wholly or mainly' outside Great Britain.[24]   The hovercraft non-discrimination duty need not be observed if the British-operated craft is under contract to a foreign operator.[25]

---

22 Ss. 1, 3 and 4.
23 Parallel legislation has been enacted for Northern Ireland.
24 S. 8. *Cf. Haughton* v. *Olau Line (UK) Ltd* [1986] 2 All E.R. 47.
25 This also applies to Government vessels; s. 75(4).

A second, more contentious, exception was granted to British shipowners employing personnel who apply, or are engaged, for employment on board ship outside Great Britain.[26] Shipowners wrung this concession from the Government by the argument that their profitability depended on the employment of lower-paid crews from overseas countries. The Act gives the Secreatary of State power to repeal this exception at any time.[27]

Incidentally, it is also unlawful to discriminate in the provisions of goods, facilities and services on and in relation to, a British ship.[28]

Anyone wishing to complain that he has been discriminated against can file a suit against the employer in an industrial tribunal.[29] If the complaint is well founded the tribunal has power to make a number of orders, choosing that which it considers just and equitable: it can do no more than declare the rights of complainant and respondent; it can order the respondent to pay compensation to the complainant, including compensation for injured feelings; or it can order the respondent to take action that will obviate or reduce the adverse effect of discrimination.[30] What Parliament had in mind when empowering the tribunal to make the third kind of order was presumably improving the terms of employment or furnishing better opportunities for promotion.

The Sex Discrimination Act 1975 contains corresponding provisions in respect of sex discrimination.[31]

Any form of discrimination is forbidden against members of the European Economic Community, for the Treaty of Rome enshrines in its Articles 48 to 51 the free movement of workers. At least one case has been won by a ship's master in France; a French nationality requirement of French law was declared illegal.[32] For obvious reasons, however, shipowners must be able to insist on crew members understanding enough English to understand orders given to them, unless in the

26 S.9.
27 S. 73. See L. Lustgarten, *Legal Control of Racial Discrimination,* (1983), pp. 143-145. There are now, apparently, fewer than 3000 Indians employed on British ships. The GCBS has a fund of £15 million which is available for distribution to Indian seamen when a satisfactory scheme can be agreed; *The Observer,* 1 September 1985, Kitchen (1980), pp. 61–62. See also Section 9.4.3(b). *infra.*
28 Ss. 20, 27(4).
29 S. 54.
30 S. 56.
31 Especially s. 10. See *Haughton* v. *Olau Line (UK) Ltd* [1986] 2 All E.R. 47 and Kitchen (1980), pp. 173–178.
32 *Commission of the European Communities* v. *The French Republic* (1974) 14 Common Market Law Reports 216.

circumstances orders can be given in the language of the foreign crew member.[33]

9.1.3 SOCIAL SECURITY

Under the social security legislation, employed earners who comply with the prescribed conditions are entitled to unemployment, sickness, industrial injury, invalidity, severe disablement and many other benefits.[34] One of the conditions is residence in Great Britain, which means that special arrangements have to be made for mariners, who in the nature of things spend long periods outside the country.[35]

Broadly, a mariner is entitled to benefits if he serves in a British ship, or if he serves in another ship but the contract of employment was concluded in the UK and the shipowner has a place of business in this country.

To claim unemployment benefit persons must normally be 'available' for work in Great Britain,[36] but a mariner is deemed to be available during periods of absence from Great Britain.[37] However, days in periods of paid leave are not treated as days of unemployment.[38] Most mariners are entitled to industrial injuries benefits[39] unless, for example, the ship is not employed exclusively in the UK and their contracts were made outside the UK or the employer has no place of business in Great Britain.[40] The benefits are payable even if an accident happens outside the UK, or while the mariner is being repatriated, or is assisting in an emergency involving another ship.[41] Similar conditions apply to the entitlement to sick pay.[42]

33 Merchant Shipping Act 1970, s. 48.
34 Social security legislation is a jungle of statutes and regulations. Students should consult Pollard (1977), or A. Ogus and E. Barendt, *The Law of Social Security* (1982). For details of benefits payable as a result of industrial injuries or death, see Section 9.6, *infra*. Many changes in law and practice will be made by the Social Security Act 1986.
35 Social Security Act 1975, ss. 2, 1(3)(a) and 129, as amended.
36 S. 17.
37 Social Security (Mariners' Benefits) Regulations 1975 (S.I. No. 529), reg. 6(1). Under reg. 6(3) rights to benefit are unaffected by payment of Establishment Benefit under the Merchant Navy Established Service Scheme.
38 *Ibid.*, reg. 2.
39 Social Security (Employed Earners' Employments for Industrial Injuries Purposes) Regulations 1975 (S.I. No. 467), reg. 4, Sch. 2, Part I.
40 *Ibid.*, reg. 5, Sch. 2, Part II.
41 Social Security (Industrial Injuries) (Mariners' Benefits) Regulations 1975 (S.I. No. 470), regs 2, 3; amended 1983 (S.I. No. 136).
42 Social Security and Housing Benefits Act 1982, as amended by the Social Security Act 1985: Statutory Sick Pay (Mariners, Airmen and Persons Abroad) Regulations 1982 (S.I. No. 1349), reg. 6. These matters will be dealt with in Section 9.6, *infra*.

Mariners, like most other people, must make contributions to the social security scheme.[43] There are special rules for calculating their earnings (for earnings related contributions) to take account of, for example, short voyages or advance wages.[44] They are only obliged to pay contributions if they are domiciled or resident in Great Britain.[45] However, there are a large number of reciprocal agreements on social security with other countries.[46]

Again, regard must be had to EEC legal provisions designed to aid the free movement of workers by removing restrictions on their social security entitlements while working in other member states.[47]

It may well happen that while the mariner is away on a voyage the Department of Health and Social Security or a local authority have to make payments to his dependants, for instance, by way of supplementary benefit. Where that happens the Department or the local authority can order the shipowner to retain a proportion of the mariner's wages with a view to public funds being reimbursed. Actual reimbursement depends on the order of a magistrates' court, and if no such order is made the deduction has to be returned to the wage earner.[48]

The recent conflict in the Falkland Islands highlighted the risks to merchant seamen injured in wartime. Statutory powers were given at the time of the 1939-45 war for schemes concerning pensions and allowances to be made for their benefit.[49] A number of schemes have been made, e.g. the War Pensions (Mercantile Marine) Scheme 1964.[50] This applies to any member of the Merchant Navy or sea fishing service whose disablement or death is directly attributable to a war injury sustained, or detention suffered, by reason of his service as a mariner in a British ship.[51] There is a similar scheme for naval

---

43 Social Security (Contributions) Regulations 1979 (S.I. No. 591), case C, regs 86–89, as amended, e.g. by the Social Security Contributions Act 1982, Sch. 1.

44 Regs 87–98, as amended by the Social Security (Contributions) (Mariners) Amendment Regulations 1982 (S.I. No. 206).

45 Reg. 87. Note also regs 89, 93 for employers' contributions.

46 Made under the Social Security Act 1975, s. 143, e.g., the Social Security (New Zealand) Order 1983 (S.I. No. 1894).

47 Treaty of Rome, Art. 51; Reg. 1408/71 (O.J. 1971 L149), especially Arts 13, 14.

48 Merchant Shipping Act 1970, s. 17; Merchant Shipping (Maintenance of Seamen's Dependants) Regulations 1972 (S.I. No. 1635), amended 1972 (S.I. No. 1875).

49 Pensions (Navy, Army, Air Force and Mercantile Marine) Act 1939, amended, the Pensions (Mercantile Marine) Act 1942.

50 S.I. No. 2058, amended 1972 (S.I. No. 1434).

51 Arts 2, 4. Note that compensation may be payable by the NMB, see Section 9.4.4, *infra*.

auxiliaries.[52] The Merchant Shipping (Compensation to Seam – War Damage to Effects) Scheme 1982[53] allowed for compensation to be paid to mariners whose effects suffered war damage while they were in the service of a British registered ship during the Falklands conflict. The claims for personal effects, uniforms and tools were limited to £1470 in total and had to be presented within six months of being suffered. Presumably similar schemes would be used in the (unhoped for) event of any future conflicts.

The road is now clear for a discussion of the special rules governing employment in the merchant service. The law has been materially transformed in some respects by the Merchant Shipping Acts 1970 and 1974, the former having been drafted following the report in 1967 of a court of inquiry, chaired by Lord Pearson; it was appointed after the seamen's strike in 1966.

9.2 GENERAL MERCHANT SHIPPING PROVISIONS

9.2.1 MANNING AND CERTIFICATION GENERALLY

Before discussing the conditions of service of master and crew we must note a set of provisions applying generally to all those serving in ships. The Merchant Shipping Act 1970 groups these provisions under the heading 'Manning and Certification'.[54]

These sections add to what has been explained in Chapter 8, for both sets of rules are designed to ensure safety at sea. In the preceding chapter, rules relating to the construction and maintenance of the ship were set out. Most studies over the years have suggested that the biggest cause of marine accidents is human error. For a long time training was left entirely to the owners, but in line with modern trends and the increasing sophistication of equipment which crews must operate, public regulation has become equally important. The rules now to be discussed aim at making sure that those manning the ship

---

52 War Pensions (Naval Auxiliary Personnel) Scheme 1964 (S.I. No. 1985), amended 1972 (S.I. No. 1436).

53 S.I. No. 1023.

54 Ss. 43–51. Students should note that this Act did not come into force immediately, but has been introduced piecemeal by Orders issued by the DoT. It is necessary to consult the latest commencement order to be up to date: see e.g. the Merchant Shipping Act 1970 (Commencement No. 9) Order 1982 (S.I. No. 1617).

have had the training required to operate the ship safely and that shipowners engage sufficient numbers of such qualified persons.

Everyone knows that many professions and occupations can be followed only by men and women who have passed examinations showing that they are suitably qualified. Nearly always, however, the employer decides how many of such qualified persons he will employ in his business. Not so in the shipping industry. Since the seaworthiness of a ship depends as much on the ship's soundly constructed hull and equipment as on its adequate manning, the State has for a very long time enacted legislation on manning requirements; in other words, it has told shipowners how many qualified crew they must engage before sending their ships to sea. It is the Secretary of State for Transport who is responsible for making regulations dealing with both the number of persons required on board ship and the standards of competence they should have.[55]

However, first it will be necessary to look at a recent international development.

9.2.2 THE STCW CONVENTION 1978

In 1978 after many years' preparation an international conference, convened by IMO, in association with the International Labour Organisation (ILO), agreed the International Convention on Standards of Training, Certificate and Watchkeeping for Seafarers (STCW).[56] The STCW Convention 1978 entered into force on 28 April 1984 and state parties are obliged to pass laws to give effect to the Convention and its Annex in order to ensure that seafarers on board ships are qualified and fit for their duties – from the point of view of safety and the environment.[57]

The Annex contains Regulations with specific chapters devoted to the master-deck department; the engine department; the radio department; special requirements for tankers; and proficiency in survival craft. These chapters lay down basic principles as well as providing a syllabus for the training of each type of seafarer, which varies with the type and

55 Merchant Shipping Act 1970 s. 43. Not surprisingly fees are payable for examinations, and, indeed, for a wide range of formal merchant shipping activities from surveying to the engagement and discharge of seamen: see, e.g. the Merchant Shipping (Fees) Regulations 1985 (S.I. No. 1607) 1986 (S.I. No. 837).
56 See Singh (1983) Vol. 3, p. 1884; S. Sadek, 'The STCW Convention 1978', in S. Mankabady (ed.), *The International Maritime Organisation* (1984), 194 *et seq.*
57 Art. I.

size of ship.[58] For instance, under Chapter II masters must observe principles relating to watch arrangements; fitness for duty; navigation; navigational equipment, duties and responsibilites; lookout; pilotage; and protection of the marine environment, To obtain STCW certificates, masters must satisfy administrations as to medical fitness, minimum periods of sea-going experience and their ability to pass an examination based on the appropriate syllabus.[59] The syllabus for masters and chief mates of ships of 200 GRT and above contains 19 major headings and a daunting array of subjects – from navigation, ship handling and fire prevention to meteorology, medical care and maritime law![60] Existing certificates are valid under the STCW Convention. Indeed, states may continue to issue certificates in accordance with their previous practices to seafarers who had already started their sea service before the Convention came into force in those states.[61] The Convention allows states to control standards by checking on the certificates of seafarers or ships in their ports.[62] If there are deficiencies, the master and the flag state should be notified in writing.[63] Failure to correct the deficiencies which could pose a danger to persons, property or the environment obliges states to detain the ship until the deficiencies are remedied.[64]

An important requirement of the Convention is that states should promote refresher and updating courses and that officers should be required to undergo medical and proficiency tests at least every five years.[65]

The UK has ratified the STCW Convention 1978 and Regulations have been issued by the DoT to bring our law into line with it. Thus the Merchant Shipping (Certification and Watchkeeping) Regulations 1982[66] came fully into force at the same time as the STCW Convention. These Regulations apply to UK sea-going ships (other than fishing vessels and pleasure craft) and non-UK sea-going ships in UK waters.[67]

58 Reference should also be made to the detailed guidelines contained in the Resolutions adopted at the Conference.
59 Art. VI, reg. II/2. STCW Certificates must be in English, or have an English translation, reg. I/2.
60 Appendix to reg. II/2.
61 Art. VII, although this practice cannot continue for longer than five years.
62 Art. X. The grounds for suspicion are stated in reg. I/4, e.g. the fact of a collision, or illegal discharge of oil.
63 Art. X, and reg. I/4.
64 *Ibid.*
65 Regs II/5, III/5, IV/2.
66 S.I. No. 1699, which came fully into force at the same time as the STCW Convention, See also 1984 (S.I. Nos. 94–97), referred to in Section 9.2.4, *infra*.
67 Reg. 3.

9.2.3   THE UK WATCHKEEPING REQUIREMENTS

Under the Merchant Shipping (Certification and Watchkeeping) Regulations 1982[68] masters and engineering officers are under a duty to ensure that the watchkeeping arrangements are in accordance with the principles in the Schedules and the operational guidance specified in Merchant Shipping Notices.[69] Masters must also arrange an effective watch in port, particularly where dangerous cargoes are concerned.[70] Masters and engineers who contravene these provisions commit an offence.[71]

9.2.4   THE UK CERTIFICATION REQUIREMENTS

(A)   CERTIFICATES OF COMPETENCE OR SERVICE

A number of sets of Certification Regulations have been made of which the most important are: the Merchant Shipping (Certification of Marine Engineer Officers) Regulations 1980[72] and the Merchant Shipping (Certification of Deck Officers) Regulations 1985;[73] the Merchant Shipping (Engine Room Watch Ratings) Regulations 1984;[74] the Merchant Shipping (Navigational Watch Ratings) Regulations 1984;[75] the Merchant Shipping (Tankers – Officers and Ratings) Regulations 1984;[76] the Merchant Shipping (Certificates of Competency as A.B.) Regulations 1970;[77] the Merchant Shipping (Certificates of Proficiency in Survival Craft) Regulations 1984;[78] the Fishing Vessels (Certification

68 S.I. No. 1699.
69 Reg. 4, Sch. 1; reg. 5, Sch. 2. The Schedules correspond to regs II/1 and III/1 of the STCW Convention. M.S. Notices Nos M. 1102, 1103.
70 Regs 6 and 7.
71 Reg. 13, which provides for fines of up to £1000 and/or imprisonment for up to two years. See also Section 9.2.4(a) *infra* for offences by masters who allow uncertificated officers to stand watch.
72 S.I. No. 2025. Replaced from 15 December 1986 by the Merchant Shipping (Certification of Marine Engineer Officers and Licensing of Marine Engineer Operators) Regulations (S.I. No. 1935). Note also the Merchant Shipping (Musters and Training) Regulations 1986 (S.I. No. 1071).
73 S.I. No. 1306.
74 S.I. No. 95, M.S. Notice No. M. 1095.
75 S.I. No. 96, M.S. Notice No. M. 1096.
76 S.I. No. 94, M.S. Notice No. M. 1091.
77 S.I. No. 294, amended 1984 (No. 97).
78 S.I. No. 97, M.S. Notice No. M. 1092.

of Deck Officers and Engineer Officers) Regulations 1984;[79] the Merchant Shipping (Certification of Ships' Cooks) Regulations 1981.[80]

The Engineer and Deck Officer Regulations revoked and re-enacted previous Regulations[81] but with a number of important differences. Thus, the Deck Officer Regulations apply to all UK ships, including passenger ships, tugs and sail training ships, as well as to foreign ships which carry passengers within the UK.[82] Ships under 80 GRT (except pleasure craft) are no longer exempt. However, the Regulations do not apply to ships which stay within the limits of what are called 'smooth or partially smooth waters'.[83] These are designated by separate Rules[84] and consist essentially, of harbour and coastal areas. The Navigational Watch Ratings Regulations apply to all UK ships of 200 GRT or more (other than fishing vessels and pleasure craft) which go beyond smooth or partially smooth waters.[85]

Likewise the Engineer Officer Regulations apply to all UK ships (except fishing vessels and pleasure craft) having registered power of 350 kW or more.[86] The Engines Room Ratings Regulations apply to all UK ships, with a registered power of 750 kW or more which go beyond smooth or partially smooth waters.[87] The Tanker Regulations apply to all UK sea-going tankers.[88]

The Deck Officer Regulations create five classes of certificates of competency.[89] Class 1 applies to master mariners and Classes 2 to 5 to other categories.[90] Master and tugmaster certificates also have command endorsements showing whether they qualify for shorter or longer voyages.[91] The Engineer Officer Regulations create four classes of certificates of competence and a new category of licensed engine operator (for ships with under 750 kW power).[92]

79 S.I. No. 1115. Note the M.S.A. 1970 (Commencement No. 10) Order 1986 (S.I. No. 2066).
80 S.I. No. 1076, M.S. Notice No. M. 965.
81 1977 (S.I. No. 2072), amended 1979 (S.I. No. 599); 1980 (S.I. No. 2026).
82 1985 (S.I. No. 1306) reg. 3.   83 Ibid. and reg. 2.
84 1977 (S.I. No. 252), amended 1978 (S.I. No. 801), 1984 (S.I. No. 955).
85 1984 (S.I. No. 96), reg. 3.
86 1980 (S.I. No. 2025), regs 3, 2. These Regulations apply to sail training ships over 80 GRT with engines and to unregistered ships which are wholly owned by a UK citizen or UK company, as defined in the Merchant Shipping Act 1979, s. 21(2). See now 1986 (S.I. No. 1935)
87 1984 (S.I. No. 95), reg. 3.   88 1984 (S.I. No. 94), reg. 3.
89 1985 (S.I. No. 1306), reg. 4.   90 Ibid.
91 Reg. 7. Note that the 1985 Regulations allowed certificates of competency and command endorsements to be issued subject to limitations as to area of operation, description of ship, or the deck officer's capacity in that ship (reg. 4).
92 1986 (S.I. No. 1935) Parts II and III.

The Regulations allowed for mariners with existing Certificates of Competence to be treated as having equivalent qualifications under the new Regulations.[93] There were also provisions for equivalent 'certificates of service' to be issued to those with relevant sea-going experience.[94]

The DoT is responsible for setting the standards of competency and holding examinations.[95] The standards are specified in the Department's Merchant Shipping publications,[96] which are amended by Merchant Shipping Notice: syllabuses and specimen examination papers are also available.[97]

An important new requirement in both sets of Officer Certificate Regulations is that certificates of competency and service will only remain valid for sea-going service if the holder can continue to comply with such standards and conditions as to medical fitness and competency as are specified.[98] This enables the UK to satisfy the STCW Convention requirements.[99]

It should also be noted that there must be specially trained officers on ships carrying dangerous cargoes in bulk.[1] Also, under the Merchant Shipping (Navigational Equipment) Regulations 1984[2] ships must have

93 E.g., 1985 (S.I. No. 1306), reg. 5; 1980 (S.I. No. 2025), reg. 6; Merchant Shipping Act 1894, ss. 93, 96, 414. Note 1986 (S.I. No. 1935).

94 E.g., 1985 (S.I. No. 1306), regs 5(2), 5(7), 6(2); 1980 (S.I. No. 2025), regs 6(2), 7(2). Certificates of service could also be issued under the Merchant Shipping (Certification and Watchkeeping Regulations) 1982 (S.I. No. 1699), subject to conditions specified in Merchant Shipping Notices; regs 9, 2. The relevant experience must have been achieved at the latest by 1 September 1981 (in the case of the 1980 Regulations) and 1 January 1983 (in the case of the 1982 Regulations), unless the Secretary of State considered the conditions had been substantially complied with: see M.S. Notice No. M. 1087. Note 1986 (S.I. No. 1935).

95 Merchant Shipping Act 1970, s. 43; 1985 (S.I. No. 1306), reg. 6(1); 1980 (S.I. No. 2025), reg. 7(1). See also M.S. Notice Nos M. 952, 1182. 1970 (S.I. No. 294), reg. 4; 1984 (S.I. No. 94), reg. 5, M.S. Notice No. 1091; 1984 (S.I. No. 95), reg. 5, M.S. Notice No. 1095; 1984 (S.I. No. 96), reg. 5, M.S. Notice No. 1096.

96 *Certificates of Competency in the Merchant Navy-Deck Officer Requirements, Certificates of Competency in the Merchant Navy: Marine Engineer Officer Requirements*, HMSO (as amended by M.S. Notices, e.g. No. M. 1172), reg. 2 of the Engineer and Deck Officer Certification Regulations. See also M.S. Notices cited in fn. 95, *supra*.

97 *Ibid.*, e.g. *Examinations for Certificates of Competency in the Merchant Navy-Deck Syllabuses and Specimen Papers*.

98 1985 (S.I. No. 1306), reg. 10(2); 1980 (S.I. No. 2025), reg. 9(2). [1986 (S.I. No. 1935)]

99 See Section 9.2.2, *supra*.

 1 1980 (S.I. No. 2025), reg. 13; 1985 (S.I. No. 1306), reg. 18. [1986 (S.I. No. 1935)]

 2 S.I. No. 1203.

qualified radar operators[3] and, where appropriate, persons qualified in the operational use of automatic radar plotting aids.[4]

It is now an offence for a deck officer to act as a master or second in command if he is uncertificated:[5] likewise for engineer officers who act as Chief Engineer Officer, or Second Engineer Officer.[6] The master who permits a deck officer or rating without the relevant certificate to be in charge of a navigational watch or to have duties in connection with tanker cargo, or cargo equipment, also commits an offence.[7] Both master and chief engineer commit offences if uncertificated engineers or ratings have the engineering watch.[8]

(B) CERTIFICATES OF HEALTH

Not only should seafarers be competent, they should also be healthy. The UK has ratified the ILO Convention Concerning Minimum Standards in Merchant Ships 1976, which came into force on 28 November 1981.[9] To give effect to that Convention[10] the Merchant Shipping (Medical Examination) Regulations 1983[11] were issued. These apply to UK sea-going ships of 1600 GRT and over, other than fishing vessels, pleasure craft and offshore installations. They prohibit the employment of seafarers who do not hold valid medical certificates.[12] These are valid for different maximum periods depending on the age of the seafarer: for those under 18 it is one year; for those between 18 and 40 it is five years; for those 40 and over it is two years.[13] If an approved medical practitioner reasonably believes that there has been a significant change in the seafarer's medical fitness he must inform the person concerned and may

3 Regs 20, 22.
4 Regs 41, 42. See further on training, M.S. Notice No. M. 1159; on the use of radar and electronic aids to navigation, M.S. Notice No. M. 1158.
5 1985 (S.I. No. 1306), reg. 19(1).
6 1980 (S.I. No. 2025), regs 14(1), 15(1). See now 1986 (S.I. No. 1935).
7 1985 (S.I. No. 1306), reg. 19(2); 1984 (S.I. No. 96), regs 4(2), 6; 1984 (S.I. No. 94), regs 4(2), 6.
8 1980 (S.I. No. 2025), reg. 14(2); 1984 (S.I. No. 95), regs 4(2), 6. See fn 72, p. 120
9 ILO, *Maritime Labour Conventions and Ratifications*, (1983); Singh (1983) Vol. 3, p. 2208.
10 Art. 2(a) and the Appendix of which require that states enact laws which are substantially equivalent to the ILO Medical Examination (Seafarers) Convention 1946 – which the UK has not ratified; Singh (1983) Vol. 3, p. 2041.
11 S.I. No. 808, in force 1 July 1983, amended 1985 (S.I. No. 512); also M.S. Notice No. M. 1179.
12 Reg. 4.
13 Reg. 8.

suspend or cancel the certificate.[14] A seafarer aggrieved at these actions does have a right of review.[15] There are powers of inspection of ships to see if a seafarer's certificate is satisfactory. If it is not, the ship could be detained, but only if the state of the seafarer's health is such as to cause serious risk to the safety and health of those on board if the ship sailed.[16]

Min Manning from Feb 1992

9.2.5 THE UK MANNING REQUIREMENTS

The Merchant Shipping (Certification and Watchkeeping) Regulations 1982[17] put a duty on an employer to ensure that the ship carries sufficient qualified officers to enable the master and chief engineer to perform their watchkeeping obligations.[18] The relevant qualifications are the certification of competence or service issued under, or recognized by, the Certification Regulations,[19] certificates of service under the 1982 Regulations, or the equivalent for persons holding certificates issued abroad.[20]

The Certification Regulations specify the minimum number of deck and engineer officers which must be carried.[21] This varies with the type of ship and its trading areas. For instance, by checking simple tables one can see that a cargo ship of 1600 GRT with a registered power of 3000 kW and an unlimited trading area requires a minimum of one deck officer of each of Classes 1, 2, 3 and 4, one chief engineer and two second engineers.[22]

The DoT has power to grant exemptions, to certain ships generally, or in respect of a particular voyage.[23] Indeed reg. 17 of the 1985 Deck Officer Regulations provides that if one of the prescribed number of deck officers is not carried because of illness, incapacity or other unforeseen circumstances, then the ship may sail. However, all reasonable steps must have been taken to find a qualified replacement and the period of undermanning must not be longer than a specified period.

---

14 Reg. 9.   15 Reg. 10.
16 Regs 12, 13. See also the Merchant Shipping (Medical Stores) Regulations 1986 (S.I. No. 144) dealing with the medicines and other medical stores to be carried on UK ships.
17 S.I. No. 1699.   18 Reg. 8.
19 S.I. 1980 (No. 2025), 1985 (S.I. No. 1306): Section 9.2.4, *supra*.
20 Reg. 8, M.S. Notice No. M. 1129.
21 Part III and Sch. 1 of both the 1980 Regulations (S.I. No. 2025) and the 1985 Regulations (S.I. No. 1306). The 1985 Regulations introduced a now threefold definition of trading areas: Unlimited, Limited European and Extended European.
22 *Ibid.*
23 Merchant Shipping Act 1970, s. 44. M.S. Notice No. M. 781 gives the recommended manning levels for oil rig supply vessels.

That period varies, according to the voyage in progress, from 7 to 28 days.[24]

If a ship goes to sea, or attempts to go to sea without carrying all the officers and seamen required under the Certification Regulations the owner or master may be guilty of an offence.[25] They may also be guilty if a ship with 100 or more persons on board goes to sea, beyond the Near Continental trading area, without a ship's doctor.[26] An owner will also commit offences against the Certification Regulations if he appoints an officer to act in a capacity for which he is not certificated;[27] against the Medical Regulations if he employs seamen without valid medical certificates;[28] against the 1982 Certification and Watchkeeping Regulations if he fails to ensure that there are sufficient qualified officers available for watchkeeping duties;[29] against the Ratings Regulations if there are not sufficient ratings for the navigation or engine room watch;[30] and against the Tanker Regulations if there are not enough officers and crew to handle the cargo and cargo equipment.[31]

There is the usual power of inspection given to DoT inspectors to check that certificates on board are in order.[32] If there are deficiencies these must be notified to the master (or the flag state in the case of foreign ships).[33] There is also a power of detention if the deficiencies are not corrected and this would result in danger to persons, property or the environment.[34] In order to assist port state control of manning levels IMO recommended that ships should carry a document indicating the minimum safe manning level.[35] States could treat this as evidence of compliance with the STCW Convention 1978. The DoT

24 Reg. 12 of the Engineer Officer Regulations is to similar effect.
25 Merchant Shipping Act 1970, s. 45. See Section 25.12, footnote 24, for interpretation of 'owner or master'. Note the increase in fines under s. 43, Merchant Shipping Act 1979.
26 Merchant Shipping (Ships' Doctors) Regulations 1981 (S.I. No. 1065), reg. 2.
27 1980 (S.I. No. 2025), regs 14(3), 15(2); 1985 (S.I. No. 1306), regs 19(3), 20(2).
28 1983 (S.I. No. 808), reg. 15.
29 1982 (S.I. No. 1699), regs 8, 13(1).
30 Merchant Shipping (Engine Room Watch Ratings) Regulations 1984 (S.I. No. 95) regs 4, 6; Merchant Shipping (Navigational Watch Ratings) Regulations 1984 (S.I. No. 96), regs 4, 6.
31 Merchant Shipping (Tankers – Officers and Ratings) Regulations 1984 (S.I. No. 94), regs 4, 6.
32 Reg. 11. See Section 8.8, supra.
33 Ibid.
34 Reg. 12.
35 Resolution A. 481 (XII), 19 November 1981.

operates a voluntary Safe Manning Scheme.[36] It issues Safe Manning
Certificates to UK ships which may help them to avoid delays in
foreign ports.

Under, or inadequate, manning could be very relevant in a collision
case, but the victim would have to prove that the deficiencies caused the
loss.[37]

9.2.6   MISCELLANEOUS REQUIREMENTS

Regulations may also include nationality requirements.[38] Generally,
the crew must have a knowledge of English sufficient to understand
orders given to them; otherwise adequate arrangements for transmit-
ting orders in another language must be made. In their absence the
superintendent can forbid the ship to sail or detain her. Disobedience is
an offence.[39]

The DoT can also regulate the merchant navy uniform and distinguishing marks indicating the wearer's rank. Unauthorized wearing
of the uniform is an offence. So as not to stifle the entertainment
industry, the wearing of the uniform in any stage, film or television,
performance is allowed, so long as the uniform is not brought into
disrepute.[40]

9.2.7   UNREGISTERED SHIPS

What has been said so far applies to registered ships, but the DoT was
given the power to make regulations so that provisions in the first place
designed only for registered ships should also apply to unregistered
ships.[41] This was a wise precaution, for an unregistered ship may meet
situations requiring control. The Regulations[42] issued by the DoT
distinguish between two kinds of such vessels. Those which ought to

36 M.S. Notice No. M. 1178.
37 In one limitation of liability case the certificated second officer dropped out and
   was replaced by the only available person. He was experienced but uncertificated.
   While on watch a collision occurred due to his fault. Although liable for this
   negligence the owners were entitled to limit liability as they had not been guilty of
   'actual fault or privity' in signing him on: *The Empire Jamaica: Koninklijke
   Rotterdamsche Lloyd* v. *Western Steamship Co. Ltd* [1957] A.C. 386. See further,
   Chapter 22, *infra*.
38 Merchant Shipping Act 1970, s. 43(4).
39 S. 48.
40 S. 87: not yet in force.
41 S. 92.
42 Merchant Shipping (Unregistered Ships) Regulations 1972 (S.I. No. 1876).

have been, but are not, registered must comply with practically all the relevant provisions of the Merchant Shipping Act 1970. Ships, other than fishing vessels, which are not registered because there is no need to do so are subject to a few such provisions, which we shall encounter as this chapter proceeds: s. 27, which deals with misconduct on board; ss. 39 and 40 which, respectively, deal with a seaman's civil liability when absent without leave or found guilty of smuggling; s. 42, which defines the circumstances in which seamen may strike; and s. 62, which prescribes an inquiry in the event of the death of a member of the crew.

9.2.8 INQUIRIES INTO FITNESS OR CONDUCT

Certificated officers, and others holding certificates, must maintain standards throughout their careers. If evidence comes to hand suggesting that an officer has proved incompetent, has misconducted himself or is for any other reason, perhaps medical, unfit to discharge his duties, the DoT may appoint one or two persons to conduct an inquiry, who will pronounce on the evidence.[43] An inquiry will also be ordered where reports have come in indicating that an officer has been seriously negligent in performing his duties or that he has failed to give assistance or information after a collision.[44] Pending the outcome of the inquiry the DoT may suspend the officer's certificate, but in that event an appeal lies to the High Court or, if the inquiry is held in Scotland, to the Court of Session; either court, in a proper case, will lift the suspension.[45]

Those conducting the inquiry have all the powers of an inspector under the Merchant Shipping Act 1979.[46] The procedure is governed by Rules[47] which require the officer to receive a notice giving details of the allegations and at least 30 days notice of the inquiry.[48] The person holding the inquiry has to be a senior lawyer or judge and must sit with one or more nautical assessors who have had similar experience to the officer concerned.[49] The hearing has some of the trappings of the court room, such as the cross-examination of witnesses, but the person

---

43 S. 52.
44 *Ibid.* The post collision obligations arise under the Merchant Shipping Act 1894, s. 422: see Section 21.3, *infra.*
45 Merchant Shipping Act 1970, s. 52(1).
46 Ss. 37(4), 27, 28.
47 Merchant Shipping Act 1970, ss. 52(3), 58: Merchant Shipping (Section 52 Inquiries) Rules 1982 (S.I. No. 1752).
48 Reg. 4.
49 Reg. 6.

holding the inquiry may dispense with technical rules of evidence.[50] Although legal representation is allowed, the officer does not have to attend personally. He may make written representations which will be read out.[51]

The fact that the officer has been suspended pending the inquiry does not, of course, prejudice its result. The person holding it can, if the charge is proved to his satisfaction, suspend or cancel the certificate, according to the seriousness of the case, or merely censure the person charged.[52] A similar procedure must be followed where the holder of a certificate, other than an officer's certificate, faces investigation.[53]

Illustration: *The Empire Antelope, The Radchurch*[54]

Tribunals of inquiry appointed by the Minister of War Transport (who during the 1939-45 war was in charge of shipping, now looked after by the DoT) had suspended the certificates of two masters. Believing that their ships had been hit by torpedoes fired from a German submarine they had given orders to abandon ship; both ships carried cargoes of iron and were thus liable to sink fast. In fact, the torpedoes had missed, but had exploded sufficiently close to the vessels to damage them.

Held: The order to abandon ship was justified and not evidence of incompetence. In any event, incompetence of a kind sufficient to deprive a master of his certificate must be of some duration; a single act of incompetence must be quite exceptional to call for such severe action.

The action just described can be taken even when there has been no casualty as a result of the misconduct or incompetence. However, as we have already seen[55] once a casualty or near miss has occurred the Act envisages more formal proceedings – a preliminary inquiry by one person, to be followed, where it appears desirable, by a formal investigation. If it is likely that the question of the withdrawal of a certificate becomes an issue, this person must sit with at least two assessors.[56] In a proper case a certificate can be cancelled or suspended; where the circumstances are less serious, censure is the appropriate action to take.[57]

50 Reg. 7.
51 *Ibid.*
52 S. 52(4).
53 Ss. 53, 54, Merchant Shipping Act 1970 and s. 37(4) Merchant Shipping Act 1979.
54 [1943] P. 79.
55 See Section 8.10, *supra.*
56 S. 56(1), Merchant Shipping Act 1970.
57 S. 56(4), Merchant Shipping Act 1970.

All these proceedings are open to review. The simplest way of doing this is administrative action by the DoT. It may come to the conclusion that the person concerned received unduly harsh treatment and that, in the words of the Act,[58] 'the justice of the case requires' the return of a cancelled certificate or the lifting of a suspension. The DoT has the option to issue a lower-grade certificate for that lost, for instance, cancelling the master's but issuing a mate's certificate.

More complicated cases require a more formal review. Where new evidence has come to light, or where a miscarriage of justice is suspected for other reasons, the DoT will order a re-hearing, either by the original investigators or by the High Court or the Court of Session, as the case may be.[59]

In the absence of such an order any person affected by the original decision has the right to appeal to one of the courts.[60] This type of proceeding does not rule out criminal proceedings being taken in addition, as will be discussed later on in this chapter.

9.3   THE MASTER

After the Great War of 1914–18, when restrictions on aliens were tightened, masters and principal officers of British ships had also to be British subjects. This requirement was repealed, and the pre-1914 position restored, in 1974.[61] We have already noticed that this type of disqualification had disappeared earlier in respect of citizens of the EEC.

9.3.1   CONTRACT OF SERVICE

The master's contract of service is regulated by the general law, as sketched earlier in this chapter, and not a great deal needs to be said about it, especially in view of the Established Service Scheme that applies to shipping companies represented on the NMB. The scheme embraces all registered seafarers, including masters, and the terms of service agreements can be checked in the NMB *Summary of Agreements*.

---

58 S. 60.
59 S. 57.
60 S. 57(4).
61 When s. 100 and Sch. 5, Merchant Shipping Act 1970 came into force, although
    s. 43(4) has retained a reserve power.

Masters may be disciplined under the Merchant Navy Establishment disciplinary procedures administered by the General Council of British Shipping.[62] Failure to carry out obligations or inefficiency, or conduct prejudicial to discipline whilst employed by a shipping company (or undergoing approved training), or misconduct can result in a caution and/or suspension of benefits, or cancellation of registration.

Many NMB agreements and recommendations apply to masters entitling them to additional benefits, for instance, extra leave and special payments when discharged sick or injured abroad. Company service contracts under the Established Service Scheme require three months' notice of termination on either side.

Nevertheless, it would seem that under the Employment Protection (Consolidation) Act 1978, Part V, a master when dismissed can appeal to an industrial tribunal, alleging unfair dismissal. In such proceedings the complainant's conduct and efficiency will of course be matters of great importance. Exceptionally, even one serious error of judgment will be held sufficient ground for dismissal. The Court of Appeal, for instance, upheld the dismissal of an aircraft pilot who had landed his aircraft with seventy persons on board so heavily that it bounced twice, once as much as ten feet, so that the nosewheel assembly collapsed and the aircraft became a total loss; no one was injured.[63] In such activities, one of the judges pointed out, the degree of professional skill required was so high and the potential consequences of the smallest departure from that high standard were so serious, that one failure was enough to justify dismissal. Therefore, in the following illustration decided under the old law, the decision apparently would now be the same. In the case the question was whether the company was justified in dismissing the master summarily without notice.

Illustration: *Power v. British India Steam Navigation Co.*[64]

The plaintiff, for many years the captain of one of the defendants' passenger steamers and with a blameless record, had on one occasion, shortly before sailing, received a report that the vessel's draught was 2 ft down by the head. He took no action on the report and set sail with 440 passengers. Water entered the hold and badly damaged some valuable Persian carpets.

---

62 See Clauses 53–58 of the Established Service Scheme, NMB, *Summary of Agreements*, pp. 27–28. The code of conduct administered through the NMB Merchant Navy Disciplinary Organization does not apply to masters as they are not signed on under crew agreements: see Section 9.4.7, *infra*.

63 *Alidair Ltd* v. *Taylor* [1978] I.C.R. 445.

64 (1930) 46 T.L.R. 294. It would seem that a justified summary dismissal can never be 'unfair'.

Held: This was a grave breach of good seamanship. It was more than a mere error of judgment, being gross negligence. Summary dismissal was justified despite the previous service.

Later in this chapter we shall discuss conduct by members of the crew which is sufficiently serious to be classed as a criminal offence. The most serious offence can also be committed by the master; it is punishable with imprisonment or fine. It consists of doing something that causes, or is likely to cause, the loss of the ship, or serious damage to it, or the death or serious injury of a person on board. Omitting to do something to preserve the ship or to prevent death or serious injury is also an offence, provided the omission was deliberate or amounted to a breach or neglect of duty.[65] Bearing in mind the habits of some sailors, the Act allows a conviction where the act or omission took place while the person charged had lost his power of deliberation through the consumption of drink or a drug, the latter unless medically prescribed.[66]

In relation to the owners of the ship the master, as the owners' agent, must communicate everything that they require to know in order to conduct their business. The owners are indeed fixed with the master's knowledge of material facts, which may be of vital importance in connection with marine insurance.[67] When acting within the scope of his authority the master binds the owners, for instance, when signing bills of lading or buying stores.

The master has a number of public duties, such as reporting casualties, which are dealt with elsewhere.[68]

9.3.2 LOG BOOKS

To comply with all the regulations an official record must be kept of what happens on board or to the ship in the course of the voyage.[69] To

65 S. 27 of the Merchant Shipping Act 1970, as amended by the Merchant Shipping Act 1979. In *The Harcourt: Hodge* v. *Higgins* [1980] 2 Lloyd's Rep. 589 a master was convicted of an offence under s. 27 when an anchor light was not showing in circumstances creating danger. It was no defence that the master had retired to bed with influenza having instructed the mate to keep a proper watch. See also Section 21.2.3, *infra*.

66 S. 33.

67 *Blackburn Low & Co.* v. *Vigors* (1887) 12 App. Cas. 531.

68 See Section 8.9, *supra*.

69 S. 68, Merchant Shipping Act, 1970; Merchant Shipping (Official Log Books) Regulations 1981 (S.I. No. 569), amended 1985 (S.I. No. 1828). The Regulations do not apply to ships belonging to a general lighthouse authority, ships of less than 25 GRT or pleasure yachts: reg. 2. For fishing vessels see the Merchant Shipping (Official Log Books) (Fishing Vessels) Regulations 1981 (S.I. No. 570).

ensure uniformity in the layout and upkeep of the official log book the
DoT Regulations go into great detail. The Schedule lists 45 kinds of
entry regarding events to be recorded. Entries have to be signed –
usually by the master – and countersigned – usually by a crew member,
but where a seaman's complaint is entered, by the complainant.[70]
Matters requiring record include: convictions of crew members by a
legal tribunal; offences to be prosecuted at the end of the voyage;
breaches of the NMB Code of Conduct;[71] disciplinary offences on
board; statements on the conduct of members of the crew; cases of
illnesses and treatments; discharges of seamen abroad; and navigational
matters such as collisions. Recently, masters have also been required to
record details of the tests which must be carried out on pilot hoists[72] and
the steering gear.[73] Births and deaths must also be recorded and then
reported to the Registrar-General of Shipping and Seamen.[74]

Failure to make an entry in accordance with the Regulations can make
the master guilty of an offence.[75] The entries in the log are sacrosanct –
wilfully destroying, mutilating or making an entry illegible is also an
offence.[76] Amendment should only be by making a fresh entry.[77] The
log must be delivered to the marine superintendent when the ship first
calls at a port more than six months after the first entry, or when the last
person employed under a crew agreement is discharged.[78]

EEC Regulations require skippers to keep logs of their fish catches so
that checks can be made on the overfishing of quotas.[79] These log book
offences could result in a £1000 fine.[80]

70 Reg. 4.
71 See Section 9.4.7, *infra*.
72 Under the Merchant Shipping (Pilot Ladders and Hoists) Regulations 1980 (S.I.
   No. 543), amended 1981 (S.I. No. 581).
73 Under the Merchant Shipping (Automatic Pilot and Testing of Steering Gear)
   Regulations 1981 (S.I. No. 571).
74 Merchant Shipping (Return of Births and Deaths) Regulations 1979 (S.I. No.
   1577). These also apply to unregistered ships whose owners either reside, or have
   their principal place of business in the UK; reg. 12. See also the Hovercraft (Births,
   Deaths and Missing Persons) Regulations 1972 (S.I. No. 1513); the Offshore
   Installations (Logbooks and Registration of Death) Regulations 1972 (S.I. No.
   1542) – remember that such installations are outside territorial waters.
75 Regs 5, 11.
76 S. 68(6), Merchant Shipping Act 1970.
77 Reg. 8.
78 And within 48 hours of that time. The period is extended if there is a pending
   wages submission or an appeal against a fine; reg. 10.
79 Council Regulation (EEC) No. 2057/82, (O.J. No. L220, 29.7.82, p. 1),
   Commission Regulation (EEC) No. 2807/83 (O.J. No. L276, 10.10.83, p. 1).
80 Sea Fishing (Enforcement of Community Control) Measures 1985 (S.I. No. 487),
   Sch.

As part of the campaign to police oil pollution a separate Oil Record Book must be provided for ships of 400 GRT and above and for oil tankers of 150 GRT and above.[81] The Oil Record Book has two parts: Part I deals with machinery space operations in all ships; Part II deals with cargo and ballast operations and need only be carried on oil tankers. There are a total of 14 operations listed which must be recorded, such as the discharge of bilge water which has accumulated in machinery spaces, or the loading of an oil cargo. Specific details of these various operations must also be included, such as the time and method of discharge, or the type and quality of oil loaded. Each completed operation has to be signed by the officer or officers in charge and each completed page by the master. The idea is that if there is an oil spill the inspectors will be able to pinpoint the guilty ship by checking the Oil Record Books of ships in the area. The owner and master can be guilty of an offence, although the maximum penalty is less than that for being caught illegally discharging oil.[82]

9.3.3   AUTHORITY ON BOARD

We have left to the end the discussion of the master's overriding duty, that of the maintenance of order and discipline on board. At one time, the master's power was likened to that of a despot[83] and accounts of sea voyages in the past[84] show how arbitrarily and cruelly some masters could behave. In fact, the master was always subject to the law of the country in which his ship was registered and on the return of the ship might, and in rare cases actually did, have to face prosecution in a criminal court.[85] A civil action for damages was also possible. In what appears to be the only reported case of this kind[86] a seaman had resisted the flogging of another seaman who had committed a disorderly act and was himself flogged for disobedience by order of the master. But his action for assault was dismissed, the court holding that the master was entitled to order the flogging of the disobedient man.

---

81 Merchant Shipping (Prevention of Oil Pollution) Regulations 1983 (S.I. No. 1398), reg. 10, Sch. 2; also the Oil in Navigable Waters (Transfer Records) Regulations 1957 (S.I. No. 358); and see Section 8.5.1, *supra*.
82 Reg. 34.
83 *R.* v. *Leggett* (1838) 8 Car. & P. 191, 194; 173 E.R. 456, 457.
84 See the books by Stevenson and Dana mentioned at the beginning of Chapter 8.
85 *R.* v. *Leggett, supra; Aitken* v. *Bedwell* (1827) 1 M. & M. 68; 173 E.R. 1084.
86 *Lamb* v. *Burnett* (1827) 1 Cr. & J. 291; 148 E.R. 1430.

Corporal punishment is now forbidden. We shall discuss the modern treatment of disciplinary offences in the following section of this chapter, dealing with seamen. But the master still has the power to arrest – to put under restraint, as the Act puts it,[87] anyone on board if concern for the safety of the ship or the preservation of good order or discipline call for that action. In one case,[88] a steward won an action for damages for false imprisonment. The man was arrested following a passenger's complaint that he had indecently assaulted the passenger's daughter, but the evidence at the trial showed that the master had ordered the arrest not because he considered the man guilty of the offence but to placate the passenger.

The power to put under restraint extends not only to passengers and crew, but also to stowaways and anyone on board without the master's consent, except government service officers or anyone acting under a statutory authority, stowing away and going on board without consent being offences.[89]

9.4   THE SEAMAN

9.4.1   MODE OF HIRING SEAMEN

To prevent abuses and frauds, and the nefarious practices of the crimp who at one time entrapped and impressed seamen, the recruiting of seamen has been restricted. Only those holding a DoT licence are allowed to run this type of business, but persons in the regular employment of those requiring sea-going personnel are not caught by the licensing provisions. Contravention of this rule is an offence.[90]

A seaman 'includes every person (except masters and pilots) employed or engaged in any capacity on board any ship'.[91] Ships' officers are therefore classed as seamen: for welfare purposes the master is usually included in this category.[92]

---

87 S. 79, Merchant Shipping Act 1970. Similar powers are vested in managers of oil platforms; Mineral Workings (Offshore Installations) Act 1971, s. 5; Oil and Gas (Enterprise) Act 1982, s. 24, Sch. 3.

88 *Hook* v. *Cunard SS Co.* [1953] 1 All E.R. 1021.

89 Ss. 77, 78, Merchant Shipping Act 1970.

90 Merchant Shipping Act 1970, s. 6. This also applies to seamen engaged in the UK by a foreign ship, *R.* v. *Stewart* [1899] 1 Q.B. 964.

91 Merchant Shipping Act 1894, s. 742. Merchant Shipping Act 1970, Sch. 3, para. 4.

92 See generally Section 9.1.3, *supra*.

As in the past, only persons aged 18 or over can be employed on board a ship, though in certain capacities persons between the ages of 16–18 can also be engaged.[93]

9.4.2 THE CONTRACT OF EMPLOYMENT[94]

This has long been subject to state supervision. Conditions of service expose seamen to particular hazards often encountered far away from their homeland and the legal protection of its administration and courts. It was accordingly recognized at an early date that seamen's contracts must contain safeguards for their well-being and that when concluding the contract the seaman must know the kind of voyage he can expect.

To ensure this, contracts must be in writing and in the form approved by the DoT.[95] They are policed by the superintendents of mercantile marine, officers appointed by the DoT, who have been described as a combination of a friendly policeman and a magistrate. Formerly contracts had to be signed in his presence, but now he merely has to be informed of the intention to employ, and normally also to discharge, a seaman, thus making supervision possible.[96] The employer must also obtain the prescribed forms of contract from the officer.

The individual contracts are normally embodied in one document in respect of each ship, the crew agreement, in the past known as the ship's articles, a copy of which must be sent to the superintendent.[97]

The terms of the agreement will, of course, be contained in whichever contract form is being used and this will usually incorporate NMB Agreements, although some companies offer better terms.[98] The matters dealt with are very wide ranging, such as the nature and length of the intended voyage; the time when the seaman will report for duty; the capacity in which each member of the crew is to serve; the wages

93 Merchant Shipping Act 1970, s. 51; not yet in force.
94 See Kitchen (1980), Chapter 6.
95 There are two forms for non-fishing vessels. Form ALC/NMBl is for ships operating under NMB Conditions and Form ALC/NFDl for those which are not: Kitchen (1980), p. 345.
96 Ss. 2, 3.
97 Ss. 1 to 3; Merchant Shipping (Crew Agreements, List of Crew and Discharge of Seamen) Regulations 1972 (S.I. No. 918), as amended 1977 (S.I. No. 45). 1978 (S.I. No. 1756), 1979 (S.I. No. 1519), 1981 (S.I. No. 1789). See reg. 25 for permission to discharge in certain cases abroad without permission. Also the Merchant Shipping Crew Agreements, Lists of Crew and Discharge of Seamen) (Fishing Vessels) Regulations 1972 (S.I. No. 919), amended 1983 (S.I. No. 478).
98 See Kitchen (1980), Chapter 7.

applicable and the fines which may be payable for misconduct. Working hours for navigating and engineering cadets aged 16–18 are restricted. *Kitchen* has said about the NMB agreements that their detail, particularly in relation to entitlement to wages, reduces uncertainty so that disputes are unlikely to come before the courts.[99]

A certified copy of the crew agreement must be posted at a convenient place in the ship for reference,[1] very similar to the corresponding provision of the general law, as enacted in the Employment Protection (Consolidation) Act 1978. On demand, a seaman is also entitled to a copy of the whole, or any extract from, the agreement.[2]

Certain ships need not comply with the stringent provisions about crew agreements: ships belonging to a general lighthouse authority; ships of less than 80 registered tons and sailing solely on coastal voyages, which means between ports in the British Isles and the Republic of Ireland; pleasure yachts, unless they go abroad and employ more than four paid crew, and ships on trial voyages.[3]

Even ships bound to observe the crew agreement rules need not include in the agreements personnel not employed in navigation, but solely engaged on construction, repairs and testing, and also men and women employed by someone other than the owner to provide goods, services or entertainment on board, which is common on passenger ships.[4] But medical and catering staffs are crew.

The owner of the ship must keep a list of the crew, including the master, which should contain full details about them such as: name and address; capacity in which employed; grade and number of certificates of competency; name and address of next of kin.[5] A copy of the list must be maintained by the owner at a UK address and if he has reason to believe that the ship has been lost or abandoned he must send a copy to the superintendent.[6] Owners of pleasure yachts on coastal voyages, or voyages where there are not more than four paid crew members, do not need to have a list.[7]

99 Kitchen (1980), p. 370.
 1 1972 (S.I. No. 918) reg. 7.
 2 Reg. 8. Note that the Data Protection Act 1984 will give individuals rights of access, as from 11 November 1987, to personal information kept on machines such as computers. Users of *any* data specified by the Act *must* register with the Data Protection Registrar by 11 May 1986, or commit an offence.
 3 S. 1(5), Merchant Shipping Act 1970; 1972 (S.I. No. 918) reg. 3.
 4 Reg. 3. These categories of persons are covered by the general employment legislation.
 5 S. 69, Merchant Shipping Act 1970; Part II of the Crew Agreements Regulations 1972 (S.I. No. 918) as amended (see fn. 97 Section 9.4.2, *supra*).
 6 Regs 16, 17.
 7 S. 69(4) Merchant Shipping Act 1970, Reg. 12.

Seamen receive from the superintendent a British Seaman's Card and a Discharge Book, which records the ships in which the recipient is and has been employed, periods of work, stand-by duties and sickness and also details of training courses attended, including courses on survival at sea run by the Merchant Navy Training Board, inoculations and vaccinations, eye tests and other relevant details.[8]

9.4.3 REMUNERATION OF SEAMEN[9]

(A) EARNING OF WAGES

The most important right of the seaman under the contract is, of course, to receive the agreed remuneration. At one time, all persons who participated in a sea adventure were regarded as co-adventurers. If the voyage was unsuccessful, that is, if no freight was earned, the crew could claim no reward for their services. This was expressed by the maxim 'freight is the mother of wages'. It needs little imagination to realize that this was the cause of great hardship, and the 1894 Act provided that 'the right to wages shall not depend on the earning of freight'.[10]

The right to receive wages at the agreed rate continues in two sets of circumstances where a seaman's employment comes to a premature end.

Where his ship is wrecked or lost, the master or seaman remains entitled to his contract wages for every day of unemployment up to two months from the wreck or loss.[11] It may not always be obvious exactly when a ship was wrecked and then it is for the court to establish the material date. In one case, decided under the similar old law but still applicable,[12] the defendants' ship was driven ashore on 27 January, salvors tried to get her off, but gave up on 5 May. On that day, the

---

8 Ss. 70, 71, Merchant Shipping Act 1970: Merchant Shipping (Seamen's Documents) Regulations 1972 (S.I. No. 1295), amended 1974 (S.I. No. 1734), 1977 (S.I. No. 1181), 1978 (S.I. Nos 107, 979, 1758), 1979 (S.I. No. 1519), 1981 (S.I. No. 313)

9 See Kitchen (1980), Chapter 8.

10 S. 157(1), which was itself repealed by the Merchant Shipping Act 1970, s. 101, and 1979 (S.I. No. 809).

11 S. 15(1), Merchant Shipping Act 1970 as extended by s. 37(1), Merchant Shipping Act 1979.

12 *The Terneuzen* [1938] P. 109.

owners abandoned the ship and paid off the crew, including the plaintiff, the chief officer. He contended that he was entitled to two months'
pay from 5 May, but the defendants regarded 27 January as the relevant
date; if they were right the plaintiff had in fact received more than the
statutory minimum. The court agreed with the plaintiff. Until 5 May, it
found, the defendants still thought they would be able to continue the
voyage.

Unless otherwise agreed, the right to wages also continues where the
seaman's employment ends because the ship, while outside the UK, is
sold or ceases to be registered there.[13]

However, this right to two months' wages must not allow a seaman
to enjoy a windfall. If wreck or sale occurs less than two months before
the contractual end of the employment the right to wages continues
only for this reduced period.[14] The benefit is also lost in respect of any
day of unemployment for which suitable alternative work was offered
and unreasonably rejected or not taken up.[15]

All employed persons enjoy certain rights safeguarding their claims
for wages or salaries against their employers, but merchant seamen,
because of the nature of their calling, enjoy certain additional privileges.

Seamen must receive their wages on discharge at the latest, and the
law brings considerable pressure to bear on employers to pay punctually. Thus for any one day on which the discharged seaman remains
unpaid, up to a maximum of fifty-six days, he is entitled to his full
wages under the crew agreement. Any sum then still outstanding
carries interest at the rate of 20 per cent.[16]

Of course, these penal provisions do not operate where non-payment
is due to a mistake that is later discovered or to a reasonable dispute
between the parties about the exact sum payable. The seaman also loses
this additional benefit if he has brought about non-payment by his own
default or if non-payment is due to any other cause not being a wrongful act or default of the employer or one of his servants or agents.[17]

We have seen that the seaman can demand his discharge if his ship is
sold while abroad. If he makes that demand the employers must
arrange for his repatriation to the UK, and the right to payment and
possible additional benefits arises on his return to the UK, a common

13 S. 15(2), Merchant Shipping Act 1970.
14 *Ibid.*
15 S. 15(3), Merchant Shipping Act 1970.
16 S. 7(3), Merchant Shipping Act 1970.
17 S. 7(4), Merchant Shipping Act 1970.

sense rule, making it unnecessary to send possibly large sums of money to a country where employers have no adequate banking facilities.[18]

Detailed provisions exist for accounts of wages and authorized deductions, for such items as canteen bills, cash advances, allotments, and contributions to pension fund, charity or trade union. Wages are payable in cash, unless payment by cheque or Giro is agreed.[19]

Where the exact amount payable is disputed the parties can go to court, but they can also agree to submit the disagreement to a superintendent of mercantile marine.[20] We mentioned earlier that this officer exercises certain functions of a magistrate. If the superintendent agrees to adjudicate, his decision is final. He need not, however, accept the submissions, perhaps because the sum in dispute is very large, or because the case raises difficult issues. In that event, in the absence of settlement, a court must decide.

All this applies only to wages due under a crew agreement. The court alone has jurisdiction where a dispute about remuneration concerns the master or anyone working on board outside the crew agreement, as explained above. Where the employee's action succeeds, the court may award interest at the rate of 20 per cent unless, as in the case of crew agreements, failure to pay was due to a mistake, a reasonable dispute or the claimant's default, and not to any wrong done by the respondent or his servants or agents.[21]

(B)   SPECIAL RIGHTS

The law protects seamen against ill-considered bargains in a number of ways. Modifying the general law, any power of attorney or other authority granted by the seaman, allowing some other person to receive his wages, is revocable at any time, except where DoT regulations otherwise provide.[22] However, a seaman who wants to provide for his dependants while absent may do so by means of an allotment note.

18 S. 7(6), Merchant Shipping Act 1970.
19 Ss. 8 and 9 Merchant Shipping Act 1970; Merchant Shipping (Seamen's Wages and Accounts) Regulations 1972 (S.I. No. 1700), amended 1972 (S.I. No. 1876), 1978 (S.I. No. 1757), 1985 (S.I. No. 340), Merchant Shipping (Seamen's Wages and Accounts) (Fishing Vessels) Regulations 1972 (S.I. No. 1701), amended 1972 (S.I. No. 1877); Merchant Shipping (Seamen's Wages) (Contributions) Regulations 1972 (S.I. No. 1699), amended 1972 (S.I. Nos 1876, 1877). Also s. 24, Merchant Shipping Act 1979. Seamen are unaffected by the Wages Act 1986, see s. (30)3.
20 S. 10, Merchant Shipping Act 1970.
21 S. 12, Merchant Shipping Act 1970.
22 Merchant Shipping Act 1970, s. 11.

These notes must normally be for not more than half the contract wages; no more than two persons may be beneficiaries.[23]

There are also restrictions on the right of seamen to waive by contract their rights to salvage.[24] Seamen are further protected in that if they themselves should purport to assign future wages to creditors such assignment binds neither the seaman nor his employer.[25]

Under the general law it is possible to enforce court judgments against individuals by means of an attachment of earnings order. This directs an employer to deduct sums before paying the employee his wages. Such an order cannot be made in respect of wages payable to a seaman, unless he is a seaman of a fishing boat.[26] The exception is where, e.g., a spouse or children seek to enforce maintenance orders.[27] A public authority which incurs expenditure for the maintenance of a seaman's dependants may also be able to direct the employer to retain a proportion of the seaman's wages.[28]

In common with other employees, seamen, including the master, also enjoy privileges in the event of the owner's insolvency. They can claim preferential payment before the general trade creditors, subject however to important limits regarding the amount of outstanding pay and the time prior to insolvency in which it was earned.[29]

However valuable these preferential rights, their efficacy depends on sufficient assets being available, and to guard against their absence merchant seamen enjoy the additional powerful safeguard of a right *in rem*, a lien,[30] that is a right to payment out of ship and freight, including freight due from sub-charterers.[31] Such an order can also be made where the owner is not insolvent.

Proceedings begin with the issue of a writ by the unpaid seaman against the owner. Arrears recoverable are not restricted to those accumulated up to the time of the writ, but where the contract of employment is terminated later the lien covers wages accumulated up to termination.

23 Merchant Shipping Act 1970, s. 13. Merchant Shipping (Seamen's Allotments) Regulations 1972 (S.I. No. 1698), amended 1972 (S.I. Nos 1876, 1877).
24 Merchant Shipping Act 1970, s. 16. See further Chapter 24. *infra*.
25 S. 11(1)(a), Merchant Shipping Act 1970.
26 Attachment of Earnings Act 1971, s. 24(2)(c).
27 S. 24(2)(c) as amended by the Merchant Shipping Act 1979, s. 39.
28 Merchant Shipping Act 1970, s. 17; Merchant Shipping (Maintenance of Seamen's Dependants) Regulations 1972 (S.I. No. 1635), amended 1972 (S.I. No. 1875).
29 Companies Act 1985, s. 614, Sch. 19; Bankruptcy Act 1914, s. 33; Insolvency Act 1976, s. 1. These provisions will be replaced by the Insolvency Act 1986, ss. 175-6, 328, 386-7, Sch. 6, from 29 December 1986.
30 See Chapter 7; s. 16, Merchant Shipping Act 1970.
31 *The Andalina* (1886) 12 P.D. 1.

Illustration: *The Fairport*[32]

The master and chief officer of a Panamanian vessel issued a writ for outstanding wages and refund of disbursements on 12 March 1965. Three days later the vessel was arrested at Dover and on 26 March the writ was amended to include all members of the crew as claimants. Master and crew were not discharged until several weeks later and the order for the sale of the vessel was made in May.

Held: The claimants were entitled out of the fund to wages due before and after the issue of the writ, for the action against the owners did not terminate the contract of employment.

If prior to the agreed termination of the contract of employment it becomes necessary to discharge a seaman out of the UK by reason of unfitness or otherwise, the master must usually obtain the written consent of the proper officer, normally a consul.[33] He must then deliver an account to the seaman.[34]

9.4.4 HAZARDOUS VOYAGES

The seaman's duties consist of doing the work for which he is engaged. If it appears in the course of the voyage that wholly uncontemplated perils arise then the seaman need not perform them unless a special reward is paid to him.

Illustration: *Palace Shipping Co. v. Caine*[35]

A British crew signed on for a voyage from Cardiff to ports within certain limits of Hong Kong. They knew that Russia and Japan were at war and that their cargo, consisting of coal, was regarded as contraband by both belligerents. At Hong Kong the master suddenly required the men to take the cargo on to a Japanese naval base, which was within the contractual limits. The crew refused to do so because that would have meant entering the war zone.

Held: The master was not entitled to force the crew to go on to the Japanese naval base; the agreement had been for a peaceful commercial voyage, and the risk of war capture and its consequences entitled the men to refuse further services.

---

32 [1966] 2 All E.R. 1026.
33 Merchant Shipping Act 1970, s. 3; Merchant Shipping (Crew Agreements, Lists of Crew and Discharge of Seamen) Regulations 1972 (S.I. No. 918) reg. 25.
34 Merchant Shipping Act 1970, s. 8; Merchant Shipping (Repatriation) Regulations 1979 (S.I. No. 97), and see Section 9.4.5, *infra*.
35 [1907] A.C. 386.

Not surprisingly, the NMB has concerned itself with situations of this type. It decided in 1973 that where the appropriate committee of the Board agrees that a ship may encounter special hazards as a result of warlike operations in a specified area, the following rules shall obtain: before a crew agreement is signed seafarers shall be advised of the special hazards to which they may be exposed; if a vessel is already en route for the area they shall be told that they are entitled to leave it at a port on the ship's route, where repatriation facilities exist or, in the alternative, they can demand additional remuneration.[36] This, of course, applies only to ships of companies who are members of the General Council of British Shipping.

9.4.5 REPATRIATION

A seaman employed on a UK-registered ship left behind at a foreign port, or shipwrecked, must be repatriated and, pending repatriation, maintained by his employer.[37] A corresponding duty rests on employers in respect of seamen engaged abroad and left behind in a UK port.[38] The superintendent or other proper officer, for instance, a consular officer, must be informed, and if the employer fails in his duty these officers must take the action required.[39]

The seaman is not entitled to an unlimited holiday at his employer's expense. The latter's obligations cease if the seaman refuses reasonable alternative employment, or reasonable arrangements made for his return; or if he disappears for over three months after having been left behind.[40]

Leaving behind a seaman requires recording[41] in the log together with a statement regarding the wages owed. Within 28 days of his

---

36 NMB, *Summary of Agreements*, p. 70. For a voyage to Kharg Island in Iran a VLCC's crew asked for a bonus of US $100 000 or more in return for risking an Iraqi missile attack, see, e.g., *Fairplay* 14 October 1982. The NMB has agreed to make payments to those killed, injured or detained as a result of warlike operations while engaged on normal commercial voyages. Dependants of a deceased seafarer could receive the following benefits: £43 000 (officer); £35 000 (petty officer); £26 000 (rating or cadet); NMB, *Summary of Agreements*, p. 71, and see Kitchen (1980), p. 377.

37 Merchant Shipping Act 1970, ss. 2, 4, 62, 63; Merchant Shipping (Repatriation) Regulations 1979 (S.I. No. 97), reg. 3. The maintenance can even extend to legal expenses where the seaman is charged with a crime arising out of his employment.

38 Reg. 2.

39 Regs 4, 7.

40 Reg. 3; Merchant Shipping Act 1970, s. 63.

41 Reg. 4.

return home he is entitled to receive his wages and an account.[42] He is also entitled to have his property returned.[43]

The employer must also bear reasonable expenses incurred abroad when seamen require medical attention. This includes the provision of dentures and spectacles and, when the patient dies, burial or cremation expenses.[44] The property of the deceased must be taken in custody and on return handed to the personal representatives.[45] These provisions also cover the master.[46]

With the approval of the NMB, shipowners have arranged in respect of tonnage entered in a Protection and Indemnity Association to extend their obligations to seamen left behind by making special payments to those who are sick or injured and discharged abroad.[47] These payments are subject to certain conditions. One of these is that the person concerned shall not have brought about his disability by his own wilful act or default, or his own misbehaviour. To make sure that the term misbehaviour is not interpreted too narrowly the rule expressly excluded contracting venereal disease from the misbehaviour concept. It is worth mentioning that before the 1970 Act wilful act or default led to the loss of the statutory right to have medical expenses paid and until 1923 venereal disease was included in that disqualification.

A seaman who has been dismissed for failure to comply with certain provisions of the NMB Code of Conduct may have to make a contribution towards his repatriation expenses.[48]

Those subscribing to the NMB rules also undertake to make every effort to repatriate seafarers abroad whose wives or children and, in the case of single men, parents, are dangerously ill.[49]

9.4.6 STRIKES

(A) MARINERS

The question whether merchant seamen should be allowed to strike remained contentious for a long time; casting one's mind back to earlier

42 Reg. 11; ss. 7, 8 Merchant Shipping Act 1970.
43 Reg. 16.
44 Reg. 2; Merchant Shipping Act 1970, s. 26.
45 Merchant Shipping Act 1970, ss. 65, 66; Merchant Shipping (Property of Deceased Seamen) Regulations 1972 (S.I. No. 1697), amended 1972 (S.I. Nos 1876, 1877).
46 Merchant Shipping Act 1970, s. 67.
47 NMB, *Summary of Agreements*, p. 67.
48 Merchant Shipping (Seamen's Wages and Accounts) (Amendment) Regulations 1978 (S.I. No. 1757), and see Section 9.4.7, *infra*.
49 NMB, *Summary of Agreements*, p. 68.

times it is no surprise that in those days many regarded a striking seaman as a mutineer. This concept was abandoned by the Merchant Shipping Act 1970, but the right of a seaman on a UK ship to strike remains subject to moderately stringent conditions.

A dispute must be a trade dispute; notice of intention to strike must be given to the master at least forty-eight hours before the planned walk-off, during which period the ship must not be taken to sea; the strike notice is effectual only if given while 'the ship is in the UK and securely moored in a safe berth'.

The definition of 'trade dispute' has become fearfully complex,[50] but it essentially refers to a dispute connected with one or more of the following matters: terms and conditions of employment; engagement, termination or suspension of employment; allocation of work or duties as between workers or groups of workers; matters of discipline; membership or non-membership of a trade union; facilities of trade union officials; and negotiation or consultation machinery.

A dispute remains an industrial one 'even if it relates to matters outside Great Britain'. These words were originally intended to legalize action against multi-national companies by co-ordinated sympathetic action of workers in several countries. But the Employment Act 1982, s. 18 has restricted the definition so that the persons taking action in the UK must be likely to be affected themselves by the outcome of the dispute. Purely political matters – very hard to define – are excluded.

Since strike notice can be validly given only while the ship is in a UK port,[51] strikes while the ship is abroad are unlawful. The employer could also sue those concerned for damages. Thus when, early in 1973, some 200 crew walked off the Shaw Savill liner *Ocean Monarch* in a foreign port, the owners were obliged to repatriate them, but to recoup expenses they deducted £50 from each man's wages.[52]

A seaman who persistently and wilfully neglects his duty, or disobeys lawful commands; or who takes joint action with other seamen while the ship is at sea to disobey lawful commands, or to neglect duties or to impede the progress or navigation of the vessel, commits a criminal offence.[53]

Students should also be aware of recent controversial changes in industrial law designed to make trade unions more democratic. The

50 Trade Union and Labour Relations Act 1974, s. 29, as amended by Trade Union and Labour Relations Act 1976, s. 1., Employment Act 1982, s. 18: see the *Encyclopedia of Labour Relations Law*, 2-1281 for a full analysis of the provisions.
51 Merchant Shipping Act 1970, s. 42.
52 *The Observer*, 4 February 1973.
53 Merchant Shipping Act 1970, s. 30, as amended by the Merchant Shipping Act 1974, s. 19, the Merchant Shipping Act 1979, Sch. 6.

Employment Act 1980, s. 1 allowed unions to be reimbursed by the Government for the costs of secret ballots taken e.g., to decide on strike action. The Trade Union Act 1984, Part II, removed the legal immunity of trade unions which called strikes without having the support of a pre-strike ballot. Part I provided for secret ballots for trade union elections. But these matters are largely outside the scope of this work. However, the changing climate of employment law is best demonstrated by the ITF campaigns.

(B)   THE ITF DISPUTES

The International Transport Workers Federation (ITF) dates back to 1896, but from 1948 it has maintained a campaign against flag of convenience (FOC) shipping. This is the practice by which shipowners 'flag out'[54] their ships to countries such as Liberia or Panama in order to take advantage of lower costs, in particular for crewing.[55] Part of the ITF campaign has been directed at substandard ships, but mostly it has been designed to raise the wages of 'crews of convenience'[56] and thus, indirectly, to protect the jobs of mariners in more developed countries.

The ITF issues 'blue certificates' to vessels in respect of which there is a special ITF agreement[57] concerning minimum wages, holidays, hours and conditions as well as contributions by the owner to the ITF's Seafarers' International Assistance, Welfare and Protection Fund. The ITF enforces its policy by 'blacking' ships which cannot produce a blue certificate to one of its inspectors. This means that port workers, such as dockers and tug crews, refuse to let the vessel leave until ITF conditions are met, including payments to the ITF's Welfare Fund as well as back pay.[58] Because of the great costs of delaying a ship, the

---

54 Northrup and Rowan (1983). See Section 3.1.2, *supra*.

55 FOC shipowners have been accused of cutting costs to the detriment of safety and FOC ships have figured prominently in casualty statistics.

56 This has not always been popular with the crews or governments of less developed countries as their opportunities for future employment are affected, see *The Nawala: N.W.L. Ltd* v. *Nelson and Laughton* [1980] 1 Lloyd's Rep. 1, 4. See also Section 9.1.2, *supra*.

57 For an example see, *The Universe Sentinel: Universe Tankships Inc.* v. *I.T.W.F.* [1982] 1 Lloyd's Rep. 1.

58 This averaged US $55 154 per ship in 1981, see Northrup and Rowan (1983), pp. 117, 122. It was reported recently that in 1983 the ITF distributed £7.8 million to seamen around the world but that its Fund stood at over £23 million: *The Observer* 1 September 1985.

owners often agree to pay up because legal action can be time-consuming.[59]

In the UK shipowners and the ITF have fought running battles through the courts, but the tide has swung against the ITF with the introduction of recent employment legislation. In the past, trade unions were granted wide immunity from suits in tort.[60] The immunity also applied to individual trade union members if they acted in contemplation or furtherance of a trade dispute.[61] This meant that if the ITF blacked, or threatened to black, a ship the owners could take no legal steps to stop them.[62] However, the protection did not extend to demands, involving economic duress, for contributions to the Welfare Fund.[63]

The Employment Act 1980 removed an individual's legal immunity from suit in relation to 'secondary' action.[64] Essentially, secondary action is where pressure is put on a person who is not directly a party to the trade dispute.

Illustration: *The Hoegh Apapa: Merkur Island Shipping Corporation* v. *Laughton, Shaw and Lewis*[65]

A Liberian registered ship with a Filipino crew docked in Liverpool. The ITF persuaded the tug men to 'black' the ship and prevent her sailing. The shipowners were responsible under the time charterparty for time lost due to such action and claimed from the ITF damages for the tort of interfering with the performance of a contract – in this case the time charter contract.

Held: (House of Lords): That the ITF had prima facie committed the tort. The actions would have been protected under the 1974 Act, but they were 'secondary' under the 1980 Act as the dispute was with the shipowners. The charterers who had contracted for the tugs were not party to that dispute.

---

59 *Ibid.*
60 Trade Union and Labour Relations Act 1974, s. 14.
61 *Ibid.*, s. 13. The definition of trade dispute in s. 29 was enlarged by the Trade Union and Labour Relations (Amendment) Act 1976, s. 1(d) to include those relating to disputes *outside* the UK: this assisted international action such as that taken by the ITF.
62 *The Nawala* [1980] 1 Lloyd's Rep. 1.
63 *The Universe Sentinel* [1982] 1 Lloyd's Rep. 1.
64 S. 17. S. 16 deals similarly with secondary picketing, i.e. picketing at a place different to that where one works.
65 [1983] 2 Lloyd's Rep. 1. The facts occurred before the commencement of the 1982 Act, *infra*.

The Employment Act 1982 went further and greatly narrowed the definition of trade dispute.[66] It removed the immunity of individuals where pressure is put on the outside suppliers of an employer who uses non-union labour.[67] Section 15 removed the complete immunity of the trade union itself – as well as that of employers' associations – so that, broadly, the union has only the same limited immunities of an individual. Certain acts are taken to be done by the union if they are authorized or endorsed by a responsible person, e.g. an official of the union.[68] However the union is given a special limit of liability for actions in tort by s. 16.[69] The limit varies according to the size of the union, but is £10 000 for a union with less than 5000 members and £250 000 for a union with 100 000 or more members.[70]

The combination of these laws has rendered the ITF very vulnerable in the UK to action in tort for the interference by unlawful means with the performance of a contract. Moreover, the absence of any provision in its rules for secret pre-strike ballots could make action by the ITF unlawful under the Trade Union Act 1984, s. 10.[71]

9.4.7 DISCIPLINE

When, earlier in this chapter, discussing the authority of the master, we made it clear that, to enforce that authority and to enable him to perform his duty to maintain order and safety, certain disciplinary powers must be vested in him. In distant days these powers were very wide indeed and often arbitrarily exercised, although even in the nineteenth century the courts, where they had a chance, curbed excessive action by the master.[72] But a code was not enacted until much later and

---

66 S. 18. The dispute must now be between workers and *their* employer. *Cf. The Nawala* [1980] 1 Lloyd's Rep. 1 where the ITF had represented 'workers' generally.
67 S. 14. Note also s. 19.
68 S. 15. The acts are essentially those specified in s. 13 of Trade Union and Labour Relations Act 1974, e.g. inducing another person to break a contract, or interfering with its performance.
69 The limit does not apply to personal injury claims or those arising out of its ownership or use of land (e.g. if the union's head office collapsed on a passer by).
70 But judgments cannot be enforced against the union's welfare fund or political funds which are not used to finance strikes, s. 17.
71 See *The Uniform Star: Shipping Company Uniform Inc. v. I.T.F.* [1985] 1 Lloyd's Rep. 173.
72 Section 9.3.3, *supra.*

was contained in the Merchant Shipping Acts 1970 and 1974, and in the Merchant Shipping (Disciplinary Offences) Regulations 1972.[73]

Apart from any civil liability which a seaman may incur by wrong doing, to be discussed later, discipline on board is enforced in two ways. Certain acts of indiscipline are so serious that they constitute criminal offences, to be tried by the ordinary courts on the ship's return. Other breaches are best dealt with promptly and on the spot by the master or any officer to whom the master has delegated his powers. The two categories overlap, for the master can treat a criminal offence, for instance, disobeying a lawful command, as a mere breach of discipline. Such action precludes later criminal prosecution in line with the general rule that no one must be in double jeopardy regarding punishment.[74]

First, the criminal offences. The most serious is when a seaman's actions are likely to cause the loss of the ship; or serious damage to the ship or to equipment; or the death or serious injury of any person on board. There is an offence if these acts (or omissions) are deliberate, a breach or neglect of duty, or if the seaman is under the influence of drink or drugs at the time.[75]

Following some rather spectacular cases of drunkenness on board fishing vessels it is an offence for a seaman to be under the influence of drink or drugs so that his capacity to perform duties on board such vessels is impaired.[76] Both these are serious offences and could result in imprisonment and/or a fine. It is a defence if drugs are taken under medical prescription.[77]

We now pass on to breaches of discipline which are not criminal, for which the master was able to impose a fine. The master could only exercise these powers against seamen who were not offi- cers.[78] Misconduct on the part of an officer on board was reported to the DoT, which had power to cancel or suspend a guilty officer's certificate, a far more severe punishment than a mere fine which leaves the status of the person concerned unaffected.

---

73 (S.I. No. 1294), amended 1972 (S.I. No. 1876), 1974 (S.I. No. 2047), 1978 (S.I. No. 1754), 1979 (S.I. No. 1519).

74 S. 37, Merchant Shipping Act 1970.

75 S. 27, as amended by the Merchant Shipping Act 1979, s. 45, Sch. 6.

76 S. 28, as amended by s. 45(2), the Merchant Shipping Act 1979, Safety at Sea Act 1986. Before the 1979 amendment it was an offence for all seamen to be under the influence.

77 S. 33, Merchant Shipping Act 1970. Note also the offence of persistently or wilfully neglecting duties or disobeying lawful commands, s. 30; see Section 9.4.6, supra.

78 1972 (S.I. No. 1294) as amended, regs 1, 2. But for the position as from 1 January 1986, see fn 84, infra.

A fine could not be imposed by masters of fishing vessels, pleasure yachts, ships of less than 200 registered tons engaged solely on coastal voyages, or ships on coastal sea trials.[79]

Misconduct liable to be dealt with in this context included wilfully striking any person or disobeying a lawful command; being absent from duty without reasonable cause, or asleep while on duty; as a result of drink or drug behaving in a disorderly manner, or being unfit to perform the allotted duty; possessing offensive weapons without consent; damaging or interfering with someone else's property;[80] failing to comply with orders designed to protect vulnerable or dangerous cargoes or stores, for instance orders not to smoke or use unprotected lights in certain places.[81]

Fines imposed for these offences, which were strictly limited, were deducted from the wages and later paid over to a superintendent or proper officer, to whom also an appeal lay against the fine.[82] In the ordinary way, disciplinary action had to be taken within 24 hours of the offence. The seaman had the right to a hearing before the master and could take along a friend to advise.[83]

For some time, seamen have considered this authoritarian method of imposing fines on those who have run foul of the disciplinary system on board ship, and indeed the very vagueness of that disciplinary system, out of keeping with modern concepts of justice. Accordingly, s. 23, Merchant Shipping Act 1979, envisages a radical reform. From 1 January 1986 ss. 34 to 38, Merchant Shipping Act 1970 (which provided the basis for the disciplinary Regulations) will cease to be law.[84]

Instead of the vague system of discipline the conduct of seamen will be defined by a code, to be approved by the Secretary of State. Instead of the master's right to fine, the master or owner will have the right to complain to a shore-based tribunal about a seaman's breach of the code of conduct. The tribunal, after hearing the complaint, and finding it proved, will have the power, according to the seriousness of the seaman's conduct, to warn or reprimand him or to recommend to the Secretary of State the withdrawal of the seaman's discharge book, for a period or permanently. This will debar the offender from work as a seaman, for without the discharge book a person seeking employment

79 Reg. 2.
80 Reg. 3.
81 Reg. 4.
82 Merchant Shipping Act 1970, ss. 34, 35 and 38; regs 8, 10–12. The fines were strictly limited in amount.
83 Regs 6, 7.
84 Merchant Shipping Act 1979 (Commencement No. 9) Order 1985 (S.I. No. 1827).

as a seaman and anyone employing him will commit an offence. Of course, regulations will provide for appeals against the tribunal decision. Corresponding provisions will apply to fishing vessels.

In 1978 the NMB published a 'Code of Conduct for the Merchant Navy' which is incorporated into agreements subject to NMB terms. If the crew agreement, approved by the Secretary of State, is one to which the NMB agreement on disciplinary procedures applies and which requires the seaman to comply with the Code of Conduct, then the Disciplinary Offences Regulations did not apply.[85]

The Code distinguishes between acts of misconduct which are so serious as to justify immediate dismissal and those of a lesser degree of seriousness which call for warnings or reprimands.[86] Amongst the grounds for dismissal forthwith are: assault; wilful damage to ship or any property on board; theft or possession of stolen property; possession of offensive weapons; persistent or wilful failure to perform duty; unlawful possession or distribution of drugs; conduct endangering the ship or persons on board; combination with others at sea to impede the progress of the voyage or the navigation of the ship; disobedience of orders relating to the safety of the ship or any person on board; to be asleep on duty or fail to remain on duty if such conduct would prejudice the safety of the ship or any person on board; incapacity to carry out duties to the prejudice of the safety of the ship or of any person on board; smoking near dangerous cargoes or in prohibited areas; intimidation, coercion and/or interference with the work of other employees; behaviour which seriously detracts from the safe and/or efficient working of the ship, or the social well being of others on board; allowing unauthorized persons to be on board while at sea; repeated commission of minor acts of misconduct after warnings have been given.

Examples of lesser acts of misconduct would include minor thefts; unsatisfactory work performance; poor time-keeping; stopping work early; failure to report for work without a satisfactory reason; absence without leave; offensive or disorderly behaviour.

The Code lays down a set of clear and fair procedures for dealing with breaches. An investigation will take place on board ship. The master

85 Merchant Shipping (Disciplinary Offences) (Amendment) Regulations 1978 (S.I. No. 1754).

86 NMB, *Summary of Agreements*, pp. 76–77. Note that cases of misconduct or inefficiency not arising out of employment whilst on a crew agreement (e.g. a drugs offence while on shore leave) will be dealt with under the Merchant Navy Establishment disciplinary procedure laid down in Clauses 53–58 of the Established Service Scheme; NMB, *Summary of Agreements*, pp. 27–28: see Section 9.3.1, *supra*.

may warn, reprimand or dismiss the seaman. Where the continued presence of the offender on board would be detrimental, the master can arrange for the dismissal to take effect at the next port of call for repatriation to the UK. Otherwise, the dismissal will be reported to a shore-based Disciplinary Committee established by the NMB.

Nothing in the Code prejudices a seaman's right to bring proceedings for unfair dismissal before an industrial tribunal.[87] In this case the Disciplinary Committee can adjourn its proceedings until the Industrial Tribunal reaches its decision.

There is a right of appeal from a local Disciplinary Committee to a Central Disciplinary Committee and if the latter is unable to reach a decision the matter will be referred to an Appeals Tribunal. Amongst the penalties which can be imposed by the Committees or the Appeals Tribunal is the power to recommend that a seaman surrender his discharge book.[88] The Secretary of State can then demand that the book be surrendered to him, either temporarily or permanently.[89]

9.5 MARINERS' CIVIL LIABILITY

Mariners may incur liabilities under the general law of contract or tort, but we must distinguish between claims by third parties and claims by shipowners.

Claims by third parties will usually be based on the tort of negligence. Even though a mariner is negligent during the course of his employment he can still be sued individually by any person who is injured. This may not be financially worth while unless the mariner is particularly wealthy. The victim may hope that the shipowner will stand behind the mariner. In that case the latter may try to rely on exemption clauses in contracts made by the victim with the shipowner. These are called 'Himalaya' clauses as they arose from a case where a master and bosun were held liable to a passenger who fell off a gang plank for their negligence in mooring the ship.[90] Properly drafted Himalaya clauses seek to make the crew party to contracts made by the

---

87 *Ibid.*, p. 79; the Employment Protection (Consolidation) Act 1978, Part V.
88 NMB, *Summary of Agreements*, p. 85.
89 Merchant Shipping (Seamen's Documents) (Amendment No. 3) Regulations 1978 (S.I. No. 1758).
90 *The Himalaya: Adler* v. *Dickson* [1955] 1 Q.B. 158, and see Section 18.1, *infra.*

shipowner as well as giving them the same exemptions and limitations. They are often found in bills of lading and towage contracts.[91]   But suing the crew and not the owner must be recognized for what it is – a tactical legal device to avoid exemption clauses and limitation of liability.

Next we must consider claims by the shipowner against the crew. Technically an employer may be entitled to an indemnity from his employee where the latter's negligence has made the employer vicariously liable to some third party.[92] However, in practice, the employer's insurers (who would normally pay for the liability) do not insist on enforcing the indemnity without the employer's consent unless there has been some evidence of collusion or wilful misconduct by the employee.[93]

The owner of the ship is also entitled to damages from the seaman for breach of the employment contract if the seaman is absent from the ship when required by his contract to be on board, unless the absence was due to an accident, mistake or some other cause beyond his control. Even then the seaman must show he took all reasonable precautions to avoid being absent.[94] Absence without leave used to be an offence. It ceased to be that in 1974, following pressure from the National Union of Seamen.

According to a 1975 decision of the NMB, wages may be lost under the crew agreement for being absent without leave, refusal or neglect of work and incapacity for work which is caused by illness or injury brought about by the seaman's own wilful misconduct.

An owner is entitled to make deductions from wages for the actual expenses caused by the seaman's absence without leave.[95] This cannot exceed £200 for any number of breaches even if the absence causes greater loss.[96] However, if the employer suffers financial loss as a result

91 See Sections 11.5, 20.1.3, 23.4, *infra*. Note also the use of 'circular indemnity clauses' where, for instance, a cargo-owner promises in the bill of lading that he will not sue any employees or subcontractors of the shipowner and will provide an indemnity to the latter if he does. The shipowner can then go to court to get an order stopping the continuation of the suit. e.g. *The Elbe Maru* [1978] 1 Lloyd's Rep. 206.

92 *Lister* v. *Romford Ice and Cold Storage Co. Ltd* [1957] A.C. 555: see Section 21.1, *infra*.

93 R. Lewis, 'Insurers Agreements not to Enforce Strict Legal Rights: Bargaining with Government and in the Shadow of the Law' (1985) 48 M.L.R. 275.

94 Merchant Shipping Act 1970, s. 39.

95 Merchant Shipping Act 1970, s. 9: Merchant Shipping (Seamen's Wages and Accounts) Regulations 1972, reg. 5. The employer must be satisfied on reasonable grounds that there has been a breach of the crew agreement.

96 Reg. 6, as amended by 1985 (S.I. No. 340).

of other breaches of the crew agreement he is entitled to a further maximum of £200.[97]

A seaman must also provide compensation for any penalty incurred by the owner as a result of infringements of the immigration regulations of any country committed when the seaman is absent without leave.[98] Finally, the seaman must compensate the owner if the latter suffers loss or expense as a result of smuggling.[99]

9.6 COMPENSATION FOR INJURIES AT WORK

Health and safety provisions designed to prevent accidents have already been discussed.[1] Failure to discharge these duties may be an offence, but does not necessarily itself form the basis of a civil action.[2]

If despite preventive measures the master or a seaman is injured he has remedies at his disposal. Apart from rights derived from the social security legislation, anyone injured at work can bring an action for negligence against his employer who is, of course, also answerable for the negligence of a fellow crew member; this is called vicarious liability.[3]

To make sure that employers have the funds required to meet a damages award they are compelled to insure against that risk.[4] Shipowners usually belong to a mutual insurance association – their Protection and Indemnity (P & I) Club. Since membership covers such risks they are normally exempted from the compulsory insurance provisions.[5]

---

97 Regs 5, 6, as amended by 1985 (S.I. No. 340). The crew agreement may limit this amount. See *Kitchen* (1980), pp. 602–605.
98 Merchant Shipping Act 1970, s. 41.
99 S. 40. Smuggling may, in some circumstances, result in a fine or the forfeiture of the ship, Customs and Excise Management Act 1979, ss. 88–90, 141–143.
1 See Section 8.7, *supra*.
2 The Health and Safety at Work Act 1974, s. 47 makes it clear that no new liabilities are created by the Act. There is no equivalent provision in the Merchant Shipping Act 1979, ss. 21, 22, or the regulations made under them.
3 See Section 21.1, *infra*. For the principles of negligence see a textbook on Torts, e.g., *Clerk and Lindsell on Torts* (15th edn 1982, with 1985 Supplement).
4 Employer's Liability (Compulsory Insurance) Act 1969.
5 Employer's Liability (Compulsory Insurance) Exemption Regulations 1971 (S.I. No. 1933), reg. 3(x); also 1971 (S.I. No. 1117), amended 1974 (S.I. No. 208), 1975 (S.I. Nos 194, 1443).

An action for negligence lies where the defendant owes a duty to the plaintiff, has failed to discharge this duty, and the plaintiff is injured as a result. The shipowner, by virtue of his contract with those manning the ship, owes them the duty to provide a seaworthy, properly equipped and manned ship. In short, he must create safe working conditions. It was proved that he had failed to do so in a case where the plaintiff, a deck officer on board a hovercraft, was injured. A lorry on the flight deck needed relashing, which the officer attempted, and in doing so he suffered injury as the result of the strong vibration of the craft. The court found negligence proved, in that the plaintiff had not been instructed in what to do in the circumstances which he encountered. He should have been told to report to the captain, who would then have altered course and slackened speed to lessen vibration and thus reduce the risk of injury.[6]

The shipowner's liability for the negligence of his employees exists also *vis-à-vis* third parties, not members of the crew manning the defendant's ship.

Illustration: *Crashley v. W. J. Woodward Fisher Ltd*[7]

The master of a tug towing barges made a careless mooring manoeuvre, as a result of which a lighterman in one of the barges in tow of the tug was injured.

Held: The owners of the tug were liable to pay damages to the lighterman.

The plaintiff in negligence actions is faced with the difficulty of furnishing sufficient facts in evidence to prove the defendant's negligence. Thus, where a seaman was drowned when the defendant's trawler capsized in severe weather in the North Sea, the deceased's widow lost her action for damages because she was unable to prove that the master's navigation had been faulty.[8] She was, of course, entitled to social security benefit, but this is usually lower than the damages awarded for negligence.

In certain cases the plaintiff is relieved of this burden of proving negligence, namely, where the circumstances in which the accident happened can in the first place be explained only by the existence of negligence on the part of the defendant. In such circumstances the event speaks for itself or, in lawyer's language, *res ipsa loquitur*. It is then for the

6 *Noseda* v. *Hoverlloyd Ltd* [1974] 1 Lloyd's Rep. 448.
7 [1962] 2 Lloyd's Rep. 284.
8 *Waddy* v. *Boyd Line Ltd* [1966] 1 Lloyd's Rep. 335.

defendant to shoulder the burden of proof, to disprove, if he can, his own or his employee's negligence.

Illustration: *Foulder v. Canadian Pacific S.S. Ltd*[9]

A steward in one of the defendants' vessels was severely scalded by grossly overheated water coming out of a shower he was using and extensive plastic surgery was required.

Held: The shipowners were liable, for this accident could not have happened had those in charge of the equipment taken the required care; there was no need for the plaintiff to furnish evidence of a particular careless action. The accident spoke for itself. The plaintiff was awarded £8400 damages, including damages for pain and suffering.

This case illustrates two further points of importance in actions for personal.injuries. The first is the duty imposed on employers by Act of Parliament to provide safe working conditions for employees. Such statutory duties are absolute, that is, the employee injured as a result of the breach of that duty need not prove negligence at all, nor can the employer exonerate himself and escape liability by proving that the breach of duty was not due to his own or another employee's negligence.

In *Foulder's* case this absolute duty of the employers to provide safe working conditions was based on reg. 24 of the Merchant Shipping (Crew Accommodation) Regulations 1953,[10] which obliged the owner to provide washing facilities. Thus, the court held, even in the absence of *res ipsa loquitur*, the plaintiff would have won his case without affirmatively proving the negligence of any particular member of the crew. A shipowner may be deemed negligent if a crew member is injured as a result of a defect in the ship's equipment, even if the defect was caused wholly by some third party, such as a shipbuilder.[11]

The other point illustrated by the case relates to the defendants', the employers', defence of contributory negligence. The employer may well admit negligence or breach of a statutory duty, but he may be able to prove that the injury, or at any rate part of it, would not have happened had not the plaintiff himself also been negligent, had he not by his conduct contributed to the accident. Originally, where the

9 [1968] 2 Lloyd's Rep. 366.
10 S.I. No. 1036. Since repealed by 1978 (S.I. No. 795) as amended, see Section 8.6, *supra.*
11 *The Derbyshire* [1986] 1 Lloyd's Rep. 418 (reversed 190 LMNL 12/2 (1987); see Section 6.4, *supra.*

defendant was able to prove any contributory negligence on the part of
the plaintiff, the latter's action was dismissed. The Law Reform (Contributory Negligence) Act 1945 remedied this state of affairs which
could lead to unfair results. Now the judge can apportion the blame.
According to the degree of negligence he can, for instance, say that
plaintiff and defendant were equally to blame, in which case the plaintiff
will get only half his damages. The judge is also free to rule in a proper
case that the plaintiff's contributory negligence was so slight that it
should fairly be disregarded. In *Foulder's* case, the judge took that
course, rejecting the defendants' contention that the plaintiff could at
any rate have reduced the severity of the scalding by first testing the
water coming out of the shower nozzle.

On the other hand, contributory negligence was upheld where a
seaman was injured by a fall into an unfenced open hatchway, since by
looking where he was going he could have prevented the fall.[12] Again, a
lighterman standing in the bows of one of two lighters being towed
abreast, and in charge of these lighters, was injured when the pin on the
dolly, a rectangular bollard bolted to the barge, broke and caused the
tow rope to backlash. His action for damages against the owners was
dismissed on the ground that it was the accepted duty of the lighterman
in charge of barges to see to it that this particular part of the towing
arrangements was safe.[13] In this case, then, the defendants were acquit-
ted of any negligence and the accident was attributed solely to the
negligence of the plaintiff.

It is thus evident that a plaintiff in an action for negligence or for
breach of a statutory duty often finds it very difficult to win an action,
quite apart from the delay necessarily occasioned by the parties' need to
discover and assemble the evidence which they want to lay before the
court. That is why industrial accident insurance was introduced, so that
payment of insurance benefit can follow promptly on injuries suffered
at work. Before 1946 this was effected by the Workmen's Compensation Act 1906, but that legislation was replaced by the modern method
adopted by the National Insurance (Industrial Injuries) Act 1946, based
on the report of Lord Beveridge made during the 1939–45 war. The
basic law is now contained in the Social Security Act 1975, ss. 50–78.[14]

12 *Dew* v. *United British S.S. Co.* (1929) 139 L.T. 628.
13 *Hardy* v. *Thames & General Lighterage Ltd* [1967] 1 Lloyd's Rep. 228.
14 As amended and extended by statutes, e.g. the Social Security and Housing
   Benefits Act 1982, and Regulations, e.g. the Social Security (General Benefit)
   Regulations 1982 (S.I. No. 1408). See generally, Pollard (1977).

The availability in some cases of remedies both under the Act and under the common law led to a new problem. To what extent can an employer held liable in an action for negligence or breach of a statutory duty be allowed to say: 'Very well, I am liable, but surely the damages awarded against me should be reduced by the amount received by the plaintiff under the social security legislation'. This question of social policy has been solved by enacting that in such circumstances damages payable by the employer should be reduced by one-half of the insurance benefits received by the plaintiff.[15]

Under the 1975 Act all persons employed in Great Britain are compulsorily insured against 'personal injury . . . by accident arising out of and in the course of employment',[16] and the State accepts the obligation of acting as insurer. An accident was defined in a case decided under the earlier Workmen's Compensation Act as 'any unexpected personal injury resulting to the workman in the course of his employment from any unlooked-for mishap or occurrence.'[17]

This definition excludes disease unless caused by some particular unexpected event. Thus where a seaman on board a ship calling at West African ports, where he was specially exposed to infection, died of yellow fever, the House of Lords considered this an 'accident arising out of his employment'.[18]

The basic benefits payable as a result of industrial injury are disablement benefit and industrial death benefit.[19] The separate 'industrial injury benefit', which was paid at a higher rate than ordinary sickness benefit, was abolished in 1983.[20] However, a person who becomes incapable of work as a result of injury or catching a disease at work may be entitled in the first instance to statutory sick pay and then to sickness

15 Law Reform (Personal Injuries) Act 1948, s. 2, as amended.
16 S. 50(1).
17 Per Lord Shand, in Fenton v. Thorley & Co. [1903] A.C. 443, at p. 451.
18 Dover Navigation Co. v. Isabella Craig [1940] A.C. 190. The Act provides in s. 50(3) that once an accident has happened in the course of employment, it is deemed also to have arisen 'out of' it, unless evidence to the contrary is produced. See further, Pollard (1977), Chapter 5.
19 Social Security Act 1975, s. 50(2). Changes to both will be made by the Social Security Act 1986.
20 Social Security and Housing Benefits Act 1982, s. 39.

or invalidity benefit.[21] Sickness benefit is a contributory benefit[22] but if an employed earner is incapable of work as a result of an industrial injury he is deemed to satisfy the contribution conditions.[23]

The statutory sick pay scheme is a recent development designed to put financial obligations on employers when employees become incapable of work.[24] For the first three days no sick pay is due.[25] Thereafter, sick pay must normally be paid by the employer for up to 28 weeks, after which the employee will be entitled to sickness benefit from the state.[26]

Regulations[27] allow mariners to claim sick pay even though they do not fulfil the normal requirement of being employed in Great Britain. Essentially they must work on board a British ship, or one where there is some close connection with the UK, e.g. where the employer has his principal place of business there.[28]

The industrial injuries benefits may be payable to mariners even if the accident or disease occurs while the person is outside Great Britain.[29] It is relevant to mention diseases because the Social Security Act 1975

21 Social Security Act 1975, ss. 14, 15. The benefits are uprated every year and any figures given here will be subject to change: therefore they are illustrative only. From July 1986 the Social Security Benefits Uprating Order 1986 (S.I. No. 1117) provided per week for sickness benefit of £29.45 and invalidity pension of between £37.05 and £38.70: there are, however, extra allowances for dependants.

22 S. 12. The industrial injuries benefits are non-contributory and a claim could theoretically be made on the first day of employment. However, the claimant must be an 'employed earner' as defined in ss. 2, 51 and the Social Security (Employed Earners' Employments for Industrial Injuries Purposes) Regulations 1975 (S.I. No. 467), amended 1980 (S.I. No. 1714), 1983 (S.I. No. 1738), 1984 (S.I. No. 303). Certain disabled persons may be entitled to a non-contributory 'severe disablement allowance' under the Health and Social Security Act 1984, s. 11, and the Social Security (Severe Disablement Allowance) Regulations 1984 (S.I. No. 1303).

23 S. 50A, inserted by the Social Security and Housing Benefits Act 1982, s. 39.

24 Social Security and Housing Benefits Act 1982.

25 S. 5(1).

26 Ss. 5, 3. The period was extended from 8 weeks as from 6 April 1986 by the Social Security Act 1985, Part III. Thereafter he will transfer to the long-term invalidity pension. Employers can recoup the payments from the Government by making deductions from National Insurance contributions, s. 9. From 6 April 1986 an employee earning more than £74.50 per week would be entitled to £46.75 sick pay, Statutory Sick Pay Uprating Order 1986 (S.I. No. 67).

27 Statutory Sick Pay (Mariners, Airmen and Persons Abroad) Regulations 1982 (S.I. No. 1349).

28 Reg. 9.

29 Social Security (Industrial Injuries) (Mariners' Benefits) Regulations 1975 (S.I. No. 470), amended 1983 (S.I. No. 186). They also apply to pilots who normally ply their trade out of British ports, reg. 4.

allows benefits to be paid to persons who catch certain prescribed diseases at work in the same way as if they had been injured.[30] The diseases are those which arise as a risk of particular occupations. The Regulations set out the particular disease and the occupations for which they are prescribed.[31] Of particular reference to seamen might be those diseases arising from the handling of, or exposure to, certain chemicals.

Disablement benefit is payable where the loss of physical and mental faculty is not less than 1 per cent, but is only available 90 days after the accident.[32] For disabilities of under 20 per cent a disablement gratuity is payable, usually as a lump sum, depending on the extent of the disability.[33] Where the disablement exceeds 20 per cent, a disablement pension is payable, again dependent on the extent of disability.[34] There are a number of supplements[35] payable in addition to the disablement benefit of which the special hardship allowance is the most important. It allows an extra sum to be paid to take into account reductions in earnings of particular employees.[36]

The death benefit is payable to relatives, such as wives, parents and children and in some circumstances to cohabitees who have looked after the deceased's children.[37]

To entitle the worker to the various industrial injuries benefits the accident must have happened while he was engaged on the work for which he was employed. There are, however, three important exceptions to this rule, all of them of importance to seamen. In the first place, benefits will be paid to a worker who is injured while trying to save life or serious damage to property in an emergency.[38] For instance, a worker on board an ocean liner received compensation for injuries received when trying to protect two women passengers against

30 Ss. 76–78.
31 Social Security (Industrial Injuries) (Prescribed Diseases) Regulations 1980 (S.I. No. 377), amended 1980 (S.I. No. 1493), 1982 (S.I. No. 249), 1983 (S.I. Nos 185, 1094), 1984 (S.I. No. 1659), Sch.1.
32 Social Security Act 1975, s. 57. The Social Security Act 1986, s. 39, will increase the minimum to 14 per cent.
33 S. 57(5); Social Security (Claims and Payments) Regulations 1979 (S.I. No. 628), reg. 20. The maximum amount from July 1986 was £4200, Sch. 4, Social Security Benefits Uprating Order 1986 (S.I. No. 1117). These figures are uprated annually.
34 S. 57(6). The maximum amount from July 1986 was £63.20 per week.
35 See ss. 58–66.
36 S. 60. The maximum supplement from July 1986 was £25.28.
37 Ss. 67–75. The widow's pension is payable at a higher rate for the first 26 weeks after death, s. 68. In July 1986 this initial rate was £54.30. The benefit will be abolished by the Social Security Act 1986, s. 39.
38 Social Security Act 1975, s. 54; 1975 (S.I. No. 470), reg. 3.

assault.[39] Although after the event it may appear that no emergency in fact existed at the time or, at any rate, the lives or property which the worker tried to save were not in danger, he will not forfeit this remedy provided he 'supposed' there was an emergency or 'thought' that danger threatened the persons or the property for whom he went into action.[40]

The second exception refers to journeys to and from work. Difficult questions may arise, for instance, when a member of the crew goes ashore on private business. At what precise moment does he lose his insurance cover on leaving the ship, or regain it on returning? The Act provides[41] that accidents during the journeys in transport provided by the employer – and ships, vessels and hovercraft are expressly included – count as work so that if, for instance, a ship's boat capsizes while taking seamen on shore leave they or their dependants are entitled to the benefits.

Lastly, there is the question of misconduct. We have seen that in a common law action for negligence the plaintiff loses his right to damages, in whole or in part, if he has himself contributed to the accident. This rule is inappropriate in a social insurance scheme designed to protect employed persons, among other things, against foolish or careless disregard for their own safety. It is accordingly provided that disobeying instructions or regulations does not lead to loss of benefit if the act leading to the accident was done in the course of employment and for the purposes of, or in connection with, the employer's trade or business.[42]

Thus a seaman injured in a fire which he had caused by smoking contrary to instructions during work on board is entitled to industrial injuries benefits, but not a seaman who is injured while taking a ship's boat for a secret trip to the shore. The latter may be entitled, however, to sickness benefit.[43] A seaman injured while being carried in a liberty boat to or from shore also qualifies for the industrial injuries benefits and the same applies, for example, to a steward who, in an actual or supposed emergency, does something falling in the province of engine-room staff and who is injured in the process.

Finally, any employee, including a seaman, is entitled to industrial injuries benefits if he is injured by the misconduct of a fellow employee,

39 *Culpeck v. Orient Steam Navigation Co.* (1922) 15 B.W.C.C. 187.
40 S. 54. Similar problems arise in the law of general average; see Chapter 15, *infra*.
41 S. 53.
42 S. 52.
43 S. 14, although he may be disqualified for up to six weeks because of his own misconduct, Social Security (Unemployment, Sickness and Invalidity Benefit) Regulations 1983 (S.I. No. 1591), reg. 17.

which includes skylarking, provided the injured seaman neither induced nor contributed to the misconduct; in other words, he must not have taken part in the game.[44]

Generally speaking, seaman not domiciled or ordinarily resident in the UK are not insured under this scheme, but these exceptions do not apply to persons domiciled or ordinarily resident in countries with which reciprocal agreements have been concluded.[45]

Disputes about industrial injuries benefits will be handled in the first instance by an insurance officer. Medical questions about disablement or disease can be referred to a medical board and a medical appeal tribunal, from which there can be appeals on a point of law to the National Insurance Commissioner.[46] The Secretary of State for the Department of Health and Social Security may refer questions of law to the High Court (or, in Scotland, to the Court of Session).[47]

9.7 MARINERS' WILLS

One last point should be noticed. As seamen, a term which here also comprises the master, may meet with sudden emergencies, the law has granted them special privileges for disposing of their property by will. In the ordinary way, a testator must make a formal will; he must have his signature attested by two witnesses, present at the time of signing, and themselves signing or acknowledging the will as witnesses in the presence of the testator.[48] Moreover, a will can only be made by a person who has attained the age of 18 years.[49] These provisions have been relaxed for 'seamen being at sea'. Under the combined operation of the Wills Act 1837, and the Wills (Soldiers and Sailors) Act 1918, a will made in such circumstances need not be attested; it may even be verbal, and seamen at sea may make a will although under age. Such informal wills remain valid until revoked like any other will, notwithstanding that the testator returns home and dies on shore.[50] However, the testator must be actually at sea when making the will; if he has been

44 S. 55.
45 S. 131.
46 Ss. 108, 112.
47 S. 94. A claimant can only use such an appeal on very limited questions, such as whether he is an 'employed earner'.
48 Wills Act 1837, s. 9, as amended by the Administration of Justice Act 1982, Part IV, s. 17.
49 Family Law Reform Act 1969, ss. 1 and 3.
50 *In the Goods of Spratt* [1897] P. 28.

discharged from the ship and makes the will while in hospital he does not come withing the Acts, and an informal will is invalid.[51] On the other hand, a seaman is still regarded as being at sea while he is a member of the crew of a ship which is permanently stationed in a harbour,[52] and a sailor in the Royal Navy was held to have been at sea, although when making the will he was on leave shortly before rejoining his ship in wartime.[53]

Merchant seamen, especially those discharged abroad and in a hospital there, may also benefit from the Wills Act 1963. This provides that a will shall be treated as properly executed if its execution conformed to the internal law in force in the territory in which it was executed.

51 *In the Estate of Thomas* (1918) 34 T.L.R. 626. Similarly, if he makes the informal will while on leave, after being discharged from one ship and before receiving instructions to join another, and is not part of the complement of the ship: *In re Rapley decd* [1983] 1 W.L.R. 1069.

52 *In re Goods of McMurdo* (1867) L.R. 1 P. & D. 540.

53 *In re Goods of Newland* [1952] P. 71.

PART TWO
THE CARRIAGE OF GOODS BY SEA

WE have tried to show in the first part of this volume what conditions a person must satisfy before he can become a shipowner and what he has to do before he can attempt to use a ship as a going concern. We have also attempted to show to what uses a ship can be put as a means of private gain, as investment, and as a security to those who have dealings, or otherwise come into contact, with the ship and her owner. We now proceed to the subject of how to run the ship as a trade undertaking. In doing so, we are not concerned with the business aspects. Nor shall we deal with certain phenomena of importance in shipping which are common to other branches of commercial and industrial activity, such as the organization of groups and combines. Though this subject gives rise to important legal considerations, it cannot be regarded as part of the law of shipping.

While the law relating to the running of ships is largely founded upon contract and can only be properly appreciated by those who have soundly grounded themselves in that branch of legal study, it has been moulded by, and adjusted to, the practical considerations to which the actual business of shipping has inevitably given rise. The following pages will therefore provide, in some measure, a reflex of economic phenomena, and it is suggested that many of the legal rules, which may at first sight appear somewhat technical, are more comprehensible if studied in the light of the actual business and requirements of shipping.

10

THE CONTRACT OF AFFREIGHTMENT

10.1 INTRODUCTORY

10.1.1 THE BUSINESS BASIS

EXCEPT FOR the law of marine insurance, the law relating to the contract of affreightment is perhaps the most difficult subject in the province of shipping law. The difficulties arise in the first place from the use of two entirely different forms of contract, the charterparty and the bill of lading. In the second place we have the multiplicity of risks to which goods travelling at sea are exposed. Then there is the complicated process of loading and discharging the vessel, which gives rise to many legal problems, especially that of demurrage, hardly met with in land transport.

Another difficulty which might easily appear puzzling should be explained at the outset. It is well known that a contract of carriage is usually preceded by a sale of goods and that the person who contracts with the shipowner for the carriage of goods may be either the seller or the buyer. If the initial sale is one on so-called f.o.b. terms, the seller's part is performed when he has put the goods free on board the ship. In that case the contract of carriage will normally be made by the buyer. On the other hand, when the sale is c.i.f. the seller bears the cost of insurance and freight and the buyer takes delivery abroad at the end of the transport. Here it is usually the seller who contracts with the shipowner for the conveyance of the goods.

In this volume, we are not concerned with the relationship between the seller and the buyer or with the allocation between them of responsibilities for the shipping arrangements. From the point of view of carriage, the sale contract commonly attached to the contract of affreightment is material only in so far as it determines the identity of the party contracting with the carrier.

10.1.2   COMMON AND PRIVATE CARRIERS

It is now necessary to draw attention to a few points relating to the law of carriage in general, and the special features of the law relating to sea carriage. From early times there is found a distinction between common carriers and private carriers. Though it is difficult to define precisely the term 'common carrier', we may nevertheless say that he is a person, or an association of persons, following the public vocation of a carrier, and in the course of his business holding himself out to take goods of everybody, provided he has room in his conveyance, at a standard, or at least at a reasonable rate. The private carrier, on the other hand, reserves the right to carry or not as he chooses and to make a different bargain every time, e.g. a furniture remover. The common carrier is under a duty to accept goods tendered to him for carriage. If he unlawfully refuses goods he commits a criminal offence and, at the same time, is liable in damages to the goods' owner. The principal test is always this: Did the carrier generally reserve to himself the right of rejecting goods irrespective of his conveyance being full or empty, or was he in the habit of accepting goods whenever there was space available? In the first case he is a private, in the second a common carrier.

Illustration 1: _Ingate v. Christie_[1]
The defendant had the word 'lighterman' posted up over the door of his office. It was proved that he carried for anyone who engaged his craft.

Held: He was a common carrier.

Illustration 2: _Belfast Ropework Co. v. Bushell_[2]
The defendant was a haulage contractor. With his own two lorries, as well as with others which he hired when necessary, he was in the habit of carrying sugar from Liverpool to Manchester. There he invited offers of goods for the return journey, but he proved in evidence that he rejected offers which in respect of rate, route, or class of goods were not satisfactory.

Held: He was not a common carrier.

1 (1850) 3 C. & K. 61.
2 [1918] 1 K.B. 210.

Though in modern times of diminishing importance, the law relating to the common carrier must still be covered in a work of this nature, for it is the basis on which modern law is built.

The first question then is: under what circumstances may the common carrier lawfully refuse offers? This he may do when the offer relates to goods of a kind which he does not profess to take, or where the goods cannot be conveniently carried in his conveyance. Again where the common carrier plies on a customary route and is offered goods for carriage to a place off that route, he is not bound to accept. He is also entitled to refuse goods tendered at an unreasonable time, either too long or too shortly before the conveyance is due to start.[3] Moreover, the common carrier will not be forced to undertake journeys involving unreasonable risks, or where the freight is not tendered in advance. However, in sea carriage it has become usual in practice to pay freight on delivery at the port of destination.

10.1.3   ABSOLUTE LIABILITY

The most important rule is that the common carrier is absolutely liable for the safety of the goods entrusted to him. He is to all intents and purposes an insurer of the goods. The private carrier, on the other hand, is only liable when loss or damage results from his negligence. The common law admitted only a few exceptions to this strict rule establishing the liability of the common carrier. Thus where loss or damage is caused directly by some elemental force, the onset of which could either not be foreseen or not be reasonably guarded against, such as lightning, heavy fall of snow, or an exceptional tempest, it is held to be due to an *Act of God*, for which man is not responsible. Likewise, if the loss is occasioned by the *Queen's Enemies*, that is the armed forces of a power at war with the United Kingdom, the carrier is excused. It is doubtful whether this exception would cover loss by pirates. *Inherent vice* of the cargo, e.g. perishable quality, and *defective packing* are other exceptions.

Illustration: *Nugent v. Smith*[4]
A mare was carried by a common carrier from Aberdeen to London. The ship encountered more than ordinary bad weather, and the mare took fright, struggled and kicked, and died in consequence.

3 *Nicholls* v. *North Eastern Railway Co.* (1888) 59 L.T. 137.
4 (1876) 1 C.P.D. 423.

Held: The carrier was not liable, because the loss was due partly to the Act of God and partly to inherent vice of the mare.

The last ground on which a common carrier may excuse himself for loss of cargo is a *general average sacrifice*.[5]

10.1.4   EXCEPTION CLAUSES

It was but natural that from early days the shipowner endeavoured to mitigate the strict liability of the common law. This he did by inserting exception clauses in charterparties and bills of lading, in other words by making a special contract with the shipper. It is perhaps surprising that the courts should have upheld such bargains limiting the liability of common carriers who were after all recognized as exercising a public calling. Whatever may have been the reason, the courts took a different attitude and special bargains were in fact allowed.[6] This had the effect that to a certain extent the common law relating to common carriers was displaced by contractual terms. In other words, there was a tendency to substitute a liability for negligence, or even complete exemption, for the absolute liability prevailing at common law, but in sea carriage such exceptions did not become common before the nineteenth century.

10.1.5   LIMITATION BY STATUTE

The legislature did not at first concern itself with the law relating to sea carriage. Parliament's first interference occurred in the eighteenth century[7] and then was in favour of shipowners. The provisions of that early statute have since been substantially re-enacted by ss. 502 and 503 of the Merchant Shipping Act 1894[8] and concerned the limitation of the shipowners' liability for damage caused by fire on board and for loss of valuables which had not been declared, as well as the new idea of limiting the amount payable according to the tonnage of the vessel.

Subsequently, private contracts went far beyond these limitations. Far-reaching exceptions were inserted in charterparties and bills of lading. With regard to the former no serious objections could be raised. The charterparty, as we shall presently see, is a purely personal contract

---

5 See Chapter 15, *infra*.
6 See e.g. *Southcote's Case* (1601) 4 Co. Rep. 83 C.
7 7 Geo. 2, Chapter 15 (1734).
8 For a more detailed discussion see Section 11.4.2(ii) and Chapter 22.

between shipowner and charterer, and nobody except the charterer himself was inconvenienced by a mitigation of the shipowners' liability. The position was different in respect of bills of lading. As will be explained later, a bill of lading contract binds not only shippers and shipowners, that is, the immediate contracting parties, but also the consignee abroad and his assignee, as well as to a certain extent bankers who take up such documents as securities for loans granted to their customers. For this reason a strong movement for legislative action developed with a view to standardizing those contracts. At the same time it was felt that isolated action by the United Kingdom could not remove the existing grievances inasmuch as the greater part of sea carriage is international and largely subject to foreign laws. Accordingly, at a meeting of the International Law Association, held at the Hague in September 1921, a representative body of interested parties, including British merchants and shipowners, agreed on a number of rules, henceforth known as the Hague Rules, which were subsequently enacted in the UK by the Carriage of Goods by Sea Act 1924, since replaced by the Act of 1971.

10.2 CARRIAGE OF GOODS BY SEA ACT 1971

The original Hague Rules relating to bills of lading improved the legal situation of owners of goods shipped under bills of lading, and this has been maintained. Although the Rules do not force the shipowner back to his absolute liability as an insurer that prevailed at common law, granting him a number of immunities, the owner of goods no longer faces the carrier without legal protection when concluding a contract. The carrier's right to exclude his liability altogether has ended. The parties are not allowed to contract out of the terms of the Rules, except to improve the rights of the cargo-owner. Moreover, those terms which give the carrier immunity in certain circumstances are very strictly construed by the courts.

The Rules endured unaltered for about fifty years, by which time their amendment had become desirable in view of practices which had developed in the interval. Following a conference at Visby, in Sweden, the Rules were amended by the Brussels Protocol of 1968,[9] and are now known as the Hague–Visby Rules or the Amended Hague Rules. They are embodied in the Carriage of Goods by Sea Act 1971 as the Schedule

9 Treaty Series, Misc. No. 14 (1968), Cmnd. 3743.

to that Act. Since the ratifications of this international convention required by the Brussels Protocol[10] were slow in being effected, the Act did not come into force until 1977. The Act was also amended by the Merchant Shipping Act 1981, section 2 of which implemented the Brussels Protocol of 1979 and substituted special drawing rights for the units of limitation used in the 1971 Act.

The structure of the original Hague Rules has been maintained, including the numbering of the Articles, so that it is easy to discover what changes have been made.[11]

Three points, in particular, required amendment, the most important being the limit of the shipowner's liability for loss of cargo or damage to it. Under the old Rules his maximum liability was £100 per package or unit, terms that will be explained later. The dramatic fall of the value of sterling made that figure quite inadequate and this was recognized at an early date, when shipping, cargo and insurance interests agreed on a voluntary gold clause. But a more formal arrangement was called for, an arrangement subsequently altered by the Brussels Protocol of 1979.

Closely connected was a practice that sprang up in the 1950s and was upheld in the case of *Adler* v. *Dickson*.[12] Where cargo was lost or damaged through the negligence of the shipowners' servants, cargo-owners hit on the idea of avoiding the receipt of limited compensation from the shipowner by suing the servants themselves; since the cargo-owner had contracted with the owners and not with their servants the action was laid in tort, and it followed that the servants were unable to invoke the contractual limitation which the owners were allowed to plead if sued in contract.

Now, as was explained during the passage of the Bill through Parliament,[13] no shipowner could watch his employees being made bankrupt, and so they paid the unlimited damages which the negligent employees had been held liable to pay. In those cases, therefore, the careful balance between shipowners' and cargo-owners' interests was

---

10 Art. 13. The countries in which the Hague–Visby Rules are in force are: Great Britain and Northern Ireland, The Isle of Man, Bermuda, British Antarctic Territory, British Virgin Islands, Cayman Islands, Falkland Islands, Falkland Islands Dependencies, Gibraltar, Hong Kong, Montserrat, Turks and Caicos Islands, Belgium, Denmark, Ecuador, Egypt, Finland, France, German Democratic Republic, Italy, Lebanon, The Netherlands, Norway, Poland, Singapore, Spain, Sri Lanka, Sweden, Switzerland, Syria, Tonga.
11 The Rules are analysed by Mr. Anthony Diamond, Q.C., in Lloyd's of London Press, *The Hague–Visby Rules*, 1977; also [1978] 2 L.M.C.Q. 225.
12 [1955] 1 Q.B. 158; Section 18.1, *infra*.
13 Lord Diplock, Hansard, Lords, Vol. 316, Cols 1032 et seq.

upset; a coach and four was driven through the Hague Rules. The 1968 Brussels Protocol, in common with other international transport conventions, allows shipowners' servants or agents, if sued in tort, to avail themselves of the same limitations as their employers.[14] This provision should put an end to the practice of suing employees rather than the employers.

Lastly, we have the new mode of transport by containers, in which often quantities of individual packages are stowed. Did the limitation of the shipowners' liability apply to the whole container or to the individual packages stowed in it? Some clauses in bills of lading were drafted making the answer to the question depend on whether or not the contents in a container were enumerated in the bill of lading. That was satisfactory as a temporary expedient, but legislative action was called for, and taken.[15]

10.2.1 WHERE THE ACT APPLIES

(1) The 1971 Act applies, whether or not the bill of lading refers to the Rules, to carriage of goods by sea from a port in the United Kingdom, which in this context includes the Isle of Man, the Channel Islands and dependent territories specified by Order in Council;[16] it applies even if the port of destination is also in the United Kingdom, so long as the contract of carriage provides expressly or by implication that a bill of lading will be issued.[17] Those voyages of the coasting trade where bills of lading are not customary, probably the majority, thus remain outside the scope of the Act, as was the case in the past, although the coasting trade is not expressly referred to, as was the case under the 1924 Act.

(2) The Act also applies to carriage between any ports in different states, provided the bill of lading is issued in a state that has ratified the Protocol (Art. X(a)); carriage from a port in a contracting state to a port in another state (Art. X(b)); or from a port in any state to a port in another state, where the parties to the contract have agreed on its being governed by the law of a state that has adopted the Hague–Visby Rules or enacted legislation giving effect to them (Art. X(c)), a frequent term

---

14 1971 Act, Schedule, Art. IV bis, Rule 2. The position of stevedores, usually independent contractors engaged by the shipowner, remains unchanged, Section 20.1.3. The courts have, however, discovered devices which might extend exclusion clauses contained in the contract of carriage even to independent contractors.

15 Art. IV, Rules 5 and 6.

16 Ss. 1(3) and 5.

17 S. 1(3) and (4).

in commercial contracts. In any of these cases the nationalities of ship, carrier, shipper, consignee or other interested persons are irrelevant.

(3) Where the contract is governed by United Kingdom law the Hague–Visby Rules also apply where the parties expressly agree that a bill of lading or a non-negotiable receipt subject to the Rules shall be issued.[18] The General Council of British Shipping has drafted such a non-negotiable receipt for use by its members, and H.M. Customs have agreed to accept this type of document as evidence of export for the purposes of Value Added Tax.[19]

(4) Deck cargo and live animals. Under Art. I(c), of the Schedule of the Act, live animals and cargo stated as being carried on deck, and actually so carried,[20] are excluded from the definition of 'goods', as was the case under the old Rules. In countries, therefore, which only enact the rules, without other national legislation, the Hague Rules do not apply to this type of cargo. This means, for instance, that a cargo-owner claiming compensation for loss or damage need not bring his action within the short period stipulated in Art. III, Rule 6. On the other hand, it would seem that shipowners are allowed to negotiate whatever terms relating to liability the cargo-owner will agree to.

Where, however, the Hague–Visby Rules apply to a contract under s. 1(6) of the 1971 Act, the definition of 'goods' in the Rules is widened to include live animals and cargo stated to be carried, and actually carried, on deck.[21] In other words, live animals and such deck cargo are treated in the same way as other goods.

This means, of course, that in a litigation it may become material to decide whether a particular contract of carriage is governed by British or a foreign law, thus impairing the uniformity desired to be achieved by the Rules. Here we encounter the phenomenon known as conflict of laws, so called because two laws conflict, contend for recognition, and it is for the court to resolve the conflict by deciding which is the proper law to apply in the case before it. This problem is beyond the scope of this volume, but it is worth remembering that factors determining the decision, apart from agreement between the parties mentioned under (2) above, include the flag under which the ship sails and the place

18 S. 1(6). For a non-negotiable receipt to be governed by the Rules, the clause incorporating the rules need not contain the words 'as if the receipt were a bill of lading': *The Veschroon* [1982] 1 Lloyd's Rep. 301.

19 1977 L.M.C.L.Q. 305.

20 A bill of lading clause, 'steamer has liberty to carry goods on deck', does not amount to a statement that they are so carried, so that the Hague Rules apply, *Svenska Traktor A.B.* v. *Maritime Agencies* [1953] 2 All E.R. 57.

21 S. 1(7).

where the contract is made.[22] The problem, despite the uniform Hague and Hague–Visby Rules, will continue to complicate disputes, as it has done in the past. For instance, many countries are slow in ratifying conventions – the USA did not ratify the 1921 Hague Rules until 1936, twelve years after the United Kingdom – and for many years the original Hague Rules and the amended Rules in force since 1977 are bound to exist side by side. Judicial interpretation of individual provisions is also apt to create case-law discrepancies between states that have adopted the Rules.[23]

10.2.2 NO CONTRACTING OUT

As has already been mentioned, the Rules, where they apply, are obligatory, strict law, and the shipowners cannot vary their terms by contract to the detriment of shipper or consignee. Any clause in a contract reducing the shipowner's liability below the standard set by the Rules is void, and this includes a clause purporting to give the carrier the benefit of a cargo-owner's insurance.[24] But clauses by which he accepts increased liabilities are, of course, valid.[25] We shall see later that a most important duty of the shipowner is that to exercise due diligence to make his ship seaworthy. He cannot shift his responsibility by a clause to the effect that a surveyor's certificate shall be regarded as conclusive evidence of seaworthiness; it is of course evidence, though evidence that can be rebutted. Again, a clause disclaiming liability for incorrect delivery unless packing or marking conform to higher than normal standards cannot be relied upon by the shipowners.[26] In *William D. Branson Ltd* v. *Jadranska Slopodna Plovidba*,[27] a Canadian court held that a clause, 'carrier not responsible for deterioration', could not be relied upon where the goods had deteriorated as a result of bad stowage, for which the carrier is liable under the Hague Rules.

22 *The Assunzione* [1945] P. 150.
23 Giles, *Uniform Commercial Law* (1970), and in *Liber Amicorum* for Ernst J. Cohn, p. 43 (1975).
24 Art. III, Rule 8: this article has also been used to avoid exclusive jurisdiction clauses which would divert disputes away from UK courts and the Hague–Visby Rules: see *The Morviken* [1983] 1 Lloyd's Rep. 1 and *The Benarty* [1983] 2 Lloyd's Rep. 50.
25 Art. V.
26 *Scrutton* (1984), p. 443.
27 [1973] 2 Lloyd's Rep. 535.

10.3   THE TWO FORMS OF CONTRACT

10.3.1   THE CHARTERPARTY

We have already mentioned the two forms of contract embodied in charterparties and bills of lading respectively. What is the difference between the two? To put it broadly a charterparty is a contract between the charterer and the shipowner, by which the former hires from the latter the use of the ship, either for a certain length of time – say, twelve months – when it is called a time charter,[28] or for a certain voyage, when it is called a voyage charter; this latter may be out and home, usually called a 'round voyage'. The charter may be an ordinary hire just as the hire of any moveable thing, for instance, a motor car for an excursion, or it may be in the nature of a lease by which the owner grants or demises the entire control and possession of the ship to the charterer (charter by demise). This type of charterparty is appropriate when a shipowner is desirous of augmenting his fleet, or where a person wishes to obtain full temporary possession of a ship, as when fitting out an expedition for exploration.[29] The demise charterer is in a position similar to the leaseholder of land, that is to say, he is for all practical purposes, except registration, the temporary owner of the ship. Accordingly, the duties and rights of the owner are performed and exercised, respectively, by him. He is bound by a salvage award, and it is on his behalf that the master signs bills of lading,[30] for master and crew are his, and not the owner's servants. During the duration of a charter by demise the owner's right is to be paid the hire or, as it is sometimes confusingly called, the chartered freight. He is not allowed to interfere in any way with the management of the ship, except in so far as the terms of the charterparty itself permit. If the ship earns a salvage award the charterer by demise is entitled to it.[31] The common form of charterparty is that used between the shipper of goods and the shipowner.[32]

---

28 Some difficult problems relating to time charters are discussed, for instance, in *Time Charters: Why the Confusion?*, Lloyd's of London Press, March 1977. A. Wilford, T. Coughlin, N.J. Healy and J.D. Kimball, *Time Charters*, 2nd edn, Lloyd's of London Press (1982), dealing mainly with the New York Produce Exchange form.

29 *Sea and Land Securities* v. *William Dickinson* [1942] 2 K.B. 65, at p. 69.

30 *Scrutton* (1984), p. 50.

31 *Elliott Steam Tug Co.* v. *Admiralty* [1921] A.C. 137.

32 See Appendix 2 for a precedent of a charterparty.

(A)   SIMPLE CHARTER

The goods-owner is only concerned with the transport of his goods, and is so far from wishing to concern himself with the management of the ship, which is after all not the business on which he is engaged, that he is, in fact, desirous of securing the services of the shipowner in the control and management of the vessel. He wants the full carrying space of the ship to be at his disposal and he wants to be able to choose the port or ports at which the vessel will load or discharge, and to have her proceed on her way with due dispatch. Beyond this he has no concern. He may be likened to a person taking a furnished service flat, in contradistinction to the charterer by demise, whom we have compared with the tenant of an empty house which he furnishes and into which he puts his own servants. Sometimes, however, the charterer may, so to speak, sublet the space which he has engaged, possibly because he finds he has no available cargo, or perhaps because he sees the chance of making a profit. This he can do either by sub-chartering the vessel to another shipper or by loading goods belonging to several other shippers on separate contracts of carriage evidenced by bills of lading.

In spite of this clear theoretical distinction it is sometimes difficult in practice to tell into which class a particular charterparty falls. This may be of great importance, for the charterer by demise is responsible for the ship and, for example, for any damage caused by her to other shipping or property. The difficulty arises because shipowners anxious about possible depreciation of a valuable and rather vulnerable type of property very often insist by the terms of the contract on retaining a certain control, for example, by the appointment of the senior officers. This may give rise to disputes as to whether the management has ever passed to the charterer.

Illustration: *Baumwoll Manufactur von Carl Scheibler v. Furness*[33]

Furness let a ship on charter to Gilchrest, and the charterparty provided, *inter alia*, that the charterers should pay for all provisions and wages of the captain, officers, engineers, firemen and crew; that the captain should be under the orders and direction of the charterers as regards employment, agency or other arrangements; that the charterers should indemnify the owner for liability incurred under bills of lading signed by the captain; that the owner had the right to appoint the chief engineer, and the duty to insure, and to keep in an efficient state, hull and machinery. Scheibler's shipped cotton at New Orleans for Bremen under bills of lading, some of which were signed by the captain; these bills did not refer to the charterparty nor did the shippers

33 [1893] A.C. 8.

have notice of its terms. The cotton was lost after the ship had foundered owing, it was alleged, to unseaworthiness. In this section only the question was tried whether owner or charterer should be liable if unseaworthiness were proved.

Held: The intention and effect of the charterparty was that the owner parted with possession and control of the vessel, and amounted therefore to a charter by demise. The rights the owner retained were comparable to those exercised by the owner of leased property. In these circumstances the captain was the charterer's and not the owner's agent, so that the latter was not liable.

(B) FORM OF CHARTERPARTY

The word 'charterparty' is derived from *carta partita* (divided document) which refers to the ancient practice of writing out the terms of the contract in duplicate on one piece of parchment and then dividing it down the middle, thus providing each party with a copy. It is therefore not surprising to observe that to this day, despite the absence of a rule requiring the written form,[34] most negotiations by telephone or telex will eventually lead to the formal drawing up of a written charterparty, with standard terms and riders attached. Whether or not the parties can be said to be contractually bound before they sign the charterparty will depend in large part on the intentions of the parties and the circumstances of the case.[35]

If a ship is owned by several owners, a part-owner who has not consented is not bound by the charterparty. He cannot prevent the ship from sailing, but he may sue the other owners for a bond securing his share. He then has no part in profit or loss of the chartered voyage.[36]

The actual terms of the contract contained in a charterparty are very varied and complicated, and some of them, though naturally couched in different language, are common to most charterparties. Others depend very much on the type of trade on which the vessel is engaged. Some big shipping companies have their own form of charterparty.[37] Similarly, some very large shippers will only charter on the terms of

---

34 Cf. a dictum by Slesser LJ in *Cory* v. *Dorman Long & Co. Ltd* (1936) 55 Ll. L.R. 1, 5. For instances of charterparties concluded orally, see *Biddulph* v. *Bingham* (1874) 2 Asp. M.L.C. 225; *Colvin* v. *Newberry* (1832) 1 Cl. & F. 283.

35 *Sociedade Portuguesa de Navios Tanques Limitada* v. *Hvalfangerselskapet Polaris A/S* [1952] 1 Lloyd's Rep. 407.

36 *Scrutton* (1984), p. 23.

37 E.g. INTERTANKTIME 80, produced by INTERTANKO.

their own standard form.[38] Again the shipowners engaged in a particular trade, such as the Baltic wood goods trade, may agree to use a standard form of charterparty. These standard forms are more frequently than not amended and added to by what have come to be called 'rider-clauses', which themselves give rise to numerous problems of interpretation.[39]

10.3.2 BILL OF LADING

The charterparty evidences the hire of an entire ship, or at any rate a large part of her such as a hold. It is clearly not a suitable form of contract for a person who wishes to send a small parcel of goods. Such a person must look out for a ship which is carrying general cargo to the port to which he wishes to send his goods. A vessel of this kind may be sailing regularly along a certain line of ports at advertised times, when she is called a liner, or from port to port looking for cargo, when she is called a tramp. Such ships are still called by lawyers 'general ships' and the owner is a 'common carrier'. The contract of affreightment is in this case made (or more strictly, evidenced) by a bill of lading which is usually issued after the loading of the goods. However, even in the case of chartered ships a bill of lading is invariably issued; it is then not used as evidence of the terms of a contract but as evidence of the shipment of goods, i.e. as a receipt. Moreover, unless it is a 'straight' bill of lading intended for use exclusively between the shipper and the consignee, the bill of lading has by mercantile usage come to represent the goods in such a way that the transfer of it to a third party may transfer to the latter the property in the goods and the right to receive delivery of them from the ship at her port of discharge. This very valuable quality on which the legal machinery of overseas commerce has largely been built up is obviously just as useful to charterer-shippers as to shippers on general ships. For suppose an English importer buys a shipload of timber from Finland. He charters a ship, thus arranging for its transport to the UK. At the moment of his doing so he may not yet know to whom he is going to resell the goods but he expects to dispose of them to an ultimate buyer. The transport takes some days. During that period the importer will try to effect the resales, so that on the arrival of the ship in England the ultimate buyer can take delivery immediately. To this end the importer must have some means of transferring the cargo while

38 Shellvoy 4.
39 See 'Non-charters – the Rider Syndrome', by Albert Morris, Charterparties Conference, Lloyds of London Press (1982).

afloat to his buyer. This is done by means of the bill of lading, which the importer will transfer to the buyer. The latter will, on arrival of the ship at her port of discharge, present the bill of lading to the master and obtain delivery of the goods.

(A)   FUNCTIONS OF BILL OF LADING

Thus a bill of lading performs three separate functions: (a) It is evidence of the terms of a contract of affreightment; (b) it is evidence of the shipment of goods; (c) it is evidence that its holder has the right to claim possession of the goods it represents and that he might, in certain circumstances, have the property therein; that is, it is a document of title.

The contracts contained in bills of lading are frequently as long and complicated as those in charterparties.[40] All important shipowners have their own forms of bill of lading specially adapted for the trade in which they engage.[41] Small shipowners occupied with a particular trade often combine to draw up a common standard form. Bills of lading used when there is a charter party will often be very short, since as we have seen their function in such cases is usually that of a receipt and document of title.[42] Like charterparties, modern bills of lading are always printed.

(B)   BILLS OF LADING IN SETS

The bills of lading are issued to the shipper in sets of three or four; if three copies are issued, one is retained by the master or broker; two copies are dispatched, one usually by express mail, to the buyer, or to any other addressee of the cargo, i.e. the consignee. If the shipper and the consignee have agreed to use a letter of credit as a method of payment, the copies would be tendered to the shipper's bank together with the other shipping documents in return for the price for the goods shipped. By the endorsement and delivery of the bills of lading to any sub-buyer, the latter as assignees steps into the consignee's shoes and, on arrival of the ship at the port of destination, the sub-buyer can take immediate delivery on presenting the bills of lading representing the lot he has purchased from the importer, who will usually be the consignee.

40 See Appendix 6.
41 E.g. ACL Bill of Lading.
42 E.g. INTANKBILL 78, intended for use with the INTERTANKVOY 76 Tanker Voyage Charterparty.

10.3.3 RELATIONSHIP BETWEEN CHARTERPARTY AND BILL OF LADING

The relationship between the two contracts may be puzzling, especially when both documents are in use at once. The co-existence of two apparently equally contractual documents has given rise to many technical difficulties. The principal question is always: Who is liable and who is entitled under the contract of carriage? In other words, whom, shipowner or charterer, do shipper and consignee hold responsible for the safe arrival of the goods? Who, owner or charterer, is entitled to the freight? In order to answer these questions it may be useful to set out the various possibilities. There are normally four and they follow naturally from what we have just said about the operation of the entire contract.

(i) The contract of carriage may be between the owner of a general ship and the shipper. A charterparty is not then used and the contract is evidenced in the bill of lading. This happens in almost all cases where goods are shipped by a liner.

(ii) The contract of carriage may be between shipowner and charterer under an ordinary form of charterparty. Here a bill of lading will be issued when the cargo is loaded, but it will generally take effect as a receipt, not as a contract.

(iii) The contract may be between charterer by demise and shipper. Here there is a contract in the nature of a lease, not a contract of carriage, unless and until one be entered into between the charterer and some other shipper, when it will fall under (i) or (ii) above, depending on whether the charterer puts up the ship as a general ship or not. The contract of carriage is then, of course, between charterer and shipper.[43]

(iv) Where the charterer under an ordinary charterparty does not ship goods himself, but transfers his right to do so to somebody else, there will normally be both a charterparty and a bill of lading issued by the shipowner or by the charterer, or by agents for either to the shipper, and it is when that happens that the chief difficulties arise. The most fruitful cause of trouble lies in the differences between the terms of the two documents.

(v) Finally, it may even happen in exceptional cases that in respect of the same voyage the contract of carriage in respect of one parcel of goods is made between shipper and shipowner, and in respect of another parcel between shipper and charterer. Thus one bill of lading might be issued by the owner and one by the charterer, the master

---

43 *Samuel & Co.* v. *West Hartlepool Steam Navigation Co.* (1906) 11 Com. Cas. 115.

signing them being the agent once of the owner and once of the charterer.[44]

Difficulties may be experienced in cases (iv) and (v), for it may be uncertain whether the shipper contracted with the owner or with the charterer. This is a question of fact to be decided by looking at all the circumstances of the case. A common instance of such difficulties is, for example, where a charterer is only a broker who guarantees cargo for vessels which he undertakes to load.

CESSER CLAUSE

Normally a charterer who transfers his space to a shipper is only too anxious to drop out of the transaction provided his profit is assured. This means that he is content to leave the work of carrying to the shipowner, and the bill of lading will accordingly be issued on the latter's behalf and will constitute the contract of carriage except in so far as it may expressly incorporate the terms of the charterparty. This result is usually brought about by inserting what is called a 'cesser clause' in the charterparty. It is provided by such a clause that the shipowner shall have a lien on the cargo for freight, dead freight and demurrage, and that the charterer's obligation to pay freight is accordingly to cease as soon as a full cargo is shipped. At that moment, of course, the right of lien will come into existence.[45] A cesser clause takes, as a rule, some such form as: 'This charter being entered into on behalf of others, all liability of the parties signing to cease after shipment of cargo, in consideration of which it is agreed that for the payment of all freight, dead freight, and demurrage, the said owner shall have an absolute lien and charge on the said cargo.[46]

44 *Wilston S.S. Co.* v. *Weir & Co.*, *infra; The Okehampton* [1913] P. 173, *per* Hamilton LJ at p. 181.
45 Compare *Samuel & Co.* v. *West Hartlepool Steam Navigation Co.*, *supra; Wilston Steam Ship Co.* v. *Weir & Co.* (1925) 31 Com. Cas. 111.
46 See generally *Scrutton* (1984), p. 178 *et seq.*

11
RIGHTS AND DUTIES OF THE PARTIES TO THE CONTRACT OF AFFREIGHTMENT

HAVING examined the methods by which contracts of affreightment are entered into we must come to the kernel of the matter, the rights and obligations of the parties in connection with the actual transport of the goods, including loading and discharge. We shall attempt to make this matter clear in the light of the general principles of law relating to the distinctions between express and implied terms,[1] and between conditions and warranties,[2] and to the basic rules of bailment. We shall then proceed to examine the more important modifications introduced by the common forms of contract, used at the present time, and by the rules of the Carriage of Goods by Sea Act 1971.

11.1   EXPRESS AND IMPLIED TERMS

Charterparties invariably contain a large number of terms expressly agreed to by the parties, contained both in the standard forms used in the market and in the special riders agreed to between particular owners and charterers. These express terms will deal with such matters as the termini or the period of the charter, the rate of freight or hire, the allocation of costs for loading and discharge and so on. However, parties cannot be expected always to provide for all eventualities and the law recognizes this by allowing for the implication of terms by the courts. Certain terms will invariably be written into the charterparty by

1 See Section 4.2.2.
2 *Ibid.*

the courts because they are so common and fundamental that their omission from the charterparty is assumed to be inadvertent: in this way, certain terms have, through judicial policy, become permanent fixtures in charterparty law.

It must be borne in mind, however, that the court will not make a contract for the parties, and no term will be implied merely because it would have been reasonable for the parties to insert one to that effect. Only if terms 'are necessary to give such business efficacy to the contract as the parties must have intended'[3] does the court see its way to imply a term. The most important of these implied terms are the following.

11.1.1   SEAWORTHINESS

By entering into a contract to carry goods in his ship whether under a charterparty or as a common carrier, a shipowner undertakes that his ship is seaworthy. Yet charterparties also contain the express term that the ship is 'tight staunch and strong and in every way fitted for the voyage', and it may well be asked why, in view of these clear words, the courts should have found it necessary to imply a warranty of seaworthiness. The answer is that the express undertaking, as the context shows, can only refer to the condition of the ship at the time when the charter contract is concluded; the 'voyage' for which the ship is to be 'in every way fitted' can therefore only be the preliminary voyage from where the ship happens to be to the port where the cargo is taken on board.[4] The charter is silent on the condition of the ship when it sails with cargo from the loading port, and the implied term as to seaworthiness applies to this cargo-carrying voyage, actually, to its beginning. The owner cannot be held responsible on this score for unseaworthiness supervening during the voyage.

11.1.2   DUE DISPATCH

It is also an implied term of every contract of affreightment that the ship will commence and carry out her voyage with reasonable diligence.

3 *Scrutton* (1984) p. 81.
4 *Carver* (1982), para. 625; as to the preliminary voyage, see *infra*, Section 12.2.

11.1.3   PROPER ROUTE

The law also implies a term imposing on the carrier the obligation to carry out the agreed voyage by the proper route, i.e. that the ship will not deviate.

It should be observed that at common law the parties to a contract of affreightment have full freedom to alter, vary, cut down or exclude any one of these implied terms, and, in practice, this is very commonly done. It was the regular practice until, as we shall see further in more detail, the Carriage of Goods by Sea Act 1924, now the Act of 1971, considerably modified the shipowner's freedom of contract in certain respects.

11.2   CONDITIONS, WARRANTIES AND INTERMEDIATE TERMS

Mention of the terms as to proper route recalls the distinction, already referred to in the context of the sale of ships, between conditions and warranties, a distinction once thought to encompass all contractual promises until the discovery of innominate terms by Diplock L J in *The Hong Kong Fir.*[5] We have already explained how these three types of obligation differ in terms of the remedies arising from their breach. Suffice it here first to raise a note of caution and then to apply the distinction to contracts of carriage.

This somewhat difficult branch of the law is made more confusing by the inveterate habit, now too much ingrained to be capable of alleviation, among both businessmen and lawyers, of referring to many of these conditions as warranties. Readers familiar with the law of contract must be on the look-out for this use of the word. Secondly, in order to illustrate the distinction between the three types of term in contracts of carriage, one need only contrast the undertaking as to seaworthiness to the duty to proceed by the proper route. Breach of the first obligation – an intermediate term – will only entitle the shipper to terminate the contract where he has been deprived of substantially the whole benefit of the contract; whereas breach of the second – a condition – will entitle the shipper to terminate the contract however trivial the effects of the breach.

5 *The Hong Kong Fir, Hong Kong Fir Shipping Co. Ltd* v. *Kawasaki Kisen Kaisha Ltd,* [1962] 2 Q.B. 26.

We have seen that the duty to proceed on the contract voyage is a condition implied into every contract of carriage; but there are other conditions which are expressly stipulated in the contract of carriage, particularly where that contract is contained in a charterparty. It will be obvious on consideration that it is of the greatest importance to cargo-owners, who are concerned with marketing or perhaps manufacturing programmes, to be able to rely implicitly upon statements made by the shipowner concerning the position of his ship during the preliminary negotiations, and on the conclusion of the contract these statements become part of its terms. They are almost invariably construed by the courts as conditions.

The most important of the conditions of this type usually appearing in a contract of affreightment are as follows.

11.2.1 NAME AND NATIONALITY OF THE SHIP

The ship actually used for the fulfilment of the contract must correspond in name and nationality to that under which she was chartered or put up as a general ship. This appears to be a continuing condition, at any rate in the case of nationality, so that it is a breach of contract to sell the ship to a foreigner during the currency of the contract.[6] But the sale of a ship to a British subject is usually not a breach of the charterparty.

11.2.2 WHEREABOUTS OF THE SHIP

A statement as to the whereabouts of the ship at the time of making the contract is considered a condition,[7] since it is of the utmost importance to charterer and shipper that they should know when loading of the cargo can begin and when it is likely to arrive at the port of destination. Where the ship is described as being 'expected to be' or 'expected to arrive' at a particular port on a particular date, and it is not, then there is no breach by the shipowner if the shipowner could reasonably have expected the vessel to be at the appointed place at the appointed time.[8]

---

6 Isaacs v. McAllum [1921] 3 K.B. 377.
7 Behn v. Burness (1863) 3 B. & S. 751; Corkling v. Massey (1873) L.R. & C.P. 395.
8 The Mihalis Angelos, Maredelanto Compania Naviera S.A. v. Bergbau-Handel G.m.b.H. [1971] 1 Q.B. 164.

11.2.3   CLASS OF SHIP

As the general condition and nature of the ship are important factors to be considered by the charterer, a statement in the charterparty of her class on Lloyd's Register of Shipping is construed as a condition. Lloyd's Register of Shipping is a society which was formed primarily for the benefit of shipowners, merchants and underwriters. Its object is the survey and classification of ships, as e.g. 100 A.1, and the annual publication of the Register Book which contains particulars about all vessels of a certain size. The statement in a charterparty of a ship's class on the Register is a condition only to a limited extent. It does not mean that the vessel must retain the class during the currency of the contract. Nor is it permissible for the charterer to go behind the statement in the Register and allege a breach of the condition by reason of the fact that the ship is not in a state which justifies its class. In other words, this condition is performed if the ship was in fact classed as stated at the time when the charterparty was made, and the condition is not broken if the ship was wrongfully classed as it was.[9]

11.2.4   TONNAGE

Apart from nationality and class the charterer will wish the contract to be for a certain size of vessel. This is measured by so-called registered tons, that is, the tonnage for which cargo-space is available on board. Unless special words are used, a representation of the ship's registered tonnage is construed not as a condition to be complied with literally, but merely as a description.[10] Where the real tonnage is at variance with that stated in the charterparty, the question arises whether the description of a chartered ship has been so widely departed from as to make it wholly different from that promised in the charterparty. Sometimes one finds in a charterparty a guarantee of the ship's 'dead weight capacity'. In the ordinary way this only refers to her abstract lifting capacity and does not contain any sort of promise that the ship is capable of carrying any particular cargo to the extent of that weight.[11] On the other hand, where not only the cargo intended to be loaded was mentioned, but where the charterer before the contract was made gave measurements of bulky machinery and the shipowner had promised that it could be stowed in the hold, it was held that such a

9 *Scrutton* (1984), p. 76.
10 *Barker* v. *Windle* (1856) 6 E. & B. 675.
11 *Millar & Co.* v. *S.S. Freden* [1918] 1 K.B. 611.

promise went beyond a guarantee of an abstract lifting capacity. In addition, the shipowner impliedly promised that the special cargo could be carried by his ship.[12]

11.3   SEAWORTHINESS

It is convenient here to consider the obligation of seaworthiness in a contract of affreightment[13] rather more closely.

In the first place it is necessary to realize that the service of carriage involves two matters which are in essence distinct:

(1) the transport of the goods from one place to another;
(2) the keeping of them safe and undamaged during this operation.

The ship is in a sense a warehouse and the shipowner a warehousekeeper as well as a carrier. The carrier's dual function makes it necessary to refer briefly to the general law on bailment.

The legal term used to denote a person who has the possession of another man's goods is 'bailee'. The carrier is a bailee. The law of bailment is very largely taken up with the question of how far the bailee is responsible for the safety of the goods which are in his custody. The rule is that an ordinary, or 'common', bailee, as he is called, must take reasonable care of the goods. If they are lost or damaged through failure on his part to exercise such care he will be responsible to the owner for damages. Failure to take reasonable care when there is a duty to do so constitutes an unlawful act, the tort of negligence, and the law of bailment is therefore largely concerned with the application of the law of negligence.

There are, however, two particular types of bailment where the law insists on a higher standard of care, viz. the innkeeper and the common carrier. We have already seen that the sea carrier who puts up a general ship will usually be a common carrier. As such, his duty to provide a seaworthy ship is a strict duty: the carrier undertakes that his vessel *is* seaworthy, not that he has taken reasonable precautions to ensure that it is seaworthy. We have also seen, however, how this strict liability of the common carrier can be mitigated by private contracts or by legislation. Thus clause 2 of the Gencon charterparty imposes liability for

---

12   *Mackill* v. *Wright Bros. & Co.* (1888) 14 App. Cas. 106, 120.

13   The obligation is relevant to contracts of carriage contained in charterparties or bills of lading and to contracts of marine insurance, and in principle the duty has the same content in all these contracts: A.L. Smith LJ in *The Vortigern* [1899] P. 140, 157.

unseaworthiness only where it is caused by 'personal want of due diligence on the part of the Owners or their Manager'. Again, where the contract is evidenced by a bill of lading governed by the Carriage of Goods by Sea Act 1971, or where rules contained in that Act are incorporated into a charterparty, the carrier need only 'exercise due diligence to make the ship seaworthy'.[14]

The carrier's dual role also makes it necessary to distinguish between two aspects of seaworthiness and between seaworthiness and bad stowage. The duty to provide a seaworthy ship involves:

(a) the duty to provide an efficient instrument of sea-going transport – seaworthiness pure and simple; and
(b) the duty to provide a safe warehouse for the cargo – sometimes called cargoworthiness.

This latter aspect of the duty of seaworthiness needs to be kept separate – for reasons which have to do with the effect of exception clauses and which will be explained at a later stage – from

(c) the duty properly to stow the cargo.

We are now in a position to discuss these questions in somewhat more detail.

11.3.1   SEAWORTHINESS PURE AND SIMPLE

To be seaworthy a vessel 'must have that degree of fitness which an ordinary, careful and prudent owner would require his vessel to have at the commencement of her voyage, having regard to all the probable circumstances of it'.[15] A ship is efficient as an instrument of transport if hull, tackle and machinery are in a state of good repair, if she is sufficiently provided with fuel and ballast and is manned by an efficient crew.

Illustration: *The Roberta*[16]
In engaging the engineer of a ship the owner had not inquired about his qualifications. He was, in fact, wholly incompetent.

Held: The ship was unseaworthy by reason thereof.

14 Carriage of Goods by Sea Act 1971, Schedule, Art III, r. 1.
15 *McFadden* v. *Blue Star Line* [1905] 1 K.B. 697, at p. 706.
16 (1938) 60 Ll. L.R. 85; 58 Ll. L.R. 159, 177.

While seaworthiness covers more than the physical state of the ship, it is now clear that the term does not impose an obligation on the carrier to ensure that the wages paid to the seamen on board the vessel have been approved by the International Transport Workers Federation.[17]   The degree of seaworthiness varies in relation to the contemplated voyage. Crossing the Atlantic Ocean calls for stronger equipment than sailing across the English Channel.

11.3.2   CARGOWORTHINESS

Cargoworthiness means in the first place that the vessel must be sufficiently strong and equipped to carry the particular kind of cargo which she has contracted to carry, and her cargo must be so loaded that it is safe for her to proceed on her voyage.

Illustration: *Kopitoff v. Wilson* [18]
Iron armour plates which had been loaded broke loose in rough weather, and went through the ship's side.
Held: She was not cargoworthy.[19]

In the second place the ship must be equipped not only to carry the contract cargo, but also to prevent its deterioration during the voyage.

Illustration 1: *Cargo on The Maori King v. Hughes* [20]
A cargo of meat was carried from Australia to Europe. At the beginning of the voyage the refrigerating machinery was defective, and owing to that defect broke down during the voyage.
Held: The ship was not cargoworthy.

Illustration 2: *Tattersall v. National S.S. Co.* [21]
Where a cattle transport ship is not disinfected after an outbreak of foot and mouth disease, the ship is not seaworthy in the sense of being cargoworthy.

17 *The Derby, Alfred C. Toepfer v. Schiffahrtsgesellschaft G.m.b.H. v. Tossa Marine Co. Ltd* [1985] 2 Lloyd's Rep. 325.
18 (1876) 1 Q.B.D. 377.
19 For a comparison of the two concepts, see *Werner v. Bergensk Dampskibsselskab* (1926) 42 T.L.R. 265.
20 [1895] 2 Q.B. 550.
21 (1884) 12 Q.B.D. 297.

Illustration 3: _Stanton_ v. _Richardson_[22]
The ship was perfectly capable of carrying a cargo of wet sugar, but the ship's pumps were not able to deal with the moisture, though good for any other purpose.

Held: The ship was not cargo- or seaworthy, and the charterer might throw up the charter.

11.3.3   BAD STOWAGE

Stowage of cargo may be inefficient in that goods which should be stowed separately are stowed in the same hold. When damage is thereby caused to the cargo the question arises whether the ship, though its safe navigation has not been impaired, has become unseaworthy in the sense of being uncargoworthy. That is to say, the vessel may not be in every way fitted to take on board the contract cargo. On the other hand, the stowage may be such that though bad it leaves the ship in a cargoworthy condition.

Illustration 1: _The Standale_[23]
A cargo of grain in bulk was stowed in the hold without adequate protection having been taken against its shifting.

Held: This mode of stowage made the ship unseaworthy.

Illustration 2: _The Thorsa_[24]
Chocolate was stowed in the same hold with gorgonzola cheese. On arrival the chocolate was tainted with cheese.

Held: The ship was cargoworthy, because the stowage did not endanger the safety of the ship. The ship was fit to receive the cargo. The stowage of chocolate and cheese in the same hold could not constitute a breach of the warranty of seaworthiness, but was simply bad stowage.

Illustration 3: _Elder Dempster & Co._ v. _Paterson Zochonis_[25]
A ship had no 'tween decks', but keep holds. At the bottom of the holds were stowed casks containing palm oil, and on the top of them bags with palm kernels. The weight of the kernels crushed the casks and the owners (bill of lading holders) sued the shipowners for damages; they contended that the

22 (1874) L.R. 9 C.P. 390 (Ex. Ch.).
23 (1938) 61 Ll. L.R. 223; _cf._ also _Kopitoff_ v. _Wilson_ (1876), 1 Q.B.D. 377.
24 [1916] P. 257.
25 [1924] A.C. 522.

ship, not being fitted with 'tween decks', was not cargoworthy for casks of palm oil.

This contention was rejected by the House of Lords, which held that at the time when the casks were loaded the ship was perfectly fitted to receive them; it was owing to the particular method of stowing kernels on top of the casks that the damage occurred. Therefore the damage was not due to unseaworthiness, but to bad stowage, which was one of the excepted perils. 'I think,' said Lord Sumner,[26] 'that the ship's design, with her peculiarities and, if you will, her defects, was no more than a *causa sine qua non*', and not a *causa causans*.

It may be noted as indicative of the great difficulty of this particular case that it was argued twice over in the House of Lords and that the decision in the end was that of a majority.

The last case illustrates the need for a distinction to be drawn between the types of breach, even though both involve facts which appear at times to be remarkably similar. The consequences of a decision one way or the other are far-reaching. Contracts not governed by the Hague–Visby Rules usually contain an exception clause protecting the shipowner against liability for bad stowage, while one protecting him against unseaworthiness is less common. In *The Thorsa* and the *Elder Dempster* cases the contract of affreightment contained bad stowage but not unseaworthiness clauses. Had the courts decided that the ships had been unseaworthy, these clauses would not have applied and the shipowners would have been held liable. As it was, they effectively pleaded these clauses and thus escaped liability. Moreover, in contracts governed by the Hague–Visby Rules, the distinction is important because while a carrier in breach of his duty 'properly and carefully . . . [to] stow' is none the less entitled to the protection of the exceptions in Art. IV 2, a carrier in breach of his duty to make his ship seaworthy is not.

A word should be added about the meaning of the term 'properly and carefully . . . [to] stow' as used in Art. IV 1 of the Hague–Visby Rules. The question has arisen whether the word 'properly' added to 'carefully' does not impose a more stringent duty on the carrier. The following argument has been presented. Suppose a carrier stows and carries a cargo carefully according to his lights, but in fact additional precautions would have been required to prevent damage. In such circumstances his conduct has been careful, but has it also been proper? The answer is that if stowage and carriage are done according to

26 At p. 549.

accepted standards, but the unusual nature of the cargo, unknown to anyone, would have required greater precautions, the carriage or stowage has been done 'properly'.

Illustration: *Albacora S.R.L. v. Westcott & Laurence Line Ltd* [27]

A consignment of wet salted fillets of ling was shipped from Aberdeen to Italy and arrived seriously damaged by bacteria, which multiplied rapidly above a certain temperature. It was subsequently established that this type of cargo could not be carried on the particular voyage at the particular season without refrigeration, but no one had realized this at the material time. This was an unusual cargo for the particular kind of voyage, and the consignor did not contend that the ship's officers concerned with the loading ought to have been aware of the danger. He also conceded that the carrier's conduct had been careful. The cargo-owners, however, contended that nevertheless stowage and carriage had not been done 'properly'.

Held: The carrier was not liable. The cargo-owners' contention was unreasonable. The cargo was carried 'properly' as long as the carrier adopted a system which was sound in the light of all the knowledge which he had or ought to have had about the nature of the goods. In this particular case the carrier had no reason to suppose that the cargo required any different treatment from that which it had in fact received.

11.3.4   EXCLUDING LIABILITY FOR UNSEAWORTHINESS

The undertaking of seaworthiness can only be cut down, where it can be cut down at all, by express words clearly releasing the shipowner from his obligations. [28] A mere right given to the charterer to inspect the vessel before loading and to satisfy himself that she was fit for the contract cargo does not free the shipowner from his obligation to provide a cargoworthy ship.

Illustration: *Petrofina S.A. of Brussels v. Compagnia Italiana Trasporto Olii Minerali of Genoa* [29]

The charterparty of a tanker which was to carry a cargo of benzine provided in clause (1) that the ship was to be 'in every way fitted for the voyage and to be maintained in such condition during the voyage'. By clause (16) the master was bound to keep tanks, pipes and pumps clean. Finally, a clause

---

27 [1966] 2 Lloyd's Rep. 53.
28 *Shawingian, Ltd v. Vokins & Co.*, [1961] 3 All E.R. 396, illustrates the effect of the exclusion of liability under the London Lighterage Clause.
29 (1937) 53 T.L.R. 650 (C.A.).

(27) was inserted according to which the steamer should be clean for the cargo in question to the satisfaction of the charterer's inspector. On discharge the benzine was discoloured, and on the evidence this was the fault of the steamer. The shipowner, however, pleaded clause (27), and contended that he was only bound to keep the tanks clean to the satisfaction of the charterer's inspector, and the latter had in fact expressed his satisfaction.

Held: That clauses (1) and (16) contained an express warranty of sea-, ie cargoworthiness, and that clause (27) far from derogating from that warranty, only gave an additional right of inspection to the charterers. Without express words to this effect, the satisfaction of the inspector could not be relied on as a discharge of the shipowner's obligation to provide a seaworthy ship.

11.3.5   STATUTORY SEAWORTHINESS

In addition to the general regulations for securing the safety of shipping, which we have already discussed, there has for some time been a new development among maritime countries. Regulations are made which are intended to secure the safety of ships engaged in certain trades to which it has been found that danger attaches, e.g. petrol or grain in bulk. These regulations have been referred to in some detail in Chapter 8. As an instance we may refer to the use of shifting boards for the carriage of grain in bulk which is compulsory in certain states.[30] The immediate effect of the breach of such regulations by a shipowner may be to prevent his ship from proceeding from the state in question by refusal of clearance certificates, or to subject him to a penalty when the vessel arrives at a port of such a country without having complied with the said regulations. Whether his failure to comply with such a regulation amounts to a breach of the condition of seaworthiness is not clear. Shifting boards, though prescribed by port regulations, need not necessarily be required in the eye of a prudent owner to make the ship in every way fitted to encounter the probable perils of the contemplated voyage, for not all states have adopted the same view of the matter, and accordingly prudent owners must be allowed to differ. Thus it is arguable that the breach of such regulations need not at the same time constitute a breach of the charterparty or the bill of lading. But British courts have always tended towards the strict view of the shipowner's obligation and it would seem that regulations of this type indicate a standard of seaworthiness which ought to be observed.

A question may also arise in cases where such regulations exist in one country but not in another as to who, shipowner or charterer, is to pay

30 Merchant Shipping (Safety Convention) Act 1949, s. 24.

for the cost of complying with them. This would appear to depend on whether the provision is necessary in the first instance in order that the shipowner may comply with the terms of his contract. In this connection *Rederi A/B 'Unda' v. Burdon & Co.*[31] is an interesting illustration, though it turns to some extent on the precise words used in the charterparty.

Illustration: *Rederi A/B 'Unda' v. Burdon & Co.*

A Swedish ship was chartered by British shippers. Swedish law required shifting boards for the contemplated bulk grain cargo, but the charterparty did not refer to Swedish law; it only provided that the owners should 'maintain (the ship) in a thoroughly efficient state in hull, machinery, and equipment for and during the service with dunnage mats, shifting boards (as far as on board), etc.'; the owners further warranted the vessel in 'every way fitted to carry bulk and general cargoes'.

On these words it was **held** that the owners had to pay for additional shifting boards which were required under Swedish law.

11.3.6   THE SEAWORTHINESS UNDERTAKING AND BILLS OF LADING

Where the Carriage of Goods by Sea Act 1971 applies, the implied term of seaworthiness is abolished;[32] and there is substituted for it the obligation[33] 'to exercise due diligence to make the ship seaworthy, to properly man, equip, and supply the ship, make the holds, refrigerating and cool chambers, and all other parts of the ship in which goods are carried, fit and safe for their reception, carriage, and preservation'. Not only has the carrier himself to be diligent, but the same duty rests on his servants and agents.[34] The net result is to equate the position of the carrier broadly speaking with that of the common bailee or private carrier, and to make him responsible in negligence. But this obligation he cannot evade by further qualifying terms in his contract.

To say that the carrier must answer for the negligence of his servants and agents seems simple enough. But the meaning of the word 'agents' gave rise to doubts, which were resolved only thirty-seven years after the Act came into force. What was in doubt was whether an independent contractor employed by the shipowner to overhaul or repair his ship was to be considered his agent. We have already seen that the

31 (1937) 57 Ll. L.R. 95.
32 Carriage of Goods by Sea Act 1971 s. 3; Sch., Art. IV, Rule 1.
33 *Ibid.*, Sch., Art III, Rule 1(a).
34 *Angliss & Co.* v. *P. & O.S.N. Co. Ltd*, [1927] 2 K.B. 456.

purchaser of a new ship can rely on the shipbuilders, and that cargo--owners suffering damage as a result of the builders' negligence have no remedy against the shipowner.[35]

In *Angliss & Co.* v. *P & O*,[36] where this point was decided, Wright J used picturesque language to make his point. He said that the old rule that the shipowner was absolutely liable for the seaworthiness of his vessel was well suited:

'. . . to more simple days when ships were not very complicated wooden structures of a few hundred tons; but in modern times, when ships are complicated steel structures full of complex machinery, the old unqualified rule imposed too serious an obligation on carriers by sea, and I think that the new Acts have intended to emphasize the specialization which has developed in modern times, and to emphasize the distinction between the carrier and shipbuilder, and limit the carrier's obligation to due diligence in his capacity as carrier.'

These words were for a long time thought to protect the shipowner not only in respect of a new vessel but also when he sent his ship to a yard for repair or overhaul. That this is not so, and that the shipowner as carrier is liable to his cargo-owners also for the negligence of a carefully selected, reputable ship repairer, was finally decided by the House of Lords in *Riverstone Meat Co. Pty Ltd* v. *Lancashire Shipping Co. Ltd*.[37]

In that case tinned food, shipped from Sydney to London under bills of lading, was found on discharge to be damaged by seawater that had entered the holds through defective inspection covers of storm valves. Before the outward voyage the vessel had passed through a special survey performed by a reputable firm of ship repairers selected by the shipowners' marine superintendent. After the Lloyds surveyor's inspection, a shipyard fitter closed the inspection covers but failed to secure the nuts adequately, an omission impossible to discover by visual inspection. On the homeward voyage the working of the ship in rough weather loosened the nuts and seawater entered. No one else – certainly no employee of the shipowners – had been negligent. Even so, the House of Lords held that the shipowner had failed to prove that he had exercised due diligence to make the ship seaworthy: the repairer was to be regarded as his agent for the purposes of the statute, and he was therefore responsible for the negligence which occurred in the repairer's yard. *Angliss's* case was good law in respect of new vessels, but once the shipowner had commissioned the ship for cargo-carrying, anyone

35 *Supra*, Section 5.4.
36 [1927] 2 K.B. 456, at p. 461.
37 [1961] 1 All E.R. 495.

working for him became his agent. In the words of Lord Radcliffe,[38] where the shipbuilder was negligent, 'the causative carelessness took place at a time before the carrier's obligation under Art. III, Rule 1, had attached and in circumstances, therefore, when the builders and their men could not be described as agents for the carrier before and at the beginning of the voyage to... make the ship seaworthy'.

Viscount Simonds[39] quoted Brown J in *The Colima,*[40] an American case decided under the Harter Act, the forerunner of the British Carriage of Goods by Sea Act. Reason and sound policy, Lord Simonds quoted Brown J as saying, led to the conclusion that it had not been intended when enacting the new legislation to relieve the shipowner who employed an independent contractor. All the legislation wanted to do was to relieve him of his absolute liability. As a result of that legislation, unseaworthiness caused by latent, undiscoverable defects was no cause of action against the shipowner. Such a defect is, for example, metal fatigue; another is unseaworthiness caused by a crew that held all the necessary competence certificates but was nevertheless incompetent, for the shipowner must be able to rely on qualifications acknowledged by bodies charged with holding examinations. This was the case in *Adamastos Shipping Co. Ltd* v. *Anglo-Saxon Petroleum Co. Ltd,*[41] where the engine-room crew, though qualified, was incompetent, so that the ship became unseaworthy, but the shipowner escaped liability.

The *Adamastos* case was a case of a charterparty, where normally the shipowner is absolutely liable unless he excludes such liability which, as we have seen, he is entitled to do. This particular charterparty contained an exception clause, described as 'paramount clause', providing that 'this bill of lading shall be subject to the provisions of the Carriage of Goods by Sea Act... which shall be incorporated therein'. What had happened was that a printed bill of lading clause had thoughtlessly been inserted in the charterparty. After a long legal battle it was held that, applying the canon of construction of contractual terms that a wrong description is harmless – *falsa demonstratio non nocet* – the parties had really meant to say 'charterparty' where in fact they had said 'bill of lading', and that in this case the shipowner was protected by exercising due diligence, which he had proved.[42]

38 At p. 520.
39 At p. 501.
40 (1897) 82 Fed. Rep. 665.
41 [1959] A.C. 133.
42 The paramount clause covers the whole of the Hague Rules, including the need to 'bring suit' within one year; Art. III, Rule 6. *Nea Agrex S.A.* v. *Baltic Shipping Co. Ltd,* [1976] 2 All E.R. 842.

The *Riverstone*[43] case came as a surprise to many lawyers, who up to then had thought that the distinction between absolute liability and Hague Rules liability was more marked. The decision is hard on shipowners, and the distinction made by the House of Lords between a shipowner commissioning a yard to build a ship and a shipowner commissioning a yard to overhaul a ship may appear to some as perhaps somewhat formalistic. The merit of the decision – and this should not be underrated – is that it establishes uniformity of American and English law.

11.3.7   TIME OF SEAWORTHINESS

We must now consider at what time the ship must be seaworthy, or the due diligence be exercised to make her so. Here we must remember that the moment the ship leaves port the owner is much less well placed for maintaining her in an efficient condition. He cannot inspect her nor, what is more important, can repairs of any magnitude be effected. The law takes notice of this and provides that seaworthiness need only exist at the commencement of the voyage.[44] Before the time of sailing a modified form of seaworthiness is required. While in port the vessel must be fit to lie in port and to take her cargo.

In *Maxine Footwear Co. Ltd* v. *Canadian Government Merchant Marine*[45] it was laid down that liability under Rule III of the Hague-Visby Rules begins at least when loading begins. In that case the ship caught fire while it was being loaded and it had to be scuttled. The fire was caused by the negligent use of an acetylene torch when thawing out frozen scupper pipes. It was held that the shipowners were liable to the cargo-owners whose goods had been loaded and were destroyed. The shipowners argued that Art. IV, Rule 2(b), which excludes liability in the event of fire, was an answer to the cargo-owners' action, but it was held that diligence to make the ship seaworthy at the beginning of the loading was an overriding obligation.

The rule that while in port the vessel must be fit to lie in port also applies to craft solely employed in the harbour if at different times different degrees of seaworthiness are required.

---

43 [1961] 1 All E.R. 495.
44 *The Rona* (1884) 5 Asp. M.C. 259; *McFadden* v. *Blue Star Line* [1905] 1 K.B. 697, 706. The Hague–Visby Rules do not place on the carrier the obligation to keep the ship seaworthy throughout the voyage.
45 [1959] A.C. 589.

Illustration: Reed v. Page[46]

A lighter employed for discharging a steamer in port had a carrying capacity of 170 tons. She in fact took on board 190 tons. While lying alongside the steamer in wait for a tug, the lighter sank and the cargo was lost. The cargo-owners sued the lighterers for damages.

Held: They were liable. When loading had finished a new stage of employment had begun. At that stage the lighter was unseaworthy by reason of being overloaded. She was neither fit to lie in the river nor to be towed.

(A)   REPAIRS DURING THE VOYAGE

This does not, of course, excuse the shipowner from failing to execute repairs during a voyage as far as he is reasonably able to do so. Failure to do this will amount to negligence, for it is part of his general duty to show and exercise proper competence during the voyage.

Illustration: Worms v. Storey[47]

A ship was chartered for a voyage with a cargo of coal. The vessel was seaworthy at the beginning of the voyage, but damage was done which might have been repaired during the transport. No repairs were effected and thereby part of the cargo was lost.

Held: The shipowner was negligent and liable to the cargo-owner in damages.

(B)   SEAWORTHINESS AND THE STAGES DOCTRINE

We have seen that seaworthiness is implied in charterparties, and that due diligence in making the ship seaworthy in bills of lading needs to be exercised only at the commencement of the voyage. During the voyage no such warranty applies, in the absence of special terms in the respective documents. This statement, however, requires some qualification.

There grew up in the law of marine insurance, as some mitigation of the harshness of the seaworthiness condition, what is called the doctrine of seaworthiness by stages. Under this the owner of a vessel which is prosecuting a voyage in stages, e.g. the first part down a river or over an inland sea, the next part over the ocean, is held to comply with the condition of seaworthiness if his vessel is in fact seaworthy at the

46 [1927] 1 K.B. 743.
47 (1855) 11 Ex. 427.

commencement of each stage in her voyage, so that when she commences the river stage she need not be efficient for the ocean stage.[48]

In the application of this doctrine to contracts of carriage the tendency has been to modify it so as to place somewhat greater burdens upon carriers. This has been most evident in a series of cases in which vessels have on touching coaling ports failed to take on board sufficient bunkers to reach the next coaling station. It has been held that the voyage from one coaling port to another is a 'stage', and that by commencing this 'stage' with an insufficiency of fuel on board the master has involved his owners in a breach of the undertaking.[49]

It can hardly be said that the voyage from each port of call to the next is to be regarded as a stage and, indeed, apart from such an obvious matter as bunkers, which it is submitted could have been more satisfactorily decided under negligence, there is much to be said for confining the doctrine to really marked stages such as the difference between river and ocean navigation. Seaworthiness does not depend on knowledge or due care, and to make the shipowner responsible for latent defects developing during a voyage on the ground that they existed when the vessel left some port of call where they could have been repaired, would be to place altogether too serious a burden on shipowners.[50]

A certain complication has been brought about by Art. IV, Rule 2(a) of the schedule of the Carriage of Goods by Sea Act. That article excepts the carrier's liability for loss or damage arising or resulting from 'act, neglect, or default of the master, mariner, pilot, or the servants of the carrier in the navigation or in the management of the ship'. Now in a case like *The Vortigern,* where an insufficient amount of bunker coals was loaded, the opinion has already been expressed that this would be a 'neglect or default of the master in the management of the ship',[51] and the owner, unless privy to the neglect, would not be liable. This was, indeed, thought to have been the intention of the framers of the Rules. The question remained an open one for many years. But it always seemed more reasonable to argue that without express words the Act cannot be taken to have abolished the doctrine of stages in connection with the contracts to which it applies. The obligation to exercise due diligence in and about the provision of a seaworthy ship, imposed by Art. III, Rule 1(a), is not cut down by the protection given by Art. IV,

---

48 *Bouillion* v. *Lupton* (1863) 33 L.J. C.P. 37.
49 *The Vortigern* [1899] P. 140.
50 *Brown & Co.* v. *Nitrate Producers S.S. Co.* (1937) 58 Ll. L.R. 188.
51 About the 'navigation and management of the ship' see particularly *Gosse Millard* v. *Canadian Government Merchant Marine* [1929] A.C. 223.

Rule 2(a).[52] And, indeed, the House of Lords has since decided that the master's not bunkering sufficient coal constituted lack of due diligence in making the ship seaworthy. The shipowners were liable to the cargo-owners for consequent loss.[53] The shipowner is, therefore, responsible in such a case as *The Vortigern,* unless he can show that the sailing without sufficient bunkers was not due to negligence on the part of the master or his other servants or agents, which he will not usually be able to do.

11.3.8   EFFECT OF BREACH OF THE SEAWORTHINESS OBLIGATION

The effect of a breach of the seaworthiness term can be summarized thus: where the effect of the breach is not such as to deprive the cargo-owner of substantially the whole benefit of the contract, or where despite such effect, the cargo-owner chooses not to terminate the contract, the cargo-owner can sue the carrier for damages in accordance with the contract. Thus the plaintiff's damages will be restricted by clauses limiting or excluding the carrier's liability for losses caused by unseaworthiness or any other course.

Illustration: *The Europa*[54]

Charterers sued carriers for damages in respect of loss caused to a cargo of sugar being carried between Stettin and Liverpool. The cargo was stowed in two parcels, parcel A in the 'tween decks and parcel B in a lower hold. While entering Liverpool, the vessel struck the dock wall, breaking a water-closet pipe. This allowed water to enter into the 'tween decks and damage the sugar stowed there. However, owing to a defect in the 'tween decks which existed at the time of sailing, the water seeped into the lower hold and damaged parcel B. The defendant carriers admitted liability for the loss caused to parcel B, as being due to a breach of seaworthiness; but denied liability for loss caused to parcel A, since there was an exception clause covering them against liability for loss caused by collision. The question therefore was: Did the breach of the seaworthiness duty sweep away all other terms which might give the carrier protection from liability for loss caused by events other than unseaworthiness?

Held: The breach did not have this effect – the breach made the carrier liable for loss ensuing therefrom, and left intact any exemptions existing in the contract and protecting the carrier from liability for other losses.

52 See *idem.*
53 *Northumbrian Shipping Co.* v. *E. Timm & Son* [1939] A.C. 397.
54 [1908] P. 84, followed in *Kish* v. *Taylor* [1912] A.C. 604.

Where the breach of the term does deprive the cargo-owner of substantially the whole benefit of the contract and where the plaintiff consequently terminates the contract, the legal implications of the breach may well be different, as we shall see when we deal with deviation.[55]

11.3.9 PROOF OF UNSEAWORTHINESS

Before leaving this subject, a word must be said about the proof of unseaworthiness. In the ordinary way the person relying on unseaworthiness, that is to say the charterer or skipper, must prove it. Rigid adherence to this rule would often exempt the owner from responsibility since the facts are almost entirely within the latter's knowledge. The Hague–Visby Rules have gone some way towards redressing the balance by imposing upon the owner the burden of proving that the unseaworthiness of the vessel was not caused by want of due diligence on the owner's part. This, however, still leaves the prior problem of proof of unseaworthiness, a problem which is harder on a charterer who, not covered by the Hague–Visby Rules, has to prove also that the unseaworthiness was caused by the carrier's want of due diligence where the charterparty makes the owner liable only for such failure. On the other hand, it must be said that the judges are free to draw their own inferences from a relatively skeletal framework of facts brought forward by the cargo-owner. The position was clarified in Lloyd J's judgment in *The Hellenic Dolphin*:[56]

'The cargo-owner can raise a prima facie case against the shipowner by showing that cargo which had been shipped in good order and condition was damaged on arrival, The shipowner can meet that prima facie case by relying on an exception, for example, perils at sea. The position in that respect is exactly the same whether the Hague Rules are incorporated or not. The cargo-owner can then seek to displace the exception by proving that the vessel was unseaworthy at commencement of the voyage and that the unseaworthiness was the cause of the loss. The burden in relation to seaworthiness does not shift. Naturally, the court can draw inferences: in *Lindsay* v. *Klein* the inference of unseaworthiness at commencement of the voyage was overwhelming. But if at the end of the day, having heard all the evidence and drawn all the proper inferences, the court is left on the razor's edge, the cargo-owner fails on unseaworthiness and the shipowners are left with their defence of perils of the sea. If, on the other hand, the court comes down in favour of the cargo-owners on unseaworthiness, the shipowners can still escape by proving that the relevant unseaworthiness was

55 *Infra*, at Section 14.1.1.
56 [1978] 2 Lloyd's Rep. 336, at p. 339.

not due to any want of due diligence on their part or on the part of their servants or agents.'

11.4   CARRIER'S IMMUNITIES

Parties concluding a contract of carriage by charterparty can agree on any number of clauses excluding or limiting the carrier's liability for breach of contract. Where the Hague–Visby Rules apply, the position is not so straightforward, for the Rules enumerate a catalogue of perils against which the carrier is protected.[57] Protection clauses which are wider than those allowed by the Rules are void. This is perhaps their greatest achievement. Shipper and consignee, indeed every bill of lading holder or person buying goods to be sent to him from overseas, knows that the carrier cannot overstep certain limits. No longer can he spring a surprise on seller or buyer, shipper or consignee, by protecting himself against yet another peril.

In this section, we shall examine the perils from which the Carriage of Goods by Sea Act allows the carrier to exclude liability. Perhaps the greatest practical difficulty in the way of the shipowner is the proof that the damage was caused by one of the excepted perils; before we examine the catalogue of excepted perils in detail, some attention therefore needs to be paid to the question of the burden of proof.

11.4.1   EXCEPTED PERILS AND BURDEN OF PROOF

Everyone knows that an accident may, in popular parlance, be caused by a number of factors. But in law a distinction is made which should be firmly grasped, namely, between the *causa causans,* or *causa proxima,* that is to say the last essential cause, and a *causa sine qua non,* that is, a cause which also contributed to the damage, but in an indirect and more remote manner.

Illustration: *Hamilton, Fraser & Co. v. Pandorf & Co.*[58]
Rice was shipped under a charterparty and bills of lading by the terms of which the shipowner was protected against damage occurring by 'dangers and accidents of the seas'. During the voyage rats gnawed a hole in a pipe

---

57 Art. IV, Rule 2.
58 (1887) 12 App. Cas. 518. See also *Wilson* v. *Owners of Cargo per Xantho* (1887) 12 App. Cas. 503, and 4.2 *infra.*

on board the ship, whereby seawater escaped and damaged the rice. The cargo-owners contended that the shipowners were liable, since the damage was caused by the rats and not by dangers of the seas.

Held: The shipowners were protected. The sea was the proximate cause of the damage. In the words of Lord FitzGerald, at p. 528: 'The remote cause was in a certain sense the action of the rats on the lead pipe, but the immediate cause of the damage was the irruption of seawater from time to time through the injured pipe caused by the rolling of the ship as she proceeded on her voyage.'

The mere fact that a certain peril is the proximate cause of damage does not, however, assist the shipowner if he cannot prove it, and we have already seen that he who seeks the protection of an excepted peril must prove the facts which bring the exception into operation.[59] The procedure is usually the following: when goods do not arrive, or arrive in a damaged condition, the consignees must first prove that the goods were lost or damaged on board the ship.

Illustration: *Chung Hwa Steel Products & Trading Co. v. Glen Lines*[60]

Cases containing wool gabardine did not arrive. The consignees claimed damages, and alleged that they had been pilfered from the ship.

Held: Action dismissed as they had not discharged the burden of proof. The goods had passed over railways and through a warehouse, and according to the evidence the chances were about that they were stolen at any of those places or on the ship. In order to succeed the plaintiffs should have affirmatively proved that the loss occurred on board.

But once this has been done the onus of proof is shifted, and the carrier has to prove that this loss or damage falls under one of the excepted perils.

Illustration: *White & Son v. Owners of Hobson's Bay*[61]

A refrigerated cargo of apples was shipped in good order and condition, but arrived overripe. The shipowners claimed the protection of Arts III, Rules (1) and (2) and IV, Rule (2)(m) and (q), alleging that the condition of the apples was due to inherent vice.

---

59 See *The Hellenic Dolphin* [1978] 2 Lloyd's Rep. 336, at 339, referred to above at Section 3.9.
60 (1935) 51 Ll. L.R. 248.
61 (1933) 47 Ll. L.R. 207.

Held: As they had not been able to prove that affirmatively they had not discharged the burden of proof and were liable.[62]

Finally, where the carrier invokes the general exception provided by Art. IV, Rule 2(q), he must also prove that neither the actual fault or privity of himself nor the fault or neglect of his agents or servants contributed to the loss or damage. By this sub-rule the carrier cannot, as is the case with the other exceptions, wait until the goods' owner proves negligence; if he relies on the protection of clause (q) he himself must affirmatively prove that neither he nor his agents or servants were guilty of negligence. It should also be noticed that so long as the shipowner satisfies the court that there was no negligence he need not go the lengths of proving the exact cause of the loss or damage, which may mean a considerable lightening of his burden of proof.

Illustration: *City of Baroda v. Hall Line*[63]

Sixty-six cases of bristles were shipped from Tsing-tao to London under bills of lading incorporating the Hague Rules. On arrival twenty-one cases were found to have been broken open and robbed of their contents. It was found to be a reasonable inference that the bristles had been stolen at the loading port. The defendants also proved that they had established a system of watchmen, but they failed to satisfy the court that the watching had actually been carried out vigilantly.

Held: The defendants were liable. Roche J at p. 719, agreed 'that the onus on a person relying on an exception relieving him from liability did not go so far as to make him prove all the circumstances which could explain an obscure situation', but he must affirmatively prove that he was not negligent. 'Here there was not only a duty to take general care in providing watchmen but also to take special care in seeing that the watching was vigilantly carried out. That the defendants had not done.'

11.4.2   THE CATALOGUE OF EXCEPTED PERILS IN THE RULES

It is now convenient to describe the individual exceptions granted to the shipowner by Art. IV, Rule 2 of the Schedule to the Carriage of Goods by Sea Act.

---

62 *Gosse Millard* v. *Canadian Government Merchant Marine* [1929] A.C. 223.
63 (1926), 42 T.L.R. 717 a decision on the original Hague Rules of 1921.

(I)   ACT, NEGLECT OR DEFAULT

'Act, neglect or default of the master, mariner, pilot, or servants of the carrier in the navigation or in the management of the ship.'

Here the words 'management of the ship' have given rise to important litigation. The difficulty of this clause lies in the fact that so many things are done on a ship in the course of its voyage that it is sometimes not easy to say whether any one act was done in the course of the management of the ship. We might derive some guidance from the consideration that the immunities granted to the carrier under the Hague–Visby Rules concern only the transport and not the storekeeper aspect of the carriage. In principle, therefore, no act, neglect or default can be covered by this clause unless it is one touching solely the safety of the ship and not directly or indirectly the preservation of the cargo. Accordingly, cases decided before the Act came into force should be treated with some care, for it is doubtful whether the decisions would be the same at the present day.

Illustration 1: *Gosse Millard* v. *Canadian Government Merchant Marine* [64]
A ship with a cargo of tinplates on board was damaged during the voyage. It was necessary to execute repairs at an intermediate port and these lasted for some weeks. While the repairs were being executed the hatches were left open to allow the workmen to pass in and out of the hold. Through the negligence of the shipowners' servants the hatches were not even covered when it rained so that rainwater fell into the hold and damaged the cargo.

Held: The shipowners were liable. The negligence of not covering the hatches had nothing to do with the management of the ship. 'Management of the ship' does not go much, if at all, beyond navigation. It certainly does not include stowage.

Illustration 2: *Foreman* v. *Federal Steam Navigation Co.* [65]
The servants of the shipowner were negligent in handling the refrigerating machinery.

Held: This was not negligence in the management of the ship, and the shipowners were liable.

It was rightly stressed in the judgments just referred to that if a wider construction were applied the carrier's position would be the same as, if

64 [1929] A.C. 223.
65 [1928] 2 K.B. 424.

no better than, under the voluntary bills of lading before the Act. This clause applies, for instance, if the steering gear breaks down owing to a fault in the management.[66] It is doubtful whether it covers neglect in the management of refrigerating machinery, which is used not only for the cargo, but also for the ship's stores.[67] Even where the negligence concerns navigation this clause will not protect an owner who has broken the warranty of seaworthiness, provided the latter has been a cause of the disaster.[68]

(II)   FIRE

This usual bill of lading exception will not normally add to the protection of an owner of a British ship, in view of the statutory protection granted by s. 502 of the Merchant Shipping Act 1894. That section, however, only applies where the fire takes place on board ship and will not, therefore, protect the carrier when the damage is caused, for example, by a fire on a lighter alongside: in these circumstances, the carrier will resort to his Hague–Visby Rules exception under Art. IV(2)(b) if the Rules apply. In the majority of cases, though, damage by fire on British ships is covered by the exception in s. 502, which currently excludes liability where the carrier can prove that the fire took place without the owner's actual fault or privity. The owner's position will improve considerably when s. 18 of the Merchant Shipping Act 1979 replaces s. 502 of the 1894 Act, on 1 December 1986, for under the new Act, the onus of proof is shifted to the cargo-owner, who will need to prove that the loss was caused through the owner's 'personal act or omission, committed with the intent to cause such loss, or recklessly and with knowledge that such loss would probably result'.[69]

(III)   PERILS OF THE SEA

'Perils, dangers, and accidents of the sea or other navigable waters.' This is in practice much the most important exception: it was in the early times the only one commonly dealt with. A peril of the seas is

---

66 *Bulgaris* v. *Bunge & Co.* (1932) 49 T.L.R. 237.
67 *Rowson* v. *Atlantic Transport Co.*, [1903] 2 K.B. 666. It was decided that the care of refrigerators, which were used also for ship's stores, came under management of the ship; but that case was before the Hague Rules, and since their enactment the authority of this case is somewhat impaired.
68 *Smith, Hogg & Co.* v. *Black Sea and Baltic General Ins. Co.*, [1940] A.C. 997, 1001, 1007.
69 For further discussion of the implications of this change, see *infra*, Section 22.3.4.

some occurrence of a fortuitous and accidental character of a type which is peculiarly liable to occur at sea. As Lord Herschell said,[70]

' "perils of the sea" does not cover every accident or casualty which may happen to the subject-matter (of the carriage) on the sea ... not every loss or damage of which the sea is the immediate cause is covered by these words. They do not protect ... against that natural and inevitable action of the winds and waves, which results in what may be described as wear and tear. There must be some casualty, something which could not be foreseen as one of the necessary incidents of the adventure.'

These words were spoken in an insurance case, but 'perils of the sea' has the same meaning in policies of marine insurance and in bills of lading. The subject of perils of the seas is naturally of great importance in the law of marine insurance where perils of the seas is the principal risk covered. It will be discussed further in Part 4.

(IV)   OTHER NAMED EXCEPTIONS

Paragraphs (d) to (p) contain exceptions in case of Act of God, act of war, or public enemies, arrest or restraint of princes, rulers or people, or seizure under legal process; quarantine restrictions, act or omission of the shipper or owner of the goods, his agent or representative; strikes or lock-outs or stoppage or restraint of labour from whatever cause, whether partial or general; riots and civil commotions; saving or attempting to save life or property at sea; wastage in bulk or weight, or any other loss or damage arising from inherent defect, quality, or vice of the goods; insufficiency of packing or marks, and latent defects not discoverable by due diligence, for instance, where goods are in a container.[71] Many of these expressions explain themselves, but it will be convenient to discuss a few of them.

The term 'act of war' is wider than the 'Queen's enemies' clause, which is common in British charterparties, since it includes acts of war where the carrying ship is neutral. It is narrower than the words 'consequences of hostilities or warlike operations'; for it includes only direct consequences and not accidents only indirectly connected with a

70 *Wilson, Sons & Co.* v. *Owners of Cargo Per Xantho* (1887) 12 App. Cas. 503, at p. 509.
71 *Scrutton* (1984), p. 385.

war, e.g. a collision with a warship proceeding to her station in war-time.[72]

Some difficulty may be experienced with the strike exception. In charterparties this clause can be relied on only if the stoppage is 'a general concerted refusal by workmen to work in consequence of an alleged grievance'.[73] It does not cover men leaving work for fear of disease.[74] The present exception clause, however, expressly mentions partial strikes and is thus far certainly wider. In addition, it would seem that in respect of the Hague–Visby Rules also such strikes which are not genuine labour disputes would excuse the shipowner since the clause mentions strikes arising 'from whatever cause'.

A strike, however, is liable to affect not only the cargo-owner whose cargo cannot be loaded or discharged in time, but also the shipowner whose ship is held up in port. Not only is the ship unable to earn money, but its owner also incurs heavy out-of-pocket expenses, since he must go on paying wages to his crew and dues to the port authorities. Small wonder that shipowners have tried to reduce such losses by inserting a clause in the bill of lading, allowing them to discharge cargo for a strike-bound port at 'any safe or convenient port'. The clause is known as the *Caspiana* clause, from the name of the ship in the leading case on the construction of the clause.[75] In that case a cargo destined for London, which was then strike-bound, was carried on to a continental port, from where the consignee shipped it to London when the strike was over. He tried unsuccessfully to recover the expenses thus incurred from the shipowner.

The case raises important legal problems which go beyond the scope of this work. From a business point of view, the *Caspiana* clause has the drawback of saddling the bill of lading holder with incalculable expenses; bankers, in particular were advised[76] to refuse bills with that clause offered to them as security for commercial credits, at any rate where no other security was offered. The position may have been altered, though perhaps inadvertently,[77] by the Uniform Customs and

72 *Scrutton* (1984), p. 449.
73 Per Sankey J in *Williams* v. *N.V. Berghuys* (1915) 21 Com. Cas. 253, at 257.
74 *Stephens* v. *Harris* (1887) 56 L.J.Q.B. 516.
75 *G.H. Renton & Co.* v. *Palmyra Trading Corporation* [1956] 3 All E.R. 957.
76 See A.G. Davis, *The Law Relating to Commercial Letters of Credit*, 1963, at p. 159.
77 This article, which did not appear in the previous version of the UCP, seems to have been intended to cover multimodal transport, where the final destination is unlikely to be the port of discharge. The section, indeed, appears to be a consequential extension of Art. 25(b)(iii), which applies an identical rule to transport documents other than marine bills of lading.

Practice for Documentary Credits (1983), which provide in Art. 26(b)(iii) that banks will not reject, unless otherwise stipulated in the credit, a bill of lading indicating a place of final destination different from the port of discharge. Whatever the position of traders and bankers holding bills containing the *Caspiana* clause, shipowners have resolved any difficulties by taking out cover provided for the purpose by the Shipowners Mutual Strike Insurance Association (Bermuda Ltd).

(V)   THE GENERAL EXCEPTION: 'ANY OTHER CAUSE . . '

This catalogue is followed by a general clause: 'Any other cause arising without the actual fault or privity of the carrier, and[78] without the fault or neglect of the agents or servants of the carrier.' The words 'any other cause' in this clause are very wide, but they are not intended to give protection against all risks. They are construed according to a well-known rule, called *ejusdem generis*. This rule provides that where special words are followed and amplified by general words the latter are to be confined in their application to things of the same kind *ejusdem generis* as the preceding specific words. In the words of Scrutton,[79] 'The question is whether a particular thing is within the *genus* that comprises the specific things. It is not a question whether the particular thing is like one or other of the specified things. The more diverse the specified things the wider must be the *genus* that is to include them: and by reason of the diversity of the *genus* that includes them may include something that is not like any one of the specified things.' Here the specific words are so numerous that it should be very difficult to find an all-embracing *genus*. For this reason it has been suggested that it is 'necessary to give these words the wider interpretation and thus to exclude the responsibility of the carrier in all cases where neither he nor his servants are at fault'.[80]

Moreover, difficulties have sometimes arisen in connection with this clause with regard to the words 'servants of the carrier'. Generally, a servant is said to be a person working under the principal's control. The word 'servant', therefore, does not include an independent contractor, who is his own master as regards control and arrangement of the work.

---

78 The Act reads 'or', but it was laid down in *Hourani* v. *Harrison* (1927) 32 Com. Cas. 305, that this is an error and should read 'and'.

79 p. 218.

80 *Scrutton* (1984), p. 450.

In respect of the present clause 'servant' would thus not include stevedores, who are independent contractors: the carrier would consequently never be held liable for losses caused by independent contractors, so long as he could prove that his own servants or agents were blameless. On the other hand it has been said that[81] 'both at common law and by Rule 2 of Article III the carrier's duty was to "discharge" the goods which he had carried, and if he chose to employ an independent contractor to carry out the duty for him the independent contractor became his agent or servant within the meaning of the subsection'.

The courts have sought to reconcile these opposing principles by drawing a subtle distinction of questionable merit. An independent contractor is treated as a servant or agent for the purposes of Art. IV(2)(q) only if he causes loss while performing the tasks for which he was engaged: in such circumstances, the carrier will be deprived of his protection under Art. IV(2)(q) if he cannot prove that the independent contractor was blameless. On the other hand, if the loss arose through an action which did not come within the independent contractor's remit, then under general principles, the carrier is not liable for such loss, so long as he can prove that his servants and agents, properly so called, were not to blame.

Illustration: *Leesh River Tea Co. v. British India Steam Navigation Co.*[82]
When calling at an intermediate port to discharge some cargo and load some fresh cargo, the shipowner employed a stevedoring company. One of its servants stole a brass plate, which was a cover giving access to a storm valve and removal of which was liable to admit seawater to the hold. The theft was not discovered because the opening was overlaid by fresh cargo, and the ship accordingly sailed in an unseaworthy condition. Water entered the hold, and the owner of the original cargo suffered damage. The cargo-owner sued for damages, and the shipowner pleaded in defence that the damage had occurred without the actual fault or neglect of his servants or agents.

Held: The court upheld this defence, Sellers LJ saying (at p. 597) that 'the circumstances here seem to create one of the perhaps rare occasions when Art. IV, Rule 2(q) can be invoked'.

81 *Per* Mackinnon J in *Heyn* v. *Ocean Steamship Co.* (1927) 43 T.L.R. 358.
82 [1966] 3 All E.R. 593.

Where, as in *Heyn* v. *Ocean Steamship Co.*,[83] stevedores employed to handle cargo stole cargo the defence was not available to the shipowner. In the *Leesh* case, however, the thief's employment had merely provided him with the opportunity to steal the coverplate; the theft was not done for the purpose of unloading or loading. Accordingly, the thief in this case was not the shipowner's agent when he stole.

11.5   LIMITATION OF LIABILITY UNDER THE HAGUE–VISBY RULES

Whenever the carrier falls short of performing his duties prescribed in Art. III he must compensate the cargo-owner for the latter's loss, the value of the goods at the point of discharge being the measure. But this does not mean full compensation, at any rate, in the ordinary way. In common with international conventions relating to carriage by land and by air, a maximum liability has been laid down so as not to inflict on the carrier crippling losses. This is one of the reasons why cargo-owners almost invariably insure cargoes in their own names, thus covering the margin between limited compensation and true value.

The consignor can, of course, before shipment, declare the nature of the cargo and its value and insist on this declaration being included in the bill of lading. In that case any loss must be fully paid for, unless the carrier disproves the valuation.[84] But where the consignor simply fails to make that declaration or the carrier refuses to carry the goods on those terms, the maximum amount which the carrier is bound to pay in the event of loss or damage is 666.7 units of account per package or unit or two units of account per kilo in gross weight carried, whichever is the higher. The trouble will sometimes be that the weight of a package or unit is not known. The unit of account here referred to is the special drawing right of the International Monetary Fund, which establishes its value from day to day.[85] The SDR replaces the Poincaré franc used by the Hague-Visby Rules and the sterling amounts used by the Hague Rules. Care should be taken to use the appropriate unit of limitation operating under the relevant convention applying to each case.[86]

83 *Supra*, fn. 81.
84 Art. IV, Rule 5(a), (f) and (h).
85 One SDR was equivalent to £0.760157 on 13 September, 1985.
86 See Chapter 10, fn. 10.

United Kingdom courts have rarely had occasion to interpret the corresponding clause in the earlier version of the Hague Rules.[87] Other countries have had a more confusing experience in that the terms 'unit' and 'package' were variously defined. These problems of interpretation can only be referred to briefly in this work.

In the first place, it must be said that while the weight limitation is clearly more appropriate in bulk cargoes, this does not preclude its use in the case of pieces of cargo shipped individually or collectively. The choice of limitation – package/unit or weight – depends on the mathematical result ('whichever is the higher') and not on the type of cargo. Thus in the case of a piece of equipment weighing more than 333.3 kilos, it is clear that the applicable method of computation is the weight limitation. There is said, however, to be a further complication: in the case, say, of bagged sugar, which of the two figures is to apply, the package/unit limit, based on the number of bags, or the weight unit, based on the overall weight? Mr Diamond[88] suggests that 'this question ought to be answered by reference to the bill of lading', i.e. where the bill gives the number of bags the package/unit limit is used, and when it does not the weight limit is used. The previous edition of this work adopted this view; it is suggested with respect, however, that the plain wording of the Rules dictates an answer which is in terms independent of the bill of lading and based simply on giving the greater award of damages to the cargo-owner.

The container presents a similar problem. Is it a package, or are the parcels stowed in it packages? In the former case compensation may well be derisory.

The Hague–Visby Rules adopt the common-sense solution.[89] They provide: 'Where a container, pallet or similar article of transport[90] is used to consolidate goods, the number of packages or units enumerated in the bill of lading as packed in such article of transport shall be deemed the number of packages or units for the purpose of this paragraph as far as these packages or units are concerned. Except as aforesaid such article of transport shall be considered the package or unit.'

Thus where the bill of lading is made out in respect of 'one container containing typewriters', the 666.67 or 2 units of account, as the case may be, need be paid only once; but where the bill of lading is for 'one

---

87 One example is *Studebaker Distributors Ltd* v. *Charlton Steam Shipping Company* [1938] K.B. 459.
88 Diamond, *loc. cit.*, 12.
89 Art. IV, Rule 5(c).
90 In a proper case this can cover LASH (lighter aboard ship) and BACAT (barge aboard catamaran).

container containing 100 typewriters' we have 100 packages, and in an extreme case 100 times the maximum liability.

There is another problem relating to containers to which, given the scope of this work, only brief reference can be made.[91] Bills of lading covering goods packed in containers frequently describe the cargo as 'one container said to contain 100 typewriters'. This type of description raises two questions which ought to be kept distinct. The first is whether the 'said to contain' description weakens the strength of the carrier's representation in the bill of lading as to the quantity of goods shipped: we shall see[92] that as between the shipowner and the shipper, the figure given in the bill constitutes prima facie evidence that goods were shipped on board in that quantity; whereas as between the shipowner and the endorsee of the bill, the figure constitutes conclusive evidence of that fact[93] where the Hague–Visby Rules apply. The problem raised by the 'said to contain' clause in this context is whether it alters this position in any way: suffice it to say at this juncture that the better opinion appears to be that it does not. The second question relates specifically to the issue of limitation here under discussion: where the bill says 'one container said to contain 100 typewriters', are we to use 1 or 100 as our multiplier for the purposes of Art. IV 5(c)? If the 'said to contain' clause is seen as an attempt to avoid the rigours of Art. IV 5(c) by suggesting a multiplier of 1 for limitation purposes while in the same breath giving the impression that the bill gives a representation that 100 typewriters have been shipped, then it would appear that the clause does not alter the operation of Art. IV 5(c): that is to say, once the figure 100 is mentioned, then that figure is the operative figure for limitation purposes. Three arguments support this view. The Rules give the carrier the opportunity not to enumerate the quantity of goods shipped where he is in no position so to emunerate:[94] where this is the position, the carrier ought to exercise that option rather than enumerate 100 typewriters and then insist that what was really meant was one container. In so far as the 'said to contain' clause is used as a device to reduce the amount of damages recoverable under Art. IV, the clause can be struck down by Art. III 8, which prohibits clauses lessening liability under the Rules. Moreover, it appears[95] that even if the clause alters the evidentiary strength of the representation in the bill

91 For a detailed study of this issue, see Schacar, The Container Bill of Lading as a Receipt (1978-9), 10 J.M.L.C. 39.
92 Section 13.1.
93 Art. III.4, Hague–Visby Rules.
94 Art. III.3.
95 Diamond, loc. cit., p. 13.

of lading, this would not necessarily mean that the lower multiplier is to be preferred to the higher for purposes of limitation: Art. IV 5(c) speaks simply of 'packages or units enumerated in the bill of lading as packed', and not of packages warranted to have been shipped.

Limitation of liability is a privilege, which must not be enjoyed by the undeserving. The Rules, therefore, provide[96] that 'neither the carrier nor the ship shall be entitled to the benefit of the limitation of liability . . . if it is proved that the damage resulted from an act or omission of the carrier done with intent to cause damage, or recklessly and with knowledge that damage would probably result'.

The words describing such reprehensible conduct are the modern version, more generally understood, of what in England in the past, in a related context, was described as wilful misconduct. The convention regulating international carriage of goods by air[97] contains words identical to those used by the Hague–Visby Rules to characterize the acts or omissions of the carrier; the convention regulating international carriage of goods by road[98] uses the words 'wilful misconduct'. Even so there is a distinction to be drawn in this regard between the road and air conventions and the sea convention. The air and road carrier loses the limitation benefit not only when he himself is guilty of wilful misconduct, but also when his servants or agents can be blamed in the same way. This is an important difference, clearly intended by those drafting the Hague–Visby Rules, for the Athens Convention on the carriage of passengers[99] also leaves out the words 'or his servants or agents' used in the two other conventions. Had the omission of those words in the Hague–Visby Rules been by inadvertence it can be assumed that those drafting the Athens Convention would have restored them.

Another difference between the two sets of conventions has also been noticed.[1] While wilful misconduct deprives the air and road carrier not only of his limitation benefit, but also of his right to plead the defences otherwise at his disposal, it deprives the sea carrier only of his limitation benefit. This distinction, it is submitted, is one which makes no practical difference whatsoever. The question whether the carrier is to be deprived of the benefit of limitation because of wilful misconduct assumes that he has been found to be liable for the loss, limitation only

96 Art. IV, Rule 5(e).
97 The Warsaw Convention, brought into force in the UK by the Carriage by Air Act 1961.
98 The CMR Geneva Convention, brought into force in the UK by the Carriage of Goods by Road Act 1965.
99 See Chapter 18, infra.
 1 Scrutton (1984), p. 456.

arising as an issue after liability has been established. Once liability has been established, it must follow that none of the exceptions in Art. IV 2 applies: if one of the exceptions did apply, then there would be no liability, and no question of limitation – much less of breaking it – would arise. Thus Art IV. 5(e) in terms deprives the carrier of limitation not because the exceptions are intended to survive wilful misconduct, but only because the exceptions are *ex hypothesi* inapplicable if and when the question of breaking limitation arises for discussion. Again, in common with road and air carriers, the sea carrier guilty of wilful misconduct is protected by the Hague–Visby time-bar[2] not because Art. IV 5(e) does not in terms deprive him of its protection, but because the time-bar goes to liability and its effects are therefore determined long before the issue of limitation – and of the possiblity of breaking it – arises.

The real difficulty in construing this provision is presented by the words 'act or omission *of the carrier*' and 'knowledge that damage would probably result'. The carrier himself is, of course, almost invariably a company, and the wilful misconduct leading to the carrier's loss of the protection of limitation must be attributed to an individual. The question as to how this is done will be dealt with later. The requirement of 'knowledge that damage would probably result' again causes problems of interpretation: while it is clear that putting a cargo of bundles of paper on deck during a storm would be accompanied by the necessary mental element, the application of those words to any particular set of facts is not always so easy. These questions are discussed more fully elsewhere.[3]

The mental elements described in Art IV 5(e) deprive not only the carrier but also his servants or agents where they are guilty of wilful misconduct. For under the Rules they too can be sued in tort. Article IV-bis envisages actions against the carrier's servants or agents[4] and allows them to plead their employer's defences. They lose this right, and also the limitation privilege, if they are guilty of wilful misconduct. The defences which they may lose through such conduct are those of negligence in the navigation or management of the ship and fire in Art. IV, Rule 2, and of the time-bar in Art. III, Rule 6.[5]

2 Diamond, *loc. cit.,* 20.
3 See Sections 22.2.4 and 22.3.4.
4 The benefit of Art. IV-bis, Rule 2 is not conferred on independent contractors, such as stevedores, unless they are direct employees of the carrier, or on managing or ship's agents. The position of stevedores is examined at greater length at Chapter 20.
5 Diamond, *loc. cit.,* p. 19.

If there is no wilful misconduct we may get the odd result that the master can rely on his employer's defences while the employer himself cannot do so. Suppose loss of goods is due to a combination of negligent navigation and unseaworthiness of the ship, the owner having failed to exercise due diligence to make the ship seaworthy. In that event the owner has no defence to the cargo-owner's action, but the master can successfully plead his employer's defence of negligent navigation.[6]

A long time ago an ingenious attempt was made to obtain unlimited damages by suing the carrier in tort, thus excluding the possibility of the carrier's pleading his contractual defences. But the court would not listen to this argument. To allow such actions, it was held, would amount to defeating the spirit of the Hague Rules.[7] Now Art. IV-bis, Rule 1 provides expressly that the carrier or his servants can plead all defences granted by the Rules and also limit the liability whether the action is framed in contract or in tort.

11.6 LOWER LIABILITY BY SPECIAL CONTRACT

Only under one condition is the shipowner permitted, if he desires it, to reduce his liability within the general limits of public policy, namely, where no bill of lading is issued in respect of the cargo, but a document marked 'non-negotiable' and containing the special conditions under which the carriage will be performed.[8] The special conditions may refer to the carrier's rights and responsibilities in respect of such goods, or to the obligations with regard to seaworthiness of the vessel and the exercise of due diligence by his servants or agents.

If the article stopped short here there would be the obvious danger of shipowners endeavouring to make a habit of entering into special contracts. To prevent such possible abuse Art. VI contains a proviso according to which a special contract is only permissible provided the shipments are not 'ordinary commercial shipments made in the ordinary course of trade, but only other shipments where the character or condition of the property to be carried, or the circumstances, terms and conditions under which the carriage is to be performed, are such as

6 Diamond, *loc. cit.*, p. 19; Art. IV, Rules 1 and 2(a), and IV-bis, Rule 2.
7 *Elder Dempster & Co.* v. *Paterson, Zochonis & Co.*, [1924] A.C. 522.
8 Art. VI.

reasonably to justify a special agreement.[9] As far as we know it has not yet been decided what exactly the term 'ordinary commercial shipment' means. It will in any case be a question of fact to be decided on the evidence. A special contract will be justified by the condition of the goods or by the circumstances under which they are carried. For instance, under Art. IV, Rule 6, the carrier has a right to refuse the carriage of inflammable, explosive or dangerous goods, and that may be an instance where a special contract would be justified.

The reason why the Act prohibits the issue of a negotiable[10] bill of lading where carrier and shipper have made a special contract seems pretty clear. A bill of lading, as we have seen, is transferable. Many persons may become holders of it who have no opportunity of consenting to special conditions. Therefore, where such conditions are made the Act ensures a real agreement between the parties, and prevents the extension of special clauses to unknown persons.

11.7   LIMITATION OF ACTIONS

Generally speaking, English law allows claims for damages to be made at any time within six years, but trade calls for a shorter period, for businessmen must know for certain what claims may be made against them. Actions on many commercial contracts must, therefore, be brought within a far shorter period, and the contract of affreightment is no exception. Clearly, a shipowner will want to make his own inquiries before vital evidence is lost, and to do so claims against him must be made promptly. Indeed, contracts of affreightment frequently provide that claims must be made within one month from the discharge of the cargo or even before its removal from the ship, although no legal proceedings need be begun as early as this. The Carriage of Goods by Sea Act deals with both matters. Where it applies, the consignee or his successor in title must inform in writing the carrier or his agent at the port of discharge of apparent loss or damage, before the goods are removed from the ship; non-apparent damage must be notified within three days of delivery.[11] In the absence of notice, the carrier can treat removal as prima facie evidence of good delivery, so that a consignee who nevertheless later sues the shipowner has a heavy burden of proof to discharge; for not only must he convince the court that loss or

9 Art. VI, proviso.
10 See *Scrutton* (1984), p. 461.
11 Carriage of Goods by Sea Act 1971, Schedule, Art. III, Rule 6.

damage has occurred, but also that this happened while the goods were still on board and not after unloading.

Any action of this kind must be brought within one year of delivery.[12] Where the consignee sues for the loss of goods, time begins to run from the date when the goods should have been delivered. In one set of circumstances the one-year limitation period is extended, namely, where the cargo-owner brings an action for indemnity against a third party.[13] Suppose a carrier has issued a through a bill of lading. At a transit port he ships the goods with a local carrier who issues his bill of lading to the first carrier; the latter is then the cargo-owner *vis-a-vis* the second carrier. If the goods are damaged while in the care of the second carrier their owner must sue the first carrier under the through bill of lading and, supposing this action succeeds, the first carrier can claim that the second carrier indemnifies him. This action for an indemnity is subject to the period of limitation prescribed by the law of the country in which the court hears that case, in any event not less than three-months from the date of the settlement of the first claim.[14]

---

12 *Ibid.* The words are 'suit is brought', which includes, in addition to an action in court, a notice or request for arbitration: *Nea Agrex S.A.* v. *Baltic Shipping Co. Ltd* [1976] 2 All E.R. 842.

13 Art. III, Rule 6-bis.

14 *Scrutton* (1984), p. 442.

12
PRELIMINARY VOYAGE AND LOADING

In the case of charterparty contracts, which are usually made a substantial period in advance of the time fixed for loading, the vessel will very likely be at some other port or even on the high seas when the contract is signed. The ordinary form of charterparty contains a term under which the first duty of the shipowner is to send his vessel to the port of loading. This voyage is called the preliminary voyage. It is necessary from the charterer's point of view that he should be able to calculate the date at which the vessel will reach her loading port so that he may have the cargo prepared. We have already seen[1] that it is for this reason that statements on the position of the vessel at the time of chartering are regarded as conditions. Similarly the law imposes upon the shipowner the obligation to prosecute the preliminary voyage with due or reasonable dispatch.

12.1 CANCELLING DATE

The terms of the charterparty frequently impose the same obligation in some such terms as 'with due dispatch' or 'with all convenient speed', but they may go further and impose a final date by which the vessel must reach her port. This will be construed as a condition, and if it is not complied with the charterer may throw up the contract. Such date is called the 'cancelling date', because its effect is to give to the charterer an option to cancel. It is a question of construction of the charterparty how far, if at all, the application of the 'cancelling date' is affected by the exceptions clause normally found therein.

1 Section 11.2.2.

Illustration: *Smith* v. *Dart*[2]

A charterparty provided for the ship to go to a safe port, to arrive there, and be ready to load by a certain date, and then to proceed on her voyage proper. The charter contained an exception clause protecting the shipowner *inter alia* against delay owing to perils of the sea, and a cancelling clause. Owing to the dangers of the sea the ship, though she had arrived at the loading port by the date fixed in the contract, was not ready to load. Thereupon the charterers cancelled the charterparty. The shipowners, however, contended that they were not entitled to do so as the delay was due to excepted perils.

Held: The charterers were entitled to cancel. The exception clause only protected the shipowners from having to pay damages for delay; it did not apply to the cancelling clause which gave the charterers an absolute right to cancel the charterparty.

In exceptional cases the cancelling clause may be qualified, for instance, by denying a charterer the option to cancel where the ship's late arrival is due to the Queen's enemies. Yet to have this effect, and to exclude the rule in *Smith* v. *Dart*, the qualification must be closely related to the cancelling clause.

Illustration: *Granger* v. *Dent*[3]

The ship was to proceed to a loading port on the coast of Malabar and 'be ready to load the said cargo on or before the 28th day of November, 1827 (unless she shall have been prevented by stress of weather or other unavoidable impediment), then and in such case, it shall be at the option of the (charterers') factors or agents . . . either to load or not to load'. The vessel was delayed first by adverse wind and later by having to call at an intermediate port for repairs to her rudder. The delay could have been avoided by extraordinary measures, such as employing a tug and, later, using ship's boats to speed discharge at the last port before sailing for the loading port.

Held: The cancelling clause could not be exercised, the 'impediment' could not be 'avoided' without unusual exertion, and this the captain was not bound to use.

12.2   EXCEPTION CLAUSES AND THE PRELIMINARY VOYAGE

The exception clause has, however, the very important function of protecting the shipowner against an action for damages for delay at the

2 (1884) 14 QBD 105.
3 (1829) M. & M., 475.

suit of the charterer. This is clear where certain perils are declared in the charterparty to be 'always excepted'.[4] On the other hand, where the contract provided for certain perils to be 'always excepted during the voyage' the matter seemed at one time to be not free from doubt. It was argued that 'voyage' meant the voyage with cargo on board, and did not cover the preliminary voyage. But for some time past it has been held that 'voyage' means the whole chartered voyage, thus covering the preliminary voyage.[5] This stage may be very short, as where the ship is already at the loading port, but has to be moved from her present berth or anchorage to the loading berth. If on this short stage damage befalls the vessel or delay is caused through excepted perils the charterer cannot claim damages.[6]

It should be borne in mind that the exception clause only applies if the ship has actually entered on her chartered voyage. It does not protect the shipowner before that event. Suppose a ship is engaged on a certain chartered voyage when a new charterparty is made, to take effect after the first chartered voyage is performed. The second charter provides for the ship to start loading at a certain date and contains an exception clause. Owing to 'excepted perils' the ship cannot complete her previous charter in time to commence the second charter punctually. In this case the shipowner is not protected. He must pay the second charterer damages for delay – for when the perils occurred the ship was not yet engaged on her chartered voyage.[7]

12.3   NOMINATION OF LOADING PORT

The preliminary voyage will usually be to a port or ports specified in the contract; but the charterparty may give the charterer the option to name a port, or to proceed to a 'port or ports as ordered'; this may be necessary, e.g., if the charterer is not himself the shipper. It will be appreciated that such an option must be exercised within a reasonable time, for if the vessel is kept waiting, heavy overhead charges are incurred. Sometimes the contract will itself specify a period within which it must be exercised. If the charterer fails to give the orders within such period as not to frustrate the commercial object of the charterparty, this would be such a substantial breach of contract as to give the

---

4 *Carver* (1982), para. 628.
5 *Hudson* v. *Hill* (1874) 43 L.J. C.P. 273.
6 *Barker* v. *M'Andrew* (1864) 34 L.J. C.P. 191, see especially *per* Willes J, at p. 194.
7 *Harrison* v. *Garthorne* (1872) 26 L.T. 508.

shipowner the right to repudiate, or he may proceed with the contract and hold the charterer liable for any damages which he may suffer.[8]

12.3.1   SAFE PORT

Some ports are notoriously dangerous to shipping under certain conditions of weather and season, and the shipowner invariably protects himself by a term in the contract[9] that the port is to be a 'safe' port. Difficult questions arise with regard to what is a 'safe' port, not least because a port can be unsafe also on political grounds, such as war or blockade.[10]

These questions have recently attracted the attention of the courts largely as a result of the impact on shipping movements in the Gulf of the war between Iran and Iraq. Discussions about the warranty typically start with an examination of its definition given by Sellers LJ in 1958:[11] 'a port will not be safe unless, in the relevant period of time, the particular ship can reach it, use it and return from it without, in the absence of some abnormal occurrence, being exposed to danger which cannot be avoided by good navigation and seamanship'. The main problem has arisen in connection with the words 'the relevant period of time': when should the nominated port be safe? At the time of its nomination, at the time of the vessel's arrival, at both times, or throughout the interval between the two? After the decision of the House of Lords in *The Evia*,[12] the position appears to be that the port must, at the time of nomination, be prospectively safe, that is to say, it must be likely to be safe at the time of arrival. Thus it need not actually be safe at the time of nomination; nor need it be safe before arrival: at both those times, however, it should be likely that it will be safe at the time of arrival. Conversely, if at the time of nomination, the port is prospectively unsafe, the time charterer[13] is in breach of what Lord

---

8 *Sieveking* v. *Maas* (1856) 6 E. & B. 670, considered in *The Timna* [1970] 2 Lloyd's Rep. 409, confirmed at [1971] 2 Lloyd's Rep. 91.

9 It is probably true to say that where the charterer does not expressly undertake to nominate only safe ports, there is an implied obligation so to do: see *Scrutton* (1984), p. 125.

10 See generally, *Scrutton* (1984), p.125 *et seq*, *S.S. Knutsford* v. *Tillmans* [1908] A.C. 406.

11 *The Eastern City, Leeds Shipping Company Ltd* v. *Société Française Bunge* [1958] 2 Lloyd's Rep. 127 at 131.

12 *The Evia, Kodros Shipping Corp.* v. *Empresa Cubana de Fletes,* [1983] 1 AC 736.

13 There is a suggestion in Lord Roskill's speech, *loc. cit.* at 765 that the position might be different in the case of voyage charterparties; but see *Scrutton* (1984) at p. 127.

Roskill called his 'primary obligation' to nominate a safe port; if between nomination and arrival, the nominated port ceases to be prospectively safe, the time-charterer is in breach of what was called his 'secondary obligation' to re-nominate[14] another port, itself prospectively safe at that time. The secondary obligation to re-nominate a port survives entry into a port which, though safe on entry, becomes unsafe after entry, at any rate where it is physically possible for the vessel to leave the first port. Their Lordships' distinction between the primary obligation to nominate, and the secondary to re-nominate, a safe port has helped to focus attention on the options actually available to the vessel in the circumstances of each case: altogether a more fruitful and pragmatic inquiry than the well-nigh insoluble question as to what makes an occurrence abnormal in such a way as to exonerate a charterer from breach of the warranty.[15]

12.3.2   AS NEAR AS SHE CAN SAFELY GET

The obligation to go to a safe port is often qualified by the further proviso 'or as near thereto as she can safely get'. It has been held that a ship can only get to a port 'safely' if she can proceed to and leave the harbour at her laden draught of water. This applies both to loading and discharging. Thus the vessel is not bound to load in port so much of her cargo as will enable her to cross a bar, and the rest outside the harbour; if that procedure is necessary, it is not a port to which the ship can 'safely' get.[16]

12.4   SHIPPER'S DUTY TO LOAD

We have now reached the stage when the preliminary voyage under the charterparty is over and the shipowner has duly provided a vessel ready to load and otherwise complied with the conditions of the charterparty as to seaworthiness and other matters. The position is henceforward,

---

14 Re-nomination might, of course, solve one problem but raise others, to which brief reference was made by Lord Roskill, *loc. cit.* at 765; see again, *Scrutton* (1984) *loc. cit.*

15 Before reaching the House of Lords, two judges, Goff J and Ackner LJ had found the charterer to be in breach, the Iran-Iraq War not being an 'abnormal occurrence', and two, Denning MR and Shaw LJ, had exonerated the charterer, the war being an 'abnormal occurrence'.

16 *Shield* v. *Wilkins* (1850) 5 Ex. 304; *The Alhambra* (1881) 6 P.D. 68.

generally speaking, the same under both types of contract of affreightment, except that some matters arise more commonly under charterparty contracts.

Loading itself falls into several stages, and in order to ascertain whose duty it is, that of the shipper or of the shipowner, to take the next step at any one stage one needs to have regard to the terms of the agreement between the parties and to any applicable custom in the port or the trade. Naturally, the greater part of the burden falls on the shipowner. In order to get a clear idea of the distribution of duties we must keep in mind that there is one dividing line that clearly marks the end of control by shore parties, namely, the ship's rail. Generally speaking, the shipper has to bring the cargo to the ship's rail; it depends on the contract whether the ship's rail must be 'alongside' a quay, or whether the consignor is bound to bring the cargo to the ship in lighters. The greater part of the operation is normally performed by the shipowner after the shipper has brought the cargo 'alongside' to the quay or on to lighters, whichever the contract prescribes.

The most crucial factor in loading as indeed in discharge, is its duration, but before we come to questions of time, we must say something about the nature of the shipper's duty to provide a cargo for loading, and about the position of dangerous goods.

12.4.1   PROVIDE A CARGO

The shipper must provide the amount and, if it is material, the kind of cargo specified in the contract, or he may have to pay damages for space not used; this type of damages is known as dead freight. The cargo must reasonably comply with the terms of the charterparty, the charterer must bring it to the loading place, and he must perform his part of the operation of putting the cargo on board the vessel.

If the charterer refuses to load, the shipowner may treat this as a repudiatory breach of contract,[17] but he may also await the running out of the time allowed for loading, and so give the charterer a chance of changing his mind. The last course may be somewhat perilous, for during the intervening period the contract may become frustrated, or some other occurrence excuse the consignor from the duty to perform his obligations. For example, it has happened that during this time war broke out and frustrated the contemplated voyage. This frustration discharged the contract automatically, and the shipowner had no action for damages against the charterer, which he would have had if he had

17 *Hochster* v. *de la Tour* (1853) 2 E. & B. 678.

accepted the refusal as final.[18] Where the charterparty contains a cancelling date, and the charterer has not supplied a cargo by that time, the shipowner is not at liberty to call upon the charterer to declare whether he will load the vessel or not.[19]

12.4.2   DANGEROUS GOODS

The cargo must not be of a 'dangerous' type, that is, it must not be of a kind which can cause damage to any of the parties engaged in the common adventure of the voyage. It has always been a breach of a shipper's common law duty to ship such goods without disclosing their character.

Illustration: *Bamfield v. Goole & Sheffield Transport Co.*[20]

The defendants delivered to the plaintiff's husband, who was the owner of a barge, a quantity of ferro-silicon for carriage. The goods were delivered as 'general cargo' and the defendants did not know, and could not reasonably be expected to know of the dangerous character of the goods. The same applied to the plaintiff's husband. Owing to poisonous gases which the ferro-silicon gave off the plaintiff's husband was killed, and the plaintiff, who was assisting her husband in the management of the keel, was seriously injured.

Held: The defendants were liable. In the first place they should have described the cargo as 'ferro-silicon' and not as 'general cargo'. Moreover (*per* Fletcher Moulton LJ, and Farwell LJ), a consignor impliedly warrants that the goods are not dangerous unless the carrier knows or ought to know of their dangerous character.

The Merchant Shipping Act 1894[21] also makes provision for such cases. If the shipment of dangerous[22] goods is desired, the shipper must distinctly mark their nature on the outside of each package and give written notice to the shipowner or master of their dangerous character, as well as the name and address of the sender. A penalty may be imposed in the event of a breach of that duty, and a person knowingly sending dangerous goods under a false description also incurs a penalty.[23] If

18 *Avery* v. *Bowden* (1856) 6 E. & B. 953, 962.
19 *Moel Tryvan S.S. Co.* v. *Weir* [1910] 2 K.B. 844; *Scrutton* (1984), p.123.
20 [1910] 2 K.B. 94.
21 S. 446 *et seq.*; and Merchant Shipping (Safety Convention) Act 1949, ss. 23, 24, and the current regulations thereunder, 1981 (S.I. No. 1747), 1986 (S.I. No. 1069).
22 S. 446(3) M.S.A. 1894.
23 S.447, M.S.A. 1894.

dangerous goods are shipped without having been marked and their nature is discovered during the voyage, the master may throw them overboard, or an Admiralty Court may direct how they shall be disposed of.[24]

The Hague–Visby Rules go even further. Under Art. IV Rule 6, 'inflammable explosive or dangerous' goods taken on board without knowledge of their nature and character, and without the consent of the master or of the carrier or his agent, may be landed, destroyed or rendered innocuous anywhere without any right of the goods' owner to claim compensation. Moreover, 'the shipper of such goods shall be liable for all damages and expenses directly or indirectly arising out of, or resulting from, such shipment'. It has even been decided that goods may be dangerous though they are not inflammable or explosive or noxious, but only endanger the free movement of the ship and cause unreasonable delay.

Illustration: *Mitchell, Cotts & Co. v. Steel Bros. & Co.*[25]

A cargo of rice was shipped from England to Piraeus. The shippers knew that it could not be discharged there without the permission of the British Government. This permission had not been given on shipment, but the shippers thought they might procure it in time. In fact it was not given at all, and the ship was in consequence delayed. The shipowner did not know, and could not reasonably be expected to know, that permission was necessary.

Held: The delay arose from breach by the shippers of their duty towards the shipowner. The latter was entitled to claim damages for the delay.

12.5 TIME TAKEN FOR LOADING

Naturally, and especially in modern times, the period for loading is carefully regulated. Freight rates are closely calculated, and the overhead expenses incurred during even a short delay in loading or discharging would soon eat up the shipowner's profits, except, that is, in time charters, where the charterer pays by time and where consequently the shipowner is not as interested as he would otherwise be in delays caused by the charterers. Thus voyage charters[26] invariably, and

24 *Ibid.*, ss. 448, 449.
25 [1916] 2 K.B. 610. Merchant Shipping (Dangerous Goods) Regulations 1981 (S.I. No. 1747), 1986 (S.I. No. 1069).
26 See Gencon cl. 6 and 7 in Appendix 5.

bills of lading[27] on occasion, place the responsibility for dispatch on the shipper and, with certain limitations which we shall discuss, make him responsible for such delays as may occur. This is done through the use of clauses providing for laytime, imposing liability for demurrage and allowing for payment of dispatch-money. Stated briefly, laytime is the period which the cargo-owner can use for loading and/or discharge. Should more time be used than the period allotted, the cargo-owner may be liable for demurrage, an amount of liquidated damages stipulated in the contract. On the other hand, should a period shorter than the laytime be used, the cargo-owner may be entitled to dispatch-money, payable by the carrier generally at half the rate at which demurrage is calculated.

12.5.1   WHEN LAYTIME STARTS – THE ARRIVED SHIP PROBLEM

The lay-days begin to run against the shipper as soon as the ship arrives and gives the shipper notice of readiness; they begin to run against the receiver[28] of the goods as soon as the ship arrives. This seems straightforward enough, but the problems caused by congestion in ports require a slightly more elaborate examination of this question. Our starting-point is to bear in mind the existence of two types of voyage-charter, the 'berth' charterparty and the 'port' charterparty. This distinction raises one difference which is interesting as a matter of fact and another which raises somewhat difficult questions of law.

In a 'berth' charterparty, the charterparty will provide for the ship to proceed to a named berth or quay, that is to say to the spot where she can receive the cargo. Here, as soon as the ship arrives at the berth and gives its notice of readiness, where required, the lay-days start running against the shipper who is, at the same time, under a duty to start loading the cargo. However, in large ports and docks it is not always possible for the charterer to name beforehand, months in advance when the charter is made, the precise loading-spot. What he will do is merely to contract for the ship to proceed to a port or dock – hence 'port' charterparty – and to reserve his right of selecting a loading-spot once the ship has arrived at the port. In this case, laytime starts running

---

27 See, for example, cl. 15 in VISCONBILL and additional clause A in CONLINEBILL. Laytime and demurrage clauses could also, of course, be incorporated from a charterparty into a bill of lading, in which case the liability to load within the laytime and to pay demurrage in default is devolved to the bill of lading holder.

28 See *Scrutton* (1984), p. 294.

against the shipper as soon as the ship arrives at the port; however, since he is in no position to ship the goods before the selected loading-spot becomes available, the charterer cannot be said to be under a duty to load until that time. In other words, whereas in a 'berth' charterparty, arrival, commencement of laytime, and the duty to load coincide in time, in a 'port' charterparty they do not: arrival and commencement of laytime coincide, but the duty to load starts later.

We have seen that once the ship has 'arrived', laytime begins to run and on its expiry before loading or discharging is completed the charterer must pay the shipowner demurrage to compensate him for the lost time during which he must pay his crew and other expenses and cannot enter a new contract earning him freight. This is true both of 'berth' and of 'port' charterparties: this, however, is where the similarity ends. While the moment of arrival is evidently clearly discernible in a 'berth' charterparty – the time at which the ship reaches the agreed berth – the moment of arrival is less easily identifiable in a port charterparty. If a port is congested the ship may have to wait a considerable time until she reaches her loading or discharging position, and the question arises which of the parties should bear the risk involved in this waiting period: the owner who must sail to a port as ordered or the charterer who gives the order and might be expected to discover conditions at the port he chooses? In other words, who bears the cost of the waiting time? In the case of congestion in a 'berth' charterparty it is clearly the shipowner who bears the cost, laytime being triggered only on arrival at berth. In a 'port' charterparty it was of crucial importance for the courts to establish precisely the moment of a vessel's arrival.

After some vacillation the legal position was finally determined by the House of Lords in *S.L. Oldendorff & Co. G.m.b.H.* v. *Trade Export S.A.*[29] In that case Lord Reid laid down: 'Before a ship can be said to have arrived at a port she must, if she cannot proceed immediately to a berth, have reached a position within the port where she is at the immediate and effective disposition of the charterer. If she is at a place where waiting ships usually lie, she will be in such a position unless in some extraordinary circumstances proof of which would lie in the charterer.'[30]

In that case, the *Johanna Oldendorff* was held to have arrived at the port of Liverpool/Birkenhead when, by order of the port authority, she had anchored at the Mersey Bar, within the port's legal limits and a usual waiting place.

29 [1974] A.C. 479.
30 *Ibid.* at p. 535.

Being within port limits was clearly crucial to Lord Reid's test for arrival of a vessel. Thus it could be said that the test itself depends on another intractable question, that of defining the limits of a port. Lord Reid, however, was of the view that this would cause little problem, 'except perhaps in some cases'.[31] The limits of a port appear to enclose 'the area within which a port authority exercises its various powers'.[32] Thus, where a ship bound for Brake, one of the four ports on the Weser, in Western Germany, was compelled to wait at anchor at the Weser lightship, which was outside the port limits, she was held not to have arrived, although she had reached the usual waiting area.[33] The position at the Weser ports, as at other ports, is thus difficult, for the owner, by force of circumstances, is prevented from arriving simply because the usual waiting area lies outside the legal limits of the port for which he is bound.

To avoid the loss which delay may cause the shipowner, charterparties often contain a clause by which the charterer agrees to treat the ship as arrived when she reached a waiting area even though it lies outside the port: 'time lost in waiting for berth to count as loading time.'[34] Such a clause exists for the Weser ports but, unluckily for the owner, it had not been inserted in the particular charterparty. This illustrates how alert shore-based shipping staff must be when handling even such a routine transaction as the issuing of a charterparty. On the other hand, where a shipowner does protect his interests by inserting such a clause, the running of time against the shipper remains subject to any exceptions which are included for his benefit in the charterparty. Thus where holidays are excluded from laytime, they are not counted as laytime even where it runs against the shipper under a 'time lost' clause before the arrival of the vessel: the effect of the clause is to work a fiction whereby laytime is considered to have started, not to have ended, with consequent loss of exceptions.[35]

12.5.2   LENGTH OF LAYTIME

The next question is: how much time is the shipper entitled to for his lay-days? The modern tendency is to define this period very carefully,

---

31 Ibid. loc. cit.
32 Ibid. loc. cit.
33 Federal Commerce & Navigation Co. Ltd v. Tradax Export S.A., [1977] 2 All E.R. 849.
34 Gencon, cl. 6. Charterers are sometimes in a position to extract from their shipowner a clause effecting the opposite result: 'delay shall not count as used laytime'. See The Laura Prima [1982] 1 Lloyd's Rep. 1.
35 The Darrah, Aldebaran Compania Maritima v. Aussenhandel A.G. [1977] A.C. 157.

because with a big ship one day either way may mean a substantial sum. Hence the charterparty will normally fix a period of so many days, as 'ten days to load', or, as is more usual, fix a rate for loading, as 'to load at the rate of 200 tons per day', which enables the number of days to be calculated. Such charterparties are called 'fixed time' charterparties.

Owing to the value of time in the case of big ships, numerous points involving fractions of days have been litigated; the following points should be noticed.

(a) Days are whole days, i.e. of twenty-four hours.

(b) A day starts at midnight. This means that the shipper is not bound to pay for the day the ship arrives unless, of course, he uses it. This point, however, may be dealt with by the terms of the charterparty.

(c) Fractions of days count as whole days. This means that if there are ten lay-days and the loading takes ten days and a few hours the shipowner is entitled to damages for one day's delay. Very troublesome questions, however, have arisen in connection with contracts providing for an average rate of loading.[36]

(d) In the absence of contrary stipulation or custom the lay-days run consecutively without intermission, and if loading proves impossible on some of them it is so much the worse for the shipper. It is common, however, to make provision against this in respect particularly of weather and holidays. The most convenient phrase stipulates that the lay-days shall be 'weather working days', which means all days on which work is ordinarily done on the spot, excluding days when weather makes work impossible.

12.5.3   LEVEL OF LIABILITY TO LOAD WITHIN LAYTIME

The obligation to load within the lay-days provided by a fixed time charterparty is absolute, subject to any mitigating exceptions in the contract. This means that, in the ordinary way, the charterer must pay demurrage though he is prevented from loading by causes over which he has no control, in other words, where there exists an impossibility.[37] For instance, demurrage has to be paid where the delay was caused by other shippers not getting their goods out of the way in time for the charterer to commence operations.[38]

36 *Yeoman* v. *The King* [1904] 2 K.B. 429; *Houlder* v. *Weir* [1905] 2 K.B. 267.
37 *Postlethwaite* v. *Freeland* (1880) 5 App. Cas. 599, at p. 608.
38 *Porteus* v. *Watney* (1878) 3 Q.B.D. 223, 534.

On the other hand, the duty to load within the laytime is not so strict as to impose an unreasonable burden on the charterer.

Illustration: *Lewis v. Dreyfus*[39]

A ship was chartered to load at a port where there existed three different methods of loading. A ship might lie in the river and load from lighters. Secondly she might go into dock and load from the dock warehouse; thirdly, she might lie alongside a bank of the river and load by manual labour. The charterers exercised their option in favour of the first method. Owing to frost a temporary delay occurred in the process of loading. Had the charterers switched over to one of the other methods the frost would not have prevented the operations, but they did not do so. The shipowners claimed demurrage, but the charterers relied on a clause in the charterparty according to which detention by frost or ice was not to count as lay-days. The shipowners replied that the charterers could have prevented the delay by choosing another method, and could therefore not rely on the clause.

Held: Action dismissed. Once the charterers had exercised their option and had selected a method they were not bound to avoid a mere temporary obstruction by adopting another method. Even if they had been bound to select another method they would have been entitled to a reasonable time in which to change their plans. No demurrage would become payable until that reasonable time had expired. In the present case the obstruction by frost was removed before a reasonable time had elapsed.

Just as in other cases of strict liability, it has become very usual to insert exception clauses in the charterparty. These vary considerably in scope and they have to be construed with great care in each individual case.

In the absence of clear words, showing a contrary intention, an exception clause relates only to such impediments of loading as arise in the port.

Illustration: *Coverdale v. Grant*[40]

A charterparty contained the clause excepting liability for delay owing to 'frost or other unavoidable accidents preventing the loading'. The goods were stored at some distance from the port and it was intended to bring them there by canal. This proved impossible because the canal became frozen over, but frost would not have prevented the loading in the port.

39 (1926) 31 Com. Cas. 239.
40 (1884) 9 App. Cas. 470.

Held: This impediment was not covered by the exception clause, and the shipowner was entitled to demurrage.

Where it is customary to bring the goods from places situated some distance from the port, the exception clause will be given a wider meaning to cover impediments during the transit to the port.

Illustration: *Smith v. Rosario Nitrate Co.*[41]

The exception clause in the charterparty protected the charterer against 'restraint of princes or rulers, political disturbances and impediments'. It was customary in that instance to bring the nitrate direct by rail from the mine to the ship. The cargo arrived late at the port because the railway was in the hands of troops during a civil war, but no such restraint existed at the port.

Held: The charterer was covered by the exception clause and not bound to pay demurrage to the shipowner.[42]

The occurrence of excepted perils does not *ipso facto* discharge the charterer from his duty of paying demurrage. If he claims the protection of an exception clause he must not only prove that one of the excepted perils has occurred, but also that the perils affected the loading operations.

Illustration: *Elswick S.S. Co. v. Montaldi*[43]

A charterparty contained an exception clause protecting a charterer *inter alia* against strikes. After operations had commenced, a strike broke out, but at that moment the charterer was already behind the time. The strike further delayed the work.

Held: The strike excused the charterer only to the extent to which the delay was actually caused by the strike. He was liable to pay demurrage in respect of the previous delay.

12.5.4   ONCE ON DEMURRAGE ALWAYS ON DEMURRAGE

It may happen that after the lay-days have expired and demurrage has become payable, one of the excepted perils arises. It has been argued

41 [1894] 1 Q.B. 174.
42 Other examples in *Carver*, paras. 1063 *et seq.*
43 [1907] 1 K.B. 626.

that in such an event no demurrage is payable while the excepted peril exists. To accept this argument would be unfair to the shipowner, for if the charterer had performed his obligation in time the perils would not have had any effect on the loading. Indeed the courts have rejected the charterer's contention. On the contrary, they have held that in the ordinary way once demurrage has become payable no excepted peril can have any effect on the charterer's duty to pay demurrage. The excepted perils have arisen too late; they no longer present an obstacle to operations which should have been completed before. 'Once on demurrage always on demurrage.' It is otherwise if the exception clause clearly indicates the intention that no demurrage shall fall due in those circumstances.

Illustration: *Lilly & Co. v. Stevenson & Co.*[44]

Under a charterparty a ship was to load a cargo of coal at a certain port in sixty hours. If loading should take longer, demurrage was to be payable at so much per hour 'unless detention arises from a strike … at any works, mine or mines with which the vessel may be booked … lay-days to count from the time the master has got ship reported, berthed, and ready to receive cargo'. The ship was berthed on 14 November, but no cargo was ready for her and loading did not begin until 22 November. Next day a strike of colliery workers broke out and lasted till 11 December. During that period loading was suspended. Loading was completed on 15 December.

Held: The lay-days began on 14 November. Consequently demurrage became payable after 60 hours, i.e. from 16 November at 6 p.m. However, the strike clause protected the charterers from paying demurrage during the continuance of the strike, i.e. from 23 November to 11 December.

12.5.5   NO FIXED TIME AGREED

In the preceding pages we have only dealt with charterparties fixing a definite time for loading. We now turn to those contracts of affreightment where the shipowner has not stipulated for the loading to be completed within a fixed period. This may happen in one of two ways. The charter may be silent altogether on that point, or contain general, indefinite words. For instance, it may be provided that the ship shall be loaded with 'customary dispatch', or 'as fast as steamer can load'.

---

44 (1895) 122 R. 278. The principle applies, it appears, not only to excepted perils, but also to other periods during which laytime does not run: *The Tsukuba Maru* [1979] 1 Lloyd's Rep 459 and *The Altus* [1985] 1 Lloyd's Rep. 423.

In cases of this kind the charterer is not permitted to extend the loading period as long as he likes. The law implies a term in the contract stipulating that the loading should be completed within a reasonable time. What is a reasonable time is always a question of fact. It depends on the existing as opposed to normal circumstances at the loading port and on the custom of the port.[45]

Illustration: *Hulthen* v. *Stewart*[46]

A charterparty provided for the vessel to discharge in London 'with customary steamship dispatch as fast as the steamer can deliver during the working hours of the respective ports, but according to the custom of the respective ports'. The vessel was ordered to the Surrey Docks, which were at that time crowded. There existed a scarcity of quay berths and lighters. The charterers used all reasonable means to expedite discharge.

Held: They were not liable for demurrage.

12.5.6   DEMURRAGE AND DAMAGES FOR DETENTION

As we have seen, most charterparties will give the charterer a fixed period for loading and discharge: the many difficulties which may impede those operations may, however, force the charterer to go beyond the permitted lay-days and two questions will then arise. Firstly, how is the shipowner to be compensated for the delay; secondly, how long a delay should the shipowner tolerate before he orders his vessel away in search of another fixture?

Before we examine these two questions, it would be useful to have a brief look at what the market does. The parties may have agreed in advance that a number of days – commonly called 'demurrage days' – will be available to the charterer. Thus Clause 7 of the Gencon Charter grants the charterer 'ten running days on demurrage at the rate stated . . .' On the other hand, the parties may have stipulated for the payment of demurrage in the charterparty without having fixed a period of extra loading days. Thus Beepeevoy 2 at Clause 18 states simply that 'Charterers shall pay demurrage at the rate of US $ . . . for all time that loading and discharging . . . exceeds the allowed laytime specified in Clause 15 hereof'.

Returning now to the first question we have mentioned, where the lay-days have lapsed, the ship is now said to be 'on demurrage': the

45 *Scrutton* (1984), 320 *et seq.*
46 [1903] A.C. 389.

charterer has now incurred a liability to pay the shipowner the amount agreed in the charterparty as the demurrage rate – in effect an agreement to pay liquidated damages. Where the parties have agreed on a fixed number of demurrage days, the agreed rate of demurrage will govern the charterer's liability for the agreed period; where the parties have not agreed on a fixed number of demurrage days, the agreed demurrage rate may, as we shall see, govern the charterer's liability for a longer period. In either case, however, the charterer may be liable for an amount greater than that provided for as demurrage where loss of another character[47] has been caused through delay. This head of damages – damages awarded for delay outside the demurrage clause – is called damages for detention.

Illustration: *Akt-Reidar* v. *Arcos Ltd*[48]

A ship was chartered for the carriage of a cargo of timber to an English port. The charterparty provided for a fixed loading time and for the payment of demurrage thereafter. The loading time was exceeded. Had the loading been completed within the lay-days, the ship would have been able to load a full and complete cargo for discharge in England. However, because of the delay the ship could only load a lesser amount of timber, if it was to comply with s. 10 of the Merchant Shipping Act 1906, which lays down conditions for the discharge of timber at British ports during a certain part of the year. The charterers admitted liability for demurrage, but the shipowners sued for dead freight in respect of the amount not loaded due to the delay.

Held: The shipowners were entitled to damages as compensation for the additional loss consequent upon detention of the vessel.

The second question we need to consider is whether there comes a time when loading or discharge has gone so far beyond the laytime that the shipowner ought not be be expected to be content with his right to demurrage, but ought to be allowed to order his vessel away in search of a more fruitful fixture. If and when such a time arrives, there then arises an incidental question: in the circumstances envisaged, what compensation can the shipowner claim from the charterer?

Where no 'demurrage days' have been agreed upon, the shipowner can repudiate the charterparty and order his vessel away where the delay is so long that the whole purpose of the contract is defeated.[49] Moreover, in these circumstances, the shipowner is not bound to accept

---

47 *Akt-Reidar* v. *Arcos Ltd* [1927] 1 K.B. 352 at 366, *per* Sargant LJ
48 [1927] 1 K.B. 352.
49 *Universal Cargo Carriers Corporation* v. *Citati* [1957] 2 Q.B. 401.

the liquidated damages fixed in the demurrage clause. He can claim all the damages he has suffered. However, to deprive the charterer of the demurrage clause protection, a very serious matter, the shipowner must clearly terminate the charterparty once it has become clear that the delay for which the charterer is responsible amounts to more than the contemplated delay and in effect constitutes a repudiatory breach of the contract. If, though aware of the repudiatory breach, the shipowner continues the charter he can only claim the agreed demurrage.

Illustration: *Suisse Atlantique v. Rotterdamsche Kolen Centrale*[50]

In December 1956, the owners chartered their ship to charterers for two years to carry coal from the USA to Europe on consecutive voyages. The charterers agreed to load and discharge at specified rates, any extension of time being paid for at the rate of 1000 dollars a day. By September 1957, there had been such exorbitant delay as to entitle the owners to repudiate the contract, but in October they agreed to let the charter run on. Subsequently, the charterers made eight round voyages. In the end the owners, who had in fact suffered damage in excess of the agreed demurrage, claimed the entire damage.

Held: This claim failed, and the charterers need only pay 1000 dollars demurrage for each day lost. Had the owners repudiated the charter in 1957, as they were entitled to do, they would have ended the contract, including its demurrage clause, and could have recovered all the damage they had suffered. The owners had, however, allowed the charter to continue, so that the demurrage clause, with its agreed damages, was preserved.

Where 'demurrage days' have been agreed upon, then it would appear that although the charterer is entitled to the agreed period on demurrage, this period does not circumscribe, without more, the time which he may use for loading or discharge. Before he orders his vessel away, the owner, here too, must be satisfied that the delay is such as to defeat the commercial object of the contract, and this test may require a longer wait than, say, the ten demurrage days provided for in the Gencon charter. Between the lapse of the agreed demurrage days and the time at which the delay becomes repudiatory, it seems here that the shipowner ought not be be restricted to his remedy for demurrage: a charterer on the Gencon form, say, has only 'bought' ten days' worth of delay at the demurrage rate and no more; beyond that , the owner ought to be able to recover the real amount of the loss caused by the detention.

50 [1967] 1 A.C. 361.

When the delay eventually assumes repudiatory proportions, the owner can then elect to terminate the charterparty and sue for damages, again unrestricted by the provision relating to demurrage.

12.6   STOWAGE

Having received the cargo over the ship's rail or otherwise as customary or as provided by the contract it becomes the carrier's duty to stow it. This task was originally performed by the shipowner, but in large modern ships is usually performed by stevedores.[51] Stevedores are experts in loading and discharging cargoes. They are independent contractors, but the carrier cannot avoid the responsibility for stowing the cargo, which is his at common law, by employing an independent contractor unless, of course, his contract enables him to do so. Though the carrier may have to answer the goods' owner, he will in his turn be able to sue the stevedores if they have caused damage to the cargo through their negligence. If the contract of carriage is not the shipowner's contract,[52] the latter may be responsible to the goods' owner for the stevedores' negligence in stowing the cargo.

The shipowner may – and usually does – insert a clause in the bill of lading exempting himself from liability for bad stowage. Where no such exemption is agreed upon the shipper may nevertheless lose his right to recover if he himself superintends the stowage and makes no complaint at all, or complains of some defects and not of those which are patent.[53] Moreover, if the shipper is previously warned how his cargo is going to be stowed and he raises no objection, he cannot afterwards complain of the stowage even if it is bad.[54]

In both of the last-mentioned cases the shipper has waived his remedy, but it would seem that in the absence of express agreement, the consignee or the latter's assignee are not bound by such waiver.[55]

As between shipowner and charterer the question who is responsible for the bad stowage depends on the terms of the charterparty.[56] We need not discuss the cases on this subject in any detail. It will, on the whole,

---

51 See generally Section 20.1, *infra*.
52 See *supra*, Section 10.3.3.
53 *Ohrloff* v. *Briscall* (1866) L.R. 1 P.C. 231; *Upper Egypt Produce Exporters* v. *Santamana* (1923) 14 Ll. L.R. 159, 163.
54 *Major* v. *White* (1835) 7 Car. P. 41.
55 *Upper Egypt Produce Exporters* v. *Santamana, supra; Scrutton* (1984) p. 170; but see *Ohrloff* v. *Briscall, supra.*
56 *Union Castle S.S. Co.* v. *Borderdale Ship Co.* [1919] 1 K.B. 612.

depend on whether the charterer or the shipowner has the right to appoint the stevedores and at whose risk the loading is to be effected. In any case, whoever is primarily liable has a remedy over against the stevedore.

12.6.1 DECK CARGO

In the ordinary way, cargo must be stowed in the holds and other usual carrying places, not on deck, where it is exposed to greater risks.

If nevertheless the carrier does stow goods on deck he prima facie commits a breach of his contractual duty. Should subsequently the goods arrive damaged the exception clauses in the contract will no longer protect him, for these apply only so long as he performs the contract. In that event, since the special contract falls to the ground, the carrier would revert to the position of a common carrier and be liable for loss or damage, unless these are caused by one of the common law exceptions.[57] In this sense, unauthorized carriage of cargo on deck is akin to deviation, and its effect on exception clauses in the contract needs to be considered in the light of developments in the law on deviation.[58]

Certain kinds of bulky cargo, such as timber, railway engines and containers, cannot be, or are not customarily, stowed in the holds. They are carried on deck and are stated in the contract of carriage to be so carried. The Hague–Visby Rules exclude such cargoes from their operation, Art. I(c) saying: ' "goods" includes goods, wares, merchandise, and articles of every kind whatsoever except live animals and cargo which by the contract of carriage is stated as being carried on deck and is so carried'. In other words, where the parties agree on cargo being carried on deck the Rules do not apply, the carriage being governed by the common law, which will allow the parties to agree in the bill of lading on exceptions giving the shipowner a greater degree of protection than that afforded by the Hague–Visby Rules.

This is a curious result and where British law applies, Art. I(c) has been in practice excluded. According to s. 1(6) and (7) of the 1971 Act, where the bill of lading or non-negotiable receipt provides that the Hague–Visby Rules shall govern a contract of carriage relating to live animals or deck cargo, the Rules shall apply 'as if Art. I(c) did not exclude deck cargo and live animals'. These curiously drafted words

---

57 See Section 10.1.3 *supra. Newell* v. *Royal Exchange Company* (1885) 33 W.R. 868
      (C.A.), affirmed *Royal Exchange Company* v. *Dixon* (1886) 12 App. Cas. 11.
58 See Chapter 14 *infra*, particularly fn. 13.

mean in effect: where you have a bill of lading or non-negotiable receipt that expressly declares the Rules the law governing the contract, and that document is made out in respect, say, of railway engines, to be carried on deck, the Rules apply if the engines are so carried. If they are lost or damaged in transit the carrier can rely on his immunities under Art. IV and no more, just as where cargo is carried below deck. He cannot bargain for more extensive relief.

13

THE BILL OF LADING

ONCE the cargo is taken on board, the bill of lading is issued to the shipper. We have already[1] mentioned this document in passing. At this stage it becomes necessary to discuss the law relating thereto in somewhat greater detail.

13.1   THE BILL OF LADING AS A RECEIPT

The original function of the bill of lading was that of a receipt. It commences with the words 'shipped' or 'received', and then proceeds to enumerate the goods according to quantity, description and shipping marks.[2] The bill of lading was originally issued by the master at the time when the goods were shipped. In modern times, however, when the goods are put on board the mate usually issues an informal receipt, which is later exchanged for the bill of lading.[3] Until the issue of the latter the shipowner will usually hold the goods on the terms of his usual bill of lading, and this is sometimes expressly provided for in the mate's receipt.[4] Despite the clear connection between the bill of lading and the mate's receipt there are important distinctions between the two documents to which we shall return in due course.[5]

The receipt function of the bill of lading raises issues which go to the quantity of the goods shipped and to the apparent condition in which they were shipped. We shall be dealing with these two aspects of the receipt function in turn. First, however, a word needs to be said about the legal basis upon which that receipt function rests and about the way in which the law has developed over the years in this regard.

1 Section 10.3.2.
2 See example Appendix 6.
3 See generally *Carver* (1982), para. 416.
4 *De Clermont v. General Steam Navigation Co.* (1891) 7 T.L.R. 187.
5 Section 13.3.4.

13.1.1 EVIDENTIARY VALUE OF THE RECEIPT

Disputes between shipowner and cargo-owner arise perhaps most frequently over the question whether goods have been delivered short, or have been damaged during carriage. It is here that the statements about the goods appearing in the bill of lading become very important. The obligation on the carrier is obviously to deliver what he received as he received it, but just as obviously the next question is – and this presents the real difficulty – on whom does the law place the burden of proof. Since the goods' owner claims that the goods were not delivered as received it is for him to prove this contention, and he can do so most easily by referring to the carrier's receipt for the goods, namely, the bill of lading.

Now a receipt is prima facie evidence of the truth of the statements which it contains. If the person who issued it claims that it is wrong, it is for him to prove the error. The carrier, therefore, who delivers to the cargo-owner a smaller number of packages, or a less weight of goods than was acknowledged in the bill of lading, or goods torn and dirty when he had issued a bill of lading which had made no mention of such defect on receipt, will find it very difficult to resist a claim for damages. In order to do so successfully he must prove affirmatively that the bill of lading was wrong: that he delivered all he received, or that the goods were torn and dirty when received on board the ship. Such proof may be very difficult and expensive, involving perhaps the taking of evidence in a foreign port; it may indeed be unobtainable, in which case liability is effectively established and the carrier can only escape if he can find protection in one of the exceptions applicable to his contract.

Difficult though it may be for the carrier to free himself of the representations on the face of the bill, it was still, before more recent developments in the law, technically possible for him to do so if he could lay his hands on evidence which could unsettle the statements appearing on the bill. Where this occurred, the carrier was at a considerable advantage over the endorsee of the bill, who in the majority of cases was the party who effectively suffered the loss but who again in the majority of cases was the party least able to collect or contradict evidence about the quantity and apparent condition of the goods on shipment.

So far as concerned the apparent condition of the goods on shipment, the common law moved to redress the balance by making the statements in this connection on the bill conclusive in favour of endorsees who could show that they had accepted the bill on the faith of its representation that the cargo was in apparent good order and condition when shipped.

Illustration: *Compañía Vascongada v. Churchill*[6]

Timber shipped under a bill of lading with the clause 'shipped in good order and condition; quality unknown', was in fact badly stained and saturated with petroleum when brought alongside for shipment. This condition was apparent and noticed by the master, but he signed a clean bill.

Held: The words 'good order and condition' amounted to a representation as to the actual appearance of the goods when shipped. The endorsee of the bill of lading had taken it upon the faith of such representation, and therefore the carrier was estopped from denying that the damage was caused on board his vessel. Nor could he rely on the words 'quality unknown'. 'Quality' differed from 'condition'. The latter was something apparent, while the former referred to something that was usually not apparent, at any rate to an unskilled person. The master of a ship is expected to notice the condition of goods, but not their quality.

In spite of such cases, the position of endorsees and of bankers holding bills of lading in security under letters of credit was still not entirely satisfactory. There were still two problems in need of solution. In the first place, it was still possible for the carrier so to phrase his bill of lading as to dilute the strength of its representations in such a way as to make a bill in the hands of the endorsee conclusive evidence of very little at all. Thus in the *Compañía Vascongada* case itself, the carrier attempted to escape liability by pleading a clause in the bill saying 'quality ... unknown' and the attempt was only unsuccessful because Channel J was able to find a distinction between the word 'quality' and the word 'condition'.[7] Secondly, whereas it was clear that endorsees could hold carriers to their bill of lading statements relating to the condition of the goods on shipment, it was not at all beyond dispute whether the same was true of statements relating to the quantity of goods shipped.[8]

Attempts to solve these problems were made first in the Hague Rules, then in the Visby amendments to those Rules.[9] The Hague Rules sought to avoid the first problem described above by stipulating what the bill must say about quantity, order and condition. Thus, in cases where the Rules apply[10] the carrier shall on demand by the shipper issue a bill of lading showing:

6 [1906] I K.B. 237.
7 See *ibid.* at 245.
8 See Section 13.1.2, *infra*.
9 See Section 10.2, *supra*.
10 See Section 10.2.1, *supra*.

(a) the leading marks necessary for identification of the goods;
(b) either the number of packages or pieces, or the quantity or weight, as the case may be;
(c) the apparent order and condition of the goods.[11]

Since it would delay the process of loading considerably if the carrier had to verify all these particulars, the shipper must furnish them to the carrier in writing, and is taken to guarantee that they are correct.[12] Should the carrier, however, have reasonable grounds for suspecting that these particulars are wrong, or have no opportunity of checking them, he need not set them out in the bill of lading.[13]

As far as concerns the second problem we have referred to, the Visby amendments to the Hague Rules made it clear that, where the Rules applied, the binding force accorded to statements as to apparent order and condition by the common law in cases such as *Compañía Vascongada* v. *Churchill*[14] was also to be given to statements as to quantity. Thus, where the Visby Rules apply, proof contradicting statements as to quantity is inadmissible against an endorsee of the bill in good faith.[15]

Now that we have looked at the basis upon which and the contexts within which the bill of lading is considered to be a binding receipt, we shall turn our attention to a number of special problems relating first to quantity then to condition.

13.1.2   STATEMENTS AS TO QUANTITY

(A)   NON-SHIPPED AND PARTIALLY SHIPPED GOODS

We have seen that the reason why a cargo-owner can sue the shipowner on the basis of bill of lading statements as to quantity is that the bill is considered to be a binding receipt or acknowledgement as to shipment on board the carrier's ship. The bill becomes the carrier's receipt as a result of the master's signature: the assumption throughout is that the master acts within the scope of his authority in signing the bill and that therefore the master's bill is the owner's bill.

11 Carriage of Goods By Sea Act 1971, Sch., Art. III, Rule 3.
12 COGSA 1971, Sch., Art. III.5.
13 *Ibid.* III.3.
14 See fn. 6, *supra*.
15 COGSA 1971, Sch., Art. III.4.

This manner of thinking has led to what is known as the rule in *Grant* v. *Norway*:[16] stated briefly, the rule is that the master has authority to bind his owner by his receipt only in cases where he has actually received the goods for carriage.

Illustration: *Grant v. Norway*

The master of a ship signed a bill of lading acknowledging that 12 bales of silk had been shipped in good order and condition. In fact the silk had not been shipped. The merchants to whom the bill of lading was issued endorsed it to the plaintiffs as security for a debt. The debt was not paid, and the plaintiffs sued the shipowner for damages.

Held: The action was dismissed. The master's authority extends only to acts which are usual in the employment of ships. It is not usual that bills of lading are signed for goods not on board the vessel. The master had therefore no authority to sign the bill in question, and his signature did not bind the shipowner, his principal. A bill of lading is not conclusive evidence against the latter.[17]

The rule, though firmly entrenched in the law, has not consistently received unqualified support,[18] the main problem with the rule being that it deprives the endorsee of the protective force of the bill of lading at precisely the time when he needs it most, i.e. when he has innocently purchased a bill of lading and no goods at all are delivered. The distaste generally felt for the rule in *Grant* v. *Norway* has led to three attempts to circumscribe its effect.

Firstly, it would appear possible to argue[19] that the rule in *Grant* v. *Norway* does not apply to circumstances where the shipowner loads part of the cargo onto his vessel: thus in this case, the master's signature would bind the carrier in an action for short delivery.

Illustration: *Rasnoimport v. Guthrie and Co.*[20]

The defendants, acting as agents for the shipowners, signed a bill of lading for 225 bales of rubber shipped in the *Demodocus*. In fact, only 90 bales

16 (1851) 10 C.B. 665.
17 See also *Heskell* v. *Continental Express* [1950] 1 All E.R. 1033, where a shipper sued a ship's loading broker for, inter alia, breach of warranty of authority in issuing a bill of lading for goods which had not been shipped. The shipper failed because there was no contract on which he could have sued the shipowner and therefore no loss ensued from the broker's breach of warranty of authority.
18 See *Scrutton* (1984), p. 112 and Carver in On Some Defects in the Bills of Lading Act 1855 at (1890) 6 L.Q.R. 289, at 302. See also Reynolds at (1967) 83 L.Q.R. 189, *The Nea Tyhi* [1982] 1 Lloyd's Rep. 606 at 610, 1 and The Saudi Crown [1986] 1 Lloyd's Rep. 261.
19 See *Scrutton* (1984) at p. 115, fn. 72; *cf. Carver* (1982) at pp. 73, 4.
20 [1966] 1 Lloyd's Rep. 1.

were shipped, and the plaintiffs, endorsees for value of the bill of lading, claimed damages for the value of the 135 bales which had not been delivered.

Held: The plaintiffs were entitled to recover on the ground of the defendants' breach of warranty of authority, for they only had authority to sign bills of lading for goods actually shipped. It was immaterial that when signing the bill of lading they had been neither negligent nor fraudulent, and had acted according to the practice of the loading port.

This restriction on the rule does not, of course, help endorsees suing carriers in case of non-delivery. Two statutory restrictions, one of more considerable import than the other, were needed to assist such an endorsee. First, the 1968 Visby amendments to the Hague Rules, as we have already seen earlier in this chapter, made conclusive in the hands of endorsees statements as to quantity contained in bills of lading.[21] This, however, does not cover all cases: firstly, of course, carriers are not caught by the effect of Art. III.4 where the Rules do not apply; secondly it is possible, as we shall see later in this chapter, for them to evade the effect of that article where the bill of lading contains a 'weight and quantity unknown' clause. In either of these two cases, it would appear that the endorsee's only remedy lies against the actual signatory of the bill of lading under s. 3 of the Bills of Lading Act 1855 which provides that

'every bill of lading in the hands of a consignee or endorsee for valuable consideration representing goods to have been shipped on board a vessel shall be conclusive evidence of such shipment against the master or other person signing the same, notwithstanding that such goods may not have been shipped, unless such holder of the bill of lading shall have actual notice at the time of receiving the same that the goods had not been in fact laden on board.'

A master faced with an action under this rule can only defend himself by proving that the misrepresentation 'was caused without any default on his part, and wholly by the fraud of the shipper or of the holder, or some other person under whom the holder claims'. If this defence succeeds the consignee or endorsee can sue the person who perpetrated the fraud or deceit. It must be noticed, however, that this liability does not extend to the shipowner: it is a remedy primarily against the master and thus may be of little practical value since the master will rarely be good for the amount required to compensate the receiver of non-delivered goods.

21 COGSA 1971, Sch., Art. III.4.

(B) 'WEIGHT AND QUANTITY UNKNOWN' CLAUSES

We have seen that the binding force which gives value to the receipt function of the bill of lading has been a feature of the document for a very long period. Consequently, carriers have for many years made a practice of inserting in the bill of lading some such term as 'weight and quantity unknown', indicating that the statement as to quantity appearing on the face of the bill is not to be relied upon and thus taking the teeth out of the binding force of the document.

The result at common law is clear: the inclusion of these words in the bill of lading very largely destroys its value as a receipt, except in so far as it remains evidence that some goods have been shipped, goods said by the shipper to amount to the figure mentioned in the bill of lading, but in respect of which the carrier makes no admission as to quantity or weight. The result is that the burden of proving what actually was shipped is shifted back to the shipper.

Illustration: *New Chinese Antimony Company v. Ocean SS Co.*[22]

A bill of lading presented to and signed by the shipowner's agent stated that 937 tons of ore had been shipped on board. The bill of lading contained the clause 'weight, measurement, contents and value...unknown'. A quantity less than 937 tons was delivered and the shipper claimed damages for short delivery.

Held: In view of the 'weight, etc., unknown' clause the bill of lading was not even prima facie evidence against the shipowner that the 937 tons had been shipped, and that the burden of proving how much ore had been shipped was on the shipper.

The plaintiff in *New Chinese Antimony* was the shipper of the goods: it appears that at common law, the endorsee of the bill of lading too is prejudiced by the 'weight and quantity unknown' clause; in the light of such a clause, it is not easy to discover a representation that the goods were shipped in the quantity stated and it seems that there is no such representation favouring the shipper and neither is there one favouring the endorsee.

Where the Hague or Hague–Visby Rules apply, we have seen that the shipper is entitled to demand, under Art. III. 3 of the Rules, the issue of a bill which states, without qualification, 'either the number . . . or the quantity, or weight, as the case may be'. Where the shipper makes such a

22 [1917] 2 K.B. 664.

demand, the carrier must delete the clause here under discussion, and the bill of lading regains its receipt value in the shipper's hands and its conclusive status in the endorsee's hands. The problem is that the Rules give the right to demand compliance with Art. III. 3 to the shipper, who is unlikely to exercise his rights under this article so long as the carrier gives him a bill of lading which he, the shipper, can tender to his buyer for payment of the purchase price for the goods.[23] Where the shipper does not oblige the endorsee by demanding of the carrier a bill complying with Art. III. 3, it would appear that despite the fact that the bill is conclusive evidence in the endorsee's hands, this is of little practical effect as it is only conclusive evidence of what the bill itself says, which in the circumstances is not a lot.

(C) 'SAID TO CONTAIN' CLAUSES

We have seen[24] that bills of lading covering goods carried in containers frequently describe the goods in terms such as 'one container said to contain 100 typewriters'. We said in Chapter 11 that this practice raises two issues, one of which we have already looked at in some detail, i.e. the effect of such a description on limitation of liability. The question which concerns us here is whether description in 'said to contain' terms in any way prejudices the position of the shipper or the receiver of goods by weakening the strength of the representation that, for example, 100 typewriters have been shipped. It is suggested that in either case, the answer, at any rate where English law governs, is that the cargo-owner is prejudiced by the 'said to contain' description, which is to be considered as having the same effect as the 'weight and quantity unknown' clause considered above. Thus as between carrier and shipper, the bill is prima facie evidence that the container is said to contain 100 typewriters, thus making no clear representations that 100 typewriters have been shipped; and as between carrier and endorsee the bill is conclusive evidence again simply of the fact that the container is said to contain 100 typewriters, not of the fact that it does. If this is the correct view, then shippers would be well-advised to exercise their right under Art. III. 3 of the Hague Rules to demand a bill containing a firm representation as to the quantity shipped. It must be said, before leaving this issue, that an alternative view has been cogently put forward

23 It appears from *The Galatia* [1980] 1 All E.R. 501, that such a clause does not entitle a c.i.f. buyer to reject the bill of lading against the seller. See for a closer study of the problem referred to in the text, *Carver* (1982), pp. 365-368.
24 Section 11.5 *supra*.

elsewhere,[25] mainly on three grounds. To allow the carrier to escape
from liability through the subterfuge of a 'said to contain' representation would be 'contrary to the whole economy of the Hague Rules'.[26]
The clause would frustrate the central purpose of the Visby amendment
to Art. III.4 of the Rules, which was intended to improve the position of
endorsees of bills of lading; it would consequently be in breach of Art.
III.8 of the Rules, the provision which avoids contractual clauses
inserted to evade the Rules; finally, it would render otiose the facility
given to the carrier by Art. III.3 of the Rules to make no representation
at all as to quantity where he 'has no reasonable means of checking' that
quantity. While this may be the preferable view in terms of policy, it is
difficult to assert, in the absence of clear judicial authority, that this is
the correct view in English law.

(D) CONCLUSIVE EVIDENCE CLAUSE

Sometimes a 'conclusive evidence clause' is inserted in the bill of lading,
a practice which is common particularly in the wood trade. The effect of
such a clause is to make the quantity as set out in the bill of lading an
admission binding both parties. This means that neither party can go
behind the statement in the bill – by alleging that more or less than
stated was in fact shipped – except, of course, where fraud can be
proved.[27]

13.1.3 APPARENT ORDER AND CONDITION – CLEAN BILLS OF LADING

Bills of lading normally start with the admission that the goods they
cover have been shipped in 'apparent good order and condition'. The
effect of this representation, where unqualified, is to raise a prima facie
presumption that the goods were so shipped where the shipper sues the
carrier for delivery of damaged goods, and to raise an irrebuttable
presumption to that effect where endorsees who have acted to their
detriment on the faith of the statement sue the carrier for delivery of
damaged goods.[28] Where a carrier issues a clean bill in circumstances
properly calling for a claused bill, any indemnity extracted from the

25 W. Tetley, *Marine Cargo Claims,* (2nd edn), 1978, pp. 105-110.
26 *Ibid.* at 108.
27 *Lishman* v. *Christie & Co.* (1887) 19 Q.B.D. 333. As to the method of proof see
    Royal Commission on the Sugar Supply v. *Hartlepools Seatonia S.S. Co.,* [1927] 2 K.B.
    419.
28 See Section 13.1.1.

shipper in consideration for the issue of a clean bill is unenforceable.[29] The admission can, of course, apply only to the outward appearance of the goods, since the carrier has no means of judging their internal condition and quality; and the courts have held this to be the correct view of the matter.

Illustration: *The Peter de Grosse*[30]

A bill of lading acknowledged the receipt of goods 'shipped in good order and condition...weight contents and value unknown'. The goods were delivered dirty externally and damaged, obviously from some external source.

Held: The bill of lading was evidence that the goods had been shipped externally in good condition to the eye. The carrier, to escape liability, must prove that the goods were in fact shipped in bad condition externally. Unless he discharges this burden, the inference of the bill of lading is that the goods were damaged while in the carrier's possession.

Moreover, it is also possible for the carrier to qualify his admission by entering a note of anything appearing to be wrong with the goods at the time when they are shipped, e.g. 'two packages torn and dirty'. When a bill of lading contains a qualification of this kind it is said to be 'claused'; without such a statement it is said to be clean.[31]

Although it is possible for carriers so to clause their bills as to qualify their statement about the apparent good order and condition of the cargo, such a qualification needs to be very specific in terms if it is to achieve the result desired by the carrier. Thus the courts have been extremely rigorous in their treatment of terms such as 'condition' or 'quality' or 'condition and quality unknown', much more rigorous, it must be said than they have been in their treatment of equivalent clauses qualifying the statement as to quantity. The courts have been happy to consider the term as similar to an exception clause and thus to interpret the words used very precisely away from the admission that the goods were shipped in apparent good order and condition. Thus, where the bill said simply that the quality of the goods was unknown, this was held to refer simply to internal quality and was therefore not intended to qualify the acknowledgement that the goods had been shipped in

29 *Brown Jenkinson* v. *Percy Dalton* [1957] 2 Q.B. 621 and *Scrutton*, (1984), p. 112.
30 (1875) 1 P.D. 414.
31 For more examples of clauses which render a bill unclean, see INCOTERMS CIF, and the Uniform Customs and Practice for Documentary Credits s.34; see also *The Galatia* [1980] 1 All E.R. 501.

apparent good order and condition.[32] This, however, did not prevent the courts in a case decided only sixteen years later that the result was the same when the carrier had taken care to qualify his admission of shipment with the words 'quality, condition... unknown'.[33]

13.2 THE BILL OF LADING AS EVIDENCE OF CONTRACT WITH THE CARRIER

We have seen above that the original function of the bill of lading was that of a receipt. The bill of lading then became the document in which the terms of the contract were set out. As soon as shipowners took to qualifying their common law obligations as carriers they took the obvious course of stating these exceptions on the bill of lading; these became standardized in course of time and bills of lading were printed. It should be noticed that the bill of lading is only evidence of the contract between shipowner and shipper, not the contract itself. Additional terms may be incorporated from the charterparty, from advertisements and similar notices, or even from oral evidence that they were agreed. Moreover, terms actually contained in the bill of lading may be varied orally, and such variations are enforceable.[34] All this, however, applies only between the immediate parties to the contract, carrier and shipper. Third parties, such as consignees or their assignees, who acquire rights by way of endorsement of the bills of lading, are entitled[35] and required[36] to assume that it contains within its four corners either all the terms of the contract or at any rate references to other documents where such terms may be found. Even between the immediate parties an unusual clause in the bill of lading in small print, for example one which provided for exempting the shipowner from paying contributions in general average, will not be enforced,[37] unless it is proved that the shipper was aware of it. On the other hand, an endorsee may even be bound by a term that is not expressly stated, but only implied, in the bill of lading, if it arises from a practice with which

32 See *Compañía Vascongada* v. *Churchill,* fn. 6 *supra.*
33 *The Tromp* [1921] P. 337.
34 E.g. a deviation clause was negatived by an oral promise to follow a direct route: *Owners of Cargo ex S.S. Ardennes* v. *Owners of S.S. Ardennes* [1951] 1 K.B. 55.
35 See *Leduc* v. *Ward* (1888) 20 Q.B.D. 475.
36 *The 'El Amria' and the 'El Minia'* [1982] 2 Lloyd's Rep. 28.
37 *Crooks & Co.* v. *Allan* (1879) 5 Q.B.D. 38; see *Richardson* v. *Rowntree,* [1894] A.C. 217.

he is familiar, and it is immaterial whether shipper or consignee, from whom he derives his title, knew of the practice.[38]

It is, of course, obvious that once the bill is issued the terms of the bill of lading operate. But the question arises whether it should not also have retrospective effect. The contract of affreightment which the bill evidences is concluded long before its issue. Scarce shipping space must be booked long in advance, and pressure of work at the shipping office may delay the issue of the bill of lading until after the ship has sailed. During that interval shipper and shipowner have to perform many operations under the contract, which give rise to rights and liabilities. Under the contract cargo is provided in time for loading, the cargo is taken on board and stowed – but on what terms?

In one case goods were damaged while being hoisted on board from the quay, and the shipowner invoked a limitation of liability clause applicable under the Hague Rules to the bill of lading. The owner of the goods strongly objected because the bill had not yet been issued, but Devlin J held that its terms nevertheless applied.[39]

'When parties enter into a contract of carriage in the expectation that a bill of lading will be issued to cover it they enter into it upon the terms which they know or expect the bill of lading to contain. Those terms must be in force from the inception of the contract; if it were otherwise the bill of lading would not evidence the contract but would be a variation of it.'

13.3   THE BILL OF LADING AS A DOCUMENT OF TITLE AT COMMON LAW

It was early found convenient to use a copy of the bill of lading as a document ordering delivery of the goods at the port of discharge. This came about in the following way. Originally, merchants travelled with their goods on board the same vessel, but when they ceased to do so it became necessary to devise some means by which the carrier could be enabled to deliver the goods to the proper person. The simplest thing was to send a copy of the bill of lading under separate cover so to speak, and even by a different ship if there was a faster one going, to the shipper's agent at the port of delivery. Eventually, when goods were shipped direct to buyers, the bill of lading was sent to them and the buyers were made consignees of the goods. In the bill of lading,

38 *Gonzales* v. *Nourse* [1936] 1 K.B. 585.
39 *Pyrene Co.* v. *Scindia Navigation Co.*, [1954] 2 Q.B. 402, 419. *Cf. Raymond Burke Motors Ltd* v. *The Mersey Docks and Harbour Board Co.* [1986] 1 Lloyd's Rep. 155.

therefore, the carrier began to agree to carry the goods, say to Antwerp, and there deliver them not only (a) to the shipper but, alternatively (b) to the shipper's order, so that the shipper could, by endorsing on the document an order that the goods should be delivered to the buyer, enable the latter to get the goods himself; or (c) to a named consignee. These three options shared the common feature that the bill operated as a document entitling delivery only in favour of the shipper or the shipper's buyer. The function of the bill as a document of title came fully into its own when a fourth option came into general use, i.e. when the carrier agreed to deliver the goods to the consignee or to his order, thus enabling the initial buyer to transfer, by endorsement of the bill to successive buyers, the right to delivery of the goods by the carrier.

The bill of lading thus came to represent the goods in respect of which it was issued: it came to be treated as 'the keys of the warehouse'.[40] This does not mean that the ownership in the goods necessarily passes from shipper to consignee by transfer of the bill: the question of passage of ownership is a matter to which the contract of sale will normally address itself and the manner of dealing with the bill of lading may or may not be an important factor in answering that question.[41] What the transfer of a negotiable bill of lading does pass is constructive possession, i.e. the right to demand of the carrier the delivery of the goods on presentation of the bill of lading. The question which then arises is: delivery on what terms? Before we deal with this question in detail we should refer to three other matters relating to this function of the bill.

13.3.1 'RECEIVED FOR SHIPMENT' BILLS

Goods are frequently left with the shipowner's agent at the port of loading prior to the arrival of the vessel at that port. On occasion, the agent will issue to the shipper a bill of lading stamped 'received for shipment' thus qualifying the usual statement that the goods have been 'shipped in apparent good order and condition'. The essence of the function of the bill as a document of title is the transfer of constructive possession, i.e. the transfer of the right to demand possession of the goods from the carrier. The function consequently assumes that the carrier is in actual possession of the goods and it follows that a bill which merely witnesses the fact that the goods were received with a view to shipment cannot be a document of title at common law. This is

---

40 *Sanders* v. *Maclean* (1883) 11 Q.B.D. 327 at 343.
41 *Scrutton* (1984), pp. 186, 187.

why cases dealing with the international sale of goods have held that a
received for shipment bill is not good tender as between seller and buyer
unless this has been previously agreed by the parties.[42] Where the
Hague Rules apply, the law of carriage of goods by sea has responded to
the problem which the practice causes traders by giving the
shipper[43] the right to demand that the date of actual shipment be noted
on the bill, thus converting a received for shipment bill into a shipped
bill.

13.3.2   BILLS IN SETS

Bills of lading are usually made out in sets of three, one being retained
by the shipper, the other travelling with the goods and the last being
sent to the consignee. One would have thought that this practice
encourages fraud, but in fact very few cases seem to have occurred. In
one of these, *Glyn Mills* v. *East & West India Dock*,[44] the consignee
possessed himself of two copies of the bill of lading, pledged one with
his bankers as a security for an overdraft and used the other to obtain
delivery of the goods on arrival. An action by the bankers against the
warehouseman for damages for wrongful delivery was dismissed. In
the words of Lord Blackburn (at p. 611):

'Where the person who produces a bill of lading is one who – either as being the
person named in the bill of lading which is not endorsed, or as actually holding
an endorsed bill – would be entitled to demand delivery under the contract,
unless one of the other parts had been previously endorsed for value to someone
else, and the master has no notice or knowledge of anything except that there
are other parts of the bill of lading, and that therefore it is possible that one of
them may have been previously endorsed, I think the master cannot be bound,
at his peril, to ask for the other parts.'

42 *Diamond Alkali Co.* v. *Bourgeois* [1921] 3 K.B. 443; *Yelo* v. *S.M. Machado & Co.
   Ltd,* [1952] 1 Lloyd's Rep. 183. See, however, for a contrary view, the Privy
   Council's judgment in *The Marlborough Hill* v. *Cowan & Sons* [1921] A.C. 444, a
   case made much of by *Scrutton* (1984) at pp. 383, 4 and distinctly preferred by
   Carver at para. 1613 and Sassoon (1984) at pp. 115-120. *Cf. Benjamin* (1981) at
   p. 766. It is clear that at any rate where Incoterms are incorporated into the
   contract of sale, tender of a received for shipment bill is bad tender in a c.i.f.
   contract. Incoterms, CIF, A7.
43 Art. III.7. The shipper is likely to exercise his rights under this article so as to
   avoid rejection of the bill by his buyer: see fn. 42 above and *cf.* Section 13.1.2(b),
   supra. Another incentive is provided where the shipper expects payment by letter
   of credit, for under the UCP, the paying bank will only accept received for
   shipment bills where the date of actual shipment is noted on the bill: aliter, with
   transport documents other than bills of lading, see UCP Art. 27.
44 (1882) 7 App. Cas. 165.

13.3.3 MODES OF TRANSFER

Bills of lading may be issued in various forms. The goods may be made deliverable 'to order' – the usual practice – or 'to bearer'. Only 'order' bills require endorsement, constructive possession in goods covered by 'bearer' bills passing by mere delivery.

FORM OF ENDORSEMENT

An endorsement is effected in two ways, viz.: the person to whose order the goods are made deliverable may simply write his name on the back of the instrument; this is called an endorsement in blank. The important point to notice about this is that an endorsement in blank converts an order instrument into a bearer instrument. Hence any further transfer may be effected by mere delivery.

Illustration:
Bill of lading to 'Smith & Co. or order'. This is an 'order' bill requiring endorsement, if Smith & Co, wish to transfer it to a purchaser of the goods. They endorse 'Smith & Co.' without mentioning the name of the purchaser. The latter can sell the goods by mere delivery, for the bill has become a 'bearer' bill.

The endorsement may be an endorsement to some named person or persons. This is called a 'special' endorsement.

Illustration:
Suppose the above goods are bought by Brown's, Ltd, then the endorsement in full would read 'Deliver to Brown's, Ltd, or order. (Signed) Smith & Co.'

It should be noted that the transferee of a bill of lading under an endorsement in blank can restrict the endorsement and thereby reconvert the 'bearer' bill into an 'order' bill.

Illustration:
In our first example the purchasers are in fact Brown's, Ltd. They can restrict the transfer by writing over the signature of Smith & Co. 'Deliver to Brown's, Ltd or order.'

13.4   THE BILL OF LADING AND THE TRANSFER OF THE CONTRACT OF CARRIAGE

We have seen[45] that the transfer of the bill of lading passes to its holder the right to demand possession of the goods from the present possessor of the goods, the carrier; that in this sense the bill is the key to the warehouse in which the goods lie. This is not the same as saying that property in the goods passes with the bill, that being a matter depending in the last analysis on the intention of the parties to the contract of sale, the transfer of the bill being but one of a number of factors evidencing such intention. Neither is it the same as saying that the contract concluded between the carrier and shipper is, by transfer of the bill and of constructive possession to the consignee, passed to the latter. Both the consignee and the carrier may wish to be bound to each other by contract: the consignee, because contract may provide him with his only cause of action against the carrier; and the carrier, because if he is to be sued at all by the consignee, contract would provide him with exceptions and limitations agreed to in the bill of lading. The doctrine of privity of contract stands in the way of such a contract, but solutions side-stepping this doctrine have been found both by Parliament and by the courts.

13.4.1   THE BILLS OF LADING ACT 1855

This Act established beyond doubt that the consignee who holds a bill of lading is liable for payments stipulated in the bill of lading, although he was not, originally, a party to the contract evidenced in the bill. Under the Act, the transfer of the bill of lading assigns the contract of carriage if the transferee owns the goods at the time of suit. Thus the consignee named in the bill of lading to whom the property has passed and an endorsee who has acquired property take the benefits and the burdens[46] of the contract of carriage contained in the bill of lading, as if this had actually been made with them.

The emphasis is on the acquisition of property. Where a bill of lading holder acquires a title short of the full property, the Act does not apply and he incurs no liability under the contract of carriage.

45 Section 13.3, *supra*.
46 Section 1 *The Blue Wave* [1982] 1 Lloyd's Rep. 151.

Illustration: *Sewell* v. *Burdick*[47]

Machinery was shipped to a Black Sea port under a bill of lading making goods deliverable to shippers or assigns. The shipper endorsed the bill to his banker as security for a loan. He then disappeared. The goods were warehoused on arrival, and after one year, in accordance with Russian law, sold to pay for customs and other charges; they realized no more than the sums owing under these heads. The shipowner then sued the bankers, as bill of lading holders, for the freight.

Held: The action was dismissed because the bankers were not owners of the bill of lading and had not claimed the goods.

On the other hand, it would appear that for the Act to apply it is not necessary for the property in the goods to pass at the same time as the endorsement of the bill of lading. If contemporaneous transfer of property and the bill of lading were required, then the Act would be rendered useless in the large number of cases where the contract of sale specifies the moment at which property in the goods is to pass, which moment may well be one other than the time of transfer of the bill. The position seems to be that the Act applies so long as the passage of property and the transfer of the bill of lading both occur because of the same contract of sale.[48]

Finally, it must be said that where the Act applies, the shipper – the original party to the bill of lading contract – does not drop out. He remains responsible, by virtue of Section 2 of the Act, although he will not normally be called upon to discharge his contractual obligations unless and until the receiver of the goods fails to do so.

13.4.2 THE RULE IN *BRANDT* v. *LIVERPOOL*[49]

We have seen that there are two limitations on the application of Section 1 of the Bills of Lading Act: the cargo-owner must hold a bill of lading, and full property must vest in him. In situations where a party with an interest in the cargo cannot for lack of either of the above requirements, bring himself within the Act, is there any other way in which a contract can be constructed between such party and the carrier, to their mutual benefit? The courts gave an affirmative answer, some time before the

---

47 (1884) 10 App. Cas. 74

48 See *Pacific Molasses Co. and United Molasses Trading Co. Ltd* v. *Entre Rios Compañía Naviera S.A.*, *The San Nicholas* [1976] 1 Lloyd's Rep. 8 and *The Sevonia Team* [1983] 2 Lloyd's Rep. 640 at 643. The major works in the area are in disagreement: see *Carver* (1982) at p.98 and *Scrutton* (1984), at p.27.

49 [1924] 1 K.B. 575.

enactment of the Bills of Lading Act in circumstances which, since 1855, would be covered by that Act. In a series of cases, the courts decided that where a bill of lading holder presented the bill and obtained possession of the goods from the ship, it might be possible to hold that he had thereby accepted the responsibility for fulfilling the contract, and also the carrier would then be bound to respect its terms *vis-à-vis* the bill of lading holder.

Illustration: *Stindt* v. *Roberts*[50]

Cattle bones were shipped to Hull under bills of lading providing for demurrage. This became payable because discharge was delayed. The assignee of bills of lading refused to pay the demurrage.

Held: He was liable to the shipowner for the payment of demurrage.

This device, whereby a contract was effectively created where none existed, survived the enactment of the Bills of Lading Act and remained useful where, for one reason or another, that Act could not apply. So much was hinted at by Lord Selborne in *Sewell* v. *Burdick*,[51] the House of Lords case which interpreted the property requirement in Section 1 of the Act. At page 86 of the report, Lord Selborne said:

'The endorsee by way of security, though not having the property passed to him absolutely and for all purposes by the endorsement and delivery of the bill of lading while the goods are at sea, has a title by means of which he is enabled to take the position of full proprietor upon himself, with its corresponding burdens, if he thinks fit; and that he actually does so as between himself and the shipowner, if and when he claims and takes delivery of the goods by virtue of that title'.

The point was taken up by the Court of Appeal in *Brandt* v. *Liverpool* in 1923.

Illustration: *Brandt* v. *Liverpool, Brazil and River Plate Steam Navigation Co.*[52]

Shippers of bags of zinc endorsed the bills of lading to the plaintiffs as pledgees. Arrival of the cargo was delayed because part of it had got wet and had to be reconditioned. The pledgees finally took delivery and paid the

50 (1848) 17 L.J.Q.B. 166.
51 (1884) 10 App. Cas. 74.
52 [1924] 1 K.B. 575. For another illustration of the principle, see *Cremer* v. *General Carriers* [1974] 1 W.L.R. 341, particularly at 348-350, where the implied contract was used by a plaintiff who held not a bill of lading, but a ship's delivery order.

freight and, under protest, the shipowner's charges for reconditioning the cargo. These they sought to recover.

Held: The action succeeded. They had taken delivery of the goods against payment of freight, for which they were liable, and were consequently entitled to those terms of the bill of lading which conferred rights on them.

It is now clear[53] that the promise to pay outstanding freight is not necessary for the implication of a *Brandt* v. *Liverpool* contract: it is enough that demurrage or other charges remain outstanding and that the plaintiff undertakes to pay them. Neither is it necessary for the plaintiff physically to possess the bill on delivery of the cargo, so long as he gives the carrier an undertaking to surrender it on arrival.[54] On the other hand, it is not clear whether a court can find a *Brandt* v. *Liverpool* contract where there are no charges yet to be paid by the cargo interests under the contract of carriage; nor whether such a contract can be said to exist where the goods have been lost. In either case, there would seem to be little content to the promises said to support the implied contract. On the other hand, at any rate, in the second case, it appears hard to deny cargo interests who, for reasons which will presently become clear, may have no action in tort, a cause of action in contract in precisely the sort of circumstance where a remedy is most sorely needed, i.e. where the goods have been lost while in the carrier's custody. The better opinion, it is suggested, is that in this case, it would be possible to support a *Brandt* v. *Liverpool* contract by implying a promise on the part of the carrier to discharge liabilities under the contract in lieu of making delivery of the goods, e.g. to pay damages.

13.4.3   ACTIONS IN TORT

While Section 1 of the Bills of Lading Act and the rule in *Brandt* v. *Liverpool* go a long way towards providing cargo-interests with *locus standi* in an action in contract against carriers, there may still be parties wishing to sue for damage to goods who cannot bring themselves within either of these two exceptions to the doctrine of privity. Thus the

53 *The Elli 2* [1985] 1 Lloyd's Rep. 107 at 111, 2 and 115, 6.
54 *Ibid.*

holder of a delivery order,[55] unacknowledged by the carrier, has no contract with the carrier and is thrown upon his remedy, if any, in tort. When he seeks redress in tort, however, the holder of such a document may find that even this path is closed by a rule preventing the recovery of pure economic loss in tort. Stated briefly and in the context of this area of shipping law, the rule is that a party can only sue a carrier in tort for loss of or damage to goods through negligence if he can prove that, at the time of loss or damage, he had a proprietary interest in the goods. It may be difficult, or indeed impossible, for a plaintiff to discharge this burden of proof, either because he cannot indicate with any certainty when during transit the loss or damage occurred, or because the contract of sale indicates that property is to pass after discharge of the goods.

It is difficult to examine the rule and its application in shipping law to any depth, without doing violence either to the general nature of this work or to the judicial erudition which has recently gone into the resolution of the dispute in a case called *The Aliakmon*.[56] Suffice it therefore to say that prior to the decision of the House of Lords in that case commercial men had to live with different answers given by courts of first instance to the central question of tortious recovery against carriers by certain receivers of goods: the judgments against recovery were *The Wear Breeze*[57] and *The Elafi*[58] and those for were *The Irene's Success*[59] and *The Nea Tyhi*.[60] Lord Brandon's speech in *The Aliakmon* states the law to be very much against recovery, his Lordship finding little reason to depart, in circumstances described as being 'of an extremely unusual character',[61] from principles accepted both in general tort law and in cases relating specifically to maritime incidents.

55 These are documents used where goods are shipped in bulk under one bill of lading and are then allocated to several purchasers, each of whom receives a delivery order. There are two main types of delivery order, broadly those acknowledged by the carrier and those not so acknowledged: otherwise known as ship's and bare delivery orders respectively. For a more detailed account of these documents, see Benjamin pp. 780–788. The problem discussed in the text relates to bare delivery orders.

56 *Leigh & Sillavan Ltd* v. *Aliakmon Shipping Co. Ltd* [1986] 2 All E.R. 145.

57 [1969] 1 Q.B. 219.

58 [1981] 2 Lloyd's Rep. 679.

59 [1982] Q.B. 481.

60 [1982] 1 Lloyd's Rep. 606.

61 [1986] 2 All E.R. 145 at 156g.

13.5 DOCUMENTS OF TITLE UNDER THE SALE OF GOODS ACT 1979

Thus far we have been examining the bill of lading as a document of title in the context of its ability to transfer constructive possession of the goods it covers and, in certain circumstances, contractual rights against the carrier. There is, however, another sense in which a bill of lading, here in common with another host of documents,[62] is a document of title: in certain circumstances the holder of a bill of lading can have a better title to it than his fraudulent transferor, such that the holder's title prevails over that of the rightful owner. This is so because as a result of s. 9 of the Factors Act 1889 and s. 25 of the Sale of Goods Act 1979, even an unauthorized transfer to a bona fide buyer for value usually confers a good title on the latter. Only where a bill of lading had been stolen – and no such case appears to have been reported – does a bona fide purchaser for value acquire no title. Lord Campbell CJ in *Gurney v. Behrend*[63] explained the law in these words:

'A bill of lading is not, like a bill of exchange or promissory note, a negotiable instrument, which passes by mere delivery to a bona fide transferee for valuable consideration, without regard to the title of the parties who make the transfer. Although the shipper may have endorsed in blank a bill of lading deliverable to his assigns, his right is not affected by an appropriation of it without his authority. If it be stolen from him, or transferred without his authority, a subsequent bona fide transferee for value cannot make title under it, as against the shipper of the goods'.

That was decided before the Factors Act and the Sale of Goods Act, and it is now only safe to rely on the words in the judgment which relate to a theft of the document. The strong position of a bill of lading holder is illustrated by the following cases.

Illustration 1: *Lickbarrow v. Mason*[64]
The buyer endorsed the bill of lading to a bona fide endorsee for value. The seller stopped the goods *in transitu* (because the buyer was insolvent – see *infra* Chapter 14) and claimed the goods from the endorsee.

62 See s. 1(4) of the Factors Act 1889.
63 (1854) 3 E. & B. 622, at p. 634.
64 (1793) 1 Smith L.C., 13th edn, 703.

Held: The original seller had lost his right. Buller J said, at p. 747: '... (the buyer) having transferred the goods again for value, I am of opinion that (the original seller) had neither property, then, nor a right to seize *in transitu'*.

Illustration 2: *The Argentina*[66]

The seller sent the bill of lading to his agent, with instructions not to deliver it to the buyer without first receiving payment. The buyer gave the agent a bill of exchange, which later turned out to be worthless, and promised immediate payment in cash. On the strength of this he was given the bill of lading, which he promptly endorsed to a bona fide endorsee for value. The buyer became bankrupt.

Held: The buyer, having acquired the bill of lading with the consent of the seller's agent, had conferred a good title on the endorsee.

13.6   IDENTITY OF SHIPPER

It will be clear in a general way from the preceding pages who are the parties to the contract of carriage, but it is now necessary to examine this matter somewhat more closely. On the one side there is, of course, the shipper and on the other the carrier and we start here with the shipper. Where the shipper sells the goods c.i.f., the past few pages have shown how it is that the buyer becomes a party to the shipper's contract of carriage. With f.o.b. sales, however, the position is not so simple, for it depends very much on the type of f.o.b. sale we are dealing with. We have seen[67] that where such a contract is made it is the buyer who normally makes the arrangements for the carriage of the goods which the seller has contracted to deliver free on board; but it has been said[68] that 'the f.o.b. contract has become a flexible instrument' and there are various ways in which a seller f.o.b. too may be a party to the contract of carriage with the carrier. In *Pyrene Co.* v. *Scindia Navigation Co.*[69] the seller had bought a fire tender, which was still his property, alongside the ship. While the tender was being lifted by the ship's tackle it slipped back on the quay and was badly damaged. The shipowner admitted liability, but claimed that he could limit this in accordance with Art. IV, Rule 5, of the Schedule to the Carriage of Goods by Sea Act, which was incorporated in the bill of lading. To this the seller objected, arguing

---

65 (1867) L.R. 1 A. & E. 370.
66 Section 10.1.1, *supra*.
67 *Per* Devlin J in *Pyrene Co.* v. *Scindia Navigation Co.* [1954] 1 Q.B. 402 at 424.
68 See fn. 67, *supra*.

that he was not party to the bill of lading contract and that he could accordingly recover the full damage which he had suffered. But it was held that the shipowner was entitled to limit his liability, for the seller was bound by the terms of the bill of lading. Devlin J found that there were three types of f.o.b. contract. In the classic type, the seller procures a bill of lading as agent for the buyer, and is directly a party to the contract of carriage, 'at least until he takes out the bill of lading in the buyer's name'. In the second type, the f.o.b. seller takes a bill of lading from the carrier in his own name and then transfers it to the buyer, who becomes a party to the carriage contract in much the same way as in a c.i.f. contract. In the third type, the buyer, through his agent at the port of loading, obtains the bill of lading from the carrier, the seller's only documentary duty being to obtain the mate's receipt and surrender it to the buyer's agent, thus enabling the latter to exchange the receipt for the bill of lading. Devlin J found that the sale in the case before him fell within the third class, which clearly raised problems of privity. Despite these difficulties, the court found that even in the third class of case, it was the intention of all parties concerned that the sellers should be part of a contract in which they were so closely – as a matter of fact, if not technically as a matter of law – involved.

13.7 BILLS OF LADING UNDER CHARTERPARTIES – IDENTITY OF TERMS AND OF CARRIER

It has already been suggested[69] that the use by carriers and traders of charterparties on some occasions and of bills of lading on others was one cause for the complexity surrounding the law on the carriage of goods by sea. It will come as no surprise, therefore, that the use of both documents within the same set of circumstances provides us with one of the most intricate parts of the subject.[70]

The issue of bills of lading pursuant to charterparties raises two distinct questions, which may or may not arise in tandem. The first is: what are the terms of the contract of carriage, the charterparty terms or the bill of lading terms? The second is: who is the carrier where goods are carried on a chartered ship? There are two situations to bear in mind:

69 Section 10.1.1, *supra*
70 In a general work of this nature, it will not be possible to give other than a brief statement of the position. For fuller accounts, see Goode (1982), pp. 603–607, *Carver,* (1982), pp. 514–544 and *Scrutton* (1984), pp. 58–74.

first, where a charterer holds a bill of lading; second, where a third party holds a bill of lading. In the first situation, only the first problem arises, it being clear that the charterer contracts with the shipowner from whom he has chartered the vessel. In the second situation, however, it is equally clear that both problems might arise, the third party seeking guidance as to whom to sue and on what terms.

We shall be looking at each of the problems we have described above in succession, but before we do so it may be instructive to inquire why it is that, at first sight somewhat curiously, traders in goods should make use both of charterparties and of bills of lading within the same transaction. A moment's reflection on the functions of a bill of lading will provide the answer. We have seen earlier on in this chapter that the bill of lading is a receipt for goods, a document of title and evidence of the contract of carriage. Only this third function does the bill share with a charterparty. Thus whether or not the shipper is the charterer, that is to say, whether we are dealing with a c.i.f. sale or an f.o.b. sale, the traders need a bill of lading because they need a receipt and a document of title, particularly if it is likely that the goods will be sold on while in transit. Moreover, a charterer needs a bill of lading whether or not he carries his own goods on the chartered ship; for where he does not, that is to say where he is simply providing a service to other traders for a profit, these other traders – his customers – will themselves require bills of lading which confirm receipt of their goods and which can be sold on down a string.

13.7.1   IDENTITY OF TERMS

The question as to whether the terms of a contract of carriage are to be sought in a bill of lading or in a charterparty needs to be examined in both of the situations described above, i.e. both where the bill is in the hands of a charterer and where it is in the hands of a third party.

(A)   WHERE A CHARTERER HOLDS A BILL OF LADING

Where a charterer takes a bill of lading directly from a shipowner, it appears that usually[71] their contract is contained in the charterparty and

---

71 See *Guillischen* v. *Stewart Bros* (1884) 13 Q.B.D. 317 and the detailed examination of this case in the context of the rest of the case-law in *Scrutton* at pp. 61, 62.

that the bill of lading is, as between themselves, only a receipt and a document of title, such that a shipowner sued by the charterer for damage to goods could not plead in his defence an exception clause contained in the bill of lading but not in the charterparty.[72] As was said by Lord Esher MR:[73]

'where there is a charterparty, as between the shipowner and the charterer the bill of lading may be merely in the nature of a receipt for the goods, because all the other terms of the contract of carriage between them are contained in the charterparty; and the bill of lading is merely given as between them to enable the charterer to deal with the goods while in the course of transit'.

Where the charterer takes the bill of lading not directly from the shipowner, but indirectly, via the shipper of the goods or via another holder of the bill, the position is slightly less straightforward. This situation may arise where a buyer f.o.b. charters a vessel for the carriage of goods he has bought and the bill is issued by the shipowner to the seller–shipper, who then transfers the bill to the buyer–charterer. It may also arise where the charterer, having simply provided a service to traders by shipping *their* goods rather than his, subsequently buys the bill or bills of lading covering the goods on the vessel chartered to him. Prior to the decision of the Court of Appeal in *The President of India* v. *Metcalfe Shipping Co. Ltd,*[74] the accepted position[75] was that where a charterer took a bill of lading other than directly from a shipowner, the bill of lading became the document defining the contractual relationship between those parties. In the *President of India* case, the charterers, buyers of goods f.o.b. were in dispute with the shipowners as to the quantity of goods delivered, but had allowed the limitation period running against them to lapse. They sought arbitration, which was provided for in the charterparty but not in the bills of lading which the charterers had taken from the shippers of the goods, their sellers. The shipowners argued that their contract with the charterers, who were endorsees of the bills of lading, was to be found in the bills, which contained no arbitration clause; but this was rejected by the Court of Appeal. The decision led to a change of view in both of the major works in the area, the position now being accepted that the charterparty governs the relationship between the shipowner and the charterer in the

---

72 *Rodocanachi* v. *Milburn* (1886) 18 Q.B.D. 67.
73 *Leduc* v. *Ward* (1888) 20 Q.B.D. 475 at 479.
74 [1970] 1 Q.B. 289.
75 *Carver,* 11th edn, p. 340; and *Scrutton,* 17th edn, p. 46.

circumstances here discussed.[76] This may be said, however, to draw the authority of the *President of India* case too far. As Fenton Atkinson LJ accepted in his judgment in that case,[77] 'the relations between shipowners, charterers and shippers respectively are to be determined as a question of fact upon the documents and circumstances of each particular case,' and it may be that the proper distinction to draw is not between the documents themselves but between the circumstances in which those documents are issued and used. Thus where, as in the *President of India* case, the charterer takes the bill directly from the shipper, his seller, it is clear that the endorsement of the bill to the charterer is very much an incident of the contract of sale and is in no way intended by any of the parties to alter, much less to supplant, the contractual arrangements between the shipowner and the charterer, contained in the charterparty.[78] On the other hand, where a charterer had originally taken goods on board a general ship, simply as a service to other traders, and has subsequently bought goods thereon in respect of which he now wishes to sue the shipowner, it is clear that the charterer and the shipowner have been brought back into contractual contact through the bill of lading, a contract in this case separate from and unconnected to the original charterparty, and that the bill should govern their relations at any rate where the charterparty contains a cesser clause.[79]

(B)   WHERE A THIRD PARTY HOLDS A BILL OF LADING

We must now ask, what is the position of the consignee where he is not the same person as the charterer? In the ordinary way, the consignee has no knowledge and no means of knowledge of the terms of the charterparty. The only contract of which he is aware is the bill of lading which

76 *Carver*, (1982) at p 516; *Scrutton* (1984) at p 59, 'at least where the charterparty provides that bills of lading are to be signed "without prejudice to this charterparty".' *Sed quaere* whether the ratio of the *President of India* case can be so restricted: see *Intercontinental Export Co. (Pty) Ltd v. Mv Dien Danielsen* 1982 (3) S.A. 534, reversed on other grounds at 1983 (4) S.A. 275.

77 See fn. 74 at p.310.

78 Indeed, under Incoterms, an f.o.b. seller is not expected to endorse a bill of lading to his buyer: rather is he to provide the 'customary clean document in proof of delivery' and to 'render the buyer ... every assistance in obtaining a bill of lading,' i.e. generally to tender a mate's receipt. On the other hand, as we have seen, there are a number of variants of the f.o.b. contract: see Section 13.6, *supra*.

79 See *Calcutta S.S. Co. Ltd. v. Andrew Weir & Co.* [1910] 1 K.B. 759, a case 'explained' in the *President of India* case, but described as 'unreliable' in the current edition of *Carver*, (1982) at p. 516.

he holds, and this is the only contract by which he is bound unless, of course, it contains a term incorporating the conditions of the charter-party, a situation raising its own problems, which we shall discuss presently. This has been well put by Lord Esher.[80] 'Where the bill of lading has been endorsed over, as between shipowner and the endorsee (i.e. consignee), the bill of lading must be considered to contain the contract, because the former has given it for the purpose of enabling the charterer to pass it on as the contract of carriage in respect of the goods.' The position has been made still clearer by Lord Atkin, when he explained the rights and duties of bill of lading holders under the Bills of Lading Act 1855:[81] 'The consignee has not assigned to him the obliga-tions under the charterparty nor, in fact, any obligation of the charterer under the bill of lading, for *ex hypothesi* there are none. A new contract appears to spring up between the ship and the consignee on the terms of the bill of lading'.

Although it is clear that the consignee's contract is contained in the bill of lading which he holds, the position may be slightly complicated where the bill of lading seeks to incorporate terms contained in the charterparty. Questions then arise as to which parts of the charterparty[82] are incorporated into the bill and according to which criteria, questions which, because of recent case-law in the area, had best be examined in the context first of incorporation in general and then of incorporation of arbitration clauses.

(i) Incorporation in general

An incorporation clause does not, without more, put the cargo-owner on notice of the whole contents of the charterparty so as to make him liable to perform them. Were it otherwise, the law would be particularly hard on consignees who appear to have no means of obtaining sight of the charterparty so as to examine its terms.[83]

---

80 *Leduc* v. *Ward* (1888) 20 Q.B.D. 475.
81 *Hain S.S. Co.* v. *Tate & Lyle, Ltd* (1936) 52 T.L.R. 617, 620.
82 Another problem, which arises where a vessel has been chartered several times over is: Which charterparty? The normal rule appears to be that the reference is to the head charter: see *The Sevonia Team* [1983] 2 Lloyd's Rep. 640.
83 It is not clear whether a c.i.f. buyer can demand, absent special agreement, tender of a copy of the charterparty by his seller. *Cf.* Sassoon p. 92, 3 and *Benjamin*, (1981), pp. 876–8. It is clear, however, that where Incoterms apply, the seller must so tender 'if the bill of lading contains a reference to the charterparty', in which case the buyer should be careful to give instructions in this direction to the banks paying under a letter of credit, who would otherwise be barred by the U.C.P. from accepting a bill 'subject to a charterparty': Art. 26 (c)(i) U.C.P.

On the other hand, the principle is not applied so rigidly as to ignore the fact that a number of standard charterparty clauses relating to shipment, carriage and discharge[84] are in such common use that they are to be deemed to be within the ken of carriers and traders alike. Given certain requirements, such terms may readily be incorporated into bill of lading contracts so as to bind consignees or other bill of lading holders. The requirements for such incorporation are best described in terms of two questions as suggested by Sir John Donaldson MR in *The Miramar*:[85]

'The first question is: Is the wording of the bill of lading contract wide enough to produce a prima facie, or a contingent, or a tentative incorporation of the whole or specific parts of the charterparty? The second question, and it only arises if the answer to that is "Yes", is: If so, do the tentatively incorporated parts have to be rejected as being insensible or inapplicable either because of their subject-matter or because of their wording?'

The courts are careful to examine the incorporation clause against the first question and the clause sought to be incorporated against the second; it is probably[86] accurate to say that where there is a doubt as to incorporation, the courts are likely to find against it. Thus in the *Miramar* itself, although the incorporation clause was wide enough for the purposes of the first question,[87] the charterparty clause sought to be incorporated by the shipowner imposed liability on the charterer and none of the nine judges dealing with the case was prepared to manipulate the meaning of the word 'charterer' to mean 'consignee' through incorporation.

(ii)   Incorporation of arbitration clauses

Arbitration clauses are clauses by which parties to a contract agree, in advance of any dispute arising, to refer any disputes which may arise to arbitration. Whether or not an arbitration clause governs the relations between two parties, and if so the modalities of time and place regulating such arbitration,[88] are questions of considerable importance to

---

84 *The Garbis* [1982] 2 Lloyd's Rep. 283 at 287.
85 [1984] 1 Lloyd's Rep. 142 at 143, approved at [1984] 2 Lloyd's Rep. 129.
86 *The Miramar* [1984] 2 Lloyd's Rep. 129 is the latest House of Lords pronouncement on the issue. For reasons which we need not go into, it was not necessary for their Lordships to overrule earlier cases, which ought nonetheless to be treated with some care since their Lordships decision: see *Scrutton*, (1984), pp.63-5.
87 'All the terms whatsoever'.
88 See, for an example of a case where the arbitration clause in a bill of lading differed from that contained in the charterparty under which it was issued, *The Roseline* 1985 A.M.C. 551.

parties to a contract of carriage of goods by sea: arbitration clauses are keys with which parties may open or close the doors to litigation in the UK, and the problem of when and how a bill of lading can incorporate a charterparty arbitration clause has consequently given rise to much discussion in the courts.[89]

The problem is discussed on the basis of the same two questions asked by Sir John Donaldson MR in *The Miramar*,[90] i.e. description and consistency. An accurate statement of the law might read as follows. For a charterparty arbitration clause to be incorporated into a bill of lading, one would need either an incorporation clause in the bill specifically incorporating the charterparty arbitration clause; or an incorporation clause in the bill, drawn in considerably wider terms, *and* a clear indication in the charterparty arbitration clause that it is intended to apply both to disputes arising under the charterparty and to those arising under the bill of lading. Problems are clearly more likely to arise in the second alternative rather than in the first. What is meant by an incorporation clause 'drawn in considerably wider terms'? Or, more particularly, would a clause seeking to incorporate 'all conditions as per charterparty' describe an arbitration clause so as to get it through the first hurdle of incorporation? It now appears clear that it would not.[91] So far as concerns the second hurdle of incorporation, consistency, it probably follows from judicial attitudes in *The Miramar*[92] that a charterparty arbitration clause referring charterparty disputes to arbitration cannot be manipulated in such a way as to include bill of lading disputes within its remit. It is not, however, altogether clear whether the same may be said of an arbitration clause in the charterparty which talks about disputes arising under 'this contract'.[93]

13.7.2   IDENTITY OF THE CARRIER

Where the aggrieved holder of the bill of lading is not the charterer, we have already seen that he must ask himself not only which terms does he

---

89 For a more detailed discussion, see Incorporation of Charterparty Arbitration Clauses by Enid A. Marshall in 1982 J.B.L. 478, and *The Varenna* [1983] 1 Lloyd's Rep. 416 and [1983] 2 Lloyd's Rep. 592.

90 Discussed at Section 13.7.1(b)(i), *supra*.

91 See *The Varenna*, *supra* at fn. 89, and *cf. The Emmanuel Colocotronis (No. 2)* [1982] 1 Lloyd's Rep. 286

92 [1984] 2 Lloyd's Rep. 129.

93 Staughton J in *The Emmanuel Colocotronis (No. 2)* incorporated such a clause into a bill of lading. It is submitted that the judgments in *The Varenna* are not necessarily inconsistent with this aspect of Staughton J's judgment.

sue on but also whom is he to sue: is it to be the shipowner or the charterer? It has long been recognized that this is a question upon which it is difficult to draw any clear, or at any rate binding, guidance from the decided cases. Thus in 1906, Walton J said:[94]

'Upon this point...the authorities appear conflicting...[T]he question is really a question of fact depending upon the documents and circumstances in each case, [and] it may be that the apparent conflict arises mainly from the fact that the documents and circumstances are different in different cases'.

Subject to this caveat, it is true to say that in the large majority of cases, the contract of carriage is made not with the charterer, but with the shipowner. It must be remembered that the bills of lading are issued by or in the name of the master who is normally the servant and agent of the owner. This is also a fair result from the point of view of the shipper of cargo. Like every other person who makes a contract, he wishes to know the identity of the other party, for on this depends the question against whom he can assert his rights under the agreement. If goods are loaded on board a ship in pursuance of a contract of carriage the normal inference to be drawn by the shipper is that he has contracted with the shipowner. His identity he knows or has the means of ascertaining. Unless special circumstances prevail the shipper will not be able to find out who the charterer is, and very often will not know and not even be interested whether the ship is under charter. In the absence, therefore, of such special circumstances, the shipper may assume that the master is the agent of the owner.[95] So strong is this presumption that it applies even where the bill of lading is signed by the charterer, at any rate where the signature is expressed to be 'for the captain and owner'.[96]

Neither is the presumption unsettled by a clause stating that master and crew are the servants of the charterer, a so-called 'employment and indemnity' clause. Such a term is inserted in order to relieve the shipowner from liability for torts committed by those persons while the charterer has control of the vessel. It makes, however, no difference to the shipper. In the case under consideration he knows nothing of the

94 *Samuel & Co.* v. *West Hartlepool Steam Navigation Co.* (1906) 11 Com. Cas. 115 at 125. See also *Scrutton* (1984) at pp. 68-71.
95 *Manchester Trust* v. *Furness* [1895] 2 Q.B. 539, *per* Lindley LJ.
96 See *Tillmans & Co.* v. *S.S. Knuttsford, Limited* [1908] 1 K.B. 185, confirmed by C.A. [1908] 2 K.B. 385 and by H.L. [1908] A.C. 406. But see *The Venezuela* [1980] 1 Lloyd's Rep. 393. *Cf. The Nea Tyhi* [1982] 1 Lloyd's Rep. 606, where the charterers' agents' signature, without the qualification 'for Master' was held none the less to bind the shipowners.

charterparty or its contents, and in spite of that clause the master will usually sign bills of lading as agent for the owner who is, after all, responsible for the carriage of the cargo. But the charterparty will then also contain a clause by which the charterer undertakes to indemnify the owner for any liability he may incur towards shippers, consignees or bill of lading holders; for as regards these persons the master remains the agent of the shipowner,[97] and the latter is in the first place liable notwithstanding his contract with the charterer.

Again, a restriction in the charterparty as to the forms of bill which may be used pursuant thereto does not, in the ordinary way, deflect a cargo-owner's action away from the shipowner where the charterer uses another type of bill. The charterparty may provide for the use of a certain form of bill of lading, such as the standard form in a particular trade. This means that the master's authority is limited to the signing of bills of lading in that particular form. The shipper may not know that the master's authority is so limited, for in the ordinary way the master has authority to sign any form of bill of lading. Therefore, as a rule, the master binds the shipowner even if a form is used which is not author-ized by the charterparty.[98] But if the shipper does know the terms of the charterparty, he is, or should be, aware that to sign a bill of lading other than in the particular form provided for is beyond the master's auth-ority, in which event the shipowner is not liable to the shipper, but the charterer is.

Finally, it would appear that a charterer may ensure that the shipowner rather than he will be treated as the carrier in any action by a cargo-owner by inserting a so-called 'demise-clause' into any bill of lading he issues.[99] Such a clause puts the plaintiff on notice that where the issuer of the bill does not own the vessel on which the goods are carried, the cargo-owner's contract is with the owner rather than with the issuer of the bill. Such use of the demise-clause seems to be well received by the courts in the United Kingdom,[1] although it has fared rather more badly elsewhere.[2]

97 *Manchester Trust* v. *Furness, supra.* fn.95.
98 This would be the sort of case where an employment and indemnity clause would give the owner a right of recourse against the charterer: see *Kruger* v. *Moel Tryvan S.S. Co.* [1907] A.C. 272.
99 The original purpose of these clauses had more to do with the extent of the protection given by ss. 502 and 503 of the M.S.A. 1894: see *Scrutton,* (1984), pp. 70-1 and *Carver* (1982), pp. 526-7.
 1 See *The Berkshire* [1974] 1 Lloyd's Rep. 185, particularly at 187-8; *The Vikfrost* [1980] 1 Lloyd's Rep. 560 and *The Henrik Sif* [1982] 1 Lloyd's Rep. 456.
 2 For a comparative review of judicial attitudes and for a robust attack upon the validity of the clause, see Tetley, *Marine Cargo Claims* (1978), pp. 88-96.

Despite the strength of the presumption that a cargo-owner contracts for the carriage of goods with the shipowner rather than the charterer, there are circumstances in which the courts can be persuaded that the reverse is the case. The clearest such circumstance arises where the vessel is let to the charterer under a demise charterparty.[3] Again, even in the absence of a demise charter, where a charterer leads a cargo-owner to believe that he, rather than the shipowner, is the appropriate defendant in an action for damage to goods, and where, in reliance on this belief, the cargo-owner allows the time bar in the shipowner's favour to run against him, the charterer cannot plead that he is not the appropriate defendant: he is put in the position of a demise-charterer by the doctrine of estoppel.[4] It is also clear that where the charterer's form of bill is used, it is likely that the contract of carriage is concluded with the charterer.[5] On the other hand, it does not necessarily follow that the charterer's signature on the bill makes him the carrier rather than the shipowner.[6]

13.8   BILLS OF LADING AND COMBINED TRANSPORT

Where it is impossible to find a ship bound for the consignee's port, the carrier may reserve to himself in the bill of lading a liberty to tranship the goods on another vessel, in which case both consignor and consignee will be keen to ensure that the carrier undertakes responsibility for the goods from port of loading to the consignee's port, i.e. beyond the point of discharge from the first vessel used. The same type of inquiry will arise where it is envisaged that the carriage of the goods from consignor to consignee will involve transport not only by sea but also by other means. It is clear that in both sets of circumstances, transhipment and multimodal transport, very troublesome problems may arise.

Firstly, we have questions akin to those discussed in the context of bills of lading issued pursuant to charterparties: who is, or possibly in this case who are, the carrier or carriers? Does the shipper contract with one carrier or with several? If with several, which regime governs

---

3 See Section 10.3 above and *Baumwoll* v. *Furness* [1893] A.C. 8.

4 *The Henrik Sif* [1982] 1 Lloyd's Rep. 456. For a case where the same doctrine applied to a booking-note, see *The Uhenbels* [1986] 2 Lloyd's Rep. 294.

5 *Samuel & Co.* v. *West Hartlepool Steam Navigation Co.* (1906) 11 Com. Cas. 115 and *The Venezuela* [1980] 1 Lloyd's Rep. 393.

6 See *The Okehampton* [1913] P. 173 and cases cited at fn. 96 above.

disputes relating to the loss of or damage to the goods?[7] In particular, what defences can be pleaded by each carrier against the cargo owner? Secondly, even if the shipper contracts with one carrier, leaving the latter to make his own arrangements for the carriage of the goods on other legs, does the same legal regime apply throughout the transit?[8] Thirdly, in the case of multimodal transport undertaken by one operator, who may or may not himself be a carrier, what type of document does he issue and how close is it in terms of its legal significance to an ocean bill of lading?

It can cause no surprise that this field is largely unexplored by judicial decisions, parties preferring settlement to litigation where there is so little material on which to base the chance of success. International agencies have, however, been very active in seeking to establish a uniform regime governing multimodal transport: the efforts of the Comité Maritime International led to the draft TCM convention, which was never actually finalized and which was superseded by the UNCTAD Convention on International Multimodal Transport of 1980.[9] This Convention, though, has not received the required number of accessions for its coming into force. In the absence of much judicial or legislative guidance, such development as there has been is due largely to the ability of people in the trade to adapt their documents and practices in order to accommodate the multimodal carriage of goods, commonly in containers. The lead was given by the International Chamber of Commerce in 1973: faced with the failure of the TCM draft, the ICC[10] published a voluntary code for combined transport entitled Uniform Rules for a Combined Transport Document. This envisages, as the title implies, the issue of a Combined Transport (CT) document by a Combined Transport Operator (CTO), either in negotiable or non-negotiable form. The CTO may himself be a carrier or he may be a forwarding agent who arranges the required modes of carriage. Of course, these Rules have no statutory force. They operate by virtue of the contract made by the consignor and the CTO. Under the Rules, the CTO who issues the document 'undertakes to perform and/or in his own name to procure performance of the combined transport' (Rule 5(a)). This means that in respect of certain stages the

---

7 Where the C.M.R. Convention governing the International Carriage of Goods by Road applies, its rules would normally govern the carriage of the goods throughout the course of transit: see Carriage of Goods by Road Act 1965, Sch. Art. 2.

8 See, for example, *Mayhew Foods* v. *O.C.L.* [1984] 1 Lloyd's Rep. 317.

9 See Goode (1982) at pp. 637-9.

10 I.C.C. Publication 273; the current version is I.C.C. 298, published in 1975.

CTO will himself be the consignor *vis-à-vis* a particular carrier whom he engages; an inland CTO will thus be the consignor *vis-à-vis* the sea carrier, who will issue his bill of lading to the CTO. As against the cargo-owner the CTO assumes liability for the goods throughout the entire transport (Rule 5(e)).

When the stage of transport where the loss or damage occurred is known, the CTO's liability to the consignor is determined – under what is known as the 'network principle' – by the international convention or domestic law applicable (Rule 13); naturally the CTO, if that stage is performed by someone other than himself, can recoup from that particular carrier the compensation paid to the goods-owner.

Where the stage of transport is not known, Rules 11 and 12 apply. They contain a selection of rules from international transport conventions which have proved fair and reasonable. Compensation is limited to 30 gold francs per kilo gross weight (unless a higher value has been declared), the limit of the Hague Rules, prior to the SDR protocol of 1979. The carrier has a complete defence where, for example, an act or omission of consignor or consignee has caused the loss or damage, or where that was the result of such factors as inherent vice of the goods, labour disputes, inevitable accident or a nuclear incident.[11]

The pattern outlined by the Rules has been followed in a number of combined transport documents, either through incorporation[12] or through simple imitation.[13] These documents, occasionally going under the name of combined transport bills of lading, are constrained to exist within a legal tradition which still sees the orthodox ocean bill of lading as its centrepiece. The main problem with container bills is the doubt which surrounds their negotiability as documents of title in international trade: they commonly affirm that the goods have been received by the combined transport operator for shipment, and not that they have actually been shipped on board a vessel.[14] If this means that such documents are not documents of title at common law, then their

---

11 For details see Giles, 'Combined Transport' (1975), 24 *International and Comparative Law Quarterly*, 379; *International and Comparative Law Quarterly*, 443; Lloyd's of London Press, Through Transport: Problem Areas. Seminar, June 15/16, 1978.

12 COMBIDOC, issued by the Baltic & International Maritime Conference and the International Shipowners' Association in 1977.

13 COMBICONBILL, issued by BIMCO in 1971, based largely on the TCM draft, a forerunner of the ICC Rules; or the ACL bill, which follows the Rules, with some variations.

14 See *Scrutton* (1984), pp. 382-384 and Sassoon, (1984) pp. 129-30, for a fuller discussion of these problems. For 'received for shipment' bills of lading, see Section 10.3, *supra*. It would appear that noting the date of actual shipment on a combined transport document would cure the defect referred to in the text.

role in the passage of constructive possession or property, their operation under s.1 of the Bills of Lading Act 1855 and the validity of their tender under c.i.f. sales are all subject to question. Again, however, it appears that the practice of the trade, and its wide acceptance of combined transport documents, may gradually lead to a new understanding of this area of the law. It cannot be without significance that these documents are accepted as negotiable by their users, and commonly describe themselves as such on their face.[15] Moreover, newer forms of c.i.f. and f.o.b. contracts, adapted to the practices of the container trade, are emerging which move away from the traditional point of the ship's rail and which talk of the 'usual transport document' rather than the bill of lading.[16] Finally, and perhaps in the long run most significantly, the use of combined transport documents under letters of credit is now unequivocally sanctioned by the Uniform Customs and Practice for Documentary Credits.[17]

15 See COMBIDOC and COMBICONBILL.
16 See the terms CIP, Carriage and Insurance Paid to, and FRC, Free Carrier Named Point in INCOTERMS, 1980, ICC Publication
17 ICC Publication 400, in force since October 1984.

14
THE VOYAGE

WE HAVE now completed the loading of the cargo and it next falls to consider the voyage itself. Like the loading, the voyage must be performed with reasonable dispatch.[1] Indeed, the problems here are identical with those discussed above.[2] In both cases, where the delay is such as to frustrate the business purpose of the adventure, the contract may be discharged. Where the delay is caused by the breach of contract of either of the parties, the innocent party may treat the contract as terminated and sue the other for damages. Where, on the other hand, the frustrating delay is caused through the default of neither of the parties, the contract is automatically ended through the doctrine of frustration under which, ordinarily speaking, rights and remedies under the contract are 'frozen' as at the moment of frustration.[3]

Illustration: *Embiricos v. Reid & Co.*[4]
There was a charterparty of a Greek ship. After a small portion of the cargo had been loaded war became imminent between Greece and Turkey.

Held: Charterers were entitled to cancel the charterparty, the adventure was frustrated, and the part-execution of the contract was no obstacle.

In this chapter, we shall be dealing mainly with delay resulting from the most obvious breach of a contract of carriage of goods by sea, deviation from the contract voyage.

1 See *Scrutton* (1984) pp. 90–92.
2 See Section 12.5 *supra*.
3 Where the Law Reform (Frustrated Contracts) Act 1943 applies, the situation is different in that the courts are given jurisdiction to adjust the position between the parties through monetary compensation. The Act, though, only applies to time and demise charterparties so far as contracts of carriage by sea are concerned. For a more detailed account of the operation of Frustration in this area, see *Scrutton* (1984), pp. 92–101.
4 [1914] 3 K.B. 45; compare *Maritime National Fish Co.* v. *Ocean Trawlers* [1935] A.C. 524.

14.1   DEVIATION

Naturally, if the ship is to perform the voyage with reasonable dispatch she must not deviate from the contract route. Effect has been given to this very reasonable proposition by the courts in a number of decisions relating both to carriage and insurance, which have established what is a somewhat artificial, and certainly a very rigorous, doctrine of deviation under which the master is held strictly to the proper route. This doctrine in its more modern manifestation has pressed hard on shipowners, and it has long been common to modify the legal rules by the terms of the contract of affreightment while the law has itself been somewhat relaxed under the Carriage of Goods by Sea Act.

The first question then is concerned with the proper route. What is the proper route? This may be laid down in express terms in the contract, but except in cases where a charterer wishes to load or discharge at a succession of ports this is not common. Normally the contract simply stipulates the port of departure and the port of destination, and the proper route between these two *termini* is that which is nautically usual.[5]

14.1.1   EFFECT ON EXCEPTED PERILS

The importance of the doctrine of deviation lies in the possibly serious consequences for the shipowner, particularly on the exception clauses in the contract of carriage which the shipowners insert to mitigate their common law liability. These apply only so long as the carrier performs the contract; as soon as the ship deviates, owners lose their right to rely upon them.

Illustration: *Joseph Thorley Ltd v. Orchis S.S. Co.*[6]
A bill of lading contained a clause exempting the shipowner from liability for loss arising from negligence of stevedores employed by him in discharging the ship. Having deviated from the proper route the shipowner was held to be debarred from relying on the clause for his protection. *Per* Fletcher Moulton LJ at 669: 'a deviation is such a serious matter, and changes the character of the contemplated voyage so essentially, that a shipowner who has been guilty of a deviation cannot be considered as having performed his part of the bill of lading contract, but something fundamentally different. He

5 *Evans* v. *Cunard S.S. Co.* (1902) 18 T.L.R. 374.
6 [1907] 1 K.B. 243, 660; and see *Hain* v. *Tate & Lyle* (1936) 52 T.L.R. 617.

therefore cannot claim the benefit of stipulations in his favour contained in the bill of lading'.

Deviation is thus said to displace the terms contained in the contract of carriage, including the catalogue of exceptions contained in Art. IV of the Hague–Visby Rules[7] where these apply. This, in turn, means that the shipowner is thrown back on his strict common law liability as an insurer unless, of course, the cargo-owner waives his right to treat the contract as repudiated.

Even at common law, the shipowner has five defences with which to defeat a cargo-owner's claim for damages: Act of God, the Queen's enemies, inherent vice of the goods, defective packing or general average sacrifice. Yet these are valid defences for a shipowner who has performed his contract. If he has broken it by deviation they fail,[8] unless the shipowner can prove that the loss was as likely to occur on the proper route as it did on the deviating one.

Illustration: *Morrison & Co. v. Shaw Savill & Albion Co.*[9]
Wool was shipped from New Zealand to London. The bill of lading was headed 'direct service between New Zealand and London', and contained the clauses: 'with liberty on the way to London to call and stay at any intermediate port or ports . . .'. In addition to the wool the ship also took on board a parcel of meat for France with orders to deliver it at Le Havre before going to London. On proceeding to Le Havre, and when eight miles from there, the ship was torpedoed by a German submarine and sank with the cargo. In an action by the holders of the bills of lading issued in respect of the wool it was proved that proceeding to Le Havre was outside the proper route on a voyage from New Zealand to London, but that at the time in question there was no greater likelihood of danger from submarines in going there than in going to London direct.

Held: The shipowners were liable to pay damages. Le Havre was not an 'intermediate' port, and the shipowners could not avail themselves of the exception of King's enemies as they could not prove that the loss would have occurred regardless of the deviation.

Now, in the USA it has been argued for some time, although it is still a matter of some controversy, that the defence of excepted perils should only be lost through deviation if the loss actually resulted from the

7 See Section 11.4.2 *supra*.
8 *International Guano* v. *MacAndrew & Co.* [1909] 2 K.B. 360.
9 [1916] 2 K.B. 783.

deviation.[10] For instance, deviation may have lengthened the voyage so much that perishable cargo actually perished.

This line of thought, it has been suggested, has since received support from s. 1(2), Carriage of Goods by Sea Act 1971, which provides that the amended Hague Rules shall have 'the force of law', so that they are no longer to be treated as merely contractual terms. If the Rules have the force of law they rank as a statute, and the statute would govern the relationship between the parties when the contract between them collapses in terms of the common law[11] by the goods' owner's decision to repudiate the contract. Thus the exceptions in Art. IV are now a statutory provision, not a contractual term that can be ousted by deviation. It is now arguable, though a firm statement must await a judicial pronouncement, that unauthorized deviation deprives the shipowner of his defences under Art. IV only where the loss or damage was the result of the deviation (Art. IV(4)).[12] Even then, certainly in an English court hearing a case of a bill of lading issued in the United Kingdom, the shipowner can rely on the time limit for actions to be brought against him provided for in Art. III, Rule 6, third paragraph, which grants this limit 'in any event'.[13]

Now it is undisputed that the exemption clauses cease to operate in respect of damage caused during the deviation, and also after the ship has regained its proper course. But what happens if the cargo has been damaged by an excepted peril before the ship deviates? Although this is not beyond dispute, it seems clear that the carrier can rely on exception clauses in respect of events preceding deviation. As Lord Maugham said in *Hain S.S. Co.* v. *Tate & Lyle*,[14] the cargo-owner, in this particular case the charterer of the ship, is entitled to treat the contract as at an end 'as from the date of the repudiation', in other words, from the moment of deviation.

10 Gilmore and Black, *The Law of Admiralty*, 2nd edn, pp. 180 *et seq.* (1975). See also *Benedict on Admiralty*, Volume 2A, paras 121 and 128 (6th edn) and *Admiralty and Maritime Law, Cases and Materials*, Schoenbaum and Yiannopoulos, 1984, pp. 420–424. For a Privy Council decision in the same direction in a case on appeal from Canada, see *Paterson S.S. Co.* v. *Robin Hood Mills* (1937) 58 Ll. L.R. 33.

11 *Thorley* v. *Orchis* and *Hain* v. *Tate & Lyle*, see fn. 6 *supra*.

12 It is also arguable that the exception clauses in the contract would survive deviation even where Art. IV.2 does not have the force of law, e.g. when the Hague–Visby Rules do not apply or when they are incorporated into a charterparty as a matter of contract. See *Photo Production* v. *Securicor Transport* [1980] 1 Lloyd's Rep. 545 and The Future of Deviation in the Law of the Carriage of Goods, C.P. Mills, (1983) 4 L.M.C.L.Q. 587.

13 *Scrutton* (1984), pp. 263, 456. See *The Antares* (No. 2) [1986] 2 Lloyd's Rep. 633.

14 (1936) 52 T.L.R. 617; *Carver* (1982) para. 1200.

14.1.2   EFFECT ON FREIGHT

The question of deviation is also of importance from the point of view of the freight. A shipowner, who by deviating from the contract route has repudiated the contract, cannot claim to be remunerated thereunder. Does this mean that he can claim nothing at all? There is no express authority on the point, but the position seems to be this:[15] where the cargo-owner does not treat deviation as a repudiation of the contract, he must pay the full freight. Even where he treats deviation as repudiation, but the goods reach their destination, liability for freight remains, though not for the contract freight; after all, the shipowner has broken his contract. At the same time, he has essentially performed his obligation to carry, and therefore deserves reasonable freight on a *quantum meruit* basis.

14.1.3   JUSTIFIABLE DEVIATION

Given that deviation may strongly impair the carrier's right to freight and his protection by contractual and statutory immunities, a carrier who has deviated will try to bring himself within one of the cases where deviation is allowed by the common law, the Hague–Visby Rules or the contract itself.

(A)   DEVIATION ALLOWED AT COMMON LAW

Even at common law, deviation was allowed under certain conditions. The master was allowed to deviate in order to save life at sea, or where he received credible information that by pursuing the contract route ship or cargo will run into imminent danger by icebergs, pirates or hostile capture.[16] Again, a deviation was considered reasonable when it was made in order to effect repairs at a port of refuge, and this was so even if the repairs had become necessary through the initial breach of the warranty of seaworthiness.

Illustration: *Kish v. Taylor, Sons & Co.*[17]
A ship was overloaded and thereby became unseaworthy. While on her voyage this unseaworthiness made it necessary to put into a port of refuge for repairs. The question arose whether this deviation was excused.

15 *Scrutton* (1984) p. 262; *Hain* v. *Tate & Lyle, supra.* fn. 6.
16 *Carver* (1982), para, 1169; *The Teutonia* (1872) L.R. 4 P.C. 171.
17 [1912] A.C. 604, see particularly Lord Atkinson, at p. 618 *et seq.*

Held: It was. The fact that it was caused by initial breach of the contract did not make an otherwise reasonable deviation unreasonable. The reason is that the breach of the warranty of seaworthiness does not set aside the contract and relegate the shipowner to the status of the common carrier. Moreover, 'it is the presence of the peril and not its causes' which justifies deviation. The master is not to choose between alternatives of unseaworthiness and not breaking the contract, thus increasing maritime perils.

(B)   DEVIATION ALLOWED BY THE HAGUE–VISBY RULES

It will be noticed that the common law rule did not extend to the saving of property. This was regarded as unreasonable, and it was left to the Hague Rules, and now to the Hague–Visby Rules, to permit in the case of contracts to which they apply deviations for the saving of property. [18]

The Rules also permit other 'reasonable deviations'. In *Stag Line* v. *Foscolo, Mango & Co.* [19] Lord Atkin laid down [20] that to be reasonable a deviation need not only be made in the joint interests of ship and cargo, or to avoid an imminent peril.

'A deviation may, and often will, be caused by fortuitous circumstances never contemplated by the original parties to the contract; and may be reasonable, though it is made solely in the interests of the ship or solely in the interests of the cargo, or indeed in the direct interest of neither: as for instance where the presence of a passenger or of a member of the ship's crew was urgently required after the voyage had begun on a matter of national importance; or where some person on board was a fugitive from justice and there were urgent reasons for his immediate appearance. The true test seems to be what departure from the contract voyage might a prudent person controlling the voyage at the time make and maintain, having in mind all the relevant circumstances existing at the time, including the terms of the contract and the interests of all parties concerned, but without obligation to consider the interests of any one as conclusive'.

(C)   DEVIATION ALLOWED BY A 'DEVIATION' CLAUSE

We have already seen that it is usual to cut down the shipowner's liability for deviation by a clause in the bill of lading, the so-called 'deviation clause'. This clause is usually very far-reaching. As its terms

---

18 Carriage of Goods by Sea Act 1971, Sch., Art. IV, Rule 4.
19 [1932] A.C. 328; see for facts, p. 280, *infra*.
20 At p. 343.

are drawn up entirely for the shipowner's benefit it is construed strictly against him.[21] Many cases have gone against shipowners for this reason.

Illustration 1: *United States Shipping Board v. Bunge y Born*[22]

A deviation clause in a charterparty from River Plate to Malaga and Seville gave 'liberty to call at any port or ports in any order for the purpose of taking bunker coals or other supplies'. Oil fuel was taken in at Rio de Janeiro. After discharging cargo at Malaga the ship had enough oil fuel left to take her to Seville, but no farther, and as no oil fuel was to be had at Malaga or Seville the ship deviated to Lisbon.

Held: This deviation was not covered by the clause. This had to be construed as referring to ports on the line of the contract route, and as the shipowners had not taken all necessary steps to obtain a sufficient supply of oil the deviation could not be said to be reasonably necessary in a business sense.

Illustration 2: *Stag Line v. Foscolo, Mango & Co.*[23]

A bill of lading for goods shipped from Swansea to Constantinople gave 'liberty to call at any ports in any order for bunkering or other purposes . . . all as part of the contract voyage'. When the vessel sailed from Swansea, engineers were taken on board to test certain newly installed machinery. The ship deviated to St Ives in order to drop the engineers after their tests had been completed. Before the vessel regained the contract route she was wrecked.

Held: The deviation did not come within the clause. The words 'other purposes' should be construed in their context as meaning calls at a port for some purpose having relation to the contract voyage. The engineers had been taken on board quite independently from any purposes connected with the contract voyage.

Per Lord Atkin, at p. 341: 'The purposes intended are business purposes which would be contemplated by the parties as arising in carrying out the contemplated voyage of the ship. This might include in a contract other than a contract to carry a full and complete cargo a right to call at port or ports on the geographical course to load or discharge cargo for other shippers. It would probably include a right to call for orders. But I cannot think that it would include a right such as was sought to be exercised in the present case to land servants of the shipowners or others who were on board at the start to adjust machinery, and were landed for their own and their owners' convenience because they could not be transferred to any ingoing vessel'.

21 The rule of construction applied is called *contra proferentem*. It means in these cases that if there is any possible ambiguity about the meaning the one which is least favourable to the shipowner will be taken.
22 (1925) 31 Com. Cas. 118.
23 [1932] A.C. 328.

The deviation was also held not to be 'reasonable' within the meaning of Art. IV, Rule 4, of the Hague Rules.

The deviation clause most commonly met with, viz. 'with liberty to call at any port or ports in any order', gives comparatively little latitude, for it has been construed to mean only any ports which are normally passed in the ordinary course of the voyage.[24] Moreover, the courts will thwart attempts by carriers to avoid such a strict construction by a clause stipulating that any deviation will be deemed to be within the contract voyage. It appears that such an artificial extension of the contract voyage will be ignored, at any rate where the carrier deviates in such a way as to frustrate the commercial expectations of the cargo-owner.

Illustration: *Connolly Shaw v. A/S Det Nordenfjeldske D/S*[25]

Lemons were shipped from Palermo to London under a bill of lading containing a deviation clause in the following terms: 'Nothing in this bill of lading (whether written or printed) is to be read as an engagement that the said carriage shall be performed directly or without delays, the ship is to be at liberty, either before or after proceeding towards the port of delivery of the said goods, to proceed to or return to and stay at any ports or places whatsoever (although in a contrary direction to or out of or beyond the route of the said port of delivery) once or oftener in any order backwards or forwards for loading or discharging cargo, passengers, coals, or stores, or for any purpose whatsoever whether in relation to her homeward voyage or to her outward voyage, and all such ports, places, and sailings shall be deemed included within the intended voyage of the said goods.' Before proceeding to London the vessel deviated to Hull. In spite of the delay thereby occasioned, the lemons arrived in London in good condition, but in the interval the price of lemons had fallen. The endorsees of the bills of lading sued the shipowner for the damages they had suffered owing to the change of market conditions which had occurred during the delay.

Held: Action dismissed. The deviation to Hull was covered by the clause. Though its wide terms would not have prevented the contract from being discharged if the purpose of the contract had been frustrated, the delay occasioned by the deviation to Hull in the present case had not in fact frustrated the adventure.

24 *Glynn* v. *Margetson* [1893] A.C. 351. Where the Hague–Visby Rules apply, of course, the clause can only be used in a 'reasonable' way under Art. III, Rule 4.
25 (1934) 50 T.L.R. 418.

One last point deserves at least a passing notice. We have already seen that an endorsee of a bill of lading is entitled to hold the carrier to the terms of the bill of lading, unaffected by any special terms agreed to between the carrier and the original shipper not apparent on the bill: thus, the shipper's prior agreement to what would otherwise be a deviation does not bind an endorsee.[26] By the same token, it should be pointed out here that the waiver of a deviation by the endorser of a bill does not bind the endorsee who is free to repudiate the contract, putting in jeopardy the carrier's right to the protection of the contract.[27]

14.1.4 DAMAGES

Where the cargo-owner has suffered damage through deviation or delay the question arises of how much of the damage he can recover. For many years it was believed that the measure of damages where a contract of affreightment has been broken is more restricted than in the law of contract generally. Not until 1967 did the House of Lords, in line with decisions in the USA, lay that ghost. It is now clear that the breach of a contract of affreightment, like the breach of any other contract, entails the payment of any damage that is not too remote.

Illustration: *Koufos v. Czarnikow Ltd*[28]

A cargo of Hungarian sugar was carried in a chartered vessel from Constanza in the Black Sea to Basra on the Persian Gulf. In breach of the charterparty the ship was diverted to Berbera to load additional cargo, and it also called at Abadan for bunkers. As a result ship and cargo arrived at the destination nine days late, and during these nine days the value of sugar in the Basra market had declined.

Held: The owners were responsible not only for the interest on the value of the sugar during the period of delay, but for the difference in the market price of the sugar between the contract date of delivery and the actual date of delivery. The shipowner knew, or could be reasonably assumed to know, that there existed a market for the cargo he carried, so that delay was 'not unlikely' to result in loss to the cargo-owner if the market price declined, as it did in this particular case.

26 See Section 13.2 *supra.*
27 *Hain S.S. Co.* v. *Tate & Lyle* see fn. 6, *supra.*
28 [1969] 1 A.C. 350.

14.2   STOPPAGE *IN TRANSITU*

At any time after he has received possession of the cargo the shipowner, or the master on his behalf, may be faced by a demand to deliver the goods to a third party claiming the right to stop them in transit. This may happen in this way. The cargo has been the subject-matter of a sale and is on its way from the seller to the buyer. While in transit the seller hears that the buyer has become insolvent. If the seller is still unpaid it would be very hard on him if he were bound to deliver the goods to the buyer despite the latter's insolvency. The seller is therefore given the right to order the shipowner or the master of the ship not to deliver the goods to the purchaser, but to redeliver them to him. This is called stoppage *in transitu*; the rules relating thereto, however, are part of the law of sale, and go beyond the scope of this volume.[29]

Whether or not the right of stoppage exists may be an exceedingly difficult question of law, and it is one which the shipowner must solve correctly. If he refuses delivery to a seller entitled to it he is guilty of conversion; yet if the carrier redelivers to a vendor not entitled to it, this too amounts to conversion. In circumstances like these, where property is claimed by two or more persons from the person in possession, the latter may use a special procedure, called interpleader proceedings. The possessor, in this case the shipowner, takes out what is called an interpleader summons; that is to say, he starts legal proceedings by calling on seller and buyer to bring their case before the court which will then decide whether the seller's stoppage was justified. The shipowner in effect declares that he is ready to hand over the property to the party the court holds is entitled to it; thereby he avoids the risk of giving possession to the wrong person, and compels buyer and seller to fight out their dispute between themselves.[30] The shipowner, who has no interest in the goods apart from costs, is enabled to drop out. Alternatively, the carrier may safely hold the goods at the seller's disposal if the latter provides a banker's indemnity to hold him harmless in case of claims by the buyer or some other person claiming through him. Before the shipowner delivers up the goods to the seller he is entitled to demand the expenses caused by the stoppage.

29 Sale of Goods Act 1979, ss. 44–6. See *Benjamin* (1981), pp. 583–601.
30 Rules of the Supreme Court, Order 17.

14.3   AUTHORITY OF THE MASTER[31]

14.3.1   CARRIER'S AGENT

During the voyage a number of emergencies may arise. A deviation may become necessary, the ship may need repairs, the cargo may deteriorate and make advisable an immediate sale short of the port of destination, or salvage agreements may become necessary. The person to decide what is to be done in all those circumstances is obviously the master, and his authority is a dual one. In the ordinary way he is, of course, the agent of the shipowner, and as such he is authorized to take all steps which are necessary to carry out the contract of affreightment between ship- and cargo-owner.

If, however, extraordinary steps of the kind just indicated become necessary, the master has power to bind the shipowner only if the situation is such as to constitute him an agent of necessity. That is to say, there must be a necessity to take a certain decision, and it must be impossible to communicate with the owner so that his instructions can arrive in time.

14.3.2   CARGO-OWNER'S AGENT

The master also binds the charterer for the provision of necessaries which by the charterparty must be borne by the charterer, e.g. the purchase of bunkers. Apart from that, the master may also be the agent of all the cargo-owners in respect of the cargo on board his vessel. While there it is in the master's custody, and it is only natural that the master should in certain circumstances be entitled to act on behalf of the cargo-owners. This he may do only as agent of necessity and with a view to benefiting the cargo. It should be borne in mind that the impossibility of communicating with consignees of cargo may be established more easily in the case of a tramp steamer or liner where there are many cargo-owners than in the case of a chartered vessel which has on board only the charterer's goods. On the other hand, communication is now very much easier, and the master's responsibility has materially diminished. These topics have accordingly lost much of their old importance and need not be dealt with at length.

31 *Scrutton* (1984), p. 254, *et seq.*

Illustration: *Australasian Steam Navigation Co. v. Morse* [32]

A ship with a cargo of wool on board was wrecked shortly after she had left the loading port. The wool was transhipped and brought back to the loading port. There it was found that the wool was damaged, dirty and wet, and on Saturday, 23rd December, Lloyd's agent advised an immediate sale, which was fixed for Tuesday, 26th December. The wool belonged to 23 owners, most of them at the port of destination, 200 miles away. No letter could reach them in time, neither would a telegram have been any good owing to Sunday and Christmas Day and the mercantile habits at the place where the cargo-owners lived.

Held: This was a case where the master by a sale of the cargo could, as agent of necessity, bind the cargo-owners.

In these circumstances the master also has the power of binding ship and cargo-owners by bottomry and respondentia bonds,[33] but under modern conditions there is hardly ever need for these expedients.

32 (1872) L.R. 4 P.C. 222.
33 See Section 6.8 *supra*.

15
GENERAL AVERAGE

WE NOW turn to the last problem arising on the voyage. Suppose in a gale it becomes imperative to lighten the ship by throwing overboard part of the cargo, and by doing so the ship is saved, and so are the interests of other persons interested in the commercial venture on which the ship is engaged, that is, as a rule, the shipowner, the other cargo-owners and the persons entitled to the freight to be earned on the voyage. Suppose, on the other hand, that part of the cargo is lost as the result of an accident for which nobody is responsible. Clearly, the two accidents merit different treatment; in the last-mentioned case there is a loss pure and simple, in the former we have a loss that was occasioned deliberately and designed to prevent greater loss. This difference is, and has been from early days, reflected in the legal treatment accorded to the two cases.

Where the loss is due to an accident pure and simple it lies where it falls, that is, in the above example it is borne by the owner whose cargo is lost, though as we have seen he may have a right over against the carrier; where, however, the loss has been effected purposely, for the benefit of all interested, it would be unfair to let the ordinary rule govern the case; and other interests which have been saved must contribute to make good the loss. This is the doctrine of general average, so-called because the loss is borne proportionately by all the parties involved.[1] In the old days, when merchants travelled with their goods, general average was agreed between master and merchant when the danger arose. Later, general average was said to be founded on an implied contract between carrier and cargo-owners or on equity and

---

1 The expression 'particular average', which is used to denote loss to individual private, or 'particular', interests, as opposed to general average, is confined to marine insurance: see Section 29.9.2.

natural justice.[2] The position is exactly the same where, without there being any actual sacrifice of property, there is an expenditure of money in the same set of circumstances and with the same object. This is a general average expenditure, and the parties benefited must contribute towards reimbursing the party who has made it, usually the shipowner.[3]

This is, in a nutshell, the idea underlying general average. To prevent confusion, we must realize that the term is used in three distinct, though connected, senses, viz., to denote the act of making the sacrifice, the loss sustained by the sacrifice, and the contributions levied on the adventure to recoup the loser.[4]

15.1 HISTORY — THE YORK – ANTWERP RULES

The problem which general average seeks to solve is probably as old as seafaring. It was known certainly to the Greeks, probably to the Phoenicians. The oldest law dealing with general average is the law of the Rhodians which has been preserved by the fact that it was reproduced in the *Digest* of the Roman Emperor Justinian.[5] This law has become part of most modern laws, among them the common law of England. It has now received a statutory definition in s. 66 of the Marine Insurance Act 1906.

Though the principles of the law are common to all maritime countries, important differences exist which make for uncertainty especially as general average adjustments may have to take place in various countries.[6] This gave rise to very troublesome problems under

---

2 *Lowndes and Rudolf* (1975) paras 9 *et seq.*, 39 *et seq.* 'The principles upon which contributions become due does not appear ... to differ from that upon which claims of recompense for salvage services are founded.' *Per* Lord Watson, in *Strang., Steel & Co.* v. *Scott & Co.* (1889) 14 App. Cas. 601, 608.

3 For an example, see p. 292 *infra*.

4 *Carver* (1982) para. 1351.

5 *De lege Rhodia de jactu*, Book XIV, Title 2, para. 1: *Lege Rhodia cavetur, ut, si levandae navis gratia iactus mercium factus sit, omnium contributione sarciatur, quod pro omnibus datum est.* This is provided in the Rhodian Statute on jettison: if goods are thrown overboard in order to keep the ship afloat, the loss incurred for the benefit of all concerned shall be made good by a contribution of all co-adventurers.

6 The process of working out the entitlements of the parties who have suffered from a general average sacrifice and the liabilities of those who have benefited is called an adjustment, and the professional men who undertake such work are known as average adjusters.

conflict of laws. British and foreign shipowners, merchants, underwriters and average adjusters have therefore collaborated, and after joint deliberations produced a standard set of rules relating to general average. These rules are known as the York – Antwerp Rules, so called from the seats of the conferences which first brought them into being. The first York Rules date from 1864, and the first York – Antwerp Rules from 1890. Following two revisions, the present Rules date from 1974, when they were agreed at a conference in Hamburg, so as to keep in step with changed commercial procedures and shipping techniques and to simplify the work of average adjusters. In some countries, this code is given statutory force by legislative enactment, but in the United Kingdom and the USA the Rules are put into operation as contractual terms in charterparties and bills of lading.[7] Where they are not so incorporated the general law still prevails. Average in the Marine Insurance Act is based on the common law. The York – Antwerp Rules are, however, in such common use that we propose to devote our attention to a discussion of them.

The scheme of the Rules is to start off with a Rule of Interpretation, followed by seven rules, lettered A to G, setting out general principles. The lettered Rules are followed by twenty-two numbered Rules covering special circumstances. For some time doubts existed as to what was the relation between the lettered and the numbered Rules particularly whether a contribution was due when the event came within the numbered rules but not within the lettered. Roche J in *The Makis*[8] decided that the event had to be covered by the lettered rules if it was to require general average contribution. The trade countered with what came to be known as the Makis Agreement, whereby parties agreed that it was enough if the event was covered by one of the numbered rules. The Makis Agreement was effectively adopted by the York–Antwerp Rules when they were revised in 1950. After providing for the adjustment of general average according to the Rules to the exclusion of inconsistent law and practice, this Rule provides: 'Except as provided by the numbered Rules, general average shall be adjusted according to the lettered Rules.'

---

7 *Lowndes and Rudolf* (1975) paras 518-24.

8 *Vlassopoulos* v. *British & Foreign Marine Insurance Co.* [1929] 1 K.B. 187: see *Lowndes and Rudolf* (1975) paras 545-549 and *Scrutton* (1984) pp. 500-1.

15.2   CONDITIONS OF GENERAL AVERAGE – GENERAL AVERAGE ACT

Rule A lays down that 'there is a general average act when, and only when, any extraordinary sacrifice or expenditure is intentionally and reasonably made or incurred for the common safety for the purpose of preserving from peril the property involved in a common maritime adventure'. This Rule brings out several of the essential features of general average.

15.2.1   DANGER

Both at common law and under Rule A, actual danger must exist if a sacrifice or expenditure is to be treated as a general average act, and this condition is also adopted by the Marine Insurance Act 1906.[9] Thus, if a sacrifice was made at a time when there was no danger, though the master of the ship was under the impression that a danger existed, the loss was not regarded as a general average loss.

Illustration: *Watson v. Firemen's Fund Insurance Co.*[10]
The master of a vessel mistakenly but reasonably believed that there was fire in the hold. He turned steam into it with a view to extinguishing the fire, and thereby damaged the cargo.
Held: The loss was not a general average loss.

This may create a dilemma for the master where circumstances prevent him from conducting a close inspection, and writers, with this in mind, have criticized this interpretation of Rule A. On the other hand, Rule V protects the master when, in a situation of actual danger, he makes a sacrifice that later turns out to have been unnecessary.

The position is the same under US law.[11] In one case decided under that law[12] it was also held that for general average rules to come into play the ship must be in actual danger, and it does not matter if the master is mistaken about the real source of danger and orders not altogether appropriate action to be taken.

9 S. 66: 'sacrifice ... incurred ... in time of peril'.
10 [1922] 2 K.B. 355.
11 *Lowndes and Rudolf* (1975) para. 50.
12 *The Wordsworth* (1898) 88 Fed. Rep. 313.

In practice, two sets of circumstances, superficially identical, may be on different sides of the border line. In one case the ship is, and in the other it is not, in danger.

Illustration: *Vlassopoulos v. British & Foreign Marine Insurance Co.*[13]

While a ship was engaged in loading cargo at Bordeaux the foremast broke, fell on the main deck and caused a derrick to fall into the hold. The ship was at no time in danger, but she was moved into a wet dock for repairs. After completion she finished loading and put out to sea. There she fouled submerged wreckage and damaged the blades of her propeller. This accident rendered the vessel unfit to encounter the ordinary perils of the sea, and she put into Cherbourg for inspection and repairs, these being necessary for the common safety of ship, cargo and freight.

Held: Expenses at Bordeaux were not general average expenditure, since the ship was at no time in danger. But the expenses at Cherbourg were general average expenditure, for the interests in the adventure were in danger. *Per* Roche J, at p. 200: 'Peril, which means the same thing as danger, is the word used in the General Rule A, just as it is the word used in the Marine Insurance Act 1906, s. 66. The phrase is not "immediate peril or danger". It is sufficient to say that the ship must be in danger, or that the act must be done in order to preserve her from peril. It means, of course, that the peril must be real and not imaginary, that it must be substantial and not merely slight or nugatory. In short, it must be a real danger.' At p. 199 the learned judge had said that it was not necessary for the ship to 'be actually in the grip, or even nearly in the grip, of the disaster that may arise from a danger. It would be a very bad thing if shipmasters had to wait until that state of things arose in order to justify them doing any act which would be a general average act.'

This case, and especially the proposition of law laid down in it, has been followed in *Daniolos v. Bunge & Co. Ltd.*[14]

15.2.2   GENERAL AVERAGE ACTS

Supposing then that danger exists, what acts can be done which the law will recognize as general average acts? There are two, as we have already mentioned: an extraordinary sacrifice, or a like expenditure. These must now be discussed. First it should be noticed that both sacrifice and expenditure must be extraordinary. This means that what is done to escape the calamity is something not incidental to an ordinary voyage of

13 [1929] 1 K.B. 187, decided under the 1924 Rules.
14 (1937) 59 Ll. L.R. 175, 177, affirmed (1938) 62 Ll. L.R. 65.

the kind on which the ship is engaged. The borderline is finely drawn as appears from the following illustrations.

Illustration 1: *Wilson v. Bank of Victoria* [15]

A sailing ship with an auxiliary engine was so damaged by perils of the sea that she had lost all her sailing power. She therefore proceeded under her auxiliary steam, and the expenses of her voyage were thereby increased by £1400. These the shipowner endeavoured to spread over the interests involved.

Held: He could not do so, for the expenditure was not extraordinary.

Illustration 2: *Robinson v. Price* [16]

A ship sprang a leak while at sea and was kept afloat only by constant pumping, the pumps being driven by the donkey engine. The coal, which was sufficient for an ordinary voyage, ran short, and ship's spars and cargo were used for fuel.

Held: This was an extraordinary sacrifice and the damage was to be made good by general average contribution.

(1) JETTISON

The best-known form of sacrifice is jettison of the cargo in order to lighten the ship and keep her afloat.

Deck cargo is nearest at hand when jettison becomes necessary, and for this reason the owner of jettisoned deck cargo could in the old days never expect a contribution from the other interests. Of course, if his cargo was in fact saved he had to contribute to the other interests. [17]

In course of time, it became usual for certain cargoes, for instance, timber and, later, containers to be carried on deck, and indeed to adapt or build ships for those purposes. That is reflected in the modern York – Antwerp Rules. Rule I provides that 'no jettison shall be made good as general average, unless such cargo is carried in accordance with the recognized custom of the trade'. The Rule does not mention deck cargo specifically, but it follows from its wording that jettisoned cargo carried on deck in accordance with a recognized trade custom ranks as a general average loss. Thus, only such cargo does not so rank that is not stowed

15 (1867) L.R. 2 Q.B. 203.
16 (1876) 2 Q.B.D. 91. 205.
17 *Lowndes and Rudolf* (1975) 106.

in accordance with a custom, and that applies both to deck and under-deck cargo.[18]

Other sacrifices are the burning of spars and cargo after the ship had sprung a leak and additional fuel was required to work the pumps;[19] again, where a vessel had stranded[20] and in an endeavour to refloat her the engines were intentionally overstrained and additional coal was burnt, the shipowner was held entitled to contribution in general average.[21]

Finally, damage inflicted on third parties, such as pier and dock-owners, may constitute a general average sacrifice, and all parties must contribute to the damages which one of them becomes liable to pay.

Illustration: *Austin Friars S.S. Co.* v. *Spillers & Bakers*[22]

A ship had stranded in the Severn; she was seriously damaged, and ship and cargo were in imminent danger. The vessel was got off with the assistance of tugs. The pilot intended to take her into dock, which involved her striking a pier, since she was difficult to handle, having no steam of her own and only her hand-steering gear available. The ship hit the pier and inflicted £5000 worth of damage, which the shipowner had to pay to the pier owners.

Held: This was a general average act, it was a reasonable thing to do in the interests of ship and cargo, and the latter had to contribute.

(II)   EXPENDITURE

The other form a general average act may take is special expenditure. As was pointed out above, the expenditure, in order to qualify for contri-bution, must occur in the same sort of circumstances as the sacrifice. But this is not altogether true; for the actual expenditure, that is, the payment, is usually made long after the measures for the safety of ship, cargo and freight have been taken. Suppose a steamer develops engine trouble preventing her from reaching port under her own steam; if the master enters into a salvage agreement with another vessel whereby this vessel is to tow the disabled steamer, the remuneration payable to the salvors may be a general average expenditure though payment is made when there is no longer any danger of the adventure failing. But not every salvage agreement is covered; the other conditions necessary to

18 *Lowndes and Rudolf* (1975) 611, 612.
19 *Robinson* v. *Price* (1876) 2 Q.B.D. 295: York–Antwerp Rules, Rule IX.
20 This does not include bumping the ground, see *The Seapool*, [1934] P. 53, 62.
21 *The Bona*, [1895] P. 125; Rule VII.
22 [1915] 1 K.B. 833, affirmed [1915] 3 K.B. 586.

qualify for general average must, of course, also subsist. If it turns out that the salvage agreement was unreasonable,[23] that is, for example, if there existed at the time no extraordinary peril, the shipowner alone has to bear the costs.[24] Even if the master acted reasonably in incurring expenses for the common safety, it does not follow that the whole amount must be contributed to by the other interests.[25] It may have been reasonable to make a towage agreement, but the sum promised to the tug may have been unreasonably high.[26]

Other very important instances of general average expenditure are necessary repairs and other expenses incidental thereto. A ship may have to put into a port of refuge for repairs without which the voyage cannot be completed. When entering and leaving the harbour port charges, pilotage and towage fees are incurred; moreover, cargo may have to be temporarily discharged to enable workmen to reach the damaged part of the ship, and where this happens payments must be made for discharging, lighters, warehousing and reloading.

Again, the first port of refuge may have inadequate repair facilities, so that the damaged ship needs towing to a suitable port.[27] Which of these expenses qualify for general average treatment?

Purists may entertain doubt because some of the expenses are incurred when the ship is no longer in actual danger. Most doubts are now set at rest by Rule X, which provides that all these expenses, including those at the second port of refuge, are general average expenses.

15.2.3   VOLUNTARY, OR INTENTIONAL ACT

To qualify for contribution, sacrifice or expenditure must be voluntary, to use the words of the common law and s. 66 (2) Marine Insurance Act, or intentional, to use those of the York – Antwerp Rules; both words have the same meaning.

This principle is strictly applied. For instance, fire breaks out on board, a serious danger to ship and cargo, and everything done to extinguish the fire, which includes beaching or scuttling the ship, is allowable, for those acts are intentional. But damage done by smoke and heat alone does not attract a contribution (Rule III), for the fire

23 Chapter 24, *infra.*
24 *Société Anonyme Nouvelle d'Armement* v. *Spillers & Bakers* [1917] 1 K.B. 865.
25 *Anderson, Tritton & Co.* v. *Ocean S.S. Co.* (1884) 10 App. Cas. 107.
26 A clause by which the tow promises to indemnify the tug for damage sustained while towing the endangered ship was held reasonable in *Australian Coastal Shipping Commission* v. *Green,* [1971] 1 Q.B. 456.
27 Though repairs have become easier since spare parts can now be flown in speedily.

engendering smoke and heat was not intended. Of course, smoke created by pumping water on the fire was created intentionally, but no one can distinguish between smoke created by fire and smoke created by water. So all smoke damage must be borne by whoever owns the affected property.

Again, suppose part of the ship, for instance masts, have been carried away by the storm; they overhang the side of the ship and though still connected with it are effectively lost. Then the master gives the order to cut those overhanging parts away – surely an intentional act, and yet the cutting away is not a general average loss (Rule IV). Why not? Because what was cut away was already lost involuntarily when the order was given.

This strict interpretation of the term 'intentional' does not, however, mean that the order to sacrifice or to incur expenditure must lead to the exact loss contemplated when the order was given.

Illustration: *M'Call & Co. v. Houlder Bros* [28]

A ship's propeller sustained damage so that the ship ceased to be navigable and the master put into a port of refuge for repairs. There was a perishable cargo on board which could not be warehoused. In order to facilitate repairs the master set the ship down by the head with cargo on board. The tipping of the ship caused seawater to run into the hold and to damage part of the cargo. It was contended that this was not a general average loss inasmuch as the damage to the cargo had not been foreseen as a consequence of the tipping of the ship, and that the damage to the cargo was not incurred voluntarily.

Held: It was 'not necessary that a particular loss should have been contemplated if it be incidental to the general average act'.

The act must be ordered by the person in control of the vessel. This is, in the ordinary way, the master, who in this respect is the agent of all parties concerned. [29] It makes no difference that the actual order is given by some other authority, provided the master sanctions it.

Illustration: *Papayanni v. Grampian S.S. Co.* [30]

A fire broke out on board, and the master put into port where the fire increased so that he sent for the captain of the port. The latter ordered the scuttling of the ship, and the master believed this course to be best in the

28 (1897) 2 Com. Cas. 129.
29 *Anglo-Argentine Live Stock & Produce Agency* v. *Temperley Shipping Co.* [1899] 2 Q.B. 403, 409.
30 (1896), 1 Com. Cas. 448.

interests of ship and cargo, raised no objection, and in the opinion of the court, sanctioned it and thereby made it his own. It was therefore held to be voluntary.

In an old case[31] it was also held that where the master was taken prisoner, and the ship was in control of a prizemaster and both the latter and mate together ordered a jettison for the common safety, this act was ordered by the proper person.

15.2.4   REASONABLE ACT

In carrying out the general average act the master must act reasonably in the interests of all concerned, even if his act is one of considerable hazard.

Illustration: *The Seapool* [32]
A ship with a cargo of coal on board was anchored off the pier. A sudden gale sprang up causing the ship to drag her anchor. There was a danger of the ship losing the propellers and possibly breaking her back. The master accordingly decided to put the ship broadside against the pier, using the latter as a lever so as to get the ship's head into such a position that he could steam out to sea. The operation was successful, but through bumping the ground and grinding the pier, £14 000 damage was caused to ship and pier.

Held: The action taken by the master was reasonable in the circumstances and the loss was a general average loss.

15.2.5   COMMON SAFETY

The act must have been done 'for the common safety for the purpose of preserving from peril the property involved in a common maritime adventure'. Common safety, or common benefit, as the common law terms it, means safety or benefit to all parties interested in the adventure. In one case,[33] where the cargo was removed from a stranded vessel into lighters, not with the object of lightening the ship, but of preserving the cargo, and subsequently expenses were incurred for getting the ship off, it was held that the cargo put into lighters need not contribute. Wills J laid down:[34] 'If the object of the removal has been the lightening of the ship for the common safety, and the object of effecting the

31 *Price* v. *Noble* (1811) 4 Taunt. 123.
32 [1934] P. 53.
33 *Royal Mail Steam Packet Co.* v. *English Bank of Rio* (1887) 19 Q.B.D. 362.
34 At p. 372 *et seq.*

removal in such a fashion as to avoid jettison has been to do to that which must be got overboard something less wasteful than actual jettison, there seems to be no reason whatever for drawing a distinction between such a case and that of actual jettison, so far as liability to general average is concerned. But if the lightening of the ship formed no part, or no appreciable part, of the purpose for which the removal was effected, if the object of the removal was not to minimize the cost of jettison but to get out of harm's way the thing removed and to prevent it from being or remaining at risk at all, it seems to me that a different result may very well ensue, and that a portion of cargo landed under such circumstances may well be regarded as separated from the adventure, and no longer liable for contribution. There is authority for saying that the purpose for which an act causing loss is done may determine whether it constitutes general average or not.'[35]

15.2.6   TIME OF LOSS

In order to be a general average loss, the loss must have happened during the adventure, and it is useful to remember that this is not terminated until the discharge of the cargo has been completed. Thus where 1300 tons had already been discharged, and only 100 tons remained on board, and fire broke out in the hold which made it necessary to pour in water, thereby damaging the cargo, it was held that the shipowners were liable to contribute to the damage.[36]

15.2.7   LOSS DIRECT CONSEQUENCE

A master's general average act may lead to many kinds of loss, not all of which can be allowable, just as damage caused by a common law tort may be too remote to qualify for compensation, as will be explained when we discuss collision damage in Chapter 21. Under Rule C of the York–Antwerp Rules, a general average contribution can be claimed only for the direct consequences of a general average act, that is, those which flow in an unbroken sequence from the act, as opposed to indirect consequences, where the sequence is broken by an intervening extraneous cause. In the case where this was laid down[37] the ship was carried from her moorings in a storm. A tug was signalled to tow her to safety and was engaged under United Kingdom Standard Towing

35 See also *Iredale v. China Traders' Insurance Co.* [1900] 2 Q.B. 515.
36 *Whitecross Wire & Iron Co.* v. *Savill* (1882) 8 Q.B.D. 653.
37 *Australian Coastal Shipping Co.* v. *Green* [1971] 1 Q.B. 456.

Conditions, which contained a clause obliging the tow to indemnify the tug for loss or damage suffered as a result of the towage operation. After a ten-minute tow the line parted and wrapped itself round the tug's propeller, which in turn led to the loss of the tug. Under the indemnity clause the tow was liable to pay for the tug's loss, and this payment was held to be a direct consequence of the general average act, namely, the engagement of the tug to guard the ship against a marine danger, and for this expenditure the owners were entitled to a general average contribution. Since this case was decided the new Rule VI expressly provides that salvage expenditure, whether by contract or otherwise, is allowable.

Rule C declares not allowable, as not being direct consequences of the general average act, loss or damage to ship or cargo through delay or loss of market suffered by the cargo.

15.2.8 SUCCESS

Finally, both at common law and under the York–Antwerp Rules, contribution can be demanded only if the general average act is successful, in other words if the adventure as a whole has really been saved; otherwise the loss lies where it falls. The whole idea underlying the doctrine of general average is that it is just that those whose property has been saved should contribute to those whose property has been sacrificed to save theirs. If the sacrifice is not successful, in the sense that no property escapes the dangers from which the sacrifice was intended to save it, this does not apply.

It is convenient here to mention a special problem. What happens if the general average act has been successful, but subsequently, owing to new causes, ship and cargo are lost?

Suppose a ship has suffered a general average loss, for instance, in the form of expenses incurred at a port of refuge for repairs, and incidental expenses, and subsequently ship and cargo are totally lost before the destination is reached. The question arises as to whether the interests which have benefited by the general average expenditure must still contribute though subsequently this benefit has been lost. The answer is that no contribution is due.[38]

At first sight this might seem inequitable, but the reason is fairly clear. Every maritime adventure is, to a certain extent, governed by a rule of limited liability; in principle no co-adventurer is supposed to

---

38 *Chellew* v. *Royal Commission on the Sugar Supply* [1921] 2 K.B. 627, *per* Sankey J [1922] 1 K.B. 12. *Lowndes and Rudolf* (1975) paras 809, 811.

lose directly more than the amount originally staked. In other words, if a party to the adventure, say, a cargo-owner, is called upon to make a payment directly arising from the adventure, such as a general average contribution, he must be able to make the payment from the goods on board, out of the fund that has been saved by the general average act. If after the general average loss, but before the end of the adventure, the cargo originally liable is lost, there is no longer any fund out of which the cargo interest can pay its contribution.

15.3   WHO MUST CONTRIBUTE?

Having thus determined the conditions under which an act amounts to a general average act, and the sacrifices and expenses that are apportionable, we now proceed to inquire what interests are liable to contribute to the general average loss.

Now, as we have seen, there are in the normal case three interests engaged in the adventure, namely, the ship, the cargo and the freight. The position of ship- and cargo-owners is easy to understand; but when we come to freight it may not, at first sight, appear that there is reason to distinguish this from the shipowner's interest, for it is he who receives the freight. This may, of course, be so, but not necessarily, since the person entitled to the freight may be the charterer, and even if the owner of the ship and the person entitled to the freight are identical it is still necessary to distinguish between ship and freight. The reason briefly is this: it is one thing to suffer a loss as shipowner because, say, the engines were overstrained; it is another matter not to receive freight on jettisoned cargo.[39] The position will perhaps become clearer if we disregard, for the time being, the persons who have to contribute, and look at ship, cargo and freight as if they were persons or interests; in doing so no confusion is likely to arise where two interests happen to be united in the same individual.

15.3.1   LIVES

Ship, cargo and freight are liable for contribution to a general average loss. Everything not falling within this category need not bear any share in the loss though other interests are in fact involved in the adventure. This applies first of all to lives.[40] Neither passenger nor crew need

39 For example, ship and freight may be insured with different underwriters.
40 *Lowndes and Rudolf* (1975) para. 439.

contribute, for the life of man has no assessable value, it cannot be part of a fund out of which the contribution can be paid.

15.3.2 PASSENGERS' LUGGAGE

Probably by reason of its negligible value or the difficulty of assessing it, passengers' luggage is free; similar considerations apply to mails and, perhaps, passengers' luggage stored in the hold.[41]

15.3.3 SEAMEN'S WAGES

Finally, seamen's wages do not form part of the fund that contributes to a general average loss.

15.3.4 SHIP

As regards the ship, it should be remembered that the shipowner's liability is excluded in case of fire on board,[42] and if the general average loss occurred owing to a fire the shipowner might say that as he is not liable in damages, neither need he contribute to the loss as general average contribution. But it has been held that this defence does not avail the shipowner, since s. 502 of the Merchant Shipping Act has no application to general average.[43]

15.3.5 CARGO

No particular difficulty exists with regard to the cargo owner's duty to contribute, though valuation is complicated.[44] Mails, because of valuation difficulties, do not, in practice, contribute.[45] The cargo cannot escape contribution merely because the general average loss was occasioned by one of the perils excepted in the bill of lading.[46]

Of course, if we speak of a general average contribution this contribution cannot be expected to cover the whole value of the loss. For it is the very idea of general average to distribute such loss equally, and if the owner of jettisoned cargo were fully compensated, he would suffer no

41 *Lowndes and Rudolf* (1975) paras 441, 444. Rule XVII.
42 Merchant Shipping Act 1894, s. 502.
43 *Greenshields, Cowie & Co.* v. *Stevens & Sons* [1908] A.C. 431; *Tempus Shipping Co.* v. *Dreyfus* [1931] 1 K.B. 195; [1931] A.C. 726.
44 *Lowndes and Rudolf* (1975) paras 416-18, 810.
45 *Lowndes and Rudolf* (1975) para. 814.
46 *Lowndes and Rudolf* (1975) para. 68.

loss at all, but the contributory interests would do so to the extent of their contribution.

15.4 GENERAL AVERAGE AND CARRIER'S FAULT

Of course, a party who is responsible for the loss he has suffered cannot claim contribution though it may have been a general average loss, as where damage to the ship was due to starting on the voyage in an unseaworthy condition, or without due diligence having been exercised to make her seaworthy, where the Carriage of Goods by Sea Act 1971 applies.[47] Indeed in most cases where the right to contribution was disputed, the defence has been the actionable fault of the party seeking contribution, for instance the unseaworthiness of the ship,[48] or the carrier's deviation.[49] But where the party claiming contribution, though having occasioned the loss, has contracted out of his liability by exception clauses in the contract of carriage, or where the party is exempted by statute, e.g. under s. 502 of the Merchant Shipping Act 1894, his right to claim general average is not lost.[50]

Illustration: _Dreyfus & Co. v. Tempus Shipping Co._[51]
A ship took on board bunker coal which was unsuitable; the ship was therefore unseaworthy. Fire broke out in the bunker and general average expenditure was incurred to save ship and cargo. The cargo owners refused to contribute and based their refusal on the contention that the ship was unseaworthy.

Held: Shipowners entitled to contribution, since under s. 502 of the Merchant Shipping Act 1894, they were not liable for damage caused by fire; moreover the unseaworthiness was not the cause of the casualty.

15.5 GENERAL AVERAGE BOND

So far we have seen that the duty to contribute to a general average loss was founded either on a term in the contract of affreightment implied by the common law, or expressly inserted into it by reference to the

---

47 _Schloss v. Heriot_ (1863) 14 C.B. N.S. 59.
48 _The Admiral Zmajevic_ [1983] 2 Lloyd's Rep. 86.
49 _The Daffodil B_ [1983] 1 Lloyd's Rep. 498.
50 _The Carron Park_ (1890) 15 P.D. 203; _Bulgaris v. Bunge & Co._ (1932) 49 T.L.R. 238; _Tempus Shipping Co. v. Louis Dreyfus & Co._ [1931] 1 K.B. 195 (C.A.); [1931] A.C. 726 (H.L.).
51 [1931] A.C. 726.

York – Antwerp Rules or some other system. Sometimes, however, an express contract is made before the cargo is delivered at the port of destination by making the cargo-owners sign a general average bond. The rights and duties created by such a bond are specially important where the contract of affreightment had been previously discharged, for instance by deviation, and no claim for general average contribution could any longer be founded on the contract.[52] Again, where cargo-owners, other than shippers, had signed a Lloyd's Average Bond it was held that they were bound by the term in the bill of lading providing for general average to be determined according to general average rules, and could not be heard to say that, as they were not parties to the original contract, they were only liable at common law.[53] Finally, such bonds may carry with them advantages relating to time-bars. Thus, although a general average dispute in principle arises out of the contract of carriage and is therefore subject to a time-bar in an arbitration clause, the alteration of such a contract by a separate undertaking to pay general average is not subject to that time-bar but to the general periods of limitation governing contracts.[54] Moreover, agreement to the Lloyd's Average Bond may have the effect of postponing the commencement of limitation from the time of the general average event to the time of final adjustment, the bond being 'a fresh agreement which stands on its own independently of the bill of lading'.[55]

15.6 ASSESSMENT OF CONTRIBUTION

The general average loss must be borne by all who are interested proportionately.[56] This involves the fixing of values on the basis of which the contribution is assessed. As any contribution must come out of the fund saved, it is natural that the material value is the saved value, that is, the value at the port of destination, even though since the general average loss the relative values of ship and cargo have substantially changed.[57] The estimation of these values, including the items to be

---

52 *Hain S.S. Co.* v. *Tate & Lyle Ltd* (1936) 52 T.L.R. 617, 620. *Reardon Smith Line* v. *Black Sea & Baltic General Insurance Co.* (1937) 57 Ll. L.R. 241.

53 *Thomson* v. *Micks, Lambert & Co.* (1933) 47 Ll. L.R. 5.

54 *Union of India* v. *E.B. Aaby's Rederi A/S* [1975] A.C. 797.

55 *Castle Insurance* v. *Hong Kong Islands Shipping Co.* [1983] 3 W.L.R. 524 at 533.

56 *Birkley* v. *Presgrave* (1801) 1 East 220, 228.

57 *Lowndes and Rudolf* (1975) para. 811. *Fletcher* v. *Alexander* (1868) L.R. 3 C.P. 375; *Henderson* v. *Shankland* [1896] 1 Q.B. 525 (C.A.); York – Antwerp Rules, 1950, Rules XVI and XVII.

allowed, is expert work, and is invariably carried out by professional men, called average adjusters.[58] Their practice, however, varies from country to country, as also do the various laws. Where, therefore, the port of destination is a foreign port the foreign average statement is only binding if the contract of affreightment so provides.[59] These difficulties are overcome by agreeing on the application of the York–Antwerp Rules, which not only lay down principles of general average, but also establish a system of adjustment. Thus under Rule XIII certain deductions from the cost of repairs of the ship are made in respect of 'new for old',[60] one-third for vessels built more than fifteen years before the casualty, and Rule XVII provides for cargo to contribute on the basis of the invoice value, and the ship without taking account of its charter value, a solution that simplifies adjustment compared with earlier practice, when the market value determined calculation.

Each interest which has suffered a general average loss becomes a creditor of the interests saved and has a direct claim against each of them for a *pro rata* contribution towards his indemnity, which can be enforced by action as well as by lien.[61]

General average contributions may, of course, be sued for in the courts, with interest at 7 per cent (Rule XXI), but special remedies have been developed to meet the situation; just as in other branches of law the person entitled to general average contribution is given the means of safeguarding himself against possible failure by the contributors.

First in importance ranks the lien. It is exercised by the master, who is regarded as the agent of all the parties for the purpose of enforcing the lien; as such he is bound to take reasonable steps for safeguarding their interests.[62] Strangely enough, general average did not come within the jurisdiction of the Admiralty Court,[63] so that contributions had to be sued for at common law. It follows that the lien against a contributor is not in the nature of the wide maritime lien; rather is it a possessory lien,[64] which is discharged when possession is given up.

---

58 But the shipowner is not bound to employ them; he may draw up the average statement himself. *Wavertree Sailing Ship Co.* v. *Love* [1897] A.C. 373.

59 *Harris* v. *Scaramanga* (1872) L.R. 7 C.P. 481; *De Hart* v. *Compañia Anónima de Seguros 'Aurora'* [1903] 2 K.B. 503; *The Mary Thomas* [1894] P. 108; *Green Star Shipping Co.* v. *London Assurance* (1931) 39 Ll. L.R. 213, 219.

60 See also Rule XVIII.

61 *Strang, Steel & Co.* v. *Scott & Co.* (1889) 14 App. Cas. 601.

62 *Kemp* v. *Halliday* (1866) L.R. 1 Q.B. 520; *Strang Steel & Co.* v. *Scott & Co.* (1889) 14 App. Cas. 601.

63 *The Constancia* (1845) 4 Notes of Cases, 677; *The North Star* (1860) Lush. 45.

64 Per Lord Tenterden, *Scaife* v. *Tobin* (1832) 3 B. & Ad. 523.

The actual exercise of the lien, e.g. on cargo, would usually, especially in modern times, work great hardship; the process of working out, or adjusting, the amounts owing by way of contribution from the various interests involved is a lengthy one and may take some months. The courts have, therefore, decided[65] that the master sufficiently discharges his duty if he accepts a sufficient deposit in cash or other suitable security for the amount owing. In practice the security takes the form of a Lloyd's Average Bond, so called from the fact that it was drafted under the auspices of Lloyd's.

It can be seen that the general average rules are complex, and a little thought will disclose that average adjustments, involving as they do difficult valuations, are protracted and costly. For some time it has therefore been discussed whether it would not be better to abolish the general average concept, let the loss lie where it falls as elsewhere, so that any loss is covered by insurance. Remember that general average became a problem many centuries before insurance had been developed as a refined and comprehensively used instrument.

We cannot go into this argument, but only wish to indicate that those believing in the need to retain general average argue that in fact not all interests in jeopardy in a sea adventure are fully insured. Besides, they point out that abolition would confront the master with additional problems; after the event he may face complaints that he had deliberately favoured, say, his owner's interests at the expense of those of cargo owners.[66]

---

65 *Strang* v. *Scott, supra*; *Crooks* v. *Allan* (1879) 5 Q.B.D. 33; *Nobel's Explosives* v. *Rea* (1897) 2 Com. Cas. 293.
66 *Lowndes and Rudolf* (1975) paras 39 *et seq*.

16
JOURNEY'S END: DISCHARGE, DELIVERY AND PAYMENT

THIS BRINGS us to the end of the voyage, and we arrive at the port of destination; there the carrier must discharge the goods from the ship and deliver them to the consignee. In practice, these acts are often difficult to keep apart, but the lawyer should always distinguish between them. If we speak of discharge we refer to technical questions, for instance: where should the ship unload, and when? And: who is to bear the expense incidental thereto? Questions of delivery, on the other hand, are: who is authorized to receive the cargo, and from whom can the shipowner demand the payment of freight?

16.1 DISCHARGE

First as to discharge. The problems arising under this head resemble those discussed in the section on loading; and reference should be made to those pages.[1] Nevertheless a few points can be dealt with more conveniently here.

It is the duty of the master to discharge at the place fixed by the contract of affreightment but, just as in the case of loading, it is often impossible to determine long in advance the actual berth or quay where discharge is to take place, and difficult questions may arise. Still, it seems clear that in the case of a general ship, that is, a ship not sailing under charter and having on board goods belonging to a number of consignees, the master has a right to determine the place of discharge; but this right may be limited by a custom of the port.

If the ship sails under charter, several cases must be distinguished. The charterer may also be the consignee and as such hold all the bills of

1 See particularly Section 12.5.

lading; where that happens he determines the place of discharge. On the other hand, if charterer and consignees are not identical the bill of lading holders may agree on the spot where they desire to take delivery; in case of disagreement the charterer seems to have an unfettered right of selecting the spot.[2]

Next, the ship must be made ready to discharge and here, too, the contract of affreightment or the custom of the port may lay down special rules.

When discussing the process of loading we drew attention to the fact that this was a joint operation of shipper and carrier; similarly, when discharging a ship, carrier and consignee must co-operate. The line of demarcation between the two spheres of control is again the ship's rail, and it is, therefore, the duty of the consignee, or his assign, to take delivery there. It depends on the terms of the charterparty or bill of lading whether the ship's rail must be 'alongside', that is to say, of the quay or warehouse, or whether loading and discharging will take place from and into lighters.[3] As was said in an old case,[4] a bill of lading 'is merely an undertaking to carry from port to port. A ship trading from one port to another has not the means of carrying the goods on land; and, according to the established course of trade, a delivery on the usual wharf is such a delivery as will discharge the carrier.'

Still, as was pointed out above, the material documents must be read in the light of the custom of the port, unless the latter is expressly excluded by the contract or is otherwise inconsistent with it.

Illustration: *Brenda S.S. Co. v. Green*[5]

The charterparty read: 'The cargo to be brought to and taken from alongside steamer at charterer's risk and expense, any custom of the port notwithstanding.'

2 *The Felix* (1868) L.R. 2 A. & E. 273; *George Ireland & Sons* v. *Southdown S.S. Co.* (1926) 32 Com. Cas 73; *Co-operative Wholesale Society* v. *Embiricos* (1928) 30 Ll. L.R. 315.

3 *Cf. Fitzgerald* v. *Lona* (Owners) (1932) 49 T.L.R. 77: bill of lading provided for discharge of timber on quay and/or lighter at consignee's 'selection'. The consignee selected lighters, but on arrival of the ship a strike of lightermen had broken out and the discharge on quay was the only available method. It was held that the ship was entitled to discharge on quay, for 'selection' meant selection subject to the means selected being available.

4 *Hyde* v. *Trent & Mersey Navigation Co.* (1793) 5 T.R. 397, *per* Buller J.

5 [1900] 1 Q.B. 518.

Held: The shipowner was only bound to deliver over the ship's rail, and was not bound by any custom of the Port of London requiring a shipowner to do work outside the ship.

However, though the custom of the port may extend the actual work to be performed by one of the parties, usually the shipowner, it does not, as a rule, saddle that party with greater expenses.

Illustration: *Palgrave, Brown & Son v. S.S. Turid*[6]

A ship was chartered to carry timber to Yarmouth, where the cargo was to be delivered 'always afloat ... cargo to be ... taken from alongside the steamer at charterer's risk and expense as customary'. When the vessel arrived at Yarmouth, it appeared that, if keeping 'always afloat', she could not come nearer than 13 ft from the quay. The custom of the port provided a rule for this case: a wooden staging was erected between ship and quay over which the stevedores, who were employed by the shipowners, carried the cargo, and deposited it not less than 10 ft from the edge of the quay; the additional cost was borne by the shipowner. They paid under protest, and sued the charterers for the difference between the cost of delivering over the ship's rail and that actually incurred by reason of the mode of discharge adopted in this case.

Held: The action succeeded, since the custom of the port was inconsistent with the provision in the charterparty that the cargo should be taken from alongside at charterer's expense. *Per* Lord Birkenhead, LC, at p. 404: 'The word "alongside" if it does not suggest actual contact, does at all events suggest close contiguity, and not the less so because the ordinary obligation of the shipowner is admittedly only to deliver to the consignee the cargo his ship carries at ship's rail. A contract which requires delivery elsewhere extends this legal obligation.'

The shipowner, at his expense, has to deliver the cargo over the ship's rail as he received it – in bulk, if loaded in bulk; in bags, if received in bags. Suppose, however, there are port regulations prescribing that certain types of cargo may only be delivered in a certain state, and suppose, further, the cargo on board the ship is not in such a state. Who has to bear the cost of adapting the cargo to the port regulations? This question was discussed in *British Oil & Cake Mills v. Moor Line*.[7] There a cargo of oil seeds had been shipped in bulk, but the regulations at the port of destination allowed discharge in bags only. Clearly, before unloading could begin the oil seeds had to be bagged. Both the shipowner and the cargo-owner were anxious to avoid payment of the

6 [1922] 1 A.C. 397; Cp. *Dalgliesh S.S. Co.* v. *Williamson* (1935) 52 Ll. L.R. 87.
7 (1936) 41 Com. Cas. 3.

cost of bagging, and an action was brought. The court held that the cost was to be borne by the shipowner, for the bagging must necessarily take place on board the vessel, before the cargo passed the ship's rail, in other words within the shipowner's sphere of influence.

On the other hand, at another port it was customary for grain cargoes, unless discharged by suction direct into silos, to be first bagged on board by the receiver, the cost of bagging to be borne by shipowners and cargo-owners in equal shares. This custom was upheld.[8]

With regard to the actual work of discharging, this has been said to be a joint operation of shipowner and consignee. The former has completed his part of the process when his crew or his stevedore men are in a position to offer delivery to the consignee over the ship's side.[9] As was said by Lord Esher, MR,[10] the shipowner 'has performed the principal part of his obligation when he has put the goods over the rail of his ship; but I think he must do something more – he must put the goods in such a position that the consignee can take delivery of them.'

So far we have only dealt with the respective duties of carrier and recipient of cargo. But we have seen above that there may be a charter where the charterer is neither shipper nor consignee. In that case it is necessary to determine who, shipowner or charterer, has to bear the cost of the expenses which according to the preceding pages fall on the carrier. The common law rule is that in principle these duties fall on the shipowner. Very clear words are necessary to shift it on to the charterer. Where the charterparty provided that 'cargo (was) to be loaded, stowed and discharged free of expense to steamer, with use of steamer's winch and winchman if required', the expenses were indeed made charterer's expenses. But the words were not clear enough to convert the shipowner's duty into a charterer's duty. Though the charterer had to compensate the ship for expenses, the actual work done was still the ship's work. This has a very important consequence. It happened in this very case that the ship was damaged through the negligence of the stevedores and the men working a crane, both of whom were appointed and paid by the charterer. On the strength of the above clause the shipowners sued the charterers for compensation. However, it was held that the discharging was still the ship's work; though the work was paid for by the charterers it was under the entire control of the shipowner, and the charterers were therefore not responsible for the negligence of the stevedores and crane men.[11]

8 *A/S Sameiling* v. *Grain Importers (Eire) Ltd* [1952] 1 Lloyd's Rep. 313.
9 *Langham S.S. Co.* v. *Gallagher* (1911) 12 Asp. M.C. 109.
10 *Petersen* v. *Freebody & Co.,* [1895] 2 Q.B. 294, 297.
11 *Ballantyne* v. *Paton,* [1912] S.C. 246.

16.2   DELIVERY

Closely connected with the question of discharge is that of delivery of the cargo to the consignee.

We have already explained in some detail the functions of the bill of lading,[12] and it follows from those functions that the consignee named in the bill of lading, or an assign to whom it has been endorsed, may claim the goods from the master. The fact that the person entitled to receive the cargo will almost invariably have the bill of lading furnishes a very useful piece of machinery for ensuring that delivery is made to the right person. As we have seen, bills of lading are issued in sets of three; nevertheless, the master is entitled to deliver the goods to the first claimant, who produces a bill of lading which is in order provided he has no notice of any other claim to the goods.[13]

It may, of course, happen that, fraudulently or otherwise, another copy has been assigned to somebody else, but such assignee has no remedy against the carrier. He must hold his assignor responsible.[14]

If a bill of lading is lost, or has not arrived, the master may deliver against security, which usually takes the form of a letter of indemnity from a banker. Delivery without such an indemnity in these circumstances endangers the shipowner's right to any protection otherwise granted to him by the contract of carriage.[15] On the other hand, where the master receives instructions from a time-charterer to deliver cargo without presentation of a bill if lading, it appears that the time-charterer is liable to the shipowner for any ensuing loss even in the absence of an indemnity extracted by the master from the time-charterer.[16]

There is no rule of law making it obligatory on the master to advise the consignee of the arrival of the goods, unless custom or a term in the contract introduce such a duty in an individual case.[17] The reason is, perhaps, that as it is customary for the consignee to assign bills of lading to persons unknown to the carrier, the master cannot be expected to know whom to advise of the arrival. It is, therefore, left to the consignee or his assign to find out for himself when the ship has actually

---

12 See Chapter 13 *supra*.

13 *Glyn, Mills & Co.* v. *East & West India Dock Co.* (1882), 7 App. Cas. 591. See Section 13.3.2 *supra*.

14 *London Joint Stock Bank* v. *Amsterdam Co.* (1916), 16 Com. Cas. 102.

15 *Sze Hai Tong Ltd* v. *Rambler Cycle Co. Ltd* [1959] A.C. 576. But see *Photoproduction* v. *Securicor Transport* [1980] A.C. 827, if Lord Denning's judgment in the *Sze Hai Tong* case can be traced to the now discredited doctrine of fundamental breach.

16 *The Sagona* [1984] 1 Lloyd's Rep. 194.

17 *Harman* v. *Mant* (1815), 4 Camp. 161.

arrived, but the shipowner must not be guilty of a wrongful act that would prevent the consignee from discovering what the position is.

Illustration: *Bradley v. Goddard*[18]

The charter of a ship provided that the ship should be addressed 'to charterer's agents'; in breach of this undertaking it was addressed by the shipowners to other agents. They gave no notice to the consignees, and the latter's inquiries at the office of the charterers' agent were naturally unsuccessful. Delay resulted, and the shipowners sued the consignees for demurrage.

Held: Action dismissed, the liability to demurrage arose from the shipowner's own breach of contract.

Once the ship has arrived the lay-days begin to run and the same problems arise, especially with regard to the payment of demurrage, as have been discussed in connection with loading. Thus, though the lay-days may have begun, the consignee must in the ordinary way, be granted a non-frustrating time for delivery.[19] But shipowners are naturally anxious to start unloading as soon as possible; for one thing, they wish to have their ship free at the earliest possible moment; apart from this they desire relief from their responsibility for the goods. To meet this demand the following clause, known as the *London Clause,* has for many years been commonly inserted in bills of lading:

The shipowner shall be entitled to land these goods on the quays of the dock where the steamer discharges immediately on her arrival, and upon the goods being so landed the shipowner's liability shall cease. This clause is to form part of this bill of lading, and any words at variance with it are hereby cancelled.

If the consignee fails to take delivery, whether because he cannot pay the freight or for some other reason, he becomes liable to pay demurrage. But the shipowner cannot wait for an unlimited period; he must consider both his and the cargo-owner's interests. As far as he himself is concerned, the demurrage may not compensate him for the actual loss he suffers, for instance, by not being ready to enter in time on the next chartered voyage. Moreover, and in this respect the shipowner must have regard even to the defaulting cargo-owner's interest, there is a rule of law that anybody entitled to damages must not act selfishly, but must try to mitigate the damage.[20] Consequently, even though the consignee

18 (1863) 3 F. & F. 638.
19 Section 12.5, *supra.*
20 See *Scrutton* (1984), pp. 395–399.

takes no action at all the master may not only be entitled, but bound, to discharge the goods and to warehouse them in a statutable warehouse, that is, in a warehouse, where the shipowner's lien is preserved.[21] The expense of warehousing falls, of course, on the cargo-owner.[22]

16.3   PAYMENT: FREIGHT AND HIRE

We have watched the progress of the goods from loading to discharge and delivery, and it will now be convenient to examine the question of the remuneration for the hire of the ship or the carriage of goods, for it is at this stage that the obligation to pay usually becomes effective. This remuneration is called the freight or, in the case of charterparties, charter hire and sometimes chartered freight.[23] The subject suggests a subdivision into four parts, viz. as to the time when freight becomes payable, what circumstances excuse the charterer or cargo-owner from paying freight, who is entitled to the freight, and who is liable for its payment? We shall end with a brief note about dead freight.

In this volume we cannot discuss at any length questions of a business character. It is well known that freight for the hire of a ship under charterparty will be calculated for a voyage, when there is a voyage charter, or for a specified time, when there is a time charter. In respect of bill of lading freight for the carriage of goods we find freight measured according to the weight, quantity or measurement of the cargo. Finally, it should be recalled that there is a real freight market, just as there is a market for the sale of certain kinds of goods. Therefore, if no amount has been agreed upon one may always determine a reasonable sum as remuneration according to the state of the market, and can thus determine what were the current rates for the shipment of goods on the trade routes in question at the time of shipment.

16.3.1   WHEN PAYABLE

We now turn to the examination of the problems we have set ourselves, and the first to present itself is: when is the freight payable? The answer

---

21 Merchant Shipping Act 1894 s. 494; Compare *Smailes* v. *Hans Dessen* (1906) 12 Com. Cas. 117, which actually decided whether demurrage was due.

22 See generally ss. 492-501, MSA 1894 and *Scrutton* (1984), pp. 300-304.

23 It is usual to refer to payment in time-charterparties as hire, and in voyage-charterparties as 'freight'. The reason for the use of two terms signifying essentially the same thing is largely to do with the issues of deduction, as to which, see further this section.

is, in principle, when the shipowner or carrier has performed his services under the contract, that is, on delivery of the goods. In the case of a time charter, however, payment is made according to the contract, typically every thirty days.[24] Where hire is paid at regular intervals during the currency of the charterparty, failure to do so[25] entitles the owner to withdraw the ship from the charterer and it has been held that this right is not subject to the equitable jurisdiction of the courts to grant relief from forfeiture, a time-charterparty differing essentially from a lease.[26] Neither is the right to withdraw necessarily prejudiced by the purported acceptance of the hire instalment by the shipowner's bank;[27] nor is it precluded by the mere passage of a limited time without withdrawal.[28] For the shipowner to be held to have waived his right to withdraw what is required is 'evidence, clear and unequivocal, that such acceptance has taken place, or, after the late payment has been tendered, such a delay in refusing it as might reasonably cause the charterers to believe that it has been accepted'.[29] A charterer wishing to prevent withdrawal of the vessel, particularly tempting to a shipowner against a rising hire market, would be well advised to have a special clause inserted giving some lee-way for payment, a clause which has come to be known as the 'anti-technicality clause'.[30]

Time-charters usually contain a clause under which the charterer undertakes to pay the hire punctually and regularly. What is punctual payment? It is now clear that payment is effected only when 'what the creditor receives is the equivalent of cash, or as good as cash'.[31] Thus in

24 See e.g. Baltime, line 30.
25 Or, in some charterparties, 'on any breach', which means, it seems, any breach not involving the non-payment of a sum of money, unless, it would appear, such non-payment amounted to an unjustified refusal to pay. See *The Tropwind* [1977] 1 Lloyd's Rep. 397 and *The Athos* [1983] 1 Lloyd's 127, for what was called construction 'by instalments' of a clause the drafting of which 'leaves a great deal to be desired', *per* Purchas LJ at 142 and 144.
26 *The Scaptrade* [1983] 2 Lloyd's Rep. 253.
27 *Tha Laconia* [1977] A.C. 850.
28 *The Mihalios Xilas* [1979] 2 Lloyd's Rep. 303.
29 *The Laconia*, see fn. 27 *supra*, *per* Lord Wilberforce, at 871.
30 'When hire is due and not received the owners before exercising the option of withdrawing the vessel from the Charterparty, will give Charterers forty-eight hours notice . . . and will not withdraw the vessel if the hire is paid within these forty-eight hours.' See *The Afovos* [1983] 1 Lloyd's Rep. 335 and *The Rio Sun* [1982] 1 Lloyd's Rep 404, both of which indicate that the courts are as rigorous in interpreting anti-technicality clauses in charterer's interests, as they are in interpreting withdrawal clauses in shipowners' interests.
31 *Per* Bridge in *The Chikuma* [1981] 1 Lloyd's Rep. 371 at 375, following *The Brimnes* [1972] 2 Lloyd's Rep. 465, approved at [1974] 3 All E.R. 88.

The Chikuma, a purported payment to a shipowner's bank which
would only allow the immediate use of the funds by the shipowner
subject to certain conditions was not payment within the relevant clause
of the New York Produce Exchange time-charterparty. It is interesting
to note that the new NYPE form, known as ASBATIME, now makes
it clear that payment must be made 'in funds available to the owner on
the due date'.[32]

Naturally, the chartered ship must be redelivered to the owners when
the time for which it has been chartered has expired though, bearing in
mind the uncertainties of sea voyages, one finds clauses giving a few
days' latitude beyond the actual expiry date. In a case where redelivery
was as much as thirty-five days late – the ship had actually sailed on her
last voyage so late that it was clear she could not make the redelivery
port in time – the charterers had to pay hire for the excess period. They
were quite prepared to do so at the charter rate, but that did not satisfy
the owners; since the charter hire had been agreed, market rates had
risen steeply and the owners wanted to be paid at the market rate
prevailing on the day of redelivery. The owners succeeded.[33] It seems[34]
to follow that, had the market rate fallen, the charterers would have
been allowed to benefit from the fall.

As regards charterparties and also bills of lading, shipowner and
carrier may not wish to forgo their claims to freight until the completion of the adventure. They may, to be able to finance the voyage,
bargain for payment of the whole or part of the freight in advance. On
the other hand, to meet port dues and other expenses incurred at the
port of loading it may be agreed that the charterer shall lend certain
sums to the master on the security of the freight. In either event, care
should be taken to make quite sure what was the true intention of the
parties; whether or not a payment by the shipper at the time of loading
or, for that matter, at any time prior to the delivery of the cargo at the
port of destination, is a true advance freight, or constitutes but a loan by
the shipper to the carrier.[35] This depends on the construction of the
words used. The parties are apt to leave the matter ambiguous,
although the question is important, for suppose the goods are lost on
the voyage by excepted perils, then if, it is a true advance freight, which

32 ASBATIME, line 116.
33 *Marbienes Compania Naviera S.A.* v. *Ferrostaal A.G.* [1976] 2 Lloyd's Rep. 149; see
    also *Attica Sea Carriers* v. *Ferrostaal A.G.* [1976] 2 All E.R. 249.
34 But see the discussion of *The London Explorer* [1972] A.C. in *Carver* (1982), pp.
    463-469.
35 *Allison* v. *Bristol Marine Insurance* (1876) 1 App. Cas. 209, 217, 233.

had become due, though not paid, prior to the loss, the carrier is entitled to the freight.[36]

Illustration 1:   *Bryne* v. *Schiller*[37]

A charterparty provided 'freight to be paid thus: £1200 to be advanced the master by freighter's agent at Calcutta, and to be deducted with 1¼ per cent commission on the amount advanced, and cost of insurance from freight on settlement thereof, and the remainder on right delivery of the cargo at port of discharge, in cash'. The ship was lost on the voyage.

Held: The shipowners were entitled to keep the £1200 paid, since this amount was intended to be advance freight, but they could not claim the remainder.

Illustration 2:   *Manfield* v. *Maitland*[38]

'Freight to be paid, half in cash on unloading and right delivery of cargo, and the remainder by bill in London at four months date. The captain to be supplied with cash for ship's use.' The master received £219 from the shippers under the last clause. The ship was lost on the voyage.

Held: There were no clear words in the charterparty showing that the sum was intended to be advance freight. The shipowner must repay the £219 to the shipper; this was a loan by the shipper to the shipowner, and not in the nature of advance freight.

It is common sense that advance freight can be demanded only as long as the voyage has not been abandoned, though a clause in a charterparty may be so worded that a different result would seem to follow.

Illustration: *Smith* v. *Pyman*[39]

A charterparty contained the clause: 'One-third freight, if required to be advanced, less 3 per cent for interest and insurance.' After the ship had been lost on the voyage, the shipowner 'required' an advance.

Held: Action dismissed. No requirement under the charter could be made when it was clear that the voyage could not be performed.

---

36 See previous note: otherwise in Scots Law: *Cantiere San Rocco* v. *Clyde Shipbuilding Co.* [1924] A.C. 226. It is here that the cargo-owner must protect himself by insuring the goods.
37 (1871), L.R. 6 Ex. 20, 319.
38 (1821) 4 B. & Ald. 582.
39 [1891] 1 Q.B. 742; but compare *Oriental S.S. Co.* v. *Taylor* [1893] 2 Q.B. 518.

Again, it must be borne in mind that, although ordinarily the carrier is not entitled to the freight until he has performed his part of the bargain, he will have a good claim to it if he is prevented from performing his part by acts of the shipper, consignee or other bill of lading holder. Thus, though freight becomes payable on discharge, the carrier has an action for the freight if he is ready to give delivery but the consignee does not take it within a reasonable time.[40] The same applies if the carrier, owing to excepted perils, cannot reach the port of destination, and the cargo-owner does not take delivery elsewhere and fails to give instructions to the master. In both cases the latter may deal with the goods as he considers best in the interests of the parties concerned, which includes, if that be expedient, the carrying of the goods back to the original loading place or the forwarding of them to another convenient port; in such circumstances the carrier is entitled to damages for breach of contract, commonly described as back freight,[41] because it will amount to the freight which would have been earned on carrying a similar quantity of goods back to the port in question.

Likewise, freight becomes payable when the delivery cannot be effected solely by default of the freighter;[42] this may happen where the latter fails to name a safe port to which the ship is to proceed.[43]

Sometimes there is a stipulation for the payment of freight at a gross sum for the use of an entire ship or a portion thereof. In this case the shipowner is entitled to the sum agreed though a short quantity of goods is shipped, or even if no goods are shipped at all. Where a short quantity has been loaded the shipowner, in order to recover the lump freight, must deliver some part of the goods shipped, but a short delivery, however serious, will not deprive him of it; he may, of course, be subject to a counter-claim for damages.[44]

16.3.2   EXEMPTIONS

So far we have only heard of the shipowner's or carrier's right to the freight. Under what circumstances, we now ask, is the other party excused? The answer seems, at first sight, fairly simple. The carrier is

40 *Duthie* v. *Hilton* (1868) L.R. 4 C.P. 138, 143; *Cargo ex Argos* (1873) L.R. 5 P.C. 134.
41 *Cargo ex Argos* (1873) L.R. 5 P.C. 134.
42 *Cargo ex Argos* (1873) L.R. 5 P.C. 134; *Cargo ex Galam* (1863), 2 Moo. P.C. N.S. 216; *The Soblomsten* (1866) L.R. 1 A. & E. 293.
43 *The Teutonia* (1872) L.R. 4 P.C. 171; *Aktieselskabet Olivebank* v. *Dansk Fabrik*, [1919] 2 K.B. 162.
44 *Thomas* v. *Harrowing S.S. Co.*, [1915] A.C. 58.

not entitled to his freight if he has broken the contract. But not all failures of performance on the part of the carrier result in a loss of freight. Where the carrier is ready to deliver at the port of destination, but the goods are in a damaged condition, though in substance still the same merchandise, freight becomes payable in full, though the consignee may have an action for damages. These, however, he must claim separately and may not deduct from the freight.

The reason for this has been explained in this way.[45] In freight cases, as in bills of exchange cases, the good conduct of business requires strict adherence to the terms of the contract regarding payment of freight. This rule, though well established, has been criticized as unfair, but has been reaffirmed by the House of Lords in *The Aries*[45] as recently as 1977. Not only is the charterer unable to deduct from the freight,[46] but he may find that the carrier's right to sue for the unpaid freight survives his own right to cross-claim for damage to the goods. The carrier's action is subject to the period of limitation governing most contracts, six years, but, as we have just seen, the cargo-owner must bring his damages action within one year. So if the carrier sues after the one year the cargo-owner's action is time-barred. This is serious. Generally, in the law of contract, a party whose action is time-barred only loses his remedy, that is, the initiative to bring an action. His right remains, and if sued by the other party he can plead his right by way of set-off. The Hague Rules time-bar, on the other hand, in common with the corresponding time-bars for claims against air and road[47] carriers, not only kills the remedy; it also extinguishes the right, which means that a cargo-owner sued for withheld freight can no longer plead his damages claim in defence; he has lost it.[48]

An action for freight can, however, be maintained only so long as the goods discharged are still the same merchandise as that shipped; sometimes they are so damaged that this is no longer the case. Whether the

---

45 *Henriksen's Rederi A/S* v. *T.H.Z. Rolimpex*, [1973] 1 All E.R. 721, *per* Lord Denning MR. This case was approved in *Aries Tanker Corp.* v. *Total Transport Ltd.* [1977] 1 All E.R. 398.

46 Unless expressly allowed by the charterparty: *The Olympic Brilliance* [1982] 2 Lloyd's Rep. 205; *cf.* the position of a time charterer, who, since the Court of Appeal's judgment in *The Nanfri* [1978] Q.B. 927, has a right to deduct from freight a reasonable estimate in respect of claims against the shipowner connected with the use of the ship, thought not, for example in respect of claims for damage to goods or short-delivery. *The Nanfri* went to the House of Lords on another point: [1979] A.C. 757. The difficult question of deductions from hire in time-charters is dealt with generally in *Scrutton* (1984) at pp. 361–364.

47 *R H & D International Ltd* v. *I.A.S. Animal Air Services Ltd* [1984] 1 W.L.R. 573.

48 *Henriksen's Rederi A/S* v. *T.H.Z. Rolimpex* [1973] 1 All E.R. 721.

goods are merely damaged or are no longer of the same kind is a question of fact to be answered in a commercial, not in a chemical sense.

Illustration: *Asfar v. Blundell*[49]

Dates had been shipped under bills of lading making the freight payable on right delivery. The ship sank on the voyage, but was later raised and brought into port. There it was found that owing to the influx of seawater the dates had become one fermenting mass, which could no longer be sold as dates, though it was still of considerable value for distillation into spirit.

Held: Since the goods had ceased to be of the same merchantable kind, no freight was payable in respect of them.

Scrutton[50] suggests that if the consignees actually take delivery they ought to pay freight, a proposition which seems difficult to refute.

Where a lump sum freight is not stipulated, the carrier is only entitled to freight calculated *pro rata* on the quantity of cargo delivered, so that if there is short delivery the freight payable will be proportionately less.[51]

A point of considerable importance was brought out in the following case. Goods were shipped to the same consignee under several bills of lading. On arrival it so happened that whereas on some of the bills of lading there was a short delivery, on others there was an over-delivery, and the carrier contended that he was entitled to set off one against the other. It was held, however, that as every bill of lading constitutes a separate contract no right of set-off existed, but the consignees had to pay freight on over-deliveries and to give credit to the carrier for the value thereof. At the same time they were entitled to damages for the short deliveries irrespective of the fact that they actually received over-deliveries on other bills of lading by the same vessel.[52] On the face of it this might seem a narrow decision, but as bills of lading, though addressed to the same consignee, are on arrival of the ship often in the hands of different bill of lading holders the result seems on reflection satisfactory.

49 [1896] 1 Q.B. 123. Compare *Duthie* v. *Hilton* (1868) L.R. 4 C.P. 138, where owing to the entry of seawater a cargo of cement had become concrete.
50 P. 342, fn. 64, where he doubts the correctness of *Asfar* v. *Blundell* on this ground. But see *The Caspian Sea* [1980] 1 Lloyd's Rep. 91, at 95, for an alternative view.
51 *Ritchie* v. *Atkinson* (1808) 10 East. 295; *The Norway* (1865) 3 Moore P.C. N.S. 245; *Spaight* v. *Farnworth* (1880) 5 Q.B.D. 115; *Mediterranean Co.* v. *Mackay* [1903] 1 K.B. 297.
52 *'Estland' (Owners)* v. *Hillas & Co.* (1936) 54 Ll. L.R. 98; *The Nordberg*, [1939] P. 121.

DELIVERY SHORT OF PLACE OF DESTINATION

As the contract of carriage is for the conveyance of the goods from one port to another, no freight is payable if the port of destination is not reached, unless this is due to the default of the cargo-owner. By the same token, a vendor who stops the goods in transit is liable for the whole freight.[53] On the other hand, where through the fault of the shipowner goods cannot be carried to their destination, for instance, because as a result of initial unseaworthiness the ship has to proceed to an intermediate port for repairs, and the goods are accordingly landed elsewhere, the shipowner is responsible to the bill of lading holders for the cost of transhipment and carriage on in another ship to their destination.[54]

Sometimes, however, when goods have been carried part of the way, and further prosecution of the voyage has become impossible,[55] for instance because of a blockade or ice at the port of delivery, the goods' owner will accept delivery at an intermediate port. The question then presents itself whether freight calculated *pro rata* for the voyage actually accomplished becomes payable. This will only be so where there is a clear agreement by the goods' owner to pay. Such an agreement may be express or implied, though it is often difficult to decide when to imply it. Acceptance of the goods by their owner at the shipowner's request at an intermediate port does not by itself imply a contract for *pro rata* freight.[56] It should be borne in mind that a contract to be valid presupposes a voluntary agreement of the parties. Likewise, where a contract is to be implied the parties must have been in a position that they might have come to a valid agreement. 'There must,' in the words of Scrutton,[57] 'be such a voluntary acceptance of the goods by their owner, at a port short of their final destination, or such a dealing, or neglect to deal with them there, as to raise a fair inference that the further carrying of the goods was intentionally dispensed with by the goods' owner.' But a promise to pay *pro rata* freight will be implied only if the cargo-owner has the opportunity to choose between the port of destination and another port, as the following case illustrates.

---

53 *Booth S.S. Co.* v. *Cargo Fleet Co.* [1916] 2 K.B. 570.
54 *Monarch S.S. Co.* v. *Karlshamns Oljefabriker* [1949] A.C. 196.
55 The following rules have not been affected by the Law Reform (Frustrated Contracts) Act 1943; see s. 2 (5) *(a)* of that Act and Chapter 14, fn. 3 *supra.*
56 *The Soblomsten* (1866) L.R. 1 A. & E. 293; *Metcalfe* v. *British Iron Works* (1877) 2 Q.B.D. 423.
57 P. 344.

Illustration: *St. Enoch S.S. Co. v. Phosphate Mining Co.* [58]

Goods were shipped in 1914 from Florida to Hamburg. During the voyage war broke out between Great Britain and Germany and, since the consignees were British subjects, the delivery of the goods at Hamburg had become illegal. The ship was, therefore, diverted, and the goods delivered to the owners at Manchester.

Held: The shipowners were not entitled to any freight. They could not claim the contract freight because the contract voyage had not been completed. Nor were they allowed *pro rata* freight; no new contract could be inferred under which the goods' owners agreed to take delivery at Manchester instead of at Hamburg.

This rule, which only in rare cases entitles the shipowner to *pro rata* freight, though the goods' owner receives the goods perhaps little short of their destination, is a harsh one. True, it is based on the general principle that a person undertaking to do a certain piece of work earns remuneration only if he completes it. Nevertheless, the absence of any exception in favour of carriers seems contrary to common sense although, of course, the shipowner can, and often does, protect himself by taking out an insurance against loss of freight.

16.3.3   WHO IS ENTITLED TO SUE?

Doubts may sometimes arise as to who is the proper person to sue for the bill of lading freight. In principle the shipowner is entitled to the freight, for as a rule the master signs bills of lading as agent of the owner. Where the ship is chartered by demise, or control and management of the ship have otherwise been transferred to the charterer, or where the latter has expressly signed the bills of lading, either himself or by his agent, in such a way as to render the charterer the carrier,[59] then it is the charterer's right to bring an action for the freight.

Shipowner and charterer, or sometimes also the loading broker, as those originally entitled to the freight, may assign it to a third person, who is usually a creditor, and then the latter stands in the shoes of the original parties.[60] Finally, a mortgagee who has taken possession of the ship,[61] becomes entitled to the freight that the ship is in the course of

---

58 [1916] 2 K.B. 624.

59 See Section 13.7.2 *supra*.

60 Very difficult questions may arise on assignment. See for a case of assignment of freight *Smith v. Owners of S.S. Zigurds and her freight* [1934] A.C. 209.

61 Section 6.6.2 *supra*.

earning, but he is not entitled to freight due prior to his taking possession, but still unpaid.[62]

16.3.4 WHO IS LIABLE?

Where there is a charter the charterer is liable for freight. With regard to
the carriage of goods, it is the person who has made the contract, that is
the shipper, unless the contract frees him from this obligation.

Apart from the shipper the consignee, to whom the property in the
cargo has passed and who is an endorsee of the bill of lading, is liable for
the freight though he is not a party to the contract of carriage; his
liability is established by the Bills if Lading Act 1855.[63] By that Act
rights and duties of the original contract pass to the consignee as if he
were a party to it. The same applies to a bill of lading holder, to whom
the bill of lading has been endorsed, provided the property in the goods
mentioned in the bill of lading has passed to him. The effect of the
statute is not, however, to substitute the consignee's or endorsee's
liability for that shipper, who is, after all, the original party. In the
absence of a term in the contract relieving the shipper from liability after
shipment he remains liable to the carrier until consignee or bill of lading
holder have paid the freight.[64]

The carrier has thus a double remedy for the freight though, of
course, he can only claim it once. In addition, as long as the cargo
remains on board ship, the carrier has at common law a lien over it for
freight and general average contributions. This is a possessory lien, so
called because it lasts only so long as the person claiming it continues in
possession of the goods. The lien for freight operates only if the freight
falls due on delivery of the cargo. If the shipowner has agreed to
payment at a later date he bears the risk, and he is bound to deliver the
goods and loses his lien.

DEAD FREIGHT

Usually freight is payable only on goods actually shipped, but where in
a charterparty the charterer has agreed to load a full and complete cargo
and has broken this promise by loading less than the ship can hold, he
becomes liable to pay damages for breach of contract. This is called
dead freight; in other words the charterer in such circumstances must

---

62 *Shillito* v. *Biggart* [1903] 1 K.B. 683.
63 S. 1. See Section 13.4.1 *supra*.
64 Bills of Lading Act 1855 s. 2.

pay freight for the space not used. However, at common law no right of lien exists for dead freight over the goods actually carried, but this is often specially granted by the terms of the contract of affreightment.[65]

The same applies to demurrage and port charges, even though the charterer has agreed to pay them. The reason for this difference is probably that at law only such charges shall be secured on the cargo as are intimately connected with the carriage. In the case of dead freight no goods are actually shipped, and the above-mentioned special contractual lien extends to goods for which no dead freight is payable, and similar considerations apply to demurrage and port-charges.

---

65 *McLean* v. *Fleming* (1871) L.R. 2 Sc. & Div., 128.

17
THE HAMBURG RULES

For some time, the developing countries complained that the Hague Rules unfairly protected the shipowner, placing too heavy a burden on the shipper. Those countries are predominantly shippers although, ironically, some of them are anxious to build up their own merchant fleet.

Responding to the call for reform, the United Nations Commission for International Trade Law (UNCITRAL) worked for several years on a new convention, and the terms of the United Nations Convention on the Carriage of Goods by Sea were at last settled at a conference of plenipotentiaries from seventy-eight states, and observers from shipping, trade and insurance interests, held in March 1978 at Hamburg. Fittingly, this new convention is known as the Hamburg Rules.[1]

Seen from one angle, the Hamburg Rules do no more than bring sea carriage of goods into line with the carriage of goods by air, road and rail, and also the carriage of sea passengers, a not unwelcome change. Seen from the angle of shipping interests, however, the new Rules make profound changes, summed up in the 'Common Understanding', contained in Appendix II of the Final Act of the conference, which is, of course, not a legal provision. It reads as follows:

It is the common understanding that the liability of the carrier under this Convention is based on the principle of presumed fault or neglect. This means that, as a rule, the burden of proof rests on the carrier but, with respect to certain cases, the provisions of the Convention modify this rule.

The Hamburg Rules have dismantled the system of carrier's duties and immunities contained in Articles III and IV of the Hague Rules. No longer are the individual duties, for instance, regarding seaworthiness, proper loading and stowage, enumerated. Instead, Art. 5(1) of the Hamburg Rules provides that the carrier shall be liable for loss, damage or delay while in charge of the goods 'unless [he] proves that he, his

---

1   UN General Assembly. A/Conf. 89/13-30th March, 1978. For a penetrating critique of the Hamburg Rules, see William Tetley, 'The Hamburg Rules – A Commentary' [1979] 1 L.M.C.Q. 1.

servants or agents took all measures that could reasonably be required to avoid the occurrence and its consequences'. The corresponding Art. 20 of the Warsaw Convention has been construed very strictly in the courts of various countries.

Article 5 (1) of the Hamburg Rules also shows that the catalogue of defences in Art. IV of the Hague Rules has gone. Neglect of master and crew in the management of the ship will no longer be a defence, nor will perils of the sea, unless reasonably required preventive measures can be proved. Act of God as a cause of loss, or acts of war and related causes, will no longer only themselves have to be proved, but the carrier will also have to prove that it was beyond his power to avert all the consequences of the occurrences.

Likewise, the defence of fire has been cut down; it ceases to be a defence if the claimant – for once not the carrier – can establish negligence of carrier, servants or agents not only in respect of the outbreak of the fire but also in respect of 'measures that could reasonably be required to put out the fire and avoid or mitigate its consequences'.

Live animals are now included in the 'goods' definition, but the carrier is protected against 'special risks inherent in that kind of carriage' (Arts 5 (5) and 1 (5)). Where, in breach of agreement, cargo is carried on deck, consequences resulting solely from that fact, for instance rusting, must be compensated for. To be valid against a consignee without notice an agreement to carry on deck requires mention in the bill of lading (Art. 9).

The carrier escapes liability if loss, damage or delay is caused by measures to save life, or by reasonable measures to save property, at sea (Art. 5 (6)). Nor is the carrier liable for that part of damage caused by a third party, say, by collision for which both are to blame, if he can prove what proportion of the damage is attributable to the third party (Art. 5 (7)).

The limits of liability are calculated no longer in gold francs, but, like the Hague–Visby Rules since 1979,[2] in units of account, equal to special drawing rights (SDR) of the International Monetary Fund as follows: 835 u/a per package or other shipping unit or 2.5 u/a per kilogram gross weight, whichever yields the larger sum. The limit of liability for delay is two-and-a half times the freight for the goods delayed, but not in excess of total freight agreed for the whole carriage (Art. 6).

The liability of the shipper, for instance, where he ships dangerous goods, the carrier's loss of the limitation privilege in the event of wilful misconduct, bill of lading requirements and container shipments remain much on the Hague Rules lines.

2   See Section 11.5 *supra*.

The following changes of detail are sufficiently important to mention: the notice of apparent damage which the consignee must give may also be given on the day following delivery, and the period of notice of non-apparent damage is extended from three to fifteen days (Art. 19); the time-bar for action or arbitration request is extended from one year to two years (Art. 20). Jurisdiction clauses are outlawed to all intents and purposes, claimants having a choice between courts in the country where the defendant has his principal place of business or his habitual residence, where port of loading or discharge were situated, or where the parties had agreed that disputes should be settled (Art. 21). Interim proceedings are allowed in the court of a country where the defendant ship or a sister ship has been arrested.

Where a charterparty contains an arbitration clause this must in future, to be binding on a consignee without notice, be mentioned as 'a special annotation' in the bill of lading (Art. 22 (2)).

The coming into force of this convention will bring about important changes for the shipping industry and in the ratio of hull and cargo insurance, a problem commented on by Lord Diplock, during the second reading of the Carriage of Goods by Sea Act 1971.[3] Probably much against its sponsors' intention the uniformity of the law (Art. 3) may also be disturbed. Other shipping conventions took care that they should come into force not only when a certain number of states had ratified, but when those ratifying accounted for a big percentage of the world's tonnage. The second requirement is not contained in Art. 30, which provides that twenty ratifications – no matter how small the state or its fleet – shall lead to the convention coming into force. It is now clear that several important maritime nations have held back, retaining the Hague Rules.[4]

3 Hansard, H.L. vol. 316, col. 1042.
4 An interesting account of the genesis of the Hamburg Rules, including the atmosphere during the negotiations, and of the principal changes of the law, will be found in John C. Moore, *The Hamburg Rules*, 10 Journal of Maritime Law and Commerce, 1 (1978). The countries which have so far ratified the Hamburg Rules are: Barbados, Chile, Egypt, Hungary, Lebanon, Morocco, Romania, Tanzania, Tunisia, Uganda.

PART THREE
THE RUNNING OF THE SHIP

18

THE CARRIAGE OF PASSENGERS

18.1   GENERAL PRINCIPLES

THE CONTRACT of carriage of passengers by sea is an ordinary contract for the conveyance of persons. Much of the law governing the contract of passage is the common law that applies to all contracts, for instance, the rules governing offer and acceptance, which demand agreement between the parties. In one case, a shipowner intended to sell an ordinary return ticket from London to Australia, but the passenger was under the impression that she was booking for a pleasure cruise. It was held that there was no contract as the parties had not reached an agreement on the same terms. However, the passenger by her subsequent conduct had acquiesced, e.g. by remaining on board for the whole voyage.[1]

Shipowners must also beware of the Trade Descriptions Act 1968 which, among other things, makes it an offence for persons engaged in trade to describe services offered to the public in a misleading manner. Advertisements must not contain prices that are lower than those actually charged, and facilities offered must actually be provided.[2]

In common with other business undertakings, shipowners and transport operators, when contracting with customers, are forbidden to discriminate on the grounds of colour, race or ethnic or national origins; this includes segregating passengers.[3] Owners of ships carrying passengers must also comply with the requirements of the Immigration

---

1 *Macmillan v. Orient Steam Navigation Company Ltd* (1935) 51 Ll.L.Rep. 93.
2 Trade Descriptions Act 1968 s. 14.
3 Race Relations Act 1976 ss. 20(2)(f), 27. S. 57(4) allows compensation for injured feelings.

Act 1971. They must only call at a specified port of entry[4] and at designated control areas for embarkation and disembarkation.[5] They must also, if required, provide a passenger and crew list.[6] The master should not allow persons to disembark without complying with the immigration procedures.[7] Owners or masters who contravene the requirements may be guilty of an offence.[8] There is a special exception for crewmen as they would normally expect to leave the UK with the ship.[9]

A shipping company provides a 'service' to passengers and thus the Supply of Goods and Services Act 1982 will apply.[10] For instance, it will be an implied term that the owner will carry out the service with reasonable care and skill.[11] However, until the Unfair Contract Terms Act 1977, shipowners were entitled to insert the widest possible exemption clauses into their passenger contracts. Thus the next-of-kin of a passenger who, on a voyage from Rio de Janeiro to Southampton, was thrown overboard and drowned in a collision caused by the negligent navigation of the vessel lost their action against the shipowners. They had protected themselves by a clause in the contract excluding liability 'for any loss or damage arising from the perils of the sea or from any act, neglect or default whatsoever of the pilot, master, or mariner'.[12] Again, a passenger injured when a chair on which she was sitting in the ship's dining room collapsed under her also lost her action for damages; she was bound by a clause in her ticket excluding compensation for injury sustained by 'any cause whatsoever'.[13]

To deal with these very wide clauses the courts adopted a number of legal devices to protect claimants, some of which are still relevant today. The owners must, for instance, take reasonable steps to bring to the attention of the passenger the fact that a ticket contains contractual

---

4 Sch. 2, para. 26 (1); the Immigration (Ports of Entry) Order 1972 (S.I. No. 1668), amended 1979 (S.I. No. 1635).

5 Sch. 2, para. 26(2).

6 Sch. 2, para. 27(2), the Immigration (Particulars of Passengers and Crew) Order 1972 (S.I. No. 1667), amended 1975 (S.I. No. 980).

7 Sch. 2, para. 27(1).

8 S. 27.

9 S. 8.

10 There is power under s. 12 to exempt categories of services from the Act. Although the international carriage of passengers was mentioned as a possible example for exemption no such order has yet been made.

11 S. 13.

12 *Haigh* v. *Royal Mail Steamship Co.* (1883) 52 L.J.K.B. 640.

13 *Budd* v. *P & O* [1969] 2 Lloyd's Rep. 262. *Cf. The Eagle: Hollingsworth* v. *Southern Ferries* [1977] 2 Lloyd's Rep. 70.

terms.[14] Moreover, this must be done before the contract is concluded. In one case, terms contained in a ticket did not form part of the contract where they were mailed to the passenger two days after he had made a reservation and paid his deposit.[15] The contract had already been concluded. In order to by-pass the terms one passenger successfully sued, in tort, the master and boatswain of the P & O liner *Himalaya*.[16] They were not entitled to the benefit of the carrier's exemption clauses as they were neither parties to the contract, nor did the ticket purport to exempt *their* liabilities. As a result of this case, properly drafted Himalaya clauses were inserted in most carriage contracts to give employees and subcontractors contractual protection.[17]

18.2 THE ATHENS CONVENTION 1974

18.2.1 INTRODUCTION

However, as with other parts of the law, these wide exclusion clauses have become bad memories as a result of radical changes made by statute. The Unfair Contract Terms Act 1977 regulated the wide exclusion clauses found in contracts generally and, in particular, those made by consumers. However, the Act[18] did allow shipowners to restrict their liabilities to the extent permitted by the Athens Convention relating to the Carriage of Passengers and their Luggage by Sea 1974. This regulates the liability of the carrier for death, personal injury and damage to luggage. Pending the coming into force internationally of the Athens Convention, the Merchant Shipping Act 1979, s.16 gave power for an Order in Council to be made giving the Convention the force of law in the UK, subject to modifications. That power has been exercised[19] and the provisions of the Convention[20] have had the force of law for contracts made on or after 1 January 1981.

---

14 *Richardson Spence & Co.* v. *Rowntree* [1894] A.C. 217.

15 *The Dragon: Daly* v. *General Steam Navigation Co. Ltd* [1979] 1 Lloyd's Rep. 257.

16 *The Himalaya: Adler* v. *Dickson* [1955] 1 Q.B. 158.

17 See Section 20.1.3, *infra* and Section 11.5, *supra*: also W. Tetley, 'The *Himalaya* Clause – Heresy or Genius' (1977) 9 J.M.L.C. 111.

18 S. 28. See Section 4.2.3, *supra*.

19 The Carriage of Passengers and their Luggage by Sea (Interim Provisions) Order 1980 (S.I. No. 1092).

20 As contained in the Merchant Shipping Act 1979, Sch.3.

18.2.2   APPLICATION

When the Convention is internationally in force it will apply to international carriage involving ships flying the flag of state parties; or where the contract was made in a state party; or where the place of departure or destination is a state party.[21] However, under the interim regime of s. 16, the rules of the Convention are only to apply to: (i) international carriages, if the contract is made in the UK, or the place of departure or destination is in the UK; (ii) domestic carriages, if the place of departure or destination is in the area consisting of the UK, the Channel Islands and the Isle of Man and there is no intermediate port of call outside that area.[22]

The provisions of the Convention thus apply to nearly all journeys to and from the UK, including, e.g. ferry trips in either direction across the Channel,[23] or from Southampton to the Isle of Wight. A passenger who made a booking in the UK for a Mediterranean cruise would also be covered. However, the Convention will not be applied to a contract of carriage which is not for reward.[24] Nor does it apply to nuclear damage,[25] as this is normally covered by specific provisions in international convention or national law.[26]

The Convention defines 'passenger' as 'any person carried in a ship' under a contract of carriage and also persons who, with the carrier's

---

21 Art. 2. The Convention will be brought fully into force in the UK by ss. 14, 15 of the Merchant Shipping Act 1979. The Convention will take precedence over the provisions of the Unfair Contract Terms Act 1977, see s. 29 of the 1977 Act. Article 22 gives states the right not to apply the Convention when passenger and carrier are its own nationals. The UK has, however, applied the Convention domestically, as will be seen. The Convention becomes effective on 28 April 1987.

22 1980 (S.I. No. 1092), Art. 2.

23 The definition of international carriage in Art. 2 of the 1980 Order and Art. 1.9 of the Athens Convention 1974 is wide enough to cover day trips including a port of call in France.

24 Merchant Shipping Act 1979, Sch. 3, Part II, para. 9. Presumably a non-reward 'contract' must be one for a nominal consideration, as the concept has little meaning in English law. In this case – as with a gratuitous carriage (eg on board a friend's yacht) – we assume that the ordinary provisions of the Unfair Contract Terms Act 1977 would apply. Section 2(1) would make void any notice which purported to exclude liability for personal injury. This seems to have the ironic result that the 'voluntary' carrier would not be entitled to the Athens Convention limits, *infra*. It may be that a 'non-reward contract carrier' could argue that s. 28 of the Unfair Contract Terms Act 1977 might still entitle him to incorporate a notice restricting his liability to Athens Convention levels.

25 Art. 20.

26 E.g., the Paris Convention 1960; the Nuclear Installations Act 1965, as amended by the Nuclear Installations Act 1969, the Energy Act 1983. See Section 25.2.3, *infra*.

consent, accompany live animals or vehicles, for instance, on roll-on, roll-off ferries.[27] This is important because, in such cases, contracts are made only in respect of the goods, i.e. the vehicles or animals, and not expressly in respect of drivers or herdsmen or grooms. 'Luggage' does not include goods carried under a charterparty or bill of lading, or live animals – so pet dogs are not luggage.[28] 'Loss of or damage to luggage' includes pecuniary loss resulting from it not being redelivered to the passenger within a reasonable time after the ship's arrival, but not delay caused by labour disputes.[29]

The period of coverage is the period of 'carriage', which means from the moment of embarkation to that of disembarkation, including carriage by tender, if that stage is included in the price of the contract ticket.[30] In contrast to the corresponding provision relating to the air carrier, the shipowner is not liable for anything happening to the passenger while the latter is at a marine terminal or station building or waiting on the quay. Luggage is covered as soon as the carrier has taken it in charge,[31] which will usually be on the passenger's arrival at the terminal.

The Convention rules come into play in relation to 'international carriage', i.e. where ports of departure and destination are in two different states or even where the same port is that of departure and destination, provided there is port of call in another state,[32] a rule important to cruise passengers.

18.2.3 LIABILITY

The shipowner's liability for a passenger's death or injury and for lost or damaged luggage depends on any of those events being 'due to the fault or neglect' of the carrier or of his servants or agents in the course of their employment.[33] Thus is, for example, a passenger has temporarily disembarked at a port and is there assaulted by an inebriated member of the crew on shore leave, he cannot sue the shipowner; while on shore leave, whatever the mariner does is not done in the course of his employment. The shipowner would be liable if, for example, a crew

27 Art. 1(4).
28 Art. 1(5).
29 Art. 1(7).
30 Art. 1(8).
31 *Ibid*.
32 Art. 1(9).
33 Art. 3(1).

member failed to warn a passenger to keep clear of ropes while unmooring took place.[34]

As always, the burden of proof is most important, and the Convention is specific on this point. The passenger must prove that the incident on which he bases his claim occurred in the course of carriage[35] – that he has contracted food poisoning while on board or that his luggage has been tampered with.[36] When it comes to the fault or neglect issue a distinction is made. If the loss or damage occurs in connection with shipwreck, collision, stranding, explosion, fire or a defect in the ship and the result is personal injury or loss or damage to cabin luggage, the fault or neglect of the shipowner or a servant or agent is presumed.[37] He can rebut the presumption, for instance, by proving that a collision was solely the fault of the other vessel.[38] Where anything happens to luggage stowed in the hold, the shipowner's fault or neglect is always presumed.[39]

The carrier incurs no liability in respect of monies, negotiable securities, jewellery or other valuables, unless they are deposited for safe-keeping.[40] Even if such articles are deposited, liability is restricted to the Convention limits[41] unless a higher value has been agreed.[42]

18.2.4   LIMITATION[43]

Like other international regimes dealing with specific aspects of carriage, such as the Hague Rules,[44] the Athens Convention allows the shipowner to limit his liability. It is clear that the Athens Convention limits are rather low and need to be increased. This is one reason why

---

34 *Cf. The Dragon* [1979] 1 Lloyd's Rep. 257. Under Art. 11 a servant or agent of the carrier, acting within the scope of his employment, is entitled to all the defences and limits open to the carrier himself. This removes the need for *Himalaya* Clauses.

35 Art. 3(2). He must also prove the extent of his loss.

36 Art. 3(3).

37 *Ibid*.

38 In an English court the claimant might also benefit from the *res ipsa loquitur* (the event speaks for itself) rule of the common law, reversing the burden of proof. It applies where prima facie the damage is the defendant's fault, e.g. in a case of food poisoning.

39 Art. 3(3).

40 Art. 5.

41 Arts 5, 8(3). The exclusions allowed under the Merchant Shipping Act 1894, s. 502 (now under the Merchant Shipping Act 1979, s. 18) are subject to the Athens Convention provisions, Merchant Shipping Act 1979, Sch. 3 Part II, para. 12: see also Section 22.4.

42 Art. 10.

43 Art. 6; Sch. 3 Part II, para. 3.

44 See Section 10.2, *supra*.

many countries have not ratified it, although states are allowed to fix higher death or personal injury limits for carriers who are nationals of that state.[45] The limits, which are subject to the global limits of liability of a shipowner,[46] are at present expressed in gold francs, but when the 1976 Protocol to the Athens Convention comes into force the special drawing right (SDR) of the International Monetary Fund will be used.[47] The limits are given below, with the sterling equivalents of the gold franc figures.[48]

Table 1: Limits of Liability under the Athens Convention 1974

Claim	Special Drawing Rights	Gold francs	Sterling
Death or personal injury to passenger	46 666 SDR	700 000 gf	£38 173.40
Loss/damage to cabin luggage per passenger	833 SDR	12 500 gf	£681.67
Loss/damage to vehicles/contents per passenger	3333 SDR	50 000 gf	£2 726.67
Loss/damage to other luggage per passenger	1200 SDR	18 000 gf	£981.60
Deductible allowed for vehicle	117 SDR	1 750 gf	£95.43
Deductible allowed for luggage	13 SDR	200 gf	£10.91

45 Art. 7. The limit of £38 173 per passenger for death claims seems grossly inadequate. It can be increased by the Secretary of State, Sch. 3 Part II, para. 4.
46 Merchant Shipping Act 1979, Sch. 3, Part II, para. 12; and see Chapter 22, *infra*.
47 S. 14(3), Sch. 3, Part III, and see Section 22.2.5, *infra*.
48 Themselves calculated by reference to the SDR value of a gold franc, see the Merchant Shipping (Sterling Equivalents) (Various Enactments) Order 1986 (S.I. No. 1777), effective from 7 November 1986. The orders are made subject to Merchant Shipping Act 1979 Sch. 3 Part II, para. 5. When the 1976 Protocol is in force a new Art. 9 will be inserted in Sch. 3, Part I (by Sch. 3, Part III, para. 3). This will require the SDR conversion to be made on the day of judgment. This is important because exchange rates may vary drastically between casualty, judgment and settlement. For the payment of interest, see *Jefford* v. *Gee* [1970] 1 All E.R. 1202 and the Administration of Justice Act 1982, s. 15; and Section 21.6.4 *infra*.

The carrier loses his right to limit if it is proved that the damage resulted from an act or omission of the carrier done with the intent to cause such damage, or recklessly and with knowledge that such damage would probably result.[49] This definition is explained in detail later,[50] but an example of such conduct might be where a shipowner sent the ship to sea knowing that it had no lifebelts.[51] Servants or agents can invoke the limits unless they themselves have been guilty of intentional or reckless conduct.[52]

18.2.5 JURISDICTION AND EXEMPTION CLAUSES

In the past, passengers have often been prejudiced by shipowners inserting in tickets a jurisdiction clause, that is, a clause compelling claimants to sue in a particular court, usually at the place where the shipowner has his principal place of business. For him this was convenient because all legal matters were thus concentrated in one office. For passengers, however, chiefly those resident abroad, this could be very inconvenient and costly, since they must then sue in a country where court procedure and language differ from their own. In extreme cases such a clause can in practice amount to a denial of justice. Following the example of the Warsaw Convention on air carriage, the Athens Convention has now outlawed such a clause and given the claimant several options.[53] He can, at his discretion, sue the defendant in one of the following courts: at the place of the defendant's principal place of business; at the place of departure or that of destination; at the place of the claimant's domestic or permanent residence, provided the defendant has a place of business in that state; or the place where the contract was made, also provided the defendant has a place of business in the state. Of course, once the incident leading to the claim has happened, both parties can agree to have their dispute decided in any court or by arbitration.[54]

---

49 Art. 13(1).
50 See Section 22.3.4, *infra* for the identical provision in the 1976 Limitation Convention. See also Section 18.4 *infra*.
51 For further examples from the Warsaw Convention relating to Carriage by Air (Carriage by Air Act 1961) see Giles, *Uniform Commercial Law,* pp. 140 *et seq.* Note that under the Warsaw Convention the carrier loses his right to limit if the servant or agent is guilty of such misconduct. At sea, under the Athens Convention, the Hague–Visby Rules and the Global Limitation Conventions it is only the misconduct of the carrier *himself* that disentitles him, see Sections 22.2.4 and 22.3.4 *infra*.
52 Art. 13(2).
53 Art. 17. See also Section 1.8, *supra*.
54 See Section 1.2, *supra*.

The shipowner cannot contract out of this or any other article in the Convention.[55] This means that clauses like those in *Haigh's* and *Budd's* cases[56] would be void. And in a case like *Budd* v. *P & O* the shipowner would only win in the unlikely event of his proving that no negligence on the part of himself or his servants made the chair unsafe.[57]

Many of the Convention provisions will be completely unknown to the ordinary passenger. It is convenient to note here that the carrier is required by Order to give notice to passengers of specific provisions of the Athens Convention.[58] Notice has to be given before departure and, where practicable, it must be given on the ticket itself. Notification has to be given of Arts 5, 7, 8, 15. But it is sufficient if the notice states that: the Athens Convention may be applicable; in most cases the Convention limits the carrier's liability; the Convention presumes luggage has been delivered undamaged unless written notice is given to the carrier.[59] Failure to comply with the Order is an offence.[60]

18.3   OTHER LIABILITIES TO PASSENGERS

The Athens Convention 1974 regulates the carrier's liability for personal injury, death and damage to luggage. It does not cover many other matters relating to the contract between the carrier and the passenger. These may still be dealt with by express terms in the contract, subject to the provisions of the Unfair Contract Terms Act 1977.[61]

A cruise which does not come up to agreed specifications may give the passenger a right to damages for the lost holiday and all the mental distress, inconvenience, upset, disappointment and frustration that could result.[62] The shipowner might try to allocate a cabin inferior to

55 Art. 18.
56 See Section 18.1, *supra*.
57 See Section 18.2.3, *supra*. Of course, the passenger could be guilty of contributory negligence: the Law Reform (Contributory Negligence) Act 1945. But *cf. The Shinjitsu Maru No.5: A.B. Marintrans* v. *Comet Shipping Co. Ltd* [1985] 3 All E.R. 442, holding the Act applies to tort, not contract, claims.
58 Sch. 3, Part II, para. 11, Carriage of Passengers and their Luggage by Sea (Interim Provisions) (Notice) Order 1980 (S.I. No. 1125).
59 *Ibid.*, Art. 2.
60 *Ibid.*, Art. 3.
61 The implied terms as to service may be varied, subject to the 1977 Act; see the Supply of Goods and Services Act 1982, s. 16.
62 *Jarvis* v. *Swan's Tours Ltd* [1973] Q.B. 233; *Jackson* v. *Horizon Holidays* [1975] 3 All E.R. 92.

that promised in the contract, or to change materially the itinerary of a cruise or abandon it altogether. The shipowner may insert a clause which tries to exclude or restrict his liability for such breaches, or which allows him to render a contractual performance substantially different from that which was reasonably expected of him, or to render no performance at all for all or part of his contractual obligation. In these cases the clauses will only be valid if they are reasonable.[63]

Reasonableness will be determined by the court. The shipowner[64] must convince the court that it was fair and reasonable to include the term in the contract, taking into account the circumstances existing at the time it was made. Thus, it might be reasonable to exclude liability resulting from a hijacking, but not, perhaps, if the owner knew that he had no security precautions. Where the owner accepts liability but wishes to limit it contractually, e.g. to a refund of passage money, the court must bear in mind what resources are available to the shipowner to meet claims and the extent to which he is able to cover himself by insurance.[65] The court can thus take account of the contingent liabilities of the business and recognize a difference between a large passenger liner and a small harbour cruiser.

Charterparties have already been dealt with in connection with the carriage of goods.[66] These documents are also used when passengers are to be carried, e.g. where a ship was chartered to cruise in the Solent when the naval review was held to celebrate the coronation of King Edward VII.[67] Far lower down the scale we find the informal hiring of rowing boats and dinghies. It is convenient to touch on this topic in the present context because consumer protection problems also arise. We should note that although the Unfair Contract Terms Act 1977 does not apply generally to charterparties, it will do so to some extent so far as consumers are concerned.[68]

In a contract for hire of a boat there is an implied condition that the supplier has the right to hire out the goods and that the hirer will have 'quiet possession' of them.[69] The supplier would be in breach if, e.g., possession of the boat was retaken by a mortgagee of whose existence the hirer was unaware. Like sale contracts,[70] the goods must also

---

63 Unfair Contract Terms Act 1977, ss. 3, 11.
64 S. 11(5).
65 S. 11(4), cf. Sch. 2.
66 See Section 10.3.1, supra and Part 2 generally.
67 Herne Bay S.S. Co. v. Hutton [1903] 2 K.B. 683.
68 Sch. 1, para. 2.
69 Supply of Goods and Services Act 1982, s. 7.
70 See Section 4.2.2, supra.

correspond with their description[71] and be of merchantable quality.[72] So the hirer of a leaking motor boat would probably be entitled to his money back and damages for ruined clothes. As against consumers these terms cannot be excluded.[73] Damage to consumers' property caused in other ways by the negligence of the supplier, e.g. in giving incorrect operating instructions, can be excluded in so far as the terms stand the test of reasonableness.[74] Liability for personal injury and death caused by negligence cannot be excluded.[75] The same rules would apply to the chartering of hovercraft.

18.4   HOVERCRAFT

The Athens Convention 1974 excludes air cushion vehicles, i.e. hovercraft, from the definition of 'ship'.[76] This is not surprising because hovercraft are monsters, partaking of the features of ships, aircraft and land vehicles. Bearing this in mind, the UK by the Hovercraft Act 1968, has provided that the carriage of passengers and their luggage by hovercraft shall be covered by the Carriage by Air Act 1961 and the Carriage by Air (Supplementary Provisions) Act 1962.[77] This is so whether the carriage is international, e.g. across the Channel, or at home, e.g. between the Isle of Wight and the mainland.

The carrier[78] is made liable for the death or personal injury of a passenger where accidents occur on board the hovercraft or during embarking or disembarking and for baggage lost or damaged during carriage.[79] Apart from proving contributory negligence of the passenger,[80] the carrier's only defence is to show that he and his servants or agents took all reasonable measures to avoid the damage or that it was

71 Supply of Goods and Services Act 1982, s. 8.

72 S. 9.

73 S. 17, inserting a new s. 7(3A) in the Unfair Contract Terms Act 1977.

74 Unfair Contract Terms Act 1977, s. 2(2).

75 S. 2(1).

76 Art. 1(3).

77 But as applied by the Hovercraft (Civil Liability) Order 1986 (S.I. No. 305). Note that major changes in air law will be effected when the Carriage of Goods by Air and Road Act 1979 is brought fully into force. See generally, *Shawcross and Beaumont, Air Law* (4th edn, 1977 with reissues).

78 1986 (S.I. No. 1305). Sch. 4(1), Part I (B) of the Order contains the relevant parts of the 1961 Act as amended. Note that a plaintiff can sue an actual or contracting carrier, Sch. 4, Part II, Art. VII.

79 See Sch. 4(1), Part I (B), Arts 17, 18.

80 Sch. 4(1), Part I (B), Art. 21.

impossible for him or them to take such measures.[81] This reverse burden of proof may be very difficult to satisfy. In March 1985 the hovercraft *Princess Margaret* crashed into the breakwater at Dover, causing four deaths and 36 injuries amongst her 370 passengers. Although there was a strong wind the captain complained of a loss of power. To escape liability the operators would have to show that this was not caused by any faults in maintenance and that the hovercraft was sufficiently powerful for the particular service conditions.[82]

The carrier is allowed to limit his liability to: £34 412 for each passenger, unless a higher sum is agreed; £246 for baggage in charge of the carrier, e.g. hand luggage; and £246 for baggage left in charge of the carrier.[83] A vehicle is not treated as baggage for these purposes.[84] The *carrier* loses his right to limit if it is proved that the damage resulted from an act or omission of the carrier, his *servants or agents*, done with intent to cause damage or recklessly and with knowledge that damage would probably result.[85] If the servants or agents *themselves* are sued they are entitled to limit.[86]

18.5   COMBINED TRANSPORT

What happens when there is a combined transport, e.g. rail and sea carriage from Victoria Station in London to Dover, thence by ship to Calais and finally, again by rail to Paris? The rail stages are regulated by the Convention concerning the International Carriage by Rail (COTIF) 1980,[87] as enacted by the International Transport Conventions Act

81 Sch 4(1), Part I (B), Art. 20.
82 Note that Art. 20 of the Warsaw Convention on which the 1981 Act is based uses the expression 'necessary' while the 1979 Order substitutes 'reasonable' measures—a requirement that is less strict.
83 Art. 22.
84 1986 (S.I. No. 1305) Art. 5. For the carriage of goods in hovercraft, see Sch. 4(2).
85 For an analysis of a similar provision, see Section 22.3.4, *infra,* but note that with hovercraft the carrier loses his right to limit if his employees have been guilty of such misconduct. This will make it much more difficult for the hovercraft operator to limit his liability to his passengers than the operator of a ship. However, for personal injury, death or property claims by third parties other than passengers the hovercraft operator is entitled to the global limits of liability, see Sections 22.2.5 and 22.3.5, *infra.*
86 Sch. 4(1), Part I (B), Art. 25A.
87 Convention relative aux transports internationaux ferroviaires (COTIF), Cmnd 8535. These railway provisions will presumably have greater importance for the UK if a Channel railway tunnel is built.

1983, s. 1.[88] COTIF set up an Intergovernmental Organization whose aim is to establish a uniform system of law for the carriage of passengers and goods by rail. The carriage of passengers is subject to the uniform rules, known as the CIV, which are contained in Annex A of COTIF. The CIV deal with general matters, e.g. the rights of railways in relation to passengers who are drunk or have no tickets and the rights of passengers when connections are missed.[89] They also regulate liability.

The CIV system of liability is very similar to that for hovercraft described above, with the railway being liable for damage or injury unless it can show that the accident was caused by unavoidable circumstances not connected with the operation of the railway.[90] There is a limit of liability of 70 000 SDR (£53 211 for death or personal injury[91] and 700 SDR (£532) per passenger for damage to hand luggage.[92] There is a similar system of liability for registered luggage, although the railway is not liable if it can show that the loss or damage arose from, e.g. inadequate packing.[93] For loss of registered luggage the railway must pay for the amount of loss up to a limit of 134 SDR (£25.85) per kg. of gross mass missing, or 500 SDR (£380) per item of luggage.[94] If the amount of loss cannot be established the railway must pay liquidated damages of 10 SDR (£7.60) per kg., or 150 SDR (£114) per item.[95] There are also limits for loss caused by delay to registered luggage.[96] For the loss of a vehicle there is a limit of 4000 SDR (£3041).[97] The railway cannot rely on the limits if the loss or damage arose from 'wilful misconduct or gross negligence' on the part

88 Repealing the Carriage by Railway Act 1972, as from 1 May 1985, see s. 11; International Transport Conventions Act 1983 (Certification of Commencement of Convention) Order 1985 (S.I. No. 612).

89 Uniform Rules concerning the Contract for International Carriage of Passengers and Luggage by Rail (CIV), Arts 10, 12, 16.

90 Art. 26.

91 Art. 30. For explanation of SDR, see Section 22.3.5. Rate calculated at 13 September 1985. The SDR conversion must be made on the day of judgment, s. 5, International Transport Conventions Act 1983.

92 Art. 31.

93 Art. 35(3).

94 Art. 38(1)(a).

95 Art. 38 (1)(b).

96 Art. 40.

97 Art. 41(3). There is a limit of 700 SDR (£532) for loss or damage, caused by the fault of the railway, to items left in the vehicle, Art. 41(4).

of the railway.[98] Contract terms which attempt to reduce the liability of the railway are void.[99]

The railway rules do not apply to damage arising in the course of carriage by road or shipping services.[1] But where railway vehicles are carried by ferry the CIV apply to accidents arising out of the operation of the railway, e.g. where a passenger is injured within or while entering or leaving a carriage.[2] Where there is combined carriage by hovercraft and other modes of carriage, the hovercraft rules only apply to the carriage by hovercraft.[3] The same is true for carriage with an air leg.[4] The Convention on the Contract for the International Carriage of Passengers and Luggage by Road incorporated in the Schedule to the Carriage of Passengers by Road Act 1974, has a similar system of liability to the other Conventions.[5] It applies to carriage by road,[6] but where the vehicle is taken on board ship the Convention (like the rail Convention) applies to incidents connected with the carriage by vehicle, e.g. injuries while entering or leaving the car or bus.[7] Power is given to regulate by Order any conflict between the Convention and other transport conventions.[8]

The Athens Convention 1974 does not apply when the carriage is subject to a civil liability regime under the provisions of another international transport convention which has mandatory application to the

---

98 'Wilful misconduct' is an expression reasonably familiar in English law as it was used in many of the nineteenth-century railway cases where the companies were not allowed to rely on exemption clauses in their contracts with customers if railway employees had been guilty of such conduct. It would probably be interpreted in a similar manner to the intention/reckless test described elsewhere; see Section 18.2.4, *supra* and Section 22.3.4, *infra*. 'Gross negligence' is not a recognized concept in English law, and derives from the French *'faute lourde'*. It seems to describe conduct which is less than intentional or reckless, but more than 'mere' negligence, i.e. that case which the least careful and most stupid persons would not fail to give to their own property, *Metall A.G.* v. *Ceres* [1977] 1 Lloyd's Rep. 665, 671-2.

99 Art. 32.

1 Art. 33(1).

2 Art. 33(2).

3 The Hovercraft (Civil Liability) Order 1979 (S.I. No. 305), Sch. 4(1), Part I, Art. 31.

4 Carriage by Air Act 1961, Sch. 1, Art. 31.

5 It has limits of 250 000 gold francs per passenger and luggage limits of 500 gold francs for each piece of luggage (2000 gold francs maximum per passenger), see Arts 13, 16. The Act is not yet in force.

6 Arts 1, 2.

7 Art. 3. It must be emphasized that we are dealing with combined transport – i.e. under a single contract. Where a passenger takes a coach, or buys an ordinary train ticket, to Dover and arranges the ferry contract separately then only the Athens Convention applies.

8 S. 7.

sea stage.[9] But a clause in the contract of carriage stating that the provisions of another convention (e.g. CIV) are to apply has the effect of making that other convention apply mandatorily.[10]

9 Merchant Shipping Act 1979, Sch. 3, Part I, Art. 2(2). See the Carriage of Passengers by Road Act 1974, *infra*.
10 Sch. 3, Part II, para. 2.

19

PILOTAGE

When a ship comes from the high seas, approaches her port, and especially when she enters harbour, local knowledge of the water is essential to avoid accidents. To this end every harbour authority has power to make by-laws for the traffic within its jurisdiction; they take precedence over the general regulations for navigation made on the basis of international agreement.[1] Naturally, masters and navigating officers of merchant ships cannot be expected to know the navigation rules of every harbour at which they may call on their voyage. Their ships must, therefore, engage the services of local pilots to guide them when entering or leaving a port, or navigating therein.

We must consider the organization of pilotage services and then the rights and liabilities of pilots. The law on the subject was consolidated in the Pilotage Act 1983 but a further change is expected in 1987.[2]

19.1 PILOTAGE ADMINISTRATION

19.1.1 LOCAL ADMINISTRATION

The British Isles are divided into pilotage districts in each of which there is a pilotage authority.[3] The authorities have wide powers to make by-laws,[4] subject to the control of the Secretary of State.[5] One of their main functions is to provide for the examination and licensing of pilots to ensure that they are qualified for their tasks.

---

1 See Rose (1984), Geen and Douglas (1983), and Section 21.2, *infra*.
2 A Pilotage Bill 1986 aims to reduce the cost of pilotage to the trade. Many of the arrangements described in Sections 19.1, 19.2 will be replaced.
3 Existing pilotage districts and authorities continued in being, Pilotage Act 1983, s. 1: Trinity House operates as a pilotage authority in 'Trinity House Outport Districts', Pilotage Act 1983, s. 27. One function of the 1986 Bill is to transfer responsibility for pilotage services to local 'competent harbour authorities'. These may subcontract the services, e.g. to Trinity House.
4 S. 15. Existing by-laws were preserved by s. 69(1), Sch. 2.
5 S. 16.

19.1.2 CENTRAL ADMINISTRATION

The Secretary of State for Transport has wide powers over pilotage[6] and he can make pilotage orders to establish, abolish or rearrange pilotage districts or authorities;[7] to define the limits of pilotage districts; to appoint committees to which authorities may delegate functions; to provide for compulsory pilotage; to authorize by-laws for the granting of pilotage certificates; to make other provisions he considers 'necessary or expedient.'

19.1.3 PILOTAGE COMMISSION

The Merchant Shipping Act 1979 constituted a 'Pilotage Commission' and this has been preserved by the 1983 Act.[8] The Commission is largely supervisory in function.[9] It must advise the Secretary of State, pilotage authorities, dock and harbour authorities, pilots and shipowners on a wide range of pilotage matters. These include: securing by means of pilotage the safety of navigation in UK ports and waters; ensuring that efficient pilotage services and equipment are provided; ensuring that the terms of service of pilots are fair; promoting uniform standards in the qualification and training of pilots.[10]

The Commission may be given additional functions by the Secretary of State.[11] This power has been exercised in order to allow a scheme to be made for compensating pilots for lost income as a result of, in particular, the granting of pilotage certificates to EEC nationals.[12] The Commission must keep under review the provision of pilotage in non-compulsory areas.[13]

The Commission has the power to establish pension and compensation schemes for pilots or former pilots and may take over the existing pilots' benefit fund.[14]

6 S. 9.
7 E.g., the Swansea and Port Talbot Pilotage Order 1985 (S.I. No. 831), establishing a new single district and authority for those two areas.
8 S. 1. However, it will be abolished when the Pilotage Bill 1986 becomes law.
9 It has a duty to provide annual reports, s. 8.
10 S. 5.
11 S. 5(2).
12 S. 5(3), Pilotage Commission (Additional Function) Order 1982 (S.I. No. 883) – originally made under the Merchant Shipping Act 1979, s. 4.
13 S. 6.
14 S. 7.

The Commission is entirely independent of the Crown and does not act as its servant or agent.[15] It has between 10–15 members, including a chairman.[16] To ensure that there is a wide cross-section of informed opinion the Secretary of State may appoint any person with special knowledge or experience (e.g., in training or engineering) likely to be of value. But there must be at least one member from the following groups: licensed pilots; persons with wide practical experience of the management of ships; persons with wide practical experience of the administration of pilotage services; persons with wide practical experience of the management of docks or harbours.[17]

19.1.4   LICENSING AND CERTIFICATION OF PILOTS

As we have noted, one of the main functions of pilotage authorities is to license pilots who have obtained certain qualifications.[18] Unlicensed pilots nevertheless exist and may be employed if no licensed pilot responds to the pilotage request signal[19] and offers his services in time.[20] A licensed pilot is entitled to supersede an unlicensed one.[21] A master who knowingly engages an unlicensed pilot after a qualified pilot has offered his services commits an offence.[22] In one case, a pilot told a master at 1540 that it would be unsafe to leave that evening, but that he would return at 0645 the next morning. It was held that there had been no 'offer' as the suggestion was unreasonable.[23]

Although pilotage provides a useful form of local employment its main function must be to ensure safe navigation of ships. In many cases, ships call regularly at certain ports and their officers do not really need the help of pilots. Before the 1914–18 war it was the practice of Dutch shipowners, plying regularly to English ports, to require their masters or mates to qualify as pilots so as to save time and pilotage dues. But

---

15 S. 2(4).
16 S. 2(1).
17 *Ibid.*
18 Ss. 12, 15(1)(a).
19 S. 49, Merchant Shipping (Pilotage Signals) Order 1970 (S.I. No. 1952).
20 *Montague* v. *Babbs* [1972] 1 All E.R. 240 decided that an offer must be specific: showing the flag at the pilot station is not enough.
21 S. 36.
22 S. 36(4), as does the unlicensed pilot, s. 36(3). It does not matter that the unlicensed pilot was unremunerated, *Lister* v. *Warne* (1935) 53 Ll. L. Rep. 96.
23 *The Ignition* [1983] 1 Lloyd's Rep. 382.

restrictions were later put on the issue of certificates to aliens.[24] After the accession of the UK to the EEC these discriminatory restrictions were no longer sustainable.[25] Pilotage authorities now have the power to grant pilotage 'certificates' to masters and first mates who pass an examination to show they have the necessary skill, experience and local knowledge.[26] However, the certificates can only be granted to Commonwealth citizens and EEC nationals and in respect of a ship registered in the EEC.

As a result, many European masters and mates applied for certificates. Trinity House was concerned that this would result in a significant drop in income for itself and its pilots. To provide some protection for pilots, pilotage authorities can refuse to grant certificates if the Pilotage Commission thinks that there are enough licences or certificates in force in the area[27] and the Secretary of State has power to revoke, on similar grounds, certificates already issued. However, this protection is not meant to be open ended and is designed to 'phase-in' the use of certificates by EEC nationals.[28] Moreover, the reduced amount of shipping in British ports is likely to lead to a radical drop in the number of pilots required. This will, itself, result in a decline in the role of Trinity House. There is a right of complaint to the Secretary of State from a pilotage authority's decision to refuse to examine, or grant a certificate to, a candidate.[29] Pilots whose licences are suspended, revoked, or not renewed or returned, can appeal to a court.[30]

19.1.5   PILOTAGE CHARGES

The Pilotage Commission is financed by a levy on pilotage authorities, based on their receipts.[31]

---

24 See the Pilotage Act 1913, s. 25; Aliens Restriction (Amendment) Act 1919, s. 4.
25 See Art. 7, Treaty of Rome.
26 S. 20, The certificates can only be granted to Commonwealth citizens and EEC nationals and in respect of a ship registered in the EEC, s. 20(2). The certificates are valid for 12 months, but they can be renewed, s. 20(4).
27 S. 21(1).
28 *The Dana Anglia* [1982] 2 Lloyds Rep. 14, 27; s. 21(3).
29 S. 25.
30 S. 26.
31 S. 3. See, e.g., the Pilotage Commission Provision of Funds Scheme 1986 (Confirmation) Order 1986 (S.I. No. 402).

Pilotage authorities derive income by charging the users of pilotage services,[32] in accordance with a prescribed list of charges.[33] Non-payment of pilotage charges can be expensive as the charges may be increased on a sliding scale which could add 30 per cent to the charges if they are unpaid after five months.[34] The pilotage authority has no general right to demand pilotage dues if a ship has been navigated without a pilot in a compulsory pilotage area. The questions whether dues are payable and whether an offence has been committed by the master are entirely separate of each other.[35]

Pilots will be paid according to rates fixed by pilotage authorities in their by-laws.[36] Obtaining a charge by wilful misrepresentation is an offence[37] and a licensed pilot who demands or receives an amount greater (or less) than allowed by law is also guilty.[38]

Owners or masters are liable for a licensed pilot's charges.[39] Moreover, inward charges may be recoverable from such consignees or agents as have paid, or made themselves liable to pay, any *other* charges for the ship in the port of destination.[40] A similar liability for outward pilotage charges is placed on consignees or agents at the port of departure.[41] This could be a very costly obligation, particularly for ships' agents. However, they do have the right to retain the charges, and expenses, out of monies received from the shipowner on account.[42]

Charges for licensed pilots may be recovered by way of summary proceedings in a magistrate's court,[43] provided that they have been

32 S. 14. Any balance left after paying an authority's expenses is applied to the benefit of pilots, s. 18. Pilots' benefit funds are not subject to attachment in legal claims brought against the authority, s. 59.
33 S. 14(d): Pilotage Charges Regulations 1980 (S.I. No. 1234). The fees are a not inconsiderable part of a shipowner's expenses as shown by the dispute in *The Dana Anglia* [1982] 2 Lloyd's Rep. 14. The Danish ferry company was paying £300 for each movement (i.e., a £600 turnround fee) as opposed to £6 per movement for certificated pilots: this had cost £100 000 in what appeared (p. 15) to be a five-month period.
34 Pilotage Charges Regulations 1980 (S.I. No. 1234), reg. 4.
35 *Muller & Co.* v. *Corporation of Trinity House* [1925] 1 K.B. 166. It is arguable that s. 14(1)(b) (first introduced in the Merchant Shipping Act 1979, s. 9) may give the authority power to charge if it can be said that the ship has not complied with by-laws dealing with 'requests for pilots'.
36 S. 15(1)(f), pooling of charges, with general consent is allowed, s. 15(1)(g).
37 S. 53, see also s. 54.
38 S. 64. Masters may also commit offences under this section.
39 S. 63(1)(a).
40 S. 63(1)(b).
41 S. 63(1)(c).
42 S. 63(2).
43 S. 63(1), in the same way as fines under the Merchant Shipping Act 1894, s. 681(2).

demanded in writing.[44] Unlicensed pilots must sue at common law, as indeed may licensed pilots if they wish.[45] The contract will usually be with the shipowner, through the agency of the master. The shipowner must be sued in an ordinary debt action, usually in the county court.

As noted earlier,[46] there is probably no maritime lien for pilotage, although there is a statutory right of action *in rem*.[47]

19.2   COMPULSORY PILOTAGE[48]

Under modern conditions, it would be unsafe to leave the decision whether or not to take a pilot to the discretion of ships' masters, and in many districts pilotage has been made compulsory, for instance, in the whole of the Port of London.

The Pilotage Act 1983 imposes various obligations in respect of compulsory pilotage. There are two possible regimes, that might apply. The existing regime[49] dates from the Pilotage Act 1913,[50] although a separate new regime may be applied, in whole or in part, from a day to be appointed.[51]

19.2.1   THE 'OLD' REGIME

Within the compulsory area ships must be under the pilotage of a licensed pilot or a certificated master or mate.[52] Once an 'offer' has been made by a licensed pilot it is an offence to navigate the ship in the district.[53] A ship 'navigates' even where it is being moved within a harbour, e.g. from one mooring to another, or into or out of a dock.[54] However, by-laws may provide otherwise[55] and movements within closed dock systems are exempted.[56]

44 S. 63(1).
45 *The Ambatielos; The Cephalonia* [1923] P. 68.
46 Section 7.1.2, *supra*.
47 Section 7.2, *supra*; Supreme Court Act 1981, ss. 20(2)(1), 21(4).
48 Geen and Douglas (1983), Chapters 1, 6; Rose (1984), Chapter IV.
49 S. 31.
50 S. 11 as amended by the Merchant Shipping Act 1979, s. 8.
51 Pilotage Act 1983, s. 30.
52 S. 31(1).
53 S. 31(2).
54 S. 38.
55 *Ibid.*, as in the Port of London, see *Montague* v. *Babbs, supra* and *McMillan* v. *Crouch* [1972] 3 All E.R. 61.
56 S. 39.

There are a number of other exceptions to the requirement that licensed pilots must be engaged where pilotage is compulsory. We have already noted that a master (if uncertificated[57]) may engage an unqualified person or sail the ship himself if no reasonable offer is made.[58] Where the signal for a pilot is unanswered it would clearly be unreasonable to expect the master to wait for a licensed pilot if to do so would expose his ship to danger by wind or currents.[59] These preconditions are unlikely to exist when a ship is about to leave the harbour and one may assume that departure will nearly always be delayed until a qualified pilot arrives.[60]

The most important exception refers to what the Pilotage Act 1983 terms 'excepted ships'.[61] These are ships belonging to Her Majesty; fishing vessels of which the registered length is less than 47.5 metres; ferry boats plying as such exclusively within the limits of a harbour authority; ships of less than fifty tons gross tonnage; ships exempted by a by-law made by a pilotage authority;[62] tugs, dredgers, sludge-vessels, barges and other similar craft belonging to a harbour or dock authority whilst employed on statutory duties within the limits of such authority.[63]

No passenger ships may be exempted.[64] This covers not only what is commonly regarded as a passenger ship. It has been held that drivers of lorries carried on a roll-on, roll-off ferry, in this case between Newcastle upon Tyne and Denmark, are passengers, although the ferry makes no additional charge for the carriage of the drivers.[65] A local exemption order accordingly did not apply to such ferries. The decision was based on the Merchant Shipping Act 1894, s. 267, which defines a passenger as anyone on board except the master, crew or owner and the latter's family and servants.

Under by-laws in force when the Pilotage Act 1983 came into effect a pilotage authority may exempt from compulsory pilotage;[66] ships

---

57 See Section 19.1.1, *supra*.

58 Once an offer has been made there is a heavy onus on the master to say that he is within an exception to the statute: *Buck v. Tyrrel* (1922) 10 Ll.L. Rep. 74, 76. *cf.* Rose (1984), p. 30.

59 *R v. Neale* (1799) 8 T.R. 241, 101 E.R. 1367. *Cf. Phillips v. Headlam* (1831) 2 B. & Ad. 380, 109 E.R. 1184 which surprisingly indicates that failure to have a qualified pilot may make a ship unseaworthy under its insurance policy; see Section 30.1.2, *infra*.

60 But *cf. The Ignition, supra.*

61 Pilotage Act 1983, s. 31(3).

62 *Ibid*. Naval vessels may employ pilots: *The Truculent* [1951] 2 Lloyd's Rep. 308.

63 S. 32.

64 S. 31(1).

65 *Clayton v. Albertson* [1972] 3 All E.R. 364.

66 S. 31(3)(e), Sch. 2, para. 1.

trading coastwise and home trade ships trading otherwise than coast-wise;[67] vessels ordinarily employed within the seaward limitations of a harbour authority.[68]

19.2.2 THE 'NEW' REGIME

The circle of excepted ships will be considerably narrowed as soon as the new regime under the Pilotage Act 1983, s. 30 comes into force. Since 1913, when the excepted categories were defined, the size of ships contained in the category of excepted ships and their engine power have substantially increased. As a result, their ability to cause damage has also substantially grown. The vessels listed in the previous section[69] will no longer be allowed as a matter of course to sail in pilotage areas without pilots; nor will fishing vessels longer than 47.5 metres be allowed to do so. Automatic exemption for pleasure yachts was removed in 1979.[70]

Of course, there is nothing to stop pilotage authorities making specific exceptions in by-laws to take account of local conditions and the type, size and cargo of the ship.[71] And ships belonging to Her Majesty need not employ a pilot. The generality of this provision seems to mean that Royal Fleet Auxiliaries, that is, merchant ships manned by civilian crews, and operated by the Ministry of Defence to supply Royal Navy ships with fuel, food, stores and ammunition, are also exempted.

All other ships navigating in a compulsory pilotage district will have to carry a licensed pilot and, if by-laws so provide, an assistant;[72] the latter need not be a licensed pilot, but may have qualifications defined by a by-law of the district. A ship whose master or first mate possesses a pilotage certificate for the district in question need not employ another pilot.[73] But he must be acting bona fide as master or mate.[74]

---

67 The latter include ships employed in trading, or going within the UK, the Channel Islands, and the Isle of Man, and the Continent of Europe between the River Elbe and Brest inclusive; and see the Merchant Shipping Act 1894, s. 742. N.B. the Pilotage Act 1913, s. 11(5), now repealed.

68 Thus the picturesque sailing barges in the Thames, the Blackwall ferry, and coastal tramp steamers may have been exempted.

69 Previously listed in the Pilotage Act 1913, s. 11(4) and (5).

70 Merchant Shipping Act 1979, s. 8(1): most would be exempt in any event under the 50 ton exemption in s. 31.

71 S. 30(4).

72 S. 30(2)(a).

73 S. 30(2)(b).

74 Ibid.

Even in a pilotage district where there is normally no compulsion to employ a pilot the master of a ship may be ordered to employ a pilot where the navigation of the ship is materially affected by a defect of its hull, machinery or equipment and the port authority has requested the pilotage authority to order the master to take a pilot on board.[75]

Failure to employ a pilot in accordance with the above provisions is an offence, unless the master proves that he navigated his ship 'only so far as was necessary to avoid serious danger to the ship'.[76] This may happen when severe weather makes waiting for a pilot impracticable, and indeed hazardous.

Finally, one should note that even where pilotage is not compulsory it may be advisable. In order to increase safety and reduce pollution an EEC directive has required states to encourage ships only to use fully qualified deep-sea pilots in the North Sea or English Channel.[77]

19.3   PILOT'S RESPONSIBILITIES

What is the pilot's standing on board ship? His rights and duties there are the same whether pilotage is compulsory or voluntary, whether he is licensed or unlicensed. At one time his duties were very wide, but the Pilotage Act of 1913 (and now the Act 1983) adapted the pilot's position to that of the continental countries.

This means in legal terms that the pilot is not the sole directing authority on board and does not oust master and mate as he used to do. He is charged with the safety of the ship, being bound to use diligence and reasonable skill in the exercise of his important functions. But he is charged with pilot's duties only[78] and he is entitled to the same assistance by the crew as are captain and officers when no pilot is on board.[79] Master and crew remain responsible, and it would seem to follow from the tenor of the decisions to be dealt with below that the master may, and even must, state his opinion to the pilot in matters of importance.[80] The pilot does not supersede the master in the command of a vessel, but acts as his adviser.[81] Still, he is an adviser whose advice should be followed. Master and navigating officers must in the ordinary

75 S. 30(3).
76 S. 30(6).
77 Council Directive of 21 December 1978 (79/115/EEC), M.S. Notice No. M. 1001.
78 *The Alexander Shukoff* [1921] 1 A.C. 216.
79 *Ibid.*
80 See particularly *Kedroff* v. *Owners of S.S. Cranley* (1920) 5 Ll. L. Rep. 303, 304.
81 *The Nord* [1916] P. 53, 54.

way abide by his decision as, after all, the pilot has the knowledge of the locality. Only quite exceptional circumstances would enable the master to overrule the pilot's orders,[82] for instance if it would involve the infringement of collision regulations.[83]

The pilot is not concerned with matters of detail. For instance, if on board the tow, he need not direct every little helm movement of the tug.[84]

19.4   PILOTAGE LIABILITIES

19.4.1   PILOT'S LIABILITY

As the pilot has the principal control of the operation it follows that he will be liable to the ship and to third parties for failure to exercise reasonable skill, care and prudence. However, a licensed pilot will be entitled to limit his liability, as will harbour authorities.[85]

19.4.2   SHIPOWNER'S LIABILITY FOR PILOT

We now have to consider whether the pilot's presence makes any difference in the event of claims being made against the shipowner for damages for negligent navigation or, conversely, where the shipowner makes a claim against a third party and is faced by the defence of contributory negligence of the pilot.

In the course of his duties the pilot often exposes the ship entrusted to his care to dangers known to him. Indeed it is because of these very dangers that he is engaged. This consideration is important. Suppose, as happened in an old case,[86] a dock, which was opened to the public, was not yet cleared, and a ship while under pilotage suffered damage thereby. The dock-owners replied to a claim for damages by the shipowners that the pilot, who was the shipowner's agent, knew of the dangerous character of the dock, had voluntarily exposed the ship to that danger, and had thus forfeited any claim for damages on the part of the ship. The court, however, held the dock-owners liable. 'Where

82   *The Prinses Juliana* [1936] P. 139, 149, 153.
83   *The Ripon* (1885) 10 P.D. 65: See Section 21.2 *infra*.
84   *The Sinquasi* (1880) 5 P.D. 241.
85   S. 42 and see Sections 22.2.1 and 22.3.1, *infra*.
86   *Thompson* v. *North Eastern Railway Co.* (1860) 2 B. & S. 106, 121 E.R. 1012.

danger has been created,'[87] said Cockburn CJ, 'by the wrongful or negligent act of another, if a man, in the performance of a lawful act, voluntarily exposes himself to that danger, he is not precluded from recovering for injury resulting from it, unless the circumstances are such that the jury are of opinion that the exposing himself to that danger was a want of common or ordinary prudence on his part'.

We have seen that the pilot's negligence exposes him to an action for damages by the ship he controls and by a third party. The action against him will, however, not be of any great value, since the amount of damages will usually by far exceed what a pilot can pay. Therefore, a third party usually will try to make the ship liable for the pilot's negligence.

Where the pilotage is voluntary, the question presents no difficulties. There is no doubt that the pilot in this case is treated as if he were the employee of the shipowner and that the latter is liable for the former's unlawful act committed in the course of his employment.

Where pilotage is compulsory, shipowners formerly argued that as they did not engage the pilot of their own free will and choice, but were forced to take anybody offering himself and were not allowed to control his actions, the compulsory pilot could not be regarded as their employee.[88] This was the view taken by the common law and statute and, as a consequence, shipowners were not liable for the compulsory pilot's negligence.[89]

Article 5 of the 1910 Collision Convention made it clear that there should be no distinction between compulsory and voluntary pilotage where liability arose because of the fault of the pilot. When the Pilotage Act 1913 restricted the pilot to pilot's duties and the master and crew were no longer divested of their obligations, the defence of compulsory pilotage was abolished.[90] It is now provided that 'the owner or master of a vessel navigating under circumstances in which pilotage is compulsory shall be answerable for any loss or damage caused by the vessel or by any fault of the navigation of the vessel in the same manner as he would if pilotage were not compulsory'.[91]

---

87 At p. 115. Cf. *Workington Harbour and Dock Board* v. *Towerfield (Owners)* [1951] A.C. 112 and see Section 20.2.4, *infra*.

88 *The Chyebassa* [1919] P. 201; *The Arum* [1921] P. 12, 22.

89 Merchant Shipping Act 1894, s. 633. They remained liable, however, if the negligence of master or crew was the sole or contributory cause of the accident, or if the latter was due to the defective equipment of the ship: *The Tactician* [1907] P. 244; *The Elysia* [1912] P. 152.

90 S. 15.

91 Pilotage Act 1983, s. 35. The Pilotage Bill 1986 alters the wording, but not the effect, of this proviso.

In other words, the compulsory pilot is now treated as the owner's employee,[92] though only while on board. This may be important, for it means that the shipowner cannot claim from the pilotage authority for damage done to his own ship. He is also liable for damage done to third parties by the fault of the pilot.[93]

Further, under the law of agency, a principal who admits his negligence out of court must allow this admission to be used as evidence against him at the trial. Likewise, if the principal's servant admits that he was negligent, his statement is evidence against the principal when the action is heard.[94] But the servant's statement binds the principal only if he was a servant at the time when he made such a statement.[95] Now in one collision case the pilot after having gone ashore had made a report to Trinity House, and the other party tried to put this report in as evidence against the shipowner. That was held inadmissible. The employment had ceased when the report was made and it could not be treated as evidence against the owners.[96]

Does anything remain of the compulsory pilotage defence? Theoretically it could still be run in an English court in respect of collisions in foreign countries where the defence is still available.[97] This is because the Pilotage Act 1983 only applies to the UK (including Northern Ireland).[98] But, if such countries exist, they are few and far between.

In cases decided on the law applicable before the abolition of the defence it was held that owners were not liable for the faults of a pilot imposed by compulsion of the Admiralty under the Defence of the Realm Regulations,[99] or by charterparty.[1] It is clear that the effect of the Pilotage Act 1983, s. 35 is to abolish the defence, whether the pilotage is compulsory under local or Public Act, or some other method.[2]

More difficult is the question whether an owner is responsible for damage caused when his master obeys directions given by persons who

92 *Clark v. Hutchinson* [1925] S.C. 386; 21 Ll. L. Rep. 169.
93 Including damage done to an authority's own works: *Workington Harbour and Dock Board v. Towerfield (Owners)* [1951] A.C. 112; see Section 20.2.4, *infra*.
94 *Halsbury's Laws of England*, Vol. 17, para. 72.
95 *The Prinses Juliana* [1936] P. 139.
96 *Ibid., Halsbury's Laws of England*, Vol. 17, para 163, *cf.* Rose (1984), pp. 33–34.
97 *The Arum, supra; The Alexander Shukoff* [1921] A.C. 216.
98 S. 70.
99 *The Penrith Castle* [1917] P. 209, 216–217.
 1 *The Arum, supra.*
 2 *The Chyebassa* [1919] P. 201, 203.

are not 'pilots'. Under the Dangerous Vessels Act 1985, s. 1[3] a harbour master may give directions to masters (but not pilots[4]) to move their vessels. Under the Prevention of Oil Pollution Act 1971, s. 12[5] the Secretary of State may give quite specific directions to masters,[6] or take over control of the ship himself. Under both Acts damage could be caused to third parties by following such directions. It is unlikely that these directions could be considered as 'pilotage' within s. 35. Liability would then depend on proof of fault in the ordinary way and it is doubtful whether there could be such liability if a master, taking all reasonable precautions,[7] obeyed an order and caused loss. The master would have little choice because failure to obey directions is an offence.[8] Where the Secretary of State took over possession of the vessel, the owner would cease to be liable as he would with a demise charterer. But if a person was imposed on board to give orders to the master and crew then this person would probably be treated as a pilot, and the owner would be responsible.

19.4.3   MASTER'S LIABILITY

In the preceding pages we have touched incidentally on the legal position of the master while a pilot is on board. No doubt his responsibility is now heavier than it was prior to the Pilotage Acts. As the pilot is only charged with pilotage duties, and these are to be exercised rather by way of advice than command, the master can no longer escape liability by abstaining altogether from watching the navigation.[9] When and how far he is bound to interfere depends on the circumstances of each case.[10] If the pilot was negligent, the owners are now always liable. So whatever the master does or omits to do while a pilot is on board is material with regard to his own personal liability.

---

3 See Chapter 8, *supra*.

4 Defined as 'a person not belonging to the vessel who has the conduct of it', s. 1(1).

5 See Section 25.1.3, *infra*.

6 There is no specific exclusion of 'pilots', but it is unlikely that a pilot would be considered as a 'master'.

7 Dangerous Vessels Act 1985, s. 5(2), Prevention of Oil Pollution Act 1971, s. 14(3).

8 Dangerous Vessels Act 1985, s. 5(1), Prevention of Oil Pollution Act 1971, s. 14(3).

9 *Marsden* (1961), para, 293.

10 See, e.g., *The Prinses Juliana, supra; The Ape* (1915) 31 T.L.R. 244.

20

HARBOUR AND
ANCILLARY SERVICES

APART FROM activities such as pilotage and towage (which are dealt with separately in Chapters 19 and 23), a number of other important services are undertaken for the benefit of ships. We will deal briefly with some of these services here.

20.1 STEVEDORES

20.1.1 EMPLOYMENT

Stevedores are a reminder that Spain was once a great seafaring nation, for the name 'stevedores' is a derivation from the Spanish *estibar* which signifies to pack tight.[1]

The men doing the actual work, the employees of the stevedoring firms, are known as dockworkers or dockers. Their working conditions are governed by the Dockworkers (Regulation of Employment) Act 1946, the main feature of which was the abolition of the objectionable method of casual employment practised in the past.[2] The contracts of registered dockworkers, like those of seamen manning United Kingdom registered ships, are not governed by the contracts of employment legislation. Nor, in common with seamen, do certain other provisions of the Employment Protection (Consolidation) Act 1978 apply to them.[3]

In speaking of stevedores we must, however, not only think of the men who do the actual work. These men are usually employees of a

1 Stevedores are already mentioned in the 13th century Catalan *Consulat del Mar*. See T. Twiss, *The Black Book of the Admiralty* (1875).
2 As regards other connected questions, see the Dock Work Regulation Act 1976.
3 See s. 145, and Section 9.1, *supra*. The Ports (Finance) Act 1985 enables grants to be made to the National Dock Labour Board to reduce the number of registered dock workers. The Dockyard Services Act 1986 deals with 'privatization'.

stevedoring firm, and it is the firm whom the ship or charterer engages to load or unload the cargo.[4]

The contract between ship or charterer with the stevedoring firm is an ordinary contract for work and labour. It is governed by the general law of contract, and there are only a few points to notice.

20.1.2   THE STEVEDORING CONTRACT

(A)   PARTIES

The first point of interest is: who are the parties to the stevedoring contract? On the one hand there are the stevedores and on the other the ship. Yet behind the ship there may be either of two different persons, the owner or the charterer. The question we have to decide is therefore which of these two parties is the employer. This is, of course, easy to determine if either of the two come into the open and engage the stevedores. In a foreign port, however, this will normally not happen, but the agreement may be made by the master of the ship and the question then arises whether the master acted as the agent of the owner or the charterer. It will be recalled that when dealing with the contract of affreightment we met with a similar problem. There we saw that the master, in the ordinary way, dealt with the shipper of goods as agent of the owner of the ship with whom the contract was made, as the owner was the ostensible principal of the master. If, however, the charter was by demise, the master represented the charterer and the latter was bound by the contract with the shipper.

The position is much the same with regard to a stevedoring agreement. Indeed, it has been decided that in the ordinary way, it is the shipowner and not the charterer who derives rights and incurs obligations under the contract.[5]

(B)   CONTENTS

We need not elaborate the contents of the stevedoring contract. Often there exists a standard form which is drawn up by the stevedore firms at

---

4 For the licensing of employers of dockworkers, see Docks and Harbours Act 1966, s. 1 et seq.

5 Eastman v. Harry (1876) 33 L.T. 800; 3 Asp. M.C. 117. In practice the charterparty may often make a distinction between who is to nominate or pay for the stevedores (e.g., the charterer) and who is liable for their faults (e.g., the owner). A time charter may provide that the charterer has to pay for stevedore damage and continue to pay hire during repairs, see e.g., The Nicki R. [1984] 2 Lloyd's Rep. 186.

a particular port. These provide for working conditions, method of remuneration and similar matters.

A usual term in a stevedoring contract is for the ship to pay to the stevedores a certain sum for standing by if loading or discharging operations must be temporarily interrupted by reason of rain, bad weather or the like. In one case, where the contract contained a term to this effect, something rather unusual happened. The stowage plan, indicating the situation in the ship's hold of the individual parcels of cargo, turned out to be incorrect. This held up the discharge, and the stevedores claimed remuneration for the additional time involved. They did so on the analogy of the rain and bad weather clause. It was true that no additional remuneration had been expressly agreed upon for the special contingency. However, they asked the court to imply a term to that effect. Now, it is well settled that the court will never imply an additional term in a contract merely because it might appear reasonable to do so. Only where it is necessary for the business efficacy of the agreement will the court say: Very well, though the parties did not agree expressly on this point, any reasonable man, who had applied his mind to the possibility of these circumstances arising, would have made this or that arrangement, and imply a term to that effect. In this case, however, the court declined to imply a term for payment of additional remuneration in case of a hold-up by reason of an incorrect stowage plan. The contract was perfectly workable without such a term. Its absence showed that the stevedores took the risk of any delay other than that caused by bad weather; it could not be said that without implying such a term the contract would lack business efficacy.[6]

If provided for, what is called 'danger money' may also be claimed by the stevedores where loading or discharging is specially dangerous, and it has been held that such additional remuneration is payable though no danger in fact exists, but is reasonably apprehended by the stevedores' men.[7]

20.1.3 STEVEDORES AND LIABILITY

Suppose a stevedore damages cargo; is the owner of the ship liable to the cargo-owner? For the purposes of the Carriage of Goods by Sea Act, 1971, the stevedores are normally the carrier's servants, and the

---

6 *Lampson Bros* v. *Lilley & Co.* (1936) 54 Ll.L.R. 331.

7 *Brown* v. *A/S Chr. Christensen Rederi* (1937) 57 Ll.L.Rep. 127. The basis of the extra payment is, apparently, that the stevedores are being asked to do more than the contract requires them to do; *cf.* Section 24.4 *infra*.

shipowner or charterer, as the case may be, is vicariously liable for damage done by them.[8] Of course, owner or charterer may claim indemnity from the stevedoring firm.

A term will often be found in a charterparty providing whose servants, owner's or charterer's, the stevedores are to be. Such a term, naturally, only operates between the parties to the charterparty and does not bind strangers. Thus if stevedores are agreed to be the charterer's servants, nevertheless the owner must compensate cargo-owners for damage done by stevedores, but for this payment he can recoup himself against the charterer.[9]

Owners of cargo, negligently damaged by stevedores, can proceed against them in tort. This is often a device to avoid the exceptions and limitations in the bill of lading. Shipowners have tried to protect stevedores against such suits by bill of lading clauses giving stevedores the same defences as those enjoyed by sea carriers. The trouble is that stevedores are not original parties to contracts evidenced by the bill of lading, and there have been doubts whether they furnish consideration for the promise that they can use the carrier's defences.[10] Moreover, Art. IV bis (2) of the Hague–Visby Rules, which confers the right to such defences on the servants of the carrier, expressly excludes agents who are independent contractors, and stevedores certainly fall into this category.

However, it appears that the problems may be overcome by the use of suitably drafted Himalaya clauses[11] in the bill of lading which bring the stevedores within the contract by making the carrier their agent. The Privy Council has held in two decisions[12] that stevedores employed by the carrier will normally and typically be allowed by such a clause to the defences and immunities conferred by the bill of lading on the carrier.[13] Although the courts will not be looking for fine distinctions to

8 *Hourani* v. *T. & J. Harrison* (1927) 32 Com. Cas. 305; *Heyn* v. *Ocean S.S. Co. Ltd* (1927) 43 T.L.R. 358. But the carriage contract may put the loading and discharging responsibility on the cargo-owner, *Pyrene Co.* v. *Scindia Navigation Co.* [1954] 2 Q.B. 402.

9 *Harris* v. *Best Ryley and Co.* (1892) 7 Asp. M.C. 272; *Ballantyne* v. *Paton & Hendry* [1912] S.C. 246.

10 See *Midland Silicones Ltd* v. *Scrutton's Ltd* [1962] A.C. 446, a House of Lords case that decided against the stevedores.

11 See Sections 18.1 and 11.5 *supra*.

12 *The Eurymedon* : *New Zealand Shipping Co. Ltd* v. *Satterthwaite Co. Ltd* [1974] 1 Lloyd's Rep. 534; *The New York Star* : *Salmond & Spraggon (Australia) Pty Ltd* v. *Port Jackson Stevedoring Pty Ltd* [1980] 2 Lloyd's Rep. 317.

13 *Ibid.*, per Lord Wilberforce, at p. 321. Apart from the exceptions, the stevedore may wish to rely particularly on the Hague–Visby Rules time bar : see Chapter 26, *infra*.

diminish this general principle, it will still be necessary to peruse the bill exceptions closely to see whether they do apply, especially to negligence otherwise than in loading or discharge.[14] A simpler device is for the carrier to include a 'circular indemnity' clause in the bill whereby the cargo-owner undertakes not to sue any subcontractors of the carrier. If he does so, the carrier can apply for an injunction to stop him.[15]

The stevedores' employer is, of course, liable vicariously for a tort committed by his employee, for instance, when the latter negligently injures a fellow employee. Where stevedores are employed by a port authority, which lends them to ships for loading or unloading, the authority remains the employer, and it, not the ship, is vicariously liable for the stevedores' negligence; it makes no difference that in matters of detail the ship's officers give orders to the men.[16]

20.2 HARBOURS AND ASSOCIATED FACILITIES[17]

20.2.1 LIABILITY OF OPERATORS

The principal problem to be discussed is the liability of those in charge of harbours, docks, piers, lighthouses and waterways for damage which may befall ships making use of them, and the liability of ships for damage they cause there.

Where a shipowner contracts with a ship repairer for the dry-docking of his vessel, or where he contracts for loading or discharging cargo at a private jetty, the ordinary rules of the law of contract apply. In the absence of express terms the dock or pier owner has no absolute duty of making the premises safe.[18] All he has to do is to take reasonable care to make the dock or pier safe for the contracted user. He is no longer free to exclude his liability without limitation. That for death and personal

14 Cf. Raymond Burke Motors Ltd v. The Mersey Docks and Harbour Company [1986] 1 Lloyd's Rep. 155. See also Miida Electronics Inc. v. Mitsui O.S.K. Lines Ltd, (1986) 175 L.M.N.L. (Canada) and e.g. B. Elliott v. J.T. Clark [1983] A.M.C. 1742 (USA).
15 The Elbe Maru [1978] 1 Lloyd's Rep. 206; Sidney Cooke v. Hapag-Lloyd [1980] 2 N.S.W.L.R. 587 (Australia).
16 Bhoomidas v. Port of Singapore Authority [1978] 1 All E.R. 956 (Privy Council).
17 See Douglas (1983).
18 Pyman S.S. Co. v. Hull & Barnsley Railway Co. [1914] 2 K.B. 788, affirmed [1915] 2 K.B. 729.

injury caused negligently cannot be excluded at all, and any exclusion or restriction of liability for negligently caused damage to property must be reasonable.[19]

The duty to take care is implied from the mere relationship of the parties. In a well-known case[20] wharfingers contracted with a ship for goods to be discharged at their jetty which extended into the River Thames. At low tide the vessel necessarily took the ground. The river bed was uneven and the vessel on taking the ground suffered damage. As the bed adjoining the jetty was vested in the harbour authority, the wharfingers had no control over it. Nevertheless they were held liable. Granted, they had no control over the bed of the river, but they had the means of ascertaining whether it was safe for a vessel of the kind to take the ground. Failure to take reasonable care to see that the berth was safe, or to warn users if it was not, amounted to breach of an implied term in the contract.

Where a ship sails into a canal which is not in the nature of a public waterway, or a dock, the ship is entitled to expect a reasonable degree of safety. Anyone going on to land, and this includes a ship canal or dock, can demand that the occupier takes reasonable care to make it safe.[21] Thus, in particular, the canal owner is under the duty to warn ships of hidden dangers which are, or ought to be, known to him. For instance, the canal owner need not remove wreckage, but he must buoy it so as to warn users of the canal.

Where authorities, or companies set up by statute, own docks or canals, for instance, the British Waterways Board[22] or Associated British Ports,[23] the statutes by which they are established invariably provide that reasonable care must be taken in making navigation safe. In other words, the position is the same as that obtaining where a special contract exists between private parties.[24] If ship or cargo are damaged by the ship running on to a mudbank[25] or by striking a boiler from old wreckage,[26] the authorities are liable if they have been negligent, and it

19 Unfair Contract Terms Act 1977, ss. 2, 11.
20 *The Moorcock* (1889) 14 P.D. 64.
21 Occupiers Liability Act 1957, ss. 1, 2; Occupiers Liability Act 1984, s. 1. *Slater* v. *Clay Cross Co. Ltd* [1956] 2 Q.B. 264.
22 Set up under the Transport Act 1962, also Transport Act 1968, ss. 43, 48 and Part VII.
23 Set up under the Transport Act 1981, Part II, and Schs 3,4.
24 *Mersey Docks & Harbour Board Trustees* v. *Gibbs* (1866) L.R. 1 H.L. 93; *The Orita; Pacific Steam Navigation Co.* v. *Mersey Docks & Harbour Board* (1925) 22 Ll.L.Rep. 383.
25 *Gibbs'* case, *supra*.
26 *The Orita*, *supra*.

may be said that a high standard of care is required in such cases. Statutory corporations, like private owners, are also liable for the negligence of their servants.[27] In certain circumstances they may also be liable vicariously for the negligence of an independent contractor, for instance, if a harbour or canal is a public highway.[28]

Even where the waterway itself is not vested in the authority, but where the latter is only under a duty to provide beaconage against payment of dues, the same liability exists. But if it can be proved that the accident to the ship happened though the authority had taken all reasonable precautions, no liability arises.[29]

Note that persons or authorities having the control or management of docks, piers or harbours will usually be entitled to limit their liabilities for damage caused to vessels or goods on board.[30]

20.2.2 NAVIGABLE HIGHWAYS

Where the public enjoys the rights of navigation – an arm of the sea, a river or other piece of water – we speak of navigable highways. The right to navigate is a right of way, and it follows that the owner of the sea or river bed, in whom property is vested, can erect structures, provided these do not interfere with navigation.[31] As regards the riparian owner, he is entitled to prohibit landing, unless a special custom to the contrary is proved. The right to use the public waterway only exists for moving along, or anchoring,[32] afloat. Grounding is usually not permitted, and the surveyor of the waterway can claim damages from the ship, provided that the grounding was not due to lack of care on his own part.[33] However, in special circumstances, for instance where the waterway is too long for the vessel to pass through on one tide, a right of taking the ground between two tides must be

27 *Gibbs'* case, *supra*. Deliberate misuse of statutory powers by an authority acting with malice, or with full knowledge that it does not possess the power, could give an injured third party the right to damages, *The Mihalis: Micosta S.A.* v. *Shetland Island Council* [1984] 2 Lloyd's Rep. 525.

28 *Gray* v. *Pullen* (1864) 5 B. & S. 970; 122 E.R. 1091.

29 *St Just S.S. Co.* v. *Hartlepool Port & Harbour Commissioners* (1929) 34 Ll.L.Rep. 344; *The Neptun* (1937) 54 T.L.R. 195.

30 See Sections 22.2.6 and 22.3.6.

31 *Tate & Lyle Industries Ltd* v. *Greater London Council* [1983] 2 A.C. 509 where a jetty owner recovered dredging expenses made necessary because of the construction of ferry terminals which caused siltation. See also Jowitt, *Dictionary of English Law* (2nd edn, 1977).

32 *Gann* v. *Free Fishers* (1866) 11 H.L.C. 192.

33 *The Carlgarth* [1927] P. 93, at p. 107 *et seq.*

conceded.[34] Obstructing navigable water is a public nuisance and anyone suffering particular damage as a result has a right of action.[35]

20.2.3   WRECK RAISING

Closely connected with the duty to use reasonable care in keeping the
fairway safe is the power of the harbour authorities to remove wrecks
and to raise[36] or even destroy them.[37] In the meantime they must light
and buoy them to warn vessels navigating in the vicinity. Most statutes
give harbour authorities the power to charge the necessary expenses of
wreck raising against the owner of the wreck,[38] and in default of
payment sell it and pay over the surplus to him.[39] These powers are
normally available even though the ship sank without any negligence
on her own part.[40] A shipowner will not usually be able to limit his
liability for such claims.[41]

If damage is caused to a third party by reason of unsufficient precautions, or while the wreck is being recovered, the authorities are
liable both for their own negligence and for that of any independent
contractor they employ.[42] The owner of the wreck is apparently not
liable if he has abandoned possession and control of the wreck without

34 *Colchester Corporation* v. *Brooke* (1845) 7 Q.B. 339.

35 *Rose* v. *Miles* (1815) 4 M & S 101, 105 E.R. 773. A private dock to which
   shipowners have a statutory right of access under the Harbours, Docks and Piers
   Clauses Act 1847, s. 33, does not become a public highway, *Anglo-Algerian S.S.
   Co. Ltd* v. *The Houlder Line Ltd* [1908] 1 K.B. 659.

36 Harbours, Docks and Piers Clauses Act 1847, s. 56. This Act does not apply
   automatically in British Ports. It has to be incorporated in local Acts, which may
   often extend the basic powers, see Douglas (1983), at p. 38. For the power to order
   the removal of dangerous vessels which are not sunk, stranded or abandoned, see
   Section 8.8.3, *supra*. For salvage claims by harbour authorities, see Section 24.4.3,
   infra.

37 Merchant Shipping Act 1894, ss. 530–534, *cf. The Crystal* [1894] A.C. 508.

38 E.g., *The Putbus: Owners of Zenatia* v. *Owners of Putbus* [1969] 2 All E.R. 676. The
   harbour authority may also claim for its expenses in negligence against vessels
   responsible for the sinking, including the sunken vessel; see *The Kylix and
   Rustringen* [1979] 1 Lloyd's Rep. 133.

39 S. 530; *cf. The Countess: Mersey Docks and Harbour Board* v. *Hay* [1923] A.C. 345.

40 E.g., *The Arabert* [1961] 2 All E.R. 385. These expenses could form part of the
   sunken ship's claim against a vessel at fault, subject to limitation of liability, see
   Chapter 22, *infra*.

41 See Sections 22.2.3, and 22.3.3.

42 *Dormont* v. urness Railway Co. (1883) 11 Q.B.D. 496. For oil pollution liabilities
   caused during wreck removal, see Chapter 25, *infra*. The Secretary of State can
   designate a prohibited area around a dangerous wreck under the Protection of
   Wrecks Act 1973, s.2.

intending to take it over again,[43] or if he has transferred the control to port authorities.[44]

20.2.4 LIABILITY OF SHIPOWNERS

We now come to the liability of owners of ships using harbours, docks or piers for damage done to such structures. Ships damaging privately owned docks are liable just as in any other case of damage, that is, for negligence. Where, however, the owners are public authorities, different considerations prevail. Such publicly owned harbours, docks and piers are dedicated to the public, and traffic depends on the facilities being available. Their damage accordingly affects not only an owner of property, but the shipping community desirous of using it. For this reason a stricter liability is imposed by statute on persons damaging public property. If a ship damages a harbour, dock or pier owned by a public authority the shipowner is liable even though his master and crew have not been negligent, provided they were still in control of the vessel.[45] Despite the strict nature of this provision it appears that there may be a defence where the damage was occasioned by an act of God or by the action of the wind and waves after master and crew had been forced to abandon the ship.[46]

20.3 LIGHTHOUSES

In principle, the superintendence and management of lighthouses is vested by statute in Trinity House, the Commissioners of Northern

---

43 *The Utopia* [1893] A.C. 492; *cf. The Snark* [1900] P. 105.
44 *The Utopia, supra.* An authority can obviously be guilty of negligence if it undertakes to light a wreck and then omits to do so, *The Douglas* (1882) 7 P.D. 151.
45 Where the Harbours, Docks and Piers Clauses Act 1847, s. 74 applies; *The Mostyn: Great Western Railway Co.* v. *Owners of S.S. Mostyn* [1928] A.C. 57; and even if the harbour authority contributed to the accident, *Workington Harbour Board* v. *S.S. Towerfield* [1951] A.C. 112. However, it seems as if the shipowner would now be entitled to bring a counterclaim against the authority for the negligence of employees, such as the harbour master, *Post Office* v. *Hampshire County Council* [1979] 2 All E.R. 818. The measure of damages under s. 74 is confined to repair and reinstatement costs and does not include consequential loss, *per* Lord Radcliffe, *Workington Harbour Board* case, *supra,* at p. 161. This would have to be claimed in negligence.
46 *River Wear Commissioners* v. *Adamson* (1877) 2 App. Cas. 743, distinguished in *The Mostyn, supra*: see also *The Octavian* [1974] 1 Lloyd's Rep. 334 (Privy Council).

Lighthouses,[47] and the Commissioners of Irish Lighthouses. The DoT has a power of inspection.[48]

Since the building of lighthouses is of national importance and may only be done according to a national scheme, a proposal to build a lighthouse anywhere in the United Kingdom must be submitted to Trinity House and approved by the DoT. Moreover, powers of compulsory purchase are vested in lighthouse authorities.[49] Light dues are payable by passing ships, and are administered according to detailed statutory provisions.[50]

47 Merchant Shipping Act 1894 Part XI, ss. 634 *et seq.*; Merchant Shipping Act 1974, s. 18; Merchant Shipping Act 1979, s. 33.

48 Merchant Shipping Act 1894, s. 636.

49 S. 639 and Lands Clauses Consolidation Act 1845.

50 Merchant Shipping Act 1894, ss. 643 *et seq.*; Merchant Shipping (Mercantile Marine Fund) Act 1898; Merchant Shipping (Amendment) Act 1920; Merchant Shipping Act 1979, s. 36(2); Merchant Shipping (Light Dues) Regulations 1981 (S.I. No. 354), amended 1986 (S.I. No. 334).

21

COLLISIONS

A COLLISION[1] between ships usually involves what is technically called a tort, that is, an unlawful act or omission on the part of someone responsible. Just as one may be liable for damages if one runs down a pedestrian with one's car, or collides with another car, so may a shipowner whose ship comes into collision with another vessel be liable to pay damages to other persons or property owners involved. Liability depends on negligence, and the important question is: what conduct, whether by act or omission, in the handling, management or navigation of a ship amounts to negligence? The answer has been given in somewhat general terms as follows: a person is negligent if he shows 'a want of that attention and vigilance which is due to the security of other vessels that are navigating the same seas'.[2] It is usual to 'personify' the ship by stating that she is at fault. However, in English law it should be remembered that this is a convenient shorthand: the liability arises as a result of the faults of individuals.[3]

21.1   VICARIOUS LIABILITY

It will be recalled that the shipowner is liable not only for his own negligence, but also for that of his servants (i.e., employees). In this connection that means the master and crew, provided the negligent act was committed in the course of the employment. This liability is called 'vicarious' (i.e., deputed) because it results *ipso facto* from his character of employer. In order to establish liability the plaintiff need not allege or prove that the shipowner himself was negligent, but simply that a contract of employment existed between the wrongdoer and the

---

1 For an admirable, comprehensive survey of the law relating to collision, covering history and comparative law see D.R. Owen, 'The origins and development of marine collision law' (1977) 51 *Tulane Law Review*, 759–1216.

2 *The Dundee* (1823) 1 Hagg. Ad. 109, 120, 166 E.R. 39.

3 The combined effect of the maritime lien and the action *in rem* may suggest that the distinction is more apparent than real: see Chapters 1 and 7, *supra*.

shipowner. This rule of law is most important in modern times. It is also eminently just; for a person employing others to work for him reaps the benefit of their work, and it is only fair that he should likewise be held responsible for the damage they inflict on others while going about their employer's business. Besides, in giving an injured third party a right of action against the employer the plaintiff has the advantage of being able to claim against a person who is probably more substantial than the actual wrongdoer.

Two questions are involved: Who for this purpose is to be regarded as a servant? What is the ambit of his employment?

21.1.1   SERVANTS

It may be difficult to determine who is to be regarded as a servant. The captain of the ship is the owner's servant, and so are all the members of the crew. Beyond this the answer is less certain, for not everyone who is employed is a servant.

We have already seen that a pilot is regarded as the shipowner's agent and the latter is responsible for the former's negligence, even if the pilotage is compulsory.[4] The reason for this rule is probably one of public policy. The damaged ship has an action against the ship at fault and is not to be put off with an action against the pilot alone. He will never have the means to make good a big loss and, if licensed, may be entitled to limit his liability to £100.[5]

This need to be able to sue somebody with a reasonable limit of liability is also relevant to towage. The owner of a big vessel which cannot leave harbour under her own power must have her towed into open waters; a bargeowner may require a tug to bring the craft upriver. Although there is nothing to stop such an owner having the towage performed by his own tugs, if he has any, in practice this work is done by independent specialists. The shipowner will make an agreement with a tugowner. Naturally, master and crew of the tug are the servants of the tugowner and not the servants of the owner of the tow. The former, and not the latter, is liable for their torts, at least in the ordinary case. The tugowner is what is known as an independent contractor, a person who carries out a given piece of work at his own discretion and, in a way, independently of his employer. Prima facie, therefore, the tugowner, while towing the tow, is responsible for any collisions which happen during the conduct of the work. This is indeed the law when , as

---

4 See Sections 19.4.2, *supra*, and 22.2.1, 22.3.1.
5 *McDermid v. Nash Dredging & Reclamation Co. Ltd* [1986] 2 Lloyd's Rep. 24 for employers's non-delegable duties to employees.

is the case with the towage of dumb barges, the whole of the motive power is in the tug.[6]

The third party may face a very low limit of liability if he sues the tug alone.[7] For this reason it has always been important for him to be able to implicate the owner of the tow as well. At one time it was said somewhat misleadingly that 'the tug is the servant of the tow'.[8] As we have seen, this is not really accurate as the tugowner is an independent contractor. But that is not to say that the tow can *never* be responsible for faults committed by the tug.

In most cases where the tow is fully manned, often with a pilot on board, it is the tow which has the nautical command of the towage. the tug would usually expect to obey the orders of the tow.[9] Clearly, a failure to control the tug, e.g. by warning it to slow down, would be negligence on the part of the tow.[10] Similarly, the tow may fail to operate properly her own engines and rudder in what is a co-operative effort. In other cases, the tow's liability will depend on the extent of its control over the tug: for instance, the tow would not expect to control the individual engine movements of the tug.[11]

The result is that in most cases it will be possible to make both the tug and the tow liable. This is very unsatisfactory from the viewpoint of the tugowner as he is liable for torts committed by the master and crew of the tug even though control has passed to the owner of the tow. It is for this reason that he will seek to obtain some form of indemnity in his towage contract.[12] However, these contractual arrangements between tug and tow would not usually affect third parties where the tug's master and crew remain the true employees of the tugowner: the tug would remain liable.[13]

Liability for negligence thus depending on control, it is understandable that even the shipowner is not liable if he has lawfully divested himself of it.

6 *The American and The Syria: Union S.S. Co.* v. *Aracan* (1874) L.R. 6 P.C. 127.
7 See Chapter 22, *infra*.
8 See *The Devonshire* [1912] A.C. 634.
9 *The Socrates and The Champion* [1923] P. 76. This would not absolve the tugowner from the negligence of the tug's master or crew.
10 *The Niobe* (1888) 13 P.D. 55, [1891] A.C. 401.
11 *The Panther* [1957] P. 143, 147.
12 See Chapter 23, *infra*, and the UK Standard Conditions for Towage and Other Services 1983 (Appendix 10). The old way of seeking indemnity was by way of a 'servant control' clause such as Clause 3, see *The Ramsden* [1943] P. 46: Clause 4 is now much more precise and renders Clause 3 (which also appeared in the 1934 and 1974 Conditions) largely superfluous.
13 *The Panther, supra; Mersey Docks and Harbour Board Ltd* v. *Coggins & Griffiths (Liverpool) Ltd* [1947] A.C. 1. *Cf.* Section 20.1.3, *supra*.

Illustration: *The Utopia*[14]

A ship had sunk in a harbour. Her owners did not abandon possession of her but agreed with the port authority that the latter should indicate the position of the wreck to prevent other ships entering or leaving the harbour from colliding with it. The port authorities failed to buoy the wreck sufficiently so that another ship collided with it and was damaged.

Held: No liability attached to either wreck or owners, since control and management of the wreck had been legitimately transferred by the owners to the port authority, acting within the apparent scope of its authority.[15]

21.1.2 SCOPE OF EMPLOYMENT

Shipowners are not liable for every wrongful act committed by their employees. There may be some acts which are completely beyond the scope of their employment. In one old case a tug-master wilfully caused damage to a sloop in an attempt to obtain £5 towage that he considered was due. The tugowners were held not liable as it was said that his unlawful act was not authorized.[16]

But in general there will be very few acts or omissions of a master in the handling of a ship for which the owner can escape liability. The fact that the owners expressly forbade a particular course of conduct, e.g. going too quickly in fog, will not of itself entitled them to claim that the master was acting outside the scope of his emplyoment.[17] This is because the master is doing what he is employed to do – navigate the ship – albeit in an unauthorized way. It would be unfair on third parties if the owners were not vicariously liable.

---

14 [1893] A.C. 492.
15 Where, however, control of the wreck was not thus transferred, but the owners employed contractors to remove it, and the latter failed in their duty, the owners of the wreck were held liable as if the contractors had been their servants. It is a public duty to keep the waterway clear, and a shipowner cannot divest himself of it by delegating the actual work necessary to an independent contractor. See *The Snark* [1900] P. 105.
16 *The Druid* (1842) 1 W. Rob. 391, 166 E.R. 619. It may be doubtful whether the same result would occur today if the tug-master's conduct was an improper mode of doing something for the owner's benefit; see generally, *Clerk and Lindsell on Torts* (15th edn, 1982 and 1985 Supp.) pp. 168 *et seq.*
17 *Cf. Limpus* v. *London General Omnibus Co.* (1862) 1 H. & C. 526, 158 E.R. 993.

21.2 COLLISION REGULATIONS[18]

21.2.1 INTRODUCTION

In the nineteenth century the introduction of fast powerful steamships hastened the need to produce clear 'rules of the road' to prevent collisions. Trinity House first produced a set of advisory regulations in 1840.[19] In 1846 Parliament enacted legislation to give statutory effect to obligations based on these regulations.[20] Over the years the regulations have been changed and brought up to date many times. Collision Regulations are now co-ordinated and revised internationally by IMO. In 1972 IMO produced the Convention on the International Regulations for Preventing Collisions at Sea. The 1972 Regulations were amended in 1981 by a Resolution of the IMO Assembly[21] and these amended Regulations have been in force since 1 June 1983. It is not much good having rules of the road if only a few people recognize them, but fortunately by 31 December 1985 there were 95 contracting states representing over 96 per cent of the world's gross tonnage. The 1972/1981 Collision Regulations are enacted in English law by the Merchant Shipping (Distress Signals and Prevention of Collisions) Regulations 1983.[22] Separate statutory instruments apply the Collision Regulations, with appropriate modifications, to seaplanes[23] and hovercraft.[24]

---

18 See R. Sturt (1984), A. Cockcroft, J. Lameijer, *A Guide to the Collision Avoidance Rules,* (1982). Many of the leading cases are usefully illustrated in H.M.C. Holdert, F.J. Buzek, *Collision Cases – Judgments and Diagrams* (1984).

19 Reproduced in 1 W. Rob. 488. *Marsden,* (1961), Chapter 23, and Sturt (1984) pp. 1 – 3.

20 Steam Navigation Act 1846.

21 This amending procedure under Art. 6 of the 1972 Convention allows amendments to be made relatively speedily. Further amendments are being considered for adoption in 1987.

22 S.I. No. 708, Sch. 1. Technically, the Regulations are not binding on ships belonging to Her Majesty (Merchant Shipping Act 1894, s. 741) but Queen's Regulations give effect to them separately: see *Marsden* (1961) p. 455.

23 Civil Aviation Act 1982, s. 97(1); the Collision Rules (Seaplanes) Order 1983 (S.I. No. 768).

24 Hovercraft Act 1968, s. 1; the Hovercraft (Application of Enactments) (Amendment) Order 1983 (S.I. No. 769).

21.2.2   CONTENT OF THE RULES

The Collision Regulations are in five parts, A to E, between them containing 38 Rules. There are also four Annexes dealing, respectively, with positioning and technical details of lights and shapes to be displayed; additional signals to be used by fishing vessels fishing in close proximity; technical details of sound signal appliances; and distress signals, such as a gun firing at one-minute intervals, continuous sounding of fog-horn and the use of flags.

This being not a navigational manual but a law book, it would be wrong to do more than indicate the content of the Rules.

Part A, Rules 1–3, is general. The Rules apply to all vessels on the high seas and in all waters connected therewith navigable by sea-going vessels, although special rules may be made for these, for instance, harbours and inland waterways.[25] Exceptions may be granted to special-purpose vessels whose structure makes compliance with all Rules impracticable.

One particular feature introduced by the 1972 Regulations was the inclusion of traffic separation schemes adopted by IMO.[26] These are vital to provide some order in areas of great shipping activity, such as the Dover Strait. The special danger of this narrow waterway is its use by ships sailing in a south-westerly and a north-easterly direction, and that both streams are crossed by the ferries connecting England and France. This crossing cannot, of course, be prevented but what has been done is to provide that the through traffic in both directions observes what may be called lane discipline: traffic in a south-westerly direction shall sail on the English, and that in a north-easterly direction on the French, side of the Strait.

The details of the schemes and any amendments adopted by IMO Resolution can be found in Admiralty Notice to Mariners No. 17.[27] Note that the 1983 Regulations do not require amendment every time IMO creates a new scheme: specification in Admiralty Notices is sufficient.[28]

Nothing in the Rules shall exonerate vessel, master, owner or crew from the consequences of neglect to comply with them or of neglect of any precaution required by the ordinary practice of seamen or by special

25 Rule 1. See the US Inland Navigation Rules 1980, and F.E. Bassett, R.A. Smith, *Farwell's Rules of the Nautical Road* (1982). Also, *The Esso Brussels* [1973] 2 Lloyd's Rep. 73 on the application of local regulations.
26 Rules 1(d) and 10.
27 As amended: this and other notices may be obtained from the Hydrographer of the Navy, Hydrographic Department, Taunton, Somerset.
28 Reg. 1(2)(b).

circumstances.[29] In other words a slavish observance of the Rules is not always enough to disprove negligence. Rule 3 includes in the definition of 'vessel', non-displacement craft, that is, hovercraft, and seaplanes on the water. A 'vessel restricted in its ability to manoeuvre' includes cable- or pipe-laying vessels, dredgers, vessels engaged in launching or recovering aircraft – they must stand in a particular position to the wind – and sometimes tugs.

Part B, which is in three sections contains the important 'Steering and Sailing Rules'. Section I deals with the general conduct of vessels in any condition of visibility. Rule 5 deals with lookout by sight and hearing 'as well as by all available means appropriate in the circumstances', which includes radar. Even under former Rules it was held that ships in fog must not rely exclusively on radar; the traditional lookout cannot be dispensed with.[30] Now, after Rule 6 has dealt with what is a safe speed, Rule 7 repeats the need to make proper use of radar, warning that decisions must not be based solely on the strength of scanty radar information. We have already mentioned traffic separation schemes and Rule 10 lays down the detailed requirements about their use. One of the 1981 amendments was to allow vessels under 20 metres in length and sailing vessels to use inshore traffic zones in all circumstances.[31] Maintenance and cable laying vessels which are restricted in their ability to manoeuvre when in a traffic separation scheme are exempted from full compliance with the Rules.[32]

Section II concerns the conduct of vessels in sight of each other. Rule 12 deals with sailing vessels on opposing courses: the windward must keep out of the way of the leeward. Rule 13 deals with overtaking: the overtaking vessel should keep out of the way of the vessel being overtaken. Rule 14 concerns a head-on situation: each vessel should alter course to starboard and pass port to port.[33] Rule 15 deals with a crossing situation: a vessel should give way to another vessel on her starboard side.

---

29 Rule 2.
30 *The Prins Alexander* [1955] 2 Lloyd's Rep. 1.
31 Rule 10(d).
32 Rule 10(k) and (l). Although vessels navigating in or near a scheme must comply with Rule 10, the other Rules apply in all respects, particularly the steering and sailing rules in Part B if risk of collision exists, *The Achilleus* [1985] 2 Lloyd's Rep. 338, 342.
33 By way of light relief reference could be made to the sketch *Port to Port* in *Misleading Cases* by A.P. Herbert. The Thames has flooded the road at Chiswick Mall where it is still tidal. A motor car and a boat meet head on. Does the rule of the road or the sea prevail? Must the two conveyances pass port to port, or starboard to starboard?

In each of these defined situations there is a 'give-way' vessel and a 'stand-on' vessel. Rule 16 requires the give-way vessel to take early and substantial action to keep clear. Rule 17 requires the stand-on vessel to maintain her course and speed.[34] Obviously, it may become apparent that the other vessel is not giving way, in which case the stand-on vessel may alter course, but not usually to port if she has another vessel on her port side.[35]

One difficulty is distinguishing between a crossing and an overtaking situation, as a vessel crossing from the starboard side would have right of way, but not if she was overtaking. The position is that the overtaking rule can apply even before there is a risk of collision (i.e. by the courses intersecting).[36] A ship is overtaking whenever she is coming up on another vessel from a position more than 22.5 degrees abaft her beam (i.e. so that at night the stern light could be seen, but not the sidelights).[37] Once the overtaking rule applies the overtaking ship cannot make herself a crossing vessel by altering course.[38]

We should also note that there are special rules for navigation in narrow channels, e.g. in ports. Vessels under 20 metres and fishing vessels are not entitled to impede the passage of larger vessels which may only be able to navigate within the channel.[39] Apart from this there is no general rule that a smaller vessel must give precedence to a larger vessel.[40]

Rule 18 requires powered vessels to keep out of the way of certain vessels, such as those restricted in their ability to manoeuvre and sailing vessels.

Section III, deals with the conduct of vessels in restricted visibility, e.g. fog: extra precautions and alertness are required.

Part C deals with lights and shapes. Rules 20 – 31 prescribe strengths and kinds of lights to be shown, e.g. by pilot vessels, vessels at anchor or stranded, tugs while towing, fishing vessels and seaplanes on the water.[41] Part D, deals with sound and light signals. Rules 32–37 prescribe equipment for such signals[42] along with the required number

---

34 Although it seems that the stand-on ship can reduce speed for the ordinary
     manoeuvre of picking up a pilot: *The Roanoke* [1908] P. 231.
35 Rule 17(a)(ii), (c). *The Otranto* (1931) 144 L.T. 251.
36 *The Nowy Sacz* [1977] 2 Lloyd's Rep. 91.
37 Rule 13(b).
38 *Cf.* Rule 13(d) and *The Nowy Sacz, supra.*
39 Rule 9.
40 See *The Toluca* [1984] 1 Lloyd's Rep. 131.
41 See also Annex 1.
42 See also the specifications in Annex III.

of whistles and blasts.[43] Part E, Rule 38, allows exemption for certain older vessels regarding lights.

21.2.3   BREACH OF THE REGULATIONS

Compliance with the Regulations is encouraged in two ways: directly, by making breach of the Regulations a criminal offence; indirectly, by making breach useful evidence of negligent navigation in a civil case for damages.[44]

The Merchant Shipping Act 1894, s. 419 made it an offence for the Regulations to be infringed by the 'wilful default' of the master or owner. Unfortunately the Act was not very clear on what happened when the master handed over the watch to another officer who then disobeyed the Regulations.[45] Section 419 was replaced by a new offence created by the 1983 Regulations. Where the Regulations are contravened, the owner, master and any person for the time being responsible for the conduct of the vessel shall *each* be guilty of an offence.[46] So an officer of the watch can be guilty of an offence in addition to the master. It is a defence for any of the persons charged to show that they took all reasonable precautions to avoid committing the offence. Thus, a master would not be guilty if he gave proper instructions to the officer of the watch. A helmsman would not normally commit an offence as he is under the orders of another person 'responsible for the conduct of the vessel'; but there may be difficulties in relation to smaller vessels where the division of responsibility is not so clear.[47]

The requirement of compliance is strict. The prosecution does not have to show that the defendant intended to break the Regulations: it is

---

43 See also Annex II.

44 The civil consequences of breaching the Regulations will be considered in Sections 21.4–21.6, *infra*.

45 In *The N.F. Tiger: Bradshaw* v. *Ewart-James* [1982] 2 Lloyd's Rep. 546 it was held that the master could not be convicted in such circumstances where he had not been at fault. A master may also be guilty of navigating without due care and attention under a local Act, e.g. The Port of London Act 1968, as in *The Varos: Slater* v. *Reed and McGrath* [1980] 2 Lloyd's Rep. 581.

46 Reg. 5. In the Crown Court a sentence of two years' imprisonment or an unlimited fine is possible: in the magistrate's court a fine can be imposed with a maximum of £50 000 (for breach of Rule 10(b)(i) dealing with traffic separation schemes), or (for other breaches) subject to the 'statutory maximum' of the Criminal Justice Act 1982.

47 Note that offences may also be committed against the Watchkeeping and Certification Regulations, see Section 9.2, *supra*.

enough to show that he intended a course of conduct which was in fact in breach.

Illustration: *The Nordic Clansman*: *Taylor v. O'Keefe*[48]

A tanker was on a voyage to ports in the Arabian Gulf which involved passing through the Strait of Hormuz – in which there was a traffic separation scheme. The master intended to anchor at the Gray Mackenzie Buoy, 22-25 miles west of the western end of the scheme. He consulted his charts and took the ship through the inshore traffic zone as he considered he was not 'through traffic'. He was prosecuted for contravening Rule 10(d) in not using the appropriate lane in the adjacent traffic separation scheme.

Held: The master's belief that he was not 'through traffic' did not, as such, make him innocent: that depended on the proper interpretation of Rule 10(d). The expression was not defined and it was up to the magistrates to decide whether the ship did or did not fall within it.

To some extent, therefore, masters may be criminally responsible if they misinterpret the Rules. It must be remembered, though, that, apart from the defence of 'reasonable precautions', the Rules themselves allow some leeway.[49] The prosecution in a case such as *The Nordic Clansman* would also need to show under Rule 10(d) that it was safe to use the main lane and that the use of the inshore zone was not 'normal'.[50] In the event of a technical infringement, the court might give a lower fine than for a deliberate infringement.

In the Dover Strait, coastguards keep a radar watch on vessels and this is recorded on tape so that incidents can be 'replayed' later to see if infringements have occurred.[51]

21.3   DUTY TO ASSIST

At this stage it is convenient to note a number of statutory duties on mariners to assist other ships, often imposed following disasters such as that involving the *Titanic*.

---

48 [1984] 1 Lloyd's Rep. 31. The case was decided under s. 419, but the essential principle will continue to apply under the 1983 Regulations.
49 Thus, Rule 2(b) requires that regard must be had to all dangers of navigation and collision and any special circumstances.
50 In fact, the master considered that using the inshore zone avoided crossing the paths of ships using the main scheme: this issue was returned to the magistrates for decision.
51 The first prosecution of a ship for contravening the separation scheme was reported in *The Times*, 23 July 1973.

Vessels in danger may make use of one or more of the distress signals set out in Annex IV of the Collision Regulations 1972.[52] The master alone has the authority to order a distress signal.[53] He shall give the order only if he is satisfied that his vessel is in serious and imminent danger or that another ship or aircraft is in that predicament and unable itself to send the signal.[54] In all cases, a second condition for the sending of a distress signal is the need for immediate assistance.

The master of any British ship on receiving a signal of distress must proceed with all speed to the assistance of the persons in distress unless: it is unreasonable or unnecessary to do so; or, he is released from the obligation because other ships are complying with the requisition; or, he is informed that assistance is no longer required.[55]

There is a general duty on masters and persons in charge of vessels to render assistance to any person in danger at sea.[56] After a collision ships are bound to exchange their names, as well as those of their home ports and the ports from which they are proceeding and for which they are bound. Moreover, they must stand by and render any assistance to each other, provided they can do so without unreasonably adding to their own danger.[57] This duty to render assistance is, however, not an absolute one. Where two ships, the *Effra* and the *Cumene,* collided, the master of the former made it clear that he considered his vessel lost and did not require the *Cumene* to stand by. In these circumstances, it was held that the *Cumene* was not bound to stand by.[58]

---

52 See the Merchant Shipping (Distress Signals and Prevention of Collision)
    Regulations 1983 (S.I. No. 708), reg. 3.
53 Merchant Shipping (Signals of Distress) Rules 1977 (S.I. No. 1010), amended 1983
    (S.I. No. 708).
54 Rule 3.
55 Merchant Shipping (Safety Convention) Act 1949, s. 22. 'Master' includes every
    person (except a pilot) having command or charge of a ship; Merchant Shipping
    Act 1894, s. 742. This would include temporary charge, *Foreman* v. *MacNeill* [1979]
    S.C. 17.
56 Maritime Conventions Act 1911, s. 6. *The Gusty and The Daniel M* [1940] P. 159.
57 Merchant Shipping Act 1894, s. 422; Collision Convention 1910, Art. 8. Note that
    IMO's International Convention on Maritime Search and Rescue 1979 entered into
    force on 22 June 1985. It is designed to improve co-operation between search and
    rescue organizations.
58 *The Effra* (1936) 77 Ll. L. Rep. 362.

The effect of providing such statutory assistance on the right to salvage will be considered later.[59] Failure to obey the various duties is a criminal offence.

21.4 LIABILITY FOR COLLISION DAMAGE

We must now consider how to establish liability for damage and loss resulting from collision.

21.4.1 ADMIRALTY COURT PROCEDURE[60]

Trials of collision actions go into very great detail, but we may note two particular differences between collision cases in the Admiralty Court and other cases, e.g. in the Commercial Court.

First, the plaintiff must file a 'preliminary act' within two months after issue of the writ and the defendant must do likewise within two months of acknowledging issue or service of the writ.[61] The 'preliminary act' is a document containing some 15 questions of fact about the collision, such as the names of the ships; the date and time of the collision; the duration and force of the wind; the course steered and lights carried; the distance and bearing of the other ship; the alterations of course made; the sound signals given and heard; the approximate angle of contact. The importance of the 'preliminary act' is that both sides are forced to commit themselves to basic facts *before* they have seen how the other side has put its case in the formal pleadings. It is regarded as a binding admission and is particularly important where the trial takes place many years after the collision when the memories of the witnesses may have faded.[62]

The second distinctive feature of the collision trial is that the Admiralty Judge is advised by two Elder Brethren of Trinity House, who sit with him on the bench. For instance, in one recent case the judge put five specific questions to the Elder Brethren concerning the safe speeds for the vessels; the action each ship should have taken; the safe passing distance both at safe speeds and the speeds at which the vessels were actually proceeding. It was clear from the answers given that both ships

---

59 See Section 24.4.1, *infra.*
60 For the jurisdiction of the court, see Section 1.3, *supra.*
61 R.S.C. Order 75 R. 18: see the White Book.
62 See *The Toluca* [1981] 2 Lloyd's Rep. 548, *per* Sheen J at p. 550.

were guilty of serious faults, e.g. by proceeding at 14 and 13 knots instead of 8 and 6 knots.[63]

The difficulty of having Elder Brethren is that they restrict the right of the parties to call expert nautical evidence and they cannot be cross-examined themselves. Some countries have chosen to do without them (e.g., Canada) while many others (particularly in Europe) have court-appointed experts who produce a report for the court.

21.4.2 STATUTORY PRESUMPTION OF FAULT

The Collision Regulations have been in force in one form or another for many years, but their relationship to a collision damage action has changed. The early statutes provided for what lawyers called a 'statutory presumption of fault' which arose where a collision had occurred and it was proved that prior to the collision one of the ships had infringed one or other of the Rules, e.g. by not carrying regulation lights.[64] The expression was not a happy one, for 'fault' connotes 'negligence'; but what the term meant was that it was presumed that the very infringement of a Rule had caused the collision. It may be recalled that at the beginning of this chapter we have said that only negligence causing the collision entails liability. Now the 'statutory presumption of fault' was rather harsh, for it is quite conceivable that the infringement of the Rule did not cause the collision, but that it would have happened even if the particular Rule infringed had been complied with. A conference in Brussels in 1910 produced the International Convention for the Unification of Certain Rules of Law Relating to Collisions between Vessels (the Collision Convention 1910). Article 6 abolished all legal presumptions of fault. This was enacted into British law by s. 4(1) of the Maritime Convention Act 1911,[65] an Act which also gave statutory effect to other provisions of the Collision Convention 1910.

It is now clear that questions of good and prudent seamanship are questions of fact, not law.[66] The burden of proof is on the party asserting negligence to prove both the breach of a duty of good seamanship and the damage suffered.[67] However, it is a matter of common

---

63 *The Roseline* [1981] 2 Lloyd's Rep. 410.

64 *Marsden* (1961) pp. 426–443.

65 S. 4(1) repealed s. 419(4), Merchant Shipping Act 1894.

66 However, there is still a presumption of fault in the USA under the rule in *The Pennsylvania* 86 U.S. 125 (1873): see W. Tetley, 'The Pennsylvania Rule – an anachronism? The Pennsylvania judgment – an error?' (1982) 12 JMLC 127.

67 *The Heranger* [1939] A.C. 94.

sense that breach of the Regulations will almost certainly be excellent evidence of negligence, particularly where a vessel is in breach of one of the defined situations, e.g. the crossing or overtaking rules.[68]

It is convenient to note here that the standard of care required is that of the ordinary (and not the extraordinary) mariner and that seamen under criticism should be judged by reference to the situation as it reasonably appeared to them at the time and not by hindsight.[69]

21.4.3   CAUSATION

We have seen that the judge may be advised that the Collision Regulations have been broken, or that ships have not been navigated in a seamanlike manner. but the mere fact that there have been such faults does not give rise automatically to liability for collision damage. The question now for the court is whether the fault actually caused or contributed to the collision. With the abolition of the statutory presumption of fault, one must no longer ask whether a failure to obey the Regulations might 'possibly' have contributed to the collision.[70] The court must examine closely the steps leading up to the collision and, it would seem, apply more strictly the maxim, *causa proxima non remota spectatur.*[71]

This imposes the duty on the judge to go through all the phases of the accident, so as to arrive at the last or operating cause, and it is often extremely difficult to determine at what moment one phase came to an end and the next began.

---

68 See, e.g. *The Roseline* [1981] 2 Lloyd's Rep. 410, 411. In *The Kylix and the Rustringen* [1979] 1 Lloyd's Rep. 133 the K had a bad lookout, attempted to overtake too closely and without an overtaking signal or prior agreement as required by by-laws. The R had a bad lookout, altered course to starboard at an improper time without signalling and failed to keep to port as required by the by-laws. The main burden of overtaking safely was on the K and the apportionment of liability was K–80%: R–20%. See also *The Achilleus* [1985] 2 Lloyd's Rep. 338 where the A was 70% to blame for being on the wrong side of a traffic separation zone and failing to give way to a crossing vessel. The C was 30% to blame for failing to have a good lookout.

69 *The Boleslaw Chobry* [1974] 2 Lloyd's Rep. 308, 316.

70 *The Enterprise* [1912] P. 207, 211; the first case to be decided under the Maritime Conventions Act 1911.

71 *Temperley* (1976), p. 112.

Illustration: *Owners of S.S. Orduna* v. *Shipping Controller*[72]

The *Orduna* and the *Konakry* were approaching each other on crossing courses. The *Konakry* had the *Orduna* on her starboard bow. Under what is now Rule 15 it was therefore the *Konakry's* duty to keep clear and the *Orduna's* duty keep her course and speed. However, the *Konakry* did nothing until she was quite close to the *Orduna*. The latter then got the impression that the *Konakry* had allowed time for going by, that she would keep her course and pass on to the *Orduna's* starboard side. Therefore the *Orduna* did not keep her course, but ported. About the same time the *Konakry* suddenly starboarded, and the *Orduna* struck the *Konakry* on the port quarter with her stem.

Held: Even while they were quite close, the two vessels were still 'crossing so as to involve the risk of collision' within the meaning of Rule 15. The ships had not yet passed into another phase, so that the *Orduna* was forbidden to change her course, and not only the *Konakry*, but also the *Orduna* was to blame.

Per Viscount Finlay, at p. 255: 'The conditions which render the Regulations for crossing ships applicable begin as soon as the two ships are approaching one another on courses which, if continued, may cause a collision. These conditions continue to subsist until the vessels have definitely passed out of the phase of crossing ships.'

It is impossible to go over all the decided cases on collision liability. They turn, more or less, on questions of fact and on the construction of the International Collision, or local harbour and dock, Regulations.

Sometimes the defendant may claim that the ship was lost as a result of some failure of the plaintiff after the collision occurred. This is called by lawyers a *novus actus interveniens* (new act intervening). Where a ship is badly holed by a collision and sinks soon afterwards as a result of water entering the hole so made, there is a prima facie case that the ship was lost as a result of the collision. It is then open to the defendant to try to rebut this prima facie case by showing that there was intervening negligence on board the plaintiff's ship which broke the 'chain' of causation.[73] But the burden is then on the defendant who must show that the plaintiff failed to take some precaution that good seamanship required, and that if it had been taken the loss would probably have been averted.[74]

An example of such a *novus actus interveniens* would be where, after a collision, there was a repeated and unreasonable refusal of salvage

72 [1921] 1 A.C. 250, Holdert and Buzek, op. cit. p. 25.
73 *The Zaglebie Dabrowski (No. 2)* [1978] 1 Lloyd's Rep. 573, 574.
74 *The Fritz Thyssen* [1967] 1 All E.R. 628, [1967] 3 All E.R. 117.

assistance so that the damaged ship became a total loss.[75] The result is that the plaintiff may only receive the notional repair costs,[76] unless it is possible to sub-apportion the damages by saying that the failure to accept assistance was partly the cause of the total loss.[77]   Before leaving this subject of the proximate cause, the application of another rule of the general law of torts to collisions at sea requires brief discussion. Generally speaking, if A voluntarily renders assistance to B and suffers injury, A cannot claim damages from B, however negligently the latter may have brought about the circumstances which impelled A to come to his rescue. The idea is that A's rescue was a new voluntary act. This act, not B's negligence, proximately caused the injury.[78] But where there is a rescuer under a legal or moral duty, any damage or injury sustained performing it flows directly from the initial negligence.[79] A collision case has illustrated this principle well.[80] The *Daniel M.* navigated negligently. She collided with the *Gusty,* and lives on board the latter were in danger. Obeying s. 6 of the Maritime Conventions Act 1911[81] the *Daphne* approached to help the persons on board the *Gusty* and suffered damage without herself being negligent. It was held that, since the *Daphne* was not a volunteer, the *Daniel M.'s* negligence had directly caused the damage to the *Daphne* and she was accordingly liable.

21.4.4   INEVITABLE ACCIDENT

Sometimes defendants try to rely on the defence of inevitable accident. This defence is available if it can be shown that the proximate cause of the accident was some external event beyond the ship's control and not to be avoided by ordinary care and skill or by common foresight.[82] An example of this might be the sudden breaking of steering gear or a sudden gale of special violence.

Where a collision results from inevitable accident no liability arises on either side. It makes no difference that prior to the inevitable accident one ship had been acting negligently – provided that this in no way contributed to the loss or damage. However, strict proof is required

75 *Ibid.*
76 *The Thuringia* (1872) 1 Asp. M.L.C. 283; *Marsden* (1961), pp. 348-9.
77 *Cf. The Calliope* [1970] 1 All E.R. 624.
78 *Cutler* v. *United Dairies* [1933] 2 K.B. 297.
79 *Haynes* v. *Harwood* [1935] 1 K.B. 146.
80 *The Gusty and the Daniel M.* [1940] P. 149.
81 See Section 21.3, *supra.*
82 *Marsden* (1961), pp. 7-12.

that the damage was not caused by any prior negligence, but by the subsequent inevitable accident. In one old case[83] the defendant ship collided with a vessel properly at anchor in broad daylight. That would have raised a prima facie case of negligence because such things do not normally happen without negligence. The defendant then claimed that there was an inevitable accident because the steering had jammed. Moreover, a new steering chain had recently been fitted. But the court held that the burden on the defendant to make out a case of inevitable accident was heavy. He had to show that the cause of the accident was not produced by him and that the result could not have been avoided. The defendant knew that such a chain might stretch and should have had the hand steering ready.[84]

It should be noted that what is ordinary diligence is determined by the circumstances of the case. Thus in darkness or thick weather a greater standard of care must be shown than during periods of good visibility, so that ordinary diligence comes to be regarded as a term of a relative nature.[85]

At common law in cases of inevitable accident the loss lies where it falls.[86] This means that the plaintiff has not proved his case, a fact which under the general law is visited by his obligation to pay the defendant's costs of the action. Admiralty Courts, however, have developed a different rule. Proof of negligence is particularly difficult in marine cases, and even less than elsewhere can the successful proof of negligence in a collision action be forecast. The Admiralty Court has therefore developed the practice that where it dismisses an action on the ground of inevitable accident, each party pays its own costs, and the unsuccessful plaintiff is not saddled with those of the defendant. But if it should have been obvious that it was an inevitable accident which caused the collision the court will dismiss the action with costs.[87]

21.5 CONTRIBUTORY NEGLIGENCE

So far we have spoken of negligence on the part of one of the colliding ships. We must now address our minds to what happens if there was negligence on the part of both vessels. Suppose in an action by ship A

---

83 *The Merchant Prince* [1892] P. 179.
84 See also *The Amoco Cadiz* [1984] 2 Lloyd's Rep. 304, Section 5.4, *supra* and Chapters 22, 25, *infra*.
85 *The Itinerant* (1844) 2 W. Rob. 236.
86 *The Dundee* (1823) 1 Hagg. Ad. 109, 120.
87 *The Innisfail* (1875) 35 L.T. 819.

against ship B, the latter admits her negligence, but goes on to plead and to prove that A's, the plaintiff's, negligence contributed to the accident; who has then to bear the loss?

21.5.1   DIVISION OF LOSS

The old rule of Admiralty law said that each party should bear half the loss. This was a rough and ready rule which often resulted in hardship to the parties. Imagine that the plaintiff's negligence was trifling, but his ship suffered damage to the extent of, say, £20 000; on the other hand the defendant's negligence was great, but the damage to his ship amounted only to £5000. What happened under the old rule was that both amounts were added up, making a total of £25 000, of which plaintiff and defendant had each to bear £12 500. That meant that, as the defendant had himself suffered only £5000 he had to pay to the plaintiff the difference between £12 500 and £5000, that is to say £7500. In the result, therefore, the plaintiff, who was guilty of that slight contributory negligence was compensated only to the extent of £7500 and had to bear £12 500 himself.

This rule was modified by the Collision Convention 1910, Art. 4 which introduced a rule based on proportionate fault. The new rule was substantially[88] enacted into British law[89] by s. 1 of the Maritime Conventions Act 1911. This provided:

'Where, by the fault of two or more vessels, damage or loss is caused to one or more of those vessels, to their cargoes or freight, or to any property on board, the liability to make good the damage or loss shall be in proportion to the degree in which each vessel was in fault.'

Thus if we take the above example and assume that the plaintiff was to blame 25 per cent and the defendant 75 per cent we get the following tabulation:

	£
Total damage	25 000
Plaintiff to bear 25%	6 250
Defendant to bear 75%	18 750
From the total the defendant has to bear	18 750
He may deduct the damage suffered by his own vessel	5 000
So that the defendant actually pays to the plaintiff	13 750

88 The Act differs in a number of significant respects from the Convention.
89 The USA is not a party to the Collision Convention 1910, but adopted a similar rule by the decision of the Supreme Court in US v. Reliable Transfer Co. Inc. 421 US 397 (1975).

It will be agreed that this is a result which conforms in a higher degree with the demands of justice.[90] Where, however, the circumstances make it impossible to establish different degrees of fault the loss is divided equally between the two ships.[91]

All this is plain sailing. There are, however, a number of special cases where the rule of the division of loss cannot be applied.

21.5.2 ALTERNATIVE DANGER

Suppose ship A manoeuvres in a negligent manner and suddenly brings ship B into grave danger. The master of the B on the spur of the moment and without time for deliberation gives an order which he believes will avert the imminent collision. In fact the order is wrong; it is the proximate cause of the collision. In those circumstances it has been held that the negligence of the master of the B shall not be counted at all; the A must bear the whole loss[92] for 'it is not in the mouth of those who have created the danger of the situation to be minutely critical of what is done by those whom they have by their fault involved in the danger'.[93]

This has been called the doctrine of alternative danger, because[94] a person chooses one danger which he believes smaller rather than continue to be exposed to one which is apparently imminent.

90 For an excellent summary of the principles, provided by an Admiralty judge who had to apply them see, H. Brandon, *Apportionment in British Courts*, (1977) *Tulane Law Review* 1025.

91 Maritime Conventions Act 1911, s. 1, proviso (a). See *The Peter Benoit* (1915) 84 L.J. P. 87; 85 L.J. P. 12. In that case the trial judge in a collision action held both ships to blame in the proportions of 20% to 80%; the Court of Appeal was of opinion that there was no evidence on which blame could be apportioned with any certainty and it therefore apportioned the liability equally between the two ships, in so far altering the trial judge's decision. See further *The Socrates and The Champion* [1923] P. 76. That was an action arising out of a collision between a tug and her tow, on the one part, and a third ship on the other. It was held that tug and tow were liable to pay damages to the third ship, but it was not necessary to apportion the damages between tug and tow. An appeal court will not normally interfere with the actual apportionment of blame fixed by the trial judge, see, e.g., *The Ercole* [1979] 1 Lloyd's Rep. 539.

92 *The Bywell Castle* (1879) 4 P.D. 219; approved in *The Utopia,* [1893] A.C. 492.

93 *United States Shipping Board* v. *Laird Line* [1924] A.C. 286, *per* Lord Dunedin, at p. 291.

94 *The Bywell Castle* (1879) 4 P.D. 219.

The doctrine has narrow limits. The owner of the B will only be able to rely on it, and thus neutralize the effect of the master's negligence, if he can prove that when taking the action the master acted, as it has been picturesquely called, 'in the agony of the moment'; for it would be unfair to call miscalculated conduct in such circumstances negligent.[95] But the danger must have been imminent and the time too short for the master to grasp the real situation. The master must have had no time to think.[96] It must be so short that he could not take considered action; he must not have acted freely but, as it were, under a natural reaction.[97] Where the danger was not imminent, or the time though short allowed for deliberation, any miscalculation on the master's part is negligence, and the rule of division of loss applies.

21.5.3 PLAINTIFF'S NEGLIGENCE SUBSEQUENT TO DEFENDANT'S

We now come to the second exception to the division of loss rule. We again proceed from the point that both plaintiff and defendant are negligent, but the defendant's negligence, in point of time, came first. Though it was a cause of the collision it was not the last or proximate cause. Rather it was the plaintiff's subsequent or contributory negligence which furnished the proximate cause. Here the defendant can no longer be said to have caused the collision. It was the plaintiff's new intervening act which did so and snapped the chain of causation.[98]

Illustration

Ships A and B collide. Both ships were negligent, but it is established that A's negligence came last. Supposing A's ship only is damaged, then if A sues B, B will not be liable to pay any damages. If both ships are damaged A will have to pay damages to B. Though both ships were negligent A had the 'last opportunity' to prevent the collision. If in the last case A sues B, and B makes no counterclaim, but only defends, then A's action will simply be dismissed. If B counterclaims or is the first to sue A, then A again gets nothing, but B will be awarded damages for the injury suffered.

---

95 *Jones* v. *Great Western Railway* (1930) 144 L.T. 194, 201, *per* Lord Warrington.
96 *Admiralty Commissioners* v. *S.S. Volute* [1922] 1 A.C. 129, *per* Lord Birkenhead.
97 *S.S. Singleton Abbey* v. *S.S. Paludina* [1927] A.C. 16.
98 *Davies* v. *Mann* (1842) 10 M. & W. 564; *The Sans Pareil* [1900] P. 267; Maritime Conventions Act 1911, s. 1, proviso (b). See Section 21.4.4, *supra.*

12.5.4 THE 'CLEAR LINE' RULE

Obviously there is but a narrow line between situations involving 'agony of the moment', 'last opportunity' and the division of loss rule generally. The court will often be in doubt whether the plaintiff's negligence was really subsequent to that of the defendant and not contemporaneous, so as to take it out of the rule. This state of affairs would be far from satisfactory, for the result will differ enormously. As we have seen in the ordinary way, that is, where the negligence of both parties was contemporaneous or where the defendant's negligence was subsequent to that of the plaintiff, the loss is divided according to the degree of fault attributable to the parties. Where the doctrine of alternative danger applies (21.5.2) the defendant bears the whole loss; and where the plaintiff's negligence is subsequent (21.5.3) the plaintiff cannot recover.

The courts are alive to the danger, and they tend to whittle down these exceptions by requiring very strong evidence to show that the plaintiff's negligence really came last. In *most* cases the negligence of both parties will be taken to be contemporaneous, thus letting in the division of loss rule. The 'clear line' rule was expounded by Lord Birkenhead:

'The question of contributory negligence must be dealt with somewhat broadly and upon common sense principles as a jury would probably deal with it. And while no doubt, where a *clear line* can be drawn, the subsequent negligence is the only one to look to, there are cases in which the two acts come so closely together and the second act of negligence is so much mixed up with the state of things brought about by the first act, that the party secondly negligent, while not held free of blame under the rule, might, on the other hand, invoke the prior negligence as being part of the cause of the collision so as to make it a case of contribution.'[99]

21.5.5 LOSS OF LIFE, PERSONAL INJURY AND CARGO CLAIMS

It should be noticed that s. 1 of the Maritime Conventions Act 1911 make no mention of loss of life or personal injury in consequence of a

---

[99] *Admiralty Commissioners* v. *S.S. Volute* [1922] 1 A.C. 129, 144, emphasis added. Where D1 and D2 collide due to the fault of both, and then, for example, D1 collides with a third ship (P), the liability for the damage caused by the second collision will normally be in the same proportions as for the first – unless D1 was negligent in failing to avoid P; see *The Vysotsk* [1981] 1 Lloyd's Rep. 439 and Section 21.4.3 *supra*.

collision. The personal representatives of a person who is killed in a collision may claim damages on behalf of near relatives of the deceased from whichever ship was negligent.[1]

The Act gives special treatment to such personal injury and death claimants by allowing them to sue the wrongdoing ships as joint tortfeasors, i.e. they are jointly and separately liable for the *whole* damage and not for their proportion.[2] If one joint tortfeasor is sued for the whole he will be entitled to contribution from the other tortfeasors in the proportion of the degree of fault attributable to the respective ships.[3]

On the other hand, innocent cargo-owners can only claim from each vessel in the proportion in which each vessel was to blame.[4] In this respect even the innocent owner of cargo is identified with the negligent vessel in which his cargo was shipped, a rule abolished for personal injuries.[5] The matter is important because the carrying ship will normally be able to exempt its own share of liability to the cargo for negligent navigation on the basis of the carriage contract.[6]

21.5.6 COLLISION OTHER THAN BETWEEN TWO SHIPS

The principal rule for the division of loss between two ships which are both at fault rests, as we have seen, on the Maritime Conventions Act

1 There was at one time a rule that he was identified with the negligence of his own carrier, but this was exploded in *The Bernina* (1886) 12 P.D. 36. As to the liability for death, see Fatal Accidents Act 1976; ss. 1 and 2, Law Reform (Miscellaneous Provisions) Act 1934.

2 Maritime Conventions Act 1911, s. 2. This may be important in practice where one ship cannot be arrested or it has a low limit of liability, see Chapter 22, *infra*.

3 Maritime Conventions Act 1911, s. 3; Crown Proceedings Act 1947, s. 6.
Likewise, an innocent ship damaged by a collision between two other ships may claim the whole damage from either of the two others: *The Devonshire* [1912] A.C. 634; *The Cairnbahn* [1914] P. 25. This is not what was intended by the Collision Convention 1910, Art. 4.

4 *The Milan* (1861) Lush, 388, 167 E.R. 167; preserved by Maritime Conventions Act 1911, s. 1.

5 *The Bernina, supra*.

6 Hague–Visby Rules Art. IV, r.2(a): See Part 2, Section 11.4.2, *supra*. As the USA is not party to the Collision Convention 1910 cargo claimants often sue there as they can recover the whole loss from the non-carrying ship under the ordinary joint tortfeasor rule. This causes great complications in settling claims, see *The Giacinto Motta* [1977] 2 Lloyd's Rep. 221.

1911. It only applies to collisions between ships,[7] i.e. not to the case where a ship collides with any other object, for instance, a pier or dock gates. There appears to be no logical or common-sense reason for this distinction. It is in fact due to historical accident, but its unfairness has been removed by the Law Reform (Contributory Negligence) Act 1945. This abolished the old common law rule which made contributory negligence, however slight, an absolute defence to an action for damages. Instead the Admiralty rule allowing for different degrees of fault is in substance applied generally. Nevertheless, collisions between ships and collisions of ships with other objects must still be distinguished, since the 1945 Act is expressly limited to non-Admiralty cases (i.e. those where S.I. of the 1911 Act does not apply).[8]

Thus collisions between ships propelled by oars, as that of a sculler and an eight on the Thames, or the collision of a ship with dock gates where both sides are to blame will be judged under the 1945 Act.[9] In the last-mentioned case one point requires consideration. As a rule, the dock and pier owner's duty will be determined by a statute imposing certain obligations of an absolute character upon these authorities, i.e., the authority will be liable for breach of statutory duty if it fails to observe such obligations even if the failure was not due to any absence of reasonable care upon its part. In this case, too, the authority can plead contributory negligence.

12.6 DAMAGES

So far we have been concerned with the question: in what circumstances is a collision a wrongful act entitling an innocent sufferer to damages from the wrongdoer? We must now discuss the problem of compensating the victim. There are two real issues: the kind of damages which may be recoverable, and how to calculate those damages.

21.6.1 REMOTENESS OF DAMAGE

Incidents involving ships may cause damage by collision or otherwise, but not every type of damage may be recovered in law. Some damages

7 According to *Edwards* v. *Quickenden* (1939) 55 T.L.R. 583, the Act does not apply to a collision between vessels propelled by oars (collision between an eight and a sculler on the Thames).
8 Law Reform (Contributory Negligence) Act 1945, s. 3.
9 Questions of contribution between tortfeasors will be dealt with under the Civil Liability (Contribution) Act 1978.

are said to be too 'remote', i.e. so removed from, or unconnected with, the original negligence that it would be unfair for the defendant to be liable for them. For instance, if a bulk vegetable oil carrier collided with a jetty so that some of the vegetable oil was spilt the defendant could hardly expect to be liable if the oil, by some freak, combined with a chemical already in the water to form a poisonous gas which injured persons nearby. The general rule in the law of tort is that the defendant is only liable if he can reasonably foresee the *kind* of damage suffered by the plaintiff.[10] It is not necessary to foresee the exact way in which the damage occurred, nor does it matter if its extent is greater than expected. Thus the vegetable oil might be expected to cause some damage to harbour facilities by fouling. But the shipowner would still have to pay if it caused pumping machinery to jam in an unusual way, or if the clean-up operations were particularly expensive. Particular diffi-culties have concerned fires following leakages of crude and refined oil from ships. While foreseeability depends on the facts of each case, in practice the shipowner will usually be liable, even if such fires are started by sparks from welding operations.[11]

21.6.2   MEASURE OF DAMAGE

Assuming that the kind of loss is foreseeable, on what principle are the damages measured? The common law rule, which also applies to collisions between ships, is that the plaintiff is entitled to be put in the position he would have been in but for the collision, so far as money can do so.[12]

It is clear that in a collision action the damage is likely to fall under one of two heads: the ship may be lost altogether, or she may require repairs. If the ship has become a total loss the defendant must replace

---

10 *The Wagon Mound (No. 1): Overseas Tankship (U.K.) Ltd* v. *Morts Dock and Engineering Co. Ltd* [1961] A.C. 388.

11 *Ibid.*, and see *The Arzew* [1981] 1 Lloyd's Rep. 142. Of course there might be a *novus actus interveniens* or contributory negligence if welding operations were undertaken knowing of the risk of fire.

12 *Cf. Admiralty Commissioners* v. *S.S. Susquehanna* [1926] A.C. 655, *per* Viscount Dunedin, at p. 661. Note also that a shipowner may be able to limit his liability by statute, in which case the fund in court has to be used to satisfy all claims. A sort of localized bankruptcy will then take place, each claimant receiving a proportion of his claim, e.g. *Stoomvart Maatschappij Nederland* v. *P. & O.* (1882) 7 App. Cas. 795. See Chapter 22, *infra*.

her. He need not pay so much as the plaintiff requires for buying a new vessel, for this would place the latter in a substantially better position than he was before the casualty. Normally, what the defendant has to pay is only the market value of the ship at the time of the collision. If the ship has no market value, evidence must be heard to establish what the value of the ship was to the owner as a going concern, and the sum thus arrived at constitutes the measure of damages.[13]

The difficulty arises in connection with the owner's loss of the use of his vessel during the period of the repairs. Generally speaking, the following considerations apply.

If the ship was under charter the owner can claim the loss of chartered freight, less disbursements, and loss through wear and tear which he has saved.[14] Irrespective of business considerations, the owner is allowed a certain amount for deprivation of the use of the ship though he can prove no special damages.[15] The fact that the owners have not got sufficient capital to replace the ship, and have to borrow at high interest or to hire another vessel, thereby suffering additional damage, does not entitle them to extra compensation. Such damage is not regarded as following directly from the wrongful act. It is too remote.[16] In the absence of a total loss the defendant must bear the cost of repairs necessary to put the plaintiff's vessel into the state it was in before the collision.[17] Though this rule looks simple enough it has given rise to a number of disputes.

In the first place it may happen that some of the repairs necessitated by the collision would have shortly had to be executed anyhow in order

---

13 *Marsden* (1961), para. 492 *et seq. The Harmonides* [1903] P1. Where persons are killed, their estates have an action under the Law Reform (Miscellaneous Provisions) Act 1934, and by dependants under the Fatal Accidents Act 1976 as amended by the Administration of Justice Act 1982, Part I. See generally, *McGregor on Damages* (14th edn 1980).

14 *The Gazelle* (1844) 2 W. Rob. 279, 166 E.R. 759; *The Philadelphia* [1917] P. 101; *Admiralty Commissioners* v. *S.S. Valeria* [1922] 2 A.C. 242.

15 *Owners of No. 7 Steam Pump Dredger* v. *S.S. Greta Holme* [1897] A.C. 596; *S.S Mediana* v. *Lightship Comet* [1900] A.C. 113; *The Astrakhan* [1910] P. 172 (Danish warship).

16 *Liesbosch (Dredger)* v. *Edison S.S. (Owners)* [1933] A.C. 449.

17 *The Bernina* (1886) 55 L.T. 781. For the heads of damage claimed in a personal injury action, see *Jefford* v. *Gee* [1970] 1 All E.R. 1202, and *McGregor on Damages.*

that the vessel could pass her regular survey. It has been held that this
fact does not entitle a defendant in a collision action to claim a reduction
of the sum he has to pay. The shipowner is entitled to a thoroughly
efficient ship, and it is not for the wrongdoer to avail himself of such an
accidental circumstance.[18]

Secondly, it is conceivable that a shipowner will combine the repairs
of the collision damage with a thorough overhaul of the whole ship. If
the cost of repair is not increased thereby the defendant cannot demand
that the costs of overhaul should be borne by the plaintiff.[19]

Finally, defendants have tried to obtain relief by the following argument. When a ship is repaired, new materials are built into it, and to this
extent the ship is more valuable after repair than it was before the
damage had occurred. For this reason, as we shall see later,[20] an insurer
is allowed to deduct the amount of appreciation from the cost of repairs,
'new for old', because under the contract of insurance he is only bound
to indemnify the assured.[21] This benefit was also claimed by defendants
in a collision action but rejected by the court. The claim against a
wrongdoer is not only for an indemnity, as under an insurance policy,
but for damages: that is to say, for the refund of those direct and natural
expenses incurred by the plaintiff which are necessary to put him into
the same position as he was in before the accident.[22]

21.6.3   ECONOMIC LOSS

Finally, we should note that negligence may affect many persons who
are not directly injured. It is rather like dropping a stone into a pond –
the ripples will range over a wide area. A collision with a bridge may
cause great damage to its structure. That would be recoverable in the
ordinary way: but what of the motorists forced to make a long detour,
or the other ships trapped up-river? The consequences for long waterways such as the Mississippi or the St Lawrence Seaway are potentially
enormous.[23] In the past one could have said with some confidence, that

18 *The Bernina, supra.*
19 *The Acanthus* [1902] P. 17; *Admiralty Commissioners* v. *S.S Chekiang* [1926] A.C. 637.
20 See Section 28.2, *infra*, but note Appendix 14, clause 14.
21 *Aitchison* v. *Lohre* (1879) 4 App. Cas. 755.
22 *The Gazelle* (1844) 2 W. Rob. 279, 166 E.R. 759; *The Bernina* (1886) 55 L.T. 781.
23 See e.g. *Bethlehem Steel Corp.* v. *St. Lawrence Seaway Authority* [1978] 1 F.C. 464 (Canada) and *The Buffalo Bridge Cases,* e.g. [1968] A.M.C. 293 (USA).

these sort of claims would not have been recoverable because they were unforeseeable or too remote: but the general law of tort is still developing.[24] However, it seems that a person is not entitled to sue for economic loss suffered because his contract with the victim of the wrong was rendered less profitable or unprofitable.

Illustration: *The Mineral Transporter: Candlewood Navigation v. Mitsui OSK Lines*[25]

D's ship negligently collided with a ship of which P[1] was the time charterer and P[2] the disponent owner. D was obliged to pay the repair costs of P[2]. While the vessel was being repaired P[1] lost profits and was also obliged to continue to pay part of the hire for the ship to P[2]. D disputed his liability for P[1]'s claims.

Held: The claim of P[1] failed. He had no proprietary or possessory interest in the vessel that was damaged:[26] his only right in relation to the vessel was contractual.

This conclusion was the result of a deliberate policy decision to limit the potential claims arising from a collision. It follows that in similar circumstances sub-charterers and persons such as stevedores, surveyors and agents would not have a tort claim against D for their lost income or wasted expenditure: nor would passengers delayed on board the damaged vessel.[27] Similarly, it seems unlikely that a person could recover damages where his ship is delayed by the negligence of another ship in damaging a lock-gate,[28] an offshore oil mooring buoy,[29] or in blocking a river.[30]

There are always exceptions to any rule. It may be that the economic loss plaintiff will have a better chance of succeeding if he can show that his property was situated in close physical propinquity to the place where the defendant's negligence had its physical effect; for instance, if

---

24 E.g., *Junior Books Ltd* v. *Veitchi Co. Ltd* [1983] 1 A.C. 520.

25 [1985] 2 All E.R. 935 (Privy Council on appeal from the Supreme Court, New South Wales). See also *The Aliakmon: Leigh and Sillavan Ltd* v. *Aliakmon Shipping Co. Ltd* [1986] 2 All E.R. 145.

26 It was also irrelevant that P[1] was in fact the owner of the vessel who had bareboat chartered it to P[2] and then taken a time charter back: P[1] was claiming for his loss as time charterer, not owner.

27 Likewise for a tugowner who loses profit on a towage contract because the tow is sunk: *S.A. de Remorquage à Hélice* v. *Bennetts* [1911] 1 K.B. 243.

28 *Anglo-Algerian S.S.* v. *The Houlder Line Ltd* [1908] 1 K.B. 659.

29 *Shell & B.P. S.A.* v. *Osborne Panama S.A.* [1982] 4 S.A. L.R. 890 (South Africa).

30 *Cf. The Maindy Manor* (1933) 45 Ll. L. Rep. 231.

his ship dredged up an oil pipeline (clearly marked on charts) which was used, but not owned, by the plaintiff.[31]

21.6.4 INTEREST

A court can give interest on a judgment debt from the date of judgment.[32] Interest may also be awarded for the period between the date when the cause of action arose and the date of judgment (or date of payment, if sums are paid before judgment).[33] Similar powers are given to arbitrators.[34] However, it seems that neither courts nor arbitrators have general power to award interest on unpaid debts *before* legal proceedings have begun.[35] There is no authority in any Admiralty case to suggest this, or that compound interest may be awarded.[36] Where a shipowner claims to limit liability and pays money to the court the victim may claim simple interest on the principal sum from the date of collision until the date of the decree of limitation.[37] In Admiralty and commercial cases it has been the practice to award interest at higher rates than found on short-term investment accounts, e.g. by awarding 'base' rate plus 1 per cent.[38]

21.6.5 DAMAGES IN FOREIGN CURRENCY

At one time English courts were only able to give damages measured in sterling converted from any foreign currency at the date of the collision.

31 See *Caltex Oil (Australia) Pty Ltd* v. *The Dredge 'Willemstad'* (1976) 136 C.L.R. 529 (High Court Australia), per Jacobs, J., at p. 604; *The Mineral Transporter, supra*, per Lord Fraser, at p. 945.
32 Judgments Act 1838, s. 17; Administration of Justice Act 1970, s. 44; and, e.g. Judgments Debts (Rate of Interest) Order 1985 (S.I. No. 437(L.3)) fixing 15% as the rate for judgments entered up after 16 April 1985.
33 Administration of Justice Act 1982, s. 15, Sch. 1, inserting a new s. 35A in the Supreme Court Act 1981. Interest must be awarded on damages for personal injuries, s. 35A(2). See also *Jefford* v. *Gee* [1970] 1 All E.R. 1202.
34 Administration of Justice Act 1982, s. 15(6), inserting a new s. 19A in the Arbitration Act 1950.
35 E.g., freight or demurrage *The La Pintada* [1984] 2 Lloyd's Rep. 9. But interest on collision damages runs from the date of collision, *The Kong Magnus* [1891] P.223.
36 *The La Pinfeda, supra.*, per Lord Brandon, at p.16. For interest on salvage awards see Section 24.8.5(b), *infra*.
37 *The Garden City (No. 2)* [1984] 2 Lloyd's Rep. 37. See pp. 407, 412, *infra*.
38 *Ibid.*

This can cause obvious hardship where the values of currencies change after that date and before any damages are paid. In *The Despina R*[39] the House of Lords held that the plaintiff was entitled to damages in the currency in which he felt the loss.

Illustration: *The Despina R*[40]

P was a Liberian company with a head office in Greece managed by agents in New York. As a result of a collision to P's ship, P incurred repair and associated expenses in Shanghai (paid in Chinese yuan); Yokohama (paid in Japanese yen); Los Angeles (paid in US dollars); and London (paid in sterling). All payments came from a dollar account in New York.

Held: P was entitled to damages measured not by the currencies immediately involved (i.e., the yuan, yen and pounds) but in the currency in which it proved it felt the loss and which it was reasonably foreseeable it would have to spend. As the currency in which P normally conducted its trading operations was dollars, the defendants had to pay damages expressed in US dollars.

This rule can cause great difficulties in deciding which currency is appropriate, as international companies may maintain accounts in many currencies. But it is for the plaintiff to satisfy the court that he felt the loss in a particular currency.[41]

---

39 [1979] 1 All E.R. 421.
40 *Ibid.* For contract claims see *The Folias* [1979] 1 All E.R. 421.
41 See J. Knott, 'The Wealth-time Continuum Revisited: Set off in Marine Collision Claims' [1981] L.M.C.L.Q. 269; *The Lash Atlantico* [1985] 2 Lloyd's Rep. 464.

22
LIMITATION OF SHIPOWNERS' LIABILITY

22.1 INTRODUCTION

WE now come to an important rule, which sets shipping apart from all other branches of industry and commerce, the rule that a shipowner can limit his liability to persons suffering loss or damage through negligent navigation or management of his ship. Broadly, when a ship collides with and damages another vessel and/or causes loss of life or personal injury to passengers or other personnel, the owner of the negligent ship need not necessarily compensate fully those who have suffered; usually he can limit his liability according to the size of his ship.

The concept goes back many centuries but its adoption and spread in Europe dates mainly from the seventeenth century.[1] The first major codification of the law was in The Maritime Ordinance of Louis XIV in 1681. The rule is probably one of the first instances of state support for its shipping industry.[2] Hugo Grotius, the great seventeenth-century international lawyer, defended it by pleading public policy, and the same view was expressed by Dr Lushington, the great English Admiralty Judge.[3] In a more recent case[4] Lord Denning MR confessed that the shipowner's right to limit his liability 'is not a matter of justice . . . [but has] its justification in convenience'.

The convenience of the rule is responsible for its survival. The modern justification is not that it would be unfair to make a shipowner pay for all the damage he has caused: it is that a shipowner can obtain adequate insurance cover for third party claims if his insurers can

---

1 J. Donovan, 'The Origins and Development of Limitation of Shipowners' Liability' (1979) 53 *Tulane Law Review* 999, 1000 *et seq.*
2 Cyril Miller, Brussels Conference of International Law Association 1962, p. 627 *et seq.*
3 *The Amalia* (1863) Br. & Lush. 151; 176 E.R. 323.
4 *The Bramley Moore: Alexandra Towing Co.* v. *Millet* [1964] P. 200, 200.

calculate their maximum exposure with certainty. Victims generally benefit if the limits are set high enough and if they can be sure that an insurer will pay their claim.

The shipowner, as has been said, can limit his total liability to all those who have suffered loss or injury to a sum of money calculated in relation to the tonnage of his ship. This sum represents a fund from which the victims of the disaster are compensated *pro rata*, being paid a proportion of their actual loss if the fund is not large enough to allow payment in full. It follows that no payment is made from the fund until all claims have been received, so that smart claimants are prevented from snatching what is available, leaving other claimants with a stale remedy.[5]

In effect, therefore, the shipowner, when sending his ship to sea, runs a calculable risk, and so does his underwriter, who is thus in a position to charge a lower premium than would be possible if the assured's liability were unlimited.

There have been two main systems of limitation in use internationally. The older system fixed the limit of liability according to the value of the ship. The trouble with this system was that it favoured the owners of old, poorly maintained ships and that if the vessel sank after a collision the limit would be next to nothing. The more modern system is based on the British nineteenth-century legislation which used the tonnage of a ship to measure her limit.[6] Attempts to produce international unity have resulted in three international conventions. The first, in 1924, did not receive widespread acceptance. The second, the International Convention Relating to the Limitation of the Liability of Owners of Seagoing Ships 1957 has over 50 state parties.[7] A number of major maritime countries, such as the USA and Greece, did not ratify this Convention and so a Convention on Limitation of Liability for Maritime Claims 1976 agreed at IMCO (now IMO) as a final attempt to achieve uniformity.[8] The 1976 Convention will enter into force on

---

5 Miller: *loc. cit.*, p. 632.
6 The *Titanic* limitation proceedings in the USA demonstrate the differences in the systems. The ship had a pre-accident value of about £1 500 000. Under the British tonnage system her limit would have been about US $3 750 000. After her loss her then US limit was US $91 805 (made up of, e.g., salved lifeboats and advance passage money). The total personal claims were US $22 000 000: see *Oceanic Steam Navigation Co.* v. *Mellor* 209 F. 501 (2 Cir., 1913), 233 US 718 (1914).
7 Cmnd 353. It entered into force on 31 May 1968. See Singh (1983) Vol. 4, p. 2976.
8 Cmnd 7035. See Singh (1983) Vol. 4, p. 2976.

1 December 1986. For those states which are parties, it will replace the
1957 Convention.[9]

The old UK law was contained in the Merchant Shipping Act 1894,
as amended. The most important amendment was the Merchant Shipping (Liability of Shipowners and Others) Act 1958 which altered the
1894 Act to give effect to the 1957 Convention. However, the Merchant
Shipping Act 1979, Sch. 4, contains the relevant provisions of the 1976
Convention and, as soon as it comes into force, the schedule will be
given the force of law by statutory instrument.[10] It will be necessary
here to consider the law under the 1894 as well as the 1979 Act for the
Merchant Shipping Act 1979, s. 19(4) will not apply the 1976 Convention retrospectively. The 1976 Convention also builds on the practice established by the earlier convention.

The questions regulated by this legislation are: who is entitled to
limit his liability? In respect of what craft can liability be limited? To
which sort of claims does the right to limit apply? And, finally, what is
the extent of limitation?

22.2   THE 1957 LIMITATION
CONVENTION: MERCHANT SHIPPING
ACT 1894

22.2.1   PERSONS ENTITLED TO LIMIT

Originally the privilege was enjoyed only by the owner of the ship
which caused the damage, but that was manifestly unfair. It meant that
where the master of the offending ship had been appointed by a charterer, thus being the charterer's servant, the charterer, unlike the
shipowner, was liable in full. The same was true of the mere hirer of a
barge whose crew had negligently caused damage to a third party. To
remedy this unfairness, the limitation privilege was extended to any
charterer (demise time or voyage) and any person interested in a ship –
in particular managers or operators.[11] The privilege also extends to any
person in possession of a ship. So a mortgagee would be able to limit his

---

9 Art 17(4). Under Art 17(1), the 1976 Convention entered into force.

10 Merchant Shipping Act 1979, ss. 17, 52. See now the Merchant Shipping Act 1979
(Commencement No. 10) Order 1986 (S.I. No. 1052), setting 1 December 1986 as
the relevant date. For casualties thereafter, see Section 22.3, *infra*.

11 Merchant Shipping Act 1894, s. 503, as amended by the Merchant Shipping
(Liability of Shipowners and Others) Act 1958, s.3.

liability for a collision occurring after he had repossessed the ship.[12] Individual employees, such as the master and members of the crew are also entitled to limit – for remember that it is usually the negligence of the master or member of the crew that causes the damage. It is only right that, if sued for their unlawful act, they should enjoy the same limitation protection.[13]

Note that a licensed pilot can limit his liability under the Pilotage Act 1983 to £100 plus the pilotage charges for the voyage.[14]

22.2.2 CRAFT SUBJECT TO LIMITATION

Turning to the ships in respect of which the privilege may be claimed it should be noticed that originally this applied only to ships as such. At a comparatively early date, however, the limitation provisions were extended to ships from the moment of launching. Now it applies to 'any structure, whether completed or in course of completion, launched and intended for use in navigation as a ship or part of a ship', the last four words presumably taking account of modern methods of prefabrication in shipbuilding.[15] Limitation could always be claimed in respect of British and foreign ships.[16] Now British ships can avail themselves of the right even if not yet registered.[17] Unfortunately it is not always clear whether certain modern structures, such as jack-up oil rigs, can be considered as ships.[18] The Merchant Shipping Act 1979, s. 41 gives the Secretary of State power to order that a thing designed or adapted for use at sea may be treated as a ship.[19] So far it has not been used. Hovercraft are subject to limitation, however.[20]

Finally, it should be mentioned that owners of docks and canals and harbour and conservancy authorities have been given the right to limit their liability to ships using their installations.[21]

---

12 *Ibid* and see Section 6.6 *supra*.

13 See Section 9.5 *supra*.

14 Pilotage Act 1983, s. 42. Under the Pilotage Act 1913 the right depended on whether he had given a bond in accordance with local by-laws, ss. 35, 17. See Chapter 19, *supra*, and fn. 86 (p. 409) *infra*.

15 Merchant Shipping (Liability of Shipowners and Others) Act 1958, s.4(1).

16 Under the Merchant Shipping Act 1894, s. 503.

17 Merchant Shipping (Liability of Shipowners and Others) Act 1958, s.4(2).

18 See also Section 24.2, *infra*.

19 See M. Summerskill, *Oil Rigs: Law and Insurance*, (1979), Chapter 2.

20 Hovercraft Act 1968, s. 1. Hovercraft (Civil Liability) Order 1979 (S.I. No. 305). See Section 18.4, *supra*.

21 Merchant Shipping (Liability of Shipowners and Others) Act 1900, s. 2.

22.2.3   CLAIMS SUBJECT TO LIMITATION

We now come to the circumstances in which the persons in control of ships, as just defined, can plead the limitation.[22] Liability can be limited in respect of claims for the loss of life or personal injury suffered by any person on board the ship and any property on board the ship.[23]

The 1957 Convention did not allow a shipowner to limit in relation to claims by his own crew if the law governing their contracts of service forbade it.[24] This protection was enacted into law,[25] but it left crews of British ships at a disadvantage until the enactment of the Merchant Shipping Act 1979, s. 35. It provides that there can be no limitation where loss of life or personal injury, or loss of or damage to property, is suffered by a claimant who is an employee whose contract of service is governed by UK law.

So far we have dealt only with the rights of persons who themselves were on board or whose property was on board the ship at fault. Questions of limitation, however, occur commonly where two ships collide or where the ship collides with a quay or other harbour installation. Those in control of the ship may then be liable to those in control and on board the other vessel or to those whose goods are on board the latter. Normally this will be a liability in tort, that is for an unlawful act, e.g. negligent navigation, but the liability may also be contractual, as where the ship collides with its tow.

In all such cases the ship at fault can limit its liability for loss of life of, or personal injury to, passengers, crew or persons on shore, as the case may be, and for property.[26] The basis of such liability will normally, but need not necessarily, be negligence, but often where liability is absolute, as where the ship damages what is called a navigable highway,[27] the same privilege of limitation applies.[28]

The negligence need not necessarily be that of the master or crew on board the ship at fault. The owner can also limit for the faults of persons

22 Merchant Shipping Act 1894, s. 502; *The Diamond* [1906] P. 282.
23 Merchant Shipping Act 1894, s. 503(1)(a) and (b).
24 Art. 1(4)(b).
25 Merchant Shipping (Liability of Shipowners and Others) Act 1958, s. 2(4), so far as concerned foreign laws preventing limits, or giving limits higher than under s. 503.
26 Merchant Shipping Act 1894, s. 503(1)(c) and (d), as amended by Merchant Shipping (Liability of Shipowners and Others) Act 1958, s. 2(1). For passenger claims see Chapter 18, *supra*. Section 503 does not apply to the limitation of liability for oil pollution: Merchant Shipping (Oil Pollution) Act 1971, s. 4(1), as to which see Chapter 25, *infra*.
27 See Section 20.2.2, *supra*.
28 Merchant Shipping (Liability of Shipowners and Others) Act 1958, s. 2(3).

not on board, provided that the wrongdoing occurred in the navigation or management of the ship or in relation to the carriage of passengers or cargo. Thus, in *The Warkworth*,[29] the ship collided with another vessel owing to a defect in its steam steering gear. This had been caused by the negligence of workmen, and a superintendent on shore, who were servants of the owner. It was held that the latter could limit his liability. This was a fault in the management of the vessel. In *The Tojo Maru*[30] a salvor was not entitled to limit when his diver operating in the sea damaged the salvage vessel. The acts were not in the 'management' of the salvage tug. This case illustrates an important point. To claim the privilege of limitation a person must satisfy the words of the statute. If he cannot do so he will be liable for the full amount of the damages.

In theory the wreck raising expenses of harbour authorities could be subject to limitation, but the UK has never brought into force the specific provisions of the 1957 Convention.[31] Nor can such claims usually be considered as an ordinary claim for damages suffered – which would be subject to limitation in the ordinary way. This is because the relevant statutory powers which allow wreck raising expenses to be reclaimed[32] are usually expressed in terms of a statutory *debt* – which is not subject to limitation.[33] Claims for damage to harbour works, basins, or navigable waterways are subject to limitation.[34]

22.2.4 LOSS OF THE RIGHT TO LIMIT

No limitation can, however, be claimed by owners or others in control who themselves were at fault. All that has been said so far applies only if the ship collided through the fault of someone for whom the owner of the ship or the other person in control was liable.

29 (1884) 9 P.D. 145.

30 [1972] A.C. 242. For the full facts see Sections 24.7.2 and 24.10.8, *infra*. For the reversal of this rule by the 1976 Limitation Convention, see Section 22.3, *infra*.

31 1957 Convention Art 1(1)(c). Merchant Shipping (Liability of Shipowners and Others) Act 1958, s. 2(2)(a). The UK made a permitted reservation to Art. 1(1)(c) when ratifying the convention. Sections 2(5) and 2(6) envisaged the establishment of a fund to compensate harbour authorities if limitation was ever allowed: but this has never happened.

32 E.g. the Harbours, Docks and Piers Clauses Act 1847, s. 56.

33 *The Stonedale No. 1 (Owners)* v. *Manchester Ship Canal Co.* [1956] A.C. 1. Each particular statutory power must be considered separately, but modern local statutes often specifically make recovery a matter of simple contract debt, e.g. the Medway Ports Authority Act 1973, s. 46(2). Douglas (1983) p. 191.

34 Merchant Shipping (Liability of Shipowners and Others) Act 1958, s. 2(2)(b). See generally on harbours Section 20.2, *supra*.

No one in control of a ship, normally the owner, can claim limitation if his 'actual fault or privity' contributed to the accident; if, in other words, negligence can be laid at the door not only of an employee but of the owner himself.[35]

Illustration: *The Lady Gwendolen: Guinness, Son and Co. Ltd* v. *The Freshfield*[36]

The Lady Gwendolen, owned by the plaintiffs, collided with and sank the defendants' vessel, *The Freshfield*, which was lying at anchor in the Mersey. Despite thick fog *The Lady Gwendolen* went at full speed, with her radar equipment switched on but not continuously manned, the master only glancing at it occasionally. [If this had been all, it would have been a clear case for allowing the owners to limit their liability, but the following facts demonstrate their own negligence in addition to that of the master.] The master had long been in the habit of sailing at excessive speed. Had the plaintiffs' marine superintendent examined the ship's log, as it was his duty to do, he would have discovered this conduct and could and should have admonished the master. In addition, the marine superintendent had failed to draw the master's specific attention to the Ministry of Transport Notice M.445, of December 1960, urging even radar-equipped vessels to go at reduced speed in conditions of poor visibility.

Held: The plaintiffs were not entitled to limit their liability since their 'actual fault or privity' had contributed to the accident. It was the duty of a reasonably prudent shipowner to appreciate the navigational problems posed by the use of radar in fog and to impress the urgency of these problems on their masters. This the plaintiffs had failed to do and they had thus themselves contributed to the collision.[37]

It will be observed that the owner in *The Lady Gwendolen* case was a limited company, which acts through its officers, and this poses the problem: How high in the hierarchy must a company's officer be for it to be said in fairness that his negligence is not only that of an employee but, as it were, the personal negligence of the company? Long ago the House of Lords laid down that where a wrong is committed by a person who 'is really the directing control and will of the corporation' – the

---

35 Merchant Shipping Act 1894, s. 503.
36 [1965] P. 294.
37 The same result may follow where the owner, contrary to regulations, appoints a non-certificated officer whose negligence causes a collision. *The Empire Jamaica* [1956] 3 All E.R. 144.

chairman, a director or managing owner of the ship – then the wrong is committed 'personally' by the company.[38]

It had been held that in the ordinary way, a shipping company's marine superintendent is not in sufficient control of the company's affairs to fix the latter with 'personal' liability,[39] and if the facts in *The Lady Gwendolen* had been only those stated above, the owners would have been entitled to limit their liability. There were, however, additional facts. Neither the company's assistant managing director in charge of shipping nor the traffic manager had displayed any interest in navigational matters, which it was their duty to do. By leaving these entirely to the marine superintendent the latter's negligence had become their own and thus the company's.[40]

Since 1948 the Crown has also been able to claim limitation in respect of H.M. Ships.[41] In 1951 a Government department tried to exercise this right for the first time when next-of-kin of civilians, who had lost their lives in a collision between a submarine and a Swedish vessel in the Thames estuary, sued the Admiralty.[42] The latter admitted 75 per cent of the blame, but brought a limitation action. The Court recognized the right to limit liability in principle but dismissed this action, because the Admiralty itself had been at fault, and not only the commander of the submarine. According to the evidence it was technically impossible to fit Regulation lights on submarines. When travelling on the surface at night their lights were so close to each other that the ship appeared to be far smaller than it in fact was. This had been a major cause of the disaster. Instructions on submarine lights were issued by the Third Sea Lord, a member of the Board of Admiralty, whose failure to obey the

---

38 *Lennard's Carrying Company* v. *Asiatic Petroleum Company* [1915] A.C. 705. Similar enquiries must be made of the structure of a state trading company, *The Garden City* [1982] 2 Lloyd's Rep. 382.

39 *Smitton* v. *Orient Steam Navigation Co.* (1907) 12 Com. Cas. 270.

40 Similarly, directors who merely send out circulars containing safety rules, without impressing on crews the need to observe them, make their company guilty of 'actual fault or privity' if the rules are disregarded; *The Anonity: Everard* v. *London and Thames Haven Oil Wharves* [1961] 1 Lloyd's Rep. 203.

41 Crown Proceedings Act 1947, s. 5.

42 *The Truculent* [1951] 2 Ll. L.R. 308, 314.

law, it was held, involved the Admiralty in the same way as a breach of duty by a director involves a limited company.[43]

Returning from corporate owners to individual owners, the following problem has arisen. What happens if the owner is also the master of the ship, and his negligence causes a collision? Can such a person limit his liability or will he be disqualified on the ground of his 'actual fault or privity'? The answer is that the decision depends on which hat he was wearing when negligent, the owner's bowler or the master's cap.

Illustration: *The Annie Hay: Coldwell-Horsfall v. West Country Yacht Charters Ltd*[44]

A collision was due to the negligent navigation of the master, who also owned the offending vessel.

Held: He was entitled to limit his liability. According to the Merchant Shipping (Liability of Shipowners and Others) Act 1958, s. 3(2), the privilege is enjoyed in respect of 'act or omission of any person in his capacity as master or member of the crew ...', and these words were wide enough to cover also a master who happens to be also the owner of the vessel. Such a person would lose the limitation privilege if his fault had been in his capacity of owner, for instance, failure to pass on or observe Admiralty or DoT instructions, or to install proper navigational equipment.[45]

One final point is in practice very important. The burden of proof is on the *shipowner* to show that he has not been guilty of 'actual fault or privity'.[46] This may be very difficult to show.

Illustration: *The Marion: Grand Champion Tankers v. Norpipe A/S*[47]

While weighing anchor the *Marion* fouled the Ekofisk oil pipeline causing over US$25 million damages. Her owners claimed to limit to £982 292. The master had been using an uncorrected chart dating back to 1953, although an up-to-date chart showing the pipeline was available in the chartroom. A

---

43 The decision would now go the other way because of Rule 1(c) of the Collision Regulations 1972, as amended *supra*, Section 21.2. When a government determines that a naval vessel of special construction (this includes a submarine) cannot fully comply with the rules with regard to visibility of lights without interfering with the vessel's military purpose, such vessel shall comply with the rules in 'the closest possible' way. Had this rule existed when *The Truculent* was decided, the question of personal fault would not have arisen, *Marsden* (1961) para. 651.

44 [1968] 1 All E.R. 657.

45 Or failure to appoint a competent engineer, *cf. The Alastor* [1981] 1 Lloyd's Rep. 581.

46 *The Norman* [1960] 1 Lloyd's Rep. 1.

47 [1984] A.C. 563.

year before the collision a Liberian Inspection had disclosed the poor state of the charts and the master had been instructed by an employee of the ship managers to remedy the defects.

Held: The failure to have a system to check on the master's corrections of charts constituted actual fault or privity: the up-dating of charts was not a matter that could be left entirely to masters. Further, the managing director of the ship managers was also guilty of actual fault as, although he was unaware of the Liberian Report, he should have had a system to ensure that such important matters were drawn to his attention while he was away on business. Finally, the owners could not prove that these faults did not cause the incident as, if there had been a proper system of supervision and reporting, the master might have changed his practices, or been sacked.

22.2.5   AMOUNT OF LIMITATION

We now come to the last question – the extent to which damages may be limited. When his privilege was first introduced in 1734[48] the value of the ship and freight was taken as the measure. As we have seen, some countries retain this rule, but in Britain a more precise method of calculation based on tonnage was introduced by the Merchant Shipping Acts of 1854 and 1862. This method was substantially re-enacted in s. 503 of the 1894 Act.[49]

The tonnage used for limitation calculations is for sailing ships the net tonnage. For powered vessels the matter is a little more complicated because one has to add to the net tonnage the engine-room space deduction (or propelling power allowance as it is sometimes called).[50] This can only be found by looking at the ship's tonnage certificate. The 1969 Tonnage Convention[51] retained the concept of gross and net tonnage, but the calculation is based on a logarithmic formula which does not record any propelling power allowance. Thus, in order to calculate the limitation tonnage of post-1982 ships under the 1957 Convention a remeasurement will be required under the old tonnage measurement system.[52] Of course this will only be necessary in the event of a particular ship being involved in a collision.

---

48 7 Geo. 2, c. 15.
49 As amended, e.g., by the Merchant Shipping (Liability of Shipowners and Others) Act 1958.
50 Merchant Shipping Act 1894, s. 503(2)(a) as amended by the Merchant Shipping Act 1984, s. 12.
51 See Section 3.4, *supra*.
52 Merchant Shipping (Tonnage) Regulations 1967 (S.I. No. 172) as amended.

A foreign ship must be measured in accordance with British law. Where this is impossible the court will give particulars of dimensions of the vessel to a DoT surveyor who will issue a certificate, stating what in his opinion the tonnage of the ship would have been if measured in accordance with British Law.[53]

The tonnage of a warship is determined by measuring it according to merchant shipping rules or directions, the Chief Ships Surveyor of the DoT estimating the tonnage according to such rules.[54]

Where a tug has one or more ships in tow it is not possible to treat the whole 'flotilla' as one unit. If the tug alone is at fault its owner is entitled to limit according to the tonnage of the tug alone,[55] even where he is also the owner of the rest of the flotilla.[56] This may be hard on a third party victim as tugs have very low limits of liability. If the victim can find faults of tug *and* tow then the limits of both will be available.[57]

To cope with the problem of small ships the 1957 Convention, Art. 3(5) provided that a ship should be deemed to have a minimum tonnage of 300 tons. But in British law the minimum only applies to personal injury and death claims.[58] Property claimants will be met by the actual limitation tonnage of the ship even if it is below 300 tons.

Until 1958 the limit of liability was £15 per ton where the claim was for damages for loss of life or personal injury only, and £8 per ton where the claim was for property damage only. The 1957 Limitation Convention did not use sterling as its unit of limitation but chose instead to have twin limits of 3100 'gold francs' and 1000 'gold francs' per ton. The DoT would then convert these figures into sterling by issuing periodic statutory instruments.[59]

This practice of using gold francs became inconvenient because of the decline in the use of gold as an international standard and uncertainties about whether 'official' or market values of gold were to be used. Rapid fluctuations of currency also meant that more statutory instruments had to be made to keep pace. So in 1979 a Protocol was added to the 1957

53 Merchant Shipping Act 1894, s. 503(2), as amended by the Merchant Shipping Act 1984, s. 12.
54 Crown Proceedings Act 1947, s. 5(5) and (6), as amended by Merchant Shipping (Liability of Shipowners and Others) Act 1958, s. 8(5).
55 *The Bramley Moore* [1964] P. 200.
56 *The Sir Joseph Rawlinson: London Dredging Co.* v. *Greater London Council* [1972] 2 All E.R. 590.
57 See, e.g. *The Smjeli* [1982] 2 Lloyd's Rep. 74.
58 Merchant Shipping (Liability of Shipowners and Others) Act 1958, s. 1.
59 *Ibid.* See e.g. the Merchant Shipping (Sterling Equivalents) (Various Enactments) Order 1984 (S.I. No. 1548) specifying the sums of £159.12 and £51.33 to represent 3100 and 1000 gold francs respectively.

Limitation Convention. This was enacted in the Merchant Shipping Act 1981, which came into force on the same date as the Protocol, 29 November 1984.[60] The Protocol substituted the special drawing right (SDR) of the International Monetary Fund (IMF)[61] for gold francs. A practitioner can obtain the correct SDR rate for a particular day by consulting the *Financial Times*.[62] The conversion is made either on the day when a limitation fund is established, or, if not, the date of judgment.[63] The 1981 Act substituted the figures of 206.67 SDR and 66.67 SDR for 3100 and 1000 gold francs respectively.[64]

Where there are personal injury or death claims only the limit is calculated by multiplying 206.67 SDR by the limitation tonnage of the ship. Where there are property damage claims only, the limit is calculated by multiplying 66.67 SDR by the limitation tonnage of the ship. It might be easier to understand if the following examples are considered:

Table 1

35 000 limitation ton ship
SDR Conversion date — 13 September 1985 = £0.760 157

Claims	Tons	SDR	£	Total
1. Personal claims only (206.67 SDR maximum)	35 000 ×	206.67 ×	0.760 157 =	£5 498 557
2. Property claims only (66.67 SDR maximum)	35 000 ×	66.67 ×	0.760 157 =	£1 773 788

It is obvious from this example that personal claimants are treated much more favourably than property claimants. It does not take much imagination to see that in a major disaster (without personal claims) the

---

60 Merchant Shipping Act 1981 (Commencement No. 3) Order 1984 (S.I. No. 1695).
61 The SDR is calculated daily by the IMF on the basis of the relative market values of a 'basket' of five currencies. The intricacies of fixing the level of the SDR are better described elsewhere see, e.g. L. Bristow, 'Gold Franc – Replacement of Unit of Account' [1978] 1 LMCLQ 31, L. Ward, 'The SDR in Transport Liability Conventions: Some Clarification', (1981) 13 J.M.L.C. 1.
62 The correct rate for 13 September 1985 was 1 SDR = £0.760 157 (*Financial Times*, 16 September 1985). A Treasury Certificate as to the correct equivalent for the SDR is conclusive, Merchant Shipping Act 1981, s. 3.
63 Merchant Shipping Act 1981, s. 1(3).
64 On 13 September 1985, 206.67 SDR = £157.10 and 66.67 SDR = £50.68.

property fund could soon be used up – particularly when a small ship is involved. Where there are several claimant they share the fund *pro rata*.

Table 2
Information as in Table 1: property claimants only

Claimant A suffers
£1 million damages
Claimant B suffers   } Total Limitation Fund = £1 773 788
£2 million damages

A gets one-third of the total   =   £591 263
B gets two-thirds of the total   =   £1 182 525

The same principle would apply if there are many personal claimants.[65]

Where there are both property *and* personal claims the calculation is a little more complicated. Essentially, the personal claimants have approximately the top two-thirds of the total fund (in fact 140 SDR) reserved solely for them. If this does not satisfy all their claims then they can also share in the remaining 66.67 SDR along with all the property claimants.[66]

Table 3
Information as in Table 1

Personal claimants suffer £6 000 000 loss   } Total Limitation
Property claimants suffer £6 000 000 loss   } Fund = £5 498 557
Personal claimants take top 140 SDR:
$$35 000 \times 140 \times 0.760 157 = £3 724 769$$
Personal claims unsatisfied: £2 275 231 } Total Fund
Property claims unsatisfied: £6 000 000   } remaining = £1 773 788

Personal and Property claims share this Fund rateably –

Personal claimants take   £487 694
Property claimants take   £1 286 094

Result:

Personal claimants receive : £3 724 769 + £487 694 = £4 212 463
Property claimants receive :   £1 286 094

65 *Glaholm* v. *Barker* (1866) 2 Eq. 598, 604. Obviously if all the claims together fall below the limit then the claimants are paid in full. The figures given are not in any sense fixed amounts of damages. They are limits on damages which have already been proved (or later will be).
66 *The Victoria* (1888) 13 P.D. 125 laid down the basic principles which are unchanged.

However, it seems that loss of life and personal injury claimants enjoy no such special priority where the owner takes no limitation proceedings, but chooses to sell the ship to satisfy all claims. In that event claims must be paid fully – if necessary from the general assets of the owner.[67] Hovercraft have limits similar to those under the 1957 Convention, but based on the maximum authorized weight of the craft.[68]

Successful claimants will also be entitled to simple interest on any sum paid into court from the date of the collision until the decree of limitation.[69] The limits of liability apply to claims arising on any 'distinct occasion'.[70] That means that if a ship on a voyage from Southampton to New York is involved in separate collisions in each port, there will be two sets of limitation funds available.

22.2.6 DOCK OWNERS;
HARBOUR AND PILOTAGE AUTHORITIES

Under the entirely separate, though similar, provisions of the Merchant Shipping (Liability of Shipowners and Others) Act 1900, owners of docks or canals, or harbour or conservancy authorities[71] are entitled to limit their liabilities for damage caused to vessels or their contents. This generous provision has a peculiar method of calculating the limit. Obviously it is not possible to measure the tonnage of a pier, so the Act fixes the limit according to 66.67 SDR per ton of the largest registered

---

67 *C.P.R.* v. *Storstad* [1920] A.C. 397.

68 Hovercraft Act 1968, s. 1. The Hovercraft (Civil Liability) Order 1979 (S.I. No. 305) Art. 6, fixed the limits of £5.50 and £1.57 per kg of maximum authorized weight, with a minimum multiplier of 8000 if the weight is less than 8000 kg. See also fn. 2, p. 414, *infra*.

69 *The Garden City (No. 2): Polish Steamship Co.* v. *Atlantic Maritime Co.* [1984] 2 Lloyd's Rep. 37, where the court awarded interest of £223 178 on a limitation fund of £395 341: the collision took place in 1969 and a payment into court was not made until 1978. A claimant who wanted compound interest would have to decide whether to accept the payment into court, or to fight on in the hope of, e.g. finding 'actual fault or privity'. See also the Administration of Justice Act 1982, s. 15, and the Judgments Act 1838, s. 17; Judgment Debts (Rate of Interest) Order 1985 (S.I. No. 437 (L.3)); Section 21.6.4, *supra*.

70 Art. 2(1); S. 503(3), Merchant Shipping Act 1894.

71 As defined in the Merchant Shipping Act 1894, s. 742. 'Dock' is defined widely in the 1900 Act, s. 2(4) to include wet docks and basins, tidal docks and basins, locks, cuts, entrances, dry docks, graving docks, gridirons, slips, quays, wharves, piers, stages, landing-places and jetties. Under s. 2(5) 'owners' includes persons or authorities having the control and management of any dock or canal. This would be relevant to determining if there was 'actual fault or privity'.

British ship which, at the time of such loss or damage occurring, is, or
within the period of five years previously has been, within the area over
which the dock owner or authority has performed any duty or exercised any power.[72]

There may be all sorts of practical problems in finding out the
identity and tonnage of the biggest ship that had visited in the given
period, although vessels built in, or merely passing through, the area
are not taken into consideration. What is clear is that the protection does
not apply to personal injury or death claims, or to claims against the
individual servants of the dock owner or harbour authority.[73] It would
extend to liabilities arising out of a harbour master's wrongful exercise
of his powers under the Dangerous Vessels Act 1985.[74] A dock owner
may claim the benefit of limitation even if in the special case he was
doing work to a ship in his dock as a ship repairer.[75]

Pilotage authorities, which are not wealthy commercial enterprises,
are given special protection by the Pilotage Act 1983.[76] The mere fact
that an authority has granted or renewed a licence does not make an
authority liable for the faults of that pilot.[77] However, they may be at
fault themselves in employing incompetent pilots. For this, as well as
their vicarious liability for the faults of pilots employed by them, they
are entitled to limit their liability to £100 plus the amount of the pilotage
charges for the voyage in question.[78] The authority might also be liable
for its own organizational faults, e.g. in failing to provide an adequate
pilotage system.[79] In such circumstances, where loss or damage is
caused to any vessel, goods on board, or any other property or rights of
any kind (on land or water, moveable or not) the pilotage authority can
limit its liability to £100 multiplied by the number of pilots holding
licences from the authority for that district.[80] The authority will not be

---

72 S. 2(1) as amended by the Merchant Shipping Act 1981, s. 1; Crown Proceedings
   Act 1947, s. 7.
73 *Mason* v. *Uxbridge Boat Centre and Wright* [1980] 2 Lloyd's Rep. 592. This was
   almost certainly due to an oversight in the Merchant Shipping (Liability of
   Shipowners and Others) Act 1958.
74 S. 2. See Section 8.8.3, *supra.*
75 *The Ruapehu* [1927] A.C. 523; *The Ruapehu (No. 2)* [1929] P. 305.
76 See p. 397, *supra,* for the pilot's individual limit of £100: and fn. 86, *infra.*
77 Pilotage Act 1983, s. 17.
78 S. 42, and see fn. 9, p. 415, *infra.*
79 *The Circassia: Anchor Line (Henderson Brothers) Ltd.* v. *Dundee Harbour Trustees*
   (1922) 38 T.L.R. 299.
80 S. 55, re-enacting provisions in the Pilotage Authorities (Limitation of Liability)
   Act 1936. See also fn. 9, p. 415, *infra.*

entitled to limit if it is guilty of 'actual fault or privity'.[81] Of course, the authority's right to limit if it is liable as *shipowner,* is unaffected.[82]

22.3   THE 1976 LIMITATION CONVENTION: MERCHANT SHIPPING ACT 1979

As noted earlier, the 1976 Limitation Convention is designed to replace the 1957 Limitation Convention internationally and on 1 December 1986, ss. 17, 19 of the Merchant Shipping Act 1979 were brought into force. Section 17 gives the 1976 Convention, as contained in Sch. 4, Part I, the force of law. This is a sensible method of drafting as it avoids the problems in the earlier legislation caused by attempts to rewrite the 1957 Convention into English legal jargon. Provisions particular to the UK are contained in Sch. 4, Part II. The main provisions of the 1976 Convention as enacted in the 1979 Act will now be considered.

22.3.1   PERSONS ENTITLED TO LIMIT

In addition to the persons entitled to limit under the 1957 Convention, Art. 1 of the 1976 Convention extends the privilege to insurers and salvors. In some countries insurers can be sued directly under so-called 'direct-action' statutes. It is now clear that they will be entitled to limit to the same extent as their insured.[83] For salvors *The Tojo Maru*[84] is reversed to the extent that they are undertaking services in direct connection with salvage operations. A salvor will be able to limit when, for instance, he puts members of a salvage team on board a stricken vessel and they cause damage or loss.[85] A licensed pilot's right to limit is unaffected.[86]

22.3.2   CRAFT SUBJECT TO LIMITATION

The right to limit applies whether the ship in question is sea-going or not.[87] Structures (completed or not) launched and intended for use in

---

81 S. 55(1), (4).   82 S. 58.

83 Art. 1(6). See generally P. Griggs and R. Williams *Limitation of Liability for Marine Claims* (1986) and *Limitation of Shipowners' Liability: The New Law* (ed. Gaskell) (1986).

84 [1972] A.C. 242, Section 22.2.3, *supra.*   85 Art. 1(3).

86 Pilotage Act 1983, s. 42: see Chapter 19 and also Section 22.3.6, *infra* The 1986 Pilotage Bill proposes a limit of £1000 plus pilotage charges.

87 Merchant Shipping Act 1979, Sch. 4, Part II, para. 2.

navigation as a ship (or a part of it) are also subject to limitation.[88] The 1976 Convention does not apply to floating platforms constructed for the purpose of exploring or exploiting the sea-bed, or its subsoil: nor does it apply to hovercraft.[89] But there is nothing to stop the UK making special provision for such platforms – as it has for hovercraft.[90]

22.3.3   CLAIMS SUBJECT TO LIMITATION

Claims which are subject to limitation include those in respect of: death or personal injury; damage to property (including harbour works) on board or in direct connection with the operation of the ship or with salvage operations;[91] loss of, or delay in, the carriage of goods or passengers; infringements of other, non-contractual, rights; wreck raising; removal or destruction of cargo; efforts by third parties to minimize loss caused by the defendant.[92] The wreck raising provision – like that under the 1957 Convention – will not be brought into force until a fund is set up to compensate harbour authorities.[93]

Article 3 excludes certain claims from limitation, e.g. those resulting from oil pollution or nuclear damage.[94]

22.3.4   LOSS OF THE RIGHT TO LIMIT

Article 4 of the 1976 Convention makes a significant change by doing away with the uncertain concept of 'actual fault or privity'. It replaces it by a test which will make it much harder to 'break' limitation. In exchange for this test – which should make most of the limits unbreakable – owners' representatives were willing to accept higher limits of liability.

---

88 *Ibid.*, para. 12.

89 Art. 15(5).

90 Hovercraft Act 1968, s. 1; Hovercraft (Civil Liability) Order 1986 (S.I. No. 1305). Merchant Shipping Act 1979, Sch. 5. The 1986 Order increases the old limits, so that hovercraft will be treated, broadly, in the same way as ships.

91 See, *The Tojo Maru* [1972] A.C. 242. Note that under the Merchant Shipping Act 1979, s. 35, claims by crew members against their owners are treated in the same way as those under the Merchant Shipping Act 1894 and are not usually subject to limitation: see Section 22.2.3 *supra*.

92 Art. 2.

93 Art. 2(d); Merchant Shipping Act 1979, Sch. 4, Part II, para. 3. This is not likely to happen.

94 Merchant Shipping Act 1979, Sch. 4, Part II, para. 4. These are dealt with under special liability and limitation regimes, e.g. the Merchant Shipping (Oil Pollution) Act 1971 and the Nuclear Installations Act 1965, Sections 25.2.2, 25.2.3, *infra*..

It must be proved that the loss resulted from the personal act or omission of the person seeking to limit, committed with the intent to cause such loss, or recklessly and with knowledge that such loss would probably result.

Under this test the burden of proof is on the *claimant*. This means that – unlike before – if there is doubt about the personal misconduct of the owner he will be entitled to limit. One might say that the 'privilege' has become a right.

The claimant must also satisfy a high degree of proof under the new test. Deliberate actions designed to cause loss will be rare, and the claimant will have to show more than mere fault of the owner (or other person seeking to limit). He will have to show 'recklessness' which is a state of mind short of intention but beyond carelessness. An example would be doing an act which created an obvious risk or turning a 'blind eye' to it – thus demonstrating a willingness to accept the risk.

This state of mind could certainly not be attributed to the ship managers in *The Marion,* considered earlier, as although they were held to be careless their intentions were always to run the ship as safely as possible. The same could be said of the owners and marine superintendent of *The Lady Gwendolen.* Her master, though, knew full well the risks of navigating at full speed in fog with poor radar monitoring and was reckless.

However, under the new Art. 4 test the claimant must show not only recklessness, but *also* 'knowledge that such loss would *probably* result'. The master of the *Lady Gwendolen* presumably thought the action he was taking in breaking the Collision Regulations involved a small risk, not a probability, of loss.[95] This 'extra' element of the test will make it impossible to break the limits, except in the most blatant of cases.

22.3.5   AMOUNT OF LIMITATION

The limits of liability under Art. 6 of the 1976 Convention will be significantly higher than under the 1957 Convention.

Limitation according to distinct occasion and tonnage is retained, but the 1976 Convention will take for its limitation tonnage the gross

95 For a similar view of the actions of an aircraft pilot, see *Goldman* v. *Thai International Airways* [1983] 3 All E.R. 693, 699.

tonnage measured under the 1969 Tonnage Convention.[96] The use of the latter Convention alone will result in some ships having a much greater tonnage for limitation purposes. Some ships, such as container ships, vehicle carriers or supply boats may have their tonnage increased by two or three times.[97]

The overall limits have been increased, but instead of the same rate per ton being payable whatever the size of the vessel, there will be a sliding scale as the size increases. The idea is to weight the limits to take account of the fact that small ships can cause great damage. The top two thirds of the limits is reserved, as before, for personal claimants and the SDR is the unit of limitation.[98] The limits are best seen in tabular form.

Table 4

Claims	Tonnage slices		SDR
A. Part reserved for	1. tonnage not exceeding	500	333 000 SDR
personal injury	AND 2. for each ton from	501 – 3000	500 SDR per ton
and death claims	AND 3. for each ton from	3001 – 30 000	333 SDR per ton
	AND 4. for each ton from	30 001 – 70 000	250 SDR per ton
	AND 5. for each ton from	70 001 upwards	167 SDR per ton
B. Other claims	1. tonnage not exceeding	500	167 000 SDR
	AND 2. for each ton from	501 – 30 000	167 SDR per ton
	AND 3. for each ton from	30 001 – 70 000	125 SDR per ton
	AND 4. for each ton from	70 001 upwards	83 SDR per ton

A simple example for 'other', e.g. property, claims will best display how the calculation is done. The basic point is that under the 1976 Convention there is not one stage in that calculation, but a number.

---

96 See Sections 3.4 and 22.2.5, *supra*. Where a ship's tonnage has not been and cannot be ascertained under the Merchant Shipping (Tonnage) Regulations 1982 (S.I. No. 841) the best available evidence of her measurements must be used for limitation purposes: see the Merchant Shipping (Liability of Shipowners and Others) (Calculation of Tonnage) Order 1986 (S.I. No. 1040).

97 See, M. Corkhill, *The Tonnage Measurement of Ships*, (2nd edn 1980), pp. 49–50.

98 The conversion date is that when the limitation fund is constituted, payment made, or security given; Art. 8. Interest on the limitation fund is set at 12 per cent, Merchant Shipping (Liability of Shipowners and Others) (Rate of Interest) Order 1986 (S.I. No. 1932).

Table 5

35 000 limitation ton ship
SDR Conversion date-13 September 1985 = £0.760 157

Claims	Tonnage slices			Tons × SDR	Total SDR
'Other'	1.	0– 500	at [fixed]	[fixed]	167 000
claims	2.	501–30 000	at 167 SDR	29 500×167	4 926 500
only	3. 30 001–35 000		at 125 SDR	5 000×125	625 000
					5 718 500

Limit: 5 718 500 SDR × £0.760 157 = £4 346 958

The principle on which personal injury or death limits are calculated is the same, although one point should be noted. Where there are personal claims *only*, the limit will be the combined total of Table 1, Parts A and B.[99] This is shown in Table 6, below.

Table 6

Claims	Tonnage slices		SDR per ton
Total fund	1. tonnage not exceeding	500	500 000 SDR
available	AND 2. for each ton from	501–3000	667 SDR per ton
Personal injury	AND 3. for each ton from	3001–30 000	500 SDR per ton
and death claims	AND 4. for each ton from	30 001–70 000	375 SDR per ton
(only)	AND 5. for each ton from	70 001 upwards	250 SDR per ton

A further example (Table 7) shows that the calculation is similar to that in Table 5.

99 This is because Art. 6 of the 1976 Convention gives only the equivalents of the 140 SDR (Table 4.A) and 66.67 SDR (Table 4.B) of the 1957 Convention.

Table 7
35 000 limitation ton ship
SDR Conversion date–13 September 1985 = £0.760 157

Claims		Tonnage slices			Tons×SDR	Total SDR
Personal injury and death claims (only)	1.	0– 500	at	[fixed]	[fixed]	500 000
	2.	501– 3 000	at	667 SDR	2 500×667	1 667 500
	3.	3 001–30 000	at	500 SDR	27 000×500	13 500 000
	4.	30 001–35 000	at	375 SDR	5 000×375	1 875 000
						17 542 500

Limit: 17 152 500 SDR×£0.760 157 = £13 335 054

A mixed personal injury/death and property claim would be dealt with in exactly the same way as in Table 3 under the 1957 Convention. The personal claimants would have sole access to the figures in Table 4A. For any shortfall they would share rateably with the other claimants the figures in Table 4B.

Salvors not operating from their own vessels are given a deemed limit of 1500 tons.[1]

The Tables show that the Convention lays down a minimum tonnage of 500 tons. The UK has fixed its own limits for small craft (of less than 300 tons) at half the Convention rates.[2]

There is also a separate limit of liability for claims by passengers against the ship in which they are being carried. This is 46 666 SDR (£35 473) multiplied by the total number of passengers which the ship is *certified* to carry, but with a maximum of 25 million SDR (£19 003 925).[3] The maximum limit would normally be relevant only in the event of a disaster to a cruise liner such as the *Queen Elizabeth 2* The passenger

1 Art. 6.3. This is the approximate size of a large salvage tug.
2 As allowed by Art. 15(2): The Merchant Shipping Act 1979, Sch. 4, Part II, para. 5, substitutes the figures of 166 667 SDR and 83 333 SDR for those of 333 000 SDR and 167 000 SDR, given in Art. 6: see Table 4, A.1 and B.1. From 1 December 1986 the hovercraft limits are set by the Hovercraft (Civil Liability) Order 1986 (S.I. No. 1305), varying with type of claim and maximum operational weight, as in Tables 4A and 4B, but with the following figures. (4A) — £142 014 (0–8000 kg); or £276 601 (if 8001–13 000 kg) with £15.98 per kg (13 001–80 000 kg) and £10.64 per kg (80 001 kg upwards). (4B) — £59 560 (0–8000 kg) or £166 378 (if 8001–13 000 kg) with £4.48 per kg (13 001 kg upwards).
3 Art. 7. Figures calculated as at 13 September 1985. The maximum is reached when there are over 535 passengers who may be carried. The Certificate is that issued under s. 274, Merchant Shipping Act 1894; Sch. 4, Part II, para. 6.

limit takes effect subject to any lower individual limit that might be available under the Athens Convention 1974.[4] It will be recalled that this Convention allows a limit of 46 666 SDR *per passenger:* the 1976 Convention overall passenger limit applies no matter how many are *actually* carried.[5]

22.3.6 DOCK OWNERS; PILOTAGE AND HARBOUR AUTHORITIES

The Merchant Shipping Act 1979 updates the Merchant Shipping (Liability of Shipowners and Others) Act 1900 in two ways. First, the actual fault or privity test is replaced by that in Art. 4 of the 1976 Convention.[6] Secondly, the limit is calculated according to the 'other claims' part of Art. 6, i.e. Table 4B.[7]

The limits of pilotage authorities under the Pilotage Act 1983[8] are unaffected, but the 1976 Convention Art. 4 test will replace 'actual fault or privity'.[9]

22.4 EXCLUSION OF LIABILITY

It is convenient to deal here with related statutory provisions that do not limit liabilities but exclude[10] them altogether. Under the Merchant Shipping Act 1894, s. 502 the owner[11] of a British ship has no liability

4 The Athens Convention rather like the Hague and Hague–Visby Rules, operates to limit each individual claim before claims are aggregated for the purposes of global limitation. See Section 18.2.4, *supra.*

5 Thus, the 1976 Convention limit for a ship certified to carry 10 passengers would be 466 660 SDRs, even if only one passenger were carried.

6 See Section 22.3.4, *supra.*

7 Merchant Shipping Act 1979, Sch. 5, para. 1, and subject to the UK small ships provisions in Sch. 4, Part II, para. 5. There may be practical difficulties in discovering the largest British ship to have visited the port, given the use of the 1969 Tonnage Convention measurement in the 1976 Limitation Convention: see Section 22.2.5, *supra.*

8 Ss. 42, 55: see Section 22.2.6, *supra.*

9 Pilotage Act 1983, s. 55(1). The Pilotage Bill 1986 proposes a limit of £1000 plus charges.

10 For the treatment of contractual exclusions of liability and the Unfair Contract Terms Act 1977, see Sections 4.2.3, 18.1, 18.2, *supra*, and 23.3 *infra.*

11 As well as charterers, managers, operators and other persons to whom the privilege of limitation was extended by the Merchant Shipping (Liability of Shipowners and Others) Act 1958, s. 8(1) and 8(4): see, e.g., Sections 4.2.3, 10.1 *supra*, and 23.3 *infra.*

where goods on board his ship are lost or damaged by fire, or water used to extinguish it.[12] The owner can rely, apparently, on this statutory exception even where the fire was caused by unseaworthiness.[13]

The same section also exempts the owner from liability if gold, silver, diamonds, watches, jewels or precious stones are lost or damaged by robbery or theft,[14] but only if their true nature and value have not been declared at the time of shipment.[15] The owner is not entitled to these s. 502 privileges if he has been guilty of actual fault or privity.[16]

Section 502 was replaced by s. 18, Merchant Shipping Act 1979 as from 1 December 1986. This substantially re-enacts s. 502, but, in particular, replaces the 'actual fault or privity test' with the intention/recklessness test from the 1976 Limitation Convention.[17]

---

12 *The Diamond* [1906] P. 282.
13 *Dreyfus* v. *Tempus* [1931] A.C. 726.
14 Theft Act 1968, s. 32. The owner is exempted even if the robbery is committed by an employee, *Acton* v. *Castle Mail Packets Co.* (1895) 1 Com. Cas. 135.
15 E.g., if the valuables are contained in a passenger's luggage, *Smitton* v. *Orient Steam Navigation* (1907) 12 Com. Cas. 270.
16 See Section 22.2.4, *supra*.
17 See Section 22.3.4, *supra*.

23
TOWAGE

23.1 INTRODUCTION

W E have already considered the tortious liabilities which a tug or tow
owner may incur towards third parties as a result of negligence.[1]

It is worth recalling that in the ordinary way the control of operations
is with the tow, and the latter will be responsible for damage which the
tug may inflict on a third party.[2] Similarly, if the tow is in charge of a
pilot the tug has to obey the latter's directions.[3]

In this chapter we are looking at the relationship of the tug to the tow
as governed by the towage contract. It is important to keep these two
issues separate because the third party will not usually be interested in
the towage contract. It may be quite common for a tug to be obliged to
pay a third party for negligence, but afterwards to be able to claim an
indemnity for this amount from the tow.

'A towage service may be described as the employment of one vessel
to expedite the voyage of another, when nothing more is required than
the accelerating (of) her progress.'[4] This is a useful definition, but
before laying down the law relating to the contract of towage it will be
convenient to picture the conditions which give rise to a towage contract. In the first place we find the towage of craft without motive
power, such as the towage of barges in a harbour. In the second place we
find increasingly the towage of ships whose engines are so strong that
their wash endangers docks, piers and smaller craft in the harbour, and
who for that reason must abandon their propelling power. Nor are such
big ships sufficiently handy for navigating in very narrow waters, and
for the purpose of docking and sailing they often require the assistance

1 See Section 21.1, *supra*.
2 *The Sinquasi* (1880) 5 P.D. 241.
3 *Spaight* v. *Tedcastle* (1881) 6 App. Cas. 217.
4 *Per* Dr Lushington, *The Princess Alice* (1849) 3 W. Rob. 138, 139, 140; 166 E.R.
914, 915.

of several tugs. Since it became possible to extract oil from the sea bed the towage of drilling rigs from shipyard to position has become common. Finally, towage may become necessary by reason of a breakdown of a ship's engines. In the last case the tug will usually have rescued the ship from danger, and the relation between tug and tow will then be governed by the law of salvage,[5] in which the general law that applies to ordinary business transactions is excluded, and a form of emergency law prevails. Here, however, we are only concerned with towage contracts proper.

23.2   IMPLIED TERMS

In practice, most towage contracts contain detailed express terms, as we shall see. If no such terms are agreed the courts may have to imply terms, as with any other contract.[6] The contract between tug and tow is one of service, and so the Supply of Goods and Services Act 1982, Part II will imply certain basic terms into the contract. Thus a tugowner must carry out the towage with reasonable care and skill[7] and within a reasonable time.[8] If the contract does not fix a price, he is entitled to make a reasonable charge.[9] Of course, if he fails to complete the contract service he will usually be entitled to no remuneration.

The courts have also implied terms into towage contracts, in favour of both tugs and tows. The owner of the tow must disclose fairly what sort of service he requires and to have the tow ready for that service.

Illustration: *Elliott Steam Tug Co.* v. *New Malden Steam Packet Co.* [10]
A tug was hired 'for towing an 800-ton lighter from West Mersea, Essex, to Chatham'. The owners of the barge failed to disclose that for several years it had been lying on a mudbank at the end of a very narrow and shallow channel and that it would be practically impossible for a tug of a size sufficient to tow such a large barge to reach the latter. The tugowners claimed damages for not being able to fulfil the contract.

5 See Chapter 24, *infra*.
6 See Sections 4.2 and 5.3.
7 S. 13. This term was also implied by the courts, *The Ratata: Preston* v. *Biornstad* [1898] A.C. 513. Failure in the duty would make the tugowner liable in damages.
8 S. 14. The contract, or the course of dealing between the parties, may fix a different time.
9 S. 15.
10 (1937) 59 Ll. L.R. 35.

Held: The action succeeded. *Per* Goddard J, at p. 39: 'It was the duty of the defendants to put the lighter into such a position that a tug of this size could take it out'. This duty they had broken and had not disclosed that the service required was more than an ordinary towage from one point to another.

Just as a shipowner, when letting his ship to a charterer, impliedly warrants that the ship is seaworthy, i.e., fit for the contemplated service, so a tug must be fit to perform the particular towage contracted for by the parties. This implied warranty of fitness not only extends to the tug itself, but also requires that crew, tackle and equipment should be equal to their task in the weather and circumstances reasonably to be expected.[11]

Illustration: *The Maréchal Suchet*[12]
A tug was supplied for the towage from Falmouth to London of the *Maréchal Suchet*. Since the tug was not fit for the voyage, a south-westerly wind drove both tug and tow to leeward so that the tow took the ground. The tug got the tow off with the assistance of other vessels and all of them claimed a salvage reward. This was rejected with regard to the contract tug, the learned judge laying down at p. 11: 'It was contended for the plaintiffs (the owners of the tug) that the contract was for a specified or named tug, the *Guiana*, and that, as the *Guiana* was supplied, the contractors fulfilled their contract, and that the owners and master of the *Maréchal Suchet* undertook all responsibility as to the efficiency of the tug. [On the evidence the learned judge came to the opposite conclusion.] The contract, therefore, was for the towage of the *Maréchal Suchet* by a tug to be supplied by the plaintiffs. This being so, the owners of the tug must be taken to have contracted that the tug should be efficient.' Only *vis major* would have excused them.

This case is not altogether conclusive, however as the decision was in a salvage case, and not, for instance, in one where the owners of the tow claimed damages against the tug.

23.3   STANDARD TOWAGE CONTRACTS
GENERALLY

In practice tugowners have been able to use their strong bargaining position in ports to insist on standard form towage contracts, such as

11 *The Maréchal Suchet* [1911] P. 1; *The West Cock*, [1911] P. 23, 208.
12 [1911] P. 1.

the UK Standard Conditions for Towing and Other Services (UKSTC). These, in very general terms, place nearly all the risks of towing on the tow.[13] Such conditions could potentially fall foul of the Restrictive Trade Practices Act 1976, but the UKSTC (1983) have been approved by the Office of Fair Trading.

Most tugowners' contracts will contain exclusions and indemnities. These, to a greater or lesser extent, will exclude the liability of tug to tow and provide that the tow shall indemnify the tug for loss suffered by the tug.

In some countries, towage contracts which purport to exclude the tug's liability for negligence may be void as being against public policy.[14] In the United Kingdom the courts have taken the view that towage agreements are made by businessmen on both sides, parties normally dealing at arms length, knowing what they are doing and capable of looking after themselves.[15]

This was a view also taken by Parliament when enacting the Unfair Contract Terms Act 1977.[16] Clauses excluding negligent liability for personal injury and death are completely void.[17] Apart from this, the basic provisions of the Act do not apply to contracts of marine towage – or salvage.[18] There is one exception: when the towage contractor (or salvor) deals with a consumer, e.g. the owner of a dismasted yacht or a pleasure boat with a disabled engine.[19] In these cases the exemption clauses will only apply if they are reasonable.[20]

It should be noted that the parties are free to exclude the terms implied by the Supply of Goods and Services Act 1982,[21] to the extent permitted by the Unfair Contract Terms Act 1977.[22]

13 As the title of the terms suggests, they also apply to other services such as tendering, but discussion here will be confined to towage.
14 *Bisso* v. *Inland Waterways* [1955] A.M.C. 899 (USA). However, the US courts will uphold a clause giving jurisdiction to the English courts even if that would mean the English courts giving effect to exclusion clauses. But, the towage contract must have been freely entered into without any element of undue pressure on the tugowner's part; see *The Chaparral: Zapata Off-Shore Company* v. *The Bremen* [1974] 2 Lloyd's Rep. 315 (Supreme Court, USA). See Section 1.8, *supra.*
15 *The President van Buren* (1924) 16 Asp. M.C. 444.
16 *Cf.* Sections 4.2.3; 18.2.5
17 S. 2(1). Note that the UKSTC (1983) no longer contain clause 4(a) (iii) of the UKSTC (1974) which was such a clause. However, no reported case deals with such an incident. See also UKSTC (1983) clause 4(e).
18 Sch. 1, para. 2(a). For salvage see Chapter 24, *infra.*
19 *Ibid.*
20 Ss. 3, 11.
21 See Section 23.2, *supra.*
22 Supply of Goods and Services Act 1982, s. 16. Again, this means that exclusions are allowed in business contracts, but must be reasonable in consumer contracts.

But for nearly all commercial towages the Act has avoided the great and damaging uncertainty which would have prevailed if every contract could, after the event, be scrutinized from the point of view of reasonableness at the suit of a disappointed party who, at the time of the contract, had no doubt that he was making a reasonable bargain. If the wide exclusions and indemnities should seem unfair on tow-owners it should be remembered that all such clauses do is to allocate risks which will be covered by insurance. Moreover, the clauses reduce the high legal costs involved in trying to establish negligence or reasonableness.

The approach of the courts will be to interpret the clauses *contra proferentem* (against the person relying on them, in this case the tugowner),[23] but otherwise to enforce them if they clearly give the tugowner the protection he alleges.[24]

23.4   THE UKSTC 1983[25]

We will now consider, briefly, some of the terms of the most widely used towage contract in British ports. It should be noted that the UKSTC have been used in many other countries, e.g. Australia and South Africa, as well as being incorporated into supply boat contracts.[26]

23.4.1   PARTIES TO THE CONTRACT

In order to apply, the UKSTC must, like any other terms, be incorporated into the contract before it is made. This is usually achieved by circulating a rate schedule containing the UKSTC (1983) to all ships' agents in a particular port.[27] When the agents then book a tug they would normally bind the shipowner to the UKSTC (1983).

The tugowner is entitled, under Clause 5, to arrange for a substitute tug to perform the service. Her owner would not normally be entitled

---

23 *The Baltyk* [1948] P. 1; *The Carlton* [1931] P. 186.

24 See generally *Photo Production Ltd* v. *Securicor Transport Ltd* [1980] A.C. 827.

25 A 1986 revision added a new clause 9 dealing with choice of law and jurisdiction; see Appendix 10.

26 E.g. SUPPLYTIME 1974. Market conditions may force tugowners to offer less onerous terms, such as the Netherlands Towing Conditions 1951. Although the UKSTC (1983) are used for ocean towages, two new international ocean towage contracts were published in October 1985. TOWCON and TOWHIRE: see Section 23.5, *infra*.

27 *Cf. Walumbra* v. *Australian Coastal Shipping Commission* [1964] 2 Lloyd's Rep. 382 (Supreme Court, Victoria).

to benefit from the contract because he was not a party to it.[28] But the UKSTC (1983) clause 5 is a type of Himalaya clause[29] and would make the substitute tugowner party to the contract, allowing him to rely on its terms. Clause 6 seeks to protect the tugowner's employees.

The towage contract might normally be expected to bind only the owner of the tow. However, it is quite common for the contract to be made by the tow's charterer, e.g., a demise or time charterer.[30] The UKSTC (1983) is a contract between the 'hirer' and the tugowner. Clause 2 provides that if the hirer is not the owner of the vessel he represents that he has authority to bind the owner. If he does not have this authority he will be liable for breach of warranty of authority, but it is unlikely that this would give the tugowner the right to arrest the *owner's* vessel.[31]

23.4.2   DURATION OF THE COVER

In some cases it was doubtful at what moment exactly the towage commenced. The towage contract may be agreed long before the service commences, but it has been decided that in the ordinary way the towage service does not commence until the tow ropes have been passed.[32] For the exception clauses to apply is it necessary, to take one extreme, that the tow rope has been secured or, to take the other extreme, is it enough that the tug has set out to meet the tow? The matter is important because the tug might be damaged before reaching the tow, or it might negligently damage the tow itself before a tow rope had been passed. The UKSTC (1983) entitle the tugowner to the special protections only during the time when he is in that area of special proximity or risk to, or from, the tow[33] – more particularly 'whilst towing'.[34] This period commences at the latest when the tow rope is passed, but it can start earlier, as soon as the tug is in a position to receive orders 'direct'. This means that those on board the tug must reasonably

28 *The Conoco Arrow* [1971] 1 Lloyd's Rep. 86.
29 See Sections 18.1 and 20.1.3, *supra*.
30 This may often happen with the towage of barges, as in the ordinary course of business the barge owner hires his barges to a carrier and it is the latter, and not the owner who in turn engages the tug; see *The Riverman* [1928] P. 33. For 'charterers' see Section 10.3.1, *supra*.
31 See Sections 1.4 and 7.2. But the *hirer's* vessels may be subject to arrest, see Section 7.2.2, *supra*.
32 *The Clan Colquhoun* [1936] P. 153.
33 Clause 4(c) (ii). Appendix 10.
34 Clauses 1(b) (iv), 4. Appendix 10.

expect the tow to give the tug an order to commence operations, e.g. pick up ropes or lines. The tug must be ready to respond to such an order if given; the tug must be within hailing distance.[35]

Illustration: *The Uranienborg*[36]

The tug arrived a short time before the towage was due to commence and while the tow was still discharging at the dock. Though the ships were in hailing distance nobody on board of either was ready to receive or give orders with regard to the picking up of lines, etc. At that moment the tug, owing to her master's faulty navigation, collided with the tow.

Held: When the collision occurred the tug was not yet in a 'position' to receive lines, and the exception clauses did not apply.

The UKSTC (1983) exceptions continue until the converse occurs, i.e. when final orders from the tow to cease operations have been carried out, or when the tow line is finally slipped, whichever is the later. The idea is that the tug shall be safely clear before the special conditions cease to operate. An accidental breakage of the tow line does not necessarily mean that it has been 'finally slipped', if the towage operation has not been abandoned.[37] Nor would the UKSTC (1983) cease to apply if the tug had been requested by the master to cast off temporarily between two berthing operations within a port.[38]

23.4.3   EXCLUSIONS AND INDEMNITIES

The UKSTC (1983) clause 4(a) excludes the tugowner's liability for damage done by the tug from any cause including negligence, or unseaworthiness[39] of the tug. Clause 4(b) makes the tow indemnify the tug for any loss or damage, including sums paid to third parties[40] and

35 *The Apollon: British Transport Docks Board* v. *Apollon (Owners)* [1971] 2 All E.R. 1223.

36 [1936] P. 21.

37 *Australian Coastal Shipping Commission* v. *P.V. Wyuna* (1964) 111 C.L.R. 303 (High Court, Australia). The tug was entitled to an indemnity for salvage expenses.

38 *Howard Smith Industries Ltd* v. *Melbourne Harbour Trust Commissioners* [1970] V.R. 406 (Supreme Court, Victoria). Under the UKSTC (1983) Clause 1(b)(iv) the tug would also be 'standing by'; see Appendix 10. This result is entirely a matter of interpretation of the particular contractual term, *cf. The Refrigerant* [1925] P. 130 (exception clauses) and *The Cap Palos* [1921] P. 458.

39 *Cf. The West Cock* [1911] P. 23, 208 where the clause in question did not exclude unseaworthiness prior to the commencement of the towage.

40 Including personal injury claims by the tug's crew, see *Knapp* v. *Port of London Authority* [1979] 1 Lloyd's Rep. 662.

damage to the tug even if both were caused by the tug's negligence. Thus, to give an extreme example, the tug could negligently cause a collision with a third vessel as a result of which all three sink: the tugowner is not liable for the tow's damage, but the tow has to pay the tugowner for the damages paid by him to the third vessel and for the cost of replacing the tug! Again it must be emphasized that the exclusion in the contract between tug and tow does not bind the third vessel. The tug must pay any damages for which it is liable and then hope to recover these by way of indemnity from the tow.

However, as already noted, the clause 4(a) and (b) claims may only be made when the tug is in a position of proximity or risk to, or from, the tow.[41] The claims are not applicable either if the *tow* can prove that they resulted *directly* and *solely* from *personal* failure of the tugowner[42] to make the tug seaworthy. This would be a very difficult burden to satisfy.

The UKSTC (1983) also exclude liability for war, strikes and delays.[43] But they do not affect any claim by the tugowner or his servants for salvage.[44]

23.5 INTERNATIONAL OCEAN TOWAGE CONTRACTS

Standard forms such as the UKSTC (1983) were devised mainly for towage services in ports although they are sometimes used for ocean towages, e.g. of oil platforms from construction site to offshore oil field. Competition for such work, especially in the North Sea, meant that tugowners could not always insist on forms giving them the wide exclusions and indemnities described in Section 23.4.3 above. This resulted in a wide variety of different contracts being negotiated. In order to provide some uniformity two new ocean towage agreements were developed in 1985, 'TOWHIRE' and 'TOWCON'.[45] These agreements resemble time and voyage charterparties in form and they contain all the detailed terms of the contract, as opposed to the UKSTC (1983) which deal with liability but not matters such as price, or the

---

41 Clause 4(c)(ii).
42 See Sections 22.2.4 and 22.3.4, *infra*.
43 Clauses 5, 7.
44 Clause 6. For the circumstances where a tug may claim salvage during the course of a towage contract, see Section 24.4.2, *infra*.
45 See BIMCO Bulletin, 5/85.

description of tug and tow. The new agreements are subject to English law and jurisdiction.

23.5.1 TOWHIRE

This is a daily hire towage agreement and Part I contains 43 boxes which must be filled in by the parties. These contain details of the tug and tow such as gross tonnage, flag and place of registry, as well as details of their respective Classification Societies and P & I liability insurers. The tow must also declare its maximum length, breadth and towing draft: the tug has to declare its indicated horsepower and certificated bollard pull. The latter may be important in assessing the tug's capacity for the operation – particularly when tugs of several operators are engaged. Other information to be recorded includes the place and date of departure; the place of destination; the contemplated route; the hire payable and details of any advance or mobilization payments.

Part II contains 25 general contractual terms. Like a time charter, it regulates the conditions of payment and additional charges or costs which arise. Thus, under clause 3 the hirer has to pay port expenses and pilotage charges. The tug and tow owners undertake to use 'due diligence' to make their vessels seaworthy,[46] although clause 14 does allow the tugowner to provide a substitute tug.

Clause 16 gives the towowner the right to cancel prior to departure (subject to a cancellation fee). Thereafter he will be liable for hire already due and to damages for lost profit. The clause also allows the tugowner to withdraw his tug from the service for five specified grounds, e.g. delays in port exceeding twenty-one days, or failure to pay hire within seven days of its falling due. But in any case the tugowner must give forty-eight hours notice of the intention to withdraw.[47]

Clause 18 deals with the respective liabilities of the owners and it is important to notice that it is significantly different to clause 4 of the UKSTC (1983). Essentially it deals with liabilities on a 'knock for knock' basis. This means that the tugowner will pay for all personal claims made by his employees (e.g. the tug's crew or a riding crew on the tow) or those on board the tug. He also pays for loss or damage to the tug *and* loss or damage caused by the *tug* to third parties, e.g. by contact with the tug or obstruction. The towowner undertakes a similar responsibility for his vessel and employees. Of course, this contract

---

46 Clauses 12, 13: and see Section 11.3.6, *supra*, for 'due diligence'.
47 *Cf.* Section 16.3, *supra*.

does not directly affect a third party: it provides a fairly simple method for allocating risks between the tugowner and the towowner. If the third party sues the tow for negligent control of the tug[48] which causes the tug to collide with the third party's vessel, the tow must pay the claim. However, it would then be entitled to an indemnity under the 'knock for knock' agreement as the damage resulted from contact with the *tug*. TOWHIRE also contains a Himalaya clause and a war clause.[49]

23.5.2   TOWCON

This is a lump sum towage agreement and many of its clauses are identical to TOWHIRE. Obviously, the main difference is that the tugowner gets paid in a different way. Clause 2 makes the lump sum fully and irrevocably earned according to the various stages specified by the parties in Box 32 on the face of the contract. Thus, the sum could be payable in instalments due, e.g. on signing the agreement, on departure, or arrival. Like voyage charters, TOWCON has to deal with the allocation of the risks of delay.[50] It allows the towowner an agreed amount of 'Free Time' (i.e., laytime) for matters such as the making up of the towage connection. Thereafter he must pay an agreed 'Delay Payment' (i.e., demurrage). Under clause 7, the towowner must give the tugowner notice, within agreed periods, as to when the tow will be ready to depart. If slow steaming is requested by the hirer, the tugowner is entitled, by clause 17, to extra compensation in the form of the appropriate 'Delay Payment'.

48 See Section 21.1, *supra*.
49 Clauses 19, 20. See also Sections 18.1 and 20.1.3, *supra*.
50 See Section 12.5, *supra*.

24
SALVAGE

24.1 INTRODUCTION

WE must now turn to a topic which is very different from those so far discussed in this work, that of salvage. Salvage originates in a sort of maritime equity; it is of very ancient date, and comes into English law from the international maritime codes which existed in all the maritime states of Europe in the Middle Ages. It is indeed a concept not familiar to the common law of England which grew up in a more limited and somewhat narrower *milieu*. Where danger of life and property on land is concerned, English law is chary of recognizing any legal duty to protect it. The common law, in principle, knows but two grounds of civil liability, namely, contract and tort. A person who on his own initiative protects another man's property, does not thereby acquire any right to reward or compensation for the loss he has suffered. Only in exceptional cases, as where the danger originated in another person's negligence, and the rescuer is under a special duty, say a policeman, may he claim to be compensated for the injury he has suffered.[1] But in no case can there be any claim to a reward.

The position is different at sea. There the right to reward for the rescue of maritime property has been recognized since the time of Rome. The right to such a reward is based on the equity that a person who has encountered a danger and has expended work and labour on another ship which has benefited by his exertions should receive some remuneration. Moreover, it is clearly public policy that such rescue work should be undertaken and rewarded in 'the general interest of ships and marine commerce'.[2] This has been recognized in modern

---

1 See Section 21.4.3, *supra* and see A.L. Goodhart, 'Voluntary Assumption of Risk', 5 *Cambridge L.J.* 192.
2 *Per* Dr Lushington, in *The Fusilier* (1865) Brown and Lush 341, 347, 167 E.R. 391, 394.

times by the imposition of the statutory duty to go to the assistance of ships in distress.[3]

The principal rules relating to the law of salvage are old, but the Brussels Salvage Convention 1910[4] provided a set of basic principles of law, most of which were already applied in English Admiralty law. Article 11 required ships to render assistance to those in danger at sea.[5] It is a necessary complement to such a duty that any service be rewarded. This reward is assessed by the Court on equitable principles which, as we shall see, have gradually been systematized: it is not based on any implied contract to pay a reasonable amount.[6] It is important always to recall the public policy element in salvage: that the courts should encourage salvors as much as possible. We shall see later that there are moves to bring salvage law more in tune with modern times, in particular by revising the 1910 Convention. The general conception of salvage has been well put in the following passage:

'The jurisdiction . . . is of a peculiarly equitable character. The right to salvage . . . is a legal liability arising out of the fact that property has been saved, that the owner of the property who has had the benefit of it shall make remuneration to those who have conferred the benefit upon him, notwithstanding that he has not entered into any contract on the subject'[7]

In speaking of salvage both the salvor's service and the salvor's reward are referred to, and for practical purposes a salvor's service has been defined as a

'service which confers a benefit by saving or helping to save a recognized subject of salvage when in danger from which it cannot be extricated unaided, if and so far as the rendering of such service is voluntary in the sense of being attributable neither to a pre-existing obligation nor solely for the interests of the salvor.'[8]

Having thus related the general underlying principles of salvage law we now proceed to a discussion of the incidents of salvage.

---

3 See Section 21.3, *supra*.
4 Convention for the Unification of Certain Rules of Law Relating to Assistance and Salvage at Sea.
5 See Section 21.3, *supra*.
6 Although there may be salvage contracts, see Section 24.9, *infra*.
7 *Per* Sir J. Hannen, *Five Steel Barges* (1890) 15 P.D. 142, 146.
8 *Kennedy* (1985) p. 8. See also Brice (1983). Salvage may apparently be earned for services in non-tidal waters, e.g. of a river or a dock, *The Goring* [1986] 1 Lloyd's Rep. 127.

24.2 MARITIME PROPERTY

24.2.1 GENERAL

The right to salvage arises only if maritime property is saved, that is ship, apparel, cargo or wreckage. Not every property in tidal waters is maritime property. This quality does not extend to buoys or other like structures, but only to vessels used in navigation. Thus, unregistered vessels such as barges and rafts are included.[9] But in *The Gas-Float Whitton (No.2)* it was held that a form of unmanned lightship, though shaped like a boat and moored in tidal waters, could not be salved as it was neither intended nor fitted for navigation. It was said that:

'It is not constructed for the purpose of being navigated or of conveying cargo or passengers. It was, in truth, a lighted buoy or beacon. The suggestion that the gas stored in the float can be regarded as cargo carried by it is more ingenious than sound.'[10]

This approach might be considered rather restrictive and it is unclear how far the many new types of oil exploration and exploitation structures are 'ships' which may be salved.[11] There is every reason in principle to consider offshore mobile structures as craft subject to salvage, particularly where they are manned: production platforms intended to be permanently fixed to the sea-bed may be another matter.[12]

Services rendered to or by an aircraft in, on or over the sea are treated as salvage if salvage would have been awarded for a vessel.[13] Thus when

---

9 *The Gas-Float Whitton (No. 2)* [1897] A.C. 337, 345.

10 *Ibid., per* Lord Herschell, at p. 343.

11 See generally M. Summerskill, *Oil Rigs: Law and Insurance* (1979), pp. 1–85. In 1977 CMI produced a Draft Convention on Offshore Mobile Craft which would have extended the provisions of Maritime Conventions to structures not permanently fixed to the sea-bed which were used for activities such as exploration, exploitation, processing, transport and storage.

12 Some production platforms are towed to the site; others are loaded onto barges and then towed out. The latter could be considered as 'cargo' for this voyage. See also the Merchant Shipping Act 1979, s. 41 and Sections 22.2.2 and 22.3.2, *supra*.

13 Civil Aviation Act 1982, s. 87(1). An aircraft, e.g. a helicopter, may also claim salvage for services rendered, s. 87(2). Both provisions of s. 87 apply to foreign aircraft.

a Harrier jump jet landed on the Spanish ship *Alraigo* in June 1983 after having run out of fuel a salvage award was in order.[14]

24.2.2   LIFE SALVAGE

With regard to the saving of life we have already noticed that a salvage reward is due to a salvor saving the lives of persons endangered on a ship. However, this needs qualification. Although the law of salvage is founded on equitable and humanitarian grounds it did not originally make provision for rewarding the salvors of human life. This is so because the reward is payable out of the property saved, a doctrine which obviously cannot apply to life salvage. In the well-known words of Brett MR:[15]

'[T]here is one element invariably required by Admiralty law in order to found an action for salvage, there must be something saved more than life, which will form a fund from which salvage may be paid, in other words, for the saving of life alone without the saving of ship, freight, or cargo, salvage is not recoverable in the Admiralty Court.'

In modern times, however, the harshness of the doctrine has been softened by the principle that if property be saved at the same time as the lives a salvage award may be made.[16] For in that case there is a fund out of which a reward may be paid.

Illustration 1:   *The Cargo ex Sarpedon*[17]
The *Sarpedon* with passengers and cargo on board was in distress, and passengers and crew as well as part of the cargo were salved by the *Calderon*. The ship and the remainder of the cargo were lost. The *Calderon* was awarded £4000 salvage remuneration, both for the salvage of the lives and the cargo. The owners of the salved cargo moved the Court to determine what proportion of that sum was due in respect of life salvage so that they might recoup themselves for that from the owners of the lost ship.

14 In fact the parties agreed to LOF arbitration at which the ship's owners and crew were eventually awarded £412 000, 123 LMNL, 19/7/1984; see Section 24.8, *infra*. For salvage of Crown Property, see the Crown Proceedings Act 1947, s. 8. Foreign states may, however, plead sovereign immunity: see Section 1.6, *supra*, e.g. *B.V. Bureau Wijsmuller* v. *USA* [1976] A.M.C. 2514. A US naval helicopter ran out of fuel in September 1985 and landed on a small car-carrier whose owners promptly engaged the same lawyer that represented the *Alraigo*! *Fairplay*, 3 October 1985, 5.
15 *The Renpor* (1883) 8 P.D. 115, at p. 117.
16 Merchant Shipping Act 1894, s. 544(1). P & I Club Rules usually cover sums due for life salvage which are not payable by underwriters.
17 (1877) 3 P.D. 28.

Held: Motion dismissed. Since the owners had lost everything they could not be made personally liable for any portion of the salvage remuneration.

Illustration 2: *The Medina*[18]

A ship was wrecked, but passengers and crew were taken off by a salving steamer, and brought to the port of destination. Thereby the passage money was earned by the owner of the wreck.

Held: The freight thereby earned constituted a fund out of which the life salvors might be paid. They had salved something more than life.

But what is the position if there are two sets of salvors, one saving only lives, the other only property? Suppose in a case like the one just related, passengers and crew were taken off by certain boats and, independently, others saved a substantial amount of the cargo. It has been held that a fund was thereby created out of which the life salvors should be remunerated.[19] The position was explained by Bagallay LJ in this way.

'The liability to pay a reasonable amount of salvage to life salvors is imposed upon owners of cargo as well as upon owners of the ship, . . . such liability is not a general personal liability to be enforced in any circumstances whether the ship and cargo are lost or not, but a liability limited to the value of the property saved from destruction . . . as regards the right of live salvors to claim a reasonable amount of salvage, it is immaterial whether the property saved from destruction has been saved by salvors, as the expression is ordinarily understood, or by other means.'[20]

It was provided that, if salvage services are rendered to a British ship anywhere or to a foreign ship in British waters, and no or insufficient property is saved, the DoT may in its discretion award a sum out of the Mercantile Marine Fund.[21]

Moreover, failure to save life if it can be done without danger to the salvor is an offence even if the services are required by subjects of an enemy state in time of war.[22]

18 (1876) 1 P.D. 272; 2 P.D. 5.
19 *Cargo ex Schiller* (1877) 2 P.D. 145, *cf. Cargo ex Sarpedon, supra.* A life salvor has priority over other salvage claimants, see Merchant Shipping Act 1894, s. 544(2).
20 At p. 157, *cf. The Fusilier* (1865), Br. & Lush 341, 167 E.R. 391.
21 Merchant Shipping Act 1894, s. 544(3). Merchant Shipping (Mercantile Marine Fund) Act 1898, s. 1 (1)(b). For financing of the Fund, see s. 676, 1894 Act. However, the s. 544 power has apparently been used only twice since 1938. The last payment was £250 in 1951.
22 Maritime Conventions Act 1911, s. 6. See also Section 21.3, *supra.*

24.3 DANGER

The property or lives must be rescued from danger. What sort of danger does the law require in order to turn an act of assistance into a salvage service? Clearly the danger must be a real one, and must not only exist in the fancy of those to whom the service is rendered. 'However a ship which might be held to be in safety if handled by a skilful master who knows the locality may be in peril if her master is not possessed of such skill and knowledge. Thus, the ignorance of persons on board may add to all the ordinary and natural perils to which a ship is prone so as to constitute the danger to the ship and property in their charge.'[23] An American court made a salvage award when the only real danger was a frightened and incompetent master.[24]

Still, this does not help in determining what is to be regarded as danger for the purposes of salvage; for a ship may be in varying degrees of danger. The courts are well aware that to lay down too strict rules would not be in the public interest since this would discourage salvors. Again, to be too liberal would incite persons to foist salvage services on ships which do not require them and thus inflict more loss than benefit on the ship- and cargo-owners; for the right to an award does not depend on the consent of those in charge of the property salved. The test which has been applied is: would the master, as a reasonably prudent man, if asked whether he required assistance, have answered: 'Yes' or 'No'?[25] The difficulty, as always where reasonable conduct is made the criterion, is to say whether in given circumstances the master should have answered the one way or the other. Decided cases, however, throw a good deal of light on the problem.

Illustration: *The Charlotte*[26]
The vessel during fog, rain, and a very high sea had got into dangerous waters through the master mistaking lights on shore. She was dragging her anchors towards the rocks and came to a stop only after the masts with the entire rigging had been cut overboard. The ship was then noticed by another ship and towed to port.

23 *Kennedy* (1985), p. 134.
24 *The Pendragon Castle* (1924) 5 Fed. Rep. (Ser. 2) 56. See generally, M. Norris, *3A Norris, Benedict on Admiralty* (1980 with supplements).
25 *The Vandyck* (1881) 7 P.D. 42; *The Emilie Galline* [1903] P. 106; *The Port Caledonia and The Anna* [1903] P. 184.
26 (1848) 3 W. Rob. 68, 166 E.R. 888.

Held: The second ship was entitled to a salvage award, for in the circumstances the ship could not have reached the port with masts and rigging gone. *Per* Dr Lushington, 'All services rendered at sea to a vessel in distress are salvage services. It is not necessary, I conceive, that the distress should be immediate and absolute; it will be sufficient if, at the time the assistance is rendered, the vessel has encountered any damage or misfortune which might possibly expose her to destruction if the services were not rendered.'[27]

The result has been summarized thus:[28]

'On the one hand, [the danger] must not be either fanciful or only vaguely possible or have passed by the time the service is rendered. On the other hand, it is not necessary that distress should be actual or immediate or that the danger should be imminent; it will be sufficient if, at the time at which assistance is rendered, the subject-matter has encountered any misfortune or likelihood of misfortune which might possibly expose it to loss or damage if the service were not rendered... [T]here must be such reasonable, present apprehension of danger that, in order to escape or avoid the danger, no reasonably prudent and skilful person in charge of the venture would refuse a salvor's help if it were offered to him upon the condition of his paying a salvage reward.'

Even if there is no danger at all, but the master wrongfully displays distress signals, or private signals which are liable to be mistaken for such, and another ship goes to the rescue she is entitled to compensation for labour, risk or other loss, and the master of the vessel displaying the signals is punishable by fine.[29]

24.4 VOLUNTARY CHARACTER OF THE SERVICE

The law of salvage only applies when there is no pre-existing duty on the part of the salvor to come to the assistance of the distressed ship. This duty may spring either from a contract between the salving and the salved vessels or from an official duty on the part of the salvors. Where such duty exists the service is not voluntary, and the law of salvage, which is an emergency law for the regulation of relations not subject to the law of contract or provision of a public nature, does not apply.

27 At p. 71 (p. 890). See also *The Phantom* (1866) L.R. 1 A. & E. 58, 60.
28 *Kennedy* (1985), p. 130.
29 Merchant Shipping (Safety Convention) Act 1949, s. 21.

24.4.1   STATUTORY DUTIES

In one sense hardly any salvage service is nowadays voluntary. As we have seen,[30] colliding vessels are bound to stand by each other and render assistance within reasonable limits; life salvage has become a statutory duty; and an obligation to render assistance is imposed by statute on all ships receiving a distress call.

However this is not the kind of duty which renders salvage involuntary within the meaning of the rule, for no person complying with those duties is officially charged with undertaking them. They remain volunteers, and if they endanger their lives and property in salvage work they may expect some reward. Indeed, Lord Stowell has defined a salvor as 'a person who, without any particular relation to the ship in distress, proffers useful service, and gives it as a volunteer adventurer, without any pre-existing covenant that connected him with the duty of employing himself in the preservation of that ship'.[31]

Accordingly, the duty to stand by under s. 422 of the Merchant Shipping Act 1894 does not preclude a salvage reward in a proper case.[32] Moreover the other statutes imposing salvage duties expressly provide that salvage remuneration may be claimed in respect of those services.[33]

Illustration: *The Tower Bridge*[34]

A ship was in grave danger in an icefield and sent out an SOS. This was answered by another vessel which at high speed and considerable risk drove her way to the ship in distress. By that time the worst danger was over and the second ship refused to stand by, but gave navigation directions enabling the first ship to reach open water.

It was held that the moral support and the giving of directions were a real salvage service, and that, under the forerunner of s. 22(8) of the Merchant Shipping (Safety Convention) Act 1949 a salvage reward could be claimed for complying with the duty imposed by the Act.

30 See Sections 21.3 and 24.2.2, *supra*
31 *The Neptune* (1824) 1 Hagg. 227, 236, 166 E.R. 81, 85.
32 *S.S. Melanie* v. *S.S. Onofre* [1925] A.C. 246, 262. This is so even where the wrongdoing ship stands by. Moreover, salvage services by the sister ship of a wrongdoing vessel may be rewarded: *The Beaverford* v. *The Kafiristan* [1938] A.C. 136.
33 Maritime Conventions Act 1911, s. 6(2); Merchant Shipping (Safety Convention) Act 1949, s. 22(8).
34 [1936] P. 30.

24.4.2 TOWAGE

A towage service may in certain events be transformed into a salvage service. In the ordinary way the tug has to perform its contractual obligations. A temporary accident necessitating an interruption of the towage and even endangering the tow will make no difference. The tug remains bound if with reasonable skill and promptitude and without herself incurring any excessive risk she can resume the towage and overcome the temporary danger.[35]

On the other hand, the accident may make the contract service impossible in the manner contemplated by the parties. Then the towage contract is suspended or discharged. Nevertheless the tug may be able to rescue the tow. In doing so the tug and her crew may incur risks not usual to simple towage, and her crew may exercise skill and promptitude beyond that normally expected from them. Obviously they deserve a reward, and this will be awarded to them in a salvage action by the Admiralty Court.

Those in charge of a tug naturally desire to see a towage converted into a salvage service; for salvage awards will usually exceed by far the towage remuneration. But the courts will only find to this effect when the following conditions are satisfied: (i) the tow was in danger by reason of circumstances which could not reasonably have been contemplated by the parties when the engagement was made and (ii) that risks are run, or responsibility undertaken, or duties performed, which could not reasonably be regarded as being within the scope of such engagements.[36]

If the tug is rendering its service under a towage contract the tug's crew cannot claim salvage[37] even, apparently, in circumstances where the services would have been salvage services if provided by a passing ship.[38]

However,

'The Court is . . . careful to scrutinize a claim for salvage by a tug engaged to tow. It is essential in the public interest, for obvious reasons, that the towage contract should not be easily set aside, and a salvage service substituted for it. A tug ought to make a clear case before she can convert herself into a salvor.'[39]

35 *The Annapolis* (1861) Lush. 355, 167 E.R. 150; *The Edward Hawkins: General Steam Navigation Co.* v. *De Jersey* (1862) 15 Moore P.C. 486, 15 E.R. 578; *The Liverpool* [1893] P. 154.
36 *The Aldora: Tyne Tugs Ltd* v. *Aldora (Owners)* [1975] 1 Lloyd's Rep. 617.
37 See *The North Goodwin No. 16* [1980] 1 Lloyd's Rep. 71.
38 *The Texaco Southampton* [1983] 1 Lloyd's Rep. 94 (Court of Appeal, New South Wales).
39 *The Maréchal Suchet* [1911] P. 1, *per* Sir Samuel Evans P at p. 12.

The tug must show that she was well equipped for the towage contract and that the additional services became necessary without any shortcomings on her part.[40]

24.4.3   HARBOUR AUTHORITIES

Similar principles apply to claims for salvage by harbour authorities:

Illustration: *The Bostonian* v. *The Gregersö*[41]

A ship stranded and obstructed the fairway in a harbour. The harbour authority was bound by statute to remove the obstruction. It sent its own tug to do so, in the course of that vessel's ordinary employment.

Held: Owner and master of the tug had not acted voluntarily, but under their contract of employment with the harbour authority. They were not entitled to salvage remuneration.

Of course, the authority may perform services beyond those required under the statute, e.g. after removing the ship from the fairway, spending time and money in patching it to prevent it sinking.[42] Such 'extra' services may entitle the authority to salvage, but a close reading of the relevant statutory provision will be necessary.

24.4.4   PILOTS

A pilot, compulsorily in charge of a disabled vessel, may convert himself into a salvor by reason of some increased risk. 'A pilot may be entitled to a salvage award where the vessel is not disabled. On the other hand, it does not follow because a vessel is disabled more or less, that any salvage award must be given.'[43] The test is not whether the vessel is in distress or damaged, but whether the risk of pilotage services was such that the pilot could not be reasonably expected to perform them for the ordinary pilot's fees, or even for an extraordinary pilotage reward.

40 *Ibid.*
41 [1971] 1 Lloyd's Rep. 220.
42 See, e.g. *The Citos* (1925) 22 Ll.L. Rep. 275.
43 *The Bedeburn* [1914] P. 146 *per* Sir Samuel Evans P. at p. 151.

Illustration: *Akerblom v. Price, Potter, Walker & Co.* [44]

In a heavy storm the ship was driven leeward in a dangerous situation, and the captain was unacquainted with the locality. Pilots who noticed the situation put off at danger of their lives. The heavy seas prevented them from boarding the vessel, but they preceded her in the pilot's boat, gave signals, and thus saved her.

Held: In the circumstances of the case the pilots had exceeded their duty as pilots and had in addition performed salvage services.

24.4.5   SHIPS' AGENTS AND PASSENGERS

Ships' agents[45] and passengers are usually not allowed salvage. But a passenger may be entitled to rank as a salvor 'if he provides a service other than for his own selfish purposes; if, when means of escape from danger for himself and his property are available, he elects to remain for the purposes of providing a salvage service; and if the service he performs is more than can justifiably be expected from a passenger in his position'.[46] On the other hand, it is no objection to a salvage claim that the salvor in performing the salvage services saved himself at the same time.[47]

24.4.6   CREW OF SALVED VESSEL

Only in exceptional circumstances will the crew of the salved vessel qualify for an award, since their contract obliges them to work for the safety of their ship.[48] To earn an award the crew must have done the salving at sea, not on the coast, e.g. by unloading cargo of a stranded vessel that would otherwise have been lost; they must have left the ship in the honest belief that they would not return, and they must have done so to save lives and by order of the master.[49]

These conditions were fulfilled in one of the great sea dramas of the 1939–45 war, when the auxiliary cruiser, *The Jervis Bay,* was sunk by a German warship while escorting a convoy in November 1940. One of the ships in the convoy, *The San Demetrio,* carrying a cargo of 11 200 tons of petrol, was set on fire, and the master, concerned for the lives of

---

44 (1880) 7 Q.B.D. 129. Also, *The Helenus and Motagua* [1982] 2 Lloyd's Rep. 261.
45 *The Purissima Concepción* (1849) 3 W. Rob. 181, 166 E.R. 930; *The Crusader* [1907] P. 196; *The Kate B. Jones* [1892] P. 366.
46 *Kennedy* (1985), p. 232.
47 *The Lomonosoff* [1921] P. 97.
48 *The Albionic* [1942] P. 81.
49 Dr Lushington, in *The Florence* (1852) 16 Jur. 572.

his crew, gave the order to abandon ship.⁵⁰ Two days later, one of the
lifeboats, manned by the second officer and fourteen others, again
sighted the tanker. Seeing it still afloat they decided to board her. Once
back the men, though all were near exhaustion and many ought to have
been in the sick bay, put out the fire, stopped the innumerable holes
which shell splinters had made in the deck, restarted the engines and
sailed the ship with her cargo 700 miles to Ireland. These heroes had
earned a salvage award.

24.4.7   ROYAL NAVY

We have noticed above that a public duty to render assistance imposed
by statute on persons engaged in shipping does not disentitle them from
claiming a reward. Originally it was otherwise if salvage services were
rendered by a person under an official duty. For this reason Her Majesty's ships, their officers and men could claim no reward for rendering of
salvage services, since under the instructions to officers and men of the
Royal Navy they must render assistance to British vessels in distress.⁵¹
In course of time, however, these rules were modified and later
reversed. For ships of the Royal Navy and their companies increasingly
undertook salvage work, especially in time of war when for various
reasons they alone could do so effectively. The first to benefit were
officers and men of Her Majesty's ships who, with the consent of the
Admiralty (now the Ministry of Defence), were granted the right to
claim salvage rewards.⁵² Nevertheless the courts do not favour such
claims and only reward special services rendered at personal risk and
outside the normal duties of the claimants.

Illustration: *The Carrie*⁵³
During the Great War of 1914–18, a Swedish vessel was stopped by a
German submarine which ordered the crew to take to the boats. Before a
torpedo was fired the submarine submerged, presumably on sighting two
British armed trawlers. The Swedish crew refused to return to their ship, and
the two trawlers towed her to port, in view of both war and sea dangers.

50 (1941) 69 Ll.L. Rep. 5.
51 *The Charlotte Wylie* (1846) 2 W. Rob 495, 497, 166 E.R. 842, 843; 13 Anne, c. 21
   (1713). See the Merchant Shipping Act 1894, ss. 557-64.
52 Merchant Shipping Act 1894, s. 557 (1), in the form established by the Merchant
   Shipping (Salvage) Act 1940.
53 [1917] P. 224: cf. *The Louisa* (1813) 1 Dods 317, 165 E.R. 1324; *The F.D. Lambert*
   [1917] P. 232; *The Gorliz* [1917] P. 233.

Held: In the circumstances officers and crews had earned salvage remuneration.

The Crown Proceedings Act 1947 reformed the whole system of actions by and against the Crown, and since 1948 not only can the Crown claim salvage like every other shipowner, but also private shipowners can claim salvage against the Crown for assistance rendered to HM ships. No action *in rem* may, however, be brought against these.[54]

24.4.8 COASTGUARDS

Coastguards are remunerated by the DoT according to a fixed scale.[55] Within their ordinary official duties they are not entitled to salvage. They will only be granted remuneration if they do more than their office demands. Probably putting out to sea at personal risk would be regarded as such an exceptional risk.

24.4.9 LIFEBOAT CREWS

The position of lifeboat crews is similar. They exist principally to save life, and for that they are remunerated by the Royal National Lifeboat Institution. If, however, they proceed to a wrecked vessel and find that life salvage is no longer required, but that their services are necessary for the salvage of property, such work is beyond their official duty and for it they rank as ordinary voluntary salvors.[56] In such a case they are taken to have borrowed the lifeboat and become personally responsible to the Institution which owns it for damage to the boat.[57]

24.4.10 NAVAL ORDERS

Another case where the operations might not, at first sight, appear to be voluntary occurs when they are directed or ordered by a third party, as by a naval officer in charge of a convoy. Yet, such orders do not make the services involuntary, for

54 Ss. 8 and 29. Supreme Court Act 1981, s. 24(2)(c).
55 Merchant Shipping Act 1894, s. 568.
56 *The Cayo Bonito* [1904] P. 310; *The Marguerite Molinos* [1903] P. 160, 164.
57 See Regulation 2.4.4.2 of the RNLI, in Brice (1983), pp. 516-7, and generally, O Warner, *The Life-boat Service,* (1974).

'the test of voluntariness is only applicable as between the salvor and the salved, and if the services be voluntary in relation to the salved, i.e. not rendered by reason of any obligation towards him, it is quite immaterial that the salvor has been ordered by someone who has control of his movements to render them'.[58]

There was in such a case no contractual or official duty towards the salved property. This became of special importance during the wars of 1914–18 and 1939–45, when mercantile shipping frequently came under the close control of the naval authorities.

Illustration: *The Kangaroo*[59]

The *Kangaroo* and the *Politician* were sailing in convoy. The *Kangaroo* developed engine trouble and dropped behind. The *Politician* thereupon offered the commander of the convoy to tow the *Kangaroo*. The offer was accepted and the naval commander ordered the towage. The *Kangaroo* was towed for 900 miles and the vessel was thus enabled to rejoin the convoy, to remain with it, and to enjoy protection against hostile attack.

Held: The *Politician* was entitled to remuneration, for the *Kangaroo* was in danger, and the voluntary character of the service was not destroyed by the orders of the naval commander to which the *Politician* was subject.

24.5   SUCCESS

As the reward, if any, is payable out of the salved property, success is necessary in order to entitle the salvor to an award: hence the expression 'no cure – no pay'. Difficulties sometimes arise in cases where several sets of salvors have taken part in salvage work; it may, for example, be doubtful whether the first set of salvors to assist the distressed vessel were really instrumental in saving her. The position is now governed by the rule laid down by Lord Phillimore, in *SS Melanie* v. *SS San Onofre*:[60]

'Success is necessary for a salvage award. Contributions to that success, or as it is sometimes expressed meritorious contributions to that success, give a title to salvage reward. Services, however, meritorious, which do not contribute to the ultimate success, do not give a title to salvage reward. Services which rescue a vessel from one danger but end by leaving her in a position of as great or nearly as great danger though of another kind, are held not to contribute to the ultimate success and do not entitle to salvage reward. In considering these

58 *Per* Pickford LJ in *The Sarpen* [1916] P. 306, 315.
59 [1918] P. 327.
60 [1925] A.C. 246, 262.

questions wherever the service has been meritorious, the court has lent towards
supporting a claim for salvage.'

Illustration 1: *The Cheerful*[61]

The *Cheerful* broke down in the Channel ten miles off Anvil Point. She was
taken in tow by the *City of Hamburg*. After several hours towing, when both
ships were off the Shambles lightship the hawser parted and the *Cheerful*
dropped anchor. She was then in a position of greater danger than before
the towage commenced. In attempting to pass another hawser, both ships
were damaged owing to unskilful though not negligent manoeuvring on the
part of the *City of Hamburg*. The latter then had to give up the salvage which
was completed by two tugs which arrived from Portland.

Held: The *City of Hamburg* was not entitled to a reward. Her services had
resulted in placing the *Cheerful* temporarily in a worse position than she was
before. No actual benefit had been conferred on the salved property.

Illustration 2: *The Marguerite Molinos*[62]

The coxswain of a lifeboat, before going out to a vessel in distress, sent a
telegram for tugs, but these were already on their way on other information.

Held: That the lifeboat was not entitled to salvage. Its message had not been
instrumental in salving the property.

24.6   THE SALVAGE REWARD: LIABILITY AND ENTITLEMENT

In the preceding pages we have shown what acts of assistance amount to
salvage services and give a right to a salvage award. Before proceeding
any further it will be convenient to ascertain who exactly are the parties
to any salvage operation. In other words, who is liable for, and who is
entitled to pay, salvage? It has already been made clear that there are two
parties to the transaction, namely the salvors and the owners of the
salved property.[63] The latter are the respective owners of the ship, cargo
and freight salved, the former are in general the owner,[64] master and
crew of the salving ship.

---

61 (1885) 11 P.D. 3.
62 [1903] P. 160.
63 Personal effects of passengers and crew do not contribute.
64 In case of a charter by demise (see Section 10.3.1, *supra*) the charterer is regarded as
    the owner, *Elliott Steam Tug Co.* v. *Admiralty* [1921] 1 A.C. 137.

24.6.1   LIABILITY FOR SALVAGE

The persons who are liable to pay for salvage are those whose interest in the property has been saved.[65] This will usually mean the shipowner and cargo-owners, but it could also extend to others, e.g. charterers, where freight, bunkers or stores are saved. Each person pays in proportion to his interest and there is no joint liability in English law for the whole.[66] This can be very inconvenient for the salvor because it means he has to obtain salvage security from each interest separately.[67]

In recent times the relative increase in the value of cargoes has meant that cargo owners are bearing an increasing proportion of salvage claims.[68] For instance, on an award of £300 000, with a ship value of £1 million and cargo values of £2 million, the ship would pay £100 000 and cargo £200 000.

24.6.2   RELATIONS BETWEEN SEVERAL SALVORS [69]

The right to salvage remuneration springs up at the moment a salvage service is commenced, though it still depends on the successful termination of the salvage. Thus the very moment a salvor has commenced salvage operations he has some right, albeit conditional, to a reward. The point is important. Though the right, at that stage, will not be of much value *vis-à-vis* the owners of the endangered property, it is otherwise on appearance of a third party. The value of salvage awards may be considerable and there is naturally keen competition to earn them. Thus a number of ships may endeavour to take part in a salvage operation, though one or two would be quite sufficient. Not only are the operations themselves thereby impeded, but also the salvors first on the spot may suffer damage in that finally they will have to share the reward with others and not get it all to themselves. Quarrels of that sort are not only unpleasant, but difficult to determine. Clearly the interests of the ship in distress must come first, and only after her safety has been

---

65 *Five Steel Barges* (1890) 15 P.D. 142.

66 *The Geestland* [1980] 1 Lloyd's Rep. 628, 630. But see now LOF clause 13, final sentence (Appendix 11) for an alteration to the specific decision.

67 In Holland, however, it seems that the shipowner is directly responsible to the salvor for all the salvage, and must rely on his right to claim general average from the cargo-owner; see I. Wildeboer, 'The CMI Draft Salvage Convention – what it omits' in *Salvage, General Average and Marine Insurance,* Conference Papers (1981). And see Sections 24.8.4, 24.9.3(a) and 24.10.5, *infra.*

68 See *Fairplay,* 24 October 1985.

69 See S. Braekhus, 'Competing Salvors' (1967) *Scandinavian Studies in Law* 65.

ensured may the interests of rival salvors be considered. The best judge of the safety of the vessel in distress is, of course, her master and as long as he is in command he determines how much assistance he requires; if he comes to the conclusion that more help than can be afforded by the salvors first on the spot is necessary, the latter have no right to exclude others who subsequently appear and offer additional help.[70] On the other hand, subsequent salvors proceeding against the wish of the captain earn no remuneration.

Illustration: *The Fleece*[71]

The ship had run on to the Gunfleet Sand where the master engaged salvors to get her off. The salvors succeeded, but as the ship was making water fast the ship was run ashore at the Maze and the original salvors were re-engaged to unload the ship. While occupied with that work a large number of men, in spite of being informed that the salvors were in legal charge with the master's consent, took forcible possession of the ship and in turn salved a quantity of cargo.

Held: The second salvors were not entitled to a reward, but the property saved by them helped to increase the reward due to the original salvors.

It is otherwise where the vessel in distress is derelict. In that case the first salvors who take possession have 'the entire and absolute possession and control of the vessel, and no one can interfere with them except in the face of manifest incompetence'.[72]

24.6.3 SALVORS' RIGHTS

Thus salvors acquire vested rights which cannot be ousted by agreements to which they are not parties[73] and which, in the case of master and crew of the salving ship, are even protected by statute.[74]

These vested rights include a maritime lien on the property saved,[75] that is to say, a right to arrest the property even if it has changed hands, to have it sold, and to satisfy their claims out of the fund in precedence

70 *Cossman v. West* (1887) 13 App. Cas. 160, 181. For the consequences of supersession, see Section 24.10.3, *infra*.

71 (1850) 3 W. Rob. 278, 166 E.R. 966.

72 *Cossman v. West, supra; The Champion* (1863) Br. & Lush. 69, 167 E.R. 303; *The Tubantia* [1924] P. 78.

73 *The Friesland* [1904] P. 345.

74 Merchant Shipping Act 1970, s. 16; *The Leon Blum,* [1915] p. 290. See Section 24.8.5(a) *infra*.

75 See Chapter 7, *supra*.

to all other previous liens on the goods. This maritime lien is considered a very good protection and salvors will, therefore, as a rule, not be allowed to retain possession of the salved property and to prevent its owners from dealing with it. This they will only be allowed to do in case of derelict property and in other cases where the security for the reward is endangered, or there are other special circumstances.[76]

Apart from this procedure *in rem,* the salvor also may proceed *in personam* against the owners of the salved property.[77] However, for reasons already indicated, he cannot, by suing the owners personally, claim a larger amount than he would have been entitled to in a suit *in rem.* The right *in personam* becomes valuable if by any means the lien over the salved property has been lost.

24.7   NEGLIGENT SALVORS

We must distinguish two different sets of circumstances: first, where a ship provides salvage services made necessary through its own conduct; secondly, where a salvor is negligent in the performance of the service.

24.7.1   NEGLIGENCE BEFORE SERVICES

It is not certain whether a ship which has negligently caused a collision may claim salvage in respect of subsequent services. The older decisions are against such claim.[78] However, certain statements made in the House of Lords suggest that these cases were wrongly decided, and support the view that salvage services deserve a reward even though they have become necessary owing to a wrong previously committed by the salvor.[79] In any event an award may be claimed for services performed by another ship in the same ownership as the wrongdoing vessel; previously it had been held that the owner of the wrongdoing vessel could not effectively claim.

---

76 *Kennedy* (1985) pp. 518-528. As to the Receiver of Wrecks, see Merchant Shipping Act 1894, ss. 518, 519, 552; Merchant Shipping Act 1906, s. 72; and see Section 24.12, *infra.*

77 See Section 1.3, *supra.*

78 *The Cargo ex Capella* (1867) L.R. 1 A. & E. 356; *The Duc d'Aumale (No.2)* [1904] P. 60.

79 *The Beaverford* v. *The Kafiristan,* [1938] A.C. 136.

Illustration: *Owners of Beaverford v. Owners of Kafiristan*[80]

A collision occurred between the *Empress of Britain* and the *Kafiristan*. The former was at least partly to blame for the casualty, and the latter was so badly damaged that she needed assistance. This was given by the *Beaverford,* which was owned by the same company as the *Empress of Britain*. The *Beaverford* towed the damaged vessel for a hundred miles when a salvage vessel took over.

Held: The owners of the *Beaverford* were entitled to an award. *Per* Lord Wright, at p. 147, 'The maritime law of salvage is based on principles of equity. There does not seem to be any reason in equity why the salved vessel...should not pay the appropriate salvage remuneration merely because the salving vessel belongs to the same owners as the other colliding vessel. That fact seems to be irrelevant so far as concerns the usefulness and meritorious character of the actual services rendered. This is not less true when the possibility of the other colliding vessel being held to blame in whole or in part is taken into account.'

To give wrongdoers the right to claim salvage seems not unreasonable. For the meritorious service deserves a reward and if the court should find that the damage is greater than the salvage then there is always room for adjusting the respective amounts.

24.7.2 NEGLIGENCE DURING SERVICES

Where the salvors are guilty of wilful or criminal misconduct they may forfeit their reward.[81] But where a salvage agreement fixing a high price is later set aside because of some form of extortion[82] this does not amount to such misconduct and the salvor will be entitled to some reward.[83] Where a salvor has performed the salvage service negligently the court may reduce his reward or deprive him of it completely. Moreover, the salvor may also face a counterclaim for damage done.

Illustration: *The Tojo Maru*[84]

The *Tojo Maru*, a tanker loaded with oil, was involved in a collision which left her with a gaping hole. A Lloyd's Open Form[85] salvage agreement was

80 [1938] A.C. 136. Generally, D.R. Thomas, 'Salvorial Negligence and its Consequences', [1977] 2 LMCLQ 167.
81 *The Neptune* (1842) 1 W. Rob. 297, 166 E.R. 583.
82 See Section 24.9.2, *infra*.
83 *The Port Caledonia* [1903] P. 184.
84 [1972] A.C. 242.
85 See Section 24.10, *infra*.

concluded with a Dutch salvage vessel. The salvors made a steel patch to cover the hole and their chief diver negligently and without orders left the salvage tug and began to bolt the patch to the ship's side before the ship had been made gas-free. An explosion occurred causing much damage, but the salvors towed the ship a long distance to a port where it could be repaired. The owners had suffered damage and loss of about £330 000, although ship and freight were still worth £1 300 000 allowing for this. The question was whether the salvors had forfeited any claim to a salvage reward and whether, in addition, they were liable to compensate the owners to the extent of £330 000.

Held: Even where the salvage is successful the owners can counterclaim for damage suffered as a result of the salvors' negligence. The salvors are entitled to offset against this the salvage remuneration that would have been due to them in the absence of negligence. The salvors were expected to be awarded a sum of not less than £125 000. So the owner was entitled to the difference between this figure (when finally determined by the salvage arbitrator) and the £330 000 damages suffered.

This was obviously a drastic result for the salvors after so much work. To make matters worse, it was held that they were not entitled to limit their liability for the counterclaim as the salvage operations did not take place on board their salvage vessel.[86]

However, the courts will be slow to impute negligence to salvors,[87] particularly non-professional salvors.[88]

24.8 THE SALVAGE REWARD: ASSESSMENT

24.8.1 GENERAL PRINCIPLES

Once the salvor's right to a reward is decided the court must make up its mind how to arrive at an equitable figure. The principal question is what should be the considerations guiding the court in arriving at the final sum awarded. It is important to note that there is no single rule for assessing salvage rewards and the duty of the court is to take into

---

86 The salvage tug would have had a limit of about £10 000. See under the Merchant Shipping Act 1894, s. 503, Chapter 22, *supra*: for the changes agreed to entitle the salvor to limit, see Sections 22.3, *supra* and 24.11, *infra*.

87 *The Tojo Maru*, *supra*, *per* Lord Reid at p. 267.

88 *The St Blane* [1974] 1 Lloyd's Rep. 557.

account many factors. It is not a simple matter of calculating hours expended in work and labour.[89]

The principles were well stated in the following passage:

'The ingredients of a salvage service are, first, enterprise in the salvors in going out in tempestuous weather to assist a vessel in distress, risking their own lives to save their fellow-creatures, and to rescue the property of their fellow subjects: secondly, the degree of danger and distress from which the property is rescued – whether it were in imminent peril and almost certainly lost if not at the time rescued and preserved: thirdly, the degree of labour and skill which the salvors incur and display, and the time occupied. Lastly, the value. Where all these circumstances concur, a large and liberal reward ought to be given; but where none or scarcely any take place, the compensation can hardly be denominated a salvage compensation; it is little more than a mere remuneration *pro opere et labore*.'[90]

It should be noted, however, that since this case more and more importance has been attached to the value of the property risked in, or at any rate occupied with, the salvage operations, and taken away from its normal work. Having regard to the high value of large modern vessels and the large freight earned, this is a reasonable and natural development.

24.8.2 VALUE OF SALVED PROPERTY

One of the main difficulties arises from the need to ascertain the value of the salved property. Beyond that no award may go. To the award every interest contributes rateably according to its salved value.[91] With regard to the ship, not only her value as a structure is considered, but her value to her owners as a going concern. Thus where she is under a profitable time charter something must be added for the present value of prospective earnings under the charter.[92] When we come to the cargo, here too the salved value is material, that is to say, the value when the salvage has come to an end, after deducting the proper expenses for unloading,

---

89 *The Rilland* [1979] 1 Lloyd's Rep. 455, 458.
90 *The Clifton* (1834), 3 Hagg. 117, *per* Sir John Nicholl at p. 121, 166 E.R. 349.
91 *Kennedy* (1985) Chapters 11 and 13, especially p. 487, *et seq.* Lloyd's figures show that in 1984 LOF awards totalling £259 000 were made in 212 cases involving property valued at £516 300 000 – a percentage award to value of 5.7%. By contrast the figures for 1964 were £2 561 000 (awards), 214 cases, £37 400 000 (values) and 6.8% (awards to values). For discussion of the LOF, see Section 24.10, *infra*.
92 *The Castor* [1932] P. 142; *The Edison* [1932] P. 52.

storage and sale.[93] Yet, if the cargo at the end of the operations is worth no more than it would have been had the service never been performed, no reward may be paid in respect of the cargo.

Illustration: *The Tarbert*[94]

A tug attempted to tow ashore a sinking vessel. During the towage the vessel struck a bank and could not be got off. Cargo of the value of £17 000 was recovered from her as she lay on the bank. It was proved in evidence, however, that had the vessel been allowed to sink in deep water, cargo of approximately equal value could have been salved.

Held: No salvage award had therefore been earned.

On the other hand, where ship and cargo were salved, but the cargo by reason of its perishable nature had really benefited to a greater extent than the ship, an award to salvors of £600 was directed to be borne as to £180 only by the ship and as to the rest by cargo and freight though, from a mere accounting point of view, the value of the salved ship was substantially higher than that of the cargo.[95]

Where a salvor has brought a cargo to a place of safety and incurs expenses in storing and looking after the goods he may be entitled to reasonable expenses from the cargo-owner.[96]

Freight contributes to the award if it would not have been earned but for the salvage operations.[97]

It is important to bear in mind that the three interests, ship, cargo and freight, are liable only for their proportion of the award so that the salvor must make all of them defendants.[98]

So far we have only discussed the interests which are liable to contribute because they themselves have benefited; but the matter does not end there. It will be recollected that salvors are also entitled to life salvage provided they have saved some property at the same time and, further, that the lives saved do not themselves pay anything towards salvage because lives have no property value and salvage is only paid out of property. The question therefore arises: who does pay for life salvage? If lives have been saved by the Royal National Lifeboat Institution

93 *Kennedy* (1985), pp. 449–452.
94 [1921] P. 372.
95 *The Velox* [1906] P. 263.
96 See *The Winson: China Pacific S.A.* v. *The Food Corporation of India* [1982] A.C. 939 where some $383 000 expenses were incurred.
97 *Kennedy* (1985) pp. 445–449 *et seq.*
98 *The Geestland* [1980] 1 Lloyd's Rep. 628; *Kennedy* (1985), pp. 487–500, see Section 24.6.1, *supra.*

no life salvage is payable at all, for the lifeboat crews are remunerated by
the Institution, and property salvors cannot claim a reward for lives
they have not saved. Where, however, lives and property are saved by
salvors other than official salvors the owners of the property salved
must at the same time pay for the life salvage, but not, this cannot be
stressed too much, beyond the amount of the property actually salved.
The result is that where ship, cargo, freight and lives are saved the three
property interests have to pay the salvors for the life salvage as well,
rateably in proportion to the value of their interests as saved.[99]
Therefore where only cargo and lives are saved, the cargo alone pays for
life salvage. This must be so because the other property interests,
namely ship and freight, are lost and in respect of them there is no fund
which could yield cash by which life salvors might be remunerated.[1]

24.8.3 VALUE OF SALVING PROPERTY

Another factor determining the award is the value of the salving vessel.
If it is small, it will neither increase nor diminish the award, but where it
is considerable, and notably where a valuable ship has been put at risk in
salving property, then this consideration will tend to increase the award
to the owners. The reason is both one of public policy and of business
necessity.[2]

As was said by Lindley LJ[3]

'The salving vessel is often herself exposed to imminent peril. . . . Hence one
element in determining the amount to be awarded for salvage services is the
value of the salving ship and cargo, which have been exposed to risk. . . . Where
the salving vessel is a large and valuable steamer, exposed to great risk, the
claims of her owner deserve very favourable attention. . . . Unless, where the
salving vessel is a valuable steamer, the remuneration awarded to her owner is
sufficient to cover this risk, owners of such vessels will naturally discourage
their employment in salvage services. . . . It is necessary that the amount of
compensation awarded to the owner of the salving ship shall, wherever practicable, be sufficient to cover the risk of damage and loss which he ran, where
fortunately none has been sustained.'

For the same reason, actual loss or damage to the salvor is taken into
account. Usually no separate award is made, as this item is included in

99 Merchant Shipping Act 1894, ss. 544-46; for jurisdiction, see Section 1.3 and
    Supreme Court Act 1981 ss. 20, 21; County Courts Act 1984 ss. 27.
1 *Cargo ex Sarpedon* (1877) 3 P.D. 28.
2 *The Werra* (1886) 12 P.D. 52; *The City of Chester* (1884) 9 P.D. 182.
3 *The City of Chester, supra*, at p. 203.

the salvage award and tends to increase it by the amount of the loss or damage.[4]

24.8.4 CONTRIBUTION OF SALVED PROPERTY INTERESTS *INTER SE*

There remains a further point for consideration with regard to the award, namely, the relationship between the salved property interests. In this connection it is necessary to recall what has previously been said about general average.[5]

Payments under a salvage award or by a shipowner under a salvage agreement may be general average expenses and there may thus arise a liability of ship, cargo and freight to contribute *inter se* (between themselves). Thus, where the shipowner paid for the cost of raising ship and cargo he is entitled to contribution from the cargo owner. However, if the accident arose by reason of the shipowner's negligence for which he is liable in law to the cargo-owner, the latter is not liable to contribute to any salvage charges which are in the nature of general average expenses.[6] But the negligence must be actionable, so that the cargo-owner is bound to contribute if, by the charterparty or the bill of lading or under the Merchant Shipping Acts, the shipowner was excused in respect of the very negligence which occasioned the accident.[7]

24.8.5 APPORTIONMENT

The last problem presented by the law of salvage proper is how the award is apportioned between the salving interests, that is, between owner, master and crew of the salving vessel or vessels.[8] This apportionment is effected in accordance with the law of the flag of the salving ship.[9] Thus, if the Admiralty Court awards salvage to a German or French ship, the questions whether a salvage service has in

---

4 Merchant Shipping Act 1894, s. 510; *Kennedy* (1985), p. 472 *et seq.* summarizing the decisions in *The Sunniside* (1883) 8 P.D. 137; *The De Bay* (1883) 8 App. Cas. 559; *The City of Chester* (1884) 9 P.D. 182. *Cf. The Ben Gairn* [1979] 1 Lloyd's Rep. 410, p. 453, *infra*.
5 Chapter 15, *supra*.
6 *The Ettrick* (1881) 6 P.D. 127.
7 *Stang, Steel & Co.* v. *Scott & Co.* (1889) 14 App. Cas. 601; *The Carron Park* (1890) 15 P.D. 203; *Louis Dreyfus & Co.* v. *Tempus Shipping Co.* [1931] A.C. 726. For the circumstances in which a shipowner is excused under the Merchant Shipping Acts, see Section 22.4, *supra*.
8 See generally, *Kennedy* (1985), pp. 501–513.
9 Maritime Conventions Act 1911, s. 7.

face been rendered, who has to contribute to the award, and how it is assessed, are determined under English law; but when it comes to apportioning the award between owner, master and crew of the salving vessel, German or French law is applicable respectively, unless the parties agree that English law shall govern also this part of the case.

(A) AGREEMENTS FOR APPORTIONMENT

In some instances the Court is never called upon to apportion the award because the parties settle among themselves how the lump sum shall be distributed between them. It was found necessary to protect the crew against high-handed actions and pressure by the owners. To achieve this end, s. 16 of the Merchant Shipping Act 1970 provides that any right which a seaman[10] may have or obtain in the nature of salvage shall not be capable of being renounced by any agreement. Nevertheless, in practice many settlements between owners, masters and crew do take place without the concurrence of the Court. There is no fault in such procedure and the Court will not disturb them provided they are equitable.[11] In this respect it has been held that agreements between owner and crew of the salving ship to the effect that the owners, before apportioning the award, should be entitled to deduct the cost of repairs and loss of profits, were contrary to the Act.[12]

A great deal of salvage work is done, of course, by specialist salvage firms.[13] In order to prevent its being contended that the ordinary agreements of service between owners and crew of such ships were hit by the above-mentioned provision, it has been specially enacted[14] that such service agreements shall not be illegal. However, this provision does not fetter the discretion of the Court in any way, and it will interfere if any one apportionment does not conform with the requirements of equity.[15]

10 That is, any member of the crew other than the master. Masters are regarded as sufficiently strong from a business point of view to look after their own interests, but in a proper case, the Court will nevertheless interfere if the agreement between owner and master is not honestly made: *The Wilhelm Tell* [1892] P. 337; *Nicholson v. Leith Salvage & Towage Co.* [1923] S.C. 409.
11 *The Afrika* (1880) 5 P.D. 192; *The Wilhelm Tell, supra.*
12 *The Wilhelm Tell, supra; The Saltburn* (1894) 7 Asp. M.C. 474.
13 A fishing trawler, where the articles with the crew provide for fishing in the North Sea and also contain terms in respect of possible salvage, is not a salvage ship: *The Wilhelm Tell, supra.*
14 Merchant Shipping Act 1970, s. 16(2).
15 *Temperley* (1976) para. 294.

(B)   APPORTIONMENT BETWEEN SALVING INTERESTS

If the Court is called upon to apportion the award between the owner, master and crew of the salving vessel it must do so under s. 556 of the Merchant Shipping Act 1894, unless this power is barred by a valid agreement. A very large number of cases have been decided on the proper method of apportionment and it would serve no useful purpose to analyse them in any detail. Suffice it to say that the Court will always have to decide whether the ship was at risk or whether the main task was performed by the skill of master and crew. Since towing has become the most frequent mode of salvage service the courts are apt to apportion a larger amount of owners than was appropriate in the days of sailing ships when the endeavour of the crew was the most vital element.[16] The owners might be awarded three-quarters of the reward, or perhaps two-thirds where, for example, a non-specialist fishing vessel performs the salvage.[17] But, of course, all depends on the circumstances of the case.

Illustration 1: *The Nicolina*[18]
A ship was discovered at sea, abandoned by her crew. The master of a passing West Indiaman carrying a valuable cargo put on board the derelict ship three members of his crew and his chief mate. The vessel was worked to safety with difficulty. The salved value was £1153. The total award was £550. Of this the owners of the salving vessel received £100. The same sum was awarded to master and first mate of the salving vessel, £150 to the three members of the crew, and £100 to the rest of the crew.

Illustration 2: *The City of Paris*[19]
The *City of Paris* was towed by the *Aldersgate,* and the *Ohio* stood by and otherwise assisted the vessel in distress. Both salving vessels were valuable steamers. Award: £600 to *Ohio,* of which £400 went to owners, £7500 to *Aldersgate,* of which £5625 were apportioned to her owners. In addition the owners of the *Aldersgate* received £500 as compensation for damage by straining of hull and engines.

16 See, e.g. *The Mungana* [1936] 3 All E.R. 670.
17 See, *The Ben Gairn* [1979] 1 Lloyd's Rep. 410.
18 (1843) 2 W. Rob. 175, 166 E.R. 720.
19 *Shipping Gazette,* W.S., 7 June 1890.

Illustration 3: *The San Onofre*[20]
The salving steamer, valued at £300 000 stood by, steered and towed (with
the assistance of another vessel) a tanker of the value of £370 000 for 1280
miles in very bad weather. Out of an award of £34 550 the sum of £32 000
was awarded to the owners.

Illustration 4: *The Ben Gairn*[21]
A trawler towed another trawler for 16 miles at night in moderately severe
seas. There was some danger to the salving vessel, and its master carried a
heavy responsibility. The salved vessel was valued at £55 000. An award of
£5400 was made, apportioned two thirds to owners and one third (£1800) to
the men. The master was awarded £650, the mate £250 and the remaining
£900 was shared between the nine crew. The owners were also awarded
£3463 as expenses for actual damage sustained by their vessel and interest.

It is usual for an award of interest to be made on the salvage award.
This may run from the termination of the services,[22] but more usually
from, e.g., 4–6 months after termination.[23]

(c)   APPORTIONMENT BETWEEN DIFFERENT
SALVORS

Also between several sets of salvors much depends on who performed
the vital or most important service, but on the whole the courts are
inclined to favour the salvors who were first on the spot.[24]

24.9   SALVAGE AGREEMENTS
24.9.1   GENERAL

In one sense most salvages of ships, other than derelicts, are performed
by 'agreement'. But in practice most salvage services are performed by
professional salvors operating under salvage contracts such as the
Lloyd's Standard Form of Salvage Agreement (LOF)[25] 1980. With the
development of telecommunications contracts may now be agreed

---

20 [1917] P. 96.
21 [1979] 1 Lloyd's Rep. 410.
22 *Ibid.*
23 E.g. *The Boston Lincoln* [1980] 1 Lloyd's Rep. 481; *The Ilo* [1982] 1 Lloyd's Rep.
   39.
24 For details, see *Kennedy*, (1985), pp. 508–510.
25 It is known as the Lloyd's Open Form as it leaves 'open' the amount of salvage
   reward, which is later determined by an arbitrator, see Appendix 11.

easily between masters, or between the salvors and the shipowners direct. Concern has been expressed that undue haggling over salvage agreements may cause vital delay in the salving of ships.[26] In reality, a contract such as the LOF 1980 can avoid disputes on the spot because the salvage award is worked out later by an arbitrator.

A salvage contract must be distinguished from a towage contract, e.g. where the tug is offered on a daily rate for straight towing. Here the tugowner would be paid for any work done, even if the ship sinks. Where a salvage agreement proper does fix a price it will usually be by reference to a lump sum, e.g. where a stranded ship must be made buoyant again and the work is of uncertain duration. A daily rate salvage agreement is possible, but less likely.[27]

In a salvage agreement the services must be rendered on a 'no cure – no pay' basis.[28] Only in such a case does the salvor acquire a maritime lien[29] and if any sum is agreed then it will be paid out of the fund actually salved.[30] As in ordinary salvage, the salvor, to be entitled to remuneration must not already be under an existing duty to do the work.[31] However, the service is not deprived of its voluntary nature because the salvor has made an agreement regulating the conditions under which he renders the salvage services.[32]

If the salvor fails to recover under the 'no cure – no pay' contract because he has not performed the exact service bargained for, he may still be able to claim an amount under the general law of salvage.

26 Allegations that the *Amoco Cadiz* went aground because of such haggling were disproved in the case as it was shown that the LOF was agreed well after the tug had a line on board, *The Amoco Cadiz* [1984] 2 Lloyd's Rep. 304. An LOF was agreed after the salvage was completed in *The Beaverford* v. *The Kafiristan* [1938] A.C. 136.

27 The only advantage of fixing a price in advance is to avoid the uncertainty and expense of having a court or arbitrator do so.

28 See e.g., *The Mark Lane* (1890) 15 P.D. 135, where an agreement to salve for £5000 or for services rendered if unsuccessful was held not to be a salvage agreement. The Court, however, awarded a reasonable sum for salvage.

29 *The Goulandris* [1927] P. 182: See Chapter 7, *supra*. Apart from the 'no cure – no pay' element the crucial distinction between salvage and towage is the element of danger; see Section 24.3, *supra*.

30 See *The Renpor* (1883) 8 P.D. 115. The agreement may, however, provide in advance that a sum greater than the (eventual) salved value should be paid, *The Inna* [1938] P. 148, *The Lyrma (No. 2)* [1978] 2 Lloyd's Rep. 30, 33: Brice (1983), p. 128.

31 See, e.g. *The Bostonian* v. *The Gregerso* [1971] 1 Lloyd's Rep. 220.

32 *Admiralty Commissioners* v. *M. V. Valverda* [1938] A.C. 173, *per* Lord Wright at p. 187.

Illustration: *The Westbourne*[33] *The Hestia*[34]

A salvage agreement was made 'no cure – no pay' to tow a disabled vessel to Gibraltar for £600. During the towage a hurricane came up, the hawser parted frequently and, finally, when only one sound rope was left, the salvor decided to tow the ship only to Cartagena. Naturally, no remuneration was due under the agreement.

Held: The Court could make an award, for the vessel was in fact salved. The sum fixed by the Court was actually higher than that originally agreed upon, namely £900.

The parties to a salvage contract are governed by the terms, express and implied, of that contract and the general maritime law of salvage only applies in so far as it is expressly or impliedly incorporated into such contract.[35] The correct approach is to determine the salvor's liability under the general English law of contract and then to see if there are any differences flowing from the special characteristics of salvage services.[36]

It may be important to decide whether a salvage service is performed under a contract (such as the LOF 1980) or not, particularly where it is alleged that the contract has been breached. But before we look at the LOF 1980 it is necessary to say a few words about the role of the Admiralty Court.

24.9.2 SUPERVISION OF THE ADMIRALTY COURT

Although salvage contracts are not contracts *uberrimae fidei*,[37] like marine insurance contracts,[38] the Court has long exercised an inherent jurisdiction to see that salvage agreements are fair. In nearly all the cases where a court has intervened it has done so because the intending salvor has demanded a high fixed price for the salvage. He may have signalled, in effect, 'no pay – no rope' and endeavoured to extort money from the ship in distress by threatening to leave her where she is until his price is paid. The Court will always scrutinize the agreement and award a lower

---

33 (1889) 14 P.D. 132.

34 [1895] P. 193.

35 *The Unique Mariner (No.2)* [1979] 1 Lloyd's Rep. 37, *per* Brandon J at pp. 50–51.

36 *The Tojo Maru* [1972] A.C. 242, *per* Lord Diplock at p. 292. Note also the effect of the Supply of Goods and Services Act 1982 and the Unfair Contract Terms Act 1977, see Sections 23.2 and 23.3, *supra*.

37 *The Unique Mariner* [1978] 1 Lloyd's Rep. 438.

38 See Section 28.3, *infra*.

sum if the agreement is obviously unfair, or the sum agreed on exorbitant.[39] Other circumstances which might encourage the Court to intervene are where there is oppression or virtual compulsion arising from the inequality in the bargaining position of the two parties concerned or collusion.[40] The Court might also intervene if one side or the other fails to disclose a material fact. Thus, if the owner or master of the vessel to be salved deceives the master of the salving ship of the true condition of the ship, the extent of the danger, or the value of the property to be salved, the Court may set aside a fixed price agreement. It may then award a sum as if no agreement had been made.[41]

We may note here that liability for death or personal injury caused by negligence cannot be bargained away in any contract.[42] In contracts made with consumers, e.g. a private boat owner, other clauses, such as indemnity clauses, must be reasonable.[43]

24.9.3   PARTIES TO THE CONTRACT

We must now consider who exactly is bound by a salvage agreement. First we must note that no salvage agreement can do away with rights vested in third parties before the agreement was entered into. Suppose a vessel begins salving operations. After a little while the masters see that it is going to be a bigger job than they expected, and the operations are discontinued in order that more help may be got. Before the services are resumed an agreement is made purporting to cover both past and future services. Now if the services rendered prior to the agreement are of assessable value, vested rights to salvage have been acquired by the salving vessel.[44] The master, by signing an agreement, cannot bargain away those rights vested in the crew and owner without being authorized to do so by those parties. In the absence of such authority any sum agreed upon only applies to subsequent services.[45]

This leads us to the question closely related to the previous one. When the masters of the salved and salving vessels sign an agreement,

---

39 *The Altair* [1897] P. 105; *The Rialto* [1891] P. 175; *The Port Caledonia and The Anna* [1903] P. 184; *Akerblom v. Price, Potter, Walker & Co.* (1881) 7 Q.B.D. 129; *The Medina* (1876) 1 P.D. 272, 2 P.D. 5.

40 *The Unique Mariner, per* Brandon J at p. 453.

41 *Ibid.; The Kingalock,* (1854) I Spinks, E & A, 265.

42 Unfair Contract Terms Act 1977, s. 2(1).

43 *Ibid.,* Sch. 1, para. 2(a).

44 This will normally not be the case where the services are continuous.

45 *The Inchmaree* [1899] P. 111.

they act, of course, not on their own account, but as agents. Now whose agents are they?

(A)   SALVED INTERESTS

The master of the salved vessel binds his owners if he acts under necessity and for their benefit.[46] He will usually have authority to accept salvage on the basis of a reasonable contract such as the LOF.[47] In principle, the cargo-owner is not bound by such a contract as he is not party to it.[48] However, in some circumstances the master will be an 'agent of necessity' and, as such, will be able to bind the cargo-owner to a contract.[49] It makes sense for the law to give a master the authority to do what is best in an emergency; but not only must the services be necessary, it must also have been impossible to communicate with the cargo-owners.[50] This would often be the case with a container ship having hundreds of cargo-owners, but not with a bulk carrier having a single cargo-owner.

It seems that where the shipowner does agree to pay a fixed price for the salvage he must, if sued by the salvor, pay the salvor the entire amount[51] and claim contribution from the cargo-owners under the law of general average. This contribution is quite independent of any salvage agreement. Even if the shipowner pays the whole of the salvage award made by the Court, he is entitled to contribution from the cargo.[52]

---

46 *The Renpor* (1883) 8 P.D. 155.

47 *The Unique Mariner* [1978] 1 Lloyd's Rep. 438, 450.

48 *The Leon Blum* [1915] P. 90, 290. The salvor would, presumably, have an ordinary salvage claim against the cargo owner.

49 See Brice (1983), pp. 194-197, 202-203. The LOF 1980 clause 17 (Appendix 11) states that the master contracts as agent for the property to be salved. If the master has no authority the salvor may be able to claim damages for a breach of a warranty of authority; see Brice (1983), pp. 203; 204.

50 Brice (1983), *The Winson: China Pacific S.A.* v. *Food Corporation of India* [1982] A.C. 939, 965.

51 *The Prinz Heinrich* (1888) 13 P.D. 31.

52 Cargo will usually be liable for its proportion of sum the agreed or paid by the owner, although the fact that the master's conduct in agreeing was reasonable is not conclusive that the whole sum paid was chargeable to general average, *Anderson Tritton & Co.* v. *Ocean S.S. Co.* (1884) 10 App. Cas. 107.

Illustration

Suppose a salvage award is made by the Court binding ship and cargo (in proportion to their values) to pay £500 (ship) and £1000 (cargo). If the shipowner pays the entire £1500 he can claim £1000 from the cargo-owners as a general average contribution. If, assuming the same services and values, there was an agreement to pay the salvor £2100, the shipowner would be bound to pay this sum. But he cannot claim a proportion from the cargo based on the sum bargained for (i.e., equivalent to £1400). For the cargo is not bound by the agreement and need only pay a reasonable contribution, as it would be assessed by the Court (i.e. £1000). The result is the same as if no agreement between salved and salvors had been made.

(B)   SALVING INTERESTS

When we turn to the salving vessel we again find that the master binds the owners provided he acts under necessity and for their benefit. It would also seem that he binds the crew if the amount is reasonable. Otherwise the crew are entitled to have their salvage awarded by the Court.[53] The power of the master may, however, not be exercised so as to bargain away vested rights.[54] The same consideration applies to an agreement made personally by the owners of the salving vessel. It binds master and crew if it is fair, but will not affect vested rights, if, for example, in ignorance of the agreement the ship has begun salvage operations.[55] It may be that a public authority has no power to enter into a 'speculative' contract such as an LOF.[56]

What has been said in this section only applies to salvage agreements between shipowners. Yet it sometimes happens that when a ship is lost the insurers, after having paid the sum insured, employ salvors to raise the ship so as to recoup themselves by selling the wreck as scrap or otherwise. Such agreements are made long after the immediate danger has passed. A court may decide that they are not salvage agreements proper, but simple employment contracts. Consequently, the salvors cannot exercise a maritime lien if after the performance of the services the insurers fail to pay the agreed remuneration.[57]

---

53 *The Nasmyth* (1885) 10 P.D. 41. See also Section 24.8.5(a), (b), *supra*.
54 *The Inchmaree* [1899] P. 111.
55 *The Friesland* [1904] P. 345.
56 *The Bostonian* v. *The Gregersö* [1971] 1 Lloyd's Rep. 220, *per* Brandon J at p. 228.
57 *The Solway Prince*, [1896] P. 120. Distinguished in *The Goulandris* [1927] P. 182.

24.10   LLOYD'S OPEN FORM SALVAGE AGREEMENT

24.10.1   INTRODUCTION

The LOF was first issued by the Committee of Lloyds in 1892, although its origin dates back to 1890.[58] It has been revised a number of times since and the most recent version is the LOF 1980. In essence, the LOF is an arbitration agreement which removes disputes about the amount of salvage payable to the calm atmosphere of an arbitrator's office in London. However, over the years other terms of importance have been grafted on to LOF and these must be considered closely. The general attitude of the courts has been to treat the LOF basically as a commercial contract for work and labour.[59] In particular, under Clause 1 the salvor agrees to use his 'best endeavours' to salve the property.

24.10.2   EFFECT OF AGREEING TO LOF

The effect of signing the LOF (or otherwise agreeing to it) would seem to put the salvor's right to salvage beyond doubt.[60] It would be very difficult for a shipowner to allege afterwards that the service was towage and not salvage. Even if the signing is, for practical purposes, conclusive of the existence of 'danger' as against the shipowner, we have seen already[61] that the cargo-owner is not necessarily bound. Further, it seems that a person who is not a volunteer[62] may have difficulties in claiming salvage under the agreement.[63] On the other hand, if the owner of a gas float (or an oil rig) specifically agrees on LOF terms that his property is to be salved, it seems fair that he should have to pay on a salvage basis. It may be, however, that if the claim was not technically salvage the salvor would be unable to assert a maritime lien.

---

58 See *Kennedy*, 4th edn (1958) p. 299; J.G.R. Griggs, 'An Examination of Lloyd's Standard Form of Salvage Agreement' [1974] 2 LMCLQ 138.
59 See Section 24.9.1, *supra*.
60 *The Beaverford* v. *The Kafiristan* [1938] A.C. 136, *per* Lord Atkin at p. 140, and Lord Wright at p. 153.
61 Section 24.9.3(A), *supra*, and clause 17, LOF, Appendix II.
62 See Section 24.4, *supra*.
63 See Brice (1983), pp. 248; 249, *The Bostonian* v. *The Gregersö* [1971] 1 Lloyd's Rep. 220.

24.10.3   SUPERSESSION OF SALVOR

A master who 'engages' a salvor on LOF terms, or otherwise, may decide to dismiss the salvor and supersede him by a different salvor. Generally speaking the master is fully entitled to decide which salvors should work on his vessel and they cannot force their services on him.[64] This is true even though they may have attached a line: the master's authority to engage or dismiss is paramount.[65] However, if the master does decide to supersede, the salvor may have lost the benefit of a large salvage award. Is he entitled to any compensation?

If the superseded salvor has already performed services which have contributed to the ultimate saving of the vessel he will be entitled to share in the award made to any later salvor.[66] But the entitlement to any further compensation will depend on whether or not there is a binding salvage contract, such as the LOF. If there is a contract the actions of the master could be considered as in breach.[67]

Illustration: The Unique Mariner (No. 2)[68]

The *Unique Mariner* went aground in 1977 while on a ballast voyage. The master requested towage assistance and the owners' representatives engaged a Fukada tug on LOF terms. Meanwhile a Selco tug had approached the *Unique Mariner* and offered her salvage assistance. The master, believing this to be the tug sent by his owners, signed an LOF. When he discovered his mistake he dismissed the Selco tug, which had started to make towing preparations. The Fukada tug arrived and successfully completed the salvage, being awarded US $28 000. The Selco tug claimed compensation for not being able to complete the service as agreed.

Held: Where salvors are engaged without any express salvage contract they are entitled to remuneration in the nature of salvage: first, for the services rendered before dismissal; secondly, by way of some compensation for the loss of opportunity to complete the service. The sum awarded is entirely in the discretion of the Court. The salvors, on the other hand, are under no obligation to continue their services.

Under an LOF contract the salvors are under a *continuing* duty to use 'best endeavours' to salve the vessel. The shipowners have a corresponding duty, by reason of an implied term in the LOF, that they will not act in such a way as

64 See Section 24.6.2, *supra*.
65 *The Loch Tulla* (1950) 84 Ll.L. Rep. 62.
66 *The Maasdam* (1893) 7 As p. M.C. 400.
67 See, e.g., *The Valsesia* [1927] P. 115.
68 [1979] 1 Lloyd's Rep. 37; see also *The Unique Mariner* [1978] 1 Lloyd's Rep. 438 for earlier proceedings upholding the validity of the LOF contract.

to prevent the salvors from performing the services which they have undertaken so long as they are willing and able to do so.

As the Selco tug was perfectly willing and able to perform the salvage, the
action of the master of the *Unique Mariner* was a repudiatory breach
entitling the salvors to damages for breach of contract. Selco were entitled to
the estimated sum they would have earned if they had been allowed to
complete the service, less deductions for risks not run and expenses and
operating time saved. There would also be a deduction for the possibility that
the operation would have failed.

The master's decision could thus be crucial. He must back his judgment in deciding whether the first salvor is powerful, or skilful, enough
to perform the service.[69] If he is wrong, his owners, may be landed with
a heavy bill for compensation, which is probably not covered by
insurance as it is contractual 'damages' and not 'salvage'.

When we look at other LOF terms we must recall that breach of them
may also result in damages.

24.10.4 TERMINATION OF LOF

The point at which salvage services cease may be important for a
number of reasons, e.g. in assessing the salvage reward or deciding
when the salvor's duties cease. Generally, salvage ceases when the vessel
ceases to be in danger.[70] Under LOF 1980 Clause 1 the salvor agrees to
use his best endeavours to salve the ship, her cargo, bunkers and stores
and take them to a named place or, otherwise, to a 'place of safety'. A
salvor is not entitled to leave the ship at a place more convenient to him
than the one specified in the contract: to do so may be breach, giving
rise to damages. Likewise, because he has a continuous duty under the
LOF he cannot simply remove his salvage tug from a difficult job on the
basis that more lucrative employment is available elsewhere. He may be
able to argue that the contract is legally 'frustrated' if performance of it
becomes radically different from that envisaged by the parties.[71] For
instance, an outbreak of fighting causing danger to the salvor would
entitle him to terminate,[72] but ordinary expected difficulties, such as
bad weather, would not be enough.

69 See, e.g. *The Zinovia* [1984] 2 Lloyd's Rep. 264.
70 *The Troilus* v. *The Glenogle* [1951] A.C. 820.
71 *Davis Contractors Ltd* v. *Fareham U.D.C.* [1956] A.C. 696, *per* Lord Radcliffe at
p. 729 and see Brice (1983), pp. 232–239.
72 See, e.g. *The Winson: China Pacific S.A.* v. *The Food Corporation of India* [1982]
A.C. 939.

Clause 2 of the LOF 1980 puts a specific obligation on the shipowner to 'co-operate fully' with the salvor. The owner will be in breach if he causes unnecessary delay, e.g. in refusing to help the salvor get permission to enter a port in the owner's country. The salvor is also entitled to make reasonable use of the vessel's equipment, provided that he does not cause unnecessary damage. Even where a salvor has brought cargo from a wrecked ship to a place of safety he still has a bailee's duty to take reasonable measures to preserve the cargo (e.g. by warehousing it) until the owners take possession.[73]

24.10.5   SALVAGE SECURITY

Although salvors have a maritime lien, they often have a problem enforcing this in practice. Under Clause 4 they can ask for security to be provided to Lloyd's, but they must not ask for an unreasonably high amount to be given.[74] The salvor also agrees not to arrest or detain the property if security is provided.[75] We have already noted that the salvors cannot force the shipowners to provide security for the proportion of the award likely to be payable by cargo,[76] although cargo may have to pay the bulk of the award. Clause 5 puts an obligation on the shipowners, before releasing the cargo, to use 'best endeavours' to ensure that the cargo owners provide security. Thus, if the shipowners allow the cargo owners to spirit away the goods in order to avoid paying for salvage, without at least warning the salvors, then the shipowners themselves will be in breach of contract. They may have to pay the salvors for cargo's proportion of salvage if the cargo owners cannot be traced. However, this simple breach of contract is not a claim for 'salvage' and so would not create a maritime or statutory lien giving the salvor the right to arrest the owner's ship.[77]

---

73 *Ibid*. The salvor should normally give possession to the cargo-owner rather than back to the shipowner.

74 *The Tribels* [1985] 1 Lloyd's Rep. 128.

75 Clause 5. Under that clause the salvor may only arrest or detain the ship if no security is provided within 14 days of the termination of services, or if the shipowner threatens to move the ship without the salvor's consent. For unauthorized detention, the shipowners would be entitled to damages for delay and any extra legal expenses involved in trying to release the vessel; *Ellerman Lines Ltd* v. *Read* [1928] 2 K.B. 144.

76 See Section 24.6.1, *supra*.

77 *The Tesaba* [1982] 1 Lloyd's Rep. 397.

24.10.6 ARBITRATION

Clause 1(b) provides that the salvage remuneration be fixed by arbitration[78] in London. Any *other* differences arising out of the agreement or operations thereunder are also to be arbitrated. Thus, allegations that the salvage tug involved in the *Amoco Cadiz* disaster was negligent and made misrepresentations *before* the LOF was agreed fell to be dealt with at arbitration and not before the US courts.[79]

The arbitration is usually heard by a Queen's Counsel experienced in maritime law. He does have the power, under Clause 10, to make an interim award so that salvors are not kept out of their money indefinitely. He may also order that one of the parties, e.g. the cargo-owner, be allowed to inspect the ship, or other property.[80]

There is a right of appeal to an appeal arbitrator – who is similarly experienced. His award is binding on all parties, represented or not. Once the award is made, Lloyd's will pay it out of the security provided.

24.10.7 POLLUTION PREVENTION

Following numerous tanker casualties where salvors faced high risks (including liability claims)[81] but low salved values, many began to question whether there was any incentive for them to get involved in such incidents. Yet it was clearly in the interests of the shipping industry and those concerned about the environment to encourage salvors to use their best endeavours to reduce pollution. The 1980 amendments to the LOF were designed to overcome some of the salvors' problems.[82] We may note two important changes.

(A) ENHANCED AWARD

Clause 1(a) puts an obligation on the salvor to use his 'best endeavours' not only to salve the ship, but also 'to prevent the escape of oil from the vessel while performing the services of salving'. Although a salvor could be in breach if he fails to fulfil this duty the idea is to give him an

78 See Section 1.2, *supra*.
79 *Amoco Transport Co.* v. *Bugsier Reederei* [1981] A.M.C. 2407.
80 *The Vasso* [1983] 3 All E.R. 211.
81 See, e.g. *The Tojo Maru* [1972] A.C. 242; *The Eschersheim* [1976] 2 Lloyd's Rep. 1; *The Amoco Cadiz* [1984] 2 Lloyd's Rep. 304.
82 See, e.g., A. Bessemer-Clark 'The Role of the LOF 1980' [1980] 3 LMCLQ 297, A. Miller, 'Lloyd's Open Form 1980, A Commentary' (1981) 12 JMLC 243.

'enhanced' (i.e., increased) award if, in saving property, he has prevented oil pollution. Enhancement already occurs with life salvage[83]
and the theory is that the enhanced award should be treated as an
ordinary salvage award, payable in the ordinary way by underwriters.[84]

(B)   SAFETY NET

Clause 1(a) continues by stating an exception to the 'no cure – no pay'
principle where the property being salved is an oil tanker laden or partly
laden with a cargo of oil. Where there is no 'success' (in the traditional
sense of some valuable property being saved) the salvor is entitled to his
reasonably incurred expenses and an increment (to represent profit) of
up to 15 per cent of these expenses. There may be no 'success' because
the tanker sinks despite much work or because a government uses its
intervention powers to destroy the tanker.[85] The salvor is only entitled
to his expenses if the lack of success was not caused by his own
negligence. The money is payable *only* by the shipowner – and not the
cargo-owner. The P & I Clubs agreed to pay for this sum, which has
been described as a 'safety net'. This is because it protects a salvor where
he has no chance of a traditional salvage award. The exact amount of the
'safety net' is a matter for the arbitrator, but the salvor knows that he
should not lose if he becomes involved in an oil tanker casualty.

24.10.8   SALVOR'S LIMITATION

As we have seen,[86] a salvor may be concerned about his ability to limit •
liability. Clause 21 of the LOF gives the salvor the protection of the 1976
Limitation Convention.[87] This means that if the salvor causes liability
to the ship or cargo owner while not operating from a salvage vessel he
will be able to limit his liability. To that extent *The Tojo Maru*[88] decision
is overcome. But a third party who is injured by the negligence of the
salvor would be able to claim full damages as clause 21 only binds
parties to the LOF contract.

83 See Section 24.2.2, *supra*.
84 See Section 30.3, *infra*. Underwriters in the London market agreed to the
   enhancement, but it appears that some overseas underwriters are less happy about
   the concept.
85 See Section 25.1.3, *infra*.
86 Section 24.7.2, *infra*.
87 See Section 22.3.3, *supra*. Now the Convention is in force, Clause 21 is not
   necessary in the UK.
88 [1972] A.C. 242.

24.11   THE DRAFT SALVAGE CONVENTION

The revisions to the LOF showed that the existing regime of the 1910 Salvage Convention was becoming out of date. In 1981 CMI[89] produced a Draft Salvage Convention for consideration by IMO. The Draft has been under consideration by IMO's Legal Committee for some time and it is to be expected that a diplomatic conference to agree a new Convention will be convened in the next few years, perhaps in 1988. We can consider, in outline only, the basic features of the consolidated working text produced by the IMO Secretariat.[90]

The Draft Convention is much more modern in form and content than the 1910 Convention. It would clearly apply, for instance, to any 'structure capable of navigation'[91] such as a semi-submersible oil rig. The Draft allows parties to 'contract out' of the Convention, e.g. by agreeing an LOF, although some countries wanted the Convention to apply mandatorily.[92] Some provisions are very similar to the 1910 Convention,[93] while others have close affinities to the LOF 1980.[94] Thus, there is an obligation on the salvor to use 'best endeavours' in the salvage and to obtain assistance from other salvors where the circumstances so require.[95] Owners are also required to co-operate fully with the salvor and to accept redelivery when reasonably requested.[96]

Both salvor and the owner and master of the vessel in distress must use 'best endeavours' to 'prevent or minimize damage to the environment'.[97] This is defined as 'substantial physical damage to human health or to marine life or resources in coastal or inland waters or areas adjacent thereto, caused by pollution, explosion, contamination, fire or similar major incidents'. It will be noted that this definition covers many more matters than mere oil pollution.

---

89 The International Maritime Committee is composed of national maritime law associations and is essentially non-governmental in nature. Its experts were responsible for drafting many maritime law conventions (such as the 1910 Collision and Salvage Conventions) before IMO – the specialized UN agency – began to take on such responsibilities.
90 LEG 55/3 Annex 1, 30 July 1985.
91 Art. 1.
92 Art. 4.
93 E.g., Art. 8, the duty to render assistance.
94 E.g., Arts 6, 7.
95 Art. 7.
96 Art. 6.
97 Arts 6(1), 7(1).

The definition is particularly relevant when considering the salvor's reward. The Draft maintains the LOF 1980 distinction between the 'enhanced award' and the 'safety net'.[98] However, the Draft allows the enhancement to take account of the skill and efforts of the salvor in preventing or minimizing damage to the environment, as defined.[99] The 'safety net', called 'special compensation' in the Draft,[1] is also more favourable to the salvor than the LOF 1980. If he carries out operations in circumstances where there is a threat of environmental damage, the salvor is entitled to his expenses – even if he has not prevented or minimized the damage.[2] If he has actually done so then he may be awarded his expenses and an increment of up to 100 per cent of those expenses.[3]

The Draft also follows the LOF 1980 by requiring security to be provided and the owner of the vessel to use best endeavours to ensure cargo owners provide security.[4] Interim payments are also possible.[5]

24.12 WRECK

24.12.1 ADMINISTRATION OF WRECKS

The Merchant Shipping Act 1894, ss. 510–537 contain provisions dealing with wreck which were mainly designed to deal with the problem of persons plundering wrecks washed ashore. The nineteenth-century solution was to give wide powers to local officials called Receivers of Wreck. At present here are just over 100 Receivers who are usually customs officers.[6] The Receivers may take command of operations to preserve the wreck and human lives. Disobeying or obstructing the Receiver is an offence.[7]

98 See Section 24.10.7, *supra*.
99 Art. 11(1)(b). It will be recalled that the LOF 1980 only recognizes the salvors' skills in reducing *oil* pollution; see Section 24.10.7, *supra*.
1 Art. 12.
2 Art. 12(1).
3 Art. 12(2). The LOF 1980 increment was 15%; see Section 24.10.7, *supra*.
4 Art. 19.
5 Art. 20.
6 Appointed under s. 566.
7 Ss. 511, 512, 514.

The Act sets up a procedure for dealing with wreck. Anyone finding a wreck in UK waters must deliver it to the Receiver.[8] This requirement also applies to wreck found or taken possession of outside UK waters and then brought into the UK.[9] Failure to comply can mean a fine and forfeiture of any right to salvage.[10] Plundering or interfering with the wreck is an offence,[11] as it is to take aboard property from a wreck in the UK.[12]

Once the Receiver takes possession of the wreck he must advertise the fact and will normally notify Lloyd's, as the insurers may be the true owners.[13] Subject to paying salvage and expenses the owner is entitled to claim the wreck.[14] Wreck unclaimed within one year of its coming into the possession of the Receiver belongs to the Crown.[15] However, in practice unclaimed wreck only brings in a few thousand pounds a year, at most. The cost of the service exceeds this by far.

The present system for administering wrecks is under review, partly because of expense and partly because modern means of communication mean that corporate owners will usually be able to make their own salvage arrangements. In 1984 the DoT issued a Consultative Document proposing changes to wreck legislation designed to protect the national heritage, but also to provide adequate recompense to salvors. It is proposed to abolish the office of Receiver, but to require all wreck found or brought within UK territorial waters to be reported to the nearest Customs and Excise Office. Wreck unclaimed within two months of the report would vest in the Crown. The Crown would then have two months to decide whether to give the wreck to a museum, subject to payment of salvage. Where no undertaking was given to a museum, title would be renounced in favour of the salvor. These changes would take account of the legislation dealing with historic wrecks.[16]

8 S. 518.
9 Merchant Shipping Act 1906, s. 72.
10 Merchant Shipping Act 1894, s. 518.
11 Ss. 519, 536. Under the Protection of Wrecks Act 1973, s. 2, the Secretary of State may designate a prohibited area around a dangerous wreck.
12 S. 535.
13 S. 520.
14 S. 521. The Receiver's fee is 7.5% of the value of the wreck, Merchant Shipping (Fees) Regulations 1985 (S.I. No. 1607), Sch. Pt. VII.
15 Ss. 521, 523. Salvors of modern wrecks could probably expect to receive 50% of the proceeds of sale (more, if heavy expenses were involved), the Crown keeping the remainder. The Crown has no rights to unclaimed wrecks outside UK territorial waters, *The Lusitania* [1986] 1 Lloyd's Rep. 132.
16 See Section 24.12.3, *infra*.

24.12.2   SALVAGE OF WRECKS[17]

Recent technological developments have meant that it is now possible for salvage operations to be undertaken on vessels which were long thought to be irrecoverable. In 1981 several tons of gold bullion were rescued from HMS *Edinburgh*, sunk while carrying it from Russia to Britain in the Second World War. The salvors were awarded compensation under an agreement with the British and Soviet Governments.[18]

In September 1985 an expedition discovered the wreck of the *Titanic* over two miles under the Atlantic.[19] Assuming the wreck could be raised a salvage claim could be made, but who would be the owners? This raises very difficult unsolved questions as to whether ownership of property can be lost by the passage of time.

In one case a submarine which had remained on the sea-bed for 25 years had not become *res nullius*.[20] This meant that the Federal Republic of Germany was able to sell its rights to a commercial salvor. On the other hand courts in the USA seem prepared to apply the law of finding to, e.g., a long lost Spanish galleon. This means that the 'finder' could claim title to the property.[21]

Illustration: *The Lusitania*[22]

In 1915 the British registered liner *Lusitania* was torpedoed and sunk in international waters. War risks insurers paid the owners, Cunard, for a total loss. In 1982, 94 items from the ship were salvaged. It was agreed that the insurers acquired legal title to the vessel, her hull, machinery, appurtenances, fixtures and fittings and the accoutrements, loose equipment, furniture or other goods owned by Cunard at the time of the loss. A dispute arose as to the ownership of the contents (both cargo and passengers' property and effects). After a lapse of 67 years it was inferred that the original owners had abandoned their property.

Held: The Crown had no right to unclaimed wreck found outside UK waters. Accordingly, the salvors, as finders in possession, had a better right to the property than all but the true owners.

---

17 See Marsden, 'Admiralty Droits and Salvage' (1899) 15 L.Q.R. 353; S. Braekhus, 'Salvage of Wrecks and Wreckage' [1976] *Scandinavian Studies in Law*, 39, Brice (1983), pp. 114-118; also Sections 24.6.2, 24.6.3, *supra*.
18 *Cf. The Egypt* (1932) 44 Ll.L. Rep. 21. Note the effect of the Protection of Military Remains Act 1986.
19 See *Sunday Telegraph* and *Observer* of 8 September 1985.
20 *Simon* v. *Taylor* [1975] 2 Lloyd's Rep. 338.
21 See, e.g. *Treasure Salvors Inc.* v. *The Unidentified Wreck and Abandoned Vessel* [1985] A.M.C. 136.
22 [1986] 1 Lloyd's Rep. 132.

So far as the *Titanic* is concerned, ownership might be claimed by the successors in title to the White Star Line[23] or by the insurers who paid out for her loss.[24] It would prove exceptionally difficult to trace ownership after all these years. The difficulties are likely to increase, particularly with the growing popularity of sub-aqua clubs. In July 1985 it was reported that divers had found over £1 million worth of coins on an East Indiaman wrecked on the Goodwin Sands in 1809.[25]

24.12.3   PROTECTION OF WRECKS

To protect historic wrecks from treasure hunters the Protection of Wrecks Act 1973 was enacted. This gives the DoT power to make protection orders and issue licences to suitable salvors. Where there is a site in UK waters containing a wreck of historical, archaeological or artistic importance a restricted area around the site may be designated by order.[26] There are about 25–30 such orders at present.[27]   For instance, they have been made in respect of *The Mary Rose,* Henry VIII's flagship lost at Spithead in 1545 and HMS *Colossus*, lost with Sir William Hamilton's collection of Greek and Roman antiquities off the Scilly Isles in 1798.[28] Applications for designation almost invariably come from the finder.

It is an offence to tamper with wrecks in restricted areas or to carry out salvage operations on them without a licence from the DoT.[29]

23 It merged with Cunard in 1934.
24 *Cf.* ss. 63, 79, Marine Insurance Act 1906 entitling the insurer to take over the interest of the assured in the subject-matter insured. In practice, cargo underwriters tend to claim rights of ownership, while hull underwriters have little incentive to do so. This is because the hull is unlikely to have any commercial value while the cargo could even increase in value.
25 *Observer* 28 July 1985. See the designation order in fn. 27, *infra.*
26 S. 1(1). Consultations usually take place beforehand with interested bodies, such as Coastguards, Trinity House and Harbour Authorities; s. 1(4). Expert archaeological advice will be sought by the DoT, which also has advice from an unofficial Advisory Committee. By s. 61(8)(b) of the Ancient Monuments and Archaeological Areas Act 1979 that Act does not apply to a site designated by the Protection of Wrecks Act 1973.
27 For a restricted area of 150 metres around a wreck off the Goodwin Sands see, The Protection of Wrecks (Designation No. 1) Order 1985 (S.I. No. 699).
28 When a site is worked out the order is revoked, as with *The Colossus*.
29 S. 1(3). Prosecutions are rare. It is difficult to obtain accurate information and the Act is theoretically 'policed' by the Receivers of Wreck. Under s. 2 there is a power to designate a prohibited area around dangerous wrecks.

The DoT issues one licence per site for competent persons to carry out salvage operations or historical research.[30] Applicants who wish to survey sites must have access to some archaeological expertise, but the requirements for an excavation licence tend to be more strict. Some licences are permanent – as with *The Mary Rose*: otherwise licences are renewed annually. In practice, licensees have to submit annual reports showing the work they have done. If little or no activity has taken place the licence may not be renewed. In practice salvors of unclaimed historic wrecks are given most or all of the net proceeds of sale in order to encourage reporting. In the case of unclaimed coins the salvors can normally expect to receive about 75 per cent of the proceeds.

Because of concern over interference with the wreckage of crashed, sunken and stranded military vessels and aircraft, the Protection of Military Remains Act 1986 was passed. In order to protect and preserve the remains the Act declares certain places to be 'protected', namely those which comprise the remains of the vessel or aircraft (or substantial parts of them) at or near the site of the casualty, or e.g. on the sea-bed.[31] The Secretary of State is given power to designate as a 'controlled site' an area around the remains, provided that less than 200 years has elapsed since the casualty occurred.[32] Controlled sites can only be designated in respect of foreign military vessels where the remains are in UK waters.[33]

The Act applies to any aircraft which crashes while in the service of the armed forces of any country.[34] Merchant vessels are not protected, whether British of foreign.[35] Where a sunken or stranded military vessel is outside a controlled site, the Act applies if the vessel itself has been designated by the Secretary of State.[36] The sinking or stranding has to have taken place after the start of World War I[37] and foreign military vessels can only be designated where the remains are in UK

---

30 S. 1(5).

31 S. 1(6).

32 S. 1(2), (4).

33 S. 1(4).

34 S. 1(1). The Act would therefore apply to aircraft such as the Wellington bomber recently raised from a Scottish loch. Hovercraft, gliders and balloons are included in the definition, s. 9(1).

35 Note that the definition of military vessel in s. 9(2) includes those being used for the purposes of the UK armed forces. This could include chartered vessels.

36 S. 1(2). Vessels can be designated even where the exact position of their remains is unknown.

37 I.e., on 4 August 1914, s. 1(3). Under s. 2(8) the Secretary of State is given power to substitute a later date.

waters.[38] Thus, in international waters, protection can only be provided for the remains of UK military vessels or aircraft.[39] In those
waters it is provided that the controlled site should not extend unduly
and, in effect, should not be more than two nautical miles wide.[40] The
remains protected include the contents of the vessels or aircraft, such as
cargo, munitions, apparel, personal effects and human remains.[41]

The Act creates a number of offences, depending on whether there is
direct or indirect interference. On a controlled site, it is an offence
physically to interfere with the remains, e.g. by tampering, moving,
removing or unearthing them, or by entering a hatch or opening in
them.[42] In a protected place, such conduct is only an offence if the
defendant believes, or has reasonable grounds for suspecting, that the
remains there are protected.[43] Also prohibited are activities aimed at
discovering and reaching the remains, such as excavation or diving or
salvage operations.[44] It is an offence to use equipment in connection
with such operations – so those on board support vessels could also be
guilty.[45] A person who shows a belief on reasonable grounds that a
place was not a protected place has a defence, but ignorance of the
existence of a controlled site is no excuse.[46] It is also a defence to show
that the interference was urgently necessary in the interests of safety or
health, or to prevent serious damage to property.[47] A specific limitation
of the Act is that in relation to remains in international waters it only
creates offences for British persons and those operating from British-
controlled ships.[48]

The Secretary of State, however, is given wide powers to issue
licences for work on remains.[49] Like the licence system under the
Protection of Wrecks Act 1973, conditions may be attached to the

38 S. 1(3). When the remains are partly in UK and partly in international waters, they
are treated as being in two separate places, s. 9(3).
39 S. 1(4), (6). Thus the Act could extend to the wrecks of HMS *Repulse* and HMS
Prince of Wales, sunk off the coast of Malaysia during World War II (assuming them
to be resting in international waters).
40 S. 1(5).
41 S. 9. Other remains within a protected place or controlled site, such as those from
a merchant vessel, may be covered under the Act, s. 2(9).
42 S. 2(1), (2).
43 *Ibid.*
44 S. 2(1), (3).
45 *Ibid.*
46 S. 2(5). The Statutory Instrument designating the site will, of course, be published.
47 S. 2(6).
48 S. 3(1). Consent of the DPP may need to be obtained, s. 3(3).
49 S. 4. See also s. 2(4).

licence,[50] e.g. so that proper respect may be shown to the human remains in what is, in effect, a war-grave. The grant of a licence does not affect the existing rights of owners of sunken property.[51] In order to police the Act wide powers are given to persons authorized by the Secretary of State to detect offences.[52] Vessels may be boarded and property seized.[53]

50 S. 4(3).
51 S. 4(6). Apart from the Crown, these owners could include foreign governments and those individuals who have bought salvage rights from states. However, it would appear that it is possible for such owners to commit offences if, without a licence, they tamper with remains.
52 S. 6. The authority must be in writing (s. 6(8)) and has to be produced on demand (s. 6(5)).
53 S. 6(3).

25

MARINE POLLUTION[1]

In recent years the dangers of marine pollution have become more apparent. The havoc caused by tanker casualties, in particular, was brought home by the wrecks of two tankers in waters close to British shores, that of the *Torrey Canyon* in 1967 off the Isles of Scilly, and that of the *Amoco Cadiz* off the coast of Brittany in 1978.[2] These disasters provided a stimulus to international action. However, it must not be thought that these incidents have been the biggest source of pollution: operational discharges must also be considered. Most attention has so far been devoted to oil, but there are many other hazardous and noxious substances being carried which could cause problems.

This subject has two main legal aspects. First, there are rules designed to prevent pollution: these are regulatory in nature and are usually enforced by the criminal law. Secondly, there are the rules designed to provide compensation for the victims of pollution: these rely on ordinary remedies such as damages obtainable in the civil courts.

25.1 PREVENTION

25.1.1 CONSTRUCTION AND SAFETY RULES

We have already considered many of the detailed rules designed to make ships, and tankers in particular, as safe and efficient as possible.[3] It is worth recalling that MARPOL 1973/78 has specific provisions on matters such as segregated ballast tanks, crude oil washing, as well as separating and filtering equipment.

---

1 For background reading, J. Bates, *United Kingdom Marine Pollution Law* (1985); D. Abecassis, *Oil Pollution from Ships – International, UK and United States Law* (1985); M. Summerskill, *Oil Rigs, Law and Insurance* (1979), Royal Commission of the Environment, 3rd Report 1972 (Cmnd 5054), 8th Report 1981 (Cmnd 8358).
2 See Sections 5.4 and 8.1, *supra*.
3 See Section 8, *supra*.

Again, we have noted efforts to provide better training for crews[4] and to designate traffic separation schemes to avoid collisions.[5]

25.1.2   DISCHARGES

Probably the largest source of oil pollution has been the discharges caused when tankers clean their tanks at sea. There were technical problems in earlier years about how tanks were to be cleaned, but many of these have been overcome with the introduction of load-on-top procedures and crude oil washing. The former method involves loading a new cargo onto the residues of the old, while the latter uses oil cargo itself, under pressure from special pumps, to clean tank walls.

The first relevant international convention in 1954, known as OilPol, introduced restrictions on the discharge of oil,[6] and was amended a number of times.[7] OilPol has now been replaced by MARPOL 1973/78 which is a comprehensive convention dealing with pollution prevention. When fully in force MARPOL 1973/78 will regulate pollution from ships whether caused by oil (Annex I), noxious liquid substances in bulk (Annex II), harmful substances carried in packaged form (Annex III), sewage (Annex IV) and garbage (Annex V). As noted already,[8] MARPOL 1973/78 and its Annex I were given effect by the Merchant Shipping (Prevention of Oil Pollution) Regulations 1983.[9] The Regulations lay down certain requirements for discharges by tankers and other ships.[10]

The scheme of MARPOL is for each state to control discharges by its own ships wherever they are, e.g. on the high seas, but to enforce the MARPOL rules against all ships in its own territorial waters.[11] For non-oil tankers (and for the machinery space bilges of such tankers)[12] a number of conditions must be satisfied before any oil,[13] or oily

---

4 See Section 9.2, *supra*.

5 See Section 21.2, *supra*.

6 See Singh (1983) Vol. 3, p. 2233. It was enacted in the Oil in Navigable Waters Act 1955.

7 In 1962, 1969, 1971.

8 See Singh (1983) Vol. 3, pp. 2272, 2424. Chapter 8, *supra*.

9 S.I. No. 1398, amended as from 7 January 1986 by 1985 (S.I. No. 2040).

10 See M.S. Notice No. M. 1141.

11 See regs 12(1), 13(1), as amended by the Prevention of Oil Pollution Act 1986. *Cf.* *The Mihalis* [1984] 2 Lloyd's Rep. 525.

12 Reg. 12.

13 Defined widely in reg. 1 to include any form of petroleum, including crude oil, fuel oil, sludge, oil refuse and refined products other than those specified in M.S. Notice No. M. 1077.

mixture,[14] is discharged into the sea. The ship must be proceeding on a voyage, outside a 'special area', more than 12 miles from land; the oil content of the discharge must be less than 100 ppm of the mixtures; and the ship must have an oil discharge monitoring and control system, oily water separating equipment, oil filtering system or other installation as required. These detailed requirements do not apply to discharges which, without dilution, have an oil content not exceeding 15 ppm of the mixture.

There are more stringent conditions to be complied with before oil-tankers can discharge oil or oily mixtures into the sea.[15] The tanker must be proceeding on a voyage, outside a special area, more than 50 miles from land; no more than 60 litres of oil per mile must be discharged; the total amount discharged must not exceed a certain proportion of the cargo of which the residue formed a part;[16] and the tanker must have an oil discharge monitoring and control system and a slop tank arrangement.

Any oil remaining on board after discharge which cannot be disposed of according to the above conditions must be retained on board and discharged into reception facilities.[17] MARPOL 1973/78 puts an obligation on states to provide reception facilities for oily wastes[18] and so the UK has enacted the Merchant Shipping Prevention of Pollution (Reception Facilities) Order 1984.[19] This requires harbour authorities and terminal operators to provide sufficient reception facilities to meet the needs of ships without causing undue delay. The reception facilities need only be provided for ships whose main purpose in being in the harbour is to use other facilities, e.g. to load or discharge their cargoes.

The 'special areas' referred to earlier are those enclosed seas where oil cannot disperse easily: the Mediterranean Sea, the Black Sea, the Red Sea and the (Persian) Gulf. Within these areas discharge is forbidden for all UK oil tankers and other ships over 400 GRT.[20] For ships under this

14 Meaning a mixture with any oil content, reg. 1.
15 Reg. 13. Clean or segregated ballast may be discharged, reg. 13(3).
16 1/15 000 for existing ships, or 1/30 000 for new ships, reg. 13(2)(e). For a new ship with a 300 000 ton cargo that would mean 10 tons: in fact several hundred tons could remain on board after discharge. New ships are all those delivered after 31 December 1979, but could include ships for which building contracts were placed after 31 December 1975, reg. 1, and see Section 8.5.1, *supra*.
17 Regs 12(5), 13(5).
18 Annex I, reg. 12. Annex II, reg. 7, (in force from 6 April 1987), will apply to wastes for chemical tankers, and see Section 8.5.1, *supra*.
19 S.I. No. 862, in force on 25 July 1984 (M.S. Notice M. 1156). This repealed the Prevention of Oil Pollution Act 1971, s. 9.
20 1983 (S.I. No. 1398), reg. 16(2), with the exception of clean and segregated ballast and a small amount of machinery bilgewater, reg. 16(3).

tonnage very limited quantities of oil may be discharged, but never less than 12 miles from land. Although the Regulations are designed mainly for ships, there are special rules for offshore installations, such as mobile, or fixed drilling or production, platforms.[21] With certain modifications they have to comply with the requirements for non-tankers over 400 GRT.

However, harbour authorities which cause oil to escape as a result of their wreck raising duties do not commit an offence unless the prosecution can show that they failed to take reasonable steps to prevent the escape.[22]

Failure to comply with the Regulations is an offence for which the owner *and* master can each be guilty of an offence.[23] Both are punishable because it is desired to prevent carelessness on the part of a master as well as to prevent collusion with the owner, who could save a great deal of time and money if the tanks were cleaned at sea.[24]

We have mentioned that contravention of these provisions is an offence. But it is a defence to show that all reasonable precautions were taken and all due diligence was exercised to avoid committing the offence.[25] Moreover, there is no offence if the discharge was necessary to save the ship or life at sea;[26] or if it resulted from damage to the ship or its equipment,[27] provided that all reasonable steps were taken afterwards to reduce the discharge and unless the owner or master acted with intent to cause loss, or recklessly and with knowledge that such loss would probably result.[28]

---

21 Reg. 30. Note also the Prevention of Oil Pollution Act 1971, ss. 1–3; Prevention of Oil Pollution Act 1971 (Application of Section 1) Regulations 1984 (S.I. No. 1684).

22 S. 7.

23 1983 (S.I. No. 1398), reg. 34(2), Prevention of Oil Pollution Act 1971, s. 2(4). The punishment could be a £50 000 fine in a magistrates' court and an unlimited fine in the Crown Court. Note also the effect of the Prevention of Oil Pollution Act 1986 s. 1.

24 Under the previous law, the master *or* owner could be guilty and in *The Huntingdon: Federal Steam Navigation Co.* v. *Department of Trade and Industry* [1974] 2 All E.R. 97, they argued that one *or* the other could be convicted, but not both. In a remarkable piece of statutory interpretation the House of Lords held that 'or' meant 'and'! Both were convicted. The matter is not entirely academic because many older regulations still use this formula. The new provision is clearer.

25 Reg. 34(3).

26 *Cf. Esso* v. *Southport Corporation* [1956] A.C. 218, Section 25.2.1, *infra*.

27 Thus, there is no criminal offence if oil is discharged as a result of a collision — even if it was caused negligently. Later carelessness is different. Of course, the master might commit a separate offence for failing to comply with the collision regulations, see Section 21.2, *supra*.

28 See Section 22.3.4 for an explanation of this expression.

Finally, mention should be made of oil pollution from pipelines and the Convention for the Prevention of Marine Pollution from Land-Based Sources 1974,[29] which has been implemented by Regulations.[30] Owners of a pipeline, and persons carrying out sea-bed operations[31] commit an offence if oil[32] is discharged into the sea both outside territorial waters,[33] and within them.[34]

25.1.3 GOVERNMENT INTERVENTION

One of the questions raised by the *Torrey Canyon* disaster was the extent to which, after a casualty, governments could intervene and control operations, particularly where foreign ships on the high seas were concerned. The *Torrey Canyon* was eventually set on fire by bombing. Many states, including the UK,[35] have asserted that there exists a customary right to take measures beyond their waters to protect those waters from actual or threatened damage.[36] To remove doubts IMO agreed the International Convention Relating to Intervention on the High Seas in Cases of Oil Pollution Casualties 1969. This enabled states to take measures on the high seas to prevent, mitigate or eliminate grave and imminent danger to coastlines or related interests from oil pollution resulting from a marine casualty: provided that major harmful consequences could reasonably be expected.[37] The power to intervene was extended by a Protocol in 1973 to a long list of dangerous or noxious chemicals other than oil.

The 1969 Convention and its Protocol have been enacted in English law by the Prevention of Oil Pollution Act 1971 and a 1980 Order.[38] Intervention action may be taken against foreign registered vessels

29 Cmnd 5803.
30 Prevention of Oil Pollution Act 1971 (Application of s. 1) Regulations 1984 (S.I. No. 1684).
31 In designated areas under the Continental Shelf Act 1964, Oil and Gas (Enterprise) Act 1982, s. 37, Sch. 3.
32 Meaning crude oil (including oil produced directly or indirectly from it), fuel oil, lubricating oil and heavy diesel oil, reg. 2 and s. 1(2) of the Prevention of Oil Pollution Act 1971.
33 Prevention of Oil Pollution Act 1971, s. 3.
34 Ss. 2, 3: *cf. Rankin* v. *De Coster* [1975] 2 All E.R. 303.
35 See Cmnd 7525, Annex 1.
36 See also Art. 221 of UNCLOS 1982, Section 2.1, *supra*.
37 Art. 1.
38 Merchant Shipping (Prevention of Pollution) (Intervention) Order 1980 (S.I. No. 1093), made under the Merchant Shipping Act 1979, s. 20. For the Convention and Protocol, see Singh (1983) Vol. 3, pp. 2454, 2482.

outside UK territorial waters when there is a grave and imminent danger of pollution – as laid down in the Convention.[39]

For all UK ships, and foreign ships in UK waters, the powers may be exercised where an accident has occurred to a ship and the Secretary of State thinks that substances from the ship could cause pollution on a large scale in the UK or its waters; and in his opinion he needs to exercise his powers urgently.[40] There is a wide power to give directions to owners, masters and salvors in possession of the vessel.[41] They may be told to: move (or not move) the vessel; take a particular route or go to a specified place; unload (or not unload) the cargo.[42] If these powers do not seem adequate the Secretary of State may take 'any action of any kind whatsoever' as respects the ship and cargo.[43] In particular, he may take over control of the ship or, indeed sink or destroy it.[44] Of course, the Secretary of State is advised by officials in the DoT and powers have been delegated to the head of the Marine Pollution Control Unit (MPCU).[45] This body, headed by a naval officer and with a permanent staff of experts, acts as a focal point of central government action.

The powers have been used twice. The tanker *Christos Bitas* went aground off Wales in October 1978. A salvage tug was ordered to hold the ship in the Irish Sea for cargo transfer operations rather than make for shelter in a British port. The tanker was eventually scuttled, but in practice all decisions were made by agreement of the owners, salvors and insurers. Agreement was facilitated because it was established that the cost of towing the wreck into port would exceed its value as scrap when salved. In May 1978 the bow of the oil tanker *Eleni V* was sliced off in a collision. The stern section was towed to Rotterdam. The bow section could not be salved and so it was towed to deep water and blown up. The owner's agents did not object.[46]

---

39 S. 16 and Art. 7 of the 1980 Order.

40 S. 12(1) and Art. 4 of the 1980 Order.

41 S. 12(2).

42 S. 12(3).

43 S. 12(4).

44 *Ibid.*

45 See s. 12(5).

46 See IMO LEG 54/4/Add. 1 (28 February 1985), Add. 2 (25 March 1985). See *The Roseline* [1981] 2 Lloyd's Rep. 410 for the *Eleni V* collision action. Also, Section 8.8.3, *supra*, for harbour master's powers to refuse entry; Section 24.10.7, *supra*, for salvage.

Failure to obey directions, or wilfully obstructing a person serving them, is an offence.[47] Directions to foreign ships beyond territorial waters can only be served on a UK citizen or company.[48]

There is no right to compensation from the Government for damage or loss caused by the exercise of the intervention powers unless the action taken was not reasonably necessary to prevent oil pollution or was disproportionate.[49] For instance, the Government would probably be liable if it destroyed a temporarily stranded tanker because a ton of oil remained on board. However, a shipowner would usually be insured against the risk of intervention damage.[50]

After the *Amoco Cadiz* disaster there were moves by a number of governments to introduce new powers to allow a coastal state to 'commandeer' salvage vessels (foreign or not), which were in the vicinity, to help reduce the risk of pollution. This suggestion is rather controversial, but it is possible that there will be moves to make the intervention powers under the 1969 Convention more explicit.

25.1.4 DUMPING

Oil pollution legislation is largely designed to prevent spillages and discharges of cargo where the main aim is to transport the oil safely between ports. A different type of pollution problem is presented by substances, such as industrial wastes, which are taken on board with the express purpose of being dumped at sea. There are two relevant international conventions, the Convention for the Prevention of Marine Pollution by Dumping from Ships and Aircraft, Oslo, 1972,[51] and the Convention on the Prevention of Marine Pollution by Dumping of Waste and Other Matter, London, 1972.[52]

These conventions were enacted into UK law by the Dumping at Sea Act 1974. This has been replaced by the Food and Environment Protection Act 1985, Part II,[53] although the effect of the Acts is similar. The

---

47 S. 14(1); although it is a defence to show all due diligence had been used or that compliance might have involved a serious risk to human life, s. 14(2).

48 1980 Order, Art. 7(3).

49 S. 13. *Cf.* The Dangerous Vessels Act 1985, s. 2, Section 8.8.3, *supra.*

50 See, e.g., Institute Time Clauses (Hulls) 1983, clause 7 (see Appendix 14), and Section 29.3.1, *infra.*

51 Cmnd 6228. This is essentially a European Convention.

52 Cmnd 6486, amended in 1978 (Cmnd 7656) to deal with incineration at sea, and 1980 (Cmnd 8555), redefining some substances covered by the Convention. See Singh (1983) Vol. 3, pp. 2522, 2536.

53 See s. 15; as from 1 January 1986.

scheme of the 1985 Act is to require a licence for eight major types of dumping activity. In outline these are: deposits of substances or articles in UK waters from any vessel, hovercraft or marine structure[54] (whenever registered); deposits anywhere in or under the sea[55] from British vessels, hovercraft or marine structures; deposits in British fishery limits[56] from foreign vessels loaded in the UK;[57] scuttling of vessels in UK waters, or anywhere if controlled from British vessels, or in British fisheries limits if controlled from foreign vessels and the vessel scuttled was taken from UK waters; the loading of a vessel, hovercraft or marine structure (or vehicle) in UK waters for deposit anywhere at sea or under the sea-bed, the towing or propelling from UK waters of a vessel for scuttling anywhere.[58] A licence is also required for the incineration of substances at sea.[59]

The scuttling provisions, which are new, are important because one of the accepted ways of dealing with a ship badly damaged after a casualty is to tow her to sea for scuttling. This happened with the *Christos Bitas* in 1978, when no port would accept the stricken tanker.[60]

Power is given to exempt operations from licensing.[61] In deciding whether to issue a licence, the licensing authority[62] must take into account the need to protect the marine environment, human health and to prevent interference with legitimate uses of the sea.[63] Account must also be taken of alternative methods of disposal.[64] The licence may be issued subject to conditions, e.g. that a scuttling shall take place at a specified place, or that operations are automatically monitored.[65] Information about the effect of dumping is vital and applicants must be willing to permit examinations and tests to be carried out both before

54 E.g., a platform or other man-made structure at sea; but not a pipe-line, s. 24. See the Petroleum and Submarine Pipelines Act 1975, Part III, as amended.
55 'Sea' includes areas, such as estuaries, submerged at mean high water spring tides, s. 24.
56 As in the Fishery Limits Act 1976.
57 E.g., by using disused under-sea mine-shafts.
58 S. 5.
59 S. 6.
60 See Section 25.1.3, *supra*; and the Dangerous Vessels Act 1985, s. 1, Section 8.8, *supra*.
61 S.7. The Deposits in the Sea (Exemption) Order 1985 (S.I. No. 1699) exempts 25 deposits including those from normal navigation or maintenance, and certain fishing wastes, drilling muds and tunnel boring equipment.
62 The Minister of Agriculture, Fisheries and Food, or the Secretary of State, s. 24.
63 S. 8(1), e.g. fishing or leisure activities.
64 *Ibid.*
65 S. 8(4): note also s. 8(12), Sch. 3 on the right to make representations in such cases.

7777777777
777

and after the dumping: they may also be required to contribute towards the expense.[66] Licences may be varied or revoked, e.g. if circumstances change, or scientific knowledge increases.[67]

It is an offence to carry out the listed activities without a licence, or to contravene the licence conditions, or to make false or reckless statements in order to obtain a licence.[68] There is a defence if the dumping took place outside UK waters under the terms of licence issued by a state party to the London or Oslo Conventions. It is also a defence for a person to prove that the operation was carried out for the purpose of securing the safety of a vessel, or of saving life *and* that he took steps within a reasonable time to inform a minister of where and how the operation took place, as well as the substances involved.[69] There is also a general defence if a person proves he took all reasonable precautions and exercised all due diligence to avoid committing the offence. This will usually be established if a person shows he acted on the instructions of an employer, or relied on misleading information supplied by others.[70] There is no defence if the operation was necessary because of the fault of the defendant.[71]

A new power is given to a minister to take remedial action, e.g. in order to protect the marine environment and human health. If a person has been convicted of an operation which made this action necessary, reasonable expenses may be recovered from him. There are also wide enforcement powers given to officers.[72]

One area of current concern is whether it is safe to dump nuclear wastes at sea.[73] The dumping of high level radioactive waste is forbidden by the London Convention.[74] Following protests by seamen, licensed dumping of low and medium-level wastes by the UK was halted, pending scientific studies. In September 1985 a consultative meeting of the London Dumping Convention rejected a proposal to resume such dumping. While this informal moratorium continues, it

66 S. 8(5), (6), (8).
67 S. 8(10), (11). The public are entitled to inspect licences free of charge, s. 14, Sch. 4.
68 Ss. 9, 21.
69 S. 9(3).
70 S. 22. But a defendant must identify the other person to the prosecution a week before the case is heard, s. 22(3).
71 S. 9(4).
72 S. 11, Sch. 2, *cf.* Section 8.8, *supra.*
73 Note the application of the Control of Pollution Act 1974, Part II to radioactive wastes by the Control of Pollution (Radioactive Wastes) Regulations 1985 (S.I. No. 708).
74 Art. IV, Annex I.

appears as if attention may be switched to land storage of radioactive wastes.

25.2   COMPENSATION

Once a casualty has occurred, many persons could suffer pollution damage and they may wish to claim compensation. Criminal prosecutions would be of little use to them, as fines are paid to the State. There are special compensation rules for oil and nuclear damage, but none, as yet, for damage caused by other pollutants. So we need to look first at the general position under the common law and then at the special rules.

25.2.1   COMMON LAW LIABILITY

At common law, a claimant would usually have to base his claim in negligence[75] – just like an ordinary collision victim.[76] He may have difficulty in proving fault,[77] or be faced with low limits of liability.[78]

Illustration: _Esso Petroleum Co. Ltd v. Southport Corporation_[79]
After a steering failure an oil tanker ran aground in a river estuary. To prevent the ship breaking its back the master ordered the discharge of 400 tons of its cargo of oil which the tide carried to the foreshore belonging to a local authority. The authority incurred substantial clean-up costs.

Held: The action for damages was dismissed. No negligence had been proved against the shipowner. Actions for trespass and nuisance also failed because the discharge was caused by the necessity of removing danger to the lives of the crew.

As we shall see, this case would be decided differently today, but not if non-oil pollution had been caused, e.g. by noxious chemicals.

75 C. Ingram, 'Oil Pollution: _Rylands_ v. _Fletcher_' [1971] N.L.J. 183.
76 See Chapter 21, _supra_.
77 _Cf. The Amoco Cadiz_, Section 5.5, _supra_.
78 See Chapter 21, _supra_. _The Torrey Canyon_ caused some £6 million worth of damage, but the applicable limit could have been about £1.25 million in English law, Ingram, _op. cit._
79 [1956] A.C. 218.

25.2.2 OIL POLLUTION DAMAGE

To remove some of the uncertainties following the *Torrey Canyon* and to provide a better deal for oil pollution victims IMCO agreed the International Convention on Civil Liability for Oil Pollution Damage 1969 (CLC).[80] This was supplemented by the International Convention on the Establishment of an International Fund for Compensation for Oil Pollution Damage 1971 (the Fund Convention).[81] These have been enacted in English law by the Merchant Shipping (Oil Pollution) Act 1971 and the Merchant Shipping Act 1974.

(A) THE CLC: MERCHANT SHIPPING (OIL POLLUTION) ACT 1971

The basic scheme of the CLC is to make a shipowner strictly liable (i.e. without proof of fault) for damage caused by oil escaping from his tanker. There are some limited defences, but the shipowner is entitled to limit his liability to amounts greater than those allowed under the 1957 Limitation Convention. He must carry compulsory insurance and claims should all be settled in one country.[82]

The CLC applies only to pollution damage caused in contracting states,[83] by tankers actually carrying oil in bulk.[84] So it does not apply to pollution damage caused by the bunkers of ordinary ships, or to tankers on ballast runs. Oil is defined as persistent oil,[85] a rather obscure technical term.[86] In general terms, gasoline, UK diesels, light gas oils and home heating oils are non-persistent, while heavy crude oils low in volatiles and aromatics, heavy lubricants, asphalt, bitumen and some bunker oils are persistent.[87] Curiously, the definition expressly includes whale oil, although fish or vegetable oils could be equally unpleasant.

---

80 Cmnd 3678; Singh (1983) Vol. 3, p. 2454: it entered into force on 19 June 1975 and has 56 contracting states.

81 Cmnd 7383; Singh (1983) Vol. 3, p. 2495: it entered into force on 16 October 1978 and has 31 contracting states.

82 For the CLC time bar, see Section 26.1.3, *infra*.

83 Art. II; Merchant Shipping (Oil Pollution) Act, s. 1. These states can be discovered by consulting IMO or the Merchant Shipping (Oil Pollution) (Parties to Conventions) Order 1983 (S.I. No. 416).

84 Art. I(1); s. 1(1).

85 Art. I(5); s. 1(1).

86 See the definition used in the Oil Pollution (Compulsory Insurance) Regulations 1981 (S.I. No. 912).

87 Explanation courtesy of Mr E.B. Cowell of British Petroleum.

The CLC does not apply to warships and Government vessels wholly engaged on public, non-commercial duties, e.g. Royal Naval auxiliaries, which service ships in distant waters.[88]

The liability is for pollution damage only,[89] i.e. contamination damage in the UK, clean-up costs and damage caused by the clean-up operation. The latter is important because detergents can cause damage. One difficulty is knowing whether the definition applies to persons who claim to suffer economic losses.[90] After the *Amoco Cadiz* disaster ruined the beaches of Brittany in 1978 claims were submitted by hotel owners and others for lost profits because tourists stayed away. Such claims are speculative at best and are unlikely to succeed in English law.[91] In one US case,[92] commercial fishermen received damages when oil pollution reduced their catches, but more recently claims by fishing leisure industries, such as bait shops and restaurants, have been denied.[93]

We noted that the owners[94] are liable even where the escape of oil happens without the negligence of themselves or their employees. However, it is a defence if the spillage of oil was caused by an act of war, hostilities, civil war, insurrection, or by an 'exceptional, inevitable and irresistible natural phenomenon'.[95] The latter expression is similar to the traditional 'Act of God',[96] but much clearer. It indicates disasters such as earthquakes, tidal waves or hurricanes – the latter, at any rate when they occur out of season. Nor is the owner responsible if the spillage resulted wholly from the act of a third person, not a servant or agent of the owner, with intent to cause damage.[97] This would cover sabotage, or terrorist attacks. A third defence is that the spillage was due wholly to the negligence or wrongful act of a public authority in not maintaining lights or navigational aids.[98] Note the word 'wholly' in these last two defences. If the sabotage or failure to maintain lights was only a contributory cause of the disaster, other factors being, say, excessive speed, unseaworthiness or lax security, the owner must pay.

88 Art. XI; s. 14. See Section 1.6, *supra*.
89 Art. I(6); s. 1(1).
90 See also *The Mineral Transporter*, Section 21.6.3, *supra*.
91 See Section 21.6.3, *supra*.
92 *Union Oil Co.* v. *Oppen* (1974) 501 F. 2d 558.
93 *Louisiana (State) ex rel. Guste* v. *M/V Testbank* (1985) 752 F. 2d 1019. *The Amoco Cadiz* damages claims for up to US $2 billion have still to be heard.
94 That means the registered owner, Art. I.3, s. 20.
95 Art. III(2)(a); s. 2(a).
96 See Section 11.4, *supra*.
97 Art. III(2)(b); s. 2(b).
98 Art. III(2)(c); s. 2(c).

He would, of course, have a right to be indemnified by the wrongdoer.[99] Moreover, any amount payable can be reduced by the claimant's contributory negligence.[1]

As part of the compromise formula which was produced at the 1969 Conference shipowners were allowed to limit their liabilities, but to much higher limits than those allowed for property claims under the 1957 Limitation Convention.[2] The limits are 133 SDR per ton up to a maximum of 14 million SDR:[3] i.e. £101.10 and £10 642 198.[4]

The Act says nothing about what happens if an oil spillage flows from a collision in which the other ship is damaged and for which the tanker is at least partly to blame. It seems to follow that the tanker must pay the pollution victims up to the CLC limits and for the damage to the other ship up to the general maritime limits.[5] This is so even if the other vessel is an oil tanker: the CLC limits are separate from the general limits.[6] If oil from both tankers caused pollution they would be jointly liable up to their respective limits.[7] However, the higher CLC limits only apply to ships of member countries of the CLC. Other countries that were parties, with the UK, to the 1957 Limitation Convention were entitled to have their ships granted the lower 1957 limits.[8] Owners are not entitled to limit if they have been guilty of 'actual fault or privity'.[9]

So that these huge payments can be met, tankers carrying over 2000 tons of oil are compelled to insure the risk.[10] The insurer may be sued directly by the claimant, but will be entitled to the owner's defences.[11] Tankers which do not have a valid certificate of insurance[12]

99 Art. III(5); s. 16.
 1 Art. III(3); s. 1(5).
 2 See Section 22.2.5, *supra*.
 3 Art. V; s. 4. The SDR was substituted for earlier gold franc figures by a 1976 Protocol to the CLC, in force from 1981 by virtue of the Merchant Shipping Act 1979, s. 38(1). For explanations of the SDR see Section 22.2.5, *supra*. For tonnage, note the Merchant Shipping (Oil Pollution) Act s. 4(2), and Section 22.2.5, *supra*.
 4 Calculated at 13 September 1985, as in Chapter 22, *supra*.
 5 Under the 1957 or 1976 Limitation Conventions, as in Chapter 22, *supra*.
 6 See the Merchant Shipping Act 1979, Sch. 4, Part I, Art. 3(b).
 7 Art. IV; s. 1(3).
 8 Art. XII; s. 8A, inserted by the Merchant Shipping Act 1974, s. 9.
 9 Art. V(2); s. 4(1). See Section 22.2.4, *supra*.
10 Art. VII; s. 10; Oil Pollution (Compulsory Insurance) Regulations 1981 (S.I. No. 912).
11 Art. VII (8); s. 12. The insurer has a complete defence if the discharge was due to the wilful misconduct of the owner himself.
12 Including one issued by other contracting states, *ibid*.

may be detained in port.[13] Failing to comply with the insurance requirements is also an offence for owners or masters.[14]

One of the principles of the CLC was to 'channel' oil pollution liability to the registered shipowner, as he carries the insurance. The owner alone has CLC liability and he cannot be sued at common law if the CLC applies.[15] The claimant is not allowed to 'by-pass' the CLC by suing the servants or agents of the owner.[16] The Merchant Shipping (Oil Pollution) Act 1971 seems to go further than the CLC by specifically exempting salvors, who might cause pollution in trying to save the ship.[17]

After the *Amoco Cadiz* disaster[18] the French claimants did not want to be bound by the CLC limits and so they sued in the US courts practically everybody in sight, including the salvors and the shipbuilders. In particular they sued the parent companies of the registered owner, which was a one-ship company.[19] As noted in an earlier chapter, the judge found the shipbuilders and the parent companies (but not the salvors) liable at common law, and without the benefit of limitation of liability.[20] The complexities of that decision are beyond this book, but it is important to note that the judge held that the parent companies were not the servants *or* agents of the one-ship company. That finding is significant because it breaks the neat channelling scheme of the CLC and may require large companies owning fleets of tankers to alter their corporate structures, or take out extra insurance. P & I Clubs now offer cover to holding companies.

(B)   THE FUND: MERCHANT SHIPPING ACT 1974

The CLC liability rules may leave pollution victims wholly without remedy, or with a claim that covers only part of their loss. But as it is often the cargo which is the real cause of the damage it is unfair for owners to carry all the responsibility. Accordingly the Fund Convention, mentioned earlier, was agreed in 1971. This established a Fund,[21] financed by levies on importers of more than 150 000 tons of oil

---

13 Art. VII (11); s. 10(8).
14 S. 10(2), (6), (7), (8). See also *The Huntingdon*, Section 25.1.2, *supra*.
15 Art. III(4); s. 3.   16 *Ibid.*
17 See, e.g. *The Eschersheim* [1976] 2 Lloyd's Rep. 1.
18 See Sections 1.7 and 5.4.   19 See Sections 5.4 and 7.2.7.
20 *The Amoco Cadiz* [1984] 2 Lloyd's Rep. 301.
21 Note that the CLC is not a fund of money, it is simply an extra liability (as with wreck raising) imposed on an owner.

per annum, the underlying idea being that those who make money by importing oil should also contribute to the alleviation of hardship created by accidents happening in connection with this dangerous commodity.[22]

Claims for compensation can be made on the Fund by pollution victims who get no satisfaction from tanker-owners, because the owners and their insurers are insolvent; or because the owners have a valid CLC defence, or can rely on the limits of liability.[23] Thus the Fund would pay if the spillage was caused by a hurricane, sabotage, or failure to maintain lights. However, it will not pay for damage caused by spillage as a result of the CLC 'war' defence, nor for damage caused by warships and other Government-owned vessels engaged wholly on public and non-commercial duties.[24] Such damage is often covered by separate Government measures.

A claimant on the Fund must be able to identify the ship from which the oil escaped[25] and the Fund may be exonerated in whole or part if he himself has been at fault.[26] The maximum liability of the Fund, in aggregate with the CLC claim,[27] is 787.5 million gold francs: £42 945 084 (from 1 December 1986).[28]

The tanker owner may himself make a claim on the Fund in two circumstances. He may claim for reasonable voluntary clean up costs incurred by him,[29] but not those caused by obeying Government intervention orders. Refundable expenses could be very heavy indeed; they may consist of remuneration paid to divers and salvors to repair holed hulls, towage of the stricken vessel to a safer place, as well as the expense of hiring booms and detergent spraying tugs. As part of the

---

22 Fund Convention, Art. 4; Merchant Shipping Act 1974, ss. 1, 2. The Fund has its headquarters in London and has the usual privileges enjoyed by international organizations in national territories; International Oil Pollution Compensation Fund (Immunities and Privileges) Order 1979 (S.I. No. 912).

23 Art. V; s. 4.

24 Art. IV, s. 4. See Section 1.6., *supra*.

25 Art. IV (2)(b); s. 4(7)(b).

26 Art IV(3); s. 4(8).

27 Art. IV (4); s. 4(10).

28 The 1976 Fund Protocol, replacing the gold francs by the SDR, is not yet in force. Reference must be made to periodic sterling equivalents orders issued by the DoT. The figure given is from the Merchant Shipping (Sterling Equivalents) (Various Enactments) Amendment Order 1986 (S.I. No. 2038). The fund originally had a limit of 450 million gold francs (£24 540 047), which was increased to 675 million gold francs (£36 801 070). From 1 December 1987 the limit will be £49 080 094. When the 1976 Protocol to the Fund is in force these figures will be converted to SDR, Merchant Shipping Act 1979, s. 38.

29 Art. IV(1); s. 4(6).

principle of sharing the loss between tanker-owner and cargo-owner the former, when faced with large CLC claims, is entitled to claim 'roll-back' relief from the Fund. This involves the Fund giving back to the owner a proportion of the sums he has paid to CLC claimants. The calculation is very complicated, but could result in a 'roll-back' of up to 37 per cent of the CLC claim.[30]

(C)   TOVALOP AND CRISTAL

Mention should be made of two schemes introduced voluntarily by the oil industry which were intended to act as a 'stop-gap' until the CLC and Fund came into force. They are still relevant for countries which have not adopted these two Conventions and for a few matters not covered by them. They are the Tanker Owners Voluntary Agreement Concerning Oil Pollution (TOVALOP) and Contract Regarding An Interim Supplement To Tanker Liability For Oil Pollution (CRISTAL). These agreements, originally introduced in 1969 and 1971, were significantly revised in 1978 and they mirror very closely the CLC and Fund, respectively. We may note, in particular, the TOVALOP limit of US $160 per ton, or US $16 800 000, whichever is the less; and the CRISTAL limit of US $36 000 000. These limits, being based on contract, are unbreakable. In at least two main respects TOVALOP is wider than CLC. It allows claimants to recover for pollution damage caused by the bunkers of a tanker on a ballast run and 'threat removal costs', i.e. expenses incurred in averting the threat of oil pollution – even if none actually occurs. Changes in 1986 are noted below.

(D)   INTERNATIONAL DEVELOPMENTS

The *Amoco Cadiz* disaster highlighted the fact that the CLC and Fund limits, although considered adequate in 1969 and 1971, had been eroded by inflation. It is interesting to note that in the period 1970–1981 the oil pollution liabilities of tanker owners were US $412 million compared

---

30 Art. 5; s. 5. He is entitled to the difference between (a) any sum paid in excess of 1500 gold francs (£81.80) per ton – up to 125 million gold francs (£6 816 680) – whichever is less, and (b) the maximum CLC limits (calculated in gold francs) of 2,000 gold francs (£98.32) – up to 210 million gold francs (£11 452 022). Sterling equivalents as per 1986 (S.I. No. 1777). The owner may lose the right to be indemnified under s. 5 if he is guilty of wilful misconduct or, if as a result of his actual fault or privity, he fails to comply with various safety regulations specified in the Merchant Shipping (Indemnification of Shipowners) Order 1985 (S.I. No. 1665), amended 1986 (S.I. No. 296).

with the US $165 million contributed by oil interests. At least US $65 million of the tanker owner figure represented no fault/doubtful fault/ pilotage cases, i.e. those for which there would have been no common law liability. Owners paid for 17 000 spills, less than one per cent of which exceeded US $120 per ton. Of the 152 expensive spills (costing US $125 000 – $10 million) 22 per cent involved tankers below 10 000 tons.[31]

IMO convened a diplomatic Conference in May 1984 and this produced a number of changes by agreeing Protocols to both the CLC and Fund.[32] The changes will now be summarized. As Table 1 shows, the limits of liability have been increased, both generally and to create a much higher proportion of liability for smaller tankers.[33] There is a new minimum limit[34] and the tonnage is to be calculated according to the 1969 Tonnage Convention.[35] The limits may only be broken by showing intention or recklessness[36] of the owner or other persons sued.

Table 1:   CLC Protocol 1984

Size of ship	SDR	1985
Minimum (ships 0–5000 tons)	3 million SDR	£2 280 471
AND (for each ton in excess of 5000 tons)	[×420 SDR]	[£319.27]
But MAXIMUM	59.7 million SDR	£45 381 372

The Fund has a new maximum of 35 million SDR (£102 621 190), but with a facility to increase it to 200 million SDR (£152 031 400). Roll-back relief is abolished.

The CLC definition of ships has been enlarged to include combination carriers on one voyage with oil residues immediately following an oil cargo voyage. Whale oil is excluded from the definition of oil and bunkers of unladen tankers are now covered. Pollution damage is redefined so that compensation for impairment of the environment,

---

31 Statistics from the International Group of P & I Clubs, quoted in 'Liability of Oil Pollution Damage', Intertanko (1984).
32 LEG/CONF.6/66 and 67, 22 May 1984.
33 Calculations as at 13 September 1985.
34 There was no such minimum limit under the CLC.
35 See Sections 22.2.5, 22.3.5, *supra*.
36 See Section 22.3.4, *supra* for a full explanation of this provision which is identical to that in the 1976 Limitation Convention.

other than loss of profit from such impairment, shall be limited to the costs of reasonable measures of reinstatement actually undertaken or to be undertaken. The geographical scope of the CLC is extended to the exclusive economic zone.[37]

The CLC channelling provisions have been tightened so that the list of persons who cannot be sued includes: the owner or members of the crew; pilots; charterers, manager and operators;[38] salvors performing salvage operations with the owners' consent or under Government instructions; persons taking preventive measures; the servants or agents of the above.

However, it must be emphasized that it may be many years before the Protocols enter into force.[39] In 1985, the oil industry came up with an agreement called PLATO (Pollution Agreement Among Tanker Owners) which was similar to the 1984 CLC Protocol. PLATO did not achieve enough support, but in 1986 a TOVALOP Supplement and a Revised CRISTAL were agreed, to become effective from 20 February 1987. The limits are similar to those in Table 1, but will be: US$3.5m, US$733 per GRT and a maximum of US$135m (CRISTAL).[40]

25.2.3   NON-OIL POLLUTION DAMAGE

We have already noted that claims for damage caused by, e.g. dangerous chemicals, will have to proceed at common law. There is an exception to this. Under the Paris Convention on Third Party Liability in the Field of Nuclear Energy 1960[41] there is strict liability on the *operator* of a nuclear installation for damage or loss carried by an incident involving radioactive nuclear substances even in the course of carriage. This Convention has been enacted into British law by the Nuclear Installations Act 1965.[42] The shipowner is not liable for nuclear

---

37 Up to 200 miles from land, see Section 2.1.
38 It is arguable that parent companies who, in effect, run the ships of their subsidiaries – as in *The Amoco Cadiz* [1984] 2 Lloyd's Rep 301 – would now be within this definition.
39 In the UK the Merchant Shipping Act 1979, s. 20 will be used to give effect to the Protocols.
40 S. 12(1) and Art. 4 of the 1980 Order.
41 Cmnd 3755, Supplemented in 1963, Cmnd 5948.
42 As amended by the Nuclear Installations Act 1969, the Energy Act 1983.

damage,[143] but the operator is entitled to limit his liability to £20 million, with the State providing additional cover up to 300 million SDR (£228 047 100).[144]

Finally, mention should be made of attempts by IMO to produce a new Convention on Hazardous or Noxious Substances (HNS). A draft HNS Convention was considered at the Diplomatic conference which agreed the 1984 CLC and Fund Protocols. However, there was much disagreement and not enough time to consider it. An amended draft will certainly be reconsidered by IMO in the near future. Suffice it to say that an HNS Convention will extend the strict liability regime to hazardous and noxious substances other than oil, but probably only those carried in bulk. This is because it may be difficult to arrange effective insurance cover for dangerous packaged cargo. There will probably be dual liability of shipowners and the shippers of goods, but agreeing the balance of liability between them will be exceptionally difficult.

If an HNS Convention is ever agreed it will probably be brought into force in the UK by an Order in Council made under the Merchant Shipping Act 1979, s. 20: no new statute is required. This provision is designed to avoid the lengthy delays that sometimes occur before pollution conventions are enacted nationally. Parliament will retain the duty and power of supervision. In certain cases the draft Order must be approved by resolution. Where such a resolution is not required either House of Parliament has power to annul the Order, but under this procedure it cannot adopt some Convention provisions and reject others.

43 S. 12(1)(b).
44 S. 16, as amended; Calculated as at 13 September 1985.

26

TIME BARS

Most legal systems fix time limits within which actions must be brought. The idea is to prevent defendants being faced with claims many years after the event, when witnesses may have disappeared, or forgotten about the incidents, and documents may be missing. Time bars encourage early, and discourage stale, claims. Technically, the claimant must make sure that his writ is issued in the given period. If a defendant leads a plaintiff to believe that he would not rely on the time bar the Court may stop him going back on his representation.[1] There are essentially two types of time bar: those which apply to specific claims and those which apply, generally, to all the others.

26.1 SPECIFIC TIME BARS

26.1.1 CARRIAGE OF GOODS

As we have seen, the Hague and Hague–Visby Rules apply a one-year limit, running from the date of delivery of goods (if damaged) or the date when they should have been delivered (if lost).[2] It should be noted that in practice 12-month extensions are often given by shipowners.[3] If ever enacted, the Hamburg Rules 1978 and the Multimodal Convention 1980 will apply a two-year limit.[4]

---

1 *The August Leonhardt* [1985] 2 Lloyd's Rep. 28. A mere misunderstanding by the plaintiff not induced or encouraged by the defendant will not be enough to create this 'estoppel'. For an application to extend the time for service of a writ, see *The Angelina the Great* [1983] 1 Lloyd's Rep. 591. For an application to join another plaintiff after expiry of the time bar, see *The Aiolos* [1983] 2 Lloyd's Rep. 25.
2 Carriage of Goods by Sea Act 1971, Sch. Art. III r.6. Note also the Hague–Visby Rules, Art. III r.6 bis limit for underwriters, *The Vechscroon* [1982] 1 Lloyd's Rep. 301. See generally Section 11.7, *supra*..
3 This will be done by those party to the British Maritime Law Association 'Gold Clause' Agreement 1977, i.e. most British owners and insurers.
4 Arts 20, 25, respectively.

26.1.2 COLLISION AND SALVAGE

The Brussels Collision and Salvage Conventions 1910 laid down a special time bar of two years for collision and salvage actions. The time was to run from two years from the date of the casualty or when the operations of salvage terminated.[5] The Maritime Conventions Act 1911 enacted these provisions in one section and in a slightly different form. The two-year periods run from the date the damage (or loss of life or personal injury) was caused, or the date when the salvage services were rendered.[6]

The Conventions leave open the question of extending the period, but s. 8 gives the Court a discretion to extend the time bar to such an extent and on such conditions as it thinks fit. Because it may be difficult in practice to start an action *in rem* the section states that the Court must extend the two-year period if there has been no reasonable opportunity of arresting the defendant's vessel, e.g. because it has never been within the UK during the two years.

The Court, in exercising its discretion to extend the time limit, will take into account whether the delay before issuing a writ is excusable, the length of that delay, and whether justice could still be done between the parties.[7] A delay of a few days or a week or two might be excusable, but one as long as four years after a collision is probably not.[8]

26.1.3 POLLUTION AND PASSENGERS

The time bar for pollution claims governed by the CLC is three years from the date of damage.[9] However, it may be that oil leaks out from a wreck many years after a sinking, so it is provided that no action can be brought after six years from the date of the incident which caused the

---

5 Collision Convention 1910 Art. 7, Salvage Convention 1910 Art. 10.

6 S. 8. The damage provision is clearer than the Convention because actual loss could occur after the initial collision has taken place. The salvage provision is rather vague, because the services may be continuous and last many days. As the Act was meant to enact the Convention it is probably acceptable to read 'rendered' as if it meant 'terminated': see *Fothergill* v. *Monarch Airlines* [1980] 2 All E.R. 696, on the interpretation of Conventions. Note also the Crown Proceedings Act 1947, s. 30.

7 *The Albany* [1983] 2 Lloyd's Rep. 195; *The Salviscount and The Oltet* [1984] 1 Lloyd's Rep. 164.

8 *Ibid.*, at p. 196. If the lawyers have been at fault in forgetting to issue the writ they could be sued for negligence.

9 Art. VIII; Merchant Shipping (Oil Pollution) Act 1971, s. 9.

damage, e.g. the collision.[10] The Fund time bar is similar.[11] TOVALOP requires written notice within one year of the incident.[12]

The Athens Convention 1974 provides a two-year limit in respect of the death or personal injury of passengers or the loss of their luggage.[13] This period is calculated from the date of disembarkation, or expected disembarkation.[14]

26.2   GENERAL TIME BARS

These are governed by the Limitation Act 1980. Contract claims must be brought within six years of breach.[15] This limit would apply, e.g. to ordinary charterparty claims. Claims for general average contributions based on liability at common law or under a general average clause in the contract of affreightment run from the date of the general average act.[16] But, where an agreement is made under a Lloyd's average bond the cause of action arises when the general average statement has been completed by the shipowner's average adjuster.[17]

Tort claims, e.g. for negligence causing property damage, also must be brought within six years of the date on which the cause of action accrued.[18] This is usually counted from the date on which the physical damage occurred, e.g. when a ship collides with a jetty. At common law, time will run even if the damage is 'latent', i.e. not discoverable until many years later.[19] This rule was criticized and the Latent Damages Act 1986 was passed to allow a three-year extension of time

10 *Ibid.*
11 Art. VI; Merchant Shipping Act 1974, s. 7. However, a shipowner claiming the 'roll-back' relief is allowed a minimum of six months from the date when he first learned of the CLC claim against him, e.g. if the CLC claim was made very late.
12 Art. VIII (c).
13 Art. 16; Merchant Shipping Act 1979, Sch. 3.
14 *Ibid.* Although if, after disembarkation, a passenger dies of injuries received, the period runs from the date of death: even then the period must not exceed three years from disembarkation. Under the CIV(Rail) Rules personal injury and death claims must be brought within 3 years: other claims should be brought within 1 year (or two in the case of wilful misconduct or fraud), see Art. 55, and Section 18.5, *supra.* See also the Hovercraft (Civil Liability) Order 1986 (S.I. No. 1305).
15 S. 5.
16 *The Potoi Chau: Castle Insurance Co. Ltd* v. *Hong Kong Islands Shipping Co. Ltd* [1963] 3 All E.R. 706.
17 *Ibid.*
18 S. 2.
19 *Pirelli General Cable Works Ltd* v. *Oscar Faber & Partners* [1983] 2 A.C. 1.

from the moment that the plaintiff knew, or ought to have known, of the damage and the identity of the defendant.[20]

Personal injury actions must normally be brought within three years.[21] However, the courts have a wide discretion to extend this short period, if it operates inequitably.[22] We may note here that an action to enforce an arbitration award must be brought within six years of the failure to perform the award.[23]

26.3   OVERLAP OF TIME BARS

Sometimes it looks as though both a special and a general limit apply. The rule is that the special limit governs. Thus a person injured in a collision with a negligently navigated ship must sue that ship within two years — and not the three years allowed under the general law.[24] However, the Maritime Conventions Act 1911 two-year damage limit only applies to claims made against another vessel at fault. Where an individual sues the carrying ship the ordinary three-year limit applies.[25] Cargo claims against the carrying ship will probably be governed by the Hague/Visby one-year period.

The two-year limit applies not only to navigational faults but also to management faults. In one case, an aircraft carrier negligently discharged water 'or other liquid' onto a barge moored alongside, which then sank. Although there was no collision the damage was 'caused by the fault' of the aircraft carrier and the two-year limit operated instead of the six-year period.[26]

20 S. 1. However, this provision also imposes a 'long stop' of 15 years from the date of the original negligence.
21 Ss. 11, 12 Limitation Act 1980.
22 S. 33. Note that an English court which is applying a foreign law, under the rules of private international law, will be bound to apply the foreign time bar; see the Foreign Limitation Periods Act 1984.
23 S. 7, *Agromet Motoimport Ltd* v. *Maulden Engineering Co. Ltd* [1985] 2 All E.R. 436.
24 E.g., *The Alnwick: Robinson* v. *Owners of Alnwick and Braemar* [1965] 2 All E.R. 569.
25 S. 8. *The Niceto de Larringa: Navarro* v. *Larringa S.S. Co. Ltd* [1965] 2 All E.R. 930. Seamen will thus be treated in the same way as ordinary employees on land – as with limitation of liability; see Sections 22.2.3, 22.3.3. Passengers to whom the Athens Convention 1974 applied would also face the two year time bar, Art. 16.
26 *The Norwhale: Owners of the vessel Norwhale* v. *Ministry of Defence* [1975] 2 All E.R. 501.

26.4   CONTRACTUAL TIME BARS

Contracting parties often insert clauses requiring notice or suit to be made within a given time — often shorter than the general limits. Strictly TOVALOP falls into this category as it is a contract. In general, parties are as free to do this as they are to exclude their liabilities altogether. But mandatory time limits, such as the one-year Hague Rules limit cannot be reduced by contract.[27]

Charterparties, which are free of such restrictions, often have limits as short as three months. But most of them provide for arbitration and the courts have wide powers to extend the time within which arbitrations must be commenced.[28] Contractual time bars are treated as exemption clauses and construed strictly against those seeking to rely on them.[29] The TOWCON and TOWHIRE agreements require notice of claims to be given within six months of delivery, or termination, of the towage and suit to be brought within one year of the time when the cause of action arose.[30]

27 See, e.g. *The Ion* [1971] 1 Lloyd's Rep. 541 and Sections 10.2.2, 11.7, *supra*.
28 Arbitration Act 1950, s. 27.
29 *The Pera* [1984] 2 Lloyd's Rep. 363. In *The Elf* 145 LMNL 23 May 1985 the Court upheld a provision in a shipbuilding contract which required all defects to be notified within a 12 month guarantee period.
30 Clause 24 in each. See Chapter 23, *supra*.

PART FOUR
MARINE INSURANCE

27

THE MARINE INSURANCE
MARKET

IN the earlier chapters we have endeavoured to give an account of the
law relating to shipping. The student will have realized that all persons
engaged in shipping constantly incur considerable risks. The
shipowner may lose his ship or he may become liable to pay damages to
another vessel or to cargo-owners. The latter, too, may suffer loss or
damage to their property, and charterers may have to compensate ship-
and cargo-owners. Clearly such damages might cripple whole undertakings, and it has long been a practice to insure against the consequences of marine perils.

Now insurance is used to cover numerous activities of civilized man,
and insurance law is part of mercantile law generally. Its importance to
those concerned with the practical aspects of shipping is such, however,
as to demand some treatment of it in a volume primarily intended for
students who are following that branch of business. Moreover, the very
interests which insurance protects have often led to a very close connection between the two branches of the law, as for example with regard to
deviation, seaworthiness and general average.

27.1   HISTORY

The actual age of marine insurance is uncertain; the Lombards in the
twelfth century probably knew it and certainly the Hanseatic League,
whose members are said to have introduced it to England practised a
form of marine insurance. As an institution, however, marine insurance
in the United Kingdom may be said to commence with the foundation
of Lloyd's, which originated in Lloyd's coffee house in the seventeenth
century. At Lloyd's also a standard marine policy was evolved, based
upon a form of words imported from Italy some 200 years earlier.
Additional words and clauses were added from time to time as necessity
arose, and the result became a somewhat cumbersome document.

From the legal point of view it was by no means praiseworthy and has been criticized by generations of judges. Sir James Mansfield CJ, once described it as 'a very strange instrument',[1] and Buller J said that 'a policy of assurance has at all times been considered in courts of law as an absurd and incoherent instrument, but it is founded on usage, and must be governed and construed by usage'.[2]

Modern judges have been no less scathing about the terminology of the Lloyd's S.G. (Ship and Goods) policy form. For example, Staughton J, in considering the term 'riot' has this to say 'nobody but a Sloane Ranger would say of this casualty: "It was a riot",' and in regard to the term 'rovers' added 'Its only current and popular meaning is, I suppose, a species of motor car'.[3] The secret of interpreting the wording of the old Lloyd's S.G. form was clearly set out by Kerr J when he said in *Shell International Petroleum Co. Ltd* v. *Gibbs*[4] 'in construing the various archaic expressions which are still to be found in this form of policy, one cannot go by their ordinary meaning in our language today, but one must treat them as terms of art and interpret them in accordance with their original meaning'.

Lloyd died in 1720, but his name has been preserved in the institution, now called the Corporation of Lloyd's. This not only conducts insurance business, but various commercial offshoots also bring out many publications covering information on shipping, the law and other matters relevant to its business.

The Lloyd's S.G. form of policy, discussed above, dates essentially from 1779 and remained in exclusive use at Lloyd's until 1982, when in response to international debate, a new form of policy document known as the MAR form was introduced.[5] After 200 years of use the S.G. policy is gradually being phased out, but at the time of writing, the old form, and derivations of it, are still to be found in the insurance markets of the world. For this reason and because many of the accepted terms and definitions from the S.G. form are incorporated in the new documents, reference will continue to be made to the old policy for some time to come. It should also be noted that it is the S.G. form which is still given as a sample form of policy in the First Schedule to the Marine Insurance Act 1906, followed by Rules for its construction, and it may be some years, if ever, before the legislators catch up with

1 *Le Cheminant* v. *Pearson* (1812) 4 Taunt. 367, at 380; 128 E.R. 372, at 377.
2 *Brough* v. *Whitmore* (1791) 4 T.R. 206, 210; 100 E.R. 976, at 978.
3 *Athens Maritime Enterprises Corp.* v. *Hellenic Mutual War Risks Association (Bermuda) Ltd* [1983] 1 Q.B. 647, at p. 661.
4 [1982] 1 Q.B. 946, at p. 990.
5 See discussion at Section 29.3.2, *infra*.

changes in commercial practice. Over the course of time, it became necessary to add to and change the terms of the S.G. policy and this was accomplished by appending sets of clauses which were updated on a regular basis. These clauses will be discussed at a later stage and compared to their modern counterparts attached to the much simplified MAR form of policy.

Marine insurance is regulated by the common law. By the end of last century the decisions of the courts had become so numerous that in the opinion of underwriters, merchants and carriers the law was no longer certain. They accordingly pressed for its codification, which was effected by the Marine Insurance Act of 1906. Its scope has since been extended to cover insurance of hovercraft.[6]

27.1.1 WHO ENGAGES IN INSURANCE BUSINESS?

The earliest insurers in England were not professional insurers. They were business men who occasionally 'took a line' in insurance, but otherwise followed their own trade. Since insurance became an established business, three groups of institutions have developed. Perhaps the most important of them is Lloyd's. Then there are the limited companies registered under the Companies Act 1985. Finally, we find a large amount of marine insurance business transacted by way of mutual insurance. Such mutual insurance associations or clubs as they are often called are non-profit-making groups of shipowners which grew up largely in the latter part of the nineteenth century, although the concept was certainly put into practice at least 100 years earlier. Traditionally, shipowners carrying on business in a certain area, say the north-east coast, formed an association, which is usually registered as an unlimited company under the Companies Act, for s. 716 of that Act declares associations of more than 20 persons illegal unless registered. Members contribute to a 'pool' of money according to the tonnage they have entered with the association and a rating factor. Claims made by the owners are compensated from the central pool, and if at the end of a policy year money is left in the pool it is returned to the members. Alternatively, additional 'calls' for contributions are made should the level of claims exceed the amount in the pool. When these clubs were first formed it was hoped to make substantial economies in respect of brokerage premiums and similar expenses. Though it is not clear how far such hopes have been realized, the business transacted by associations and clubs is certainly very useful from the point of view of the

6 Hovercraft (Application of Enactments) Order 1972 (S.I. No. 971) Sch. 1.

shipowner. They enable him to insure against a number of risks which Lloyd's underwriters or the companies either do not insure at all, or only cover on unfavourable terms. The associations also provide for assistance in cases of legal dispute.

Mutual insurance is recognized by the Marine Insurance Act and by s. (85)4, the provisions of the Act apply to mutual insurance with two exceptions. These exceptions relate to the premium[7] and the way in which provisions of the Act that may be modified by the parties can be incorporated into the rules of mutual associations.[8] As with other forms of marine insurance, a written policy is necessary but in the case of mutual insurance it must be construed in conjunction with the rules of the association.[9]

Nowadays, ships, their cargoes and freight are almost invariably insured. This was not always the case, even after marine insurance was firmly established. William Makepeace Thackeray, in *The Virginians*, describes the anxiety of a London merchant until his ship, during the war with France in the eighteenth century, had safely reached Falmouth from America. He had not insured it, 'for the rate at which ships is underwrote this war-time is so scandalous that I often prefer to venture than to insure'.

27.2 COURSE OF BUSINESS AT LLOYD'S

Before discussing the law it may be convenient to deal shortly with the course of business at Lloyd's. This institution is an association of underwriters acting in their own name and on their own account in much the same way as members of the Stock Exchange. It was incorporated by Act of Parliament as late as 1871. Before that time it was an unincorporated club whose members originally congregated in Edward Lloyd's coffee house, from the seventeenth century onwards, where they met shipowners and captains who came there in search of persons who would insure their ships and cargoes. The present corporation has strict disciplinary regulations[10] ensuring that underwriters do not underwrite more risks than they will be able to meet from their working capital. Besides, each member on election is bound to deposit

7 Marine Insurance Act 1906, s. 85(3).
8 *Ibid.,* s.85(4).
9 See *Arnould* (1981), paras 132 *et seq.*
10 Contained in the Society of Lloyd's Bylaws made by the Council of Lloyd's by authority of the Lloyd's Act 1982.

with the Committee a security, to be held in trust in case he should not be able to discharge his liabilities, and sometimes also to provide guarantors.

It is usual for a number of underwriters, say between six and ten, to form themselves into syndicates, informal associations, of which one of the associates becomes the leader, that is to say the underwriting agent for the other members. In this way much of the financial stability usually associated with a limited company is attained, and yet the flexibility of individual working is retained. As was said in a Special Report on Lloyd's published by *The Times* of 29 June, 1977: 'The cohesive anarchy of Lloyd's gives it a flexibility that cannot be matched within a more formal corporate structure. And that flexibility . . . keeps the market on its toes.'

This is what happens when a particular risk is to be insured. The prospective assured approaches the underwriters through a broker, who acts as the agent for the assured only.[11] The broker is instructed to effect a policy on a ship for, say, £500000, bound on a voyage from Liverpool to Argentina. The first thing he does is to write down the name of the ship, the proposed voyage, the sum for which he seeks insurance, in short all the essential facts, on a piece of paper, which is called the 'slip',[12] and to take it to the underwriting room of Lloyd's. There he approaches the underwriters who are leaders of a syndicate and tries to place portions of the required sum with them. The first underwriter will perhaps underwrite for £1000, the next for, say, £50000, and so on.[13] Each underwriter initials the slip, and writes down the amount up to which he and the members of his syndicate will be liable. At this point, the contract is deemed concluded as between the underwriter and assured. 'The presentation of the slip by the broker constitutes the offer, and the writing of each line constitutes an acceptance of this offer' to the extent of the written line.[14] Subsequently a signed policy is issued to the broker, who pays the premium and in turn settles with his principal, the assured.[15]

11 *Anglo-African Merchants Ltd* v. *Bayley* [1969] 2 All E.R. 421.
12 A specimen slip will be found in Appendix 2.
13 It is now more usual to express the amount taken as a percentage of the total value; see *Templeman* (1986), p. 17.
14 *General Reinsurance Corp.* v. *Forsäkringsaktiebolaget Fennia Patria,* [1983] 1 Q.B. 856, *per* Kerr LJ at 866; see also Rogers, W.V.H. (1985) Obligations at Lloyd's, 14 Anglo-American L.R., 33.
15 For a description of the process of effecting a policy at Lloyd's see *The Zephyr: General Accident Fire and Life Assurance Corp. and Others* v. *P.W. Tanter* [1984] 1 Lloyd's Rep. 58, at 65, appeal reported at [1985] 2 Lloyd's Rep. 529.

27.3   THE PREMIUM

The premium is the consideration which the assured pays the insurer
for underwriting the risk. It is not, and cannot be regarded as, a
consideration for the payment of the sum insured. Rather the premium
is the remuneration due to the underwriter for his bearing the risk.

27.3.1   RESPONSIBILITY FOR PREMIUMS

The usage of marine insurance business has produced a curious discre-
pancy between this and the other branches of insurance. The contract of
marine insurance is made, as are all other insurances, between insurer
and assured and, according to the general principles of contract law, the
assured can claim the sum insured direct from the insurer. The broker is
but a conduit pipe. However, as the broker not only makes the contract
with the insurer, but does so regularly for various assureds who are
often not even known to the underwriter, the custom developed of
making the broker directly responsible for the premium. This usage has
now become law.[16] This has two advantages. Brokers and underwriters
need not exchange numerous cash payments, relating to individual
policies, but may among themselves simply settle periodic accounts.
Moreover, brokers have a means of bringing pressure to bear on the
assured if he fails to pay the premium by withholding the policy, for the
Act has given them a lien on the latter[17]. This lien depends, of course, on
the broker's retaining possession of the policy.

In this connection it is important to notice that persons instructing
brokers to take out a policy are often themselves agents of the future
assured. In that event the following distinction must be made.

(i) If the broker is not aware that his client is an agent then the position
is exactly the same as where the client is himself the principal.

(ii) Where, however, the broker knows that his client is an agent the
lien exists only in respect of each individual policy taken out. The
broker is not entitled to exercise his lien in respect of that policy even
though the agent is in arrear with other premiums.[18] The reason can
best be appreciated by showing the different interests of assured and
broker. If A employs an agent who in turn negotiates with a broker, and
if the agent is in arrear with premiums due on a policy taken out for B,
the exercise of the broker's lien is possible even against A, who has paid

---

16 Marine Insurance Act 1906, s. 53 (1).
17 *Ibid.*, s. 53 (2).
18 *Cahill* v. *Dawson* (1857) 3 C.B. N.S. 106.

all his debts. The law in the ordinary way puts the broker's interest over that of the assured. But if the broker knows that his client is an agent he must take precautions, and it would be unfair to a principal if he had to suffer through the conduct of another principal with whom he has had no dealings.

It should be noticed that in the Lloyd's S.G. policy the underwriter acknowledges that he has been 'paid the consideration due unto us for this Assurance by the Assured'. Normally those words would operate as an estoppel, preventing the insurer from denying receipt of the premium and from suing the assured. But as it is the broker who has an action against the assured the estoppel as between the latter and the insurer cannot operate between assured and broker. Even between insurer and assured fraud could prevent the estoppel from becoming effective.[19] In the MAR policy document the wording concerning acknowledgement of payment is rather more ambiguous. In the new form, the underwriters merely 'agree' in consideration of the payment to us . . . of the premium specified in the schedule, to insure. . . '. It may be that the practical effect of these words is essentially the same as the older form of wording found in the S.G. policy, but until there is a judicial ruling on the matter some doubt would seem to remain. Actually, no payments pass between broker and Lloyd's underwriters in respect of individual contracts. Between them the custom prevails of settling the account,[20] i.e. by payment of balances at fixed intervals.

27.3.2 'PREMIUM TO BE ARRANGED' AND 'HELD COVERED' CLAUSES

The rate of premium is normally fixed at the time when the ship is insured, but it sometimes happens that the policy provides for 'a premium to be arranged'. Circumstances of the case may make this necessary, for the risks to be covered are sometimes not capable of a reliable estimate in advance so that the insurer cannot quote a premium, as when there is a sudden outbreak of piracy or a new type of cargo is to be carried. It will accordingly be agreed that the amount shall be fixed later at a sum to be arranged. If it is not found possible to agree on a rate then it is provided that a premium is payable which is reasonable in the circumstances that have prevailed.[21] This will bind the parties, unless there is a term to the contrary in the contract, and if they should not be

19 Marine Insurance Act 1906, s. 54.
20 For details see *Arnould* (1981), paras 168, 169.
21 Marine Insurance Act 1906, s. 31 (1).

able later to agree on a sum, this will be determined by arbitration or in Court. Similarly, all marine cargo policies invariably contain a 'termination of contract of carriage clause'[22] which can protect the assured where the carriage contract is terminated short of the destination, for example where the discharge port is closed down by strikes.[23] In such an event, the assured must give prompt notice and request continuation of cover whereby the insurance will remain in force. Naturally, such a variation may materially increase the insurer's risk and therefore an additional premium, 'to be arranged', becomes payable depending on the extra degree of risk which is afterwards found to have occurred.

27.3.3   RETURN OF PREMIUM

There are a number of ways in which an insurance, once agreed, may become ineffectual, for example, upon the discovery of non-disclosure or a breach of warranty.[24] Similarly, an underwriter may be freed from his obligations because the assured has no insurable interest in the subject-matter insured. Finally, a voyage may be insured which at the last moment is cancelled, or goods may be insured which are never shipped. In these circumstances the assured has paid the premium, but the insurer never incurred any risk. In other words, the assured has made payment for a consideration which has wholly failed. Under the general law of contract, payments of that nature may be recovered.[25] The Marine Insurance Act 1906[26] gives an additional statutory remedy provided there has been no fraud or illegality on the part of the assured or his agents. Sometimes the policy itself provides for a return of the premium under certain conditions.[27]

If the policy never attached then the whole premium must be returned,[28] but if the subject-matter of the insurance has once been at risk, prima facie the premium is not recoverable. Where, on the other hand, the premium is apportionable and there is a total failure of consideration in respect of an apportionable part, then a corresponding proportion of the premium can be recovered by the assured.[29] Where no

22 Institute Cargo Clauses, 1982, cl. 9.
23 See discussion at Section 29.6.2, *infra*.
24 See discussion at Sections 28.3.3 and 29.6.1, *infra*.
25 *Rowland* v. *Divall* [1923] 2 K.B. 500.
26 Marine Insurance Act 1906, ss. 82 and 84(1).
27 *Ibid.*, s. 83.
28 *Ibid.*, s. 84 (1).
29 *Ibid.*, s. 84 (2).

apportionment can be made there is no total failure of consideration, and the insurer can keep the entire premium.

Illustration

A cargo of 500 bales of cotton is insured, but only 250 bales are shipped. Half the premium must be returned since the whole risk has never attached, and there is a total failure of an apportionable part of the consideration.

With regard to insurable interest we will see that an adventure in which there is only what is called a defeasible interest may be insured. If the assured parts with his interest during the currency of the policy and no loss has occurred before the interest ceased, the premium cannot be recovered since the policy had attached.

Illustration: *Boehm v. Bell*[30]

A ship was captured and the captors insured her though their interest still depended on the decision of the Prize Court. This contingent interest was held to be a good insurable interest, and had the vessel been lost or damaged before the decision the captors could have recovered under the policy. But the Prize Court decided that the capture was illegal. The captors thereupon sued the insurers for the return of the premium.

Held: They could not recover since the whole interest had been at risk for some time, and there was accordingly no total failure of consideration.

27.4 SUPERVISION AND CONTROL OF THE MARKET

In common with other countries, the United Kingdom has made laws for public supervision of insurance business to protect those making use of this service against losses suffered as a result of unsound or fraudulent business practices. A comprehensive scheme of State supervision was not introduced until the Insurance Companies Act 1958; the law is now contained in the Insurance Companies Act 1982.

27.4.1 INSURANCE COMPANIES

The aim of the supervision, which is exercised by the Department of Trade, is to ensure that no one launches or conducts an insurance business without funds sufficient to meet expected claims. Thus, in the

---

30 (1799) 8 T.R. 154, 101 E.R. 1318; see Marine Insurance Act 1906, s.84(3)*(d)*.

initial stage, a new business requires Department of Trade authorization;[31] subsequently, any business must submit financial statements and allow inspection. In extreme cases, the Department has power to bring about the winding-up of an unsound or fraudulent business.

The 1982 Act refers expressly to those conducting marine insurance business[32] and specifically mentions insurance of ships and goods and the liability of the users of ships. Part I of the Act[33] contains the basic rule that no 'person shall carry on any insurance business... unless authorized to do so'[34] by the Secretary of State or unless exempted by the Act itself. One of the main exemptions granted by s. 2(2) is to Members of Lloyd's, a remarkable tribute to the standards upheld by that institution. The remainder of this first part of the Act is taken up with the procedure governing applications for authorization, which are set out in broad terms, the detail to be filled in by regulations made under the Act. Part II[35] of the 1982 Act creates the supervisory and regulatory system governing insurance companies and the way they undertake their business. In particular, companies are required to maintain a minimum margin of solvency (defined by s. 32(5) as the 'excess of the value of its assets over the amount of its liabilities') as specified by EEC Directive[36] and submit annual accounts to the Secretary of State. The latter has considerable intervention powers[37] in the affairs of insurance companies in the event that they do not comply with their obligations under the Act.

In addition, the Secretary of State requires such companies to undertake adequate reinsurance arrangements and seek his approval to appoint certain executives to run the company's business. Apart from corporate sanctions, action may also be taken against directors, chief executives and managers where offences under the Act have been committed with 'the consent or connivance of, or attributable to any neglect of' such persons.[38]

27.4.2   LLOYD's

While members of Lloyd's may be exempt from the need to apply for authorization from the Department of Trade to conduct insurance

31 Insurance Companies Act 1982, s.2.
32 Insurance Companies Act 1982, s. 1 and Schedule 2, Part I.
33 Ibid., ss. 1-14.
34 Ibid., s. 2(1).
35 Ibid., ss. 15-71.
36 No. 73/239, July 23 1973 (as amended).
37 Insurance Companies Act 1982, ss. 37-48.
38 Ibid., s. 91.

business, they by no means escape statutory regulation altogether. As far as the 1982 Act goes, Lloyd's members are exempt from most of the supervisory provisions in Part II[39] provided that they do comply with the requirements set out in s. 83. These include: payment of all premiums into an approved trust fund and an annual audit of every underwriter's accounts by an accountant approved by the Committee of Lloyd's. The Act also imposes an obligation on Lloyd's as a whole, to deposit annually a statement 'summarizing the extent and character of the insurance business done by the members'[40] during the preceding year. While the provisions in the Act relating to 'margins of solvency' are not applied to individual members of Lloyd's, ss. 32, 33 and 35 do apply these rules, as amended by regulation,[41] to Lloyd's as a whole. In the event of a breach of these obligations, a number of the intervention powers granted to the Secretary of State may be exercisable[42] in relation to the members of Lloyd's.

The Insurance Companies Acts aside, the members of Lloyd's are further regulated in their activities by the Society of Lloyd's Bylaws made by the Council of Lloyd's under the authority of s. 6(2) of the Lloyd's Act 1982. Such bylaws make detailed provision for and regulate the admission, suspension and disciplining of members of Lloyd's, Lloyd's brokers and underwriting agents. In addition, the bylaws also regulate the day to day business operations of Lloyd's members by prescribing, for example, limits on premium income, audit arrangements and the disclosure of interests. Breaches of these regulations are dealt with by a Disciplinary Committee with an appeal lying to an Appeal Tribunal. It can therefore be appreciated that although Lloyd's underwriters may not be burdened with many of the obligations imposed on insurance companies by the Insurance Companies Act 1982, there is nevertheless a largely internal, regulatory framework, which has been developed to preserve the reputation and confidence in the institution built up over more than two centuries.

39 *Ibid.*, s. 15(4).
40 *Ibid.*, s. 86.
41 Currently The Insurance (Lloyd's) Regulations 1983 (S.I. 1983 No. 224).
42 Insurance Companies Act 1982, s. 84.

28
PRINCIPLES OF MARINE INSURANCE

BEFORE going into details, three fundamental principles common to all types of insurance must be discussed. These are: insurable interest, indemnity and good faith.

28.1 INSURABLE INTEREST

Under this principle an assured can only recover under the policy if he has an insurable interest in the subject-matter of the insurance. In other words, a contract of insurance is binding on the underwriter only if it is made to cover an interest which the law declares to be capable of being insured. This means, as we shall see in more detail later, that the assured usually holds or expects to acquire an interest in the nature of property. It became necessary to establish this principle in order to prevent insurance from being used as a cloak for wagering. An insurance of the vessel *British Trader*, at a premium of 1 per cent for a voyage from London to New York is at first sight simply a bet of a hundred to one that the vessel will safely reach New York. What distinguishes such a contract from a bet is that the assured must have an insurable interest, or right of property, in the ship. In the early days of marine insurance no such requirement was necessary. This gave rise to grave scandals, and the law was accordingly altered as long ago as 1745,[1] so as to forbid policies by way of gaming or wagering. As will be seen later, the Act of 1745 and subsequent legislation has not prevented policies which are themselves the only proof of interest (p.p.i.) still being effected to cover legitimate commercial interests. However it is clear that no action can be maintained on such policies[2] which are binding in honour only.

1 Marine Insurance Act 1746.
2 Marine Insurance Act 1906, s. 4.

The exact significance which is to be attached to the expression 'insurable interest' is very important, and is moreover a matter not free from difficulty. 'Interest,' said Lawrence, J., in an early case,[3] 'does not necessarily imply a right to the whole or part of a thing, nor necessarily or exclusively that which may be the subject of privation. ... To be interested in the preservation of a thing, is to be so circumstanced with respect to it as to have benefit from its existence, prejudice from its destruction.'

Accordingly, s. 5 of the Marine Insurance Act 1906 enacts that 'every person has an insurable interest who is interested in a marine adventure'. That is the case notably 'where he stands in any legal or equitable relation to the adventure or to any insurable property at risk therein, in consequence of which he may benefit by the safety or due arrival of the insurable property, or may be prejudiced by its loss, or by damage thereto, or by the detention thereof, or may incur liability in respect thereof'.

It might at first sight appear that a bet of a hundred to one that the *British Trader* will safely reach New York involves a benefit or loss according as she arrives or sinks, and that therefore there is an insurable interest. But in reality there is no interest other than that created by the wager itself. An interest to be capable of insurance must be one in the adventure itself, that is to say, the assured must stand to gain by the safe arrival of the vessel or lose because of its destruction quite apart from the wager itself.

28.1.1 INTERESTS WHICH MAY BE INSURED

(A) OWNERSHIP

The most obvious case of an insurable interest is the ownership of the ship. It should be remembered that in the case of a shipping company the latter owns the ship, not the shareholders. Even the owner of practically all the shares in the company does not thereby acquire an insurable interest in the company's vessels, for the company is a legal person apart from its shareholders.[4] The latter may actually lose money if the company's ships are destroyed, for this may lead to reduced dividends or the liquidation of the company. Likewise, they may profit by the vessel's safety, for their shares may yield more profit. But the

3 *Lucena* v. *Craufurd* (1806) 2 B. & P., N.R., 269, at p. 302; 127 E.R., 630 at p. 643.
4 *Salomon* v. *Salomon* [1897] A.C. 22.

Marine Insurance Act does not say: you have an insurable interest wherever a person may benefit or lose by reason of the existence of the insured thing. The Act, in s. 5, does provide: a person must stand in a legal or equitable relationship to the property insured, and this direct relationship must cause him profit or loss according to whether or not the thing survives.

(B)   CHARTERERS

Apart from owners, many other parties may have a stake in the use and operation of ships. One of the most common relationships is that of charterer and the question therefore arises whether charterers have an insurable interest in the ship they charter. In the case of demise charterers it seems clear that the charterer has at least a possessory interest in the ship which would give him the right to insure. Indeed, standard demise charter agreements[5] can require charterers to keep the vessel insured to protect the interests of both owners and charterers.

Under time and voyage charters, however, the charterers' interest in the hull extends only to the potential liability which may arise if the ship is damaged through obeying the charterers' orders. While such liability is clearly not an interest in the way of property, the modern view is that it is sufficient 'to have a right in the thing insured, or to have a right or be under a liability arising out of some contract relating to the thing insured'.[6] In many instances it will be obvious that charterers will benefit from the preservation of the ship or suffer prejudice from its destruction and that they should be able to demonstrate an insurable interest makes good commercial sense.

(C)   MORTGAGES

It is clear from the Marine Insurance Act 1906, s. 14(1), that a mortgagee of the subject-matter has an insurable interest and may insure up to the full value of the ship but can only recover under the policy to the extent of the mortgage debt. In addition, a mortgagee commonly effects a mortgagee's interest protection insurance. This protects the mortgagee against the possibility that a hull policy taken out by the owner, and assigned to the mortgagee, may be avoided by reason of

---

5 For example, Barecon A, cl. 11.
6 *Arnould* (1981), para. 332.

some act or default of the original assured,[7] thus giving the insurer a defence under s. 50(2) of the Marine Insurance Act.

(D)   TRUSTEES

If a ship is held in trust, the trustee alone is regarded as having a legal interest and as such may insure the full value of the property which is the subject of the trust.[8]

(E)   THE ADVENTURE

A person who has no insurable interest in the ship as such may nevertheless be able to insure the adventure on which she is engaged.[9] Thus a person might be interested financially in the undertaking of laying an Atlantic cable without having any interest in either ship or cable as such. A shareholder in a limited company has only a legal interest in his shares and not in the property which it owns.[10] However, it has been held that where the company is engaged upon a business adventure such as the laying of an Atlantic cable the shareholders have an insurable interest in that adventure.[11] More recently, in the House of Lords, it has been pointed out that this earlier decision was based on the special wording of the policy[12] and the case has since been considered as of very doubtful authority.

(F)   CREDITORS

Whatever may be the case of the shareholder a creditor has no such interest even though he may know that the only chance of his loan being repaid is the successful completion of a certain voyage. Nevertheless he will not be able to insure the adventure, for he has a legal claim against the debtor whether or not profits are made. He, therefore, stands in no legal or equitable relationship to the marine adventure out of the proceeds of which he will in fact be repaid the loan. His claim is good even if the adventure fails. A creditor can only protect himself by a non-marine insurance, namely by taking out a credit insurance policy insuring the debt as such, or taking out an honour policy, so-called

7 E.g. see *The Alexion Hope* [1987] 1 Lloyd's Rep. 60.
8 *Arnould* (1981), para. 382.
9 Marine Insurance Act 1906, s. 3(1).
10 *Macaura* v. *Northern Assurance Co.* [1925] A.C. 619.
11 *Wilson* v. *Jones* (1867) L.R. 2 Ex. 139, criticized in *Arnould* (1981), para. 328.
12 *Macaura* v. *Northern Assurance Co., supra* fn.10, *per* Lord Buckmaster at p. 627.

because it is binding only in honour. This may be done by inserting the words 'interest admitted' in the policy.[13] As has already been mentioned, such policies are void under s. 4 of the Marine Insurance Act, but by no means uncommon.

(G)   LIEN HOLDERS

While creditors in general cannot show an insurable interest there is no doubt that a creditor who holds a lien on maritime property has an interest to the extent of his lien. The interest of the holder of a maritime lien will arise with the incident which brings the lien into being, for example a collision, or the completion of salvage services.[14] However, the interest of a creditor seeking a statutory right of arrest *in rem* cannot attach until, at the earliest, when a writ is issued[15] and possibly not until it is served.[16]

(H)   BUYER OF GOODS

A partial interest in the subject-matter insured is insurable,[17] as for instance an undivided interest in a parcel of goods.[18] The same applies to defeasible and contingent interests.[19] For example, a buyer to whom goods are shipped acquires under certain conditions the property as soon as the goods are shipped on board.[20] This, however, does not affect his right to reject the goods if they are not of merchantable quality. If he does so the interest of the buyer ceases. Pending this event his interest is contingent. Nevertheless such contingent interest may be insured.[21] Likewise, a buyer's interest may be defeated by stoppage *in transitu*.[22] Until the transit is completed the buyer's interest is defeasible at the instance of the unpaid seller, but this does not prevent the buyer from insuring the defeasible interest.[23]

13 *Arnould* (1981), paras 20, 386.
14 See discussion *re* liens at Chapter 7 *supra*.
15 *In re Aro Co. Ltd* [1980] 1 Ch. 196. See Section 7.2, *supra*.
16 For a contrary view see *Arnould* (1981), para. 337.
17 Marine Insurance Act 1906, s. 8.
18 *Inglis* v. *Stock* (1885), 10 App.Cas. 263, 274.
19 Marine Insurance Act 1906, s. 7.
20 Sale of Goods Act 1979, s. 18, Rule 5(2).
21 Marine Insurance Act 1906, s. 7(2).
22 See Section 14.2, *supra*.
23 Marine Insurance Act 1906, s. 7(1).

Illustration 1: *Piper v. Royal Exchange Assurance*[24]

The plaintiff bought a yacht in Norway, at seller's risk until her arrival in England. It was held that when the yacht left Norway the buyer had no insurable interest in the yacht, but possibly in her arrival.

Illustration 2: *Anderson v. Morice*[25]

A cargo of rice was insured by the buyer. Under the contract of sale the property was not intended to pass until a full and complete cargo was shipped. The rice was lost when three-fourths only were on board. It was held that the buyer had no interest.

Illustration 3: *Yangtze Insurance Association v. Lukmanjee*[26]

A cargo of teak wood was sold 'ex ship', paid for, and lost. The seller had already insured the cargo 'for and in the name or names of all or any persons to whom the same doth, may, or shall appertain in part or in all'. It was held that the buyers had an interest in the cargo when it was lost, but as there was no evidence that the insurance was effected with the intention of passing the benefit to the buyers the latter could not recover under the policy. It would have been different under a c.i.f. contract, because under such a contract the buyer takes the advantage of the insurance.

Illustration 4: *Crowley v. Cohen*[27]

Canal carriers took out a policy 'on goods'. It was held that they had an insurable interest in respect of their liability for safe carriage of goods. This interest was sufficiently described by the words 'on goods'.

28.1.2   WHEN MUST THE INTEREST EXIST?

So much as to the nature of the insurable interest. The question now arises: at what time must the assured have the interest in the subject-matter of the insurance? The problem arises in this way. Suppose the owner of a ship insures her for one year, and before the policy has expired he sells the ship. After the sale the vessel is lost. In this case the assured has an insurable interest at the time he effects the insurance, but none at the time of the loss. Conversely, suppose in the case of the yacht bought in Norway[28] the yacht had been destroyed after the risk had passed from the seller to the buyer, then the buyer would have had an

24 (1932) 44 Ll. L.R. 103.
25 (1876), 1 App. Cas. 713. Contrast *Colonial Insurance Co.* v. *Adelaide Marine Insurance Co.* (1886) 12 App. Cas. 128.
26 [1918] A.C. 585. See Marine Insurance Act 1906, s. 15.
27 (1832) 3 B. & Ad. 478; 110 E.R. 172.
28 *Piper* v. *Royal Exchange Assurance Co.*, *supra.*

insurable interest at the time of the loss, but none when the policy was taken out.

Such situations are dealt with by s. 6(1) of the Marine Insurance Act 1906 which provides: 'The assured must be interested in the subject-matter insured at the time of the loss, though he need not be interested when the insurance is effected'. It appears therefore that the material moment at which the interest should exist is the time of the loss.

This is not unjust. The law prohibits wagers and wager policies, and logically it might appear necessary to have the interest at the time when the insurance is effected, as is the case in other insurances. On the other hand, it may be very convenient to insure something in which as yet there is no interest. By doing so no interval of time elapses between the acquisition of the interest and the taking-out of the policy, and this may be useful from a business point of view. Two examples will make this clear. Where carriers wish to insure against their liability as carriers they often take out policies – say for one year – 'as interest may appear'. They may carry no goods when they effect the insurance, but the moment goods are loaded on board their conveyance the policy attaches, and they are protected from the very first moment.[29]

Again, suppose the buyer of a cargo of wheat is to take the risk under the terms of the contract of sale as the wheat is loaded on board. Obviously, the loading may last some days during which a fire might destroy the parcels on board. It would be impracticable to take out separate policies on the loading of each parcel. Therefore the whole cargo will be insured before any insurable interest has been acquired. Then each parcel is covered the moment it is loaded.[30] It is necessary, however, that there should be a genuine interest in prospect at the time when the contract is made, and not the mere expectation or hope of an interest.[31]

28.1.3   VALUE OF INSURABLE INTEREST

Any person may insure the whole of his interest. Thus the owner may insure the whole value, and the mortgagee the value of the sum advanced.[32] Indeed, s. 14(2) of the Marine Insurance Act 1906, allows that the latter may insure for the full value of the property at risk, but

29 *Crowley* v. *Cohen* (1832) 3 B. & Ad. 478; 110 E.R. 172.
30 *Colonial Insurance Co.* v. *Adelaide Marine Insurance Co.* (1886) 12 App. Cas. 128; contrast *Anderson* v. *Morice* (1876) 1 App. Cas. 713.
31 *Buchanan and Co.* v. *Faber* (1899) 15 T.L.R. 383.
32 Marine Insurance Act 1906, s. 14(1).

then becomes a trustee of the balance over and above his own interest for the other parties interested.

28.1.4 RIGHTS AGAINST THIRD PARTIES

As insurance is designed to furnish compensation for losses automatically, and independently of the solvency of any person liable, the existence of an action for damages does not prevent the person entitled to compensation from insuring. Thus where a charterer undertook to indemnify the owner for any loss, the owner was nevertheless held entitled to insure.[33] Likewise, a cargo-owner may insure though he has a remedy over, against the shipowner.[34] In such cases the assured is, of course, not entitled to keep both the damages and the insurance money, because if he gets the damages he has lost nothing, and if he gets the insurance money he has suffered no damage. As we shall see later[35] the assured may claim damages, and thus give up the insurance or take the more usual course and claim the insurance and leave the insurer to recoup himself against any third-party liable.

28.1.5 WAGERING POLICIES

All policies not covering insurable interests are wager policies and void under s. 4 of the Marine Insurance Act 1906. Section 4 is further supplemented by the Marine Insurance (Gambling Policies) Act 1909, which makes it an offence to effect such policies.

Illustration: *Gedge v. Royal Exchange Assurance*[36]
The subject-matter of the insurance was the arrival of a ship at Yokohama on a certain day, though the assured had no interest whatever in such arrival.

Held: He could not recover.

It will be clear from the foregoing that the rules as to insurable interest are somewhat strict in character. For this reason there are many commercial interests which are genuine enough and yet cannot easily be brought within the legal definition of an insurable interest. For example, the anticipated profit which a warehouseman expects from

---

33 *Hobbs* v. *Hannam* (1811) 3 Camp. 93, 170 E.R. 1317; Marine Insurance Act 1906, s. 14(3).
34 *Dufourcet* v. *Bishop* (1886) 18 Q.B.D. 373.
35 See discussion as to Subrogation at Section 28.2.1.
36 [1900] 2 Q.B. 214.

renting warehouse space and handling an import cargo[37] might be one such interest. Thus, despite the strictures of the legislation, policies which dispense with the necessity to prove interest continue to be executed and honoured in the cause of commercial necessity. Such 'honour' policies, however, continue to be void in law and no action can be maintained in the rare event of default of payment.

Similar 'honour policies' may be employed when goods are insured on shipment, whereby their value at that date is made the basis of insurance. Before their arrival the market value at the port of destination may have increased, or they may have been sold during transit. In such cases the original policy no longer affords sufficient cover, and it becomes necessary to take out an Increased Value Policy. In the ordinary way, in order to recover under this policy in the event of loss the assured would have to disclose buying and selling prices as well as the names of the parties. This is very inconvenient and contrary to business usage.[38] Instead, it has long been the practice between insurers and insured to bargain on the basis that the assured shall not be required to produce proof of his interest in the subject-matter of the policy beyond the production of the policy itself. Such insurances are called p.p.i (policy proof of interest). Akin to these, are policies which admit on their face a full interest in the assured (f.i.a.), or expressed to be without benefit of salvage to the insurer (w.b.s.). Although such conditions are in practice acted upon by underwriters, who indeed regard themselves as in honour bound to do so (whence these policies are called 'honour policies'), they remain wagers in the eye of the law. While in practical terms, the fact that such policies are considered void, may cause few difficulties there are rare circumstances where the point may be of some commercial importance. For example, the trustee in bankruptcy of an underwriter will, in the interest of all the creditors, not be allowed to pay on such policies.

While most wager policies, from the point of view of public policy, may be quite innocuous, and indeed a service to commerce, it may clearly be highly dangerous in cases where no real business interest exists at all. For this reason, as pointed out already, insurances of this latter type have been made criminal[39] not only between insurer and insured, but also on the part of the broker who acts as intermediary, so that he gets no remuneration.

---

37 *Thomas Cheshire and Co.* v. *Vaughan Bros and Co.* [1920] 3 K.B. 240.
38 It has been suggested that I.V. policies are now less common; *Arnould* (1981), para. 452. But see the specific I.V. provision in cl. 14 of the 1982 Cargo Clauses.
39 Marine Insurance (Gambling Policies) Act 1909.

28.2   INDEMNITY

Closely connected with the concept of insurable interest is the principle of indemnity, under which the assured is entitled to be compensated precisely to the extent of the loss he has suffered as a result of the occurrence of an event against which the insurer has agreed to protect him. In other words, the assured is not permitted to make a profit on the insurance. Thus, for example, the Act in s. 69 allows an insurer to deduct 'new for old' when he pays for new material to repair a ship. However, in practice, as will be seen from clause 14 of the 1983 Hull Clauses, such deductions are not generally made.

28.2.1   SUBROGATION

From the doctrine of indemnity two rules are derived. The first is that where the insurer settles for a total loss the assured must abandon what is left of the thing insured to the underwriter.[40] The other rule is expressed in the doctrine of subrogation. Under this doctrine, if the loss or damage is occasioned through the negligence or other unlawful act of a third party, so that the assured can claim damages, or if the assured has a contractual right to compensation, then the insurer is entitled to take over such rights on settling the loss,[41] though not until he has done so. If it were not for this rule the assured might make a profit out of the transaction by making a claim against his insurer as well as against the third party.

Illustration 1

A ship is damaged by collision with another vessel that is alone to blame. If the insurer pays for the damage to the innocent ship he has a right to take over the assured's claim for damages against the owners of the wrongdoing ship.

Illustration 2

Under a towage agreement the tow is bound to indemnify the tug against damage suffered by the latter in the course of the towage service. The tug is so damaged, and the insurer of the tug pays for that damage. He has a right to enforce for his own account, but in the assured's name, the tug's contractual right against the tow for the indemnity.

40 See Section 31.3, *infra*.
41 Marine Insurance Act 1906, s. 79. But note, once the assured ceases legally to exist, the insurer is precluded from maintaining an action, *Smith & Mainwaring* [1986] 2 Lloyd's Rep. 244.

28.2.2   PROBLEMS ARISING FROM SUBROGATION

Over the years a number of situations have arisen which have caused difficulty for insurers attempting to exercise their rights of subrogation. Most of these problems stem from the fact that the insurer, via subrogation, is only entitled to exercise rights already accruing to the assured and cannot therefore acquire new rights which the assured never possessed. A number of examples will serve to illustrate this point.

(A)   GIFTS AND WINDFALLS

In a case where the assured receives compensation not as a matter of right, but as a gift, the insurer, following the above principle, has nothing to which he can claim to be subrogated.

Illustration: *Burnand v. Rodocanachi*[42]
Underwriters had insured cargoes under valued policies. The cargoes were destroyed by the Confederate cruiser *Alabama*, and the insurers paid the cargo-owners the insured value, which was less than the actual value. Subsequently an Act of Congress was passed providing a fund for persons who had suffered damage and had either not been reimbursed at all or inadequately by insurers. No insurer was to receive any of the amounts paid. Nevertheless the insurers claimed to be subrogated.

Held: The payment was not designed to reduce the loss against which the insurers had indemnified the cargo owners. Therefore the payment was made as a gift and would not give rise to rights as far as the insurers were concerned. The insurers' action was therefore dismissed.

The principle of indemnity means that the assured must not make a profit at the expense of the insurer. But he is entitled to keep a windfall, that is, a benefit received whether or not he had been insured. In *Yorkshire Insurance Co. v. Nisbet Shipping Co.*[43] the insurer had paid £72 000 under a policy, following the loss of the ship after its collision with a Canadian vessel. The latter was held solely to blame, and the assured eventually received payment in Canadian dollars. Before the payment was made the pound sterling was devalued, and as a result the dollar compensation worked out at £55 000 in excess of the £72 000 received under the policy. The shipowner repaid £72 000 to the insurer, but the latter claimed also the excess. Diplock J held that the insurer was not entitled to more than he had paid under the policy. The assured's

42 (1882) 7 App. Cas. 333.
43 [1961] 2 All E.R. 487.

profit in this case was not made at the insurer's expense, but was the result of an extraneous circumstance.

(B) SEVERAL INSURERS

Difficulties sometimes arise where there is more than one insurer of the same interest. Supposing a ship has a value of £1350 and is insured for £1000 under an unvalued policy.[44] Here the owner is regarded as his own insurer in respect of the uninsured portion of £350. Suppose further that the ship collides with another vessel and becomes a total loss whereupon the underwriters pay £1000. Later the ship at fault also pays the owner £1000. Under the principle of subrogation it might seem that the insurers are entitled to the whole sum, but this is not the case, because the uninsured portion of the risk was borne by the owner. The compensation must be shared between the two in the proportion of 1000-1350ths for the insurers and 350-1350ths for the owner.[45] But where a ship insured on a valued policy is valued below her real value this rule cannot apply, as the parties through agreed valuation are prevented (estopped) from disputing the value of the thing insured.[46]

Illustration: *North of England Iron Steamship Insurance Association* v. *Armstrong* [47]
A ship was worth £9000, but under a valued policy was both valued and insured for £6000. The ship was involved in a collision and later, after £6000 had been paid in settlement for a total loss, the owners recovered £5000 from the guilty vessel. The underwriters claimed repayment of the full £5000.

Held: The insurers were entitled to receive the whole sum as the owner by his under-valuation was estopped from denying the insured value, and as between himself and the underwriter could not be treated as his own insurer for the balance between real value and insured value.

(C) INCREASED VALUE POLICIES

Another problem has arisen through the use of what are known as increased value policies. That such policies serve a useful purpose has already been explained, but they entailed a risk to the underwriters of the increased value. In one case, cargo was first insured with A, and later

44 Marine Insurance Act 1906, s. 28; see Section 29.2.2.
45 *The Commonwealth*, [1907] P. 216.
46 Marine Insurance Act 1906, s. 27(3).
47 (1870) L.R. 5 Q.B. 244, see *per* Cockburn CJ at p. 248.

its increased value only with B. Both insurers paid for the loss. Subsequently, as a result of the general average adjustment a contribution was paid to the cargo-owners who handed it over to A. The contribution was less than the amount paid by A. Nevertheless B claimed a share in the fund, but his action was dismissed. At the moment of insuring A had received a right to subrogation on the basis of the declared value; this right could not be derogated by a subsequent insurance contract between the cargo-owner and B.[48]

(D)   COLLISION LIABILITIES

A further difficulty with subrogation arises when dealing with the legal situation involving a collision for which both ships are to blame. In such cases we have seen that the loss is apportioned between the two ships according to the degree of fault.[49] Thus when A and B were equally negligent, A suffering damage to the extent of £500 000 and B to that of £250 000 then, in order to avoid cross-liabilities, only one judgment is given. In a case where each is equally to blame the ship sustaining most damage will get one-half the excess of her damage over the damage to the other ship, that is, in our example B would have to pay

	£
	500 000
less	250 000
	250 000
divided by 2	125 000

This is called the 'single liability principle'.[50]

We must now put ourselves in the position of the insurers. Assuming both ships are total losses they are subrogated to whatever the owners may receive as compensation from the other side. If in fact each party was required to pay half the damage the other one had suffered it would appear that both sets of underwriters would receive something. However, in the judgment, the two amounts are set off against one another and therefore each underwriter is only subrogated to 'a claim for half the balance of the two losses, which if his loss is the smaller will

---

48 *Boag* v. *Standard Marine Insurance* [1937] 2 K.B. 113. In respect of cargo policies, this problem has been overcome by an 'increased value' clause (cl. 14) in the 1982 clauses.

49 See Section 21.5, *supra*.

50 *The Khedive: Stoomvaart Maatschappij Nederland* v. *P. & O. Co.* (1882) 7 App. Cas. 795; *Young* v. *Merchants' Marine Insurance Co.* [1932] 2 K.B. 705.

be nothing'.[51] In our example A's insurer will, therefore, get £125 000 and B's insurer nothing.

In fact, the underwriters of the two vessels will be liable to their assureds not only for the total losses of the ships, but also under a collision clause[52] in the policies, for three-fourths of the damages payable by their respective assured to the owners of the other vessel. If the single liability principle is used to settle these liability claims, it will be seen that B's underwriter would have to pay a further three-fourths of £125 000 with no chance of subrogation set-off, and A's underwriter pays nothing extra but continues to be subrogated to the £125 000 paid by B to A. This method of calculation was felt to be inequitable by underwriters and after the judgment which affirmed the single liability principle in collision cases[53] the clause was amended such that where 'both vessels are to blame then, unless the liability of one or both vessels becomes limited by law, the indemnity under this clause shall be calculated on the principle of cross-liabilities'. Thus in our case, providing the appropriate conditions are met, B's underwriter will pay B his damage claim (£250 000) plus three fourths of the sum he would be required to pay under the principle of cross-liabilities (£250 000 × ¾ = £187 500).

While this sum is larger than under single-liability, under this method, B's underwriter becomes subrogated to the sum which A is assumed to pay B under the cross-liability principle (£125 000, being half of B's damage). Similarly, A's underwriter becomes liable for A's loss (£500 000) plus three fourths of his damages liability to B (£124 000 × ¾ = £93 750), less his subrogation right which is assumed to be the amount paid by B to A (£250 000). From this example it can be seen that use of the cross-liability principle, in combination with the doctrine of subrogation, spreads the loss more evenly over the parties involved.

Whereas the calculation of indemnities arising from collision claims is a complex task, a further arbitrariness can be introduced to the result when both ships involved in the collision belong to the same owner. It must first be remembered that the insurer is subrogated only to the legal rights of the assured. Let us then suppose that two ships of the same owner collide and that one ship is alone to blame. The ships are insured by different insurers. Here the insurers of the innocent ship cannot, in

51 *Per* Scrutton LJ in *Young* v. *Merchants' Marine Insurance Co.*, *supra*, at p. 708.
52 Known as the 'running down clause' (R.D.C.), cl. 1 of the Institute Time Clauses (Hulls) 1970 (used with the SG form) or the '¾ths collision liability clause', cl. 8 of the Institute Time Clauses (Hulls) 1983 (for use with the MAR form of policy); see Section 30.3.1(b) *infra*.
53 *The Khedive*, *supra*.

the ordinary way, after having paid the sum insured, recover damages against the insurers of the wrongdoing ship. The reason is clear: the insurer is subrogated to the assured's rights. But both ships belong to the same owner, and as nobody has a legal right against himself there is no right to which the insurer of the innocent ship can be subrogated.[54]

Insurers felt aggrieved by this state of the law. In their opinion it gave a purely accidental, and therefore unreasonable, advantage or disadvantage, as the case might be, to insurers of ships belonging to the same owners, which come into collision.

To meet this difficulty, there is inserted in hull policies a 'sister ship clause'[55] which provides that in the event of a collision between ships belonging to the same owners 'the Assured shall have the same rights under this insurance as they would have were the other vessel entirely the property of Owners not interested in the vessel hereby insured'. It should be noted that there has been no effective change in the wording of this clause between the 1970 and 1983 sets of hull clauses.

28.3   UTMOST GOOD FAITH (*UBERRIMAE FIDEI*)

The principle of good faith is common to the entire law of contract, but the law of insurance requires an even higher standard of honesty than usual. This is necessary because of the special circumstances prevailing in this trade which put the insurer peculiarly at the mercy of the assured.

28.3.1   GOOD FAITH IN ALL CONTRACTS

Under the general law no party to a contract must misrepresent essential facts to the other party. However innocent the misrepresentation, the other party can avoid the contract, if the false statement was material and had induced him to contract.[56] That is if, but for the misrepresentation, the other party could not have been reasonably expected to make the agreement. In general, only actual misrepresentations entitle the innocent party to rescind the contract. On the other hand, failure to disclose a material fact is, as a rule, unobjectionable. For example, if you

---

54 *Simpson* v. *Thomson* (1877) 3 App. Cas. 279; *Midland Insurance Co.* v. *Smith* (1881), 6 Q.B.D. 561, at p. 565.

55 Institute Time Clauses (Hulls) 1970, cl. 2 (for use with the SG form); Institute Time Clauses (Hulls) 1983, cl. 9 (for use with the MAR form).

56 For a fuller discussion of this see e.g. G.H. Treitel *An Outline of the Law of Contract*, 3rd edn (1984) p. 142 *et seq.*, Misrepresentation Act 1967.

wish to enter into a service agreement, and on inquiry wrongfully, though innocently, say that you are healthy the prospective employer may avoid the contract. On the other hand, if you are not asked about your health and do not disclose that you are a carrier of germs, the employer has no right of rescission, however material this fact may have been in his decision whether to employ you.

28.3.2 CONTRACTS 'UBERRIMAE FIDEI'

The general rule may be sufficient for ordinary contracts, but it is certainly unsatisfactory in certain cases where one party is peculiarly defenceless in case of the non-disclosure of material matters. This rule has therefore been tightened, for instance, in the law relating to limited companies,[57] and it has always been more stringent in the law of insurance. Insurance would obviously be impossible as a genuine business unless the insurer could rely upon having knowledge of all the matters known to the prospective assured and which enable him to calculate carefully the probable incidence of the risk. The Marine Insurance Act 1906 accordingly provides in s. 17 that 'a contract of marine insurance is a contract based upon the utmost good faith, and, if the utmost good faith be not observed by either party, the contract may be avoided by the other party'.

28.3.3 NON-DISCLOSURE

A person who is about to effect a policy must therefore not only make no active misrepresentations, but must also disclose to the insurer every material circumstance, that is, everything which 'would influence the judgment of a prudent insurer in fixing the premium, or determining whether he will take the risk'.[58] Disclosure must be made before the contract is made. As already explained, marine insurance business is transacted in a somewhat informal manner, and it may be some time before the policy is issued. For this reason, the moment at which the contract is actually concluded has been the subject of some debate.[59] It has therefore been provided that the contract is deemed to have been

57 Companies Act 1985, ss. 56, 66 and 67.
58 Marine Insurance Act 1906, s. 18.
59 See now *General Reinsurance Corp.* v. *Forsäkringsaktiebolaget Fennia Patria*, [1983]
   1 QB 856; see also Section 29.1.2.

concluded when the insurer has accepted the proposal, and this is commonly proved by the slip bearing the insurer's initials.[60]

Of course, in the ordinary way a person can only be expected to disclose facts which he knows,[61] but insurance business would be even riskier than it is if the prospective assured were allowed to take shelter behind his bad memory or ignorance. In the eye of the law a prospective assured is deemed to have knowledge of 'every circumstance which, in the ordinary course of business, ought to be known by him'.[62] Where an agent, e.g. a Lloyd's broker, negotiates the policy, he must disclose to the insurer every material circumstance that he should know in the ordinary course of his business and all that ought to have been communicated to him by his principal. However, if the assured hears of a material fact when it is too late to be communicated to the agent before the risk is accepted then failure to disclose, will not entitle the insurer to avoid the policy.[63]

Illustration: *Blackburn, Low & Co.* v. *Haslam*[64]

The plaintiffs were underwriters in Glasgow. They had insured a ship which had become overdue. They therefore instructed an insurance broker to effect a reinsurance. Before the broker actually made the contract of reinsurance he received independent information that the ship was lost. This was indeed the case. However, because the information was received in confidence, the broker failed to communicate the news either to his principals, or to the defendant reinsurer. The defendant refused to pay the sum insured, and the plaintiffs sued.

Held: The action was dismissed. The policy was void on the ground of concealment of a material fact by the agent of the assured.

It should be noted that what in old cases is called concealment need not necessarily mean that some material fact was deliberately or fraudulently suppressed. Concealment there means simply what now is termed non-disclosure. In the modern law fraudulent concealment gives, of course, also a right to avoid the policy. Besides, the insurer may bring an action for deceit. While the law thus imposes a heavy burden on the assured, this rule should not be unduly extended. Suppose a shipowner instructs broker A to insure his ship. A has heard that the ship is lost, but fails to communicate his knowledge to the

---

60 Marine Insurance Act 1906, s. 21.
61 *Joel* v. *Law Union & Crown Insurance Co.* [1908] 2 K.B. 863.
62 Marine Insurance Act 1906, s. 18(1).
63 *Ibid.* s. 19.
64 (1888) 21 Q.B.D. 144.

shipowner. If A takes out a policy the latter is, of course, void, for the principal is fixed with the notice possessed by his agents. In the present case the shipowner decides to take out a second policy on his ship which so far as he actually knows is still afloat. He now instructs a second broker, B, who also does not know that the ship is lost and takes out a policy 'lost or not lost'. Strictly speaking the second policy should also be voidable on account of non-disclosure. However, it has been laid down that the shipowner is fixed with knowledge only of his permanent agents, and of casual agents only in respect of the one transaction for which they are employed, but not in respect of later transactions carried out through another agent.[65] This decision helps relieve the strictness of the rule and is satisfactory because it takes account of the exigencies of business practice.

(A) FACTS WHICH ARE MATERIAL

We must now consider in more detail what kind of circumstances are material and must therefore be disclosed. This is always a question of fact. The Act is of no great assistance when we come down to individual cases. It only provides that in the absence of inquiry the following circumstances need not be disclosed[66]:

   (i) circumstances diminishing the risk;

   (ii) circumstances actually known to the insurer;

as well as circumstances of common notoriety or knowledge, and matters which the insurer ought to know in the ordinary course of business, such as trade usages[67] and political events;

   (iii) circumstances in respect of which information has been waived by the insurer.

Illustration: *Mann, MacNeal & Co.* v. *General Marine Underwriters*[68]

An American wooden four-masted motor schooner, described in her register as a gas screw auxiliary schooner, was insured for a voyage from America to France and back. The assured did not disclose to the underwriter that the cargo on the outward voyage would be 100 000 gallons of petrol in drums. On her homeward voyage the ship was lost by a peril insured against, but the underwriters contended that non-disclosure of the nature of the cargo

---

65 *Blackburn, Low & Co.* v. *Vigors* (1887) 12 App. Cas. 531, at p. 542. 'Lost or not lost' cover remains in the 1982 Cargo Clauses (cl. 11.2) but not the Hull Clauses.

66 Marine Insurance Act 1906, s. 18(3).

67 *Carter* v. *Boehm* (1766) 3 Burr, 1905, at p. 1910, 97 E.R. 1162 at p. 1164; *British & Foreign Marine Insurance Co.* v. *Gaunt* [1921] 2 A.C. 41, at pp. 59-62.

68 [1921] 2 K.B. 300.

made the policy voidable and refused payment. At the trial it was proved that petrol in drums was no unusual cargo on voyages from America to France.

Held: The absence of inquiry by the underwriter in a case like the present one amounted to a waiver of disclosure.

(iv) Circumstances which it is superfluous to disclose by reason of any express or implied warranty.

To these matters specially noticed by the Act one or two further points may be added. In life, fire and accident insurance the fact that another insurer has previously refused to insure the risk is generally regarded as a material fact which the applicant must disclose to the insurer.[69] This is not so in marine insurance, the main reason being that a marine underwriter may often find himself compelled to refuse a risk not because he considers it a bad one, but because he has reached the limit of his commitment.[70] Moreover, it should be borne in mind that what has to be disclosed are only 'circumstances', that is, facts. Therefore, mere opinions do not call for disclosure. For instance, an original insurer as a matter of opinion comes to the conclusion that he has insured a bad risk, and in order to get rid of it he re-insures it at a higher premium than he has himself received. It has been held that this need not be disclosed.[71] Nor need the assured inform the underwriter of 'loose rumours which have gathered together, no one knows how'.[72] But in the case in which Gibbs CJ spoke these words it was held that the rumour was sufficiently credible for it to be made known to the insurer, and failure to do so vitiated the policy. For the sake of caution, therefore, full disclosure of rumours is advisable.[73]

From the positive point of view it must always be remembered that the acid test is whether, had he known the facts, the underwriter would have accepted the risk, or accepted it at a higher premium. This will, if necessary, be ascertained by hearing the evidence of experienced independent underwriters. Indeed, the Court of Appeal has recently gone even further by accepting that all the underwriter need show, is that had the facts been disclosed, they would have influenced the underwriting judgment of a prudent insurer.[74] It would therefore seem that the

69 *Glasgow Assurance Corporation* v. *Symondson* (1911) 16 Com. Cas. 109, at p. 119.
70 See Section 27.4.2 *supra*, as to regulations obtaining at Lloyd's.
71 *Glasgow Assurance Corporation* v. *Symondson, supra; cf. Anderson* v. *Pacific Fire & Marine Insurance Co.* (1872) 7 C.P. 65.
72 *Durrell* v. *Bederley* (1816) Holt, 283, at p. 285.
73 *Arnould* (1981), para. 653.
74 *Container Transport International Inc.* v. *Oceanus Mutual Underwriting Association (Bermuda) Ltd,* [1984] 1 Lloyd's Rep. 476, *per* Kerr LJ, at 492; Marine Insurance Act 1906, s. 20(2), 68(2).

insurer will not even be required to prove that the undisclosed facts would have been enough to persuade him not to take the risk or to charge a higher premium.

As noted in the CTI case, the opinion of the individual underwriter, who claims that disclosure should have been made in a given case, is not necessarily conclusive. The Act aims at a more objective test by asking, not: What did this or that underwriter consider important? but: What is the view of a hypothetical 'prudent insurer' on the subject? Bearing this in mind, we may note the following points.

Only circumstances relating to the subject-matter of the insurance, the ship and the perils are material.[75] Thus, the age of the vessel is material.[76] But the misnomer of the ship seems to be immaterial at least in a policy on goods by ships to be declared, because it is the sole object of the declaration to 'earmark and identify the particular adventure to which the assured elects to apply the policy. The assent of the assurer is not required to this'.[77]

Over-valuation, particularly of ships, is not uncommon and in some cases may even be desirable. Excessive over-valuation however, may be sufficient 'to change the character of the risk from a business risk to a speculative risk'. In cases of this type it has been held that there must be disclosure of the over-valuation, otherwise the policy may be avoided by the underwriter.[78]

Illustration: *Ionides* v. *Pender*[79]

A policy for £2800 was taken out on goods valued at £2800. The real value of the goods was only £970. This over-valuation was not disclosed by the assured.

Held: That on evidence, underwriters consider it material to take into consideration whether the over-valuation is so great as to make the risk a speculative one. The lack of disclosure by the assured on this matter therefore entitled the underwriters to avoid the policy.

Again, unusual terms in a charterparty may be material circumstances. Thus, even where the policy has a wide description of voyage clause,

75 *Glasgow Assurance Corporation* v. *Symondson, supra.*
76 *Ionides* v. *Pacific Fire & Marine Insurance Co.* (1871) L.R. 6 Q.B. 674, affirmed C.A, (1872) L.R. 7 Q.B. 517.
77 *Per* Blackburn J in *Ionides* v. *Pacific Fire & Marine Ins. Co., supra,* at p. 682.
78 *Mathie* v. *The Argonaut Marine Insurance Co. Ltd* (1924) 18 Ll. L. Rep. 118, *per* Bailhache J at 121; affirmed by C.A. (19 Ll. L Rep. 64) and H.L. (21 Ll. L Rep. 145).
79 (1874) L.R. 9 Q.B. 531.

the fact that the charterparty permits the vessel to call at a little known and particularly dangerous port must be disclosed.[80]

On the other hand, the past history of the master does not call for disclosure.[81]

Briefly stated, 'those facts only are necessary to be disclosed which, as material to the risks considered in their own nature, a prudent and experienced underwriter would deem it proper to consider'.[82] It would be too much to put on the assured the duty of disclosing everything which might influence the mind of an underwriter. It may thus be seen that the test in deciding what is material is an objective one. The insurer will not be allowed to avoid a policy because in his opinion a certain fact was material. Rather must he prove that the undisclosed facts were such as to influence the judgment of a prudent insurer.

(B) EFFECT OF NON-DISCLOSURE

The effects of non-disclosure are slightly different from those in contract law generally. If material misrepresentations were made or material facts not disclosed when the contract was made the insurer may avoid the policy by resisting an action for the sum insured or by claiming back money paid in error before the misrepresentation or non-disclosure had become known to him. These rights may be exercised not only against the assured himself, but also against the innocent assignee of a policy.[83] This rule becomes specially important with regard to policies on goods, for these are commonly assigned in connection with sales together with the other shipping documents. If in such cases the consignee, as assignee of the policy, fails to recover he has a right of action over against the assignor, who will usually be the seller, but this, of course, may be much less valuable than a good insurance policy.

An insurer endeavouring to avoid the policy on such grounds must prove the misrepresentation or non-disclosure,[84] and he must also prove that it was material. Some of the cases indicate that the burden of proof as to this is not a heavy one, for it has been held that if the

---

80 *Laing* v. *Union Marine Insurance Co.* (1895) 1 Com. Cas. 11.
81 *Thames & Mersey Marine Insurance Co.* v. *Gunford Ship Co.* [1911] A.C. 529. It might, however, be evidence of unseaworthiness.
82 *Per* Blackburn J in *Ionides* v. *Pender, supra,* at p. 538; applying Duer *On Insurance,* Vol. 2, p. 388.
83 Marine Insurance Act 1906, s. 50(2); *Pickersgill* v. *London & Provincial Marine Insurance Co.* [1912] 3 K.B. 614; *The Litsion Pride* [1985] 1 Lloyd's Rep. 437.
84 *Davies* v. *National Fire & Marine Insurance Co. of New Zealand* [1891] A.C. 485.

underwriter when the action is tried has no longer any recollection of what took place in the course of the negotiations it will be sufficient if he says: I cannot have been told this material fact, for if I had been told I should never have written this policy at the ordinary rate of premium.[85]

It may of course be very difficult for an underwriter to furnish sufficient evidence of non-disclosure or misrepresentation. For this reason he may apply for an order of discovery against the assured. That is to say, he can by way of interlocutory proceedings, that is before the trial of the action, force the other side to produce on affidavit the documents which bear on the matter.[86] Over and above the ordinary action for discovery, the underwriter may be entitled to an order against the assured to produce all the ships papers. This order[87] is peculiar to actions on marine insurance policies and while general to marine insurance actions, is in practice only granted where the wilful misconduct of the assured is alleged in scuttling the ship.[88] The order is discretionary, and because of its stringent nature will not be made automatically even where the insurer alleges the assured has cast away his vessel.[89]

85 *Per* Scrutton LJ in *Williams* v. *Atlantic Assurance Co. Ltd* [1933] 1 K.B. 81, at p. 94; *Greenhill* v. *Federal Insurance Co.* [1927] 1 K.B. 65.
86 See e.g. *South British Insurance Co. Ltd.* v. *Medre* [1986] 2 Lloyd's Rep. 247.
87 R.S.C. Ord. 72, r. 10.
88 *Arnould* (1981), paras 1347 *et seq.*
89 *Probatina Shipping Co. Ltd* v. *Sun Insurance Office Ltd* [1974] 1 Q.B. 635, *per* Lord Denning MR, at p. 642.

29

THE MARINE INSURANCE CONTRACT

29.1 FORMATION OF THE CONTRACT

IN principle a contract of marine insurance is governed by the general
rules of the law of contract. Modifications, however, prevail both by
reason of the course of business peculiar to marine underwriting and to
certain statutory provisions.

29.1.1 THE SLIP AND ISSUE OF THE POLICY

The course of business varies slightly as between insurances effected by
Lloyd's underwriters and by the companies. Yet, on the whole the same
methods are used. A person desirous of insuring his ship, his goods or
the freight to be earned on a voyage instructs an insurance broker who,
in the case of a Lloyd's insurance, must be a member of Lloyd's. The
broker is furnished with all necessary particulars. He then, as we have
seen, draws up a brief standardized statement, the slip,[1] which contains
the name of the broker, the ship, the voyage or period of time, the
property to be insured and its valuation, if any, the premium, the sum
insured, and any special terms of the insurance. This slip the broker
takes round to the underwriters who if they are so minded accept the
whole or a proportion of the sum to be insured by initialling the slip.
When the total sum is underwritten the insurance, is in a sense,
complete.

Once the slip is complete it is the broker's job to arrange for the
execution of the policy in accordance with its terms. In the case of
Lloyd's policies, the broker takes the form together with the appropriate clauses to Lloyd's Policy Signing Office where it is compared with

1 See specimen slip at Appendix 12.

the original slip. Assuming all is satisfactory, the policy is stamped by the signing office and signed by its manager. The effect of this signature is the same as if each individual insurer listed in the policy had signed his own name.[2]

29.1.2 MOMENT OF FORMATION OF THE CONTRACT

The way in which marine insurance business is transacted raises a number of important legal points relating to the contract. One of the most significant is how to determine the exact moment at which the contract is concluded between the underwriter and assured. This moment is important because, among other things, it marks the point at which each is bound by the contract and signals the end of the duty of disclosure, which is relevant only up to the moment of contracting.[3] There are, then at least three stages during the transaction where it might be argued that a binding contract comes into being. These are: at the moment the underwriter initials the slip, when the last underwriter initials the slip thus completing it, and finally when the policy is issued and signed.

The Marine Insurance Act 1906 provides that 'a contract of marine insurance is deemed to be concluded when the proposal of the assured is accepted by the insurer, whether the policy be then issued or not'.[4] This provision would seem to eliminate the last of the three possible moments from the list above but use of the term 'acceptance' still leaves an element of uncertainty. In *Jaglom* v. *Excess Insurance Co.*[5] Donaldson J took the view (*obiter*) that normally no contract came into existence until the slip was fully subscribed. If this were not the case, the assured might well be put in an extremely difficult position by being bound to contracts on only part of the risk, if it proved impossible to complete the slip. The conclusion of Donaldson J on this point attracted widespread criticism and was rejected by the Court of Appeal in a later case[6] on the basis that the evidence showed it not to be in accordance with the understanding of the insurance market. Kerr LJ said in this case 'the presentation of the slip by the broker constitutes the offer, and the writing of each line constitutes an acceptance of this offer by the

---

2 *Eagle Star Insurance Co. Ltd* v. *Spratt* [1971] 2 Lloyd's Rep. 116, *per* Phillimore LJ at p. 128.
3 Marine Insurance Act 1906, s. 18(1).
4 *Ibid.* s. 21.
5 [1972] 2 Q.B. 250.
6 *General Reinsurance Corp.* v. *Försäkringsaktiebolaget Fennia Patria* [1983] 1 Q.B. 856.

underwriter *pro tanto*. The evidence in the present case clearly shows
that in the insurance market this is the intention of both parties to the
transaction, and the legal analysis must accord with their intention.'[7]
After *General Reinsurance* there appears to be no doubt that a binding
contract comes into existence as soon as the underwriter subscribes to
the slip tendered by the broker, on behalf of the assured. While the legal
analysis may thereby agree with the understanding of the market, the
decision does raise a number of important points of principle, not least
in relation to the exact legal position and effect of the slip before any
policy is issued.

29.1.3   LEGAL EFFECT OF THE SLIP

(A)   BEFORE THE POLICY IS ISSUED

The precise legal significance of the slip, before the policy document is
issued, is becoming a matter of increasing importance with the growing
practice of using slip policies, whereby no formal policy is executed,
unless specifically requested by the assured.[8] The older view on this
point is that the slip is no more than a memorandum of the insurance
contract, binding in honour only, and not legally enforceable until a
valid policy is issued. This view developed, from the decisions in a
number of old cases, that it was not possible to maintain an action on a
slip because it could not be stamped as a marine policy under the
provisions of the revenue acts then in force.[9] Further support seemed to
be given to this approach by s. 22 of the Marine Insurance Act 1906,
which states that 'a contract of marine insurance is inadmissible in
evidence unless it is embodied in a marine policy in accordance with this
Act'. Until 1959 'in accordance with this Act' meant, among other
things, that the policy had to be stamped to comply with the Stamp Act
1891 otherwise it could not be considered a marine policy.

Despite this view being taken, the slip is not regarded as a nullity. It
would bind the parties in honour so that if a loss occurred between the
initialling of the slip and the issue of the policy the underwriters would
invariably pay for the loss. Even so a policy must be issued even after
the event has happened. Therefore, while the insurers are bound in
honour to issue a policy in due course difficulties may arise if between

---

7 *Ibid.*, at pp. 866, 867.

8 See *Templeman* (1986), pp. 19-20.

9 For example, *Home Marine Insurance Co. Ltd* v. *Smith*, (1898) 2 Q.B. 351

the initialling of the slip and the issue of the policy the underwriter dies or goes bankrupt. As the executor, administrator or liquidator is only entitled to perform legal obligations of the deceased or bankrupt he may not grant policies on outstanding slips.[10]

For some time, the appreciation that the slip is binding only in honour has been under attack. With the repeal of the Stamp Act in 1959[11] the early cases have lost much of their authority. Indeed there are early decisions which indicate that, at the very least, in situations where the revenue laws did not apply, the slip might be used in an action for specific performance against the insurer to issue a policy.[12] Apart from maintaining an action on the slip in this way, modern writers have put forward the view that most ordinary marine slips for voyage and time risks fulfil the requirements of the Marine Insurance Act,[13] and can be considered policies in their own right and admissible as evidence.[14] As yet, there is no judicial authority to support this view, but if correct, it would seem to accord well with market practice and the views expressed in the *General Reinsurance* case, and at the same time overcome the difficulties created by the former approach.

(B) AFTER THE POLICY IS ISSUED

Whatever the true position of the slip before the policy is issued, there is no doubt about the ways in which it may be referred to, and its legal effect, once a formal policy document has been executed. For instance, by inadvertence the name of the ship may have been stated incorrectly in the policy,[15] or a specially agreed term not inserted.[16] Again, where the policy is issued after a loss, doubts may exist as to whether the contract was made prior to the event; or the insurer may seek to avoid the policy for non-disclosure, and the assured may allege that he heard of the fact only after the contract had been made, though before the policy was issued.[17] In such cases the contents of the original agreement

10 *In re Clyde Marine Insurance Co.* (1923) 17 Ll. L.R. 287; *In re City Equitable Fire Insurance Co.* [1930] 2 Ch. 293.

11 Finance Act 1959.

12 *Bhugwandass v. Netherlands India Insurance Co.* (1888) 14 App. Cas. 83.

13 Ss. 23, 24 and 26.

14 Arnould (1981), paras 14, 16 and 17.

15 *Ionides v. Pacific Fire & Mar. Ins. Co.* (1871) L.R. 6 Q.B. 674, at pp. 685, 686.

16 *Symington & Co.* (No.2) v. *Union Insurance Society of Canton* (1928) 45 T.L.R. 181.

17 *Cory v. Patton* (1872) L.R. 7 Q.B. 304.

and its exact date become material and the Act provides that the slip may be referred to as evidence of such facts.[18]

It should further be noticed that while the slip can be so used for the purpose of evidence it will not operate so as to override or contradict the terms of the policy, unless there is a clear case of common mistake.[19] Where that is so, and where a policy contains a clerical error the court will rectify the mistake in pursuance of its equitable jurisdiction.

Illustration: *Motteux v. London Assurance*[20]

A policy was expressed on a ship 'from Fort St George to London'. An entry in the company's books signed by the assured's agent and by two directors on behalf of the company showed that the contract was made '*at* and from'. The court rectified the mistake and allowed the assured to recover under the policy for a loss which had occurred at Fort St George.

29.2 TYPES OF POLICY

We now have to consider the policy itself. Before considering its clauses it will be convenient to mention the different kinds of policies which are used in marine insurance.

29.2.1 THE SUBJECT-MATTER OF MARINE INSURANCE POLICIES

The first distinction we have to make is between policies on ship, on goods and on freight, as well as reinsurance policies. The principal question arising under this head is: what objects are covered by the respective policies?

(A) SHIPS

Let us first consider a policy on a ship. The old Lloyd's S.G. policy provided that 'the body, tackle, apparel, ordnance, munition, artillery, boat, and other furniture' shall be covered. According to rule 15 of the Rules for Construction of Policy, in the First Schedule to the Marine Insurance Act, this includes stores and provisions of officers and the

---

18 Marine Insurance Act 1906, s. 89.
19 *British & Foreign Marine Ins. Co.* v. *Sturge* (1897) 2 Com. Cas. 244.
20 (1739) 1 Atk. 545, 26 E.R. 343.

crew[21] and, in the case of vessels engaged in a special trade, the ordinary fittings requisite for the trade, for instance refrigerating machinery, even though not on board at the time when the contract is made.[22]

The MAR form, and 1983 Institute Hull Clauses, do not specify what is covered except in so far as the subject-matter may be designated in the schedule to the policy form.[23] However, the term 'ship' is defined in rule 15 of the Rules for Construction of Policy as including 'hull, materials and outfit, stores and provisions for the officers and crew . . . the ordinary fittings requisite for the trade and also . . . the machinery, boilers, coals and engine stores'.[24]

(B) GOODS

Goods in the ordinary sense of the word are all moveable things except money, but for the purposes of a marine policy on goods the term is restricted to 'merchandise, and does not include personal effects or provisions or stores for use on board'.[25] It is, however, not sufficient to take out a policy on goods where the nature of the merchandise or the method of its conveyance involve special risks to the underwriter. For this reason it is further provided that in the absence of a commercial usage[26] deck cargo and living animals must be insured 'specifically and not under the general denomination of goods'.

(C) FREIGHT

The third interest to be protected by a marine policy is the claim to freight. This includes 'the profit derivable by a shipowner from the employment of his ship to carry his own goods or moveables, as well as freight payable by a third party, but it does not include passage money'.[27] This must be insured separately.

Care should be taken to ascertain at whose risk the freight really is, because if not at risk no insurable interest will subsist. Usually freight

---

21 But not their personal belongings, as the assured has no insurable interest in them.
22 *Hogarth* v. *Walker* [1900] 2 Q.B. 283. *Cf.* Marine Insurance Act 1906, s. 16(1).
23 See Appendix 13 for an example of the MAR form of policy.
24 Marine Insurance Act 1906, s. 30 (2) applies the Rules, subject to the provisions of the Act and unless the context of the policy requires otherwise.
25 Marine Insurance Act 1906, First schedule, Rules for Construction of Policy, rule 17. These can, of course, be insured separately.
26 *British and Foreign Marine Insurance Co.* v. *Gaunt* [1921] 2 A.C. 41.
27 Marine Insurance Act 1906, s. 90, and First Schedule, rule 16, of the Rules for Construction of Policy.

does not become payable until the voyage is completed, and it is then at the shipowner's risk. Where, however, advance freight is stipulated for and the parties have agreed that no repayment shall be made if the voyage fails, then the freight is at risk of the shipper and he is the proper person to insure.[28] It has been held, however, that advance freight may be designated in the policy simply as 'freight' and need not be specifically described as 'advance freight'.[29]

(D) REINSURANCE

Just as merchants and shipowners insure certain risks an insurer himself may consider it expedient to reinsure with another underwriter the risks he has underwritten. This he will usually do if he finds that an individual commitment is specially large or hazardous. Reinsurances were at one time illegal as wager policies,[30] but it is now provided that every insurer of a marine adventure has an insurable interest in his risk which is capable of reinsurance.[31] It is not necessary, however, for a reinsurance policy to be described as such on its face. As the risk originally insured will normally be either ship, goods or freight, the reinsurance policy need likewise only describe the subject of the original insurance. Nevertheless in special cases the original insurer might be bound as a matter of good faith to disclose to the reinsurer the fact of reinsurance, as for instance where there is something of importance in the original contract or the person of the original assured.

As a rule every reinsurance policy contains the clause: 'being a reinsurance, subject to the same clauses and conditions as the original policy, and to pay as may be paid thereon.' The last words have been construed by the courts as meaning 'to pay as the original underwriter is liable to pay thereon'. Thus where the original insurer paid the sum insured though in fact no loss had occurred the reinsurer was discharged from his obligation.[32] But where the reinsurer bound himself in the policy to accept compromises between the parties to the original insurance contract, then he cannot require strict proof of the original insurer's liability to pay provided there was a genuine compromise.[33]

On the other hand, where the original insurer becomes insolvent and the receiver pays the assured only a small portion of his claim, say, 25p

28 *Ibid.* s. 12.
29 *Hall* v. *Janson,* (1855) 4 E. & B. 500, 119 E.R. 183.
30 Marine Insurance Act 1746, s. 4.
31 Marine Insurance Act 1906, s. 9(1).
32 *Chippendale* v. *Holt* (1895) 1 Com. Cas. 197.
33 *Gurney* v. *Grimmer* (1932) 38 Com. Cas. 7.

in the £, the reinsurer must pay the whole amount to the receiver, because the original insurer, though he did not pay the whole amount, was liable to do so.[34] This case also served to outline the more general rule that actual payment of a claim under the original insurance is not a prerequisite to making the reinsurer liable under the reinsurance contract.

29.2.2 UNVALUED AND VALUED POLICIES

Although s. 27(1) of the Marine Insurance Act 1906 specifies that policies may be valued or unvalued, in practice the great majority are of the former type.[35]

(A) UNVALUED POLICIES

In order to understand the distinction between the two types of policy it is well to recall that insurance is a contract of indemnity. If a ship is insured for £100 000 without anything more, and is afterwards lost her owner is not necessarily entitled to the sum insured. He must first prove that his loss really amounts to £100 000, i.e. that the ship was worth at least this sum. If it turns out that she was worth only £50 000 this is all he can claim, for otherwise he would make a profit on the insurance.

An unvalued policy then, is one which does not specify the value of the insured subject-matter but, in the event of loss, leaves the 'insurable value' to be ascertained at a later date.[36] The items which may legitimately be taken into account when calculating the 'insurable value' of ships, cargoes or freight are laid down in s. 16 of the Marine Insurance Act 1906. For example, the 'insurable value' of cargo is defined as the prime cost of the goods (prima facie the invoice cost) plus the shipping and insurance charges. Any claim under the policy will of course be subject to the overall limit of the sum insured.

(B) VALUED POLICIES

After the destruction of the property, proof of its value may be exceedingly difficult to establish, especially in the case of a ship. In any case, obtaining such proof is likely to be expensive, since often expert

34 *In re Eddystone Marine Insurance Co.* [1892] 2 Ch. 423.
35 For an example of an unvalued policy see *Berger & Light Diffusers Pty Ltd* v. *Pollock*, [1973] 2 Lloyd's Rep. 442, at 459.
36 Marine Insurance Act 1906, s. 28.

evidence must be called. It has long been the practice, therefore, for the parties to agree on the value of the subject-matter of the insurance in advance; the insurer accepting the value put forward by the assured. The agreed valuation figure is inserted in the contract, and such a policy is then called a 'valued policy'. It is defined by s. 27(2) of the Marine Insurance Act as 'a policy which specifies the agreed value of the subject-matter insured'. This type of policy is invariably used in insurances on ships, but where the insurance is on goods or freight difficulties of proof are not so great, and while unvalued policies, are not common, they are in use.

Since the value of a ship fluctuates and is often not certain, it may happen that what the parties agree on is a figure above the actual value, and to this extent the policy is strictly speaking not a contract of indemnity.[37] This is a good example of the law allowing the needs of business to override the claims of logical conformity, for as long as the fact that there is or may be an over-valuation is known and accepted by the insurer, no harm is done. Of course, this must have its limits, and it has been held that a gross over-valuation, when not revealed to the insurer, is evidence of bad faith.[38]

A total loss under a valued policy can be speedily settled, because in the absence of fraud, the valuation is conclusive as between insurer and assured. Also, in the case of a partial loss, the adjustment is facilitated.[39] By an estoppel, the parties are prevented, as between themselves from disputing the value of the thing insured as stated in the policy.[40] This rule is of course subject to there being no lack of good faith on either side.

If one bears in mind that it is the purpose of a valued policy to facilitate the settlement of losses under an insurance, it will be readily understood that the value fixed between insurer and assured is conclusive only in respect of the insurance and not for any other purpose. The following examples may illustrate this proposition.

Illustration 1

The parties engaged in a marine adventure may become liable to pay general average contributions, the latter bearing in proportion to the values saved by the general average act. In a case like that the value fixed by the policy cannot be conclusive, because it was agreed between insurer and

---

37 *Irving* v. *Manning* (1847) 1 H.L.C. 287; *The Maira No. 2* [1986] 2 Lloyd's Rep. 12.
38 *Thames & Mersey Marine Insurance Co.* v. *Gunford Ship Co.* [1911] A.C. 529.
39 Marine Insurance Act 1906, s. 27(3).
40 *North of England Iron S.S. Ins. Assn* v. *Armstrong* (1870) L.R. 5 Q.B. 244.

assured, and cannot bind the persons to be indemnified by general average contributions since they are not parties to the insurance.

Illustration: 2 *Burnand* v. *Rodocanachi & Co.*[41]

The assured had been paid under a valued policy as for a total loss. He later received an indemnity under a special Act passed by the United States Congress. It so happened that the ship had been under-valued, and it was only by adding the indemnity that the assured was fully compensated. The insurers claimed the indemnity under the principle of subrogation. They contended that they had paid the assured all he was entitled to under the valued policy, and whatever he might receive from other sources was due to them, inasmuch as the assured had no right to claim an indemnity from the United States on another scale than that fixed in the valued policy.

Held: The valuation was only binding in respect of the insurance contract. Where the assured claimed independently from the latter he was free to make the true value the basis of his claim.

Finally, the Act provides that for the purpose of determining whether there has been a constructive total loss,[42] the valuation may be re-opened.[43] This means, as we shall see later, that an assured may claim as for a total loss not only when the ship is actually lost, but also where she is constructively lost, as by being so badly damaged that the cost of repair would be higher than her value when repaired. In the ordinary way, then, the assured, when claiming as for a constructive total loss, cannot rely on the valuation in order to prove the repaired value. However, this provision has proved inconvenient, and it is now laid down in the policy that the agreed value shall be taken as the repaired value, thus derogating from the statutory provision.[44]

(c) SEVERAL VALUED POLICIES

What is the position if a ship is insured under more than one valued policy?

The answer is simple where the valuations in the policies tally. The contract is a contract of indemnity, and the assured cannot recover more than the agreed value. Thus where the agreed value in two policies was £3000, one policy being for £1700, the other for £2000, it was held that

41 (1882) 7 App. Cas 333.
42 See Section 31.2, *infra*.
43 Marine Insurance Act 1906, s. 27(4).
44 *Angel* v. *Merchants' Marine Insurance Co.*, [1903] 1 K.B. 811; see Institute Time Clauses (Hulls) 1970, cl. 17 and 1983, cl. 19.1.

the assured could not recover more than £3000 under both policies taken together.[45]

Where the valuations differ other rules apply. In the first place it might be thought that where one and the same ship is valued differently some sort of dishonesty must exist. However, that need not be so. As was said by Pollock CB:[46] 'It certainly may happen that when a vessel is insured for a long time, or a long voyage, that most fairly and properly, most righteously and honestly, her value may not be the same at the beginning of the voyage as when she has really performed the whole of it.' Likewise in an insurance of goods the latter may increase in value during the transport, by reason of a rise of the market value at the port of discharge or for other reasons.

In *Bruce* v. *Jones*[47] a ship was insured under four policies – the first for £725 on a valuation of £3000, the second for £500 on a valuation of £3000, the third for £3450 on a valuation of £5000, and the fourth for £2400 on a valuation of £3200. The ship became a total loss, and the owner recovered £3127 under the first three policies. When he claimed under the fourth it was held that he could only recover the difference between the valuation – £3200 – and the sums received under the other policies, namely £73, the reason being that the assured can only recover the agreed value of a policy less any sums received for the same loss on other policies. Had the plaintiff in this case recovered the £3127 on policies one, two and four, and then sued on policy three, he would have had to deduct that sum from £5000, and recovered £1873.

(D) DOUBLE INSURANCE

Where the assured takes out several policies and the combined sums insured exceed the insurable value (unvalued policy) or agreed value (valued policy) of the subject-matter insured, the assured is said to be over-insured by double insurance. For instance, a shipper insures a cargo with an insurable value or agreed value of £10 000 under two policies, one for £7000 and the other for £4000. In view of the principle of idemnity, which forbids an assured to make a profit, not more than £10 000 is recoverable under both policies together. It follows that the maximum liability of the two insurers between them is only £10 000, so

45 *Irving* v. *Richardson* (1831) 2 B. & Ad. 193, 109 E.R. 1115.
46 *Bruce* v. *Jones* (1863) 32 L.J. Ex. 132, at p. 135.
47 *Ibid.*, see Marine Insurance Act 1906, s. 32, especially subs. (2)(b).

that they have received a premium for £1000 which is not at risk, and must be returned unless the assured knew of the double insurance.[48]

The law provides that the assured, if he has suffered a loss, can claim under either policy first, but when he claims under the second policy he must give credit for what he has received from the first insurer. Where the second policy is a valued one he must give credit against the value stated, and where it is unvalued against the full insurable value of the subject-matter insured.[49]

Illustration

A insures a ship worth £1 000 000 with the B company for £800 000 and with the C company for £500 000. The ship is lost. A can claim first the full £800 000 from B company and then £200 000 from C company. If he proceeds first against the latter he can recover the full amount insured, but then only £500 000 from B company. A can also proceed against both insurers simultaneously in proportion to their policies. If the policy with the C company is a valued one, A must give credit for what he has received under the first policy agaisnt this valuation. Thus, if the valuation in the policy with the C company is £1 100 000, A will receive £300 000 under this insurance, having recovered £800 000 from the B company.

Odd results may follow where valuations in the several policies vary, as was the case in *Bruce* v. *Jones*.[50] For if in the illustration the ship is valued in the B company's policy at £900 000, and in that of the C company at £1 100 000, credit must be given against these different valuations, since the latter are conclusive as between assured and insurer.

Clearly, the amount either insurer has to pay must not be determined by the whim of the assured, namely by the fact that he decided to claim first against one insurer in preference to the other. Accordingly, s. 80 of the Act provides that the insurers as between themselves must contribute rateably, and that an insurer who has paid the assured more than his proper proportion can recover the balance from the insurer who has paid less.[51]

These rules apply only where the several policies are taken out by the same assured. Where the policies cover different interests in the same subject-matter there is no double insurance and the rules of contribution between insurers do not apply.

48 Marine Insurance Act 1906, s. 84(3) (f).
49 Marine Insurance Act 1906. s. 32(2).
50 *Supra.*
51 For a discussion as to the meaning of s. 80(1), see *Templeman* (1986), pp. 440 *et seq.*

Illustration: *North British and Mercantile Insurance Co. v. London, Liverpool and Globe Insurance Co.*[52]

Goods in a warehouse were insured by their owner, and also by the warehouseman to cover his liability *vis-à-vis* the owner. The goods were destroyed and the owner's insurers paid the policy money. They then sued the warehouseman's insurers for a refund of what they had paid the owner of the goods.

Held: The action succeeded, and the defendants' contention that they need only contribute a proportion failed. This was a case of subrogation, not contribution. The insurer had to pay what without the insurance his assured would have been legally bound to pay, and since the warehouseman was liable to the owner of the goods, his insurers were liable to compensate the insurers of the owner.

29.2.3   VOYAGE AND TIME POLICIES

The period of time for which the subject-matter of the policy is covered against loss or damage is of critical importance. Insurances on cargo will naturally relate to the voyage on which the cargo moves, whereas insurances on ships may extend to cover a particular voyage or a specified length of time. In practice the distinction may not be so clear cut and policies which are a mixture of the two elements of voyage and time are not uncommon.

(A)   VOYAGE POLICIES

In a voyage policy a ship is insured for a voyage from one place to another, and the underwriter has to pay for losses happening on that voyage.

The Act defines voyage policies as contracts which insure the subject matter 'at and from' or 'from one place to another'.[53] For voyage policies on ships the time at which the policy attaches depends on which form of wording is used. Voyage policies on cargo on the other hand normally attach, in accordance with the transit clause,[54] when the goods leave the warehouse.

Voyage policies on ships are now uncommon, it being more convenient to insure for a specified period of time. Voyage policies also have the disadvantage for the shipowner that once the voyage has been agreed, any change of voyage or deviation while on the voyage, can

52 (1877) 5 Ch. D. 569.
53 Marine Insurance Act 1906, s. 25.
54 See discussion on Attachment and Duration of Risk at Section 29.4.

leave him with no insurance cover. Time policies circumvent this difficulty and, subject to the Institute trading warranties, allow the owner to trade the ship with maximum flexibility anywhere he wishes. Despite the obvious disadvantages of voyage policies they are still employed for situations where one-off trips are required, for example on a delivery voyage to a new owner or for a voyage to a repair port.

(B) TIME POLICIES

Under a time policy a ship is insured irrespective of any special voyage for a certain period. Any loss occurring when the time has expired is of course not covered by the policy. Exceptionally a complication arises. For instance, the ship is badly damaged during the currency of the policy, but survives for the time being, finally succumbing only when the time for which it is insured has run out. Must the insurers pay? The decision, it has been held,[55] depends on whether at the time the policy expires the structure is still a ship or has become a wreck. If the ship to the end of the period still floats and navigates, albeit only thanks to the continuous use of pumps, it remains a ship and is not lost. In this case a claim could only be admitted for a partial loss as unrepaired damage.[56] On the other hand, if the structure is doomed, but does not finally go to the bottom until after the time policy has expired, there has been a total loss under the policy and the insurers must pay.

Again, where there were two consecutive time policies and damage to hull was suffered under the first, but the bill of the ship repairer fell due during the second policy, the first underwriters were held liable.[57] Scrutton LJ laid down.[58] 'Only the actual loss or damage to hull from the named perils is recoverable. Loss to the shipowner's pocket is only recoverable as the measure of the actual loss or damage to hull.'

(C) MIXED POLICIES

A voyage policy rarely stands by itself. Very often a time policy is added to it by a term holding ship or goods covered during a number of days after arrival. In the absence of special terms this period remains covered though a new adventure may in fact have begun.

55 *Lidgett* v. *Secretan* (1870), 5 C.P. 190.
56 See discussion as to partial loss at Section 31.4. See also Hull Clauses, cl. 2.
57 *Hutchins Bros.* v. *Royal Exchange Ass.* [1911] 2 K.B. 398.
58 *Ibid.*, at p. 405.

Illustration: *Gamgles* v. *Ocean Marine Insurance Co. of Bombay*[59]

A ship was insured 'at and from the Port of Pomaron to Newcastle-on-Tyne, and for 15 days whilst there after arrival'; before the 15 days were up the cargo had been discharged and a new cargo was being loaded in preparation for a new outward voyage. Then the ship was damaged. The insurers disputed their liability and contended that the 15 days after arrival were intended only as a maximum period for the discharge of the cargo, but the Court held that the words must be taken as engrafting on the voyage policy a time policy for 15 days, and the insurers were liable for any loss or damage occurring during that period. It was not a time policy with reference to the voyage, but an independent time policy.

The Marine Insurance Act recognizes such policies by stating that 'A contract for both voyage and time may be included in the same policy'.[60] While a voyage policy which covers the subject-matter for a specified period after arrival is considered a mixed policy, one which covers a vessel for a period, within fixed geographical limits, has been considered a time policy.[61]

29.2.4   FLOATING POLICIES AND OPEN COVERS

One last form of policy should be noted, the so-called floating policy, and the open cover. Either is usually used by large shippers of small parcels of goods. For such persons it is often inconvenient to take out a policy on each shipment. Instead, under a floating policy, they insure all their shipments for a lump sum and every shipment declared reduces the underwriter's liability under the policy.[62]

The floating policy is subject to no time limit, although there is usually a cancellation clause, and the policy only expires once the amount insured is exhausted. Apart from the sum insured, the only other major limitation of the floating policy is to restrict the value of goods shipped in any one vessel, thus protecting the underwriter from an unexpected accumulation of risk on any particular voyage.

59 (1876), 1 Ex. D. 141.
60 Marine Insurance Act 1906, s. 25.
61 *Wilson* v. *Boag* [1956] 2 Lloyd's Rep. 564, Sup. Ct. (N.S.W.). For a case involving an example of a mixed policy see *The Al-Jubail IV: M. Almojil Establishment* v. *Malayan Motor and General Underwriters Ltd* [1982] 2 Lloyd's Rep. 637.
62 *Arnould* (1981), 274 *et seq.*; Marine Insurance Act 1906, s. 29.

All goods shipped within the terms of the policy must be declared,[63] for otherwise the assured might, by declaring only the bad risks, act unfairly towards the underwriter.

Illustration: *Dunlop v. Townend*[64]

The plaintiffs effected a floating policy at Lloyd's covering war risks only and intended to protect their interest as consignees of goods for commission and advances made to shippers. They declared most consignments, but some of them they did not declare, because the shippers gave instructions that particular shipments should be insured under the Government Scheme of war risk insurance.

Held: The instructions of the shippers made no difference, and the plaintiffs were bound to declare all shipments.

The declaration within the period prescribed by the policy is in the nature of a warranty. It is not clear whether a breach of the assured's duty to declare material facts has any further effect than to discharge the insurer from liability in respect of the shipment in question, or whether the whole policy is thereby avoided, an opinion which is perhaps unnecessarily severe.[65]

Another question which arises is whether the assured must disclose the name of the ship by which the cargo will be carried, if indeed he knows it. On principle there would not appear to be such a duty, since the insurer must be taken to have agreed to shipment on any seaworthy ship. Where, however, the goods-owner knew material facts about the vessel which was intended to carry the goods – for instance, where he had heard that the ship was to be cast away, even though he did not believe it, it was held that it was his duty[66] to disclose this circumstance when insuring.[67]

Where the declaration, though made within the agreed time limit, is made after loss the policy nevertheless covers the goods. In a certain floating policy the parties had agreed that declarations should be made 'as soon as possible after sailing of the vessel to which interest attaches'. The ship sailed on 21st August and was lost on 12th September. One day later the declaration was made and this was held not 'as soon as possible' and thus was too late, so that the insurer was not liable.[68] Lord

63 Marine Insurance Act 1906, s. 29(3).
64 [1919] 2 K.B. 127.
65 See *Arnould* (1981), para. 657, and *Leigh* v. *Adams* (1871) 25 L.T. 566.
66 *Leigh* v. *Adams, supra.*
67 *Arnould* (1981), para. 657.
68 *Union Insurance Society of Canton* v. *Wills* [1916] 1 A.C. 281.

Parmoor made it clear, however,[69] that the policy attaches immediately on loading, and that if the goods had been destroyed by fire before sailing, which is before the time fixed for the declaration, the insurers would have been liable.

The floating policy, as can be seen, is a flexible form of insurance, for on shipment nothing more onerous or time wasting than a declaration is required. A degree of rigidity is, however, introduced by the maximum amount insured under the policy, for watch must be kept that the cover does not get exhausted. This defect is absent from the even more flexible form of insurance known as an 'open cover'.[70] This, too, is a contract under which the assured must declare all shipments. It is, however, not a formal policy document as such but a permanent slip, the only limitation of which is the maximum value of shipments by any one vessel. Policies must be issued at a later stage, as required, but in the meantime the assured is issued with blank insurance certificates. As each shipment is made, the assured fills in a set of certificates and sends one copy to the brokers, which acts as a declaration of the shipment and is used for accounting purposes. The other copies will accompany the shipping documents as evidence of the insurance. Open covers are written for twelve months or for an indefinite period subject to a cancelling clause, which enables either party to terminate the arrangement. No premiums are payable before shipment and accounts between the parties are settled on a periodic basis.

29.3   FORM, STRUCTURE AND DEVELOPMENT OF MARINE POLICIES

The Marine Insurance Act 1906 imposes no conditions on the form a marine policy has to take. The only relevant provision in the Act states 'A policy may be in the form in the First Schedule to this Act'.[71] An examination of the schedule will reveal the form of policy adopted by Lloyd's and the insurance companies, the wording of which is very similar to that first settled in 1779. As already discussed, the S.G. form of policy as it became known, appears to modern readers as an antiquated document, full of quaint terminology drawn from an earlier age. Though the old-fashioned phraseology lent the document a certain

---

69 *Union Insurance Society of Canton* v. *Wills* [1916] 1 A.C. 287.
70 *Arnould* (1981), paras 165, 274. The more restrictive floating policy is now being generally replaced by the more flexible open cover.
71 S. 30(1).

charm, it was also the cause of much adverse judicial comment. The courts were by no means the only source of criticism, and for many years prospective assureds have expressed their own reservations about the difficulty of establishing exactly what risks and losses the policy covers.

It may be difficult for the person unfamiliar with the London marine insurance market, to understand why insurers should wish to retain such an unpopular form of policy. The reason would appear to be, however, that over two centuries, each word or phrase of the S.G. form has received judicial attention and interpretation, often many times over. As such, the underwriters and their representatives believed it would be impossible to modernize the form of words without losing a very large part of the certainty which attached to the policy document. Major change, they maintained, would result in a flood of unnecessary and expensive litigation.

The culmination of this battle between those for and against the S.G. form came in the late 1970s when the United Nations Conference on Trade and Development (UNCTAD) joined the cause of those seeking to change the old policy. UNCTAD proposed an international review of marine insurance policy conditions, law and practice, with a view to drawing up a standard set of marine insurance clauses, as an international model, and establishing an international marine insurance legal regime.[72] While these objectives have only been partially fulfilled, UNCTAD's ideas were sufficient to spur the London market into reviewing and updating the S.G. form and its associated clauses.

Therefore, after reigning unchallenged for over 200 years, the S.G. form and standard clauses came to be replaced in 1982 for cargo insurance, and in the following year for hull business. Its successor, the Marine Policy form or MAR form is a much simplified document with the detailed provisions of the insurance now incorporated entirely in the standard clauses which are attached to the basic policy form. Although transition to the new form is now complete, for insurance effected in the London market, it is not possible to simply discard the old S.G. policy in favour of the new. Apart from the fact that litigation arising on the old form will be passing through the courts for some years to come, the S.G. policy and the interpretation of its terms form the basis of many established principles and wordings relevant to the new policy. It is also true that many overseas markets have adopted variations of the S.G. form. Such policies will be in domestic use for some years and their

72 See UNCTAD Document TD/B/C.4/ISL/27/Rev. 1, Legal and Documentary Aspects of the Marine Insurance Contract, 1982.

effects will filter through to the London market via reinsurance business. It will therefore be appreciated that it is presently necessary to
discuss both types of policy and point out the differences where these
occur.

29.3.1 LLOYD'S S.G. POLICY

The Lloyd's S.G. Policy form[73] is designed as a single document to
cover interests in both ships and goods. Indeed in practice it was used
even more widely to insure such items as freight, profits and disbursements. Such diversity of use, without altering the wording, has
obviously brought about a further degree of difficulty in interpretation,
thus complicating the meaning of an already obscure phraseology. In
order to cope with insuring such a diverse range of interests, insurers
would add to the standard policy, clauses which related to the particular
subject-matter and risks to be covered. Such clauses were either stuck to
the policy document or 'written, printed or stamped on the margin'.[74]
By the early 1900s the variety of clauses in common use had become so
great that it was deemed necessary to produce standard sets of clauses to
cover particular types of subject-matter. The first Institute cargo
clauses, drafted by the Institute of London Underwriters, were introduced in 1912 and with modern needs, and technological change,
revised sets of clauses appeared at regular intervals.

The S.G. policy document itself consists of three separate but related
sections. The first is the insurance itself, which specifies *inter alia* the
subject-matter, names of insurers, extent of cover, value of subject-
matter and perils covered. The following section is the 'sue and labour'
clause[75] and the final part the Memorandum[76] which specifies minimum percentages (or franchise) under which claims for loss of certain
perishable commodities will not be payable.

As already mentioned, special sets of clauses designed for ships
(hulls), including yachts, different types of cargo and freight are
attached to the policy. New clauses are introduced as decisions by the
courts and new phenomena make this advisable. Indeed, the appearance
of new clauses and the new versions of existing ones reflect events in the
history of warfare, technological change and economic development.
For example, naval tactics to protect merchant shipping led to a new

73 See Appendix 15; and for construction, *Arnould* (1981), para. 83 *et seq.*
74 Ivamy (1985), p. 102.
75 See Section 30.3 *infra.*
76 See Section 30.4 *infra.*

version of the 'free of capture and seizure' clause, which in the S.G. form acted as a war risks exclusion.[77]

Examples of clauses prompted by technological and consequent legal changes are those dealing with oil pollution, a hazard covered, as we have seen, by international conventions. Now, once pollution threatens or has happened, governments may take action to prevent or mitigate pollution damage; thus when the *Torrey Canyon* stranded near the Scilly Isles in 1967, the British government ordered the destruction of the vessel by bombing, which of course ended any hope of salvage. To protect owners in such circumstances a pollution hazards clause covers the assured against 'loss of or damage to the vessel caused by any governmental authority, acting under the powers vested in it to prevent or mitigate a pollution hazard, or threat thereof, resulting directly from damage to the vessel for which the underwriters are liable under this insurance'.[78] This cover does not, however, extend to cases where the assured himself, through his negligence, caused the casualty which led to the government action.

It can therefore been seen, that in construing the S.G. Policy, great importance must be attached, not only to the wording of the document itself but also to the set of clauses which inevitably accompany it. These clauses both add to[79] and detract from[80] the obligations of the insurers under the original policy document and in order to construe the overall meaning and content of the contract both clauses and policy must be looked to.

29.3.2 MAR FORM OF POLICY

The Marine Policy Form,[81] introduced in 1982, is a much simplified document in comparison to the old S.G. form. Not only has the antiquated phraseology been removed but much of the substance of the old form, such as the list of perils and the 'sue and labour' clause, has been taken out of the policy and included in the standard sets of clauses. For this reason alone, the MAR form is more suited to insuring the differing types of subject-matter which are commonly the subject of marine insurance policies. In effect, the MAR policy document is nothing more than a schedule of the important variables concerning the

77 Now the 'war exclusion' clause (Institute Hull Clauses 1983, cl. 23).
78 Institute Time Clauses (Hulls) 1983, cl 7.
79 For example, Institute Hull Clauses 1970, cl. 7 ('Inchmaree' clause).
80 For example, Institute Hull Clauses 1970, cl. 23 ('F.C. & S.' clause).
81 See Appendix 13.

particular insurance contract to which it relates. Thus the form lists: the policy number, name of assured, name of vessel, description of voyage or period of insurance (depending on whether the insurance is a voyage or time policy), subject-matter insured, agreed value (if any), sum insured and the premium payable. These particulars are followed by any clauses, endorsements, special conditions or warranties which are deemed appropriate and are attached to the policy. It is made clear by the form that such clauses, for example, the Institute Cargo Clauses (A) 1982, form an integral part of the policy. Finally, the policy lists the underwriters, their syndicates and the percentage of the risk each is willing to bear. There is of course, space for the signature and stamp of Lloyd's Policy Signing Office or the Institute of London Underwriters, depending on whether it is a Lloyd's or company policy.

29.3.3   THE INSTITUTE CLAUSES

The important point to note about the MAR form is the complete lack of any terms or conditions relating to the duties and liabilities of the parties to the marine insurance contract. All details relating to such matters are contained in the relevant Institute clauses which are attached to the policy. It is therefore convenient here to describe briefly the main changes which have taken place with the introduction of the Institute clauses which may be attached to the MAR form of policy.

(A)   HULL CLAUSES

The Institute Time Clauses (Hulls) 1983 came into use for new insurance business on 1 October 1983. The changes introduced by the new hull clauses, while perhaps not so dramatic as for the cargo clauses, are none the less important. Perhaps the first thing to notice, is that the transfer of much of the substance of the contract from the policy to the clauses has provided a valuable opportunity to rearrange the clauses in a more logical sequence.

The 1983 clauses begin with a statement (not included in the old clauses) that the insurance 'is subject to English law and practice'. While this statement may be deleted, it is intended to make clear the point that the clauses have been drafted against the background of English law and the Marine Insurance Act 1906, and that unless the parties otherwise agree, English law should be applied even if some other jurisdiction is accepted.[82] Following this initial statement, come the clauses dealing with the conditions to be observed by the assured in order to maintain the insurance cover. One of the major changes in this section is the new provision in clause 1.3, which in the event of the vessel being sent for breaking up, reduces the insured value of the vessel to its market value as scrap at the time of any loss. The clause however has no effect on claims for collision liability, general average or salvage charges under clauses 8 and 11. Apparently it was felt necessary to add this new provision in the light of poor underwriting results on such voyages[83] and it should be noted that its application is automatic unless the assured gives the underwriter prior notice and agrees an amended form of cover. In a similar way, the scope of the 'termination' clause[84] has been extended such that cover ceases automatically on the happening of a variety of changes in the way the vessel is operated. The old clauses imposed this sanction only where the vessel is transferred or sold to new management. This provision is preserved in the 1983 clauses and in addition, any change in Classification Society, loss of class, change of flag, bareboat charter or requisition will, subject to minor reservations, have the same effect.

The second major section of the new clauses (cl. 6-8) relates to the perils which may cause loss or damage to the vessel and collision liabilities which the assured may be required to discharge. The 1983 clauses maintain the named perils approach seen in the 1970 clauses, but deleting the list of perils from the policy has had the effect of adding a list of marine perils to the clauses where they are grouped with those which were covered under the old Inchmaree clause. The change has also meant a considerable tidying up and modernizing of the list of perils which no longer include such picturesque terms as rovers, men of war, surprisals and takings at sea. 'Perils of the seas' on the other hand do reappear in the new clauses, despite the difficulty of definition, because it was agreed that they are universally recognized and should not be experimented with. One of the casualties from the S.G. form however, is the phrase 'all other perils' which has often been used to extend the notion of 'perils of the seas' to those which are *ejusdem generis* with such perils.[85] However, to help counter this loss, clause 6.1.1

82 See *The Al Wahab* [1983] 2 Lloyd's Rep. 365 and *The Stolt Marmaro* [1985] 2 Lloyd's Rep. 428; two cases where the application of English law to the S.G. form arose.

83 J.K. Goodacre, *Institute Time Clauses: Hulls – A Comparison* (1983), p. 2.

84 Institute Time Clauses (Hulls) 1983, cl. 4.

85 *Canada Rice Mills Ltd.* v. *Union Marine and General Insurance Co. Ltd* [1941] A.C. 55.

states that the insurance is to cover losses caused by 'perils of the seas, rivers, lakes or other navigable waters'. Other significant changes to the list of perils are the transfer of losses due to piracy from the list of excepted war risks to become a covered marine risk and the addition of a proviso that barratry will not be covered if there is want of due diligence on the part of the assured. This latter alteration probably does little to alter the accepted understanding that barratry will not be covered if it takes place with the privity of the assured.

Types of expense, other than loss or damage, which the assured may incur are covered by clauses 9 to 22, as are restrictions on effecting additional insurances and situations where premium may be returnable. Major changes in this section relate to: clause 12.1, which makes it clear that the deductible is not to apply to sue and labour claims and that it is the assured's duty to take action to minimize loss; clause 18, which defines more clearly the extent of underwriter's liability for unrepaired damage; clause 19.2, which clarifies the position in relation to constructive total loss and clause 21 which raises the limit on additional disbursements insurance from 10 per cent to 25 per cent of the sum insured.

The fourth and final part of the insurance (cl. 23–26) relates to specific exclusions from cover and follows a paramount clause, which in the event of inconsistency between the exclusions and any other clauses, ensures that the former prevail. The old 'free of capture and seizure' clause (F.C. & S.) has been replaced by a much simplified 'war exclusion' clause[86] which cannot be discussed in detail here.[87] The 'strikes exclusion' clause (clause 24), is a new addition to the exclusions and embraces losses caused by strikers as well as terrorists and those acting from political motives. This clause makes it clear that not only are such risks excluded from cover but that insured perils are also excluded when caused by the classes of persons mentioned above. Finally, the remaining exclusions found in the final two clauses have not been subject to any effective changes. In regard to the exclusion clauses, the overall intention is that cover shall be obtained by the assured for such perils on a back-to-back basis under the Institute War and Strikes Clauses (Hulls-Time) 1983.

(B)   CARGO CLAUSES

While the hull clauses have undergone considerable tidying up and rearrangement, and certain doubtful points have been clarified, there is

86 Institute Time Clauses (Hulls) 1983, cl. 23.
87 See discussion at Section 30.3.3, *infra*.

no doubt that the cargo clauses have undergone a far more fundamental revision of form and structure. Gone are the old distinctions of 'all risks', 'with average' (WA) and 'free of particular average' (FPA), and in their place are three sets of clauses labelled simply 'A', 'B' and 'C' which introduce a new form of cover. The 'all risks' approach is still retained in the form of the A clauses but the B and C clauses are completely new, the only difference between them being in the risks which they are intended to cover. Thus, the major change which has come about with this revision is the move away from clauses which do not offer cover for particular average (a partial loss caused by an insured peril), the so-called FPA clauses. All three sets of the 1982 cargo clauses therefore cover particular average in full.

Apart from the change of format, it became necessary in doing away with the terms contained in the S.G. form, to incorporate in modern language, the named perils and effects of the 'sue and labour' and 'waiver' clauses into the new forms. At the same time it was decided to dispense with the 'Memorandum' from the S.G. form and therefore there is no longer a franchise provision in any of the cargo clauses. In general terms it can be said that the A clauses are 'all risks' clauses, subject to named exceptions found in clauses 4, 5, 6 and 7 and that the C clauses are intended to provide for standard cover against major casualties. The B clauses hold the middle-ground, comprising as they do, the C clauses plus some additional named risks. In regard to the B and C clauses it was also felt that there would be demand for extra cover in respect of deliberate damage which is excluded. This need is provided for by the addition, at an extra premium, of the Institute 'malicious damage' clause, which has the effect of deleting clause 4.7 of the B and C clauses.

In addition to making these large-scale changes, the opportunity was taken to rearrange and group the clauses in a more logical framework, under specific headings. Thus, the order of the clauses now reads: risks covered, exclusions, duration of the insurance and matters relating to claims. Towards the end of the document various miscellaneous items are dealt with, such as the assured's duty to minimize loss and act with reasonable dispatch. The final clause repeats the provision, found at the beginning of the hull clauses, which makes the insurance subject to English law and practice.

This new layout of clauses has also allowed for additions and changes to the substance of the document and, in particular, enables attention to be drawn to the various exclusions from cover. A number of these exclusions were incorporated into the old policies by virtue of provisions in the Marine Insurance Act, but under the 1982 clauses they

have been specifically enumerated.[88] Thus we find exclusions relating
to losses attributable to the wilful misconduct of the assured, wear and
tear, inherent vice and delay. Further to these statutory exclusions new
provisions have been incorporated concerning insufficiency of packing
and losses arising from financial default of owners, managers, charterers or operators of the carrying vessel. One other new clause which is
worthy of mention is the 'insurable interest' clause[89] which repeats the
requirement laid down by s. 6 of the Marine Insurance Act, that at the
time of loss the assured must hold an insurable interest in the subject-
matter of the insurance. The second part of this clause goes on to
re-establish the 'lost or not lost' provision found in the S.G. form,
whereby the assured can recover for an insured loss during the period of
the insurance even though the loss might have occurred prior to the
conclusion of the contract. Recovery under this clause is of course
subject to the provision that the assured was not aware of such loss
before effecting the contract.

(C)   COMMODITY CLAUSES

In addition to the standard cargo clauses there is a considerable variety
of special commodity clauses, designed to complement the risks associated with particular types of cargo. During the latest round of clause
revision, strenuous attempts were made by insurers to limit the pro-
liferation of clauses for specific cargo types. These efforts have been
aided by the introduction, for the first time, of the Institute Commodity Trades Clauses, which appear in A, B and C versions in a
similar fashion to the standard cargo clauses. At the time of writing,
these standard commodity clauses have been agreed with the Federation
of Commodity Associations for the insurance of cocoa, coffee, cotton,
fats and oils (not in bulk), hides, skins and leather, metals, oil seeds,
sugar and tea. The list of such commodities insured in this way is likely
to grow as negotiations proceed with the various commodity
associations.

An examination of the Commodity Trades Clauses reveals their close
similarity to the standard cargo clauses both in terms of layout and
content. There are however a few significant differences which distinguish them from the Institute Cargo Clauses, 1982. One of the
variations worthy of mention, is the somewhat more generous wording applied to the insolvency exclusion found in clause 4.6. It will be

88 Institute Cargo Clauses 1982, cl. 4.
89 *Ibid.* cl. 11.

remembered that under the 1982 Institute Cargo Clauses, the insurer is not liable for loss or expense arising from the financial default of vessel owners or operators. Under the Commodity Trades Clauses the exclusion will only apply if, at the time of loading the assured was aware that such insolvency could prevent the normal prosecution of the voyage. A further valuable concession granted by the insurers under the revised form of exclusion is that it shall not apply to assignees who buy the cargo in good faith.

Despite the introduction of the Commodity Trades Clauses it has still been found necessary to maintain sets of clauses which relate to specific types of cargo and take account of any unusual characteristics and particular risks which attach. Thus, modified versions of the standard clauses are available for insuring shipments of a diverse range of commodities such as frozen food, coal, oil in bulk, jute and natural rubber.

29.4   ATTACHMENT AND DURATION OF RISK

It is a most important question to determine at what moment the insurance begins to run and for how long the cover lasts, or in other words when the policy attaches and the duration of the risk. If any loss occurs outside these time limits the insurer cannot be held liable, with the possible exception of losses after the expiry of a time policy where the cause of loss acted within the insured period.

29.4.1   COMMENCEMENT OF RISK

For insurances on ships, in the case of a voyage policy 'from' a certain port, the policy attaches as soon as the moorings are cast off. However, if the policy is expressed as 'at and from' a certain port, the policy attaches while the ship is in port preparatory to her voyage. The terms 'from' and 'at and from' in voyage policies are defined more precisely in rules 2 and 3 of the Rules for Construction of Policy.[90] The attachment of risk under a pure time policy is a much simpler question and occurs when the period agreed to be covered begins to run. Cargo policies, which are in essence voyage policies, used to attach from the loading of the goods onto the ship. In practice, however, the moment of attachment of risk under a cargo policy is brought forward in time by the

---

90 Voyage clauses 1983 do not give time of attachment; this is put in the MAR schedule.

transit clause (once termed the warehouse to warehouse clause) which specifies that the insurance attaches 'from the time the goods leave the warehouse or place of storage at the place named herein for the commencement of the transit' ICC 1982, cl. 8.1.[91]

29.4.2   DURATION OF RISK

Having established when the policy begins to run, the next question to be considered is when does the risk terminate? Again, under a time policy the answer is relatively simple; at the time specified in the policy. There are of course exceptions to this rule, e.g. where the assured falls foul of any stipulations contained in the 'termination clause'[92] , such as loss of vessel's class or change of flag. Such events will have the effect of reducing the duration of the risk. In contrast, under the terms of the 'continuation clause',[93] the insurance may be extended to the point of destination at the election of the assured, if on expiration of the policy, the vessel is at sea or in distress or at a port of refuge or call.

Ships insured under a voyage policy, come off-risk once they have arrived in good physical safety at the port named in the policy. The old rule developed on this matter indicates that the vessel shall only be considered arrived once she has reached the place at which ships of her type and size usually moor.[94] Apart from termination at the point of destination, a voyage policy on a ship may also be terminated by reason of a decision by the assured to change the prospective voyage or to deviate from the agreed voyage. A change of voyage occurs where the contemplated voyage is commenced but at some later stage the decision is taken to change the port of destination. In such a case the Marine Insurance Act provides that 'where there is a change of voyage the insurer is discharged from liability as from the time of the change'.[95] In fact, for this provision to operate, the vessel's course does not have to be changed, it is enough that the master has been given orders to make for a new destination. Similar provisions apply to a deviation from the contemplated voyage, even though there be no change of destination, except that the insurance will not terminate unless there is a deviation in fact.[96] Again, in practice, the assured is relieved from the effect of these stringent rules by a clause stating that the assured will be 'held covered'

---

91 See *Kallis* v. *Success Ins.* [1985] 2 Lloyd's Rep. 8 where risk never attached.
92 Institute Time Clauses (Hulls), 1983, cl. 4.
93 *Ibid.* cl. 2.
94 See Ivamy (1985), p. 119 *et seq.*
95 Marine Insurance Act 1906, s. 45(2).
96 Marine Insurance Act 1906, s.46.

provided prompt notice is given to underwriters and any necessary additional premium is paid.

Determination of the point at which a cargo policy ceases to attach is made by reference to the 'transit clause'.[97] This provides that the policy normally terminates on delivery of the cargo to consignees or into a warehouse at the named destination. Alternatively, if the assured places the cargo into a warehouse for storage, other than in the ordinary course of transit, or for allocation or distribution, the policy will cease to operate from the time of delivery to such warehouse. Finally, the clause imposes an overall time limit for cover of 60 days after completion of discharge, of the goods insured, at the final port of discharge.

29.5 ASSIGNMENT

The commercial value of every asset depends on the possibility of disposing of it, either by simple sale or by way of security for some form of loan. In the case of goods or things in possession, this is done by transferring them by sale or pledge or by creating an equitable charge. Where the asset is not a tangible thing which is capable of being physically possessed, but merely a right, though perhaps evidenced or contained in a document, its existence becomes apparent only when it is exercised, when a claim is made, or an action brought; a right is thus called a thing, or *chose*, in action. Insurance policies are such things in action. They are dealt with like other rights of that kind by a special mode of transfer, called assignment.

29.5.1 ASSIGNMENT OF MARINE POLICIES

The assignment of a marine insurance policy becomes necessary, for instance, where insured goods are sold, and the insurance is intended to be transferred from the seller to the buyer. To begin with, it has been provided that where the assured disposes of his interest in the subject-matter insured, in other words where he e.g. sells the insured ship or goods, the insurance is not assigned unless the parties have made an express or implied agreement to this effect.[98] So if no such agreement was made the policy lapses since the seller ceases to have an insurable

97 Institute Cargo Clauses, 1982, cl. 8.
98 Marine Insurance Act 1906, s. 15.

interest. If the parties intend to assign the policy together with the goods they must take care to effect the assignment either 'before or at the time' of transferring the subject-matter insured. For, to make a valid assignment, the assured must still be entitled to the insurance, a right which he loses with his insurable interest. If the seller, as an after-thought, that is when he is no longer interested in the insured goods, purports to effect an assignment, this is of no avail.[99] However, if, the insured goods are lost the right to the indemnity can always be assigned.[1]

Illustration: *Lloyd v. Flemming*[2]

Goods insured under a marine policy were lost. After the loss by perils insured against the policy together with all rights thereunder was assigned.

Held: The assignee of the policy was entitled to maintain an action against the underwriter. The reason why before loss an assignment of the policy without an interest in the subject-matter insured is invalid is that no person can recover under a marine policy unless he be beneficially interested in the subject-matter and is prejudiced by its loss. *Per* Blackburn, J., at p. 302: 'But after the loss has happened ... this reason ceases at once ... The reason of the distinction is, that after the loss the right to indemnity no longer depends on the right of property in the subject-matter of insurance, so far as it still exists, but on the right of property in the thing or the portion of the thing lost.'

Let us suppose, however, that the parties to a contract of sale of a ship have agreed at the right time that the insurance shall pass from the seller to the buyer. In that case it becomes necessary to consider the rights of the insurer. It will be readily understood that an insurer may be willing to insure the vessel of a careful owner, but might not wish to cover any subsequent owner whose reliability is not known to him. Though in general, insurances cannot be transferred without the insurer's consent, the law has taken into consideration the special nature of marine insurance and has provided that 'a marine policy is assignable unless it contains terms expressly prohibiting assignment'.[3]

A marine policy on goods is usually assignable; in fact the sale of goods by documents is the most common example where assignment of an insurance policy takes place. In the case of ships, it is usual to provide for a limitation of the right to assign. The Institute Time

99 Marine Insurance Act 1906 s. 51.
 1 *Ibid.* s. 50(1).
 2 (1872) L.R. 7 Q.B. 299.
 3 Marine Insurance Act 1906, s. 50(1).

Clauses (Hulls), 1983 provide for an automatic cancellation of the insurance if there is 'any change, voluntary or otherwise, in the owner-ship' of the vessel, unless the underwriters agree to the contrary in writing. Where, however, the ship is sold while at sea the cancellation of the policy may be deferred, if required by the assured until she reaches her port of destination or final port of discharge; clearly the new owners or managers will not normally be able to do anything that materially increases the risk while the ship is at sea. For this reason the Institute Voyage Clauses contain no corresponding term.[4]

29.5.2 FORM OF ASSIGNMENT

We now pass to the mode of assignment. The Act provides in s. 50(3) that this shall be effected by endorsement of the policy or in other customary manner. If the endorsement has been general, that is to say, if the name of the assignee is not mentioned in the endorsement, the policy may in future be assigned by mere delivery. Even where there is no endorsement it would seem that it is now a 'customary manner' to assign marine policies, at any rate, on goods, by delivery only. As was said by Roche J 'policies often are assigned otherwise than by endorse-ment'. He continued: 'In the case of c.i.f. contracts they are so often handed over without any endorsement being made upon them, that I should be surprised if it could not be proved that that is a customary manner of assigning policies'.[5] In policies on ships, an Institute clause provides that a dated notice of assignment must be endorsed on the policy, and that without such notice, the underwriters will not be bound by or recognize the assignment.[6] Further, as we have noted above the 1983 hull clauses are subject to an overriding condition that any change of ownership or management of the vessel will automatically terminate the insurance unless underwriters agree to the contrary. Thus, although goods policies are commonly assigned with little formality, the assign-ability of policies on ships is subject to much tighter control.

In all cases it is, however, necessary to satisfy the court that the transfer of a policy was intended by the parties to be an assignment.[7]

---

4 Cf. a restriction in case of a mutual insurance: *Laurie* v. *West Hartlepool Indemnity Association* (1899) 15 T.L.R. 486.

5 *Safadi* v. *Western Assurance Co.* (1933), 46 Ll. L.R. 140, at p. 144. See also *Aron & Co. Inc.* v. *Miall* (1928), 34 Com. Cas. 18, *per* Scrutton LJ at p. 20.

6 Institute Time Clauses (Hulls) 1983, cl. 5; Institute Voyage Clauses (Hulls) 1983, cl. 3.

7 *Safadi* v. *Western Assurance Co.*, *supra*; *cf. North of England Pure Oil Cake* v. *Archangel Maritime Insurance Co.* (1875) L.R. 10 Q.B. 249.

29.5.3   EFFECT OF ASSIGNMENT

Finally, we have to decide what is the effect of a valid assignment. The principal effect of an assignment is that in the event of a loss the assignee can sue the insurer in his own name,[8] irrespective of the fact that he was not interested in the subject-matter when the damage occurred.[9] The assignee's right to sue in his own name depends on his having acquired the beneficial interest in the policy.[10] It is doubtful whether the assignee of a part interest in the policy can be said to have the 'beneficial interest in such policy'. In *Williams* v. *Atlantic Assurance Co. Ltd.*,[11] Greer and Slesser LJJ held that such person was only an equitable assignee and could only sue by joining the assignor as co-plantiff. On the other hand, Scrutton LJ in the same case did not base his decision on that ground, and Roche J in *Safadi* v. *Western Assurance Co.*[12] treated the question as an open one.

As in all other cases of assignment, the insurer may not be put into a worse position by reason of a third party being substituted for the original assured. The Act provides that he 'is entitled to make any defence arising out of the contract which he would have been entitled to make if the action had been brought in the name of the person by or on behalf of whom the policy was effected.[13] Thus where an insurer is entitled to avoid the policy on the ground of non-disclosure he may do so also as against the innocent assignee.[14] Were it otherwise everybody could protect himself against the effect of non-disclosure by assigning the policy. On the other hand, the defences open against the assignee must arise 'out of the contract', that is, out of the very contract on which the assignee sues.[15] Suppose an insurer is liable to one person under two policies, A and B. He pays on A under a mistake of fact and has thus a claim for refund. If the assured sues him under B the claim for refund under A may be set off against the claim for payment under B. But if B has been assigned to an innocent assignee the refund under A cannot be thus set off, because the claim for refund does not arise out of the

8 Marine Insurance Act 1906, s. 50(2).
9 *Aron* v. *Miall, supra;* following *Lloyd* v. *Fleming* (1872) L.R. 7 Q.B. 299.
10 Marine Insurance Act 1906, s. 50(2).
11 [1923] 1 K.B. 81.
12 *Supra.*
13 Marine Insurance Act 1906, s. 50(2).
14 *Pickersgill* v. *London & Provincial Marine Insurance Co.* [1912] 3 K.B. 614; However, note now the unusual effect of cl. 4.6 of the Institute Commodity Trades Clauses, 1983, whereby the assignee appears to have been placed in a better position than the original assured, in respect of exclusion of liability for loss resulting from the financial default of a carrier of goods.
15 *The Litsion Pride* [1985] 1 Lloyd's Rep. 437, at p. 517 *et seq.*

contract sued upon.[16] In other words the contracts in such circumstances are regarded as being in water-tight compartments.

16 *Baker* v. *Adams* (1910) 15 Com. Cas. 227.

30

OBLIGATIONS OF THE PARTIES

30.1   GENERAL OBLIGATIONS OF THE ASSURED

GENERALLY speaking, a marine insurance policy contains engagements by the assured and the underwriter; the underwriter engages to pay the sum insured if the insured risk causes loss or damage, and the assured engages to pay the premium.

30.1.1   WARRANTIES

Let us first examine the obligations incurred by the assured. Apart from his duty to pay the premium and his obligation in relation to disclosure, which we have discussed, he 'warrants' the present existence of certain facts or a certain conduct for the future. These so-called warranties are conditions precedent to the insurer's liability, and the reader should take care not to confuse them with warranties which are referred to in other types of contract.[1] 'Warranties' in the Marine Insurance Act correspond to 'conditions' in the Sale of Goods Act, whereby any breach gives the insurer the right to avoid the contract. This divergence of terminology is most unfortunate. Historically it may be explained, if not excused; for the sale of goods warranties were developed much later than, and independently from, the marine insurance warranties.

A warranty is defined as an undertaking of the assured 'that some particular thing shall or shall not be done, or that some condition shall be fulfilled, or whereby he affirms or negatives the existence of a particular state of facts'.[2]

---

1 See discussion at Sections 4.2.2 and 11.2, *supra*.
2 Marine Insurance Act 1906, s. 33(1).

At this stage we are specially concerned with the last thirteen words of the definition. Suppose during the negotiations for an insurance a misrepresentation is made, but this wrong statement is not mentioned in the policy. As we have seen, the insurer is then entitled to avoid the policy if, but only if, the misrepresentation was material. But the parties may agree that the statement shall be embodied in the policy as a term thereof; if they do that the representation becomes an express warranty, and if the warranty is broken, i.e. if the representation was false, the insurer is discharged from his obligations under the policy whether or not the fact be material to the risk.[3] That may seem hard on the assured, but the answer is that he should not have allowed a term to be included in the contract which he knew or ought to have known could not be exactly fulfilled. Of course, if a warranty is broken by the assured the insurer is at liberty to waive the breach. In addition, hull policies contain a clause to the effect that, in case of a breach of certain types of warranty, the assured shall be held covered in spite of the breach, at a premium and on conditions to be agreed.[4] That is to say, the parties must agree on the payment of an additional premium, which in the event of failure to agree must be reasonable in the circumstances.

If the policy contains no such provision or, as is more likely, the assured can not bring himself within its terms, the insurer is discharged from his liability by reason of a breach of warranty. However, the time as from which he is so discharged depends on the character of the warranty. If, in the words of the Act, the assured 'affirms or negatives the existence of a particular state of facts', for instance where he warrants the special equipment of the ship, and the facts differ from the warranty then the policy never attaches. On the other hand, the assured may warrant a certain future course of action, for example, he may promise that the ship will have sailed from a certain port by a given date. Failure to comply with such a warranty discharges the insurer only from the breach, and if damage was suffered between attachment of the policy and breach the insurer is liable.[5] This is so even where at the time of the damage it is clear that the warranty cannot possibly be complied with.

Illustration: *Baines* v. *Holland*[6]

The policy provided for the insured ship to sail from New York to London via Quebec, but to leave the latter port not later than 1 November. The ship

---

3 *Ibid*, s. 33(3); see *Arnould* (1981), paras 589, 590.
4 Institute Time Clauses (Hulls) 1983, cl. 3.
5 Marine Insurance Act 1906, s. 33(3).
6 (1855), 10 Ex. 802, 156 E.R. 343.

sailed from New York so late that it was unlikely she could reach Quebec by that date. Nevertheless the insurer was held liable to pay for the loss which happened after 1 November while at sea between New York and Quebec. The reason given, was that on its true construction, the warranty as to time could only apply to that part of the voyage between Quebec and London, and that there was no time limit imposed on the earlier leg of the voyage. The decision would have gone the other way had the warranty been to the effect that the ship was to leave New York in time to be ready for sailing from Quebec by 1 November.

In order to avoid the policy actual breach of warranty must have been committed; intention alone is insufficient as long as it is revocable.[7] Here the difference between a voyage and a time policy may become important. For instance, in a time policy the assured warranted that the ship should not proceed east of Singapore. In fact, when sailing from Cardiff she was bound for Kiaochau, a port east of the agreed limit. Off the Tunis coast she was lost, and the insurers were held liable because the warranty had not yet been broken.[8] Now contrast this with a case where goods were insured not for a certain time but for a voyage from the Mersey to a port west of Gibraltar. They were, in fact, shipped from Liverpool to Cartagena, which is east of the line, but lost before crossing it. Here the court came to the conclusion that from the beginning the voyage on which the ship started differed from the one insured so that the policy never attached, and no liability arose.[9]

30.1.2 IMPLIED WARRANTIES

Every contract of marine insurance also contains implied warranties, that is to say, warranties not set out in the express words of the policy, but implied by law from the circumstances in which the bargain was effected. Such promises are implied only if they are so vital that without them the contract would not function properly.

(A) SEAWORTHINESS

The most important of the implied warranties is the warranty of seaworthiness. What this term means has been discussed above,[10] and reference should be made to what we have said there. The law under this head tallies in affreightment and insurance contracts. Only a few

---

7 *Mountain* v. *Whittle* [1921] 1 A.C. 615.
8 *Simpson S.S. Co.* v. *Premier Underwriting Association* (1905) 10 Com. Cas. 198.
9 *Simon, Israel & Co.* v. *Sedgwick* [1893] 1 Q.B. 303.
10 See Section 11.3, *supra*.

remarks need be added. We have seen that in a contract for the carriage of goods, coming within the Carriage of Goods by Sea Act 1971, the carrier undertakes that he will display due diligence to make the ship seaworthy, before and at the beginning of the voyage. In a contract of insurance the shipowner has a heavier responsibility, for the law implies in every voyage policy an absolute warranty that the ship is seaworthy at the commencement of the voyage or at the commencement of any stage of it.[11] In other words, the rule under the Marine Insurance Act corresponds with the rule of common law relating to contracts of affreightment. Thus the insurer is discharged even though unseaworthiness arises from hidden causes which no ordinary examination could possibly reveal.[12]

Still, other rules of law as well as private agreements have done much to mitigate this rigour. First, the implied warranty of seaworthiness does not apply to time policies at any particular stage of the adventure. The reason for this relaxation of the rule is that a ship may be at sea when the policy is taken out, and it is quite impossible for the assured to know anything about the state of his ship at that moment, or to take measures for making it seaworthy. However, this provision is intended to apply only to genuine cases, and where 'with the privity of the assured', the ship is sent to sea in an unseaworthy condition during the currency of a time policy, the insurer is not liable for any loss occurring by reason of the unseaworthiness.[13]

It has been explained[14] that a shipowner is 'privy' to the sending to sea of an unseaworthy ship not only if he knows that it is being done or concurs in the act, but also if he turns a blind eye, that is, will not know. The insurer is then discharged even if the shipowner has not been guilty of 'wilful misconduct'[15] or negligence. For s. 39(5) to apply, the unseaworthiness to which the assured is privy need not have been the sole cause of the casualty, as long as it was a proximate cause.[16] Moreover, the assured's knowledge must relate to that unseaworthiness which led to the casualty.

11 Marine Insurance Act 1906, s. 39.
12 See *Templeman* (1986), pp. 38, 39.
13 Marine Insurance Act 1906, s. 39 (5). *The Miss Jay Jay* [1987] 1 Lloyd's Rep. 32.
14 *Compania Maritima San Basilio S.A.* v. *Oceanus Mutual Underwriting Association* [1977] 1 Q.B. 49.
15 Marine Insurance Act 1906, s. 55(2) (a).
16 For a discussion as to the proximate cause rule, see Section 30.2.2, *infra*.

Illustration: *Thomas v. Tyne & Wear Steamship & Freight Insurance Association* [17]

The vessel was unfit for the voyage by reason of a defect in the hull as well as an insufficient crew. The assured was aware of the latter fact, but not of the former which was the cause of the loss. In those circumstances the insurer was held liable.

A second mitigation of the rule in respect of voyage policies is found in policies on goods. A shipper of goods usually has no influence whatever over the control and management of the vessel, and it would be very hard if he were to forgo the protection of his policy if the ship turned out to be unseaworthy.

Therefore, a clause is included in cargo policies whereby underwriters waive any breach of the implied warranty of seaworthiness of the vessel, and of the fitness of the vessel to carry cargo, provided that the assured or his servants are not privy to this state of affairs. [18]

(B) DEVIATION

While deviation and change of voyage have a similar effect in voyage policies to breach of a warranty, they are not normally regarded as being warranties as such. [19] However, for the purposes of our discussion, we can assume that in a voyage policy on a ship there is the equivalent of an implied warranty that the ship will not deviate from the voyage contemplated by the policy. If the vessel deviates from her course, without a statutory or agreed excuse, the underwriter is discharged from liability under the policy as from the time of deviation. [20] It can make no difference that the ship has regained her contract route by the time she sustains a loss. [21] Again though, there is an Institute clause which mitigates this strict rule, to the effect that the vessel will be 'held covered in case of deviation or change of voyage, provided notice be given immediately after receipt of advices and any amended terms of cover and additional premium required be agreed'. [22] This clause does not, however, protect the assured if he knew of the deviation from the beginning and failed to disclose it. [23]

17 [1917] 1 K.B. 938.
18 Institute Cargo Clauses 1982, cl. 5.2.
19 See *Arnould* (1981) para. 692, fn. 69.
20 Marine Insurance Act 1906, s. 46.
21 *Ibid.* s. 46(1); as to deviation see Section 14.1, *supra*.
22 Institute Voyage Clauses (Hulls) 1983, cl. 2.
23 *Laing* v. *Union Marine Insurance Co.* (1895) 1 Com. Cas. 11.

Just as deviation may be excused as between shipowner and shipper under a contract of carriage, the assured may plead lawful deviation *vis-à-vis* his insurer. Apart from terms in the policy, deviation is excused[24] where it is caused by circumstances beyond the control of the master and his employer.

Illustration: *Rickards v. Forestal Land, Timber & Railways Co. Ltd*[25]

During the 1939–45 war, German ships carrying goods of British merchants proceeded to Germany under orders from the military government. In various circumstances the goods were lost or reached Germany. The goods' owners sued the underwriters for a total loss of goods. Among other defences the underwriters pleaded deviation.

Held: Underwriters liable, since being under German orders the master could not control the movements of his ship and thus there was a lawful excuse for deviation. Nor was an additional premium payable under the 'held covered' clause.

The Marine Insurance Act provides for several other cases of justifiable deviation. These comprise: reasonable necessity to comply with an express or implied warranty or to save ship or cargo, deviation to save human life or going to the assistance of other ships in distress where human life may be in danger, or to obtain medical aid for a person on board or, finally, deviation caused by barratry, if the policy covers this peril.[26] This catalogue does not go as far as the broad exceptions which protect the carrier *vis-à-vis* the cargo-owner under the Hague–Visby Rules.[27] It would therefore be possible to have a case where the carrier was permitted to deviate under the contract of carriage, but which discharges the insurer from liability under the policy of insurance. In any event where insurance law allows a deviation, the ship must resume her course with reasonable dispatch as soon as the excuse ceases to operate.[28] Unlike voyage policies on ships, modern cargo wordings protect the assured during deviation without requiring notice or additional premium (ICC 1982, cl. 8.37).

---

24 Marine Insurance Act 1906, s. 49 (1).
25 [1942] A.C. 50.
26 Marine Insurance Act s. 49(1) (*a*) and (*c*) to (*g*).
27 Carriage of Goods by Sea Act 1971, Art. IV, Rule 4.
28 Marine Insurance Act 1906, s. 49(2).

(C)   CHANGE OF VOYAGE

Under a voyage policy, it is important to note the distinction between a deviation and the sailing of the vessel from or to a port other than that agreed in the policy,[29] and also what is called 'a change of voyage'.[30] There is a change of voyage when after the ship has sailed on the insured voyage it is decided to alter her destination, thus substituting a new voyage for the insured one.[31] Where the vessel sails for or from a port not named in the policy, the insurance never attaches. Where there is evidence of a change of voyage, a breach is committed which discharges the underwriter from his obligations, under the contract, as soon as the decision has been taken to change the destination. Only in very exceptional cases of *force majeure* will the assured be excused where the voyage is changed; for instance, if a British ship is bound for the port of a country which during the voyage becomes an enemy port the continuance of the voyage would make the latter illegal under an Act forbidding trading with the enemy, and a change of voyage would become justified.[32] As is the case with deviation, the strict rule concerning change of voyage by the assured is modified in relation to cargo policies, and a held covered clause is available. Similarly, other provisions (ICC 1982, cl. 8 and 9) give cargo-owners a measure of protection where the anticipated voyage is disrupted by the action of the carrier.

(D)   VOYAGE IS TO BEGIN WITHIN A REASONABLE TIME

Again, under a voyage policy the insured voyage must be commenced within a reasonable time, otherwise the insurer is entitled to avoid the policy,[33] and if in the course of an insured voyage reasonable dispatch is lacking without lawful excuse the insurer will be discharged from liability from the time when the delay becomes unreasonable.[34]

---

29 *Ibid.* s. 43, 44.

30 *Ibid.* s. 45.

31 For instance, in *Union Castle* v. *U.K. Mutual War Risks Assn* [1958] 1 Q.B. 380, the ship, following the closing of the Suez Canal, turned round and proceeded in the opposite direction.

32 *British & Foreign Marine Insurance Co.* v. *Sanday* [1916] 1 A.C. 650.

33 Marine Insurance Act 1906, s. 42.

34 *Ibid.* s. 48. But the assured is excused if the delay is necessary in order to comply with an express or implied warranty, as where the ship must be made seaworthy for a particular stage: Marine Insurance Act 1906, s. 39(3); *Bouillon* v. *Lupton* (1863) 15 C.B.N.S. 113.

Again, an assured under a cargo policy is protected against even unreasonable delay of the carrier by the provisions of the 'transit clause', provided that such delay is beyond the control of the assured.[35]

The reason for all these warranties is fairly obvious, for whenever the assured contravenes any of the canons of good conduct the insurer's risk may be increased, and he may be prevented from carrying on his business properly. Suppose, for example, a voyage which normally lasts a few weeks proceeds so slowly that it lasts three months. Then the insurer is saddled unreasonably long with the contingent liability under the policy; unreasonably because he may be prevented from underwriting other policies during that period since his risk limit has been reached and, because the chance of loss is materially increased the longer the cover lasts.

(E) LEGALITY

Finally, the Act mentions the implied warranty of legality of the adventure.[36] This means that the adventure must be a lawful one and that as far as the assured has control of the matter, it is carried out in a lawful manner. Again this requirement will bear more heavily on a shipowner than a cargo-owner, who has little or no control over the actions of the ship and its crew. Apart from the warranty, s. 3(1) of the Marine Insurance Act 1906 specifies that 'every lawful marine adventure' may be the subject of a marine insurance contract; implying that it is not possible to hold an insurable interest in an unlawful adventure. An adventure may be considered unlawful if prohibited by statute or contrary to good morals or public policy.[37]

30.1.3 EXPRESS WARRANTIES

Apart from implied warranties, parties may agree on any number of a great variety of express warranties to meet the requirements of the particular circumstances of the policy. Such warranties may be couched in any form of words so long as the intention can be inferred that the promises shall be in the nature of warranties. To be binding, express warranties must appear in the policy or in some document to which the policy refers.[38] Business people, however, are apt to use the word

---

35 Institute Cargo Clauses 1982, cl. 8.
36 Marine Insurance Act 1906, s. 41.
37 *Wetherell* v. *Jones* (1832), 3B. & Ad. 221, at pp. 225, 226.
38 Marine Insurance Act 1906, s. 35(2).

'warranty' in cases where it is legally speaking unjustifiable. For example, it is common to exclude a certain area or a certain period of time from the cover furnished by the policy, and the clause by which this is done is usually introduced by the word 'warranted'. While there appears to be some support from early cases that such limitations should be treated as strict warranties, the modern view is that trading limits of this nature are mere exceptions to the cover granted by the policy.[39] The implication of this view, is that where for example, a limitation is placed on the policy in the words 'warranted not in the Gulf of St Lawrence before April' and the vessel enters the Gulf in March, it does not mean there is a breach of warranty but only that the ship is not insured while in the prohibited area during March. So soon as the exclusion clause ceases to apply the cover revives.

30.2   GENERAL OBLIGATIONS OF THE INSURER

We now turn to the underwriter's engagements, and have to find out in what circumstances he is bound to pay. This is determined by the policy and the attached clauses embodying the contract of insurance.

30.2.1   INSURER'S LIABILITY FOR LOSSES

Section 55(1) of the Marine Insurance Act provides that in the absence of statutory or contractual rules to the contrary 'the insurer is liable for any loss proximately caused by a peril insured against'. What these perils are, appears of course, from the policy, and the attached standard clauses. The old S.G. policy described the perils as 'of the seas, men of war, fire, enemies, pirates, rovers, thieves, jettisons, letters of mart and countermart, surprisals, takings at sea, arrests, restraints, and detainments of all kings, princes, and people, of what nation, condition, or quality soever, barratry of the master and mariners, and of all other perils, losses, and misfortunes, that have or shall come to the hurt, detriment, or damage of the said goods, and merchandises, and ship, etc., or any part thereof'. A number of these old-fashioned perils became more picturesque than real, but they were nevertheless retained until the introduction of the new standard MAR form and clauses in 1982 and 1983. Indeed, major litigation on the definition of 'takings at sea', one of the oldest perils (which does not appear in the new forms),

39 See *Arnould* (1981) para. 692.

was in process during the introductory period of the MAR form; the House of Lords finally deciding on a meaning which required them to overrule a Court of Appeal decision which had been accepted for fifteen years.[40]

Perhaps the most important of all the perils listed in the Lloyd's S.G. form, and retained as the first peril mentioned in the Institute Hull Clauses, 1983 (for use with the MAR form) is that of 'perils of the seas'. This phrase is defined by the Marine Insurance Act 1906 as 'fortuitous accidents or casualties of the seas'.[41] Damage which is caused by 'the ordinary action of the winds and waves' is not included, for insurance is intended to cover damage arising from an untoward event, and not to provide an indemnity against natural depreciation, which business men must expect and provide for by writing off in their balance sheets. Thus the sinking of a barge if due to old age and general debility is not covered,[42] though the insurer would probably have been liable had there been any accident, despite the fact that a less rotten barge would have survived. This, of course, is subject to the warranty of seaworthiness.

The exact meaning of 'perils of the seas' has given rise to a good deal of legal argument. Scrutton LJ suggested for example 'the expression is not happy; it is not clear what kind of accident or casualty is not fortuitous, or what is an intentional accident' and then later 'it is clear that there must be a peril, an unforeseen and evitable accident, not a contemplated and inevitable result; and it must be of the seas, not merely on the seas. The ordinary action of the winds and waves is of the seas, but not a peril'.[43]

In an attempt to remove doubt the Act provides that 'ordinary wear and tear, ordinary leakage and breakage, inherent vice or nature of the subject-matter insured, or for any loss proximately caused by rats or vermin, or for any injury to machinery not proximately caused by maritime perils' shall not give rise to a claim on the policy.[44]

30.2.2 THE PROXIMATE CAUSE RULE

To make the insurer liable, the perils insured against must have proximately caused the loss.[45] We have already met with this concept when

---

40 *The Salem: Shell International Petroleum Co. Ltd* v. *Gibbs*, [1983] 2 A.C. 375.
41 First Schedule, Rule 7 of Rules for Construction of Policy; *Schloss Bros.* v. *Stevens* [1906] 2 K.B. 665, at 673.
42 *Wadsworth Lighterage & Coaling Co.* v. *Sea Insurance Co.* (1930) 35 Com. Cas. 1.
43 *Samuel* v. *Dumas* (1922) 13 Ll. L. Rep. 503 C.A., at 505; *The Miss Jay Jay, supra.*
44 Marine Insurance Act 1906, s. 55(2) (*c*). See the *Inchmaree* case, *Thames & Mersey Marine Insurance Co.* v. *Hamilton* (1887), 12 App. Cas. 484.
45 Marine Insurance Act 1906, s. 55(1).

dealing with the liability for negligence in causing a collision,[46] and have seen that it means the effective cause and not just a cause without which the loss would not have occurred. Thus where there are two, or more, interacting causes of the loss, the one which is the proximate cause will be determined by deciding 'as a question of fact' which of the causes was the 'dominant' of them.[47] Secton 55(2) of the Act recognizes that a number of causes may operate and provides that, while the insurer is not liable if the loss is 'attributable to the wilful misconduct of the assured', he must pay where an insured peril is the proximate cause, even though there would have been no loss had not master or crew misconducted themselves or behaved negligently. Neither the master's bad seamanship nor his negligent navigation disentitle the assured from recovering, provided the loss was in the end caused by something in the nature of a maritime casualty.[48] But if the circumstances causing the loss amount to wilful misconduct of the assured, or if the ship is scuttled with his knowledge or consent, the assured cannot recover, because he is not allowed to take advantage of his own wrong. In those cases the scuttling is the proximate cause and not the entry of the seawater into the holds.[49] Even an innocent mortgagee of the ship cannot claim in these circumstances.[50] However, where assureds can show on the balance of probability, that a vessel was sunk deliberately, but without their consent or knowledge, they will be entitled to recover as against the insurer for the insured peril of barratry.[51]

The question of what was the proximate cause of the loss becomes important where a policy excepts certain perils.

Illustration: *Leyland Shipping Co.* v. *Norwich Union Fire Insurance Society*[52]

A ship was insured against perils of the sea, but excepting war damage. The vessel was torpedoed by a German submarine, but towed into Havre and moored inside the breakwater. The ship had been very badly shattered by

46 Section 21.4.3.
47 *Leyland Shipping Co. Ltd* v. *Norwich Union Fire Insurance Society Ltd* [1918] A.C. 350, at 363. *The Miss Jay Jay* [1987] 1 Lloyd's Rep. 32, 36 *et seq*.
48 *Dixon* v. *Sadler* (1839), 5 M. & W. 405; *Trinder* v. *Thames & Mersey Insurance Co.* [1898] 2 Q.B. 114. *Lemos* v. *British & Foreign Marine Insurance Co.* (1931) 39 Ll. L.R. 275.
49 *Samuel* v. *Dumas* [1924] A.C. 431. H.L.
50 *Ibid*. See also *The Captain Panagos D.P.* [1986] 2 Lloyd's Rep. 470.
51 *The Michael: Piermay Shipping Co. SA* v. *Chester* [1979] 1 Lloyd's Rep. 55, affirmed C.A., [1979] 2 Lloyd's Rep. 1; See also Hazelwood, SJ (1982) Barratry – the scuttler's easy route to the 'golden prize', [1982] 3 LMCLQ 383.
52 [1918] A.C. 350.

the torpedo, and when she had been at Havre for two days her bulkheads broke in a storm and she sank.

Held: The proximate cause of the sinking was the torpedoing, which was an excepted peril, and not the subsequent breaking of the bulkheads due to the action of the sea.

Again, suppose a cargo of fruit has been insured. Owing to a peril of the sea the engine breaks down, the ship arrives late and, in consequence, the fruit has become over-ripe and worthless. It is a logical consequence of the general principle that s. 55(2) *(b)* of the Act provides that in such a case, when the last cause of the damage was delay, the insurer is not liable, irrespective of the fact that the delay had in turn been caused by perils of the sea.[53]

The lay reader may perhaps be inclined to consider the limitations just referred to as lawyers' quibbles. In truth they owe their origin to the exigencies of insurance business and experience of the shipping trade. It is quite possible to cover nearly all the perils which are normally excluded under standard form policies, but they must be mentioned specifically and an additional premium will usually be charged for the additional cover.

30.3 PARTICULAR RISKS COVERED IN MARINE POLICIES

'Perils of the seas' may be one of the most important perils enumerated in marine policies, but over the course of time its limitations have become clear. The restrictions implied by these words have led to the incorporation of various clauses over the years, designed to cover many legitimate types of loss deemed by insurers appropriate in marine policies. The Institute Clauses thus afford many examples of insurance against losses which cannot easily be considered to lie within 'perils of the seas' and it is appropriate at this point to examine some of the more important of these clauses.

---

53 *Cf. Taylor* v. *Dunbar* (1869) L.R. 4 C.P. 206, where the ship had been held up by gales and the meat cargo had consequently beome putrid and was thrown overboard. The insurer was held not liable.

30.3.1   HULL CLAUSES

Of the 26 clauses which presently make up the Institute Time Clauses (Hulls), 1983 there are three, the 'perils' clause, 'collision' clause and 'sue and labour' clause which bear a close examination. All three of these clauses have an interesting historical development and are designed to cover specific and important types of loss.

(A)   'PERILS' CLAUSE

Clause 6 of the Institute Time Clauses (Hulls), 1983 lists the primary perils against which ships are insured. Listing the perils in this way is a completely new approach, adopted for the first time in the clause revision of 1983. The list is drawn from two sources; the list of perils in the old S.G. form and the *'Inchmaree'* clause[54] perils. It should be noted, however, that the new clause is not merely a composite list of the two original sources, but that repetition has been eliminated and some of the old perils, no longer appropriate to modern conditions, have been withdrawn. In particular, it is worth pointing out that 'perils of the seas' has been extended to cover similar circumstances causing loss on rivers, lakes and other navigable waters.

In *Thames & Mersey Marine Insurance Co.* v. *Hamilton, Fraser & Co.*,[55] it was held that the insurer was not liable for damage occasioned by an explosion through a valve mistakenly being kept closed, for such an accident was not incidental to a sea voyage, it might just as well have happened on land, and was not, therefore, a peril of the seas. On the other hand, it was realized that insurance against that kind of happening was highly desirable, and a clause was subsequently drafted, known as the *'Inchmaree'* clause after the name of the ship in respect of which the problem had first arisen.

Those parts of the present 'perils' clause, which are based on the *Inchmaree* wording, have a much greater scope than the original circumstances which gave the clause its origin. Thus the second half of the perils clause now covers accidents in loading or discharging or shifting cargo or fuel; negligence or barratry of the master, officers or crew; negligence of pilots; negligence of repairers or charterers; bursting of boilers, breakage of shafts or any latent defect in the machinery or hull. Losses caused by any of the above perils are covered, unless they have resulted from a want of due diligence by the assured, owners or

54 The 'Inchmaree' clause last appeared as cl. 7 of the 1970 Hull Clauses
55 (1887) 12 App. Cas. 484.

managers. The only peril in the above list which does not originate from the '*Inchmaree*' clause is 'barratry' which is now subject to the 'due diligence' test. In order to claim for a loss by one of these perils the assured must show that the peril has proximately caused the loss. Therefore, a latent defect becoming apparent through ordinary wear and tear, and causing no other loss, is outside the scope of the insurance.[56] Similarly, where a latent defect does cause loss, other than the defect itself becoming apparent, that loss can be recovered but the cost of remedying the defect cannot.[57]

All the other *Inchmaree* perils are included in the first part of the new 'perils' clause and are no longer subject to the 'due diligence' proviso. The perils so listed comprise: explosion; breakdown of or accident to nuclear installations or reactors; contact with aircraft, land conveyance, dock or harbour equipment or installation; earthquake, volcanic eruption or lightning. A new addition to this list is contact with objects falling from aircraft or objects similar to aircraft, which it has been suggested, would include satellite or launch vehicle debris. The remaining few perils in clause 6.1 are drawn from the list in the S.G. form and consist of: fire, violent theft from persons outside the vessel, jettison and piracy. A major change in the 1983 clauses has been to reinstate piracy as a marine rather than war risk. Although it was listed as an insured peril in the S.G. form it was in fact automatically excepted in all standard marine policies by inclusion of the 'free of capture and seizure' clause (F.C. & S.).[58]

(B) 'COLLISION' CLAUSE

In an old case[59] the problem was considered which arises when the insured ship is wholly or partly to blame for a collision, and its owner pays damages to the other vessel. Can the assured recover that payment under the ordinary marine policy? The court answered this by holding that the policy covers only physical damage to the insured ship, not any liability in tort incurred by that ship to a third party. Shipowners were naturally anxious to insure against this danger and to meet this demand the collision clause,[60] also known under the old S.G. form as the

---

56 *Hutchins Bros* v. *Royal Exchange Assurance Corp.* [1911] 2 K.B. 398.
57 *Scindia Steamships (London) Ltd* v. *London Assurance* [1937] 1 K.B. 639.
58 See Section 30.4.3, *infra*.
59 *De Vaux* v. *Salvador* (1836) 4 Ad. and E. 420.
60 Now the '¾ths collision liability' clause (Institute Time Clauses (Hulls) 1983, cl. 8).

'running-down' clause (R.D.C. for short) was added to the policy.[61] The clause covers the assured for three-fourths of the damages for which he is legally liable and has paid in respect of loss or damage to another vessel[62] or property thereon, including loss of use of such vessel or property, and also salvage or general average payable in respect of those interests. The clause also covers three-fourths of the cost of legal proceedings undertaken to contest or limit liability. A proviso excludes compensation payable by the assured for removal of wrecks or other obstructions, for loss of, or damage to, property on land or on the insured vessel, and – most important – loss of life, personal injury or illness. Also excluded are any payments made by the assured in respect of pollution or contamination of any property except the vessel with which the collision occurred and any property on that vessel.

Nor does the clause cover liability incurred by the insured vessel in contract, as opposed to tort. A towage contract provided that the tow should indemnify the tug for damage suffered by the latter even if the tug was at fault. In the course of the towage, tug and tow collided, the tug being to blame, and the tow paid what was due under the contract, claiming the amount in question from marine underwriters under their insurance. It was held that in the context of the collision clause 'damages' payable under the clause meant only damages in tort, and the underwriters were not liable.[63] The same principle applied where the insured vessel had to pay an indemnity under the provisions of French law to a pilotage authority.[64]

Where both vessels are to blame and neither's liability is limited by law, the underwriters are liable to pay on the principle of cross-liabilities,[65] that is, according to the liability of each ship to the other, not according to the final balance.

(c) 'SUE AND LABOUR' CLAUSE

We now come to a clause which has given rise to quite a lot of litigation, the so-called 'sue and labour' clause. The original 'sue and labour' clause was contained in the body of the S.G. policy and supplemented by clause 9 of the Institute Time Clauses (Hulls) 1970. In the 1983 Hull Clauses the two have been amalgamated into clause 13 which is now

---

61 Marine Insurance Act 1906, s. 74.
62 Collision with a hovercraft, even where borne on its air cushion, is included: Hovercraft (Application of Enactments) Order 1972 (S.I. No. 971), Sch. 1.
63 *Furness, Withy & Co.* v. *Duder*, [1936] 2 K.B. 461.
64 *Hall Brothers S.S. Co.* v. *Young* (1939) 55 T.L.R. 506.
65 See discussion at Section 28.2.2(d).

titled the 'duty of assured (sue and labour)' clause. A simplified version of the clause appears in the various forms of the Institute Cargo Clauses.[66]

The main concept behind the clauses is expressed in a new, modern form of words in the first two sub-sections which provide:

'13.1 In case of any loss or misfortune it is the duty of the Assured and their servants and agents to take such measures as may be reasonable for the purpose of averting or minimizing a loss which would be recoverable under this insurance.

13.2 Subject to the provisions below and to Clause 12 the underwriters will contribute to charges properly and reasonably incurred by the Assured, their servants or agents for such measures. General average, salvage charges (except as provided for in Clause 13.5) and collision defence or attack costs are not recoverable under this Clause 13.'

The underlying principle of the clause is one of general application, namely, that a person entitled to an indemnity or damages must do everything in his power to avert or minimize the loss.[67] In marine disasters, however, the assured could probably do very little to reduce the insurer's liability without the outlay of money. An old case decided that the assured could not recover the money thus spent in order to minimize the loss. Hence a special clause was added to the policy under which the assured can recover costs incurred in taking measures to preserve the subject-matter insured, thereby keeping the insurer's liability under the policy as low as possible.

The clause is drafted primarily in the interest of the insurer whose liability may be substantially reduced if the assured or his servants or agents take prompt action for the safety or preservation of the subject-matter of insurance. Expenses of this kind are termed 'particular charges',[68] and may result from extraordinary efforts to save the ship, e.g. by making a salvage agreement, in costs incurred in order to recondition damaged goods, or in forwarding goods by another ship in order to save the freight. Despite expenditure which is incurred for the safety or preservation of the subject-matter insured, there may in the end be an eventual total loss. Insurers might then argue that the assured who recovers for a total loss could not also claim the particular charges above the sum insured. Such argument would, however, be short-sighted, since an assured would, under these circumstances, be very

66 See the Institute Cargo Clauses 1982, cl. 16 ('Duty of Assured').
67 Marine Insurance Act 1906, s. 78(4).
68 Ibid. s. 64(2).

reluctant to do anything, and the consequent value of the clause to the insurer would be greatly reduced. In fact, clauses 13.5 and 13.6 make it clear that 'sue and labour' cover takes the form of a separate engagement, over and above the sum insured proper. In other words, the assured can recover these so-called particular charges in spite of the fact that they were fruitless and that he received payment under the policy of the whole sum insured as for a total loss.

Clearly, this may throw a heavy burden on the insurer who may find himself liable to pay more than the sum insured, and it therefore becomes necessary to limit the said charges to reasonable proportions.[69] The reason for inserting the clause is to enable and induce the assured to do what he can for the purpose of lessening the insurer's liability. If we bear this in mind we shall have no difficulty in understanding that the sue and labour clause cannot cover charges for salvage, not arising under a salvage agreement. For where salvage services are rendered voluntarily, i.e. without first entering into an agreement, the salved ship becomes liable to pay in law and not under a contract; in other words, voluntary salvage charges become payable in law even though the assured has done nothing for the preservation of the subject-matter. The inducement held out to him by the 'sue and labour' clause was therefore not instrumental in the salvage charges being incurred. It was only another way of expressing the same idea when Lord Cairns said: 'the salvage expenses were not expenses incurred under the suing and labouring clause by the owner of the ship, but were a payment which the ship, as an actual chattel, had to submit to by maritime law, and would be obliged to make good in proceedings against the ship *in rem*.'[70] Of course, an award for voluntary salvage services may also be recovered under a policy of marine insurance, though not under the 'sue and labour' clause.[71] These 'salvage charges' as defined by s. 65(2) of the Marine Insurance Act, 1906 are recoverable, subject to the limit of the sum insured and may be reduced in respect of any under-insurance.[72]

Likewise, no general average losses or contributions may be claimed under the sue and labour clause.[73] This is perhaps less easily comprehensible for, as we have seen,[74] a general average loss is one 'voluntarily incurred for the common safety', and might thus be thought

69 Institute Time Clauses (Hulls) 1983, cl. 13.4–13.6.
70 *Aitchison* v. *Lohre* (1879) 4 App. Cas.755, at p. 767; *Kidston* v. *Empire Maritime Insurance Co.* (1866) L.R. 1 C.P. 535; *Cf.* Chapter 24, on salvage, *supra,* and ss. 64(2) and 78(1) of the Marine Insurance Act 1906.
71 Marine Insurance Act 1906, s. 65.
72 Institute Time Clauses (Hulls) 1983, cl. 11.1.
73 Marine Insurance Act 1906, s. 78(2).
74 Ch. 15, *supra.*

distinguishable from voluntary salvage charges. But though a difference certainly exists it must be borne in mind that both salvage charges and general average contributions have this in common that they arise by virtue of maritime law and not by way of deliberate contracts made by the assured or his servants or agents.[75]

30.3.2 CARGO CLAUSES

The standard clauses which are used in the case of cargo policies are radically different in nature and content from the hull clauses. These clauses reflect the circumstances that surround the movement of cargo from origin to destination (e.g. the 'transit' clause) and recongize that the cargo-owner has minimal control over the ship and the prosecution of the voyage (e.g. the 'unseaworthiness exclusion' clause and the 'change of voyage' clause). While there is no space in a volume of this nature to describe in detail each individual clause, some of the more important are dealt with below.

(A) RISKS CLAUSE

With the disappearance of the list of perils from the policy form it became necessary with the 1982 Cargo Clauses to incorporate, for the first time, a list of risks against which the cargo is covered. As already noted, the cargo clauses are issued in three versions, one of the main differences between them being the risks against which the cargo is insured. Of the three, the A clauses are the most wide-ranging, offering cover against 'all risks of loss of or damage to the subject-matter insured', subject to a list of exceptions which are contained in clauses 4 to 7.

Risks covered by the B and C clauses are enumerated individually in the 'risks' clause.[76] Unlike the hull clauses, the term 'perils of the seas' has been dropped from the cargo clauses. In its place, under the B clauses (but not C), the cargo is covered against loss or damage caused by 'entry of sea, lake or river water' into the vessel or container. The other perils which are listed and subject to the 'proximate cause rule' are: general average sacrifice, jettison or washing overboard. All the remaining B clause risks do not appear to be subject to the 'proximate cause rule' and it is only necessary that any loss or damage is 'reasonably attributable' to such perils. Included in this group are the perils of fire

---

75 *Aitchison* v. *Lohre, supra.*
76 Institute Cargo Clauses B and C 1982, cl. 1.

and explosion; stranding, sinking, grounding or capsizing of the carrying vessel; collision of the carrying vessel with other vessels or objects;
discharge of cargo at a port of distress or earthquake, volcaninc eruption
or lightning.

It should be noted that the C clause cover is not as wide ranging as the
B cover just described.

(B) 'TRANSIT' CLAUSE

The present day 'transit' clause[77] has its roots in the 'warehouse to
warehouse' clause, first introduced into cargo policies towards the end
of the ninetenth century. Prior to this, cover on goods under the S.G.
policy commenced as the goods were loaded on to the carrying vessel
and ceased as they were discharged at the port of destination.[78] Thus,
the 'warehouse to warehouse' provision was designed to cover the
goods while being moved between warehouse and ship, a period during
which the goods are vulnerable. The clause has now been incorporated
in the wider transit clause, which covers both sea and land risks.[79] This
operates 'from the time the goods leave the warehouse or place of
storage at the place named' in the policy 'for the commencement of the
transit, continues during the ordinary course of transit and terminates
either on delivery . . . at the destination named in the policy . . . or on the
expiry of 60 days after completion of discharge over-
side . . . at the final port of discharge, whichever, shall first occur'. The
clause also protects the assured in the event of delay caused by circumstances beyond his control. It should be noted, however, that the clause
merely extends the duration of cover for insured losses occurring
during delay and does not provide cover for losses proximately caused
by the delay.[80]

Under the 'transit' clause, insurance cover is maintained despite
deviation of the carrying vessel under a liberty 'granted to shipowners
or charterers under the contract of affreightment', a liberty which
cargo-owners frequently have to grant. Cover is also maintained in the
event of forced discharge of the goods, their reshipment or transhipment. Again, under the related 'termination of contract of carriage'
clause,[81] if the contract of affreightment is prematurely terminated –

77 Institute Cargo Clauses 1982, cl. 8.
78 Marine Insurance Act 1906, First Schedule, Rules for Construction of Policy, 4
and 5.
79 Ibid., s. 2.
80 Marine Insurance Act 1906, s. 55(2)(b); Institute Cargo Clauses 1982, cl. 4.5.
81 Institute Cargo Clauses 1982, cl. 9.

which happens, for example, in the event of non-allowable deviation – insurance cover automatically terminates unless insurers are given prompt notice, continuation of cover is requested, and an additional premium is paid, if required. Finally, under the 'change of voyage' clause[82], the goods remain insured, at a premium to be arranged, in the event of a change of voyage by the assured.

(C) 'SEAWORTHINESS ADMITTED' CLAUSE

This clause, which last appeared in the 1963 cargo clauses, stipulates for payment of the insurance money, although the loss of the insured goods was attributable to the misconduct of the shipowners or their servants, provided the insured cargo-owner was not privy to it. Another recognition of the fact that the cargo-owner cannot normally influence those engaged in the carriage of his goods.

A sub-clause having essentially the same effect as the 'seaworthiness admitted' clause, appears in the 1982 cargo clauses.[83] By this sub-clause the underwriters waive any breach of the implied warranty of seaworthiness, which in a voyage policy requires the vessel to be seaworthy at the commencement of each stage of the voyage.[84]   The underwriters will not waive such breach, however, where the assured or his servants are privy to the particular unseaworthiness. In a similar fashion, the sub-clause waives any breach of the implied warranty that the ship should be reasonably fit to carry the goods.[85]

(D) 'DUTY OF THE ASSURED CLAUSE'

Throughout their transit the goods are, of course, in the hands of others, whether under the contract of carriage or a warehousing contract. These contracts, along with those which involve the entrusting of goods to others, for instance, where valuables are left with bankers for safe custody or articles with a craftsman for repair, are known as bailments, and the person in temporary possession of the goods is known as the bailee. The insurer of goods in transit is of course liable to make good losses suffered by the assured as a result of the bailee's carelessness, but he can recoup himself by exercising the bailor's rights vested in the assured. To do so, and also to keep the loss as small as

---

82 *Ibid.*, cl. 10.
83 *Ibid.*, cl. 5.2.
84 Marine Insurance Act 1906, s. 39(3); see discussion at Section 30.1.2, *supra.*
85 *Ibid.*, s. 40(2).

possible, the assured must help, if he can, and the 'duty of the assured'
clause is designed, among other things, to impose on him the duty to do
so.[86] The clause declares: 'It is the duty of the Assured and their servants
and agents in respect of loss recoverable hereunder, to take such
measures as may be reasonable for the purpose of averting or minimizing such loss [note: the same thought that prompted the 'sue and labour'
clause!] and to ensure that all rights against carriers, bailees or other
third parties are properly preserved and exercised.' For instance, the
assured must not make a compromise that would prejudice the interest
of the insurer and must take care to make claims for loss or damage
within any time limits specified in contracts or statute. Where the
assured undertakes obligations imposed by this clause he does so normally to the benefit of the insurer. For this reason, the Privy Council has
recently held[87] that where the clause is silent as to who should bear the
expense of complying with such obligations, it is necessary to imply a
term that the underwriter should reimburse the assured. At least to the
extent that the expenditure relates to the preservation or exercise of
rights in respect of loss for which the insurer would otherwise be liable.

(E) OTHER CARGO CLAUSES

Other clauses covering, for instance, strikes and civil commotion, are
inserted when required. Special clauses deal with such commodities as
coal, oil and jute,[88] and include increased value clauses to take care of
price fluctuations during transit. Of great importance, since the growth
of container traffic, are the container clauses. Goods packed in them are
naturally covered by standard goods insurance. But containers often
owned by carriers, are themselves valuable pieces of equipment, and
their loss, actual or constructive, or damage to them is an interest well
worth covering by insurance.[89]

30.3.3 WAR CLAUSES

All standard hull and cargo insurances have detailed clauses which
exclude losses resulting from war risks and similar incidents.[90] Although

---

86 Institute Cargo Clauses 1982, cl. 16.
87 *The Netherlands Insurance Co. Ltd* v. *Karl Ljungberg & Co. AB* [1986] 2 Lloyd's
   Rep. 19. The ICC 1982 (cl. 16) states the assured's costs will be reimbursed.
88 See discussion on commodity clauses at Section 29.3.3, *supra*.
89 For a case involving the Institute Container Clauses see *Integrated Container
   Service Inc.* v. *British Traders Insurance Co. Ltd* [1984] 1 Lloyd's Rep. 154.
90 E.g., Institute Time Clauses (Hulls) 1983, cl. 23–26; Institute Cargo Clauses
   1982, cl. 6.

such risks are not specifically named in the policies and therefore by implication are not covered, underwriters are concerned that the risks of fire and explosion which are insured perils could be interpreted widely enough so as to include some war risks. For this reason, war risks are specifically excluded from MAR policies as they were for many years by the 'free of capture and seizure' clause (F.C. & S.) from the S.G. form. Fortunately, the old, and much debated wording of the 'F.C. & S.' clause has given way to a more modern mode of expression, which is much clearer and easier to understand.

Essentially, war risk cover is offered on a back-to-back basis, whereby all of the risks specifically excluded from the hull or cargo policy are named as insured perils in war risk policies. Thus, the Institute War and Strike Clauses (Hulls–Time) 1983, cover war, civil war, revolution, rebellion, insurrection or civil strife arising therefrom, or any hostile act by or against a belligerent power; capture, seizure, arrest, restraint or detainment and the consequences thereof or any attempt thereat; derelict mines, torpedoes, bombs or other derelict weapons of war; any terrorist or any person acting maliciously or from a political motive; confiscation or expropriation. In addition the clauses also cover loss or damage caused by 'strikers, locked-out workmen or persons taking part in labour disturbances, riots or civil commotions.[91]

The Institute War Clauses (Cargo) 1982 list similar war risks in the 'risks covered' clause except that cover is not provided for terrorists or persons acting maliciously or politically. Again, cargo war clauses, unlike the hull war clauses, do not cover strike risks and if the assured requires this type of insurance it must be entered into separately using the Institute Strikes Clauses (Cargo) 1982 which also extend to cover terrorist risks. As already noted,[92] cover against deliberate or malicious damage to cargo by vandalism or sabotage can be arranged on the B and C cargo forms by the addition of the Institute Malicious Damage Clause 1982, which has the effect of deleting clause 4.7.

Clause 3 of the 1983 War Clauses is very similar to the 1970 Institute Detainment Clause. A significant change, however, is that the new clause provides cover where the assured loses 'the free use and disposal of the vessel'. The same phrase, used by Staughton J sitting as judicial arbitrator in the *Bamburi* case,[93] has led to speculation that on a literal interpretation the 1983 War Clauses might cover blocking and trapping risks hitherto insured separately. A note of caution must however be

91 Cl. 1.
92 See Section 29.3.3.
93 See Section 31.2.1.

sounded, in that cover for a detainment is only likely to be available where it results directly from war or strikes, i.e. the types of risk these clauses are primarily intended to cover. Thus, a lengthy detainment resulting from, say, a channel blocked by a sunken vessel lost after a collision would not constitute a valid blocking claim under the War and Strikes Clauses.

30.4   S.G. FORM EXCEPTIONS

The major exception clauses found attached to the new MAR form of policy have already been dealt with above.[94] It may however be useful here, to describe briefly some of the exceptions found in the old S.G. form which are not reproduced in the MAR policy.

30.4.1   MEMORANDUM

The Memorandum was introduced as early as 1749 'to prevent the underwriters from being harassed by trifling demands, which must necessarily have arisen upon every insurance of this kind, on account of the perishable nature of the cargo'.[95] In this sense it is an exception clause. The Memorandum in the S.G. policy read as follows: 'Corn, fish, salt, fruit, flour and seed are warranted free from average, unless general, or the ship be stranded – sugar, tobacco, hemp, flax, hides and skins are warranted free from average, under five pounds per cent, and all other goods, also the ship and freight, are warranted free from average under three pounds per cent, unless general, or the ship be stranded'.

The principal difficulty presented by this Memorandum is to decide whether a loss is a total loss of the part or a partial loss of the whole. Generally speaking, a loss can only be a total loss of part if it has been separately insured and can be separately identified by packing or otherwise.

Illustration: *Hills v. London Assurance*[96]
Wheat shipped in bulk was insured for £1600 under the above exception. The vessel shipped water which had to be pumped out. During the pumping wheat to the value of about £75 was pumped out with the water and lost.

Held: This was a partial loss of the whole, and the plaintiff could not recover.

94 See, e.g. Sections 29.3.3, 30.3.2 and 30.3.3.
95 Park, *On Insurance*, p. 22.
96 (1839), 5 M. & W. 569.

It is important to note that there is no equivalent provision to the Memorandum in the 1982 cargo clauses.

30.4.2 WARRANTED FREE OF AVERAGE (FPA)

Other terms were commonly added to the S.G. policy by means of the Institute Clauses, to exclude various kinds of loss from the operation of the insurance. Thus the clause 'warranted free of average' limits the assured's right of recovery to claims for total loss. The F.P.A. clause, which is a variation of the Memorandum, excludes particular average; usually it is limited to a certain percentage, say 3 per cent, when particular average beyond such amount may be recovered under the policy. Where the policy contains the clause F.P.A. absolutely the insurer is only liable for actual and constructive total loss, general average contributions, and salvage charges.[97]

These clauses differ somewhat from the Memorandum in that they are not restricted to any particular cargo, and vary the free percentages. Moreover, whereas the Memorandum mentions only stranding of the vessel, the F.P.A. (cargo) clause adds also its sinking and burning. If the F.P.A. clause is limited to a certain percentage, general average losses may not be added to any particular average loss within the policy in order to make up the specified percentage[98]. It should be noticed that if the free percentage, or franchise as it is called, is for instance 3 per cent, then if damage is suffered to the extent of 5 per cent, the whole damage may be recovered from the insurer, and not only the 2 per cent above the franchise.[99] Where a voyage policy is taken out, successive losses on the same voyage may be added together for the purposes of reaching the franchise percentage.[1]

Illustration: *Blackett* v. *Royal Exchange Assurance Co.*[2]
Voyage policy from London to Calcutta warranted 'free from average under 3 per cent'. The vessel first lost a boat and later sustained other damage. Each loss was under 3 per cent of the insurance value, but added together the franchise was exceeded.

Held: The several losses could be added together and the whole damage could be recovered from the insurers.

97 Marine Insurance Act 1906, s. 76.
98 *Ibid.*, s. 76(3).
99 See generally *Arnould* (1981) para. 839 *et seq.*
 1 *Ibid.*, para. 849.
 2 (1832), 2 Cr. & J. 244.

In time policies on hulls to which the Institute Time Clauses (Hulls) 1970 applied, the free of particular average provision was replaced by a deductible clause, applicable to each separate accident or occurrence. This formulation gets around the difficulty of how to apply, in a time policy, the rules relating to successive losses under voyage policies. Again, it should be noted that under MAR cargo policies, all forms of standard cargo clauses now cover particular average in full. In relation to hull policies, the deductible clause has been incorporated with only minor changes into the 1983 hull clauses for use with the MAR policy.[3]

30.4.3   THE 'F.C. AND S.' CLAUSE

The F.C. and S. clause, invariably attached to S.G. policies, has often changed, and until well into the middle of the 1939-45 war it read:

'Warranted free of capture, seizure, arrest, restraint or detainment, and the consequences thereof or of any attempt thereat; also from the consequences of hostilities or warlike operations, whether there be a declaration of war or not. Further warranted free from the consequences of civil war, revolution, rebellion, insurrection, or civil strife arising therefrom or piracy.'

Since the Admiralty controlled all sailings, either in convoy or *en route* for the convoy rendezvous, every voyage was in some respect a 'warlike operation' which the marine insurer excluded from cover, and casualties such as stranding were held by the courts to be due to war risks to the great bewilderment of the marine insurance market.[4] The Government, in its capacity of war risk insurer, and marine underwriters accordingly negotiated with a view to restoring equilibrium by narrowing the operation of war risk insurance proper. The result was a new 'F.C. and S.' clause, which was inserted in all policies after 31 December, 1942. This contained before the last sentence dealing with civil war the following words:

'But this warranty shall not exclude collision, contact with any fixed or floating object (other than a mine or torpedo), stranding, heavy weather or fire unless caused directly (and independently of the nature of the voyage or service which the vessel concerned or, in the case of a collision, any other vessel involved therein, is performing) by a hostile act by or against a belligerent power; and for the purpose of this warranty "power" includes any authority maintaining naval, military or air forces in association with a power.'

---

3 Institute Time Clauses (Hulls) 1983, cl. 12.
4 See *The Coxwold: Yorkshire Dale S.S. v. Min. of War Transp.* [1942] A.C. 691.

The additional words take many cases hitherto treated as losses due to warlike operations out of the exception clause in the marine policy, and restore liability for them to the marine underwriters. Up to the end of the war no dispute leading to litigation arose on the new clause, but its effect can be illustrated by reference to the last important case decided on the 'F.C. and S.' clause as used up to the end of 1942. In *Liverpool and London War Risks Association* v. *Ocean Steamship Co. Ltd*,[5] a ship, requisitioned by the Admiralty and sailing between two war bases, was heavily laden with munitions of war; these included a bridgebuilder stowed on deck. In exceptionally severe gales, with heavy seas sweeping the decks, the bridgebuilder broke loose and damaged the hatch cover. Because of the damage sea water entered the hold. However to avoid submarines, the ship continued at high speed on a zigzag course and so much water penetrated that the ship finished the voyage 11 feet down by the head. On these facts, the House of Lords held that, although the prima facie cause of the damage was the marine perils of gales and sea, the predominant cause was the deliberately increased risk as a result of the war. This was a 'warlike operation', to which the 'F.C. and S.' clause applied, so that the marine underwriters escaped liability for the damage. Under the later version of the clause, it is submitted, the marine underwriters would be liable, for owing to the words in brackets, the nature of the voyage is immaterial and no direct hostile act was directed against the ship. If, however, the facts being otherwise identical, a submarine had actually attacked the vessel, and in trying to avoid its torpedo it had collided with another vessel in the convoy, 'direct hostile act' would have been established, the exception clause would apply and the loss would fall on the war insurers.

The 'F.C. and S.' clause has been replaced in the clauses to be attached to the MAR form by much simplified forms of war risk exclusion clauses.[6]

---

5 [1948] A.C. 243.
6 See discussion at Section 30.3.3

31

LOSSES

So far we have discussed the question: What causes of loss or damage are covered by the policy? We must now determine what kind of loss or damage occasioned by the said causes will give the assured the right of recovery against the underwriter.

31.1   ACTUAL TOTAL LOSS

The most obvious instance of the sum insured becoming due is the actual total loss of the subject-matter insured. The Act, in s. 57(1), provides that this is the case 'where the subject-matter insured is destroyed, or so damaged as to cease to be a thing of the kind insured, or where the assured is irretrievably deprived thereof'. Thus the mere sinking of a ship need not immediately constitute an actual total loss. But this will be the case if what has gone to the bottom of the sea has ceased to be a ship, or in Lord Watson's picturesque words,[1] if the ship has been 'reduced to the condition of a mere congeries of wooden planks or of pieces of iron which could not without reconstruction be restored to the form of a ship'.

Apart from the type of loss outlined above, the statute deems a ship an actual total loss when, though the ship remains in being, the owners have been irretrievably deprived of her. This happens where the vessel sinks in very deep water and is not recoverable or where she is captured and condemned or in one case where she was salved and sold under an order of the Admiralty Court for less than the salvage charges.[2]

Goods are regarded as an actual total loss as soon as they cease to be goods of the kind insured from a commercial point of view. Thus wetted rice which has been dried may no longer be of merchantable quality, and the consignee may be entitled to refuse acceptance, but it will nevertheless retain the mercantile description of rice, and therefore

1 *Sailing Ship Blairmore Co.* v. *Macredie* [1898] A.C. 593, at p. 603.
2 *Cossman* v. *West* (1887) 13 App. Cas. 160.

only be a partial loss.[3] A distinction between total and partial losses of this nature could have been critical when cargo insurance was available on F.P.A. terms, whereby particular average losses (a partial loss caused by insured perils) were excluded from the policy. However, since the introduction of the 1982 cargo clauses, the distinction has lost much of its importance as all three sets of clauses now cover particular average in full.

On the other hand, there is a total loss when the goods have ceased to answer their former description altogether.

Illustration: *Asfar & Co. v. Blundell*[4]

A policy was effected to insure a profit to be made on freight. Part of the cargo were dates which arrived at the port of destination in a damaged state whereby they still had a certain commercial value for distilling purposes but no longer answered the description of dates. Therefore no freight was payable for them and the profit on freight was lost. Consequently the insurer of the profit was liable to pay.

Had the policy in this case been one on goods there would have been a total loss, since the cargo no longer answered the merchantable description by which it was insured.

An actual total loss of freight may be more difficult to determine. Where ship or goods have been actually lost so that freight can no longer be earned, the case is simple. But freight may be actually lost even when ship and goods are still in existence, though so damaged as to entitle the assured under ship and goods policies to regard them as commercially lost and no longer of any value to him, since their reconditioning or recovery would cost more than their value when repaired. This is one example of what lawyers call a constructive total loss of ship or goods.[5] In the words of Brett J, in his famous opinion in *Rankin* v. *Potter*,[6] 'where the ship is damaged to such an extent or under such circumstances as would authorize an abandonment of the ship on a policy on the ship, and where there is no cargo on board the ship, or if on board, where none is saved with the chance of an opportunity of its being forwarded in a substituted ship. In the several states of circumstances above set forth and considered, the loss of freight on the policy on freight would be an actual total loss.'

3 *Francis* v. *Boulton* (1895) 65 L.J., Q.B. 153.
4 [1896] 1 Q.B. 123.
5 See Section 31.2, *infra*.
6 (1873) L.R. 6 H.L. 83, at p. 102.

But freight may become an actual total loss in other circumstances as was decided in *Carras v. London & Scottish Assurance Corporation Ltd*.[7] In order to appreciate its import it may be as well to recall certain matters which were the subject of discussion in the chapter on the contract of affreightment. There we pointed out that a common mode of employing a ship was by letting her out on hire under a charterparty. Now suppose a shipowner lets his ship to a charterer, the charter to commence at a certain port and a certain date. While on her way to the port a casualty happens which precludes the vessel from reaching the loading port in time. In such an event, depending on the terms of the agreement and the circumstances of the casualty, it may be that the charterparty is frustrated,[8] both parties being discharged from their obligations. In other words the owner need no longer tender the ship and the charterer is free from his obligation to pay hire. The ship may not actually be lost, even commercially, if it can be repaired at a reasonable cost; but it might be that repairs cannot be effected in time for the charter. In this situation the chartered freight is lost and where the shipowner has taken out a policy on chartered freight he will be allowed to claim as for an actual total loss of freight.[9] We thus arrive at the conclusion that an actual total loss of freight can occur where the adventure is frustrated, such that the shipowner is freed from his obligations under the carriage contract, even though ship, and possibly goods, remain in existence.

Illustration: *Carras v. London & Scottish Assurance Corpn Ltd*[10]

A ship was chartered to proceed to Valparaiso to load a cargo. The charterparty contained the usual exception clause for perils of the sea, and 20 November, 1930, was fixed as cancelling date. The plaintiff owners, insured with the defendants against loss of freight for £4000. While proceeding to Valparaiso the ship stranded on 13 November, and was abandoned to the hull underwriters four days later.

Held: As, owing to perils of the sea, the ship could not make the cancelling date or be tendered to the charterers at Valparaiso according to the contract, the charterparty was discharged by perils of the sea and the voyage was frustrated. Accordingly, there was an actual total loss of freight and the insurers were liable to reimburse the shipowners under the policy.

7 [1936] 1 K.B. 291.
8 See Section 12.4, *supra*.
9 *Arnould* (1981), para. 1166.
10 [1936] 1 K.B. 291.

31.2 CONSTRUCTIVE TOTAL LOSS

The definition of a constructive total loss given in the Marine Insurance Act is as follows:[11] 'There is a constructive total loss where the subject-matter insured is reasonably abandoned on account of its actual loss appearing to be unavoidable, or because it could not be preserved from actual loss without an expenditure which would exceed its value when the expenditure had been incurred.'

Section 60(2) goes on to illustrate two types of case:

(i) where the assured is deprived of the insured property by a peril insured against in circumstances which make it unlikely that he will be able to recover it;

(ii) when the insured property is lost or damaged and the cost of recovery or repair would be so great as to exceed the value of the property when recovered or repaired.

Each type of constructive total loss requires further illustration and discussion.

31.2.1 DEPRIVATION OF POSSESSION

Where the assured is dispossessed of his ship or goods, the test of whether there has been a constructive total loss does not rely on the simple fact of deprivation but on whether the recovery of the subject-matter is unlikely. The test is not satisfied if recovery is merely uncertain which appears to have been the position before the Marine Insurance Act 1906.[12]

Illustration 1: *Polurrian S.S. Co. v. Young*[13]
A ship was insured on a voyage from the UK to Constantinople. After leaving England war broke out between Greece and Turkey. The master of the ship was unaware of this. The Greeks captured the ship and confiscated the cargo, which consisted of coal, as contraband. The assured wished to treat the ship as a constructive total loss and gave notice of abandonment to the underwriters, but the latter refused to accept it. Subsequently the master was able to satisfy the Greek authorities that he had no knowledge of the war, and ship was thereupon released, six weeks after capture.

11 S. 60(1).
12 *Arnould* (1981), para. 1188.
13 [1915] 1 K.B. 922.

Held: This was not a constructive total loss. At the moment of commencing the action it was uncertain, but not 'unlikely' that the ship would be released.

Illustration 2:   *Rickards* v. *Forestal Land, Timber and Railways Co.*[14]

During the 1939–45 war, German ships with British-owned cargoes aboard were ordered by the military government in Germany to proceed to a German port.

Held: Once the masters of the ships decided to obey the instructions of the German government and acted on that decision, they ceased to hold the goods as bailees of the assured and became servants or agents of the German government. The assureds were deprived of possession at this time and it was then unlikely that they could recover their goods. This constituted a constructive total loss of the goods and the underwriters were liable to the cargo-owners.

Illustration 3:   *Irvine* v. *Hine*[15]

The trawler *Elswick* stranded in January 1942, and the assured claimed for a constructive total loss, arguing that he was unlikely to get her repaired within a reasonable time owing to war-time conditions and the licensing system governing ship repairs, then in force.

Held: This was not a constructive total loss under s. 60 of the Marine Insurance Act 1906. Nor could the plaintiff rely on the old common law rule which might have allowed the claim, since the definition in s. 60 was complete in circumscribing the concept of constructive total loss.

The material date at which recovery must be 'unlikely' is the date of the issue of the writ, and the facts on which the court will decide are the true facts, at that moment, as opposed to those known to the assured.[16] In practice it would seem to be extremely difficult to establish that recovery was unlikely as opposed to uncertain and the very narrow construction which this term has received from the courts is clearly shown in *Marstrand Fishing Co.* v. *Beer.*[17] There, the master and crew of a fishing vessel, *The Girl Pat,* had barratrously taken possession of her; no competent engineer was on board, and the engines had broken down twice; the master had falsified the log and had sailed without a proper chart; the rig had been altered by the addition of a bowsprit, the vessel had been repainted and the fishing numbers blacked out. All this

14 [1942] A.C. 50.
15 [1950] 1 K.B. 555.
16 *Marstrand Fishing Co.* v. *Beer* (1936) 56 Ll. L.R. 163, 173.
17 (1936) 56 Ll. L.R. 163.

had made it difficult to recognize the runaway ship even if she should reach port in spite of her defective equipment.

Nevertheless, it was decided that on a balance of probabilities it was just as likely the ship would, as would not, be recovered, and thus the insurers were held not liable to pay for a constructive total loss of the vessel.[18]

Although s. 60(2)(i) of the Act requires recovery to be unlikely, without further specification, the courts have imposed a limit in favour of the assured, that recovery must be unlikely within a reasonable time. What constitutes a reasonable time in any case will depend on the facts. In *The Bamburi*,[19] a vessel became trapped during September 1980 in the Shatt-al-Arab waterway during a war between Iran and Iraq. Notice of Abandonment[20] was tendered by the assured over a year later, when the vessel was still trapped, and declined by the underwriters. One of the questions which came before the sole arbitrator, Staughton J, was whether the vessel could be considered a constructive total loss, the owners being unlikely to recover the vessel within a reasonable time. Considering the facts, the arbitrator found that a reasonable time in these circumstances meant 12 months from the date when notice of abandonment was tendered and that in this case it was unlikely the owners would recover the ship within that period. In addition, he decided that the owners' loss of free use and disposal of the vessel amounted to a deprivation of possession under the Act, and the owners having satisfied the other criteria, the underwriters were bound to settle for a constructive total loss.

Similar considerations apply to goods, and a mere temporary detention will not be enough to show a constructive total loss. The same strict test will be applied to the facts as is employed to determine whether or not a ship is a constructive total loss.

31.2.2 DAMAGE IN EXCESS OF REPAIRED VALUE

The second type of constructive total loss differs from the previous one in that there the assured had lost possession and control of the subject-matter insured whereas here he may have both. However, in this case, owing to the cost of recovery or reconditioning, the property is as good as lost from a business point of view.

18 *Polurrian S.S. Co.* v. *Young* [1915] 1 K.B. 922, applied; see also *Captain J.A. Cates Tug and Wharfage Co.* v. *Franklin Insurance Co.* [1927] A.C. 698.
19 [1982] 1 Lloyd's Rep. 312. See also Institute War Clauses 1983, cl. 3.
20 See Section 31.3.1, *infra*.

Illustration: *Irving v. Manning*[21]

	£
A ship was valued at	17 500
She was insured for	3 000
She was damaged and her repairs were estimated to cost	10 500
The value of the ship when repaired would be	9 000

This was held to constitute a constructive total loss.

In the above illustration it would obviously be unreasonable to spend £10 500 in order to get a ship worth only £9000.

The same considerations prevail in respect of cargo. This is said to be constructively lost, if the cost of reconditioning and forwarding it to its destination would be higher than its value on arrival.[22] The test usually applied, though with a growing number of decided cases, perhaps no longer of the same importance as formerly, is: What would a prudent uninsured owner do in the circumstances? If he chooses to repair the goods and forward them to their destination the loss should be considered partial, but if he merely abandons the attempt and sells them for any residual value remaining in the goods this would be considered a constructive total loss.

Where the assured is seeking to establish a constructive total loss of his ship by this second criterion he may, in addition to the cost of repairs, take into account the cost of future salvage operations and of future general average contributions to which the ship would become liable if repaired. On the other hand, the Act specifies that in estimating repair costs 'no deduction is to be made in respect of general average contributions to those repairs payable by other interests.'[23] This sub-section appears to overrule a case,[24] decided some forty years before the Act came into being, which held that in calculating the cost of a salvage operation, which constitutes a general average expenditure, the shipowner is required to deduct from the cost any general average contribution due from the cargo. Although the point is not without doubt, it appears that *Kemp* v. *Halliday*[25] can still stand and that general average contributions by other parties to the cost of salvage must be deducted, but similar contributions to the 'cost of repairs' need not be.[26]

In the case of goods, the Act provides that a constructive total loss takes place when 'the cost of repairing the damage and forwarding the

21 (1847) 1 H.L.C. 287. Note now the effect of 1983 Hull Clauses, cl. 19.1.
22 Marine Insurance Act 1906, s. 60(2)(iii). *Arnould* (1981), paras 1223 *et seq.*
23 Marine Insurance Act 1906, s. 60(2)(ii).
24 *Kemp* v. *Halliday* (1866) L.R. 1 Q.B. 520.
25 *Ibid.*
26 See *Arnould* (1981), paras 1201, 1202.

goods to their destination' exceeds their value on arrival. Whether the 'cost of forwarding' is the entire cost of carrying the goods from the port of distress to destination, or merely the excess of this sum over the original bill of lading freight to destination is uncertain, but the former alternative seems to be preferred.[27]

31.3 ABANDONMENT

We have seen – and this fact should be constantly borne in mind – that in cases of constructive total loss something of the subject-matter insured remains which, though of no use to the assured's business, still represents a certain value. A ship, of no value to the owners, may be of value for instance to shipbreakers, and goods may be sold, though at a lower price, somewhere else than at their destination.

Since the contract of insurance is a contract of indemnity the assured is not allowed to keep what is left of the subject-matter in addition to receiving the sum insured. It is therefore provided that he must abandon the former to the underwriters so that they may have the opportunity to recoup themselves, at least in part, for the sum they paid to the assured.[28]

31.3.1 SHIP AND CARGO

The damage to constructively lost ship and cargo is very often progressive. That is to say, if steps for recovery or repair are speedily taken a greater value will be preserved. Accordingly the assured must make up his mind quickly. He must give notice of abandonment 'with reasonable diligence after the receipt of reliable information of the loss, but where the information is of a doubtful character the assured is entitled to a reasonable time to make inquiry'.[29] Failure to give notice in time does not, however, mean that the assured has lost everything; though he can no longer claim as for a constructive total loss, he remains entitled to claim compensation as for a partial one.

27 *Arnould* (1981), para. 1231.
28 Marine Insurance Act 1906, ss. 61, 62.
29 *Ibid.*, s. 62(3).

Illustration   £
A ship is valued and insured for   15 000
She is damaged and her repairs cost   10 000
Her value when repaired will be   8 000

Here the assured can treat the loss as a constructive one and claim £15 000. But this is so only if he gives notice of abandonment with reasonable diligence. If not he has lost this right, but can still claim for the partial loss of £10 000. *Note:* In modern hull practice cl. 19.1 would defeat this CTL claim.

31.3.2 FREIGHT

This need for the abandonment of what remains of the subject-matter insured has given rise to great difficulty in regard to constructive total loss of freight. The provisions of the Marine Insurance Act 1906 are of little help on this point, as no definition is offered of those circumstances which might constitute such a constructive total loss. Generally speaking, the difficulty arises because freight is not a tangible asset, as are ship and cargo, and it is hard to visualize that freight can be of no commercial value to the assured, but nevertheless of some value to the insurer. In such circumstances, it is difficult to see how notice of abandonment could possibly benefit the insurers, and if such is the case the Act frees the assured from tendering notice at all.[30] This in effect means, that in many cases, what might be thought of theoretically as a constructive total loss of freight, is treated for all practical purposes as an actual total loss.

8Another way of looking at the point is that notice of abandonment in regard to freight gives underwriters at least a chance of earning the freight which is in danger of being lost, by substituting a vessel for the one which is stranded, or by salving and provisionally repairing the stranded vessel in time. By incurring expenses beyond the means of a prudent uninsured owner they might by able to recoup themselves for at least a proportion of the sum payable on the freight policy.[31]

31.4 PARTIAL LOSS

As opposed to a total loss, the assured may only have suffered a partial loss to the subject-matter of the insurance. Although there are some

30 Marine Insurance Act 1906, s. 62(7).
31 *Rankin* v. *Potter* (1873) L.R. 6 H.L. 83, *per* Brett J at pp. 102, 103; see *Kulukundis* v. *Norwich Union Fire Insurance Society* [1937] 1 K.B. 1; *Arnould* (1981), paras 1242 *et seq.*

types of insurance which offer cover only for total losses,[32] the demise of the 'free of particular average' (F.P.A.) cargo clauses, means that the majority of all marine policies cover partial loss as well as total loss. Therefore, if the ship or goods are damaged, or only part of the freight is earned, and under the provisions of the Marine Insurance Act the assured cannot show a total loss, his loss will be treated as partial. Such losses where proximately caused by a peril insured against, and not being a general average loss, are termed particular average losses.[33] This term should not be confused with the notion of particular charges, which are recoverable as sue and labour expenses.[34]

In relation to insurances on goods, the Act expressly provides that where they reach their destination in *specie*, but cannot be identified because of the obliteration of marks, then if the assured suffers any loss at all, it shall only be a partial one.[35] Apart from damage or loss to the subject-matter, particular charges, salvage charges and some general average losses may be recovered by the assured as partial losses.[36] To determine the amount claimable for a partial loss involves distinguishing between loss caused by wear and tear or other uninsured causes and that arising from the insured perils, as it is only the latter for which the underwriter is liable. The situation becomes further confused where the assured, under a hull policy, elects not to repair damage, or a partial loss to the vessel is followed by a total loss before the first damage is made good. Consideration is given by the Act to such circumstances and in s. 69 it is provided that if the ship is partially repaired, or remains unrepaired until the end of the risk, the assured is entitled to an indemnity equal to the reasonable depreciation of the vessel arising from the unrepaired damage. This indemnity is, however, subject to a limit of the reasonable cost of repairing such damage, as specified in s. 69(1).

In the case of a vessel which is totally lost, before an antecedent partial loss is remedied, the Act provides that the insurer shall only be liable for the total loss.[37] In this context, it should be noted that if the subsequent total loss is caused by an uninsured peril, there can be no claim under the policy for either the unrepaired partial loss or later total loss.[38]

---

32 Institute Time Clauses (Hulls) Total Loss, General Average and 3/4ths Collision Liability 1983.
33 Marine Insurance Act 1906, ss. 56(1), 64(1).
34 See Section 30.3.1(c), *supra*.
35 Marine Insurance Act 1906, s. 56(5); see *Spence* v. *Union Marine Insurance Co.* (1868) L.R. 3 C.P. 427.
36 *Ibid.* ss. 64(2), 65(1) and 66.
37 Marine Insurance Act 1906, s. 77(2).
38 *Livie* v. *Janson* (1810) 12 East 648, 104 E.R. 253.

31.5 PROOF OF LOSS

As a general rule, where the policy expressly lists the insured perils, the *onus* of proving a loss within the terms of the policy falls on the assured.[39] In the ordinary way the evidence of the assured consists of the oral testimony of master or crew. However, it may be sufficient that the owner has not heard of the ship's arrival within a reasonable time.[40] There is then a presumption that the ship has become an actual total loss. Provided the assured can then show that the vessel was bound for and sailed on the voyage insured, her non-arrival will be prima facie evidence that she has been lost by perils of the seas.

31.5.1 LOSS BY ACCIDENT OR WEAR AND TEAR

Sometimes more complicated situations arise. It may be not altogether certain that the ship really met with a fortuitous accident which would allow the assured to recover for a loss caused by perils of the seas. The insurer may bring forward suggestions of the loss having been occasioned by ordinary wear and tear. Obviously it would be a great hardship for the assured, and indeed would deprive him of an important advantage of insurance, had he to prove an accident affirmatively. The law does not adopt this course. It is sufficient that 'the damage proved was such as did not occur and could not be expected to occur in the course of a normal transit'. The assured is held to have discharged his burden of proof if 'the inference remains that it (viz. the loss) was due to some abnormal circumstance, some accident or casualty'.[41]

While it may be true that the assured is not required to prove an accident affirmatively, it is well understood that 'the burden of proving, on a balance of probabilities, that the ship was lost by perils of the sea, is and remains throughout on the shipowners'.[42] In circumstances where the vessel sinks and no physical evidence remains as to the cause of loss, the discharge of the burden of proof by the assured may be extremely difficult. This difficulty is compounded where the underwriters suggest a cause of loss against which the ship was not insured, e.g. wear and tear, especially as it is not necessary for them to prove the alternative explanation, even on the balance of probabilities. Finally, it may not be

---

39 *Templeman*, p. 200 *et seq.*
40 *Arnould* (1981), para. 794; Marine Insurance Act 1906, s. 58.
41 *British & Foreign Marine Insurance Co.* v. *Gaunt* [1921] 2 A.C. 41, at p. 46.
42 *The Popi M: Rhesa Shipping Co. S.A.* v. *Herbert David Edmunds*, [1985] 2 Lloyd's Rep. 1, *per* Lord Brandon at p. 2.

possible for either side to show conclusively, even on the balance of probabilities, the true proximate cause of loss. In such a case the cause remains in doubt, and consequently the assured will have failed to discharge the burden of proof which falls upon him.[43]

Illustration: *The Popi M: Rhesa Shipping Co. S.A. v. Edmunds*[44]

The *Popi M* was lost in calm seas and fair weather, due to the sudden entry of water into the engine room through the side plating. A claim for loss by perils of the sea was made by the assured and evidence was submitted that the vessel was in a seaworthy state prior to the sinking. The assured put forward the argument that the vessel had struck a submerged object, possibly a submarine, and that this had caused the loss. In resisting the claim, the insurers contended that the loss was proximately caused by the defective, deteriorated and decayed condition of the ship's shell plating, due to age and wear and tear.

Held: The House of Lords found in favour of the insurers. This was despite the fact that the owners had succeeded before the lower courts because, on the balance of probabilities, their explanation was preferred. Their Lordships explained, that in reaching a decision as to the cause of loss, where two unlikely causes are put forward, the court is not bound to favour one or the other. In such a case it is open to the court to hold that the true cause of the loss is in doubt and therefore the owners had failed to discharge the burden of proof which was upon them.

31.5.2   WAR OR MARINE LOSS

The question of proving a cause of loss becomes of considerable importance during war, because of the universal use in all marine policies of clauses designed to exclude war risks.[45] During the wars 1914–18 and 1939–45, a scheme was evolved under which the Government took a substantial part of the burden of war risks, with the result that there were usually two separate insurances, one against the ordinary marine risks and the other against war risks.[46] When a vessel so insured went missing the question arose whether the marine or the war risk underwriters had to compensate the assured. The peacetime presumption of loss by perils of the sea loses much of its force in time of

---

43 *La Compañía Naviera Martiartu v. The Corporation of the Royal Exchange Assurance* [1923] 1 K.B. 650, *per* Scrutton LJ at p. 657.
44 [1985] 2 Lloyd's Rep. 1.
45 E.g. The 'free of capture and seizure' (F.C. & S.) clause in S.G. policies and the 'war exclusion' clause (cl. 23) in the Institute Time Clauses (Hulls) 1983.
46 For an illustration see *J. Wharton (Shipping), Ltd v. Mortleman* (1941) 57 T.L.R. 514, C.A., where the assured recovered against the marine underwriters.

war, yet although a ship might be engaged on a warlike operation, such as troop or munitions transport, she may just as well have succumbed to ordinary marine perils. In such cases the courts have in practice been able, in the light of the evidence of the collateral circumstances, such as the weather prevailing at the time, the amount of enemy activity known to have taken place on the vessel's route at the relevant date, the experience of other vessels, and like matters, to come to a decision without having to rely upon the presumption.[47]

Illustration 1: *Euterpe S.S. Co. v. North of England Protecting & Indemnity Association*[48]

The plaintiffs insured with the defendants a steamship against war risks. They also took out a marine risk policy with other underwriters. In January 1917 the vessel steamed up the east coast of England. After passing Great Yarmouth nothing was heard of her. The defendants contended that the vessel was lost owing to a peril of the sea. Evidence established that she was passing close to a minefield, that the weather was sufficiently rough to blow mines across the ship's route, but not so rough as to be likely to endanger a ship of the type insured. As no signals had been received, and no wreckage found, the ship must have met with a sudden end.

Held: Everything pointed to a loss by war perils, and the defendants were held liable.

Illustration 2: *Compañía Maritima of Barcelona v. Wishart*[49]

The *Pelayo* was insured against marine perils, excepting war perils. In November 1916 she left the Tyne with coal bound for a Spanish port and was never heard of afterwards. Evidence was given of very bad weather in the North Sea at the material time, and that several marine casualties happened to other ships. On the other hand, there was no evidence of mines having been about in the area through which the *Pelayo* was bound to sail.

Held: The loss could be explained without war perils, and the marine underwriters were held liable.[50]

---

47 *Munro, Brice & Co.* v. *War Risks Association* [1918] 2 K.B. 78, reversed in [1920] 3 K.B. 94.

48 (1917) 33 T.L.R. 540.

49 (1918) 23 Com. Cas. 264.

50 See general observations by Bailhache J, in *Munroe, Brice & Co.* v. *War Risks Association and Anchor War Mutual Underwriting Association* [1918] 2 K.B. 78 at p. 88; but note that the actual decision was overruled [1920] 3 K.B. 94.

31.5.3 SCUTTLING

The problems of evidence, and where the burden of proof lies, frequently crop up where there is a possibility that the loss of a vessel was due to scuttling. Where the assured claims for a loss by perils of the sea he must establish at least a prima facie case and show on the balance of probabilities a fortuitous accident. The burden of proof in such a case is on the assured, but if the insurer attempts to defend the action by alleging that the vessel was scuttled, with the privity of the assured, the burden of proving this lies upon the underwriter.[51]

Where it is agreed between the parties that the cause of loss is scuttling, the assured may still be able to recover under the insured peril of barratry which is defined in the Marine Insurance Act 1906, as 'every wrongful act wilfully committed by the master or crew to the prejudice of the owner'.[52] In *The Michael*,[53] Kerr J decided that to succeed in a claim for barratry the shipowner must show that the vessel had indeed been sunk deliberately, but also, on a clear balance of probabilities that the assured had in no way connived at the sinking. While the Court of Appeal affirmed Kerr J's conclusion, Roskill LJ made it clear that this must not be taken to be an approval by the Court of the learned judges views on the question of burden of proof.[54] Roskill LJ pointed to an earlier decision of the Court of Appeal in *Issaias* v. *Marine Insurance Co. Ltd*[55] which was clearly inconsistent with the reasoning of Kerr J, in *The Michael*. In the *Issaias* case it was held that where the parties had agreed the loss was by deliberate sinking, the assured was entitled to the benefit of the presumption of innocence. It was thus for the insurers to discharge the burden of proof that the assured had been privy to the scuttling. The burden of proof in such a case would appear to be a heavy one, in that the insurer is attempting to show that the shipowner has committed a crime under English law.[56]

In view of the above, the question as to where the burden of proof lies in such cases is not without doubt. If the authority laid down in *Issaias* is followed, barratry becomes an exception to the general rule that it is for the assured to establish a prima facie case of loss by an insured peril by

---

51 *La Compañía Naviera Martiartu* v. *The Corporation of the Royal Exchange Assurance, supra.*
52 First Schedule, Rules for Construction of Policy, r. 11.
53 *Piermay Shipping Co. S.A. and Brandt's Ltd* v. *Chester*, [1979] 1 Lloyd's Rep. 55.
54 [1979] 2 Lloyd's Rep. 1, at p. 12.
55 (1923) 15 Ll. L. Rep. 186.
56 The burden of proof on the prosecution in a criminal case is heavier than that on a plaintiff in a civil case. *The Captain Panagos D.P.* [1986] 2 Lloyd's Rep. 470, 511.

proving all the components which go to make up the definition of that
peril.[57] That the point still raises doubt, can be seen from the judgment
of Evans J in a recent decision, where he remarked, 'the definition of
barratry includes "to the prejudice of the owner" which suggests that
the assured must prove that he was an innocent victim'.[58] As such, he felt
that 'if unaided by authority' he would conclude, as did Mr Justice Kerr
in *The Michael*,[59] that the assured had the burden of proving they were
not privy to the casualty.

57 See Hazelwood SJ (1982) Barratry – the scuttler's easy route to the 'golden prize',
    [1982] 3 LMCLQ 383.
58 *The Captain Panagos D.P.* [1986] 2 Lloyd's Rep. 470, at 511.
59 *Supra.*

FURTHER READING

Listed below [for further reference] is a selection of works on shipping law, many of which are mentioned in this book.

Abecassis, D. and Jarashow, R., *Oil Pollution from Ships – International, UK and United States Law and Practice,* 2nd edn, (1985) Stevens & Sons, London.

Atiyah, P.S., *The Sale of Goods,* 7th edn, (1985) Pitman, London.

Bates, J., *United Kingdom Marine Pollution Law,* (1985) Lloyd's of London Press, London.

Benedict on Admiralty, 7th revised edn (1983), with Supplements.

Brice, G., *Maritime Law of Salvage,* (1983) Stevens & Sons, London.

Brown, R., *Analysis of Marine Insurance Clauses, Book 1 – The Institute Cargo Clauses,* 2nd edn, (1983) Witherby & Co., London.

Brown, R., *Analysis of Marine Insurance Clauses, Book 2 – The Institute Time Clauses – Hulls,* (1983) Witherby & Co., London.

Brown, R., *Marine Insurance, Principles and Basic Practice,* 5th edn, (1986) Witherby & Co., London.

Brown, R., *Marine Insurance, Volume 2 Cargo Practice,* 4th edn, (1985) Witherby & Co., London.

Brown, R., *Marine Insurance, Volume 3 Hull Practice,* (1975) Witherby & Co., London.

Brown, R., *Dictionary of Marine Insurance Terms,* 4th edn, (1975) Witherby & Co., London.

Brown, R. and Reed, P., *Marine Insurance,* (1981) Witherby & Co., London.

Buglass, L., *Marine Insurance and General Average in the United States,* 2nd edn, (1981) Cornell Maritime Press, Centreville, Maryland.

Clarke, M. (ed.), *Shipbuilding Contracts,* (1982) Lloyd's of London Press, London.

Cockerell, H. and Shaw, G., *Insurance Broking and Agency, The Law and Practice,* (1979) Witherby & Co., London.

Coghlin, T., Wilford, M. and Healy, N., *Time Charters,* 2nd edn, (1982) Lloyd's of London Press, London.

Colinvaux, R., *Carver's Carriage by Sea,* 13th edn, (1982) Volumes 1-2, Stevens & Sons, London.

Current Law, (monthly parts and annual volume), Sweet & Maxwell, London.

Current Law Statutes, (regular issues and annual volumes), Sweet & Maxwell, London.

Dias, R., (ed.), *Clerk and Lindsell on Torts,* 15th edn, (1982) with Supplement (1985), Sweet & Maxwell, London.

The Digest, Volumes 1-52 and supplements, [British, Commonwealth and European Cases], Butterworths, London.

Donaldson, J., Staughton, C. and Wilson, D. *Lowndes and Rudolf's Law of General Average and the York-Antwerp Rules,* 10th edn, (1975) Stevens & Sons, London.

Douglas, R.P.A., *Harbour Law,* 2nd edn, (1983) Lloyd's of London Press, London.

Gaskell, N.J.J., (ed.), *Limitation of Shipowners' Liability: The New Law,* (1986) Sweet & Maxwell.

Geen, G.K. and Douglas, R.P.A., *The Law of Pilotage,* 2nd edn, (1983) Lloyd's of London Press, London.

Goodacre, J., *Institute Time Clauses Hulls: A Comparison,* (1983) Witherby & Co., London.

Goodacre, J., *Marine Insurance Claims,* 2nd edn, (1981) Witherby & Co., London.

Goode, R., *Commercial Law,* (1982) Penguin Books, London.

Griggs, P. and Williams, R., *Limitation of Liability for Marine Claims,* (1986) Lloyd's of London Press and the Institute of Maritime Law.

Guest, A., *Benjamin's Sale of Goods,* 2nd edn, (1981) Sweet & Maxwell, London.

Guest, A. (ed.), *Chitty on Contracts,* 25th edn, (1983) 2 Volumes, Sweet & Maxwell, London.

Halsbury's Laws of England, (4th edn, 1973-1984), Volumes 1-52 with Supplements. See especially Volume 1 (Admiralty), Volume 43 (Shipping), Butterworths, London.

Halsbury's Statutes of England, (4th edn, 1985). See especially, Volume 1 (Admiralty); (3rd edn, 1968-1972) Volume 31 (Shipping and Navigation), Butterworths, London.

Halsbury's Statutory Instruments, Volumes 1-23 and Supplements. See especially, Volume 20, Butterworths, London.

Herman, A., *Shipping Conferences,* (1983) Lloyd's of London Press, London.

Holdert, H. and Buzek, F., *Collision Cases – Judgments and Diagrams,* (1984) Lloyd's of London Press, London.

Hudson, N. and Allen, J., *Marine Claims Handbook*, 4th edn, (1984) Lloyd's of London Press, London.

Hudson, N. and Allen J., *The Institute Clauses Handbook*, (1986) Lloyd's of London Press, London.

Ivamy, E., *Marine Insurance*, 4th edn, (1985) Butterworths, London.

Ivamy, E., *Encyclopaedia of Shipping Law Sources (UK)*, (1985) Lloyd's of London Press, London.

Ivamy, E., *Dictionary of Shipping Terms*, (1984) Butterworths, London.

Ivamy, E., *Chalmers' Marine Insurance Act 1906*, 9th edn, (1983) Butterworths, London.

Jackson, D., *Enforcement of Maritime Claims*, (1985) Lloyd's of London Press, London.

Jacob, J., (ed.), *The Supreme Court Practice 1985* [The White Book], 2 Volumes, Sweet & Maxwell, London.

Kitchen, J., *The Employment of Merchant Seamen*, (1980) Croom Helm, London.

Lambeth, R., *Templeman on Marine Insurance*, 6th edn, (1986) Pitman, London.

MacGregor, H., *MacGregor on Damages*, 14th edn, (1980) Sweet & Maxwell, London.

McGuffie, K., Fugeman, R. and Gray, V., *Admiralty Practice*, (1964) with Supplement (1975) Stevens & Sons, London.

McGuffie, K., *Marsden's The Law of Collisions at Sea*, 11th edn, (1961) and Supplement (1973) Stevens & Sons, London.

Mocatta, A., Mustill, M. and Boyd, S., *Scrutton on Charterparties and Bills of Lading*, 19th edn, (1984) Sweet & Maxwell, London.

Morris, J.H.C., *Dicey and Morris on the Conflict of Laws*, 10th edn, (1980) with Cumulative Supplement (1985), Stevens & Sons, London.

Mustill, M. and Gilman, J., *Arnould's Law of Marine Insurance and Average*, 16th edn, (1981) Volumes 1-2, Stevens & Sons, London.

Northrup, H. and Rowan, R., *The International Transport Workers' Federation and Flag of Convenience Shipping*, (1983) University of Pennsylvania Industrial Research Unit.

Packard, W.V., *Sale and Purchase*, (1981) Fairplay Publications, London.

Parks, A., *The Law of Tug, Tow and Pilotage*, 2nd edn, (1982) Cornell Maritime Press, Centreville, Maryland.

Percy, R., *Charlesworth and Percy on Negligence*, 7th edn, (1983) with supplements (1984) Sweet & Maxwell, London.

Pollard, D.W., *Social Welfare Law*, (1977) with supplements, Oyez, London.

Reference Book of Marine Insurance Clauses, 58th edn, (1986) Witherby & Co., London.

Rodière, R., *Droit Maritime,* 10th edn, (1986) Dalloz, Paris.

Rose, F., *The Modern Law of Pilotage,* (1984) Sweet & Maxwell, London.

Sassoon, D., and Merren, H.O., *CIF and FOB Contracts,* 3rd edn, (1984) Stevens & Sons, London.

Singh, N., *International Maritime Law Conventions,* (1983), Volumes 1-4, Stevens & Sons, London.

Singh, N. and Colinvaux, R., *Shipowners,* (1967) Stevens & Sons, London.

Steel, D., Rose, F. and Shaw, R., *Kennedy's Law of Salvage,* 5th edn, (1985) Stevens & Sons, London.

Sturt, R., *The Collision Regulations,* 2nd edn, (1984) Lloyd's of London Press, London.

Summerskill, M., *Laytime,* 3rd edn, (1982) Stevens & Sons, London.

Summerskill, M., *Oil Rigs, Law and Insurance,* (1979) Stevens & Sons, London.

Tetley, W., *Maritime Liens and Claims,* (1985) Business Law Communications, London.

Tetley, W., *Marine Cargo Claims,* 2nd edn, (1978) Butterworths, Toronto.

Thomas, D., *Maritime Liens,* (1980) Stevens & Sons, London.

Thomas, M. and Steel, D., *Temperley's Merchant Shipping Acts,* 7th edn, (1976) Stevens & Sons, London.

Tiberg, H., *The Law of Demurrage,* 3rd edn, (1979) Stevens & Sons, London.

Todd, P., *Modern Bills of Lading,* (1986) Collins, London.

Wood, P., *Law and Practice of International Finance,* (1980) Sweet & Maxwell, London.

APPENDICES

APPENDICES

APPENDIX 1
SUPREME COURT ACT
1981[1]

ADMIRALTY JURISDICTION OF HIGH COURT

20. – (1) The Admiralty jurisdiction of the High Court shall be as follows, that is to say –

   (a) jurisdiction to hear and determine any of the questions and claims mentioned in subsection(2);

   (b) jurisdiction in relation to any of the proceedings mentioned in subsection (8);

   (c) any other Admiralty jurisdiction which it had immediately before the commencement of this Act; and

   (d) any jurisdiction connected with ships or aircraft which is vested in the High Court apart from this section and is for the time being by rules of court made or coming into force after the commencement of this Act assigned to the Queen's Bench Division and directed by the rules to be exercised by the Admiralty Court.

(2) The questions and claims referred to in subsection (1) (a) are –

   (a) any claim to the possession or ownership of a ship or to the ownership of any share therein;

   (b) any question arising between the co-owners of a ship as to possession, employment or earnings of that ship;

   (c) any claim in respect of a mortgage of or charge on a ship or any share therein;

   (d) any claim for damage received by a ship;

   (e) any claim for damage done by a ship;

   (f) any claim for loss of life or personal injury sustained in

---

1 Reference should also be made to ss. 22-24 for various restrictions and definitions.

consequence of any defect in a ship or in her apparel or
equipment, or in consequence of the wrongful act, neglect or
default of –

> (i) the owners, charterers or persons in possession or
> control of a ship; or

> (ii) the master or crew of a ship, or any other person for
> whose wrongful acts, neglects or defaults the owners,
> charterers or persons in possession or control of a ship are
> responsible,

being an act, neglect or default in the navigation or management of the ship, in the loading, carriage or discharge of
goods in, in or from the ship, or in the embarkation, carriage
or disembarkation of persons on, in or from the ship;

(g) any claim for loss of or damage to goods carried in a ship;

(h) any claim arising out of any agreement relating to the carriage of goods in a ship or to the use or hire of a ship;

(j) any claim in the nature of salvage (including any claim
arising by virtue of the application, by or under section 51 of
the Civil Aviation Act 1949, of the law relating to salvage to
aircraft and their apparel and cargo);

(k) any claim in the nature of towage in respect of a ship or an
aircraft;

(l) any claim in the nature of pilotage in respect of a ship or an
aircraft;

(m) any claim in respect of goods or materials supplied to a ship
for her operation or maintenance;

(n) any claim in respect of the construction, repair or equipment
of a ship or in respect of dock charges or dues;

(o) any claim by a master or member of the crew of a ship for
wages (including any sum allotted out of wages or adjudged
by a superintendent to be due by way of wages);

(p) any claim by a master, shipper, charterer or agent in respect
of disbursements made on account of a ship;

(q) any claim arising out of an act which is or is claimed to be a
general average act;

(r) any claim arising out of bottomry;

(s) any claim for the forfeiture or condemnation of a ship or of
goods which are being or have been carried, or have been
attempted to be carried, in a ship, or for the restoration of a
ship or any such goods after seizure, or for droits of
Admiralty.

(8) The proceedings referred to in subsection (1) (*b*) are –

(*a*) any application to the High Court under the Merchant Shipping Acts 1894 to 1979 other than an application under section 55 of the Merchant Shipping Act 1894 for the appointment of a person to act as a substitute for a person incapable of acting;

(*b*) any action to enforce a claim for damage, loss of life or personal injury arising out of –

    (i) a collision between ships; or

    (ii) the carrying out of or omission to carry out a manoeuvre in the case of one or more of two or more ships; or

    (iii) non-compliance, on the part of one or more of two or more ships, with the collision regulations;

(*c*) any action by shipowners or other persons under the Merchant Shipping Acts 1894 to 1979 for the limitation of the amount of their liability in connection with a ship or other property.

(4) The jurisdiction of the High Court under subsection (2) (*b*) includes power to settle any account outstanding and unsettled between the parties in relation to the ship, and to direct that the ship, or any share thereof, shall be sold, and to make such other order as the court thinks fit.

(5) Subsection (2) (*e*) extends to –

(*a*) any claim in respect of a liability incurred under the Merchant Shipping (Oil Pollution) Act 1971; and

(*b*) any claim in respect of a liability falling on the International Oil Pollution Compensation Fund under Part I of the Merchant Shipping Act 1974.

(6) The reference in subsection (2) (*j*) to claims in the nature of salvage includes a reference to such claims for services rendered in saving life from a ship or an aircraft or in preserving cargo, apparel or wreck as, under sections 544 to 546 of the Merchant Shipping Act 1894, or any Order in Council made under section 51 of the Civil Aviation Act 1949, are authorised to be made in connection with a ship or an aircraft.

(7) The preceding provisions of this section apply –

(*a*) in relation to all ships or aircraft, whether British or not and wherever the residence of domicile of their owners may be;

(*b*) in relation to all claims, wherever arising (including, in the case of cargo or wreck salvage, claims in respect of cargo or wreck found on land); and

(c) so far as they relate to mortgages and charges, to all mortgages or charges, whether registered or not and whether legal or equitable, including mortgages and charges created under foreign law:

Provided that nothing in this subsection shall be construed as extending the cases in which money or property is recoverable under any of the provisions of the Merchant Shipping Acts 1894 to 1979.

MODE OF EXERCISE OF ADMIRALTY JURISDICTION

21. – (1) Subject to section 22, an action in personam may be brought in the High Court in all cases within the Admiralty jurisdiction of that court.

(2) In the case of any such claim as is mentioned in section 20 (2) (a), (c) or (s) or any such question as is mentioned in section 20 (2) (b), an action in rem may be brought in the High Court against the ship, or property in connection with which the claim or question arises.

(8) In any case in which there is a maritme lien or other charge on any ship, aircraft or other property for the amount claimed, an action in rem may be brought in the High Court against that ship, aircraft or property.

(4) In the case of any such claim as is mentioned in section 20 (2) (e) to (r), where –

(a) the claim arises in connection with a ship; and

(b) the person who would be liable on the claim in an action in personam ("the relevant person") was, when the cause of action arose, the owner or charterer of, or in possession or in control of, the ship,

an action in rem may (whether or not the claim gives rise to a maritime lien on that ship) be brought in the High Court against –

(i) that ship, if at the time when the action is brought the relevant person is either the beneficial owner of that ship as respects all the shares in it or the charterer of it under a charter by demise;

or

(ii) any other ship of which, at the time when the action is brought, the relevant person is the beneficial owner as respects all the shares in it.

(5) In the case of a claim in the nature of towage or pilotage in respect of an aircraft, an action in rem may be brought in the High Court against that aircraft if, at the time when the action is brought, it is beneficially owned by the person who would be liable on the claim in an action in personam.

(6) Where, in the exercise of its Admiralty jurisdiction, the High Court orders any ship, aircraft or other property to be sold, the court shall have jurisdiction to hear and determine any question arising as to the title to the proceeds of sale.

(7) In determining for the purposes of subsections (4) and (5) whether a person would be liable on a claim in an action in personam it shall be assumed that he has his habitual residence or a place of business within England or Wales.

(8) Where, as regards any such claim as is mentioned in section 20 (2) (e) to (r), a ship has been served with a writ or arrested in an action in rem brought to enforce that claim, no other ship may be served with a writ or arrested in that or any other action in rem brought to enforce that claim; but this subsection does not prevent the issue, in respect of any one such claim, of a writ naming more than one ship or of two or more writs each naming a different ship.

APPENDIX 2
BILL OF SALE

(XS 79)

<table>
<tr><td>Prescribed by the Commissioners of Customs & Excise with the consent of the Secretary of State for Transport</td><td>**BILL OF SALE**</td><td>XS 79</td></tr>
</table>

Official number	Name of ship	Number, year and port of registry

	Feet	Tenths	Sailing, steam or motor ship	Horse power of engines (if any)
Length from fore part of stem, to the aft side of the head of the stern post/fore side of the rudder stock				
Main breadth to outside of plating			Gross tonnage	Register tonnage
Depth in hold from tonnage deck to ceiling amidships..				
			(Where dual tonnages are assigned the higher of these shouldbe stated)	

and as described in more detail in the Register Book

*I/We .... — Full name(s), address(es) and occupations of individuals, OR Full name and principal place of business of body corporate

....

....

.... hereinafter called 'the transferor(s)'

in consideration of the sum of .... paid to *me/us by

.... — Full name(s) and address(es) of transferee(s) with their occupation(s) in the case of individuals and adding "as joint owners" where such is the case

....

....

.... hereinafter called 'the transferee(s)'

the receipt whereof is hereby acknowledged, transfer .... shares in the said ship and in her boats and appurtenances to the said transferee(s).

Further, *I/We the said transferor(s) for *myself/ourselves and *my/our heirs or successors covenant with the said transferee(s) and *his/their/its assigns, that *I/we have power to transfer in manner aforesaid the premises hereinbefore expressed to be transferred, and that the

same are free from encumbrances .... (if any subsisting encumbrance add 'save as appears by the registry of the said ship')

For completion when sale is by Individual or Joint Owners

In witness whereof *I/We have hereunto subsribed *my/our name(s)

and affixed *my/our seal on .... 19........

Signature(s) of transferor(s) ....

Executed by the above named transferor(s) in the presence of:—   Seal

Witness:— Name ....

Address ....

Occupation ....

Signature of witness(es) .... (if the ship is registered in Scotland two witnesses are required.)

For completion when sale is by Body Corporate

In witness whereof we have hereunto affixed our common seal on .... 19.....   Seal

In the presence of:—

Signature of witness(es) .... Status .... (director, secretary etc.)

NOTES 1. A purchaser of a registered British ship does not obtain a complete title until the Bill of Sale has been recorded at the port of registry of the ship, and neglect of this precaution may entail serious consequences.

2. Registered owners or mortgagees are reminded of the importance of keeping the Registrar of British Ships informed of any change of residence on their part.

*Delete as necessary
XS 79   F 2059 (1985)   DU 4046/85 SEPT/MJ

APPENDIX 3
SALEFORM 1983

MEMORANDUM OF AGREEMENT

Norwegian Shipbrokers' Association's Memorandum of Agreement for sale and purchase of ships. Adopted by The Baltic and International Maritime Conference (BIMCO).
Code-name
SALEFORM 1983
Adopted 1956   Revised 1983

Dated:

hereinafter called the Sellers, have today sold, and   1

hereinafter called the Buyers, have today bought   2

Classification: 3
Built: by: 4
Flag: Place of Registration: 5
Call sign: Register tonnage: 6
Register number: 7
on the following conditions: 8

1. Price   9
Price: 10

2. Deposit   11
As a security for the correct fulfilment of this contract, the Buyers shall pay a deposit of 10% —   12
ten per cent — of the Purchase Money within   banking days from the date of this   13
agreement. This amount shall be deposited with   14

and held by them in a joint account for the Sellers and the Buyers. Interest, if any, to be credited the   15
Buyers. Any fee charged for holding said deposit shall be borne equally by the Sellers and the Buyers.   16

3. Payment   17
The saids Purchase Money shall be paid free of bank charges to   18

on delivery of the vessel, but not later than three banking days after the vessel is ready for delivery   19
and written or telexed notice thereof has been given to the Buyers by the Sellers.   20

4. Inspections   21
The Buyers shall have the right to inspect the vessel's classification records and declare whether   22
same are accepted or not within   23

The Sellers shall provide for inspection of the vessel at/in   24

The Buyers shall undertake the inspection without delay to the vessel. Should the Buyers   25
cause such delay, they shall compensate the Sellers for the losses thereby incurred.   26
The Buyers shall inspect the vessel afloat without opening up and without cost to the Sellers. Du-   27
ring the inspection, the vessels's log books for engine and deck shall be made available for the Buyer's 28
examination. If the vessel is accepted after such afloat inspection, the purchase shall become definite   29
— except for other possible subjects in this contract — provided the Sellers receive written or telexed   30
notice from the Buyers within 48 hours after completion of such afloat inspection. Should notice of   31
acceptance of the vessel's classification records and of the vessel not be received by the Sellers as   32
aforesaid, the deposit shall immediately be released, whereafter this contract shall be considered null   33
and void.   34

5. Place and time of delivery   35
The vessel shall be delivered and taken over at/in   36

Time of delivery/date of cancelling: 37

The Sellers shall keep the Buyers well posted about the vessel's itinerary and estimated time and   38
place of drydocking.   39
Should the vessel become a total or constructive total loss before delivery the deposit shall immedi-   40
ately be released to the Buyers and the contract thereafter considered null and void.   41

6. Drydocking   42
In connection with the delivery the Sellers shall place the vessel in drydock at the port of delivery   43
for inspection by the Classification Society of the bottom and other underwater parts below the Sum-   44
mer Load Line. If the rudder, propeller, bottom or other underwater parts below the Summer Load   45
Line be found broken, damaged or defective, so as to affect the vessel's clean certificate of class, such 46
defects shall be made good at the Seller's expense to[1]   47

satisfaction without qualification on such underwater parts.[2]   48
Whilst the vessel is in drydock, and if required by the Buyers or the representative of the Classifi-   49
cation Society, the Sellers shall arrange to have the tail-end shaft drawn. Should same be condemned   50
or found defective so as to affect the vessel's clean certificate of class, it shall be renewed or made   51
good at the Seller's expense to the Classification Society's satisfaction without qualification.   52
The expenses of drawing and replacing the tail-end shaft shall be borne by the Buyers unless the   53
Classification Society requires the tail-end shaft to be drawn (whether damaged or not), renewed or   54
made good in which event the Sellers shall pay these expenses.   55
The expenses in connection with putting the vessel in and taking her out of drydock, including dry-   56
dock dues and the Classification Surveyor's fees shal be paid by the Sellers, if the rudder, propeller,   57
bottom, other underwater parts below the Summer Load Line or the tail-end shaft be found broken,   58
damaged or defective as aforesaid or if the Classification Society requires the tail-end shaft to be   59
drawn (whether damaged or not). In all cases the Buyers shall pay the aforesaid expenses, dues   60
and fees.   61
During the above mentioned inspections by the Classification Society the Buyer's representative   62
shall have the right to be present in the drydock but without interfering with the Classification Surve- 63
yor's decisions.   64
The Sellers shall bring the vesel to the drydock and from the drydock to the place of delivery at   65
their own expense.   66

7. Spares/bunkers etc.

The Sellers shall deliver the vessel to the Buyers with everything belonging to her on board and on   67
shore. All spare parts and spare equipment including spare tail-end shaft(s) and/or spare propeller(s),   68
if any, belonging to the vessel at the time of inspection, used or unused, whether on board or not shall   69
become the Buyers' property, but spares on order to be excluded. Forwarding charges, if any, shall be   70
for the Buyers' account. The Sellers are not required to replace spare parts including spare tail-end   71
shaft(s) and spare propeller(s) which are taken out of spare and used as replacement prior to delivery,   72
but the replaced items shall be the property of the Buyers. The radio installation and navigational   73
equipment shall be included in the sale without extra payment, if same is the property of the Sellers.   74
                                                                                                                                75

The Sellers have the right to take ashore crockery, plate, cutlery, linen and other articles bearing   76
the Seller's flag or name, provided they replace same with similar unmarked items. Library, forms,   77
etc., exclusively for use in the Sellers' vessels, shall be excluded without compensation. Captain's   78
Officers' and Crew's personal belongings including slop chest to be excluded from the sale, as well as   79
the following additional items: 80

The Buyers shall take over remaining bunkers, unused lubricating oils and unused stores and pro-   81
visions and pay the current market price at the port and date of delivery of the vessel.   82
Payment under this clause shall be made at the same time and place and in the same currency as   83
the Purchase Money.   84

8. Documentation

In exchange for payment of the Purchase Money the Sellers shall furnish the Buyers with legal Bill   85
of Sale of the said vessel free from all encumbrances and maritime liens or any other debts whatsoe-   86
ver, duty notarially attested and legalised by the   consul toget-   87
her with a certificate stating that the vessel is free from registered encumbrances. On delivery of the   88
vessel the Sellers shall provide for the deletion of the vessel from the Registry of Vessels and deliver a   89
certificate of deletion to the Buyers. The deposit shall be placed at the disposal of the Sellers as well as   90
the balance of the Purchase Money, which shall be paid as agreed together with payment for items   91
mentioned in clause 7 above.   92
                                                                                                                                93

The Sellers shall, at the time of delivery, hand to the Buyers all classification certificates as well as   94
all plans etc. which are onboard the vessel. Other technical documentation which may be in the Sel-   95
lers' possession shall promptly upon the Buyers' instructions be forwarded to the Buyers. The   96
Sellers may keep the log books, but the Buyers to have the right to take copies of same.   97

9. Encumbrances

The Sellers warrant that the vessel, at the time of delivery, is free from all encumbrances and ma-   98
ritime liens or any other debts whatsoever. Should any claims which have been incurred prior to the   99
time of delivery be made against the vessel, the Sellers hereby undertake to indemnify the Buyers   100
against all consequences of such claims.   101
                                                                                                                                102

10. Taxes etc.

Any taxes, fees and expenses connected with the purchase and registration under the Buyers' flag   103
shall be for the Buyers' account, whereas similar charges connected with the closing of the Sellers' re-   104
gister shall be for the Sellers' account.   105
                                                                                                                                106

11. Condition on delivery

The vessel with everything belonging to her shall be at the Sellers' risk and expense until she is de-   107
livered to the Buyers, but subject to the conditions of this contract, she shall be delivered and taken   108
over as she is at the time of inspection, fair wear and tear excepted.   109
                                                                                                                                110

However, the vessel shall be delivered with present class free of recommendations. The Sellers   111
shall notify the Classification Society of any matters coming to their knowledge prior to delivery   112
which upon being reported to the Classification Society would lead to the withdrawal of the vessel's   113
class or to the imposition of a recommendation relating to her class.   114

12. Name/markings   115
Upon delivery the Buyers undertake to change the name of the vessel and alter funnel markings.   116

13. Buyers' default   117
Should the deposit not be paid as aforesaid, the Sellers have the right to cancel this contract, and   118
they shall be entitled to claim compensation for their losses and for all expenses incurred together   119
with interest at the rate of 12% per annum.   120
Should the Purchase Money not be paid as aforesaid, the Sellers have the right to cancel this con-   121
tract, in which case the amount deposited together with interest earned, if any, shall be forfeited to   122
the Sellers. If the deposit does not cover the Sellers' losses, they shall be entitled to claim further com-   123
pensation for their losses and for all expenses together with interest at the rate of 12% per annum.   124

14. Sellers' default   125
If the Sellers fail to execute a legal transfer or to deliver the vessel with everything belonging to her   126
in the manner and within the time herein specified, the Buyers shall have the right to cancel this con-   127
tract in which case the deposit in full shall be returned to the Buyers together with interest at the rate   128
of 12% per annum. The Sellers shall make due compensation for the losses caused to the Buyers by   129
failure to execute a legal transfer or to deliver the vessel in the manner and within the time herein   130
specified, if such are due to the proven negligence of the Sellers.   131

15. Arbitration   132
If any dispute should arise in connection with the interpretation and fulfilment of this contract,   133
same shall be decided by arbitration in the city of[3)]   134
and shall be referred to a single Arbitrator to be appointed by the parties hereto. If the parties cannot   135
agree upon the appointment of the single Arbitrator, the dispute shall be settled by three Arbitrators,   136
each party appointing one Arbitrator, the third being appointed by[4)]   137

If either of the appointed Arbitrators refuses or is incapable of acting, the party who appointed   138
him, shall appoint a new Arbitrator in his place.   139
If one of the parties fails to appoint an Arbitrator — either originally or by way of substitution —   140
for two weeks after the other party having appointed his Arbitrator has sent the party making default   141
notice by mail, cable or telex to make the appointment, the party appointing the third Arbitrator   142
shall, after application from the party having appointed his Arbitrator, also appoint an Arbitrator on   143
behalf of the party making default.   144
The award rendered by the Arbitration Court shall be final and binding upon the parties and may   145
if necessary be enforced by the Court or any other competent authority in the same manner as a   146
judgement in the Court of Justice.   147
This contract shall be subject to the law of the country agreed as place of arbitration.   148

---

1) The name of the Classification Society to be inserted.
2) Notes, if any, in the Surveyor's report which are accepted by the Classification Society without qualification are not to be taken into account.
3) The place of arbitration to be inserted. If this line is not filled in, it is understood that arbitration will take place in London in accordance with English law.
4) If this line is not filled in it is understood that the third Arbitrator shall be appointed by the London Maritime Arbitrators' Association in London.

Copyright: Norwegian Shipbrokers' Association, Oslo.
Sole distributor in England: Messrs. S. Straker & Sons Ltd. London.
Printed and sold by Halvorsen & Larsen A.s. Oslo.

APPENDIX 4
MORTGAGE TO SECURE
ACCOUNT CURRENT:
BODY CORPORATE
(XS 81a)

Prescribed by the Commissioners of Customs & Excise with the consent of the Secretary of State for Trade

MORTGAGE (to secure Account Current, &c.)

Form No. 12A   (Body Corporate)   **XS 81a**

Official number	Name of Ship	Number, year and port of registry	Whether a sailing, steam or motor ship	Horse power of engines (if any)

		Feet	Tenths
Length from fore part of stem, to the aft side of the head of the stern post/fore side of the rudder stock			
Main breadth to outside of plating			
Depth in hold from tonnage deck to ceiling amidships			

Number of Tons
(Where dual tonnages are assigned the higher of these should be stated)

Gross   Register

and as described in more detail in the Register Book

Whereas (ᵃ) ....

....

....in consideration of the premises for ourselves and our successor, covenant

Now we (ᵇ) ....(hereinafter called the mortgagee(s)

with the said (ᶜ) ....

and (ᵈ) ....assigns, to pay to him or them or it the sums for the time being due on this security, whether by way of principal or interest, at the times and manner aforesaid. And for the purpose of better securing to

the mortgagee(s) the payment of such sums at last aforesaid, we do hereby mortgage to the mortgagee(s) ....shares, of which we are the Owner in the Ship above particularly described, and in her boats and appurtenances.

Lastly, we for ourselves and our successors, covenant with the mortgagee(s) and (ᵈ) ....assigns that we have power to mortgage in manner aforesaid the above-mentioned shares, and that the

same are free from incumbrances (ᵉ) ....

In witness whereof we have hereunto affixed our common seal on 19

The Common Seal of the ....

was affixed hereunto in the presence of (ᶠ) ....

....

....

(a) Here state by way of recital that there is an account current between the mortgagor, giving the full name of the Body Corporate together with its principal place of business, and the mortgagee(s), giving full name(s), and address(es) with their description in the case of individuals and adding "as joint mortgagees" where such is the case and describe the nature of the transaction so as to show how the amount of principal and interest due at any given time is to be ascertained, and the manner and time of payment. (b) Name of the Body Corporate. (c) Full name of mortgagee. (d) "his", "their" or "its". (e) If any prior incumbrance add, "save as appears by the Registry of the said ship". (f) Signatures and description of witnesses, i.e. Director, Secretary, etc. (as the case may be).

NOTE. *The prompt registration of a Mortgage Deed at the port of registry of the ship is essential to the security of a Mortgagee, as a Mortgage take its priority from the date of production for registry, not from the date of the instrument.*

NOTE. *Registered Owners or Mortgagees are reminded of the importance of keeping the Registrar of British Ships informed of any change of residence on their part.*

(32683)   F. 183 (Nov. 1977)

APPENDIX 5
GENCON CHARTERPARTY

1. Shipbroker	RECOMMENDED THE BALTIC AND INTERNATIONAL MARITIME CONFERENCE UNIFORM GENERAL CHARTER (AS REVISED 1922 and 1976) INCLUDING "F.I.O." ALTERNATIVE, ETC. (To be used for trades for which no approved form is in force) CODE NAME: "GENCON" Part I
	2. Place and date
3. Owners/Place of business (Cl. 1)	4. Charterers/Place of business (Cl. 1)
5. Vessel's name (Cl. 1)	6. GRT/NRT (Cl. 1)
7. Deadweight cargo carrying capacity in tons (abt.) (Cl. 1)	8. Present position (Cl. 1)
9. Expected ready to load (abt.) (Cl. 1),	
10. Loading port or place (Cl. 1)	11. Discharging port or place (Cl. 1)
12. Cargo (also state quantity and margin in Owners' option, if agreed; if full and complete cargo not agreed state "part cargo") (Cl. 1)	
13. Freight rate (also state if payable on delivered or intaken quantity) (Cl. 1)	14. Freight payment (state currency and method of payment; also beneficiary and bank account) (Cl. 4)
15. Loading and discharging costs (state alternative (a) or (b) of Cl. 5; also indicate if vessel is gearless)	16. Laytime (if separate laytime for load. and disch. is agreed, fill in a) and b). If total laytime for load. and disch., fill in c) only) (Cl. 6)
	a) Laytime for loading
17. Shippers (state name and address) (Cl. 6)	b) Laytime for discharging
	c) Total laytime for loading and discharging
18. Demurrage rate (loading and discharging) (Cl. 7)	19. Cancelling date (Cl. 10)
20. Brokerage commission and to whom payable (Cl. 14)	
21. Additional clauses covering special provisions, if agreed.	

It is mutually agreed that this Contract shall be performed subject to the conditions contained in this Charter which shall include Part I as well as Part II. In the event of a conflict of conditions, the provisions of Part I shall prevail over those of Part II to the extent of such conflict.

Signature (Owners)	Signature (Charterers)

PART II
"Gencon" Charter (As Revised 1922 and 1976)
Including "F.I.O." Alternative, etc.

1. It is agreed between the party mentioned in Box 3 as Owners of the 1
steamer or motor-vessel named in Box 5, of the gross/nett Register 2
tons indicated in Box 6 and carrying about the number of tons of 3
deadweight cargo stated in Box 7, now in position as stated in Box 8 4
and expected ready to load under this Charter about the date in- 5
dicated in Box 9, and the party mentioned as Charterers in Box 4 6
that: 7
The said vessel shall proceed to the loading port or place stated 8
in Box 10 or so near thereto as she may safely get and lie always 9
afloat, and there load a full and complete cargo (if shipment of deck 10
cargo agreed same to be at Charterers' risk) as stated in Box 12 11
(Charterers to provide all mats and/or wood for dunnage and any 12
separations required, the Owners allowing the use of any dunnage 13
wood on board if required) which the Charterers bind themselves to 14
ship, and being so loaded the vessel shall proceed to the discharg- 15
ing port or place stated in Box 11 as ordered on signing Bills of 16
Lading or so near thereto as she may safely get and lie always 17
afloat and there deliver the cargo on being paid freight on delivered 18
or intaken quantity as indicated in Box 13 at the rate stated in 19
Box 13. 20

2. Owners' Responsibility Clause 21
Owners are to be responsible for loss of or damage to the goods 22
or for delay in delivery of the goods only in case the loss, damage 23
or delay has been caused by the improper or negligent stowage of 24
the goods (unless stowage performed by shippers/Charterers or their 25
stevedores or servants) or by personal want of due diligence on the 26
part of the Owners or their Manager to make the vessel in all respects 27
seaworthy and to secure that she is properly manned, equipped and 28
supplied or by the personal act or default of the Owners or their 29
Manager. 30
And the Owners are responsible for no loss or damage or delay 31
arising from any other cause whatsoever, even from the neglect or 32
default of the Captain or crew or some other person employed by the 33
Owners on board or ashore for whose acts they would, but for this 34
clause, be responsible, or from unseaworthiness of the vessel on 35
loading or commencement of the voyage or at any time whatsoever. 36
Damage caused by contact with or leakage, smell or evaporation 37
from other goods or by the inflammable or explosive nature or in- 38
sufficient package of other goods not to be considered as caused 39
by improper or negligent stowage, even if in fact so caused. 40

3. Deviation Clause 41
The vessel has liberty to call at any port or ports in any order, for 42
any purpose, to sail without pilots, to tow and/or assist vessels in 43
all situations, and also to deviate for the purpose of saving life and/ 44
or property. 45

4. Payment of Freight 46
The freight to be paid in the manner prescribed in Box 14 in cash 47
without discount on delivery of the cargo at mean rate of exchange 48
ruling on day or days of payment, the receivers of the cargo being 49
bound to pay freight on account during delivery, if required by Cap- 50
tain or Owners. 51
Cash for vessel's ordinary disbursements at port of loading to be 52
advanced by Charterers if required at highest current rate of ex- 53
change, subject to two per cent. to cover insurance and other ex- 54
penses. 55

5. Loading/Discharging Costs 56
* *(a) Gross Terms* 57
The cargo to be brought alongside in such a manner as to enable 58
vessel to take the goods with her own tackle. Charterers to procure 59
and pay the necessary men on shore or on board the lighters to do 60
the work there, vessel only heaving the cargo on board. 61
If the loading takes place by elevator, cargo to be put free in vessel's 62
holds, Owners only paying trimming expenses. 63
Any pieces and/or packages of cargo over two tons weight, shall be 64
loaded, stowed and discharged by Charterers at their risk and expense. 65
The cargo to be received by Merchants at their risk and expense 66
alongside the vessel not beyond the reach of her tackle. 67

* *(b) F.i.o. and free stowed/trimmed* 68
The cargo to be brought into the holds, loaded, stowed and/or trim- 69
med and taken from the holds and discharged by the Charterers or 70
their Agents, free of any risk, liability and expense whatsoever to the 71
Owners. 72
The Owners shall provide winches, motive power and winchmen from 73
the Crew if requested and permitted; if not, the Charterers shall 74
provide and pay for winchmen from shore and/or cranes, if any. (This 75
provision shall not apply if vessel is gearless and stated as such in 76
Box 15). 77
* *indicate alternative (a) or (b), as agreed, in Box 15.* 78

6. Laytime 79
* *(a) Separate laytime for loading and discharging* 80
The cargo shall be loaded within the number of running hours as 81
indicated in Box 16, weather permitting, Sundays and holidays ex- 82
cepted, unless used, in which event time actually used shall count. 83
The cargo shall be discharged within the number of running hours 84
as indicated in Box 16, weather permitting, Sundays and holidays ex- 85
cepted, unless used, in which event time actually used shall count. 86
* *(b) Total laytime for loading and discharging* 87
The cargo shall be loaded and discharged within the number of total 88
running hours as indicated in Box 16, weather permitting, Sundays and 89
holidays excepted, unless used, in which event time actually used 90
shall count. 91
(c) Commencement of laytime (loading and discharging) 92
Laytime for loading and discharging shall commence at 1 p.m. if 93
notice of readiness is given before noon, and at 6 a.m. next working 94
day if notice given during office hours after noon. Notice at loading 95
port to be given to the Shippers named in Box 17. 96
Time actually used before commencement of laytime shall count. 97
Time lost in waiting for berth to count as loading or discharging 98
time, as the case may be. 99
* *indicate alternative (a) or (b) as agreed, in Box 16.* 100

7. Demurrage 101
Ten running days on demurrage at the rate stated in Box 18 per 102
day or pro rata for any part of a day, payable day by day, to be 103
allowed Merchants altogether at ports of loading and discharging. 104

8. Lien Clause 105
Owners shall have a lien on the cargo for freight, dead-freight, 106
demurrage and damages for detention. Charterers shall remain re- 107
sponsible for dead-freight and demurrage (including damages for 108
detention), incurred at port of loading. Charterers shall also remain 109
responsible for freight and demurrage (including damages for deten- 110
tion) incurred at port of discharge, but only to such extent as the 111
Owners have been unable to obtain payment thereof by exercising 112
the lien on the cargo. 113

9. Bills of Lading 114
The Captain to sign Bills of Lading at such rate of freight as 115
presented without prejudice to this Charterparty, but should the 116
freight by Bills of Lading amount to less than the total chartered 117
freight the difference to be paid to the Captain in cash on signing 118
Bills of Lading. 119

10. Cancelling Clause 120
Should the vessel not be ready to load (whether in berth or not) on 121
or before the date indicated in Box 19, Charterers have the option 122
of cancelling this contract, such option to be declared, if demanded, 123
at least 48 hours before vessel's expected arrival at port of loading. 124
Should the vessel be delayed on account of average or otherwise, 125
Charterers to be informed as soon as possible, and if the vessel is 126
delayed for more than 10 days after the day she is stated to be 127
expected ready to load, Charterers have the option of cancelling this 128
contract, unless a cancelling date has been agreed upon. 129

11. General Average 130
General average to be settled according to York-Antwerp Rules, 131
1974, Proprietors of cargo to pay the cargo's share in the general 132
expenses even if same have been necessitated through neglect or 133
default of the Owners' servants (see clause 2). 134

12. Indemnity 135
Indemnity for non-performance of this Charterparty, proved damages, 136
not exceeding estimated amount of freight. 137

13. Agency 138
In every case the Owners shall appoint his own Broker or Agent both 139
at the port of loading and the port of discharge. 140

14. Brokerage 141
A brokerage commission at the rate stated in Box 20 on the freight 142
earned is due to the party mentioned in Box 20. 143
In case of non-execution at least 1/3 of the brokerage on the estimated 144
amount of freight and dead-freight to be paid by the Owners to the 145
Brokers as indemnity for the latter's expenses and work. In case of 146
more voyages the amount of indemnity to be mutually agreed. 147

15. GENERAL STRIKE CLAUSE 148
Neither Charterers nor Owners shall be responsible for the con- 149
sequences of any strikes or lock-outs preventing or delaying the 150
fulfilment of any obligations under this contract. 151
If there is a strike or lock-out affecting the loading of the cargo, 152
or any part of it, when vessel is ready to proceed from her last port 153
or at any time during the voyage to the port or ports of loading or 154
after her arrival there, Captain or Owners may ask Charterers to 155
declare, that they agree to reckon the laydays as if there were no 156
strike or lock-out. Unless Charterers have given such declaration in 157
writing (by telegram, if necessary) within 24 hours, Owners shall 158
have the option of cancelling this contract. If part cargo has already 159
been loaded, Owners must proceed with same, (freight payable on 160
loaded quantity only) having liberty to complete with other cargo 161
on the way for their own account. 162
If there is a strike or lock-out affecting the discharge of the cargo 163
on or after vessel's arrival at or off port of discharge and same has 164
not been settled within 48 hours, Receivers shall have the option of 165
keeping vessel waiting until such strike or lock-out is at an end 166
against paying half demurrage after expiration of the time provided 167
for discharging, or of ordering the vessel to a safe port where she 168
can safely discharge without risk of being detained by strike or lock- 169
out. Such orders to be given within 48 hours after Captain or Owners 170
have given notice to Charterers of the strike or lock-out affecting 171
the discharge. On delivery of the cargo at such port, all conditions 172
of this Charterparty and of the Bill of Lading shall apply and vessel 173
shall receive the same freight as if she had discharged at the 174
original port of destination, except that if the distance of the sub- 175
stituted port exceeds 100 nautical miles, the freight on the cargo 176
delivered at the substituted port to be increased in proportion. 177

16. War Risks ("Voywar 1950") 178
(1) In these clauses "War Risks" shall include any blockade or any 179
action which is announced as a blockade by any Government or by any 180
belligerent or by any organized body, sabotage, piracy, and any actual 181
or threatened war, hostilities, warlike operations, civil war, civil com- 182
motion, or revolution. 183
(2) If at any time before the Vessel commences loading, it appears that 184
performance of the contract will subject the Vessel or her Master and 185
crew or her cargo to war risks at any stage of the adventure, the Owners 186
shall be entitled by letter or telegram despatched to the Charterers, to 187
cancel this Charter. 188
(3) The Master shall not be required to load cargo or to continue 189
loading or to proceed on or to sign Bill(s) of Lading for any adventure 190
on which or any port at which it appears that the Vessel, her Master 191
and crew or her cargo will be subjected to war risks, in the event of 192
the exercise by the Master of his right under this Clause after part or 193
full cargo has been loaded, the Master shall be at liberty either to 194
discharge such cargo at the loading port or to proceed therewith. In 195
the latter case the Vessel shall have liberty to carry other cargo for 196
Owners' benefit and accordingly to proceed to and load or 197
discharge such other cargo at any other port or ports whatsoever, 198
backwards or forwards, although in a contrary direction to or out of or 199
beyond the ordinary route. In the event of the Master electing to 200
proceed with part cargo under this Clause freight shall in any case 201
be payable on the quantity delivered. 202
(4) If at the time the Master elects to proceed with part or full cargo 203
under Clause 3, or after the Vessel has left the loading port, or the 204

PART II
"Gencon" Charter (As Revised 1922 and 1976)
Including "F.I.O." Alternative, etc.

last of the loading ports, if more than one, it appears that further 205
performance of the contract will subject the Vessel, her Master and 206
crew or her cargo, to war risks, the cargo shall be discharged, or if 207
the discharge has been commenced shall be completed, at any safe 208
port in vicinity of the port of discharge as may be ordered by the 209
Charterers. If no such orders shall be received from the Charterers 210
within 48 hours after the Owners have despatched a request by 211
telegram to the Charterers for the nomination of a substitute discharg- 212
ing port, the Owners shall be at liberty to discharge the cargo at 213
any safe port which they may, in their discretion, decide on and such 214
discharge shall be deemed to be due fulfilment of the contract of 215
affreightment. In the event of cargo being discharged at any such 216
other port, the Owners shall be entitled to freight as if the discharge 217
had been effected at the port or ports named in the Bill(s) of Lading 218
or to which the Vessel may have been ordered pursuant thereto. 219

(5) (a) The Vessel shall have liberty to comply with any directions 220
or recommendations as to loading, departure, arrival, routes, ports 221
of call, stoppages, destination, zones, waters, discharge, delivery or 222
in any other wise whatsoever (including any direction or to delay proceeding 223
mendation not to go to the port of destination or to delay proceeding 224
thereto or to proceed to some other port) given by any Government or 225
by any belligerent or by any organized body engaged in civil war, 226
hostilities or warlike operations or by any person or body acting or 227
purporting to act as or with the authority of any Government or 228
belligerent or of any such organized body or by any committee or 229
person having under the terms of the war risks insurance on the 230
Vessel, the right to give any such directions or recommendations. If, 231
by reason of or in compliance with any such direction or recom- 232
mendation, anything is done or is not done, such shall not be deemed 233
a deviation. 234

(b) If, by reason of or in compliance with any such directions or re- 235
commendations, the Vessel does not proceed to the port or ports 236
named in the Bill(s) of Lading or to which she may have been 237
ordered pursuant thereto, the Vessel may proceed to any port as 238
directed or recommended or to any safe port which the Owners in 239
their discretion may decide on and there discharge the cargo. Such 240
discharge shall be deemed to be due fulfilment of the contract of 241
affreightment and the Owners shall be entitled to freight as if 242
discharge had been effected at the port or ports named in the Bill(s) 243
of Lading or to which the Vessel may have been ordered pursuant 244
thereto. 245

(6) All extra expenses (including insurance costs) involved in discharg- 246
ing cargo at the loading port or in reaching or discharging the cargo 247
at any port as provided in Clauses 4 and 5 (b) hereof shall be paid 248
by the Charterers and/or cargo owners. and the Owners shall have 249
a lien on the cargo for all moneys due under these Clauses. 250

17. GENERAL ICE CLAUSE 251
Port of loading 252

(a) In the event of the loading port being inaccessible by reason of 253
ice when vessel is ready to proceed from her last port or at any 254
time during the voyage or on vessel's arrival or in case frost sets in 255
after vessel's arrival, the Captain for fear of being frozen in is at 256
liberty to leave without cargo, and this Charter shall be null and 257
void. 258

(b) If during loading the Captain, for fear of vessel being frozen in, 259
deems it advisable to leave, he has liberty to do so with what cargo 260
he has on board and to proceed to any other port or ports with 261
option of completing cargo for Owners' benefit for any port or ports 262
including port of discharge. Any part cargo thus loaded under this 263
Charter to be forwarded to destination at vessel's expense but 264
against payment of freight, provided that no extra expenses be 265
thereby caused to the Receivers, freight being paid on quantity 266
delivered (in proportion if lumpsum), all other conditions as per 267
Charter. 268

(c) In case of more than one loading port, and if one or more of 269
the ports are closed by ice, the Captain or Owners to be at liberty 270
either to load the part cargo at the open port and fill up elsewhere 271
for their own account as under section (b) or to declare the Charter 272
null and void unless Charterers agree to load full cargo at the open 273
port. 274

(d) This Ice Clause not to apply in the Spring. 275

Port of discharge 276

(a) Should ice (except in the Spring) prevent vessel from reaching 277
port of discharge Receivers shall have the option of keeping vessel 278
waiting until the re-opening of navigation and paying demurrage, or 279
of ordering the vessel to a safe and immediately accessible port 280
where she can safely discharge without risk of detention by ice. 281
Such orders to be given within 48 hours after Captain or Owners 282
have given notice to Charterers of the impossibility of reaching port 283
of destination. 284

(b) If during discharging the Captain for fear of vessel being frozen 285
in deems it advisable to leave, he has liberty to do so with what 286
cargo he has on board and to proceed to the nearest accessible 287
port where she can safely discharge. 288

(c) On delivery of the cargo at such port, all conditions of the Bill 289
of Lading shall apply and vessel shall receive the same freight as 290
if she had discharged at the original port of destination, except that if 291
the distance of the substituted port exceeds 100 nautical miles, the 292
freight on the cargo delivered at the substituted port to be increased 293
in proportion. 294

APPENDIX 6: ACL BILL OF LADING

BILL OF LADING

B/L No.

Reference No.

Booking No.

ACL

Shipper/Exporter

Consigned to order of

Notify address

Pre-carriage by*   Place of receipt*

Vessel   Port of loading

Port of discharge   Place of delivery*

Marks and Nos; Container Nos.	Number and kind of packages; description of goods	Commodity No.	Gross weight, kg	Cube m³

Particulars above declared by Shipper

Freight and charges $

Shippers declared value $

Subject to extra freight as per tariff and clause 6 of this B/L

CARRIER'S RECEIPT – Received in apparent external good order and condition except as otherwise noted herein the containers whose numbers are listed above said to contain the goods or in the case of breakbulk cargo the number of pieces or packages listed above, to be transported to such place as agreed, authorized or permitted herein and there to be delivered to the authorized receiver. The shipment to be transported by the ocean vessel, feeder vessel or other means of transportation (rail, truck or air), subject to the terms and conditions noted on this page and overleaf and also when applicable subject to the Carrier's published tariffs on file with the Federal Maritime Commission Washington, D.C. USA or with the Canadian Transport Commission, Ottawa, Ont. Canada, such tariffs also being available from any port agent listed on the reverse side hereof. In accepting this Bill of Lading the Merchant agrees to be bound by its terms and conditions. ACL shall have the right to ship goods in containers and to stow all types of containers on deck or under deck. In witness of the contract herein the carrier has signed (   ) original Bill(s) of Lading, one of which being accomplished the other(s) to be void.

Freight payable at   Place and date of issue

Number of original Bs/L   For

ACL

As agents only

* Applicable only when document used as Through Bill of Lading

TERMS AND CONDITIONS

1. DEFINITIONS.
In this Bill of Lading ACL means Atlantic Container Line BV and the word "Carrier" includes ACL, the vessel and any of their employees, agents, contractors or sub-contractors. The words "Carriage by Water" and "vessel" shall include any substitute vessel, feeder ship, barge or watercraft. The word "Merchant" includes the shipper, the consignee, the holder of the Bill of Lading and the owner of the goods. The words "on board" mean on board any mode of transportation used or procured by the carrier, including rail, road and air transports.

2. CONTRACTING PARTIES.
The contract evidenced by this Bill of Lading is between the Merchant and ACL/the vessel. It is agreed that only ACL and the vessel *in rem* shall be liable as carriers under this contract. Claims may be sent to any ACL office or port agent listed above.

3. RESPONSIBILITY.
I. ACL shall be responsible for the goods from the time when the goods are received by ACL at the port of loading to the time when they are delivered or dispatched by ACL at the port of discharge, and also during any previous or subsequent periods of carriage by water under this Bill of Lading, and such custody and carriage shall be subject at all such times to the Hague Rules contained in the International Convention for the Unification of Certain Rules Relating to Bills of Lading dated 25th August, 1924, as amended by the Protocol signed at Brussels on the 23rd February, 1968 (Hague-Visby Rules), or to any legislation making such Rules, whether amended by the above Brussels Protocol or not, compulsorily applicable to this Bill of Lading, including the Carriage of Goods by Sea Act of the United States, approved April 16th, 1936, which Rules and Act shall be deemed to be incorporated herein. The provisions of said Act or Rules (except as otherwise specifically provided herein) shall govern before the shipment is loaded on and after it is discharged from the vessel while the shipment is in the custody and possession of the carrier. It is agreed that such Act or Rules shall also apply to containers carried on deck and that the carrier has the right to ship goods in containers stowed on deck or under deck.

II. When either the place of receipt of place of delivery set forth herein is an inland point in the USA or Europe, the responsibility of ACL with respect to the transportation to and from the sea terminal ports will be as follows

a) Within countries in Europe, to transport the goods in accordance with any mandatory national law or in the absence thereof, subject to the inland carrier's own contracts and tariffs.

b) Between countries in Europe, to transport the goods

(1) if by road, in accordance with the Convention on the Contract for the International Carriage of Goods by Road, dated 19th May, 1956 (CMR).

(2) if by rail, in accordance with the International Agreement on Railway Transports, dated 25th February, 1961 (CIM).

(3) if by air, in accordance with the Convention for the Unification on certain Rules relating to International Carriage by Air, signed Warsaw 12th October, 1929, as amended by the Hague Protocol, dated 28th September, 1955.

c) Between points in the USA or Canada, to procure transportation by carriers (one or more) authorized by competent authority to engage in transportation between such points, and such transportation shall be subject to the inland carrier's contracts of carriage and tariffs. ACL guaranties the fulfilment of such inland carriers' obligations under their contracts and tariffs.

III. As to services incident to through transportation, ACL undertakes to procure such services as necessary. All such services will be subject to the usual contracts of persons providing the services. ACL guaranties the fulfilment of the obligations of such persons under the pertinent contracts.

IV. When the goods have been damaged or lost during through-transportation and it cannot be established in whose custody the goods were when the damage or loss occurred, the damage or loss shall be deemed to have occurred during the carriage by water and the Hague Rules as defined above shall apply.

4. DELAY.
ACL does not accept responsibility for any direct or indirect loss or damage sustained by the Merchant through delay, unless ACL is liable for consequences of delay under any laws, statutes, agreements or conventions of a mandatory nature.

5. DEFENCES AND LIMITS FOR SERVANTS, ETC.
If an action for loss or damage to goods is brought against any insurer, servant, agent, independent contractor or sub contractor, including but not restricted to stevedores, carpenters or watchman, such person shall be entitled to avail himself of the defences and limits of liability which the carrier is entitled to invoke under this contract. For the purpose of this clause all such persons are entitled to this contract made on their behalf by the carrier. The aggregate of the amounts recoverable from the carrier or from the above mentioned persons shall in no case exceed the limits provided in this Bill of Lading.

6. PACKAGE/SHIPPING UNIT LIMITATION AND DECLARED VALUE.
The carrier shall not, unless a declared value has

TERMS AND CONDITIONS *(Continued)*

been noted in accordance with the below ad valorem section of this clause be or become liable for any loss or damage to or in connection with the transportation of goods in an amount per package or shipping unit limitation amount as laid down by the Hague Rules 1924, as amended by the Hague Rules 1924, as amended by the Hague Visby Rules 1968, or any legislation making these rules or part of these rules compulsorily applicable to this Bill of Lading.

Such limitation amount according to the Hague Rules 1924, is, in the United States in accordance with the US Carriage of Goods by Sea Act US$500 and in Canada, in accordance with the Water Carriage of Goods Act Can$500.

If no other limitation amount is applicable as either set forth above or statutory, the compensation shall not, however, exceed the equivalent of 10,000 poincare francs per package or unit or 30 poincare francs per kilogram of gross, weight of the goods, whichever is higher.

The words 'shipping unit' as used in the US Carriage of Goods by Sea Act shall mean each physical unit or piece of cargo not shipped in a package, including articles or things of any description whatsoever, except goods shipped in bulk and, irrespective of weight or measurement, units employed in calculating freight charges.

AD VALOREM: DECLARED VALUE OF PACKAGE OR UNIT.

The carrier's liability, if any, per package or shipping unit in accordance with the above package limitation section of this clause may be increased to a higher value per package or shipping unit by a declaration in writing to such an effect by the shipper upon delivery to the carrier, such higher value being inserted on the reverse page of this Bill of Lading and extra freight paid. In such case, if the actual value of the goods per package or per shipping unit shall exceed such declared value, the value shall nevertheless be deemed to be the declared value and the carrier's liability, if any, shall not exceed the declared value and any partial loss or damage shall be adjusted pro rata on the basis of such declared value.

7. TIME BAR.

All liability whatsoever of the carrier shall cease unless suit is brought within 12 months after delivery of the goods or the date when the goods should have been delivered.

8. PACKING AND MERCHANT-OWNED EQUIPMENT.

The Merchant shall be liable for any loss, damage or injury caused by faulty packing of goods within containers and trailers and on flats when such packing has been performed by the Merchant or on behalf of the Merchant.

ACL does not accept responsibility for the functioning of reefer containers or trailers, not owned nor leased by ACL.

9. ROUTE.

The goods may be carried by any route whatsoever, whether or not the most direct or advertised or customary route, via any ports or places in any order whatsoever and for whatsoever purpose visited, together with other goods of every kind, dangerous or otherwise whether stowed on or under deck. Vessels may sail with or without pilots, undergo repairs, adjust equipment, drydock and tow vessels in all situations.

10. SUBSTITUTION OF VESSEL AND TRANSHIPMENT.

ACL has the right, but not the obligation, to carry the goods by any substitute vessel, or by any otyher means of transport whether by water, land or air and may discharge the goods at any place for transhipment, tranship, land or store the goods either on shore or afloat and reship or forward the same.

11. DECK SHIPMENT.

ACL shall have the right to carry the goods on deck in containers.

12. DELIVERY OF GOODS.

If the goods are not taken by the Merchant within a reasonable time of ACL calling upon him to take delivery, ACL shall be at liberty to put the goods in safe custody on behalf of the Merchant at the Merchant's risk and expence.

13. FREIGHT AND CHARGES.

a) Freight to be paid in cash without discount and, whether prepayable or payable at destination, to be considered as earned on receipt of the goods and not to be returned, goods lost or not lost.

b) Freight and all other amounts mentioned in this B/L are, at the option of ACL, to be paid in the currency named in this B/L or of the country to the port of loading or port of discharge, at the highest selling rate of exchange for banker's sight draft current on the date of the freight agreement or on the date of this B/L, or for prepayable freight on the day of loading, or for freight payable at destination on the day when the vessel is entered at the Customs House or on the date of withdrawal of the delivery order.

If ACL has consented to payment of freight and charges in other currencies than US or Canadian dollars and such other currencies are devalued before payment, then the conversion of US or Canadian currencies shall be effected at the highest bank selling rate on the date of payment.

c) All dues, taxes and charges or other expenses in connection with the goods shall be paid by the Merchant.

d) The Merchant shall reimburse ACL in proportion to the amount of freight for any increase of war risk insurance premium and war risk increase of the wages of the Master, officers and crew and for any increase of the cost for bunkers and for deviation or delay caused by war or warlike operations or by government directions in such connection.

TERMS AND CONDITIONS *(Continued)*

c) The Merchant warrants the correctness of the delcaration of contents, insurance, weight, measurement or value of the goods but ACL reserves the right to have the contents inspected in order to ascertain the weight, measurement or value for the purpose of verifying the freight basis. If on such inspection it is found that the declaration is not correct it is agreed that a sum equal either to five times the difference between the correct freight and the freight charged or to double the correct freight less the freight charged, whichever sum is the smaller, shall be payable as liquidated damages to ACL notwithstanding any other sum having been stated on the B/L as freight payable. The Merchant shall hold the carrier harmless from any fines or damages resulting from any misdeclaration of description or of weight or measurement of goods.

14. LIEN.
ACL shall have a lien on the goods or part of the goods (including any Merchant owned containers or equipment) for any amount due to ACL under this Bill of Lading (and for costs of recovering same) and shall be entitled to sell or otherwise dispose of such goods to recover any such amounts and may enforce such lien in any reasonable manner.

15. GENERAL AVERAGE.
General Average to be adjusted at any port or place at the carrier's option, and to be settled according to the York-Antwerp Rules, 1974, this covering all goods, whether carried on or under deck. The amended Jason Clause to be considered as incorporated herein. Such security including a cash deposit as the carrier may deem sufficient to cover the estimated contribution by the goods and any salvage and special charges thereon, shall, if required, be submitted to the carrier prior to delivery of the goods.

16. HINDRANCES ETC. AFFECTING PERFORMANCE.
(1) The carrier shall use reasonable endeavors to complete the transport and to deliver the goods at the place designated for delivery.

(2) If at any time the performance of the contract as evidenced by this Bill of lading is or will be affected by any hindrance, risk, delay, difficulty or disadvantage of whatsoever kind, and if by virtue of sub-clause (1) the carrier has no duty to complete the performance of the contract, the carrier (whether or not the transport is commenced) may elect to.

   (a) treat the performance of this contract as terminated and place the goods at the Merchant's disposal at any place which the carrier shall deem safe and convenient; or

   (b) deliver the goods at the place designated for delivery.

In any event the carrier shall be entitled to full freight for goods received for transportation and additional compensation for extra costs resulting from the circumstances referred to above.

17. JURISDICTION.
Disputes arising under this Bill of lading shall be determined at the option of the Merchant either by the Commercial Court in London in accordance with English law or by the US District Court for the Southern District of New York in accordance with the laws of the United States. For traffic to or from Canada, jurisdiction will be limited to the Commercial Court in London only.

18. SEPARABILITY.
The terms of this Bill of Lading shall be separable, and if any provision hereof, or any part of any provision be held to be invalid or unenforceable, such holding shall not affect the validity or enforceability of any other provision or part thereof in this Bill of Lading.

GOODS OF DANGEROUS OR DAMAGING NATURE AND RADIOACTIVE MATERIAL MUST NOT BE TENDERED FOR SHIPMENT UNLESS WRITTEN NOTICE OF THEIR NATURE AND THE NAME AND ADDRESS OF THE SENDER AND THE RECEIVER HAVE BEEN PREVIOUSLY GIVEN TO ACL. SUB-CARRIERS, MASTER OR AGENT OF THE VESSEL AND THE NATURE IS DISTINCTLY MARKED ON THE OUTSIDE OF THE PACKAGE OR PACKAGES AS REQUIRED BY APPLICABLE STATUTES OR REGULATIONS AND IN ADDITION ON EACH CONTAINER, FLAT, TRAILER ETC. A SPECIAL STOWAGE ORDER GIVING CONSENT TO SHIPMENT MUST ALSO BE OBTAINED FROM ACL. THE MERCHANT WILL BE LIABLE FOR ALL CONSEQUENTIAL DAMAGE AND EXPENSE IF ALL THE FOREGOING PROVISIONS ARE NOT COMPLIED WITH.

APPENDIX 7
GCBS WAYBILL

NON-NEGOTIABLE SEA WAYBILL

UK Customs Assigned No. SWB No.

Shipper's Reference

F/Agent's Reference

Shipper

Consignee

Name of Carrier

Notify Party and Address (leave blank if stated above)

The contract evidenced by this Waybill is subject to the exceptions limitations conditions and liberties (including those relating to pre-carriage and on-carriage) set out in the Carrier's Standard Conditions of Carriage applicable to the voyage covered by this Waybill and operative on its date of issue; if the carriage is one where had a Bill of Lading been issued the provisions of the Hague Rules contained in the International Convention for unification of certain rules relating to Bills of Lading dated Brussels, 25th August 1924 as amended by the Protocol signed at Brussels on the 23rd February 1968 (the Hague Visby Rules) would have been compulsorily applicable under Article X, the said Standard Conditions contain or shall be deemed to contain a Clause giving effect to the Hague Visby Rules. Otherwise the said Standard Conditions contain or shall be deemed to contain a Clause giving effect to the provisions of the Hague Rules. In neither case shall the proviso to the first sentence of Article V of the Hague Rules or the Hague Visby Rules apply. The Carrier hereby agrees: (i) that to the extent of any inconsistency the said clause shall prevail over the said Standard Conditions in respect of any period to which the Hague Rules or the Hague Visby Rules by their terms apply, and (ii) that for the purpose of the terms of this Contract of Carriage this Waybill falls within the definition of Article 1 (b) of the Hague Rules and the Hague Visby Rules.
The Shipper accepts the said Standard Conditions on his own behalf and on behalf of the Consignee and the owner of the goods and warrants that he has authority to do so. The Consignee by presenting this Waybill and/or requesting delivery of the goods further undertakes all liabilities of the Shipper hereunder, such undertaking being additional and without prejudice to the Shippers own liability. The benefits of the contract, evidenced by this Waybill shall thereby be transferred to the Consignee or other persons presenting this Waybill.
Notwithstanding anything contained in the said Standard Conditions, the term Carrier in this Waybill shall mean the Carrier named on the front thereof.
A copy of the Carrier's said Standard Conditions applicable hereto may be inspected or will be supplied on request at the office of the Carrier or the Carrier's Principal Agents.

Pre-Carriage by★

Place of Receipt by Pre-Carrier★

Vessel

Port of Loading

Port of Discharge

Place of Delivery by On-Carrier★

Marks and Nos;	Container No.	Number and kind of packages; Description of Goods	Gross Weight	Measurement

Freight Details; Charges etc.

RECEIVED FOR CARRIAGE as above in apparent good order and condition, unless otherwise stated hereon, the goods described in the above particulars.

| GCBS |
| SWB |
| 1979 |

711

Ocean Freight Payable at

Place and Date of issue

Signature for Carrier; Carrier's Principal Place of Business

©**GCBS 1979**

Particulars declared by Shipper

★Applicable only when document used as a Through Bill of Lading

APPENDIX 8
BILLS OF LADING ACT 1855
(18 & 19 Vict c. 111)

WHEREAS, by the custom of merchants, a bill of lading of goods being transferable by endorsement, the property in goods may thereby pass to the endorsee, but nevertheless all rights in respect of the contract contained in the bill of lading continue in the original shipper or owner; and it is expedient that such rights should pass with the property: And whereas it frequently happens that the goods in respect of which bills of lading purport to be signed have not been laden on board, and it is proper that such bills of lading in the hands of a bona fide holder for value should not be questioned by the master or other person signing the same on the ground of the goods not having been laden as aforesaid:

1. Consignees, and endorsees of bills of lading empowered to sue. – Every consignee of goods named in a bill of lading, and every endorsee of a bill of lading, to whom the property in the goods therein mentioned shall pass upon or by reason of such consignment or endorsement, shall have transferred to and vested in him all rights of suit, and be subject to the same liabilities in respect of such goods as if the contract contained in the bill of lading had been made with himself.

2. Saving as to stoppage in transitu, and claims for freight, etc. – Nothing herein contained shall prejudice or affect any right of stoppage *in transitu*, or any right to claim freight against the original shipper or owner, or any liability of the consignee or endorsee by reason or in consequence of his being such consignee or endorsee, or of his receipt of the goods by reason or in consequence of such consignment or endorsement.

3. Bill of lading in hands of consignee, etc., conclusive evidence of shipment as against master, etc. – Every bill of lading in the hands of a consignee or endorsee for valuable consideration, representing goods to have been shipped on board a vessel, shall be conclusive evidence of such shipment as against the master or other person signing the same, notwithstanding that such goods or some part thereof may not have been so shipped, unless such holder of the bill of lading shall have had actual notice at the time of receiving the same that the goods had not been in fact laden on board: Provided, that the master or other person so signing may exonerate himself in respect of such misrepresentation by showing that it was caused without any default on his part, and wholly by the fraud of the shipper, or of the holder, or some person under whom the holder claims.

APPENDIX 9
CARRIAGE OF GOODS
BY SEA ACT 1971

An Act to amend the law with respect to the carriage of goods by sea.
[8th April 1971]

BE IT ENACTED by the Queen's most Excellent Majesty, by and
with the advice and consent of the Lords Spiritual and Temporal, and
Commons, in this present Parliament assembled, and by the authority
of the same, as follows:

1.–(1) In this Act, 'the Rules' means the International Convention for
the unification of certain rules of law relating to bills of lading signed at
Brussels on 25 August 1924, as amended by the Protocol signed at
Brussels on 23 February 1968 and by the protocol signed at Brussels on
21 December 1979.

(2) The provisions of the Rules, as set out in this Schedule to this Act,
shall have the force of law.

(3) Without prejudice to subsection (2) above, the said provisions shall
have effect (and have the force of law) in relation to and in connection
with the carriage of goods by sea in ships where the port of shipment is a
port in the United Kingdom, whether or not the carriage is between
ports in two different States within the meaning of Article X of the
Rules.

(4) Subject to subsection (6) below, nothing in this section shall be taken
as applying anything in the Rules to any contract for the carriage of
goods by sea, unless the contract expressly or by implication provides
for the issue of a bill of lading or any similar document of title.

[(5) – Repealed by the Merchant Shipping Act 1981, Sch.]

(6) Without prejudice to Article X *(c)* of the Rules, the Rules shall have the force of law in relation to –

(a) any bill of lading if the contract contained in or evidenced by it expressly provides that the Rules shall govern the contract, and

(b) any receipt which is a non-negotiable document marked as such if the contract contained in or evidenced by it is a contract for the carriage of goods by sea which expressly provides that the Rules are to govern the contract as if the receipt were a bill of lading,

but subject, where paragraph *(b)* applies, to any necessary modifications and in particular with the omission in Article III of the Rules of the second sentence of paragraph 4 and of paragraph 7.

(7) If and so far as the contract contained in or evidenced by a bill of lading or receipt within paragraph *(a)* or *(b)* of subsection (6) above applies to deck cargo or live animals, the Rules as given the force of law by that subsection shall have effect as if Article I *(c)* did not exclude deck cargo and live animals.

In this subsection "deck cargo" means cargo which by the contract of carriage is stated as being carried on deck and is so carried.

2.–(1) If Her Majesty by Order in Council certifies to the following effect, that is to say, that for the purposes of the Rules

(a) a State specified in the Order is a contracting State, or is a contracting State in respect of any place or territory so specified, or

(b) any place or territory specified in the Order forms part of a State so specified (whether a contracting State or not),

the Order shall, except so far as it has been superseded by a subsequent Order, be conclusive evidence of the matters so certified.

(2) An Order in Council under this section may be varied or revoked by a subsequent Order in Council.

3. There shall not be implied in any contract for the carriage of goods by sea to which the Rules apply by virtue of this Act any absolute undertaking by the carrier of the goods to provide a seaworthy ship.

4.–(1) Her Majesty may by Order in Council direct that this Act shall extend, subject to such exceptions, adaptations and modifications as may be specified in the Order, to all or any of the following territories, that is:

  (a) any colony (not being a colony for whose external relations a country other than the United Kingdom is responsible),

  (b) any country outside Her Majesty's dominions in which Her Majesty has jurisdiction in right of Her Majesty's Government of the United Kingdom.

(2) An Order in Council under this section may contain such transitional and other consequential and incidental provisions as appear to Her Majesty to be expedient, including provisions amending or repealing any legislation about the carriage of goods by sea forming part of the law of any of the territories mentioned in paragraphs (a) and (b) above.)

(3) An Order in Council under this section may be varied or revoked by a subsequent Order in Council.

5.–(1) Her Majesty may by Order in Council provide that section 1 (3) of this Act shall have effect as if the reference therein to the United Kingdom included a reference to all or any of the following territories, that is –

  (a) the Isle of Man;

  (b) any of the Channel Islands specified in the Order;

  (c) any colony specified in the Order (not being a colony for whose external relations a country other than the United Kingdom is responsible);

  (d) any associated state (as defined by section 1 (3) of the West Indies Act 1967) specified in the Order;

  (e) any country specified in the Order, being a country outside Her Majesty's dominions in which Her Majesty has jurisdiction in right of Her Majesty's Government of the United Kingdom.

(2) An Order in Council under this section may be varied or revoked by a subsequent Order in Council.

6.–(1) This Act may be cited as the Carriage of Goods by Sea Act 1971.

(2) It is hereby declared that this Act extends to Northern Ireland.

(3) The following enactments shall be repealed, that is–

(a) the Carriage of Goods by Sea Act 1924,

(b) section 12 (4) *(a)* of the Nuclear Installations Act 1965,

and without prejudice to section 38 (1) of the Interpretation Act 1889, the reference to the said Act of 1924 in section 1 (1) *(i)* (ii) of the Hovercraft Act 1968 shall include a reference to this Act.

(4) It is hereby declared that for the purposes of Article VIII of the Rules section 502 of the Merchant Shipping Act 1894 (which, as amended by the Merchant Shipping (Liability of Shipowners and Others) Act 1958, entirely exempts shipowners and others in certain circumstances from liability for loss of, or damage to, goods) is a provision relating to limitation of liability.

(5) This Act shall come into force on such day as Her Majesty may by Order in Council appoint, and, for the purposes of the transition from the law in force immediately before the day appointed under this subsection to the provisions of this Act, the Order appointing the day may provide that those provisions shall have effect subject to such transitional provisions as may be contained in the Order.

SCHEDULE

The Hague Rules as amended by the Brussels Protocol 1968.

Article I

In these Rules the following words are employed, with the meaning set out below:

(a) "Carrier" includes the owner or the charterer who enters into a contract of carriage with a shipper.

(b) "Contract of carriage" applies only to contracts of carriage covered by a bill of lading or any similar document of title, in so far as such document relates to the carriage of goods by sea, including any bill of lading or any similar document as aforesaid issued under or pursuant to a charter party from the moment at which such bill of lading or similar document of title regulates the relations between a carrier and a holder of the same.

(c) "Goods" includes goods, wares, merchandise, and articles of every kind whatsoever except live animals and cargo which by the contract of carriage is stated as being carried on deck and is so carried.

(d) "Ship" means any vessel used for the carriage of goods by sea.
(e) "Carriage of goods" covers the period from the time when the goods are loaded on to the time they are discharged from the ship.

Article II

Subject to the provisions of Article VI, under every contract of carriage of goods by sea the carrier, in relation to the loading, handling, stowage, carriage, custody, care and discharge of such goods, shall be subject to the responsibilities and liabilities, and entitled to the rights and immunities hereinafter set forth.

Article III

1. The carrier shall be bound before and at the beginning of the voyage to exercise due diligence to –
   (a) Make the ship seaworthy.
   (b) Properly man, equip and supply the ship.
   (c) Make the holds, refrigerating and cool chambers, and all other parts of the ship in which goods are carried, fit and safe for their reception, carriage and preservation.

2. Subject to the provisions of Article IV, the carrier shall properly and carefully load, handle, stow, carry, keep, care for, and discharge the goods carried.

3. After receiving the goods into his charge the carrier or the master or agent of the carrier shall, on demand of the shipper, issue to the shipper a bill of lading showing among other things –
   (a) The leading marks necessary for identification of the goods as the same are furnished in writing by the shipper before the loading of such goods starts, provided such marks are stamped or otherwise shown clearly upon the goods if uncovered, or on the cases or coverings in which such goods are contained, in such a manner as should ordinarily remain legible until the end of the voyage.
   (b) Either the number of packages or pieces, or the quantity, or weight, as the case may be, as furnished in writing by the shipper.

(c) The apparent order and condition of the goods.

Provided that no carrier, master or agent of the carrier shall be bound to state or show in the bill of lading any marks, number, quantity, or weight which he has reasonable ground for suspecting not accurately to represent the goods actually received, or which he has had no reasonable means of checking.

4. Such a bill of lading shall be prima facie evidence of the receipt by the carrier of the goods as therein described in accordance with paragraph 3 *(a)*, *(b)* and *(c)*. However, proof to the contrary shall not be admissible when the bill of lading has been transferred to a third party acting in good faith.

5. The shipper shall be deemed to have guaranteed to the carrier the accuracy at the time of shipment of the marks, number, quantity and weight, as furnished by him, and the shipper shall indemnify the carrier against all loss, damages and expenses arising or resulting from inaccuracies in such particulars. The right of the carrier to such indemnity shall in no way limit his responsibility and liability under the contract of carriage to any person other than the shipper.

6. Unless notice of loss or damage and the general nature of such loss or damage be given in writing to the carrier or his agent at the port of discharge before or at the time of the removal of the goods into the custody of the person entitled to delivery thereof under the contract of carriage, or, if the loss or damage be not apparent, within three days, such removal shall be prima facie evidence of the delivery by the carrier of the goods as described in the bill of lading.

The notice in writing need not be given if the state of the goods has, at the time of their receipt, been the subject of joint survey or inspection.

Subject to paragraph 6*bis* the carrier and the ship shall in any event be discharged from all liability whatsoever in respect of the goods, unless suit is brought within one year of their delivery or of the date when they should have been delivered. This period may, however, be extended if the parties so agree after the cause of action has arisen.

In the case of any actual or apprehended loss or damage the carrier and the receiver shall give all reasonable facilities to each other for inspecting and tallying the goods.

6*bis*. An action for indemnity against a third person may be brought even after the expiration of the year provided for in the preceding paragraph if brought within the time allowed by the law of the Court seized of the case. However, the time allowed shall be not less than three months, commencing from the day when the person bringing such action for indemnity has settled the claim or has been served with process in the action against himself.

7. After the goods are loaded the bill of lading to be issued by the carrier, master, or agent of the carrier, to the shipper shall, if the shipper so demands, be a "shipped" bill of lading, provided that if the shipper shall have previously taken up any document of title to such goods, he shall surrender the same as against the issue of the "shipped" bill of lading, but at the option of the carrier such document of title may be noted at the port of shipment by the carrier, master, or agent with the name or names of the ship or ships upon which the goods have been shipped and the date or dates of shipment, and when so noted, if it shows the particulars mentioned in paragraph 3 of Article III, shall for the purpose of this article be deemed to constitute a "shipped" bill of lading.

8. Any clause, covenant, or agreement in a contract of carriage relieving the carrier or the ship from liability for loss or damage to, or in connection with, goods arising from negligence, fault or failure in the duties and obligations provided in this article or lessening such liability otherwise than as provided in these Rules, shall be null and void and of no effect. A benefit of insurance in favour of the carrier or similar clause shall be deemed to be a clause relieving the carrier from liability.

Article IV

1. Neither the carrier nor the ship shall be liable for loss or damage arising or resulting from unseaworthiness unless caused by want of due diligence on the part of the carrier to make the ship seaworthy, and to secure that the ship is properly manned, equipped and supplied, and to make the holds, refrigerating and cool chambers and all other parts of the ship in which goods are carried fit and safe for their reception, carriage and preservation in accordance with the provisions of paragraph 1 of Article III. Whenever loss or damage has resulted from unseaworthiness the burden of proving the exercise of due diligence shall be on the carrier or other person claiming exemption under this article.

2. Neither the carrier nor the ship shall be responsible for loss or damage arising or resulting from –

(a) Act, neglect, or default of the master, mariner, pilot, or the servants of the carrier in the navigation or in the management of the ship.

(b) Fire, unless caused by the actual fault or privity of the carrier.

(c) Perils, dangers and accidents of the sea or other navigable waters.

(d) Act of God.

(e) Act of war.

(f) Act of public enemies.

(g) Arrest or restraint of princes, rulers or people, or seizure under legal process.

(h) Quarantine restrictions.

(i) Act or omission of the shipper or owner of the goods, his agent or representative.

(j) Strikes or lockouts or stoppage or restraint of labour from whatever cause, whether partial or general.

(k) Riots and civil commotions.

(l) Saving or attempting to save life or property at sea.

(m) Wastage in bulk or weight or any other loss or damage arising from inherent defect, quality or vice of the goods.

(n) Insufficiency of packing.

(o) Insufficiency or inadequacy of marks.

(p) Latent defects not discoverable by due diligence.

(q) Any other cause arising without the actual fault or privity of the carrier, or without the fault or neglect of the agents or servants of the carrier, but the burden of proof shall be on the person claiming the benefit of this exception to show that neither the actual fault or privity of the carrier nor the fault or neglect of the agents or servants of the carrier contributed to the loss or damage.

3. The shipper shall not be responsible for loss or damage sustained by the carrier or the ship arising or resulting from any cause without the act, fault or neglect of the shipper, his agents or his servants.

4. Any deviation in saving or attempting to save life or property at sea or any reasonable deviation shall not be deemed to be an infringement or breach of these Rules or of the contract of carriage, and the carrier shall not be liable for any loss or damage resulting therefrom.

(5) *(a)* Unless the nature and value of such goods have been declared by the shipper before shipment and inserted in the bill of lading, neither the carrier nor the ship shall in any event be or become liable for any loss or damage to or in connection with the goods in an amount exceeding 666.67 units of account per package or unit or 2 units of account per kilogramme weight of the goods lost or damaged, whichever is the higher.

(b) The total amount recoverable shall be calculated by reference to the value of such goods at the place and time at which the goods are discharged from the ship in accordance with the contract or should have been so discharged.

The value of the goods shall be fixed according to the commodity exchange price, or, if there be no such price, according to the current market price, or, if there be no commodity exchange price or current market price, by reference to the normal value of goods of the same kind and quality.

(c) Where a container, pallet or similar article of transport is used to consolidate goods, the number of packages or units enumerated in the bill of lading as packed in such article of transport shall be deemed the number of packages or units for the purpose of this paragraph as far as these packages or units are concerned. Except as aforesaid such article of transport shall be considered the package or unit.

(d) The unit of account mentioned in this Article is the special drawing right as defined by the International Monetary Fund. The amounts mentioned in sub-paragraph (a) of this paragraph shall be converted into national currency on the basis of the value of that currency on a date to be determined by the law of the Court seized of the case.

(e) Neither the carrier nor the ship shall be entitled to the benefit of the limitation of liability provided for in this paragraph if it is proved that the damage resulted from an act or omission of the carrier done with intent to cause damage, or recklessly and with knowledge that damage would probably result.

(f) The declaration mentioned in sub-paragraph *(a)* of this paragraph, if embodied in the bill of lading, shall be prima facie evidence, but shall not be binding or conclusive on the carrier.

(g) By agreement between the carrier, master or agent of the carrier and the shipper other maximum amounts than those mentioned in sub-paragraph *(a)* of this paragraph may be fixed, provided that no maximum amount so fixed shall be less than the appropriate maximum mentioned in that sub-paragraph.

(h) Neither the carrier nor the ship shall be responsible in any event for loss or damage to, or in connection with, goods if the nature or value thereof has been knowingly mis-stated by the shipper in the bill of lading.

6. Goods of an inflammable, explosive or dangerous nature to the shipment whereof the carrier, master or agent of the carrier has not consented with knowledge of their nature and character, may at any time before discharge be landed at any place, or destroyed or rendered innocuous by the carrier without compensation and the shipper of such goods shall be liable for all damages and expenses directly or indirectly arising out of or resulting from such shipment. If any such goods shipped with such knowledge and consent shall become a danger to the ship or cargo, they may in like manner be landed at any place, or destroyed or rendered innocuous by the carrier without liability on the part of the carrier except to general average, if any.

Article IV *bis*

1. The defences and limits of liability provided for in these Rules shall apply in any action against the carrier in respect of loss or damage to goods covered by a contract of carriage whether the action be founded in contract or in tort.

2. If such an action is brought against a servant or agent of the carrier (such servant or agent not being an independent contractor), such servant or agent shall be entitled to avail himself of the defences and limits of liability which the carrier is entitled to invoke under these Rules.

3. The aggregate of the amounts recoverable from the carrier, and such servants and agents, shall in no case exceed the limit provided for in these Rules.

4. Nevertheless, a servant or agent of the carrier shall not be entitled to avail himself of the provisions of this article, if it is proved that the damage resulted from an act or omission of the servant or agent done with intent to cause damage or recklessly and with knowledge that damage would probably result.

Article V

A carrier shall be at liberty to surrender in whole or in part all or any of his rights and immunities or to increase any of his responsibilities and obligations under these Rules, provided such surrender or increase shall be embodied in the bill of lading issued to the shipper. The provisions of these Rules shall not be applicable to charter parties, but if bills of lading are issued in the case of a ship under a charter party they shall comply with the terms of these Rules. Nothing in these Rules shall be held to prevent the insertion in a bill of lading of any lawful provision regarding general average.

Article VI

Notwithstanding the provisions of the preceding articles, a carrier, master or agent of the carrier and a shipper shall in regard to any particular goods be at liberty to enter into any agreement in any terms as to the responsibility and liability of the carrier for such goods, and as to the rights and immunities of the carrier in respect of such goods, or his obligation as to seaworthiness, so far as this stipulation is not contrary to public policy, or the care or diligence of his servants or agents in regard to the loading, handling, stowage, carriage, custody, care and discharge of the goods carried by sea, provided that in this case no bill of lading has been or shall be issued and that the terms agreed shall be embodied in a receipt which shall be a non-negotiable document and shall be marked as such.

Any agreement so entered into shall have full legal effect.

Provided that this article shall not apply to ordinary commercial shipments made in the ordinary course of trade, but only to other shipments where the character or condition of the property to be carried or the circumstances, terms and conditions under which the carriage is to be performed are such as reasonably to justify a special agreement.

Article VII

Nothing herein contained shall prevent a carrier or a shipper from entering into any agreement, stipulation, condition, reservation or exemption as to the responsibility and liability of the carrier or the ship for the loss or damage to, or in connection with, the custody and care and handling of goods prior to the loading on, and subsequent to the discharge from, the ship on which the goods are carried by sea.

Article VIII

The provisions of these Rules shall not affect the rights and obligations of the carrier under any statute for the time being in force relating to the limitation of the liability of owners of sea-going vessels.

Article IX

These Rules shall not affect the provisions of any International Convention or national law governing liability for nuclear damage.

Article X

The provisions of these Rules shall apply to every bill of lading relating to the carriage of goods between ports in two different States if:
- (a)   the bill of lading is issued in a contracting State,
  or
- (b)   the carriage is from a port in a contracting State,
  or
- (c)   the contract contained in or evidenced by the bill of lading provides that these Rules or legislation of any State giving effect to them are to govern the contract,

whatever may be the nationality of the ship, the carrier, the shipper, the consignee, or any other interested person.

[The last two paragraphs of this article are not reproduced. They require contracting States to apply the Rules to bills of lading mentioned in the article and authorize them to apply the Rules to other bills of lading.]

[Articles 11 to 16 of the International Convention for the unification of certain rules of law relating to bills of lading signed at Brussels on 25 August 1924 are not reproduced. They deal with the coming into force of the Convention, procedure for ratification, accession and denunciation, and the right to call for a fresh conference to consider amendments to the Rules contained in the Convention.]

APPENDIX 10
UK STANDARD CONDITIONS FOR TOWAGE AND OTHER SERVICES
(Revised 1983)

1. (a) The agreement between the Tugowner and the Hirer is and shall at all times be subject to and include each and all of the conditions hereinafter set out.

(b) for the purposes of these conditions

(i) "towing" is any operation in connection with the holding, pushing, pulling, moving, escorting or guiding of or standing by the Hirer's vessel, and the expressions "to tow", "being towed" and "towage" shall be defined likewise.

(ii) "vessel" shall include any vessel, craft or object of whatsoever nature (whether or not coming within the usual meaning of the word "vessel") which the Tugowner agrees to tow or to which the Tugowner agrees at the request, express or implied, of the Hirer, to render any service of whatsoever nature other than towing.

(iii) "tender" shall include any vessel, craft or object of whatsoever nature which is not a tug but which is provided by the Tugowner for the performance of any towage or other service.

(iv) The expression "whilst towing" shall cover the period commencing when the tug or tender is in a position to receive orders direct from the Hirer's vessel to commence holding, pushing, pulling, moving, escorting, guiding or standing by the vessel or to pick up ropes, wires or lines, or when the towing line has been passed to or by the tug or tender, whichever is the sooner, and ending when the final orders from the Hirer's vessel to cease holding, pushing, pulling, moving, escorting, guiding or standing by the vessel or to cast off ropes, wires or lines has been carried out, or the towing line has been finally slipped, whichever is the later, and the tug or tender is safely clear of the vessel.

(v) Any service of whatsoever nature to be performed by the Tugowner other than towing shall be deemed to cover the period commencing when the tug or tender is placed physically at the disposal of the Hirer at the place designated by the Hirer, or, if such be at a vessel, when the tug or tender is in a position to receive and forthwith carry out orders to come alongside and shall continue until the employment for which the tug or tender has been engaged is ended. If the service is to be ended at or off a vessel the period of service shall end when the tug or tender is safely clear of the vessel or, if it is to be ended elsewhere, then when any persons or property of whatsoever description have been landed or discharged from the tug or tender and/or the service for which the tug or tender has been required is ended.

(vi) The word "tug" shall include "tugs", the word "tender" shall include "tenders", the word "vessel" shall include "vessels", the word "Tugowner" shall include "Tugowners", and the word "Hirer' shall include "Hirers".

(vii) The expresion "tugowner" shall include any person or body (other than the Hirer or the owner of the vessel on whose behalf the Hirer contracts as provided in Clause 2 hereof) who is a party to this agreement whether or not he in fact owns any tug or tender, and the expression "other Tugowner" contained in Clause 5 hereof shall be construed likewise.

2.   If at the time of making this agreement or of performing the towage or of rendering any service other than towing at the request, express or implied, of the Hirer, the Hirer is not the Owner of the vessel referred to herein as "the Hirer's vessel", the Hirer expressly represents that he is authorised to make and does make this agreement for and on behalf of the owner of the said vessel subject to each and all of these conditions and agrees that both the Hirer and the owner are bound jointly and severally by these conditions.

3.   Whilst towing or whilst at the request, express or implied, of the Hirer, rendering any service other than towing, the master and crew of the tug or tender shall be deemed to be the servants of the Hirer and under the control of the Hirer and/or his servants and/or his agents, and anyone on board the Hirer's vessel who may be employed and/or paid by the Tugowner shall likewise be deemed to be the servant of the Hirer and the Hirer shall accordingly be vicariously liable for any act or omission by any such person so deemed to be the servant of the Hirer.

4.   Whilst towing, or whilst at the request, either expressed or implied, of the Hirer rendering any service of whatsoever nature other than towing:-

(a)   The Tugowner shall not (except as provided in Clauses 4 (c) and (e) hereof) be responsible for or be liable for

(i) damage of any description done by or to the tug or tender; or done by or to the Hirer's vessel or done by or to any cargo or other thing on board or being loaded on board or intended to be loaded on board the Hirer's vessel or the tug or tender or to or by any other object or property
or

(ii) loss of the tug or tender or the Hirer's vessel or of any cargo or other thing on board or being loaded on board or intended to be loaded on board the Hirer's vessel or the tug or tender or any other object or property;
or

(iii) any claim by a person not a party to this agreement for loss or damage of any description whatsoever;

arising from any cause whatsoever, including (without prejudice to the generality of the foregoing) negligence at any time of the Tugowner his servants or agents, unseaworthiness, unfitness or breakdown of the tug or tender, its machinery, boilers, towing gear, equipment, lines, ropes or wires, lack of fuel, stores, speed or otherwise and

(b)   The Hirer shall (except as provided in Clauses 4(c) and (e)) be responsible for, pay for and indemnify the Tugowner against and in respect of any loss or damage and any claims of whatsoever nature or howsoever arising or caused, whether covered by the provisions of Clause 4(a) hereof or not, suffered by or made against the Tugowner and which shall include, without prejudice to the generality of the foregoing, any loss of or damage to the tug or tender or any property of the Tugowner even if the same arises from or is caused by the negligence of the Tugowner his servants or agents.

(c)   The provisions of Clauses 4(a) and 4(b) hereof shall not be applicable in respect of any claims which arise in any of the following circumstances:-

    (i)   All claims which the Hirer shall prove to have resulted directly and solely from the personal failure of the Tugowner to exercise reasonable care to make the tug or tender seaworthy for navigation at the commencement of the towing or other service. For the purpose of this Clause the Tugowner's personal responsibility for exercising reasonable care shall be construed as relating only to the person or persons having the ultimate control and chief management of the Tugowner's business and to any servant (excluding the officers and crew of any tug or tender) to whom the Tugowner has specifi-cally delegated the particular duty of exercising reasonable care and shall not include any other servant of the Tugowner or any agent or independent contractor employed by the Tugowner.

    (ii)   All claims which arise when the tug or tender, although towing or rendering some service other than towing, is not in a position of proximity or risk to or from the Hirer's vessel or any other craft attending the Hirer's vessel and is detached from and safely clear of any ropes, lines, wire cables or moorings associated with the Hirer's vessel. Provided always that, notwithstanding the foregoing, the provisions of Clauses 4(a) and 4(b) shall be fully applicable in respect of all claims which arise at any time when the tug or tender is at the request, whether express or implied, of the Hirer, his servants or his agents, carrying persons or property of whatsoever description (in addition to the Officers and crew and usual equipment of the tug or tender) and which are wholly or partly caused by or arise out of the presence on board of such persons or property or which arise at anytime when the tug or tender is proceeding to or from the Hirer's vessel in hazardous conditions or circumstances.

(d)   Notwithstanding anything hereinbefore contained, the Tugowner shall under no circumstances whatsoever be responsible for or be liable for any loss or damage caused by or contributed to or arising out of any delay or detention of the Hirer's vessel or of the cargo on board or being loaded on board or intended to be loaded on board the Hirer's vessel or of any other object or property or of any person, or any consequence therof, whether or not the same shall be caused or arise whilst towing or whilst at the request, either express or implied, of the Hirer rendering any service of whatsoever nature other than towing or at any other time whether before during or after the making of this agreement.

(e)   Notwithstanding anything contained in Clauses 4(a) and (b) hereof the liability of the Tugowner for death or personal injury resulting from negligence is not excluded or restricted thereby.

5.   The Tugowner shall at any time be entitled to substitute one or more tugs or tenders for any other tug or tender or tugs or tenders. The Tugowner shall at any time (whether before or after the making of this agreement between him and the Hirer) be entitled to contract with any other Tugowner (hereinafter referred to as "the other Tugowner") to hire the other Tugowner's tug or tender and in any such event it is hereby agreed that the

Tugowner is acting (or is deemed to have acted) as the agent for the Hirer, notwithstanding that the Tugowner may in addition, if authorised whether expressly or impliedly by or on behalf of the other Tugowner, act as agent for the other Tugowner at any time and for any purpose including the making of any agreement with the Hirer. In any event should the Tugowner as agent for the Hirer contract with the other Tugowner for any purpose as aforesaid it is hereby agreed that such contract is and shall at all times be subject to the provisions of these conditions so that the other Tugowner is bound by the same and may as a principal sue the Hirer thereon and shall have the full benefit of these conditions in every respect expressed or implied herein.

6.   Nothing contained in these conditions shall limit, prejudice or preclude in any way any legal rights which the Tugowner may have against the Hirer including, but not limited to, any rights which the Tugowner or his servants or agents may have to claim salvage remuneration or special compensation for any extraordinary services rendered to vessels or anything aboard vessels by any tug or tender. Furthermore, nothing contained in these conditions shall limit, prejudice, or preclude in any way any right which the Tugowner may have to limit his liability.

7.   The Tugowner will not in any event be responsbile or liable for the consequences of war, riots, civil commotions, acts of terrorism or sabotage, strikes, lockouts, disputes, stoppages or labour disturbances (whether he be a party thereto or not) or anything done in contemplation or furtherance thereof or delays of any description, howsoever caused or arising, including by the negligence of the Tugowner or his servants or agents.

8.   The Hirer of the tug or tender engaged subject to these conditions undertakes not to take or cause to be taken any proceedings against any servant or agent of the Tugowner or other Tugowner, whether or not the tug or tender substituted or hired or the contract or any part thereof has been sublet to the owner of the tug or tender, in respect of any negligence or breach of duty or other wrongful act on the part of such servant or agent which, but for this present provision, it would be competent for the Hirer so to do and the owners of such tug or tender shall hold this undertaking for the benefit of their servants and agents.

9.   (a)   The agreement between the Tugowner and the Hirer is and shall be governed by English Law and the Tugowner and the Hirer hereby accept, subject to the proviso contained in sub-clause (b) hereof, the exclusive jurisdiction of the English Courts (save where the registered office of the Tugowner is situated in Scotland when the agreement is and shall be governed by Scottish Law and the Tugowner and the Hirer hereby shall accept the exclusive jurisdiction of the Scottish Courts.

(b)   No suit shall be brought in any jurisdiction other than that provided in sub-clause (a) hereof save that either the Tugowner or the Hirer shall have the option to bring proceedings in rem to obtain the arrest of or other similar remedy against any vessel or property owned by the other party hereto in any jurisdiction where such vessel or property may be found.

APPENDIX 11
LLOYD'S STANDARD FORM
OF SALVAGE AGREEMENT

LOF 1980

LLOYD'S

®

STANDARD FORM OF

SALVAGE AGREEMENT

(APPROVED AND PUBLISHED BY THE COMMITTEE OF LLOYD'S)

NO CURE—NO PAY

NOTES.
1. Insert name of person signing on behalf of Owners of property to be salved. The Master should sign wherever possible.
2. The Contractor's name should always be inserted in line 3 and whenever the Agreement is signed by the Master of the Salving vessel or other person on behalf of the Contractor the name of the Master or other person must also be inserted in line 3 before the words "for and on behalf of". The words "for and on behalf of" should be deleted where a Contractor signs personally.
3. Insert place if agreed in Clause 1(a) and currency if agreed in Clause 1(c).

On board the
Dated   19

† See Note 1 above

IT IS HEREBY AGREED between Captain†   for and on behalf of the Owners of the "   " her cargo freight bunkers and stores and   for and on behalf of

*See Note 2 above

(hereinafter called "the Contractor"*):—

1. (a) The Contractor agrees to use his best endeavours to salve the

‡See Note 3 above

and/or her cargo bunkers and stores and take them to‡   or other place to be hereafter agreed or if no place is named or agreed to a place of safety. The Contractor further agrees to use his best endeavours to prevent the escape of oil from the vessel while performing the services of salving the subject vessel and/or her cargo bunkers and stores. The services shall be rendered and accepted as salvage services upon the principle of "no cure—no pay" except that where the property being salved is a tanker laden or partly laden with a cargo of oil and without negligence on the part of the Contractor and/or his Servants and/or Agents (1) the services are not successful or (2) are only partially successful or (3) the Contractor is prevented from completing the services the Contractor shall nevertheless be awarded solely against the Owners of such tanker his reasonably incurred expenses and an increment not exceeding 15 per cent of such expenses but only if and to the extent that such expenses together with the increment are greater than any amount otherwise recoverable under this Agreement. Within the meaning of the said exception to the principle of "no cure—no pay" expenses shall in addition to actual out of pocket expenses include a fair rate for all tugs craft personnel and other equipment used by the Contractor in the services and oil shall mean crude oil fuel oil heavy diesel oil and lubricating oil.

   (b) The Contractor's remuneration shall be fixed by arbitration in London in the manner herein prescribed and any other difference arising out of this Agreement or the operations thereunder shall be referred to arbitration in the same way. In the event of the services referred to in this Agreement or any part of such services having been already rendered at the date of this Agreement by the Contractor to the said vessel and/or her cargo bunkers and stores the provisions of this Agreement shall apply to such services.

   (c) It is hereby further agreed that the security to be provided to the Committee of Lloyd's the Salved Values the Award and/or Interim Award and/or Award on Appeal of the Arbitrator

‡See Note 3 above

and/or Arbitrator(s) on Appeal shall be in‡   currency. If this Clause is not completed then the security to be provided and the Salved Values the Award and/or Interim Award and/or Award on Appeal of the Arbitrator and/or Arbitrator(s) on Appeal shall be in Pounds Sterling.

   (d) This Agreement shall be governed by and arbitration thereunder shall be in accordance with English law.

15.1.08
3.12.24
13.10.26
12.4.50
10.6.53
20.12.67
23.2.72
21.5.80

2.   The Owners their Servants and Agents shall co-operate fully with the Contractor in and about the salvage including obtaining entry to the place named in Clause 1 of this Agreement or such other place as may be agreed or if applicable the place of safety to which the salved property is taken. The Owners shall promptly accept redelivery of the salved property at such place. The Contractor may make reasonable use of the vessel's machinery gear equipment anchors chains stores and other appurtenances during and for the purpose of the operations free of expense but shall not unnecessarily damage abandon or sacrifice the same or any property the subject of this Agreement.

3.   The Master or other person signing this Agreement on behalf of the property to be salved is not authorised to make or give and the Contractor shall not demand or take any payment draft or order as inducement to or remuneration for entering into this Agreement.

PROVISIONS AS TO SECURITY
4.   The Contractor shall immediately after the termination of the services or sooner in appropriate cases notify the Committee of Lloyd's and where practicable the Owners of the amount for which he requires security (inclusive of costs expenses and interest). Unless otherwise agreed by the parties such security shall be given to the Committee of Lloyd's and security so given shall be in a form approved by the Committee and shall be given by persons firms or corporations resident in the United Kingdom either satisfactory to the Committee of Lloyd's or agreed by the Contractor. The Committee of Lloyd's shall not be responsible for the sufficiency (whether in amount or otherwise) of any security which shall be given nor for the default or insolvency of any person firm or corporation giving the same.

5.   Pending the completion of the security as aforesaid the Contractor shall have a maritime lien on the property salved for his remuneration. Where the aforementioned exception to the principle of "no cure—no pay" becomes likely to be applicable the Owners of the vessel shall on demand of the Contractor provide security for the Contractor's remuneration under the aforementioned exception in accordance with Clause 4 hereof. The salved property shall not without the consent in writing of the Contractor be removed from the place (within the terms of Clause 1) to which the property is taken by the Contractor on the completion of the salvage services until security has been given as aforesaid. The Owners of the vessel their Servants and Agents shall use their best endeavours to ensure that the Cargo Owners provide security in accordance with the provisions of Clause 4 of this Agreement before the cargo is released. The Contractor agrees not to arrest or detain the property salved unless (a) the security be not given within 14 days (exclusive of Saturdays and Sundays or other days observed as general holidays at Lloyd's) after the date of the termination of the services (the Committee of Lloyd's not being responsible for the failure of the parties concerned to provide the required security within the said 14 days) or (b) the Contractor has reason to believe that the removal of the property is contemplated contrary to the above agreement. In the event of security not being provided or in the event of (1) any attempt being made to remove the property salved contrary to this agreement or (2) the Contractor having reasonable grounds to suppose that such an attempt will be made the Contractor may take steps to enforce his aforesaid lien. The Arbitrator appointed under Clause 6 or the person(s) appointed under Clause 13 hereof shall have power in their absolute discretion to include in the amount awarded to the Contractor the whole or such part of the expense incurred by the Contractor in enforcing or protecting by insurance or otherwise or in taking reasonable steps to enforce or protect his lien as they shall think fit.

PROVISIONS AS TO ARBITRATION
6.   (a) Where security within the provisions of this Agreement is given to the Committee of Lloyd's in whole or in part the said Committee shall appoint an Arbitrator in respect of the interests covered by such security.
      (b) Whether security has been given or not the Committee of Lloyd's shall appoint an Arbitrator upon receipt of a written or telex or telegraphic notice of a claim for arbitration from any of the parties entitled or authorised to make such a claim.

7.   Where an Arbitrator has been appointed by the Committee of Lloyd's and the parties do not wish to proceed to arbitration the parties shall jointly notify the said Committee in writing or by telex or by telegram and the said Committee may thereupon terminate the appointment of such Arbitrator as they may have appointed in accordance with Clause 6 of this Agreement.

8.   Any of the following parties may make a claim for arbitration viz.:—(1) The Owners of the ship. (2) The Owners of the cargo or any part thereof. (3) The Owners of any freight separately at risk or any part thereof. (4) The Contractor. (5) The Owners of the bunkers and/or stores. (6) Any other person who is a party to this Agreement.

9.   If the parties to any such Arbitration or any of them desire to be heard or to adduce evidence at the Arbitration they shall give notice to that effect to the Committee of Lloyd's and shall respectively nominate a person in the United Kingdom to represent them for all the purposes of the Arbitration and failing such notice and nomination being given the Arbitrator or Arbitrator(s) on Appeal may proceed as if the parties failing to give the same had renounced their right to be heard or adduce evidence.

10.   The remuneration for the services within the meaning of this Agreement shall be fixed by an Arbitrator to be appointed by the Committee of Lloyd's and he shall have power to make an Interim Award ordering such payment on account as may seem fair and just and on such terms as may be fair and just.

CONDUCT OF THE ARBITRATION

11.   The Arbitrator shall have power to obtain call for receive and act upon any such oral or documentary evidence or information (whether the same be strictly admissible as evidence or not) as he may think fit and to conduct the Arbitration in such manner in all respects as he may think fit and shall if in his opinion the amount of the security demanded is excessive have power in his absolute discretion to condemn the Contractor in the whole or part of the expense of providing such security and to deduct the amount in which the Contractor is so condemned from the salvage remuneration. Unless the Arbitrator shall otherwise direct the parties shall be at liberty to adduce expert evidence at the Arbitration. Any Award of the Arbitrator shall (subject to appeal as provided in this Agreement) be final and binding on all the parties concerned. The Arbitrator and the Committee of Lloyd's may charge reasonable fees and expenses for their services in connection with the Arbitration whether it proceeds to a hearing or not and all such fees and expenses shall be treated as part of the costs of the Arbitration. Save as aforesaid the statutory provisions as to Arbitration for the time being in force in England shall apply.

12.   Interest at a rate per annum to be fixed by the Arbitrator from the expiration of 21 days (exclusive of Saturdays and Sundays or other days observed as general holidays at Lloyd's) after the date of publication of the Award and/or Interim Award by the Committee of Lloyd's until the date payment is received by the Committee of Lloyd's both dates inclusive shall (subject to appeal as provided in this Agreement) be payable upon any sum awarded after deduction of any sums paid on account.

PROVISIONS AS TO APPEAL

13.   Any of the persons named under Clause 8 may appeal from the Award but not without leave of the Arbitrator(s) on Appeal from an Interim Award made pursuant to the provisions of Clause 10 hereof by giving written or telegraphic or telex Notice of Appeal to the Committee of Lloyd's within 14 days (exclusive of Saturdays and Sundays or other days observed as general holidays at Lloyd's) after the date of the publication by the Committee of Lloyd's of the Award and may (without prejudice to their right of appeal under the first part of this Clause) within 14 days (exclusive of Saturdays and Sundays or other days observed as general holidays at Lloyd's) after receipt by them from the Committee of Lloyd's of notice of such appeal (such notice if sent by post to be deemed to be received on the day following that on which the said notice was posted) give written or telegraphic or telex Notice of Cross-Appeal to the Committee of Lloyd's. As soon as practicable after receipt of such notice or notices the Committee of Lloyd's shall refer the Appeal to the hearing and determination of a person or persons selected by it. In the event of an Appellant or Cross-Appellant withdrawing his Notice of Appeal or Cross-Appeal the hearing shall nevertheless proceed in respect of such Notice of Appeal or Cross-Appeal as may remain. Any Award on Appeal shall be final and binding on all the parties concerned whether such parties were represented or not at either the Arbitration or at the Arbitration on Appeal.

CONDUCT OF THE APPEAL

14.   No evidence other than the documents put in on the Arbitration and the Arbitrator's notes of the proceedings and oral evidence if any at the Arbitration and the Arbitrator's Reasons for his Award and Interim Award if any and the transcript if any of any evidence given at the Arbitration shall be used on the Appeal unless the Arbitrator(s) on Appeal shall in his or their discretion call for or allow other evidence. The Arbitrator(s) on Appeal may conduct the Arbitration on Appeal in such manner in all respects as he or they may think fit and may act upon any such evidence or information (whether the same be strictly admissible as evidence or not) as he or they may think fit and may maintain increase or reduce the sum awarded by the Arbitrator with the like power as is conferred by Clause 11 on the Arbitrator to condemn the Contractor in the whole or part of the expense of providing security and to deduct the amount disallowed from the salvage remuneration. And he or they shall also make such order as he or they shall think fit as to the payment of interest on the sum awarded to the Contractor.

The Arbitrator(s) on the Appeal may direct in what manner the costs of the Arbitration and of the Arbitration on Appeal shall be borne and paid and he or they and the Committee of Lloyd's may charge reasonable fees and expenses for their services in connection with the Arbitration on Appeal whether it proceeds to a hearing or not and all such fees and expenses shall be treated as part of the costs of the Arbitration on Appeal. Save as aforesaid the statutory provisions as to Arbitration for the time being in force in England shall apply.

PROVISIONS AS TO PAYMENT

15. (a) In case of Arbitration if no Notice of Appeal be received by the Committee of Lloyd's within 14 days (exclusive of Saturdays and Sundays or other days observed as general holidays at Lloyd's) after the date of the publication by the Committee of the Award and/or Interim Award the Committee shall call upon the party or parties concerned to pay the amount awarded and in the event of non-payment shall realize or enforce the security and pay therefrom to the Contractor (whose receipt shall be a good discharge to it) the amount awarded to him together with interest as hereinbefore provided but the Contractor shall reimburse the parties concerned to such extent as the final Award is less than the Interim Award.

(b) If Notice of Appeal be received by the Committee of Lloyd's in accordance with the provisions of Clause 13 hereof it shall as soon as but not until the Award on Appeal has been published by it call upon the party or parties concerned to pay the amount awarded and in the event of non-payment shall realize or enforce the security and pay therefrom to the Contractor (whose receipt shall be a good discharge to it) the amount awarded to him together with interest if any in such manner as shall comply with the provisions of the Award on Appeal.

(c) If the Award and/or Interim Award and/or Award on Appeal provides or provide that the costs of the Arbitration and/or of the Arbitration on Appeal or any part of such costs shall be borne by the Contractor such costs may be deducted from the amount awarded before payment is made to the Contractor by the Committee of Lloyd's unless satisfactory security is provided by the Contractor for the payment of such costs.

(d) If any sum shall become payable to the Contractor as remuneration for his services and/or interest and/or costs as the result of an agreement made between the Contractor and the parties interested in the property salved or any of them the Committee of Lloyd's in the event of non-payment shall realize or enforce the security and pay therefrom to the Contractor (whose receipt shall be a good discharge to it) the amount agreed upon between the parties.

(e) Without prejudice to the provisions of Clause 4 hereof the liability of the Committee of Lloyd's shall be limited in any event to the amount of security held by it.

GENERAL PROVISIONS

16. Notwithstanding anything hereinbefore contained should the operations be only partially successful without any negligence or want of ordinary skill and care on the part of the Contractor his Servants or Agents and any portion of the vessel her appurtenances bunkers stores and cargo be salved by the Contractor he shall be entitled to reasonable remuneration and such reasonable remuneration shall be fixed in case of difference by Arbitration in the manner hereinbefore prescribed.

17. The Master or other person signing this Agreement on behalf of the property to be salved enters into this Agreement as Agent for the vessel her cargo freight bunkers and stores and the respective owners thereof and binds each (but not the one for the other or himself personally) to the due performance thereof.

18. In considering what sums of money have been expended by the Contractor in rendering the services and/or in fixing the amount of the Award and/or Interim Award and/or Award on Appeal the Arbitrator or Arbitrator(s) on Appeal shall to such an extent and in so far as it may be fair and just in all the circumstances give effect to the consequences of any change or changes in the value of money or rates of exchange which may have occurred between the completion of the services and the date on which the Award and/or Interim Award and/or Award on Appeal is made.

19. Any Award notice authority order or other document signed by the Chairman of Lloyd's or any person authorised by the Committee of Lloyd's for the purpose shall be deemed to have been duly made or given by the Committee of Lloyd's and shall have the same force and effect in all respects as if it had been signed by every member of the Committee of Lloyd's.

20.   The Contractor may claim salvage and enforce any Award or agreement made between the Contractor and the parties interested in the property salved against security provided under this Agreement if any in the name and on behalf of any Sub-Contractors Servants or Agents including Masters and members of the Crews of vessels employed by him in the services rendered hereunder provided that he first indemnifies and holds harmless the Owners of the property salved against all claims by or liabilities incurred to the said persons. Any such indemnity shall be provided in a form satisfactory to such Owners.

21.   The Contractor shall be entitled to limit any liability to the Owners of the subject vessel and/or her cargo bunkers and stores which he and/or his Servants and/or Agents may incur in and about the services in the manner and to the extent provided by English law and as if the provisions of the Convention on Limitation of Liability for Maritime Claims 1976 were part of the law of England.

For and on behalf of the Contractor

For and on behalf of the Owners of property to be salved.

. . . .

. . . .

(To be signed either by the Contractor personally or by the Master of the salving vessel or other person whose name is inserted in line 3 of this Agreement.)

(To be signed by the Master or other person whose name is inserted in line 1 of this Agreement.)

APPENDIX 12: INSURANCE MARKET SLIP

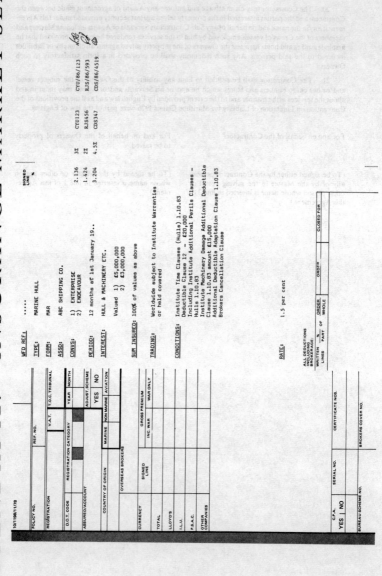

MFD REF: .....

TYPE: MARINE HULL

FORM: MAR

ASSD: ABC SHIPPING CO.

CONVS:
1) ENTERPRISE	2.136	3%	CYU/86/123 CYU123
2) ENDEAVOUR	1.424	2%	RJS/86/593 RJS456
	3.204	4.5%	CDS/86/4519 CDS347

PERIOD: 12 months at 1st January 19..

INTEREST: HULL & MACHINERY ETC.

Valued 1) £5,000,000
2) £3,000,000

SUM INSURED: 100% of values as above

TRADING: Worldwide subject to Institute Warranties or held covered

CONDITIONS: Institute Time Clauses (Hulls) 1.10.83
Deductible Clause 12 - £20,000
Including Institute Additional Perils Clauses -
Hulls 1.10.83
Institute Machinery Damage Additional Deductible
Clause 1.10.83 Amount £1,000
Additional Deductible Adaptation Clause 1.10.83
Brokers Cancellation Clauses

RATE: 1.5 per cent

SIGNED LINE % ....

10/1198D/11/78

POLICY NO.	REF. NO.		

REGISTRATION

	V.A.T.	T.O.C. TRIBUNAL

D.O.T. CODE	REGISTRATION CATEGORY	YEAR	MONTH

ASSURED/ACCOUNT		ADJUST.SCHEME
		YES NO

COUNTRY OF ORIGIN	MARINE NON MARINE AVIATION

OVERSEAS BROKERS

CURRENCY	SIGNED LINE	GROSS PREMIUM	
		INC. WAR	WAR ONLY

TOTAL		
LLOYD'S		
I.L.U.		
P.S.A.C.		
OTHER COMPANIES		

ALL DEDUCTIONS INCLUDING BROKERAGE

WRITTEN LINES	% OF PART	ORDER WHOLE	ORDER	ORDER	CLOSED FOR

C.P.A.	SERIAL NO.	CERTIFICATE NOS.
YES NO		

BUREAU SCHEME NO.		BROKERS COVER NO.

658

APPENDIX 13
LLOYD'S MARINE POLICY (MAR)

Lloyd's Marine Policy

We, The Underwriters, hereby agree, in consideration of the payment to us by or on behalf of the Assured of the premium specified in the Schedule, to insure against loss damage liability or expense in the proportions and manner hereinafter provided. Each Underwriting Member of a Syndicate whose definitive number and proportion is set out in the following Table shall be liable only for his own share of his respective Syndicate's proportion.

In Witness whereof the General Manager of Lloyd's Policy Signing Office has subscribed his Name on behalf of each of Us.

LLOYD'S POLICY SIGNING OFFICE
General Manager

This insurance is subject to English jurisdiction.

MAR
LPO 62A (1.1.82) Printed by The Carlton Berry Co. Ltd.

<u>SCHEDULE</u>

POLICY NUMBER   XYZ123

NAME OF ASSURED

        ABC SHIPPING CO.

VESSEL

      1) ENTERPRISE

      2) ENDEAVOUR

VOYAGE OR PERIOD OF INSURANCE

      12 months @ 1st January 1986

SUBJECT-MATTER INSURED

      Hull & Machinery etc.

AGREED VALUE
  (if any)

      1) £5,000,000

      2) £3,000,000

AMOUNT INSURED HEREUNDER

      100% of value as above

PREMIUM

      ......

CLAUSES, ENDORSEMENTS, SPECIAL CONDITIONS AND WARRANTIES

      As attached

THE ATTACHED CLAUSES AND ENDORSEMENTS FORM PART OF THIS POLICY

Definitive numbers of the Syndicates and proportions

The List of Underwriting Members of Lloyd's mentioned in the above Table shows their respective Syndicates and Shares therein and is deemed to be incorporated in and to form part of this Policy: It is available for inspection at Lloyd's Policy Signing Office by the Assured or his or their representatives and a true copy of the material parts of it certified by the General Manager of Lloyd's Policy Signing Office will be furnished to the Assured on application.

APPENDIX 14
INSTITUTE CLAUSES

This Appendix does not contain all the Institute Clauses but only a selection of the most important ones, namely:

Institute Time Clauses (Hulls), 1983

Institute Cargo Clauses (A), 1982

Institute Cargo Clauses (B), 1982 (Only those clauses varying from (A))

Institute Cargo Clauses (C), 1982 (Only those clauses varying from (B))

Institute Malicious Damage Clause, 1982

Institute War and Strikes Clauses (Hulls-Time), 1983

1/10/83

(FOR USE ONLY WITH THE NEW MARINE POLICY FORM)

INSTITUTE TIME CLAUSES
HULLS

This insurance is subject to English law and practice

1   NAVIGATION

1.1   The Vessel is covered subject to the provisions of this insurance at all times and has leave to sail or navigate with or without pilots, to go on trial trips and to assist and tow vessels or craft in distress, but it is warranted that the Vessel shall not be towed, except as is customary or to the first safe port or place when in need of assistance, or undertake towage or salvage services under a contract previously arranged by the Assured and/or Owners and/or Managers and/or Charterers. This Clause 1.1 shall not exclude customary towage in connection with loading and discharging.

1.2   In the event of the Vessel being employed in trading operations which entail cargo loading or discharging at sea from or into another vessel (not being a harbour or inshore craft) no claim shall be recoverable under this insurance for loss of or damage to the Vessel or liability to any other vessel arising from such loading or discharging operations, including whilst approaching, lying alongside and leaving, unless previous notice that the Vessel is to be employed in such operations has been given to the Underwriters and any amended terms of cover and any additional premium required by them have been agreed.

1.3   In the event of the Vessel sailing (with or without cargo) with an intention of being (a) broken up, or (b) sold for breaking up, any claim for loss of or damage to the Vessel occurring subsequent to such sailing shall be limited to the market value of the Vessel as scrap at the time when the loss or damage is sustained, unless previous notice has been given to the Underwriters and any amendments to the terms of cover, insured value and premium required by them have been agreed. Nothing in this Clause 1.3 shall affect claims under Clauses 8 and/or 11.

2   CONTINUATION

Should the Vessel at the expiration of this insurance be at sea or in distress or at a port of refuge or of call, she shall, provided previous notice be given to the Underwriters, be held covered at a pro rata monthly premium to her port of destination.

1
2
3
4
5
6
7

8
9
10
11
12
13

14
15
16
17
18
19

20
21
22
23

3   BREACH OF WARRANTY

Held covered in case of any breach of warranty as to cargo, trade, locality, towage, salvage services or date of sailing, provided notice be given to the Underwriters immediately after receipt of advices and any amended terms of cover and any additional premium required by them be agreed.

4   TERMINATION

This Clause 4 shall prevail notwithstanding any provision whether written typed or printed in this insurance inconsistent therewith.

Unless the Underwriters agree to the contrary in writing, this insurance shall terminate automatically at the time of

4.1   change of the Classification Society of the Vessel, or change, suspension, discontinuance, withdrawal or expiry of her Class therein, provided that if the Vessel is at sea such automatic termination shall be deferred until arrival at her next port. However where such change, suspension, discontinuance or withdrawal of her Class has resulted from loss or damage covered by Clause 6 of this insurance or which would be covered by an insurance of the Vessel subject to current Institute War and Strikes Clauses Hulls-Time such automatic termination shall only operate should the Vessel sail from her next port without the prior approval of the Classification Society.

4.2   any change, voluntary or otherwise, in the ownership or flag, transfer to new management, or charter on a bareboat basis, or requisition for title or use of the Vessel, provided that, if the Vessel has cargo on board and has already sailed from her loading port or is at sea in ballast, such automatic termination shall if required be deferred, whilst the Vessel continues her planned voyage, until arrival at final port of discharge if with cargo or at port of destination if in ballast. However, in the event of requisition for title or use without the prior execution of a written agreement by the Assured, such automatic termination shall occur fifteen days after such requisition whether the Vessel is at sea or in port.

A pro rata daily net return of premium shall be made.

5   ASSIGNMENT

No assignment of or interest in this insurance or in any moneys which may be or become payable thereunder is to be binding on or recognised by the Underwriters unless a dated notice of such assignment or interest signed by the Assured, and by the assignor in the case of subsequent assignment, is endorsed on the Policy and the Policy with such endorsement is produced before payment of any claim or return of premium thereunder.

6   PERILS

6.1   This insurance covers loss of or damage to the subject-matter insured caused by

6.1.1   perils of the seas rivers lakes or other navigable waters

6.1.2	fire, explosion	55
6.1.3	violent theft by persons from outside the Vessel	56
6.1.4	jettison	57
6.1.5	piracy	58
6.1.6	breakdown of or accident to nuclear installations or reactors	59
6.1.7	contact with aircraft or similar objects, or objects falling therefrom, land conveyance, dock or harbour equipment or installation	60 61
6.1.8	earthquake volcanic eruption or lightning.	62
6.2	This insurance covers loss of or damage to the subject-matter insured caused by	63
6.2.1	accidents in loading discharging or shifting cargo or fuel	64
6.2.2	bursting of boilers breakage of shafts or any latent defect in the machinery or hull	65
6.2.3	negligence of Master Officers Crew or Pilots	66
6.2.4	negligence of repairers or charterers provided such repairers or charterers are not an Assured hereunder	67
6.2.5	barratry of Master Officers or Crew,	68
	provided such loss or damage has not resulted from want of due diligence by the Assured, Owners or Managers.	69 70
6.3	Master Officers Crew or Pilots not to be considered Owners within the meaning of this Clause 6 should they hold shares in the Vessel.	71 72

7 POLLUTION HAZARD

This insurance covers loss of or damage to the Vessel caused by any governmental authority acting under the powers vested in it to prevent or mitigate a pollution hazard, or threat thereof, resulting directly from damage to the Vessel for which the Underwriters are liable under this insurance, provided such act of governmental authority has not resulted from want of due diligence by the Assured, the Owners, or Managers of the Vessel or any of them to prevent or mitigate such hazard or threat. Master, Officers, Crew or Pilots not to be considered Owners within the meaning of this Clause 7 should they hold shares in the Vessel.

8 3/4THS COLLISION LIABILITY

8.1   The Underwriters agree to indemnify the Assured for three-fourths of any sum or sums paid by the Assured to any other person or persons by reason of the Assured becoming legally liable by way of damages for   80 81 82 83

8.1.1   loss of or damage to any other vessel or property on any other vessel   84

8.1.2   delay to or loss of use of any such other vessel or property thereon   85

8.1.3   general average of, salvage of, or salvage under contract of, any such other vessel or property thereon,   86 87

where such payment by the Assured is in consequence of the Vessel hereby insured coming into collision with any other vessel.   88 89

8.2   The indemnity provided by this Clause 8 shall be in addition to the indemnity provided by the other terms and conditions of this insurance and shall be subject to the following provisions: 90 91

8.2.1   Where the insured Vessel is in collision with another vessel and both vessels are to blame then, unless the liability of one or both vessels becomes limited by law, the indemnity under this Clause 8 shall be calculated on the principle of cross-liabilities as if the respective Owners had been compelled to pay to each other such proportion of each other's damages as may have been properly allowed in ascertaining the balance or sum payable by or to the Assured in consequence of the collision.   92 93 94 95 96

8.2.2   In no case shall the Underwriters' total liability under Clauses 8.1 and 8.2 exceed their proportionate part of three-fourths of the insured value of the Vessel hereby insured in respect of any one collision.   97 98

8.3   The Underwriters will also pay three-fourths of the legal costs incurred by the Assured or which the Assured may be compelled to pay in contesting liability or taking proceedings to limit liability, with the prior written consent of the Underwriters.   99 100 101

EXCLUSIONS

8.4   Provided always that this Clause 8 shall in no case extend to any sum which the Assured shall pay for or in respect of   102 103 104

8.4.1   removal or disposal of obstructions, wrecks, cargoes or any other thing whatsoever   105

8.4.2   any real or personal property or thing whatsoever except other vessels or property on other vessels   106

8.4.3   the cargo or other property on, or the engagements of, the insured Vessel   107

8.4.4   loss of life, personal injury or illness   108

8.4.5   pollution or contamination of any real or personal property or thing whatsoever (except other vessels with which the insured Vessel is in collision or property on such other vessels). | 109 110

9   SISTERSHIP

Should the Vessel hereby insured come into collision with or receive salvage services from another vessel belonging wholly or in part to the same Owners or under the same management, the Assured shall have the same rights under this insurance as they would have were the other vessel entirely the property of Owners not interested in the Vessel hereby insured; but in such cases the liability for the collision or the amount payable for the services rendered shall be referred to a sole arbitrator to be agreed upon between the Underwriters and the Assured. | 111 112 113 114 115 116

10   NOTICE OF CLAIM AND TENDERS

10.1   In the event of accident whereby loss or damage may result in a claim under this insurance, notice shall be given to the Underwriters prior to survey and also, if the Vessel is abroad, to the nearest Lloyd's Agent so that a surveyor may be appointed to represent the Underwriters should they so desire. | 117 118 119 120

10.2   The Underwriters shall be entitled to decide the port to which the Vessel shall proceed for docking or repair (the actual additional expense of the voyage arising from compliance with the Underwriters' requirements being refunded to the Assured) and shall have a right of veto concerning a place of repair or a repairing firm. | 121 122 123 124

10.3   The Underwriters may also take tenders or may require further tenders to be taken for the repair of the Vessel. Where such a tender has been taken and a tender is accepted with the approval of the Underwriters, an allowance shall be made at the rate of 30% per annum on the insured value for time lost between the despatch of the invitations to tender required by Underwriters and the acceptance of a tender to the extent that such time is lost solely as the result of tenders having been taken and provided that the tender is accepted without delay after receipt of the Underwriters' approval. | 125 126 127 128 129 130

Due credit shall be given against the allowance as above for any amounts recovered in respect of fuel and stores and wages and maintenance of the Master Officers and Crew or any member thereof, including amounts allowed in general average, and for any amounts recovered from third parties in respect of damages for detention and/or loss of profit and/or running expenses, for the period covered by the tender allowance or any part thereof. | 131 132 133 134 135

Where a part of the cost of the repair of damage other than a fixed deductible is not recoverable from the Underwriters the allowance shall be reduced by a similar proportion. | 136 137

10.4   In the event of failure to comply with the conditions of this Clause 10 a deduction of 15% shall be made from the amount of the ascertained claim. | 138 139

11 GENERAL AVERAGE AND SALVAGE

11.1   This insurance covers the Vessel's proportion of salvage, salvage charges and/or general average, reduced in respect of any under-insurance, but in case of general average sacrifice of the Vessel the Assured may recover in respect of the whole loss without first enforcing their right of contribution from other parties.

11.2   Adjustment to be according to the law and practice obtaining at the place where the adventure ends, as if the contract of affreightment contained no special terms upon the subject; but where the contract of affreightment so provides the adjustment shall be according to the York-Antwerp Rules.

11.3   When the Vessel sails in ballast, not under charter, the provisions of the York-Antwerp Rules, 1974 (excluding Rules XX and XXI) shall be applicable, and the voyage for this purpose shall be deemed to continue from the port or place of departure until the arrival of the Vessel at the first port or place thereafter other than a port or place of refuge or a port or place of call for bunkering only. If at any such intermediate port or place there is an abandonment of the adventure originally contemplated the voyage shall thereupon be deemed to be terminated.

11.4   No claim under this Clause 11 shall in any case be allowed where the loss was not incurred to avoid or in connection with the avoidance of a peril insured against.

12 DEDUCTIBLE

12.1   No claim arising from a peril insured against shall be payable under this insurance unless the aggregate of all such claims arising out of each separate accident or occurrence (including claims under Clauses 8, 11 and 13) exceeds ....in which case this sum shall be deducted. Nevertheless the expense of sighting the bottom after stranding, if reasonably incurred specially for that purpose, shall be paid even if no damage be found. This Clause 12.1 shall not apply to a claim for total or constructive total loss of the Vessel or, in the event of such a claim, to any associated claim under Clause 13 arising from the same accident or occurrence.

12.2   Claims for damage by heavy weather occurring during a single sea passage between two successive ports shall be treated as being due to one accident. In the case of such heavy weather extending over a period not wholly covered by this insurance the deductible to be applied to the claim recoverable hereunder shall be the proportion of the above deductible that the number of days of such heavy weather falling within the period of this insurance bears to the number of days of heavy weather during the single sea passage. The expression "heavy weather" in this Clause 12.2 shall be deemed to include contact with floating ice.

12.3   Excluding any interest comprised therein, recoveries against any claim which is subject to the above deductible shall be credited to the Underwriters in full to the extent of the sum by which the aggregate of the claim unreduced by any recoveries exceeds the above deductible.

12.4 Interest comprised in recoveries shall be apportioned between the Assured and the Underwriters, taking into account the sums paid by the Underwriters and the dates when such payments were made, notwithstanding that by the addition of interest the Underwriters may receive a larger sum than they have paid.

13 DUTY OF ASSURED (SUE AND LABOUR)

13.1 In case of any loss or misfortune it is the duty of the Assured and their servants and agents to take such measures as may be reasonable for the purpose of averting or minimising a loss which would be recoverable under this insurance.

13.2 Subject to the provisions below and to Clause 12 the Underwriters will contribute to charges properly and reasonably incurred by the Assured their servants or agents for such measures. General average, salvage charges (except as provided for in Clause 13.5) and collision defence or attack costs are not recoverable under this Clause 13.

13.3 Measures taken by the Assured or the Underwriters with the object of saving, protecting or recovering the subject-matter insured shall not be considered as a waiver or acceptance of abandonment or otherwise prejudice the rights of either party.

13.4 When expenses are incurred pursuant to this Clause 13 the liability under this insurance shall not exceed the proportion of such expenses that the amount insured hereunder bears to the value of the Vessel as stated herein, or to the sound value of the Vessel at the time of the occurrence giving rise to the expenditure if the sound value exceeds that value. Where the Underwriters have admitted a claim for total loss and property insured by this insurance is saved, the foregoing provisions shall not apply unless the expenses of suing and labouring exceed the value of such property saved and then shall apply only to the amount of the expenses which is in excess of such value.

13.5 When a claim for total loss of the Vessel is admitted under this insurance and expenses have been reasonably incurred in saving or attempting to save the Vessel and other property and there are no proceeds, or the expenses exceed the proceeds, then this insurance shall bear its pro rata share of such proportion of the expenses, or of the expenses in excess of the proceeds, as the case may be, as may reasonably be regarded as having been incurred in respect of the Vessel; but if the Vessel be insured for less than its sound value at the time of the occurrence giving rise to the expenditure, the amount recoverable under this clause shall be reduced in proportion to the under-insurance.

13.6 The sum recoverable under this Clause 13 shall be in addition to the loss otherwise recoverable under this insurance but shall in no circumstances exceed the amount insured under this insurance in respect of the Vessel.

14 NEW FOR OLD

Claims payable without deduction new for old.

15 BOTTOM TREATMENT

In no case shall a claim be allowed in respect of scraping gritblasting and/or other surface preparation or painting of the Vessel's bottom except that

15.1 gritblasting and/or other surface preparation of new bottom plates ashore and supplying and applying any "shop", primer thereto,

15.2 gritblasting and/or other surface preparation of:

the butts or area of plating immediately adjacent to any renewed or refitted plating damaged during the course of welding and/or repairs,

areas of plating damaged during the course of fairing, either in place or ashore,

15.3 supplying and applying the first coat of primer/anti-corrosive to those particular areas mentioned in 15.1 and 15.2 above,

shall be allowed as part of the reasonable cost of repairs in respect of bottom plating damaged by an insured peril.

16 WAGES AND MAINTENANCE

No claim shall be allowed, other than in general average, for wages and maintenance of the Master, Officers and Crew, or any member thereof, except when incurred solely for the necessary removal of the Vessel from one port to another for the repair of damage covered by the Underwriters, or for trial trips for such repairs, and then only for such wages and maintenance as are incurred whilst the Vessel is under way.

17 AGENCY COMMISSION

In no case shall any sum be allowed under this insurance either by way of remuneration of the Assured for time and trouble taken to obtain and supply information or documents or in respect of the commission or charges of any manager, agent, managing or agency company or the like, appointed by or on behalf of the Assured to perform such services.

18 UNREPAIRED DAMAGE

18.1 The measure of indemnity in respect of claims for unrepaired damage shall be the reasonable depreciation in the market value of the Vessel at the time this insurance terminates arising from such unrepaired damage, but not exceeding the reasonable cost of repairs.

18.2 In no case shall the Underwriters be liable for unrepaired damage in the event of a subsequent total loss (whether or not covered under this insurance) sustained during the period covered by this insurance or any extension thereof. 232 233 234

18.3 The Underwriters shall not be liable in respect of unrepaired damage for more than the insured value at the time this insurance terminates. 235 236

19 CONSTRUCTIVE TOTAL LOSS 237

19.1 In ascertaining whether the Vessel is a constructive total loss, the insured value shall be taken as the repaired value and nothing in respect of the damaged or break-up value of the Vessel or wreck shall be taken into account. 238 239 240

19.2 No claim for constructive total loss based upon the cost of recovery and/or repair of the Vessel shall be recoverable hereunder unless such cost would exceed the insured value. In making this determination, only the cost relating to a single accident or sequence of damages arising from the same accident shall be taken into account. 241 242 243 244

20 FREIGHT WAIVER 245

In the event of total or constructive total loss no claim to be made by the Underwriters for freight whether notice of abandonment has been given or not. 246 247

21 DISBURSEMENTS WARRANTY 248

21.1 Additional insurances as follows are permitted: 249

21.1.1 *Disbursements, Managers' Commissions, Profits or Excess or Increased Value of Hull and Machinery.* A sum not exceeding 25% of the value stated herein. 250 251

21.1.2 *Freight, Chartered Freight or Anticipated Freight, insured for time.* A sum not exceeding 25% of the value as stated herein less any sum insured, however described, under 21.1.1. 252 253

21.1.3 *Freight or Hire, under contracts for voyage.* A sum not exceeding the gross freight or hire for the current cargo passage and next succeeding cargo passage (such insurance to include, if required, a preliminary and an intermediate ballast passage) plus the charges of insurance. In the case of a voyage charter where payment is made on a time basis, the sum permitted for insurance shall be calculated on the estimated duration of the voyage, subject to the limitation of two cargo passages as laid down herein. Any sum insured under 21.1.2 to be taken into account and only the excess thereof may be insured, which excess shall be reduced as the freight or hire is advanced or earned by the gross amount so advanced or earned. 254 255 256 257 258 259 260 261

21.1.4 *Anticipated Freight if the Vessel sails in ballast and not under Charter.* A sum not exceeding the 262 anticipated gross freight on next cargo passage, such sum to be reasonably estimated on the basis of the current rate of freight at time of insurance plus the charges of insurance. Any sum insured under 21.1.2 to be taken into account and only the excess thereof may be insured.

21.1.5   *Time Charter Hire or Charter Hire for Series of Voyages.* A sum not exceeding 50% of the gross hire which is to be earned under the charter in a period not exceeding 18 months. Any sum insured under 21.1.2 to be taken into account and only the excess thereof may be insured, which excess shall be reduced as the hire is advanced or earned under the charter by 50% of the gross amount so advanced or earned but the sum insured need not be reduced while the total of the sums insured under 21.1.2 and 21.1.5 does not exceed 50% of the gross hire still to be earned under the charter. An insurance under this Section may begin on the signing of the charter.

21.1.6   *Premiums.* A sum not exceeding the actual premiums of all interests insured for a period not exceeding 12 months (excluding premiums insured under the foregoing sections but including, if required, the premium or estimated calls on any Club or War etc. Risk insurance) reducing pro rata monthly.

21.1.7   *Returns of Premium.* A sum not exceeding the actual returns which are allowable under any insurance but which would not be recoverable thereunder in the event of a total loss of the Vessel whether by insured perils or otherwise.

21.1.8   *Insurance irrespective of amount against:*
Any risks excluded by Clauses 23, 24, 25 and 26 below.

21.2   Warranted that no insurance on any interests enumerated in the foregoing 21.1.1 to 21.1.7 in excess of the amounts permitted therein and no other insurance which includes total loss of the Vessel P.P.I., F.I.A., or subject to any other like term, is or shall be effected to operate during the currency of this insurance by or for account of the Assured, Owners, Managers or Mortgagees. Provided always that a breach of this warranty shall not afford the Underwriters any defence to a claim by a Mortgagee who has accepted this insurance without knowledge of such breach.

22   RETURNS FOR LAY-UP AND CANCELLATION

22.1   To return as follows:

22.1.1   Pro rata monthly net for each uncommenced month if this insurance be cancelled by agreement.

22.1.2   For each period of 30 consecutive days the Vessel may be laid up in a port or in a lay-up area provided such port or lay-up area is approved by the Underwriters (with special liberties as hereinafter allowed) (a)................per cent net not under repair — 294

    (b)................per cent net under repair. — 295

If the Vessel is under repair during part only of a period for which a return is claimable, the return shall be calculated pro rata to the number of days under (a) and (b) respectively. — 296, 297, 298

22.2   PROVIDED ALWAYS THAT

22.2.1 a total loss of the Vessel, whether by insured perils or otherwise, has not occurred during the period covered by this insurance or any extension thereof — 299, 300

22.2.2 in no case shall a return be allowed when the Vessel is lying in exposed or unprotected waters, or in a port or lay-up area not approved by the Underwriters but, provided the Underwriters agree that such non-approved lay-up area is deemed to be within the vicinity of the approved port or lay-up area, days during which the Vessel is laid up in such non-approved lay-up area may be added to days in the approved port or lay-up area to calculate a period of 30 consecutive days and a return shall be allowed for the proportion of such period during which the Vessel is actually laid up in the approved port or lay-up area — 301, 302, 303, 304, 305, 306, 307

22.2.3 loading or discharging operations or the presence of cargo on board shall not debar returns but no return shall be allowed for any period during which the Vessel is being used for the storage of cargo or for lightering purposes — 308, 309, 310

22.2.4 in the event of any amendment of the annual rate, the above rates of return shall be adjusted accordingly — 311, 312

22.2.5 in the event of any return recoverable under this Clause 22 being based on 30 consecutive days which fall on successive insurances effected for the same Assured, this insurance shall only be liable for an amount calculated at pro rata of the period rates 22.1.2(a) and/or (b) above for the number of days which come within the period of this insurance and to which a return is actually applicable. Such overlapping period shall run, at the option of the Assured, either from the first day on which the Vessel is laid up or the first day of a period of 30 consecutive days as provided under 22.1.2(a) or (b), or 22.2.2 above. — 313, 314, 315, 316, 317, 318, 319

The following clauses shall be paramount and shall override anything contained in this insurance inconsistent therewith. — 320, 321

23 WAR EXCLUSION — 322

In no case shall this insurance cover loss damage liability or expense caused by — 323

23.1   war civil war revolution rebellion insurrection, or civil strife arising therefrom, or any hostile act by or against a belligerent power   324 325

23.2   capture seizure arrest restraint or detainment (barratry and piracy excepted), and the consequences thereof or any attempt thereat   326 327

23.3   derelict mines torpedoes bombs or other derelict weapons of war.   328

24   STRIKES EXCLUSION

In no case shall this insurance cover loss damage liability or expense caused by   329

24.1   strikers, locked-out workmen, or persons taking part in labour disturbances, riots or civil commotions   330 331 332

24.2   any terrorist or any person acting from a political motive.   333

25   MALICIOUS ACTS EXCLUSION

In no case shall this insurance cover loss damage liability or expense arising from   334

25.1   the detonation of an explosive   335

25.2   any weapon of war   336

and caused by any person acting maliciously or from a political motive.   337 338

26   NUCLEAR EXCLUSION

In no case shall this insurance cover loss damage liability or expense arising from any weapon of war employing atomic or nuclear fission and/or fusion or other like reaction or radioactive force or matter.   339 340 341

CL. 280 *Sold by Witherby & Co. Ltd., London.*

1/1/82

(FOR USE ONLY WITH THE NEW MARINE POLICY FORM)

INSTITUTE CARGO CLAUSES (A)

RISKS COVERED

1   This insurance covers all risks of loss of or damage to the subject-matter insured except as provided in Clauses 4, 5, 6 and 7 below. — *Risks Clause*

2   This insurance covers general average and salvage charges, adjusted or determined according to the contract of affreightment and/or the governing law and practice, incurred to avoid or in connection with the avoidance of loss from any cause except those excluded in Clauses 4, 5, 6 and 7 or elsewhere in this insurance. — *General Average Clause*

3   This insurance is extended to indemnify the Assured against such proportion of liability under the contract of affreightment "Both to Blame Collision" Clause as is in respect of a loss recoverable hereunder. In the event of any claim by shipowners under the said Clause the Assured agree to notify the Underwriters who shall have the right, at their own cost and expense, to defend the Assured against such claim. — *"Both to Blame Collision" Clause*

EXCLUSIONS

4   In no case shall this insurance cover — *General Exclusions Clause*

4.1   loss damage or expense attributable to wilful misconduct of the Assured

4.2   ordinary leakage, ordinary loss in weight or volume, or ordinary wear and tear of the subject-matter insured

4.3   loss damage or expense caused by insufficiency or unsuitability of packing or preparation of the subject-matter insured (for the purpose of this Clause 4.3 "packing" shall be deemed to include stowage in a container or liftvan but only when such stowage is carried out prior to attachment of this insurance or by the Assured or their servants)

4.4   loss damage or expense caused by inherent vice or nature of the subject-matter insured

4.5   loss damage or expense proximately caused by delay, even though the delay be caused by a risk insured against (except expenses payable under Clause 2 above)

4.6   loss damage or expense arising from insolvency or financial default of the owners managers charterers or operators of the vessel

4.7   loss damage or expense arising from the use of any weapon of war employing atomic or nuclear fission and/or fusion or other like reaction or radioactive force or matter.

5 5.1 In no case shall this insurance cover loss damage or expense arising from

unseaworthiness of vessel or craft,

unfitness of vessel craft conveyance container or liftvan for the safe carriage of the subject-matter insured,

where the Assured or their servants are privy to such unseaworthiness or unfitness, at the time the subject-matter insured is loaded therein.

5.2 The Underwriters waive any breach of the implied warranties of seaworthiness of the ship and fitness of the ship to carry the subject-matter insured to destination, unless the Assured or their servants are privy to such unseaworthiness or unfitness.

Unseaworthiness and Unfitness Exclusion Clause

6 In no case shall this insurance cover loss damage or expense caused by

6.1 war civil war revolution rebellion insurrection, or civil strife arising therefrom, or any hostile act by or against a belligerent power

6.2 capture seizure arrest restraint or detainment (piracy excepted), and the consequences thereof or any attempt thereat

6.3 derelict mines torpedoes bombs or other derelict weapons of war.

War Exclusion Clause

7 In no case shall this insurance cover loss damage or expense

7.1 caused by strikers, locked-out workmen, or persons taking part in labour disturbances, riots or civil commotions

7.2 resulting from strikes, lock-outs, labour disturbances, riots or civil commotions

7.3 caused by any terrorist or any person acting from a political motive.

Strikes Exclusion Clause

DURATION

8 8.1 This insurance attaches from the time the goods leave the warehouse or place of storage at the place named herein for the commencement of the transit, continues during the ordinary course of transit and terminates either

8.1.1 on delivery to the Consignees' or other final warehouse or place of storage at the destination named herein,

8.1.2 on delivery to any other warehouse or place of storage, whether prior to or at the destination named herein, which the Assured elect to use either

8.1.2.1 for storage other than in the ordinary course of transit or

Transit Clause

8.1.2.2   for allocation or distribution,

or

8.1.3   on the expiry of 60 days after completion of discharge overside of the goods hereby insured from the oversea vessel at the final port of discharge,

whichever shall first occur.

8.2   If, after discharge overside from the oversea vessel at the final port of discharge, but prior to termination of this insurance, the goods are to be forwarded to a destination other than that to which they are insured hereunder, this insurance, whilst remaining subject to termination as provided for above, shall not extend beyond the commencement of transit to such other destination.

8.3   This insurance shall remain in force (subject to termination as provided for above and to the provisions of Clause 9 below) during delay beyond the control of the Assured, any deviation, forced discharge, reshipment or transhipment and during any variation of the adventure arising from the exercise of a liberty granted to shipowners or charterers under the contract of affreightment.

9   If owing to circumstances beyond the control of the Assured either the contract of carriage is terminated at a port or place other than the destination named therein or the transit is otherwise terminated before delivery of the goods as provided for in Clause 8 above, then this insurance shall also terminate *unless prompt notice is given to the Underwriters and continuation of cover is requested when the insurance shall remain in force, subject to an additional premium if required by the Underwriters,* either

9.1   until the goods are sold and delivered at such port or place, or, unless otherwise specially agreed, until the expiry of 60 days after arrival of the goods hereby insured at such port or place, whichever shall first occur,

or

9.2   if the goods are forwarded within the said period of 60 days (or any agreed extension thereof) to the destination named herein or to any other destination, until terminated in accordance with the provisions of Clause 8 above.

10   Where, after attachment of this insurance, the destination is changed by the Assured, *held covered at a premium and on conditions to be arranged subject to prompt notice being given to the Underwriters.*

CLAIMS

11 11.1   In order to recover under this insurance the Assured must have an insurable interest in the subject-matter insured at the time of the loss.

Termination of Contract of Carriage Clause

Change of Voyage Clause

Insurable Interest Clause

11.2   Subject to 11.1 above, the Assured shall be entitled to recover for insured loss occurring during the period covered by this insurance, notwithstanding that the loss occurred before the contract of insurance was concluded, unless the Assured were aware of the loss and the Underwriters were not.

12   Where, as a result of the operation of a risk covered by this insurance, the insured transit is terminated at a port or place other than that to which the subject-matter is covered under this insurance, the Underwriters will reimburse the Assured for any extra charges properly and reasonably incurred in unloading storing and forwarding the subject-matter to the destination to which it is insured hereunder. *Forwarding Charges Clause*

This Clause 12, which does not apply to general average or salvage charges, shall be subject to the exclusions contained in Clauses 4, 5, 6 and 7 above, and shall not include charges arising from the fault negligence insolvency or financial default of the Assured or their servants.

13   No claim for Constructive Total Loss shall be recoverable hereunder unless the subject-matter insured is reasonably abandoned either on account of its actual total loss appearing to be unavoidable or because the cost of recovering, reconditioning and forwarding the subject-matter to the destination to which it is insured would exceed its value on arrival. *Constructive Total Loss Clause*

14
14.1   If any Increased Value insurance is effected by the Assured on the cargo insured herein the agreed value of the cargo shall be deemed to be increased to the total amount insured under this insurance and all Increased Value insurances covering the loss, and liability under this insurance shall be in such proportion as the sum insured herein bears to such total amount insured. *Increased Value Clause*

In the event of claim the Assured shall provide the Underwriters with evidence of the amounts insured under all other insurances.

14.2   **Where this insurance is on Increased Value the following clause shall apply:**
The agreed value of the cargo shall be deemed to be equal to the total amount insured under the primary insurance and all Increased Value insurances covering the loss and effected on the cargo by the Assured, and liability under this insurance shall be in such proportion as the sum insured herein bears to such total amount insured.

In the event of claim the Assured shall provide the Underwriters with evidence of the amounts insured under all other insurances.

BENEFIT OF INSURANCE

15   This insurance shall not inure to the benefit of the carrier or other bailee. *Not to Inure Clause*

MINIMISING LOSSES

16   It is the duty of the Assured and their servants and agents in respect of loss recoverable hereunder *Duty of Assured Clause*

16.1 to take such measures as may be reasonable for the purpose of averting or minimising such loss, and

16.2 to ensure that all rights against carriers, bailees or other third parties are properly preserved and exercised

and the Underwriters will, in addition to any loss recoverable hereunder, reimburse the Assured for any charges properly and reasonably incurred in pursuance of these duties.

17 Measures taken by the Assured or the Underwriters with the object of saving, protecting or recovering the subject-matter insured shall not be considered as a waiver or acceptance of abandonment or otherwise prejudice the rights of either party.

Waiver Clause

AVOIDANCE OF DELAY

18 It is a condition of this insurance that the Assured shall act with reasonable despatch in all circumstances within their control.

Reasonable Despatch Clause

LAW AND PRACTICE

19 This insurance is subject to English law and practice.

English Law and Practice Clause

NOTE:— It is necessary for the Assured when they become aware of an event which is "held covered" under this insurance to give prompt notice to the Underwriters and the right to such cover is dependent upon compliance with this obligation.

CL. 252. *Sold by Witherby & Co. Ltd., London.*

INSTITUTE CARGO CLAUSES (B)

RISKS COVERED

		Risks Clause
1	This insurance covers, except as provided in Clauses 4, 5, 6 and 7 below,	
1.1	loss of or damage to the subject-matter insured reasonably attributable to	
1.1.1	fire or explosion	
1.1.2	vessel or craft being stranded grounded sunk or capsized	
1.1.3	overturning or derailment of land conveyance	
1.1.4	collision or contact of vessel craft or conveyance with any external object other than water	
1.1.5	discharge of cargo at a port of distress	
1.1.6	earthquake volcanic eruption or lightning,	
1.2	loss of or damage to the subject-matter insured caused by	
1.2.1	general average sacrifice	
1.2.2	jettison or washing overboard	
1.2.3	entry of sea lake or river water into vessel craft hold conveyance container liftvan or place of storage,	
1.3	total loss of any package lost overboard or dropped whilst loading on to, or unloading from, vessel or craft.	

EXCLUSIONS

		General Exclusions Clause
4	In no case shall this insurance cover	
4.1	loss damage or expense attributable to wilful misconduct of the Assured	
4.2	ordinary leakage, ordinary loss in weight or volume, or ordinary wear and tear of the subject-matter insured	

4.3 loss damage or expense caused by insufficiency or unsuitability of packing or preparation of the subject-matter insured (for the purpose of this Clause 4.3 "packing" shall be deemed to include stowage in a container or liftvan but only when such stowage is carried out prior to attachment of this insurance or by the Assured or their servants)

4.4 loss damage or expense caused by inherent vice or nature of the subject-matter insured

4.5 loss damage or expense proximately caused by delay, even though the delay be caused by a risk insured against (except expenses payable under Clause 2 above)

4.6 loss damage or expense arising from insolvency or financial default of the owners managers charterers or operators of the vessel

4.7 deliberate damage to or deliberate destruction of the subject-matter insured or any part thereof by the wrongful act of any person or persons

4.8 loss damage or expense arising from the use of any weapon of war employing atomic or nuclear fission and/or fusion or other like reaction or radioactive force or matter.

6 In no case shall this insurance cover loss damage or expense caused by

6.1 war civil war revolution rebellion insurrection, or civil strife arising therefrom, or any hostile act by or against a belligerent power

6.2 capture seizure arrest restraint or detainment, and the consequences thereof or any attempt thereat

6.3 derelict mines torpedoes bombs or other derelict weapons of war.

War
Exclusion
Clause

*Clauses which vary from the A clauses.

CL.253. *Sold by Witherby & Co. Ltd.. London.*

INSTITUTE CARGO CLAUSES (C)*

RISKS COVERED

1   This insurance covers, except as provided in Clauses 4, 5, 6 and 7 below,

   1.1   loss of or damage to the subject-matter insured reasonably attributable to

   1.1.1   fire or explosion

   1.1.2   vessel or craft being stranded grounded sunk or capsized

   1.1.3   overturning or derailment of land conveyance

   1.1.4   collision or contact of vessel craft or conveyance with any external object other than water

   1.1.5   discharge of cargo at a port of distress,

   1.2   loss of or damage to the subject-matter insured caused by

   1.2.1   general average sacrifice

   1.2.2   jettison.

---

*Clauses which vary from the B clauses.

CL.254.   *Sold by Witherby & Co. Ltd., London.*

INSTITUTE MALICIOUS DAMAGE CLAUSE

1/8/82

(FOR USE ONLY WITH THE NEW MARINE POLICY FORM)

INSTITUTE MALICIOUS DAMAGE CLAUSE

In consideration of an additional premium, it is hereby agreed that the exclusion "deliberate damage to or deliberate destruction of the subject-matter insured or any part thereof by the wrongful act of any person or persons" is deemed to be deleted and further that this insurance covers loss of or damage to the subject-matter insured caused by malicious acts vandalism or sabotage, subject always to the other exclusions contained in this insurance.

CL. 266.   *Sold by Witherby & Co. Ltd., London*

1/10/83

(FOR USE ONLY WITH THE NEW MARINE POLICY FORM)

INSTITUTE WAR AND STRIKES CLAUSES

Hulls—Time

This insurance is subject to English law and practice

1 PERILS

Subject always to the exclusions hereinafter referred to, this insurance covers loss of or damage to the Vessel caused by

  1.1 war civil war revolution rebellion insurrection, or civil strife arising therefrom, or any hostile act by or against a belligerent power

  1.2 capture seizure arrest restraint or detainment, and the consequences thereof or any attempt thereat

  1.3 derelict mines torpedoes bombs or other derelict weapons of war

  1.4 strikers, locked-out workmen, or persons taking part in labour disturbances, riots or civil commotions

  1.5 any terrorist or any person acting maliciously or from a political motive

  1.6 confiscation or expropriation.

2 INCORPORATION

The Institute Time Clauses—Hulls 1/10/83 (including 4/4ths Collision Clause) except Clauses 1.2, 2, 3, 4, 6, 12, 21.1.8, 22, 23, 24, 25 and 26 are deemed to be incorporated in this insurance in so far as they do not conflict with the provisions of these clauses.

Held covered in case of breach of warranty as to towage or salvage services provided notice be given to the Underwriters immediately after receipt of advices and any additional premium required by them be agreed.

3 DETAINMENT

In the event that the Vessel shall have been the subject of capture seizure arrest restraint detainment confiscation or expropriation, and the Assured shall thereby have lost the free use and disposal of the Vessel for a continuous period of 12 months then for the purpose of ascertaining whether the Vessel is a constructive total loss the Assured shall be deemed to have been deprived of the possession of the Vessel without any likelihood of recovery.

1
2
3
4
5
6
7
8
9
10
11
12
13
14
15
16
17
18
19
20
21

(Continued)

4 EXCLUSIONS

This insurance excludes

4.1	loss damage liability or expense arising from	22
4.1.1	any detonation of any weapon of war employing atomic or nuclear fission and/or fusion or other like reaction or radioactive force or matter, hereinafter called a nuclear weapon of war	23 / 24
4.1.2	the outbreak of war (whether there be a declaration of war or not) between any of the following countries:	25 / 26
	United Kingdom, United States of America, France, the Union of Soviet Socialist Republics, the People's Republic of China	27 / 28 / 29 / 30 / 31
4.1.3	requisition or pre-emption	32
4.1.4	capture seizure arrest restraint detainment confiscation or expropriation by or under the order of the government or any public or local authority of the country in which the Vessel is owned or registered	33 / 34
4.1.5	arrest restraint detainment confiscation or expropriation under quarantine regulations or by reason of infringement of any customs or trading regulations	35 / 36
4.1.6	the operation of ordinary judicial process, failure to provide security or to pay any fine or penalty or any financial cause	37 / 38
4.1.7	piracy (but this exclusion shall not affect cover under Clause 1.4),	39
4.2	loss damage liability or expense covered by the Institute Time Clauses—Hulls 1/10/83 (including 4/4ths Collision Clause) or which would be recoverable thereunder but for Clause 12 thereof,	40 / 41
4.3	any claim for any sum recoverable under any other insurance on the Vessel or which would be recoverable under such insurance but for the existence of this insurance,	42 / 43
4.4	any claim for expenses arising from delay except such expenses as would be recoverable in principle in English law and practice under the York-Antwerp Rules 1974.	44 / 45

5 TERMINATION

5.1	This insurance may be cancelled by either the Underwriters or the Assured giving 7 days notice (such cancellation becoming effective on the expiry of 7 days from midnight of the day on which notice of cancellation is issued by or to the Underwriters). The Underwriters agree however to reinstate this insurance subject to agreement between the Underwriters and the Assured prior to the expiry of such notice of cancellation as to new rate of premium and/or conditions and/or warranties.	46 / 47 / 48 / 49 / 50 / 51

5.2 Whether or not such notice of cancellation has been given this insurance shall TERMINATE AUTOMATICALLY 52 53

5.2.1 upon the occurrence of any hostile detonation of any nuclear weapon of war as defined in Clause 4.1.1 wheresoever or whensoever such detonation may occur and whether or not the Vessel may be involved 54 55 56

5.2.2 upon the outbreak of war (whether there be a declaration of war or not) between any of the following countries: 57 58

United Kingdom, United States of America, France, 59
the Union of Soviet Socialist Republics, 60
the People's Republic of China 61

5.2.3 in the event of the Vessel being requisitioned, either for title or use. 62

5.3 In the event either of cancellation by notice or of automatic termination of this insurance by reason of the 63
operation of this Clause 5, or of the sale of the Vessel, pro rata net return of premium shall be payable to 64
the Assured. 65

This insurance shall not become effective if, subsequent to its acceptance by the Underwriters and prior to the intended time of its attachment, there has occurred any event which would have automatically terminated this insurance under the provisions of Clause 5 above.

CL. 281 *Sold by Witherby & Co. Ltd., London.*

APPENDIX 15: LLOYD'S S.G. POLICY

(*No.*)

S.G.

Be it known that

as well in *their* own name as for and in the name and names of all and every other person or persons to whom the same doth, may, or shall appertain, in part or in all, doth make assurance and cause *themselves* and them, and every of them, to be insured, lost or not lost, at and from

Upon any kind of goods and merchandises, and also upon the body, tackle, apparel, ordnance, munition, artillery, boat, and other furniture, of and in the good ship or vessel called the

whereof is master under God, for this present voyage, or whosoever else shall go for master in the said ship, or by whatsoever other name or names the same ship, or the master thereof, is or shall be named or called ; beginning the adventure upon the said goods and merchandises from the loading thereof aboard the said ship, *as above* upon the said ship, &c., *as above* and so shall continue and endure, during her abode there, upon the said ship, &c. And further, until the said ship, with all her ordnance, tackle, apparel, &c., and goods and merchandises whatsoever shall be arrived at *as above* upon the said ship, &c., until she hath moored at anchor twenty-four hours in good safety ; and upon the goods and merchandises, until the same be there discharged and safely landed. And it shall be lawful for the said ship, &c., in this voyage, to proceed and sail to and touch and stay at any ports or places whatsoever *and wheresoever for all purposes* without prejudice to this insurance. The said ship, &c., goods and merchandises, &c., for so much as concerns the assured to this insurance are and shall be valued at

686

Touching the adventures and perils which we the assurers are contented to bear and do take upon us in this voyage : they are of the seas, men of war, fire, enemies, pirates, rovers, thieves, jettisons, letters of mart and countermart, surprisals, takings at sea, arrests, restraints, and detainments of all kings, princes, and people, of what nation, condition, or quality soever, barratry of the master and mariners, and of all other perils, losses, and misfortunes, that have or shall come to the hurt, detriment, or damage of the said goods and merchandises, and ship, &c., or any part thereof. And in case of any loss or misfortune it shall be lawful to the assured, their factors, servants and assigns, to sue, labour, and travel for, in and about the defence, safeguard, and recovery of the said goods and merchandises, and ship, &c., or any part thereof, without prejudice to this insurance ; to the charges whereof we, the assurers, will contribute each one according to the rate and quantity of his sum herein assured. And it is especially declared and agreed that no acts of the insurer or insured in recovering, saving, or preserving the property insured shall be considered as a waiver, or acceptance of abandonment. And it is agreed by us, the insurers, that this writing or policy of assurance shall be of as much force and effect as the surest writing or policy of assurance heretofore made in Lombard Street, or in the Royal Exchange, or elsewhere in London.

Warranted free of capture, seizure, arrest, restraint or detainment, and the consequences thereof or of any attempt thereat ; also from the consequences of hostilities or warlike operations, whether there be a declaration of war or not; but this warranty shall not exclude collision, contact with any fixed or floating object (other than a mine or torpedo), stranding, heavy weather or fire unless caused directly (and independently of the nature of the voyage or service which the vessel concerned or, in the case of a collision, any other vessel involved therein, is performing) by a hostile act by or against a belligerent power ; and for the purpose of this warranty "power" includes any authority maintaining naval, military or air forces in association with a power.

Further warranted free from the consequence of civil war, revolution, rebellion, insurrection, or civil strife arising therefrom, or piracy.

And so we, the assurers, are contented, and do hereby promise and bind ourselves, each one for his own part, our heirs, executors, and goods to the assured, their executors, administrators, and assigns, for the true performance of the premises, confessing ourselves paid the consideration due unto us for this assurance by the assured, at and after the rate of

IN WITNESS whereof we, the assurers, have subscribed our names and sums assured in *LONDON, as hereinafter appears.*

N.B.—Corn, fish, salt, fruit, flour, and seed are warranted free from average, unless general, or the ship be stranded ; sugar, tobacco, hemp, flax, hides and skins are warranted free from average under five pounds per cent., and all other goods, also the ship and freight, are warranted free from average under three pounds per cent. unless general, or the ship be stranded.

Now know ye that We the Assurers, Members of the Syndicates whose definitive numbers in the after-mentioned List of Underwriting Members of Lloyd's are set out in the attached Table, hereby bind ourselves each for his own part and not one for another and in respect of his due proportion only, to pay or make good to the Assured all such Loss and/or Damage which he or they may sustain by any one or more of the aforesaid perils and the due proportion for which each of us, the Assurers, is liable shall be ascertained by reference to his share, as shown in the said List, of the Amount, Percentage or Proportion of the total sum assured hereunder which is in the Table set opposite the definitive number of the Syndicate of which such Assurer is a Member AND FURTHER THAT the List of Underwriting Members of Lloyd's referred to above shows their respective Syndicates and Shares therein, is deemed to be incorporated in and to form part of this Policy, bears the number specified in the attached Table and is available for inspection at Lloyd's Policy Signing Office by the Assured or his or their representatives and a true copy of the material parts of the said List certified by the General Manager of Lloyd's Policy Signing Office will be furnished to the Assured on application.

LLOYD'S POLICY SIGNING OFFICE,

In Witness whereof the General Manager of Lloyd's Policy Signing Office has subscribed his name

on behalf of each of us.

Dated in London, the

GENERAL MANAGER.

(In the event of accident whereby loss or damage may result in a claim under this Policy, the immediate notice us given to the nearest Lloyd's Agent.)

(26-11-58)
(24-4-63)
(25-3-64)   L.P.O. 62 settlement will be much facilitated if

FOR EMBOSSMENT BY ● LLOYD'S POLICY SIGNING OFFICE

Definitive Numbers of Syndicates and Amount, Percentage or Proportion of the
Total Sum Assured hereunder shared between the Members of those Syndicates.

APPENDIX 16

INSTITUTE CARGO CLAUSES (F.P.A.).

1/1/63

1. This insurance attaches from the time the goods leave the warehouse or place of storage at the place named in the policy for the commencement of the transit, continues during the ordinary course of transit and terminates either on delivery

    (a) to the Consignees' or other final warehouse or place of storage at the destination named in the policy,

    (b) to any other warehouse or place of storage, whether prior to or at the destination named in the policy, which the Assured elect to use either

        (i) for storage other than in the ordinary course of transit

        or

        (ii) for allocation or distribution,

or (c) on the expiry of 60 days after completion of discharge overside of the goods hereby insured from the oversea vessel at the final port of discharge,

whichever shall first occur.

If, after discharge overside from the oversea vessel at the final port of discharge, but prior to termination of this insurance, the goods are to be forwarded to a destination other than that to which they are insured hereunder, this insurance whilst remaining subject to termination as provided for above, shall not extend beyond the commencement of transit to such other destination.

This insurance shall remain in force (subject to termination as provided for above and to the provisions of Clause 2 below) during delay beyond the control of the Assured, any deviation, forced discharge, reshipment or transhipment and during any variation of the adventure arising from the exercise of a liberty granted to shipowners or charterers under the contract of affreightment, but shall in no case be deemed to extend to cover loss damage or expense proximately caused by delay or inherent vice or nature of the subject matter insured.

2. If owing to circumstances beyond the control of the Assured either the contract of affreightment is terminated at a port or place other than the destination named therein or the adventure is otherwise terminated before delivery of the goods as provided for in Clause 1 above, then, subject to prompt notice being given to Underwriters and to an additional premium if required, this insurance shall remain in force until either

    (i) the goods are sold and delivered at such port or place, or, unless otherwise specially agreed, until the expiry of 60 days after completion of discharge overside of the goods hereby insured from the oversea vessel at such port or place, whichever shall first occur,

    or (ii) if the goods are forwarded within the said period of 60 days (or any agreed extension thereof) to the destination named in the policy or to any other destination, until terminated in accordance with the provisions of Clause 1 above.

3. Including transit by craft raft or lighter to or from the vessel. Each craft raft or lighter to be deemed a separate insurance. The Assured are not to be prejudiced by any agreement exempting lightermen from liability.

4. Held covered at a premium to be arranged in case of change of voyage or of any omission or error in the description of the interest vessel or voyage.

Transit Clause (incorporating Warehouse to Warehouse Clause).

Termination of Adventure Clause.

Craft, &c. Clause.

Change of Voyage Clause.

689

5. Warranted free from Particular Average unless the vessel or craft be stranded, sunk, or burnt, but notwithstanding this warranty the Underwriters are to pay the insured value of any package or packages which may be totally lost in loading, transhipment or discharge, also for any loss of or damage to the interest insured which may reasonably be attributed to fire, explosion, collision or contact of the vessel and/or craft and/or conveyance with any external substance (ice included) other than water, or to discharge of cargo at a port of distress, also to pay special charges for landing warehousing and forwarding if incurred at an intermediate port of call or refuge, for which Underwriters would be liable under the standard form of English Marine Policy with the Institute Cargo Clauses (W.A.) attached. *(F.P.A. Clause.)*

This Clause shall operate during the whole period covered by the policy.

6. No claim for Constructive Total Loss shall be recoverable hereunder unless the goods are reasonably abandoned either on account of their actual total loss appearing to be unavoidable or because the cost of recovering, reconditioning and forwarding the goods to the destination to which they are insured would exceed their value on arrival. *(Constructive Total Loss Clause.)*

7. General Average and Salvage Charges payable according to Foreign Statement or to York-Antwerp Rules if in accordance with the contract of affreightment. *(G.A. Clause.)*

8. The seaworthiness of the vessel as between the Assured and Underwriters is hereby admitted.

In the event of loss the Assured's right of recovery hereunder shall not be prejudiced by the fact that the loss may have been attributable to the wrongful act or misconduct of the shipowners or their servants, committed without the privity of the Assured. *(Seaworthiness Admitted Clause.)*

9. It is the duty of the Assured and their Agents, in all cases, to take such measures as may be reasonable for the purpose of averting or minimising a loss and to ensure that all rights against carriers, bailees or other third parties are properly preserved and exercised. *(Bailee Clause.)*

10. This insurance shall not inure to the benefit of the carrier or other bailee. *(Not to Inure Clause.)*

11. This insurance is extended to indemnify the Assured against such proportion of liability under the contract of affreightment "Both to Blame Collision" Clause as is in respect of a loss recoverable hereunder.

In the event of any claim by shipowners under the said Clause the Underwriters agree to notify the Underwriters who shall have the right, at their own cost and expense, to defend the Assured against such claim. *("Both to Blame Collision" Clause.)*

12. Warranted free of capture, seizure, arrest, restraint or detainment, and the consequences thereof or or of any attempt thereat; also from the consequences of hostilities or warlike operations, whether there be a declaration of war or not; but this warranty shall not exclude collision, contact with any fixed or floating object (other than a mine or torpedo), stranding, heavy weather or fire unless caused directly (and independently of the nature of the voyage or service which the vessel concerned or, in the case of a collision, any other vessel involved therein, is performing) by a hostile act by or against a belligerent power; and for the purpose of this warranty "power" includes any authority maintaining naval, military or air forces in association with a power. *(F.C. & S. Clause.)*

Further warranted free from the consequences of civil war, revolution, rebellion, insurrection, or civil strife arising therefrom, or piracy.

Should Clause No. 12 be deleted, the relevant current Institute War Clauses shall be deemed to form part of this insurance. *(F.S.R. & C.C. Clause.)*

13. Warranted free of loss or damage
(a) caused by strikers, locked-out workmen, or persons taking part in labour disturbances, riots or civil commotions;
(b) resulting from strikes, lock-outs, labour disturbances, riots or civil commotions.

Should Clause No. 13 be deleted, the relevant current Institute Strikes Riots and Civil Commotions Clauses shall be deemed to form part of this insurance.

14. It is a condition of this insurance that the Assured shall act with reasonable despatch in all circumstances within their control. *(Reasonable Despatch Clause.)*

NOTE.—It is necessary for the Assured when they become aware of an event which is "held covered" under this insurance to give prompt notice to Underwriters and the right to such cover is dependent upon compliance with this obligation.

CL. 31.   Sold by *Witherby & Co. Ltd., London.*

APPENDIX 17
INSTITUTE CARGO
CLAUSES (WA) 1963 cl. 5

The only clause which varies from the Institute Cargo Clauses (FPA) is clause 5 which is as follows:

5.   Warranted free from average under the percentage specified in the policy, unless general, or the vessel or craft be stranded, sunk or burnt, but notwithstanding this warranty the Underwriters are to pay the insured value of any package which may be totally lost in loading, transhipment or discharge, also for any loss of or damage to the interest insured which may reasonably be attributed to fire, explosion, collision or contact of the vessel and/or craft and/or conveyance with any external substance (ice included) other than water, or to discharge of cargo at a port of distress.

This Clause shall operate during the whole period covered by the policy.

INDEX